BIBLICAL THEOLOGY
OLD TESTAMENT

BIBLICAL THEOLOGY

VOLUME ONE
OLD TESTAMENT

15798

By Chester K. Lehman

HERALD PRESS, SCOTTDALE, PENNSYLVANIA

BIBLICAL THEOLOGY: OLD TESTAMENT
Copyright © 1971 by Herald Press, Scottdale, Pennsylvania, 15683
Library of Congress Catalog Card Number: 74-141829
International Standard Book Number: 0-8361-1633-X
Printed in the United States

Designed by Tom Hershberger

To My Students of
Theology of the Old Testament
Who through the past years have inspired me with
their interest and enthusiasm in this course.

I look back with deepest appreciation to my privilege of pursuing biblical theology courses under the late Dr. Geerhardus Vos. His simple. constructive, and conservative approach to biblical theology made a deep impression upon me. His approach was not only scholarly, but genuinely Christian. He devoted very little time to rebutting opposing viewpoints; instead, he built upon the solid foundation of the Bible itself. In all of his lectures he exhibited a depth of insight and profound understanding of the Bible that gave him the structural basis for a consistent and thoroughgoing presentation of biblical theology.

Dr. Vos's approach to biblical theology was distinctive in that it was biblically centered. He recognized that the Bible is the record of an unfolding revelation of God, progressive in nature, and culminating in the revelation of God through Jesus Christ. This viewpoint has challenged me throughout my own teaching experience and has stimulated me to concentrate my energies and thought on this discipline. Dr. Vos perceived the close interrelations among the periods of biblical history and the stages of God's revealing activity. To him, God's acts in history and His spoken words constituted divine revelation.

This basic approach to the discipline of biblical theology has served as a general guide to my own thinking. First, I accept without any reservation the Bible's claims for its origin and nature. Because of this conviction I have endeavored to present the unfolding of God's revelation as the Bible represents it. Second, I have followed to the best of my ability the accepted grammatico-historical system of interpretation. Obviously, this is an area where no one has spoken the last word. There is a continuing need for study and research in the entire field of hermeneutics.

Third, I have endeavored to appreciate the valid conclusions and contributions that may be gained from biblical criticism. Scholars have probed into problems of authorship, date of writing, occasion, purpose, literary aspects, historical backgrounds, and related matters; and, as everyone knows, serious differences of opinion and great disparity in conclusions still exist. Personally, I believe that sound biblical criticism gives adequate grounds for believing in the integrity and authenticity of the biblical records. With absolute confidence we may believe that God did reveal Himself to man and that He wrought miracles, wonders, and signs in support of this objective revelation.

Fourth, there is need for recognizing the structure of the Bible. This requires determining the relation of the Old Testament to the New Testament. There is need for laying hold of the fundamental idea of progressive revelation according to which the promises and predictions of the Old Testament have been fulfilled in the New Testament. It involves the insight to discover the grand unity of the entire Bible which centers in Christ.

Fifth, I am unreservedly committed to the Bible's claim to inspiration, in accordance with Paul's declaration, "All scripture is inspired by God"; and also with Peter's testimony that "Men moved by the Holy Spirit spoke from God." In other words, the Bible constitutes the "holy scriptures" and the "sacred writings."

With the foregoing points in mind, let me add that I have sought to give a positive and constructive approach to the discipline of biblical theology. In this effort it has been my desire to appropriate the values of divergent viewpoints or differing interpretations, even though I do not agree with the fundamental positions of such approaches. Historicism, liberalism, form criticism, dispensationalism, existentialism, neoorthodoxy, and others have all made definite contributions to the understanding of the Bible. On this account one who is committed to belief in the Bible as the record of God's revelation given through divine inspiration should accept, in all honesty, whatever truth is contributed regardless of its source. I am so grateful that practically all of the modern works on Old Testament theology hold to the grand unity of the Bible, structured on the idea that the Old Testament looks forward to Christ, who is the center of the New Testament.

In writing this book I have sought to prepare it for as wide as possible use. It should be sufficiently comprehensive and deep for seminary students and graduates. Technical problems of literary criticism, linguistic inquiries, and philosophical approaches have been held to a minimum so that the book should be serviceable to upper level students in colleges and Bible schools. Ministers who have not had the opportunity of securing advanced biblical training, and others who are devoting themselves to serious Bible study should also be able to use the book with profit.

A few details deserve attention. I have arranged the contents at the beginning of the volume with the purpose of setting forth the structural pattern of the book. This should help the reader to grasp the distinctive nature of biblical theology as a theological discipline. At the close of each chapter I have appended a limited bibliography for parallel reading by which the reader can broaden his approach to the chapter contents. At the close of the volume I have also appended a selected bibliography, including Old Testament theologies, monographs, Bible dictionaries, and Bible encyclopedias.

Throughout the book, where Hebrew words are used, I transliterated them according to Young's *Analytical Concordance* to the Bible so that the reader who has not studied Hebrew can trace the uses of a given word throughout the Old Testament. While this transliteration differs slightly from Strong's *Exhaustive Concordance* of the Bible, and from *The Englishman's Hebrew and Chaldee Concordance*, the reader should be able to use this transliteration with little difficulty.

In the preparation of this work I have sensed severe limitations due to a lack of time for depth research and study. Nevertheless, I have moved forward fully conscious of the Holy Spirit's presence and direction.

I desire to express my gratitude to Eastern Mennonite College and to the Herald Press for granting me the equivalent of a year's time for study and writing. To my students during the past forty-five years, who shared so generously and constructively in class discussions, I also feel deeply indebted.

I am grateful to Dr. Myron S. Augsburger for reading the manuscript, for passing on to me helpful suggestions, and for writing a gracious introduction.

Most of all I am indebted to my wife for her faithful labor in typing this manuscript twice. In addition, she has corrected the manuscript for grammar and composition and has made detailed suggestions for its improvement.

It is my fervent prayer that this book will prove helpful to many readers who are pursuing serious study of the Old Testament with the special objective of gaining a larger comprehension of God's unfolding revelation.

INTRODUCTION

For the past several decades there has been a renewed interest in biblical theology. In the mid-twenties Dr. Kittel said, "We have come near to apologizing for the existence of the Bible." But by the mid-thirties biblical theology came to the fore as both a method of study and a statement of content. From the concerns of evangelical church organizations to World Council affirmations there have come fresh affirmations on the primacy of Holy Scriptures. One basic affirmation that the Bible is a unity is emphasized by the World Council of Churches in principles "D" and "E," that "the center and goal of the whole Bible is Jesus Christ" and that "the unity of the Bible is the ongoing program of God's saving work." Since the Christian church believes that Jesus Christ is both Lord of the Scripture and Lord of history, the study of the Scripture is essential to understanding Jesus Christ and to understanding His work as it continues in the world through the Holy Spirit.

In one sense biblical theology is the confessional recital of the acts of God in history with the interpretation of these acts. Historical study today is concerned with the history of the idea itself, the *Sitz im Leben*. Consequently, many of the biblical theologies are expressions of the search for categories of thought native to the Bible itself. For example, Professor Walther Eichrodt concentrates on "covenant" as a category of biblical thinking. Another example is C. H. Dodd, who concentrates on "kerygma" as New Testament perspective in biblical theology.

Biblical theology as a discipline is set between systematics and exegetics. It is not to be thought of as a substitute for systematic theology but rather it aims to gather the content of revelation in the biblical form. On the one hand, exegetics is concerned with the discovery of the truth of biblical revelation in its parts, and on the other hand, systematics attempts to gather together the content of revelation and synthesize it and present it in a logical and defensible form. Biblical theology stands between these two seeking to relate the biblical parts in such a way as to be consistent with the total content of the biblical disclosure. The author of this volume, Chester K. Lehman, is uniquely qualified to present this work, having achieved his graduate degree in systematic theology and having taught both biblical and systematic theology at Eastern Mennonite College and Seminary. His keen mind, careful scholarship, and noble Christian life add dimensions of meaning to his writings for all of us who know him.

The author of this work stands in the Anabaptist/Mennonite theological tradition. In the sixteenth century the Anabaptist movement carried the principle of "sola scriptura" further than their contemporary reformers and insisted that the authority of the Scripture be seen in the total life of the disciple. This perspective did not use the Scripture as simply a basis for a doctrine of justification by faith but insisted that beyond a doctrinal confession one who relates to Christ by faith comes under the lordship of Christ. This concept of discipleship was expressed in the words of Hans Denck who said, "No man truly knows Christ except he follow Him in life." The Mennonite Church, known as the contemporary expression of this Anabaptist vision, emphasizes the lordship of Christ for daily discipleship, the implications of being a people of God in secular life. This conviction arises from a basic emphasis on the conversion experience of the believer in which one who is in Christ becomes a new creature. This is an emphasis on discipleship in grace, a relationship in which the Holy Spirit enables the disciple to live as a member of the kingdom of heaven here and now.

An essential aspect of Anabaptist/Mennonite theology is the conviction that God's self-disclosure in Scripture culminates in the person of Jesus Christ and that the Bible is interpreted properly only through Him. This has led to regarding the Bible as an unfolding revelation in which the New Testament is at a higher level than the Old Testament. In this work Dr. Lehman, as a theologian in the Mennonite perspective of theology, applies this principle of hermeneutics to Old Testament theology. This first volume of his biblical theology is a significant expression of interpreting the Old Testament in a way that is consistent with its own goal and progress as seen in the full revelation of the two Testaments. Dr. Lehman's approach is one which takes seriously the theological or biblical themes of the Old Testament and interprets them in a way consistent with the full scope of biblical revelation.

For the serious student of Scripture this volume is a most significant aid in biblical interpretation. Here one finds the evidence of scholarly work coupled with deep conviction that the Bible is the Word of God written. With a "high" view of Scripture, the Word written is here interpreted through the premises of faith which come to the fore in the Scripture itself. While Dr. Lehman has been conversant with what scholarship has to say regarding difficulties in various passages, his major emphasis is as Augustine said, "to interpret the darker passages by the more clear." The reader will be stimulated through the insights and convictions expressed in his method of analysis and interpretation.

Myron S. Augsburger
President, Eastern Mennonite College

CONTENTS

PREFACE 7

INTRODUCTION 11

PART ONE: GOD'S REVELATION THROUGH MOSES
I. NATURE AND METHOD OF BIBLICAL THEOLOGY 23
   1. Formative Ideas of Biblical Theology............................ 23
   2. Definition of Biblical Theology — A Survey of Recent Approaches
      and Definitions 26
   3. Impact of Philosophical, Critical, and Theological Thought upon
      the Study of Biblical Theology 29
   4. Bearing of Pentateuchal Criticism on Old Testament Biblical
      Theology 33
   5. Relation of Biblical Theology to Other Theological Disciplines 36
   6. Method of Biblical Theology 38
II. GOD'S REVELATION IN THE CREATION AND IN
   THE FALL OF MAN 42
   1. Introduction 42
   2. God the Creator 43
   3. God's Act of Creation 48
   4. Creation of Man 52
      a. Man, the Climax of Creation
      b. Man's Unique Dignity
      c. Cessation of Creation
      d. Religious Aspect of Creation
   5. God's First Revelation to Man 58
      a. Interpreting the Garden of Eden Narrative
      b. Meaning of the Garden of Eden Story
      c. Tree of Knowledge of Good and Evil
      d. Serpent's Encounter with Eve
      e. God's Encounter with Sinful Man and Woman
III. COURSE OF HISTORY TO THE REVELATION
   THROUGH ABRAHAM 69
   1. General Trend of the Narrative 69
   2. Offerings of Cain and Abel 69
   3. Author of Genesis Interprets Antediluvian History 70
   4. Revelation Given Through Noah 73
      a. God, His Nature and Acts
      b. Life of the People of God
      c. Noah's Worship of the Lord
      d. God's Covenant with Noah
      e. Noah's Prophetic Deliverance
   5. The Lord's Direction of History to the Call of Abraham 82
      a. Table of Nations, Genesis 10

       b. Tower of Babel and the Confusion of Tongues
       c. Election of the Shemites
       Use of the Name LORD in Genesis (Appended Note)

IV. GOD'S REVELATION THROUGH THE PATRIARCHS ·.......... 88
  1. Critical Views of the Historicity of the Patriarchs 88
  2. God's Encounters with Abraham 89
     a. The Call
     b. The Promise
     c. The Covenant
     d. The Tests
  3. Supernatural Power of God and Abraham's Response of Faith . 97
     a. The Lord Revealed as God Almighty
     b. Abraham's Response of Faith
  4. Forms of Revelation During the Patriarchal Period.............. 100
     a. Spoken Words of the Lord
     b. Appearances of the Lord
     c. Visions
     d. Dreams
     e. The Angel of the Lord
  5. Revelation in the Era of Jacob 103
     a. Continuing Principle of Election
     b. Elements of Revelation in the Life of Jacob
     c. Joseph, a Model of Moral Integrity and an Agent
       of Divine Providence

V. REVELATION IN THE ERA OF MOSES 112
  1. Place of Moses in God's Revelation 112
  2. Redemption of Israel from Egypt............................. 114
     a. Deliverance Wrought Through the Mighty Acts of God
     b. Spiritual Aspects of the Deliverance from Egypt
  3. Israel Drawn into Covenant Relationship with the Lord 118
     a. Historical Character of the Covenant
     b. The Covenant Concept
     c. Making of the Covenant
  4. Function of the Law Under God's Rule........................ 123
  5. The Decalogue 124

VI. WORSHIP IN THE ERA OF MOSES 134
  1. Introduction... 134
  2. Structure of the Tabernacle: Its Symbolism and Typical Significance . 134
     a. Pattern of the Tabernacle
     b. Symbolism of the Tabernacle Structure and Furnishings
     c. Typical Element of the Tabernacle and Its Furniture
  3. The Tabernacle, Dwelling Place of God 138
     a. Purpose of the Tabernacle Symbolism
     b. Problems Concerning the Interpretation of Symbolism
     c. Typical Significance of the Tabernacle
  4. Sacrificial System in Israel's Worship 147
     a. Background of Pre-Mosaic Sacrifices
     b. Ends or Purposes Served by Sacrifice
     c. Category of Sacrifice Expressed by Corban
     d. Materials for Sacrifice

   e. Relation Between the Offerer and His Sacrifice
   f. Steps or Stages in the Ritual of Sacrifice
   g. Day of Atonement
  5. Meaning of Uncleanness and Purification 161
  6. Life of the People of God 164
  7. Concluding Observations 165
   An Examination of Critical Opinions Concerning the Historicity
   of the Tabernacle (Appended Note) 166
VII. MOSES' FINAL EXPOSITION OF THE LAW 172
  1. Introduction 172
  2. God's Direction of the Course of Israel's History 174
   a. The Conquest Understood in the Light of God's Promises
    to Abraham
   b. Theology of the Inheritance of Canaan
   c. Ethical Aspects of the Conquest
  3. The God of Israel 176
   a. The Lord Revealed as the Only True God
   b. The Lord, the God Who Speaks to His People
   c. The Faithful God Who Keeps Covenant and Steadfast Love
  4. Deuteronomy, a Gospel of God's Redeeming Love 178
   a. Israel, the Elect of God
   b. A Faith Requiring Obedience, Trust, and Patience
   c. Love to God Manifested in Obedience
   d. Ethical Aspects of Obedience
   e. Eschatological Aspect of Israel's Faith
   f. Israel's Faith Strengthened by a Central Place of Worship
VIII. SIN AND SALVATION AS REVEALED IN
  THE PENTATEUCH 186
  1. Introduction 186
  2. Tragic Course of Sin 186
  3. Vocabulary for Sin 187
   a. *Ra*
   b. *Chata*
   c. *Chamas*
   d. *Avon*
   e. *Rasha*
   f. *Pesha*
   g. *Marah*
   h. *Asham*
   i. *Ma'al*
   j. *Qashah*
   k. *Chalal*
   l. Less frequently used words
  4. Birth of the Idea of Salvation 192
  5. Repentance and Confession of Sin 194
  6. Awakening of a Faith Relationship with God 194

PART TWO: GOD'S REVELATION THROUGH THE PROPHETS
I. THE RISE OF PROPHETISM 197
  1. Prophetism Before the Era of Moses 197

2. Manifestations of the Prophetic Gift from Moses to Samuel 199
3. Prophetic Office from Samuel to Elisha 201
    a. Samuel
    b. Nathan, Gad, Ahijah, Shemaiah, and Others
    c. Elijah, Micaiah, Elisha, and the Unnamed Prophets
II. PLACE OF PROPHETISM IN THE OLD TESTAMENT 207
1. Introduction 207
2. Concept of Prophetism 207
    a. Man of God
    b. Servant of the Lord
    c. Messenger of the Lord
    d. Mediator
    e. Seer
    f. Watchman
    g. Prophet
3. Influence of the Prophetic Concept on Old Testament Canon 210
4. Place of Prophetism in Biblical Revelation 211
    a. The Prophet, God's Spokesman to His People
    b. The Prophetic Order and the Theocratic Kingdom
    c. The Prophet, the Agent of Divine Revelation
    d. Relation of God's Revelation to Biblical Inspiration
    e. Prophetic Periods
III. NATURE OF THE PROPHETIC GIFT. 216
1. Call to the Prophetic Office 216
2. Affirmations of Real Communications from God 217
3. Analysis of the Prophetic Claims 218
    a. God's Speaking and Man's Hearing
    b. God's Showing and Man's Seeing
4. Modes of Communication Used by the Prophets 220
IV. THEOLOGY OF THE FORMER PROPHETS 222
1. Introduction 222
2. God's Revelation from Joshua to Samuel 222
    a. Fulfillment of the Promises
    b. God's Continued Action in History
    c. Worship of Israel During This Period
    d. Disclosure of God and His Nature
    e. Life of the People of God
3. God's Revelation During the Period of the Monarchy 227
    a. God and His Revelation
    b. God's Revelation Through the Davidic Kingdom
    c. God's Actions in History
    d. The Temple, the House of the Lord
    e. The Lord's Judgment on Israel
    f. The Spirit of the Lord
    g. Life of the People of God
V. GOD'S REVELATION THROUGH THE PROPHETS OF THE
    ASSYRIAN PERIOD, 746-625 B.C. 238
1. Introduction 238
    a. Problems Centering in Literary Criticism
    b. Method of Approach to Prophetic Revelation

2. The God of Israel: His Nature and Manifestations 240
   a. Joel
   b. Jonah
   c. Hosea
   d. Amos
   e. Isaiah (1 — 39)
      (1) The Sovereign Majesty of God
      (2) The Holiness and Righteousness of God
      (3) The God of Love and Mercy
      (4) The God of Judgment
      (5) The God of Creation
      (6) The God Who Acts in History
   f. Micah
3. The Spoken and Written Word of God. 251
   a. Obadiah, Joel, and Jonah
   b. Hosea
   c. Amos
   d. Isaiah (1 — 39)
4. Israel's Election Actualized by Covenant Relation with God 254
   a. Obadiah
   b. Hosea
      (1) Marriage, a Symbol of a Covenant Relation
      (2) Development of the Covenant Idea in Hosea
   c. Amos
   d. Isaiah (1 — 39)
   e. Micah
5. The Day of the Lord — Judgment 259
   a. Obadiah and Joel
   b. Amos
   c. Isaiah (1 — 39)
   d. Micah
6. The Messiah and the Messianic Kingdom 267
   a. Obadiah and Joel — The Dawn of Messianic Understanding
   b. Hosea's Messianic Understanding
   c. Amos — Messianism
   d. Isaiah (1 — 39) — The Messiah and His Kingship
   e. Micah — Messianism
7. The Latter Days — Prophetic Eschatology 274
   a. Restoration of Israel
   b. God's Redemption and Salvation
   c. Outpouring of the Holy Spirit
8. Life of the People of God. 284
   a. Joel — Call to Godly Living
   b. Jonah — Living in the Fear of the Lord
   c. Hosea — Holy Living in Reverse
   d. Amos — Unholy Living Condemned
   e. Isaiah (1 — 39) — Holy Living: Positive and Negative
   f. Micah — Godly Living in All Areas of Life
9. Nature of Sin and Man's Sinfulness 289
   a. Obadiah and Joel

     b. Hosea and Amos
     c. Isaiah and Micah
  10. Repentance, Faith, and Regeneration 293
     a. Joel's Call to Repentance
     b. Hosea's Teaching on Repentance, Faith, and Regeneration
     c. Amos's Call to Repentance
     d. Jonah's Witness to Repentance
     e. Isaiah's Teaching (1 — 39) on Repentance, Faith, and
       Regeneration
     f. Micah's Message of Repentance, Faith, and Regeneration
  11. Death and Sheol 299
VI. THEOLOGY OF ISAIAH (40 — 66) 304
  1. Introduction 304
  2. The God of Israel: His Nature 304
     a. The Sovereign Majesty of God
     b. God, the Holy One and Redeemer of Israel
     c. The God of Righteousness and Salvation
     d. The God of Love and Mercy
     e. The God of Judgment
     f. The God of History
     g. The God of Creation
  3. The Spoken and Written Word of God 313
  4. Israel the Chosen People and Servant of the Lord 315
     a. Problem of Interpreting the Servant of the Lord
     b. The Servant Concept in Israel's Early History
     c. The Servant Passages Not Quoted in the New Testament
     d. The Servant Who Shall Bear the Sin of Many
  5. The Messiah and the Messianic Kingdom 320
     a. Relating the Servant of the Lord Passages to the
       Messianic Idea
     b. New Testament Guidelines for Determining the Messianic
       Reference to the Servant of the Lord
  6. Eschatological Viewpoint of Isaiah 40 — 66 322
     a. Introduction
     b. "The Former Things" and "The Things to Come"
     c. The New Exodus: Israel's Restoration to Their Land
     d. Future Glory of Zion
VII. THEOLOGY OF THE PROPHETS OF THE CHALDEAN
    PERIOD, 625-586 B.C. 329
  1. The God of Israel 329
     a. Nahum
     b. Zephaniah
     c. Habakkuk
     d. Jeremiah
       (1) Implicit Monotheism
       (2) God the Creator
       (3) The God of Love and Mercy
       (4) The God of Righteousness and Justice
       (5) The God Who Knows All Things
       (6) The God of Power and Might

(7) The God Who Tries the Hearts
(8) The God Who Acts in History
(9) The God of Salvation
2. The Spoken and Written Word of God 336
   a. Nahum, Zephaniah, and Habakkuk
   b. Jeremiah
3. Israel's Election Actualized by Covenant Relation with God 337
4. The Messiah and the Messianic Kingdom 339
5. The Day of the Lord — Judgment 340
6. The Latter Days — Prophetic Eschatology 342
7. Life of the People of God 344
8. Nature of Sin and Man's Sinfulness 345
   a. Nahum
   b. Zephaniah
   c. Habakkuk
   d. Jeremiah
9. Repentance, Faith, and Regeneration 349
   a. Zephaniah
   b. Habakkuk
   c. Jeremiah

VIII. THEOLOGY OF THE PROPHETS OF THE BABYLONIAN
EXILE, 602-534 B.C. 353

1. Introduction 353
2. The God of Israel 354
   a. The Sovereign and Glorious Majesty of God
   b. The Living God
   c. God, the Holy One of Israel
   d. The God of Love and Mercy
   e. The God Who Judges Righteously
   f. The God Who Acts in History
   g. The God of Salvation
   h. Worship of God
   i. The Spirit of God
3. God's Revelation, the Spoken and Written Word 371
4. Israel's Election Actualized by Covenant Relation with God 373
5. The Messiah and the Messianic Kingdom 374
   a. Ezekiel's Messianic Visions
   b. Daniel, Interpreter of Messianic Dreams
6. The Day of the Lord — Judgment 377
7. The Latter Days — Prophetic Eschatology 378
   a. Ezekiel's Visions of the Latter Days
   b. Daniel's Disclosure of the Latter Days
8. Life of the People of God 383
9. Nature of Sin — Man's Sinfulness 384
   a. Ezekiel's Exposure of Sin
   b. Daniel's Understanding of Sin
10. Repentance, Faith, and Regeneration 386
   a. Ezekiel's Teaching on Spiritual Renewal
   b. Daniel's Direction of the Way to Repentance

IX. THEOLOGY OF THE PROPHETS OF THE PERSIAN
    PERIOD, 520-c.450 B.C. 390
    1. The God of History 390
        a. Haggai
        b. Zechariah
        c. Malachi
    2. The Spoken and Written Word of God 392
    3. Israel's Election Actualized by Covenant Relation with God 393
    4. The Messiah and the Messianic Kingdom 394
        a. The Forward Look of Haggai
        b. Zechariah's Messianic Predictions
        c. Malachi's Messenger of the Covenant
    5. The Day of the Lord — Judgment 399
    6. The Latter Days — Prophetic Eschatology 403
    7. Life of the People of God 403
    8. Nature of Sin — Man's Sinfulness 405
    9. Repentance, Faith, and Regeneration 406

PART THREE: THE HAGIOGRAPHA
I. THEOLOGY OF THE PSALMS 409
    1. Introduction 409
    2. Theological Aspects of Worship............................. 410
        a. The Soul's Thirst for God
        b. Praise and Thanksgiving
        c. Singing Praises to the Exalted and Enthroned Lord
        d. Prayer to the Lord
        e. Joy of Worship
        f. Living in the Presence of God
    3. The God of Israel 414
        a. The Sovereign Majesty of God Most High
        b. The Holiness and Righteousness of God
        c. The God of Love and Mercy
        d. The Goodness of God
        e. The God of Judgment
        f. The God of Creation
        g. The God of History
    4. God's Spoken and Written Word............................. 424
    5. Israel's Election Actualized by Covenant Relation with God 425
    6. The Day of the Lord — Judgment 425
    7. The Messiah and His Work 426
        a. Introduction
        b. The Suffering Messiah
        c. Rule of the Anointed One
    8. Restoration, Redemption, and Salvation of Israel 430
        a. Frequent Occurrences of Salvation Language
        b. Psalms of Spiritual Restoration and Deliverance
    9. Life of the People of God 432
        a. Ethical Ideals
        b. Some Vocabulary for the Ethically Good
        c. Trusting God in Life's Varied Experiences

10. Nature of Sin and Man's Sinfulness 434
11. Repentance, Faith, and Regeneration 435
12. Individual Eschatology 437
    a. Ideas of Death
    b. State of the Wicked Dead
    c. State of the Righteous Dead
13. Imprecatory Psalms 438
II. PROVERBS, ECCLESIASTES, SONG OF SONGS 442
1. The Proverbs 442
    a. Introduction
    b. Meaning of Wisdom
    c. Fear of the Lord
    d. The Proverbs, Foundation for New Testament Ethics
    e. Life Beyond the Grave
2. Ecclesiastes 446
    a. Introduction
    b. Voice of Experience — All Is Vanity
    c. Values of Wisdom
    d. Wholesome Advice
    e. Value of Ecclesiastes in the Perspective of Biblical Theology
3. The Song of Songs 451
    a. Introduction
    b. Theological Import of the Book
III. THE BOOK OF JOB 454
1. Introduction 454
2. Dramatic Presentation of the Story 455
3. The Book of Job — A Disclosure of Divine Providence 456

SELECTED BIBLIOGRAPHY 459

INDEX OF BIBLICAL REFERENCES 463

INDEX OF SUBJECTS 478

CHAPTER I
NATURE AND METHOD OF BIBLICAL THEOLOGY

1. Formative Ideas of Biblical Theology

"In many and various ways God spoke of old to our fathers by the prophets; but in these last days he has spoken to us by a Son, whom he appointed the heir of all things, through whom also he created the world" (Heb. 1:1). With these words the writer of the letter to the Hebrews expressed in brief yet most fundamental and significant language a primary concept of the formative ideas and structural pattern of biblical theology. The words "God spoke" lead to the very heart of this discipline. The writer hereby gave witness to the most stupendous fact of all human history. God spoke to mankind. And, further, it was by the prophets through whom God spoke. By this restrictive statement it becomes clear that God did not speak just to any one but rather to a chosen group of His servants called prophets.

In Old Testament history these prophets were the mouthpieces of God. In the most apropos times they spoke God's word to the people. These messages came in many parts and in many ways. This suggests that He used the most significant ways and means of communication to His people. The climactic manner of God's speaking was by His Son. There is a definite progress from God's speaking through the prophet to His speaking through the Son. The form of language suggests that God not only spoke *by* His Son but also *in* His Son. This suggests the organic unity of all God's revelation whether given through the prophets or through the Son. A very important chronological aspect becomes apparent in His closing words. It was in *the last days* that God spoke by a Son. This reflects a grand eschatological view of God's revealing work. The prophets looked forward to an era beyond their time which they called *the latter days*. Through the coming of the Son, this prophetic period, the latter days, took its beginning.

These definitive ideas of God's revelation to man are voiced elsewhere in the New Testament. Jesus gave a new dimension to the spoken word of God when He said, "Everything written about me in the law

. . . and the prophets and the psalms must be fulfilled" (Lk. 24:44). Jesus hereby referred to the Old Testament in its entirety. In this way He gave witness to the grand unity, the unfolding character, and the forward look of the Old Testament. The most distinctive character of this body of writings was that they looked forward to the coming of Christ. This unique character of these writings becomes greatly accentuated in the claim that everything must be fulfilled. This cannot be predicated of any other body of writings.

Paul gave a similar testimony when he declared to the people at Antioch, "We bring you the good news that what God promised to the fathers, this he has fulfilled to us their children by raising Jesus" (Acts 13:32, 33). Thus all that the Old Testament Scriptures foretold of the coming One was very appropriately known as the good news, the gospel. In his letter to the Galatians (3:15-18) Paul gave some insight into the character of the Old Testament revelation, especially on the point of its structure. He brought the promises made to Abraham and the law into perspective by stating that the latter did not annul the former. The promises could not be broken because God gave them by covenant agreement. This covenant relation between God and His people obtained supreme importance throughout biblical history and on this account the two parts of the Bible, the Old and New Testaments (covenants) respectively, bear these titles. Paul affirmed the unique nature of the Bible by his use of the expressions *the holy scriptures* and *the sacred writings*. He maintained its distinctiveness by stating that "All scripture is inspired by God." This God-breathed Scripture possesses the most extraordinary values in being "profitable for teaching, for reproof, for correction, and for training in righteousness, that the man of God may be complete, equipped for every good work" (Rom. 1:1, 2; 2 Tim. 3:15-17).

Peter gave yet another insight as to the divine character of the prophetic Scriptures. He wrote, "No prophecy of scripture is a matter of one's own interpretation, because no prophecy ever came by the impulse of man, but men moved by the Holy Spirit spoke from God" (2 Pet. 1:20, 21). These words express two aspects of the Scriptures: the divine and the human. Men moved by the Holy Spirit spoke from God, and yet men spoke.[1]

Drawing together these formative ideas concerning the process of divine revelation, we note these points: (1) God spoke to man. This speaking of God to man was divine revelation. (2) The agent of this divine revelation was the Spirit of Christ, the Holy Spirit. (3) God's speech to mankind was limited to chosen individuals, most of whom were called prophets. Being called of God they spoke from God and for this reason they possessed special authority. (4) This revelation from God was not limited to only one disclosure or to words alone. It came in many parts and in various ways. (5) God's word pertained not only to man in his then present need. It has a forward look. It was a word of promise. Its very character was eschatological. As noted earlier, the prophets looked forward to a coming age, the *latter days*, in which God would bestow upon His people untold blessings of deliverance and salvation. (6) These divine revelations centered in the good news, the gospel, and pertained to the coming One, the Messiah, the Christ, who would rule in the kingdom of God. This distinctive characteristic of the Old Testament has no parallel in any other body of writings.

(7) The biblical revelation began in the Garden of Eden when God encountered Adam and Eve after their transgression. He spoke not only words of judgment and consolation but He also implanted a hope. He promised that He would put enmity between the serpent and the woman. He would send One who would bruise the head of the serpent. Hope was built on the promise. This gives the fundamental character of divine revelation. Throughout the entire Old Testament era God continued to give many promises upon which hope could be built. (8) God's revelations were vitally bound up with covenants which He made with His people. Through these sacred agreements God drew His people to Himself. His unfolding revelation further expounded the meaning of this covenant relationship. This covenant relationship became the fundamental connection between the Old Testament and the New Testament. (9) God's revelation was closely bound up with the nature and circumstance of human history. Thus God's promises to Abraham were in a different historical setting from that of giving the law.

(10) This divine revelation possesses two general characteristics, unity and progress. The unity is found in that whether the revelation was through the prophets or through Christ, in all of it God spoke. The progress is seen in the unfolding of divine revelation throughout the entire Bible and of its coming to a climax in Christ. Naturally it becomes one of the major tasks in the study of divine revelation to gain the proper sense of relationship between unity and progress in divine revelation. (11) There is need also for determining the relation between the spoken word of God as recorded in the Bible and the written word, the Bible itself. The words of God's spokesmen — the prophets, Christ, and the apostles — are words of God. The closely related idea of the written Word as being God-breathed and so in all verity the Holy Scriptures and the sacred writings, places the written Word in the same category as the spoken word.

(12) Finally, distinctive values are ascribed to the Holy Scriptures. They possess the dynamic for instructing one for salvation. They are profitable for teaching, for reproof, for correction, and for training in righteousness. With these values the man of God may be complete, equipped for every good work.

These twelve formative ideas constitute in the large the author's concept of biblical theology. Obviously they form a distinctive approach to this study. My reason for this approach is found in what I conceive to be the Bible's own claims pertaining to the nature of its contents. By the grace of God, I shall make a strenuous effort to give an exposition of the biblical view of divine revelation. With these formative ideas of divine revelation before us, the definition of biblical theology should now be possible.

2. Definition of Biblical Theology –– A Survey of Recent Approaches and Definitions

Biblical theology is that branch of biblical interpretation which deals with the revelation of God to men in the light of the revealing activity of God, the spiritual experiences of men to whom He spoke, and the character of the written Word. This definition of biblical theology holds to the fundamental ideas of such scholars as J. H. Titcomb, G. F. Oehler, Hermann Schultz, A. B. Davidson, Geerhardus Vos, E. J. Young, and J. B. Payne. Writing in 1871, Titcomb gave a significant title to his book: *Revelation in Progress from Adam to Malachi.* He looked at the Old Testament "as containing a series of gradual and progressive revelations, which, while given from the time of Adam to that of Malachi, under every variety of circumstance, were yet marked by an organic unity of purpose which historically culminated in Christianity, and in it alone found their true meaning and fulfillment."[2]

Oehler, in his monumental work, said: "Biblical theology has the task of exhibiting the religion of the Bible according to its progressive development and the variety of the forms in which it appears. The theology of the Old Testament has therefore to follow the gradual progress by which the Old Testament revelation advanced to the completion of salvation in Christ; and to bring into view from all sides the forms in which under the Old Covenant, the communion between God and man found expression."[3]

Hermann Schultz wrote, "Biblical theology (is) that branch of the theological science which gives a historical presentation of revealed religion during the period of its growth."[4]

Vos, to whose work I am most deeply indebted, wrote: "Biblical theology is that branch of exegetical theology which deals with the process of the self-revelation of God deposited in the Bible."[5] He also noted that "the inward, hidden content of God's mind can become the possession of man only through a voluntary disclosure on God's part. God must come to us before we can go to Him." Since it is impossible for the spirit of man to penetrate into the Spirit of God, it is necessary for God to open up to us the mystery of His nature before we can acquire any knowledge concerning Him. Vos gave four main aspects which determine the study of biblical theology: (1) The historic progressiveness of the revelation process, (2) The actual embodiment of revelation in history, (3) The organic nature of the historic process observable in revelation, and (4) The practical adaptability of revelation.[6]

E. J. Young and J. Barton Payne followed in the spirit of Vos. The latter defined biblical theology simply as "the biblical history of divine redemption."[7] To Payne, biblical theology was historical, divine, and redemptive. It derived its knowledge of the will of God from the Bible.

A. B. Davidson held that "Biblical theology is the knowledge of God's great operation in introducing His kingdom among men, presented to our view exactly as it lies presented in the Bible."[8] Elsewhere he noted that God's operation extended over long periods of time and culminated in the coming of God's Son. He emphasized that Old Testament theology is a historical science and that the presentation of the Old Testament religion in Old Testament theology is genetic. Its progress was organic. He held that Old Testament theology is a development. It is completed in New Testament theology.[9]

The past fifteen years have marked a very significant revival of study of biblical theology both of the Old Testament and the New. While most of these works represent some departure from the traditional, conservative viewpoint and movement in the direction of neoorthodoxy, the most significant advance is found in a new discovery of the unity of the Bible. Though understood differently by contemporary theologians, this is the grand truth to which conservative scholars have held all through the history of the study of biblical theology. A second characteristic of most modern biblical theologies centers in a lowering of the value of the written Word. While it seems evident that some students have overstated the claims of the Bible for itself, it is apparent that many modern scholars do not accept the Bible's claims for its origin and authority. Although these scholars pay a high tribute to the fact of God's revelation to man, it is to be regretted that the Bible's claims for itself are not fully recognized. The problem centers in an overemphasis of the human side of the origin and nature of the Scriptures to a corresponding neglect or rejection of the divine aspects of these matters.

A scholar of this class is Edmond Jacob, professor of the University
of Strasbourg. "The theology of the Old Testament," said Jacob, "may
be defined as the systematic account of the specific religious ideas
which can be found throughout the Old Testament and which form its
profound unity."[10] The viewpoint of Jacob becomes clear when he says
that within the Old Testament itself it is already possible to speak of
theology. The Old Testament counts among its authors several real
theologians. By this he would have us understand that "a theology of
the Old Testament should be able to draw inspiration from those
theologians in such a way as not to fit the Old Testament into a modern
scheme or explain it according to a dialectic which is fundamentally
foreign to it."[11] The author noted further that the New Testament, too,
is the theology of the Old Testament, for its essential purpose is to show
that Jesus of Nazareth is the Christ, the Messiah promised to Israel
to whom all Scripture bears witness. Jacob insists that a theology of
the Old Testament which is founded on the Old Testament as a whole
can only be a Christology. What was revealed under the old covenant
through a long and varied history in events, persons, and institutions,
is in Christ gathered together and brought to perfection. This idea is
based upon the principle of the unity of the two Testaments and *a
fortiori* on the internal unity of the Old Testament itself. His critical
view of the Old Testament itself is reflected briefly when he says,
"The unity of the Old Testament is in no way incompatible with what
critical and historical study has revealed about the very diverse elements
that have gone into its composition, for the collections of books and
traditions have not prevented the Old Testament from remaining as one
book and the expression of one religion. That is an objectice fact and
consequently justifiable from scientific study."[12]

George A. F. Knight gave a clue to his distinctive viewpoint by
entitling his book, *A Christian Theology of the Old Testament*. He
pointed out that the Old Testament is nothing less than Christian Scripture. That is, "A theology of the Old Testament must arise out of the
combined thinking of the whole church. The Old Testament is a Book
that must be read within the walls of the Christian church since the
'church has received the Old Testament from the hand of Jesus.' Therefore an exposition of the Old Testament cannot confine itself merely to
a critical and historical analysis either of its books or its teaching."[13]
Still further expressing his viewpoint, Knight said, "This *Christian
Theology of the Old Testament* is consequently an attempt to discover
and present the total meaning of the Old Testament. It does not attempt to analyze the progressive thought of Israel about God and
about God's mighty purposes. But it does seek to discover what the

Old Testament has to say to the twentieth century in the light of the Christian revelation as a whole."[14] [15]

3. Impact of Philosophical, Critical, and Theological Thought upon the Study of Biblical Theology

Biblical theology, like any other theological discipline, has been affected by existing types of thought. It lies beyond my purpose to give a history of this discipline, but it is essential to take a look at the development of biblical theology.[16] The term "biblical theology" was used first of a collection of proof texts that were adduced in support of the doctrines of the church. It stood over against the philosophical and theological presentation of systematic theology. The Pietists used the term, as Vos said, "to voice their protest against the hyperscholastic method in the treatment of dogmatics."[17] John Phillip Gabler first spoke of biblical theology as a historical science in his Altdorf inaugural oration in 1787, "Concerning the Correct Distinction Between Biblical and Dogmatic Theology." Gabler defined the work of biblical theology as tne statement of the "Religious Ideas of Scripture as an Historical Fact, so as to distinguish the different times and subjects, and so also the different stages in the development of these ideas."[18] While it was distinctly to his credit to see the need for a historical treatment of the Bible, it is necessary to observe that he was limited by his philosophical rationalism. Vos noted this when he said: "The chief characteristic of this school was its disrespect for history and tradition, and the corresponding worship of reason as the sole and sufficient source of religious knowledge. A distinction was drawn between (a) past beliefs and usages recorded in the Bible as a matter of history, and (b) what proved demonstrable by reason."[19] Rationalistic thought has continued to impose a negative influence upon the study of biblical theology.

In such a rationalistic environment, E. W. Hengstenberg was the first to exert a positive influence on the theological treatment of the Old Testament. In his extensive four-volume work, *Christology of the Old Testament*, with all of its one-sidedness, Hengstenberg "very distinctly aimed at finding all the fundamental New Testament doctrines not in the process of growth, but ready-made."[20] Another important figure in the development of biblical theology was Johann Christian Konrad von Hofmann, who wrote an important two-volume work in 1841-44 entitled *Prophecy and Fulfillment in the Old and New Testaments.* Hofmann belonged to the Erlangen school of theology. He originated the idea of the *Heilsgeschichte Theologie* (Theology of Redemption). Writing as a historian and theologian, he saw the manifestations of God's activity in history. He demonstrated that the progress of prophecy and of history bore a close relationship. He regarded the history of Israel as a related chain of actions that led up to and prepared for Jesus Christ. "In the holy and blessed man Jesus," he said, "the history of the relation of God and man has reached its preliminary consummation."[21]

The rise of the historical-religious school had far-reaching effects upon the study of biblical theology. Through the influence of Graff, Wellhausen, Gunkel, Kuenen, Wrede, Troeltsch, and many others, the theory of evolution was applied to the development of Israel's religion. Wellhausen, in particular, conceived of Israel's religion as beginning with Animism and passing through stages of Polytheism to Henotheism and finally to Monotheism, which stage was reached only in the days of the prophets of Israel. The Bible thus is a product of human, evolutionary development. It is to be viewed only as a history of religion without any revelation of God to this nation. Obviously, this reconstruction of Israel's history according to the pattern of evolutionary development runs diametrically opposite to the Bible's own representation of itself. While modern scholarship has greatly modified the Graff-Wellhausen critical view of the Old Testament, the general impact of this theory upon biblical theology still remains. This heightens our present responsibility to gain a correct view of the Bible's representation of its own origin.

A historicism dominated by the philosophy that miracles are impossible exerted a real tyranny over theological thought. Theological writings which support the Bible's record of the miraculous have had great difficulty in securing a hearing. It is highly gratifying that acceptance of the Bible's clear presentation of supernatural events in biblical history is again gaining ground. This is made possible in part by the evident historical sense and integrity of the biblical record itself. Historicism showed itself influenced more by philosophy than by plain historical evidence. Eichrodt stated the problem very clearly when he wrote of the rediscovery of the proper approach to our task: "This is no new problem, certainly, but is one that needs to be solved anew in every epoch of knowledge — the problem of how to understand the realm of Old Testament belief in its structural unity and how, by examining on the one hand its religious environment and on the other its essential coherence with New Testament, to illuminate its profoundest meaning. Only so shall we succeed in winning back for Old Testament studies in general and for Old Testament theology in particular that place in Christian theology which at present has been surrendered to the comparative study of religions."[22]

We move forward to consider Barth and the theology of crisis, otherwise known as neoorthodoxy. Undoubtedly, Barth holds the first place among theologians of the first half of the twentieth century. He was able to capture the attention both of liberalism and conservatism. For my purpose, Barth's concept of the Word of God is of prime importance. He distinguished three senses of the Word of God. The first and highest sense was the revealed Word or the Word that God spoke. This Word is Jesus Christ. The second was the written Word, the Bible, and the third was the preached Word. My present concern has to do with the first two of these senses. To Barth the revealed or spoken word of God is alone the Word of God. The written word cannot be called, in any proper sense, the Word of God with the same meaning as the revealed or spoken word. The written word possesses the character of the revealed or spoken word only when through the written word God encounters man. This is the existential aspect of Barth's thought which he gained from Kierkegaard. Barth emphasized that God has encountered man, not only the prophets but all men throughout human history. This gives a definitely subjective turn to his thought. The Bible does not give us full truth. The encounter of God with man becomes the channel of truth, according to his theology.

Barth's thought has several important implications for the study of biblical theology. First and foremost is the positive one of his recognition of the revealed or spoken word of God. Barth recognized that God spoke to man. God, the eternal, the absolute, the wholly other, encountered man. This encounter is a genuine human experience. This is the theology of crisis.

Second, Barth held that the center of theology is Christ, the superhistorical, not Jesus, the historical. For this reason Barth rejected the historicity of the fall of man. According to his thinking, it is a superhistorical verity. On this account historical facts are nothing more than parables and demonstrations of the divine.[23]

It is at once apparent that this viewpoint is devastating to the biblical presentation of sacred history. It becomes apparent that this viewpoint makes it well-nigh impossible for us to lay hold of the spoken word of God. The spoken word of God is learned only through the divine encounter and not through the written record of His Word. But how can we gain a knowledge of the Christ and of Jesus without a written word?

Third, the low value given to the written word, for all practical purposes, robs us of the historical basis of biblical theology. With full recognition of the problems with regard to the interpretation of the biblical record, the only valid approach to biblical theology is the recognition of the internal claims which the Bible makes for itself. If some historical claims are rejected, no basis remains for accepting as historical any recorded event in the Bible. In spite of the stature of Barth, he has failed to give recognition to the uniquely divine and hence accurate character of the written word. This is not to ignore the place of critical studies of the Bible. Both lower criticism and higher criticism have a valid function in spite of the devastating effects of negative criticism.

Fourth, the recent developments of neoorthodox thought have given a commendable expression of the grand unity of the Bible. Scholars such as Baab, Eichrodt, Jacob, Knight, Vriezen, Rowley, and others are discovering that the Bible centers in Christ. The Old Testament looks forward to and prepares for the coming of Christ and the New Testament records the fulfillment of the Old. The use of the Old Testament by New Testament speakers or writers is being given very careful study. This has been the source of great enrichment of both Old Testament and New Testament biblical theology. There still remains the need of recognition by neoorthodox scholars of the biblical claim to inspiration.

Fifth, the serious implication for the study of biblical theology centers in *Form Criticism*. According to this viewpoint, oral tradition preceded the writing of the Bible. Early Old Testament history was preserved for centuries of time by oral tradition. The life and teachings of Christ were orally preserved in the church for several decades. The common outcome of this procedure is to maintain that the Old Testament contains much that is a backward projection of thought held when the historical books were written. In other words, the doctrinal content of the Pentateuch is the backward projection of the theological thought held by the prophets. The written teachings of Jesus represent the thought of the Apostolic Church at the time when the Gospels were actually written. While the general integrity of oral tradition is usually recognized, considerable freedom is taken to reject certain elements in the account which may not appeal to the student as being historical. In this way certain scholars reject all records of the supernatural. The most serious aspect of this question is seen in the rejection by some of the bodily resurrection of Jesus. These scholars fail to see that biblical writers followed a modern criterion for the writing of history, that of the validity of the testimony of eyewitnesses who are both competent and trustworthy. True indeed, the supernatural as depicted in the Bible lies beyond present human experience. But this does not make impossible the occurrence of supernatural events. When competent and honest witnesses bear testimony to the supernatural, we have adequate ground for their historicity.

4. Bearing of Pentateuchal Criticism on Old Testament Biblical Theology

It is now obviously necessary to pay some attention to the bearing of Pentateuchal criticism on our study. Students with the traditional viewpoint have held that the Pentateuch is Mosaic. This means that it is a product of the Mosaic era whether written by Moses or by others under his direction.[24]

In support of the composite character of the Hexateuch, Simpson[25] draws attention to parallel narratives and laws, inconsistencies within narratives and laws, and chronological difficulties. Following the documentary hypothesis developed by Graff and Wellhausen, he holds that the J[1] document appeared about 1000 B.C., produced by a writer whose interest was in Hebron. This was revised by J[2] about 950 in the interest of making an appeal to the people of the north after their rebellion against the House of David. The E document is much the same as J[2]. It was written about 700 and represents an attempted *rapprochement* between the north and the south. After the fall of Jerusalem in 586, another *rapprochement* was attempted through the conflating of J and E in which effort was made to preserve the salient features of each. The Deuteronomic Code was designed to provide authoritative guidance for the people of the north after the catastrophe of 722. It was accepted by the south after 586 and later combined with JE. The Priestly Code was drawn up by those who wished to make Jerusalem the religious center of Israel after the return from captivity. It was combined with JED forming the present Hexateuch (The Pentateuch plus Joshua), J.E.D.P.

The documentary theory is obviously the result of a painstaking application of literary criteria. But external evidence for this process is entirely lacking. Nowhere in the Pentateuch are we made aware of a compilation of J.E.D.P. with all the attending revisions, recensions, or editings. Neither is there any evidence in the remaining books of the Old Testament or in Jewish tradition or in the New Testament of any such growth of the Pentateuch. Not that such a growth is impossible but rather that it is a grand case of accounting for the present form and content of these books on the sole basis of stylistic criteria.

Our concern in this study is with the bearing of all this upon biblical theology. Were Adam, Noah, Abraham, and Jacob historical persons? Does the Pentateuch give authentic history? Did God reveal Himself in word and deed as recorded in the Pentateuch? Is the civil and ceremonial legislation of Exodus, Leviticus, and Numbers Mosaic? Was the tabernacle as described in Exodus actually erected as stated in Exodus 40:17-33?

Did Moses give the several addresses to Israel as recorded in Deuteronomy? These questions are crucial for the study of biblical theology. In general whoever had anything to do in producing the Pentateuch in its present form and content sought to give the impression that all of the above questions are to be answered in the affirmative. Negative answers would seem to attack the honesty of all who shared in the composition of these books. If internal claims of these books to historical validity are to be rejected, we have no scientific basis for accepting anything as genuine or authentic from these books.

Further, as to the amount or extent of oral tradition relating to earliest history, say from Adam to Noah, or from Abraham to Jacob, or the era of Moses, we have no information. We do know that there were ancient written documents such as the code of Hammurabi. But there is no record of any contemporary historical writings dealing with the materials of the Pentateuch. There are no data in the Pentateuch referring to oral tradition as the source of its contents.

A positive approach to the Pentateuchal problem may be made as follows: First, the external evidence based on the canon of the Old Testament speaks something to this question. The forming of the Hebrew canon of the Old Testament at about 250 B.C. expressed a concept of the special character of this body of writings. This can be maintained in spite of problems which have to do with the forming of the Old Testament canon. The attitude of Judaism, of Christ and the early church is expressed most compactly by Paul in the names "holy scriptures" (Rom. 1:2) and "sacred writings" (2 Tim. 3:15). These books are the only body of writings which in the language of New Testament writers or speakers can be properly labeled as coming into being through the guidance of the Holy Spirit, or as God speaking, or to which reference may be made in the words, "It is written." No external evidence exists as to how these books came into being. Our sole source of information is to be found in the books themselves.

Other external evidences for the origin of the Pentateuch are found in references to its contents in other books of the Bible. Beginning with Joshua and continuing through the books of the Kings, Chronicles, Ezra, Nehemiah, Daniel, Malachi, Matthew, Mark, Luke, John, Acts, Paul's Epistles, and Hebrews there are no less than forty references to the Pentateuch with the titles, "The Law of Moses," "The Book of the Law of Moses," "Book of Moses," and "Book of the Law of the Lord Given through Moses."[26] A number of these references do not give precisely the extent of the body of writings referred to. The nearest to the definitive idea of the content of these books is found in Luke 24:44, where Jesus referred to the threefold division of the Old

Testament. Since the Old Testament canon was then completed, the law of Moses evidently referred to the present Pentateuch. In most of the Old Testament quotations from the law of Moses, reference is specifically made to a statement from Deuteronomy. The frequency and character of the references to Adam, Noah, Abraham, Isaac, and Jacob would certainly indicate that Bible writers outside of the Pentateuch thought of these men as historical characters.

The testimony of archaeology is also very significant. Melvin Grove Kyle, who wrote more than thirty years ago, emphasized these functions of archaeology in criticism.[27] First, archaeology furnishes the true historical setting of Scripture. Second, it gives guidance to the methods of criticism; and third, it supplies facts wherewith to test theories. On the last point he added that there can be no real antagonism between the facts of archaeology and a correct literary criticism of trustworthy documents. The continuing studies of Albright, Wright, Thompson, Free, and others confirm the testimony of Kyle. The almost limitless evidence from archaeology completely confirms the historicity of the Pentateuchal contents. The value of this for biblical theology becomes apparent. Since the Pentateuch gives authentic history, we may believe that God revealed Himself in this era. Israel's God is "God who acts."[28]

By way of conclusion, external evidence with regard to the origin and nature of the Pentateuch gives solid support to the internal evidences which we shall presently note. There are no disturbing factors from such areas as the canon and text of the Old Testament, literary criticism, biblical references to the Pentateuch outside of this body of writing, nor from archaeology. We are in position to survey the internal evidence and with confidence believe this testimony or witness. The historical character of the Pentateuch becomes evident in every narrative. These marvelous stories are presented in true historical fashion. There is complete absence of myth or folklore pattern, allegorical or parabolic style. The narratives deeply root themselves in temporal, historical, geographical, economic, and cultural data. For instance, the details of the patriarchs and of the wilderness wanderings are told in the language of an eyewitness. The historical events and the law constitute so many marks and tokens of Israel's life and journey in the wilderness. They dwelt in tents. They built a tabernacle and instituted a mode of worship. All along the way the entrance to Canaan was in prospect. The addresses of Moses in Deuteronomy appropriately came at the close of his life and anticipated Israel's early entrance into the land of promise.

With respect to the indications of authorship in the Pentateuch, we must note to begin with the complete absence of any claim to authorship covering the entire Pentateuch. The viewpoint of the writer or writers is one of anticipation and preparation for entrance to Canaan. The writer does not identify himself. He refers to Moses speaking and writing the definite portions ascribed to Moses.[29] The writer represents Moses as speaking seven-eighths of Exodus and on through Deuteronomy. Moses was certainly fitted to write. In the language of Stephen, "[He] was instructed in all the wisdom of the Egyptians, and he was mighty in his words and deeds" (Acts 7:22). The most natural explanation of authorship is that one closely associated with Moses wrote under his direction and guidance. The nature of the entire narrative is that of a fellow wanderer through the wilderness. Evidence of embedded documents need not affect this view of authorship. It would seem that any view of the origin of these embedded documents which would reject their being written by competent and trustworthy recorders of oral tradition or by eyewitnesses of the events must be ruled out. It is evident that post-Mosaic materials are found in the Pentateuch. With the overwhelming evidence both external and internal for the historicity of these narratives, we can leave such matters as revisions or recensions of the original writings to further study and exploration. It does not lie beyond the possibility that manuscripts may yet be discovered which far antedate our present oldest copies of the Pentateuch. I therefore feel free to study the form and content, the nature and mode of God's revelation without dealing further with the question of embedded documents.

5. Relation of Biblical Theology to Other Theological Disciplines

Another step in orientation takes into consideration the relation of biblical theology to other closely related disciplines. It is common practice to think of four major classes of theological disciplines: first, biblical studies, often called exegetical theology; second, theological studies, including systematic theology, history of Christian thought, philosophy of religion, and sociology of religion; third, historical studies, including courses in church history; and fourth, practical studies, usually including courses in Christian education, practical theology, missions, and church music.

Biblical theology is the crowning work of the first main division, biblical studies. The subject matter of biblical studies naturally falls into four main classes. The first main class embraces foundation studies which support the historicity of the Bible. It includes courses in Bible geography, history of contemporary nations which affected Israel's history, biblical archaeology, and studies of the religion of peoples among whom Israel lived.

The second subdivision of biblical studies comprises biblical languages and biblical criticism including also biblical hermeneutics. In the area of biblical criticism we have studies of the canon of the Scripture, which relates to the books which make up the body of Scripture; the text, which seeks to determine the correct text of Scriptures; and literary criticism, which involves matters of authorship, date, and literary character of the books of the Bible. Biblical hermeneutics has to do with the science of interpretation. It includes all that must be considered when we reproduce in our own minds the thoughts of the writer as he recorded his thoughts in written language.

Biblical history may very properly mark off a third division of biblical study. Biblical history according to John D. Davis "is the record of that series of events which form the basis of the religion of the Bible."[30] This concept of biblical history is the natural stepping-stone to the proper concept of biblical theology. Among that "series of events which form the basis for the religion of the Bible" are the revealed words and acts of God. Biblical theology studies God's revelation in the setting of biblical history. It is concerned with the form, mode, content, and historical setting of this divine revelation.

It is essential to make clear the relation of biblical theology and systematic theology. A bit of confusion exists in the use of these two expressions. The use of the term "biblical theology" might imply that systematic theology is not biblical. Systematic theology by its very nature is biblical, but the approach to this discipline is different from that of biblical theology. Both of the disciplines deal with the same biblical materials. Biblical theology examines the process of the unfolding of God's Word to man. It is concerned with the mode, the process, the progress, and content of divine revelation. Systematic theology, on the other hand, looks at the total revelation of God, seeks to systematize these teachings, and to give a logical presentation of them in doctrinal form.

Thus by way of example, biblical theology studies the unfolding of divine revelation concerning the covenants recorded in the Bible. In this approach the covenants made with Noah, Abraham, Moses, and by Christ will be studied in their respective historical settings. The nature, content, and distinctive features of each are noted. On the other hand, systematic theology presents the total idea of God's covenant relation with man as it culminated in Christ. The strands of thought found in all the covenants are bound together in one grand teaching concerning God's covenant relation with man. The involvement of this doctrinal content with other great theological teachings such as the atonement, Christ's kingship, and the Lord's Supper adds breadth and depth to the meaning of this doctrine.

It is necessary to add, however, that systematic theology is broader than that outlined above. It includes a careful analysis and criticism of the great systems of Christian doctrine which commonly have the labels of Lutheranism, Calvinism, Arminianism, Anabaptism, Liberalism, Fundamentalism, Neoorthodoxy, and the like.

6. Method of Biblical Theology

The final step by way of orientation is that of giving brief consideration to the method of biblical theology. Drawing from Vos's presentation,[31] the method of biblical theology is determined in the main by the principle of historic progression. Periods or eras of divine revelation are determined in strict agreement with the lines of cleavage drawn by revelation itself. It may be very properly stated that the Bible is, as it were, conscious of its own organic being. It is aware of its own anatomy. By this approach we discover that the most fundamental line of cleavage in divine revelation centers in the several covenants which God made with man. It is this principle that Walther Eichrodt laid hold of in his great work, *Theology of the Old Testament*. Volume I, Chapter II of this work has to do with "The Covenant Relationship." This lays the foundation for his entire work.

It will be my plan after giving attention to God's revelation in the Creation to consider individually and in order the covenants made by God with Noah, Abraham, Moses, and through Christ.[32] All the teaching centering in these covenants will be considered in relation to these several covenants.

Oehler also gave some instructive insights as to the method of biblical theology.[33] He stated that the method of biblical theology is *historical-genetic.* As a historical science, it rests on the results of grammatico-historical exegesis. This task, of course, must be pursued with proper attention to the principles of hermeneutics. We need to recognize the various forms in which revelation expresses its content and comprehend these forms as *parts of an organic process of development.* As noted earlier, Oehler also stressed the point that biblical theology must view the Old Testament in the light of the completed revelation of God in Christ for which it forms a preparation. It must show how God's saving purpose fulfilled in Christ moved through the preliminary stages of this history of revelation. He stressed that the genetic method seeks to reproduce the living process of the growth of the thing itself. This method refuses to find ripe fruit where only the bud exists. It aims to show how the fruit grew from the bud; it sketches the earlier stages in a way that makes it clear how the higher stages could, and necessarily did, spring from the former.[34]

For Additional Reading and Reference:

Baab, *Theology of the Old Testament*, pp. 7-22.
Buber, *The Revelation and the Covenant*, pp. 13-19.
Davidson, *The Theology of the Old Testament*, pp. 1-30.
Eichrodt, *The Theology of the Old Testament*, Vol. I, pp. 25-35, 512-20.
Elliott, *The Message of Genesis*, pp. 1-16.
Jacob, *Theology of the Old Testament*, pp. 11-35.
Knudson, *The Religious Teaching of the Old Testament*. pp. 17-45.
Mowinckel, *The Old Testament as the Word of God*, pp. 9-41.
Oehler, *Theology of the Old Testament*, pp. 5-47.
Payne, *The Theology of the Older Testament*, pp. 15-43.
von Rad, "Genesis," pp. 13-42.
    Old Testament Theology, Vol. I, pp. 105-28.
Raven, *The History of the Religion of Israel*, pp. 5-9.
Richardson, "Genesis," I-XI, pp. 11-40.
Ringgren, *Israelite Religion*, pp. 1-8.
Rowley, *The Old Testament and Modern Study*, pp. 1-83.
Schultz, *Old Testament Theology*, Vol. I, pp. 1-85.
Smart, *The Interpretation of Scripture*, pp. 232-304.
Vischer, *The Witness of the Old Testament to Christ*, Vol. I, pp. 7-36.
Vos, *Biblical Theology — Old and New Testaments*, pp. 11-36.
Vriezen, *An Outline of Old Testament Theology*, pp. 2-126.
Weidner, *Biblical Theology of the Old Testament*, pp. 17-34.
Young, *An Introduction to the Old Testament*, pp. 109-53.
————— , *The Study of Old Testament Theology Today*.
The International Standard Bible Encyclopedia:
    Volume I
    "Archaeology and Criticism," by M. G. Kyle.
    "The Bible," by James Orr, Sec. IV.
    "Biblical Theology," by James Lindsay, Sec. II.
    Volume II
    "Criticism of the Bible," by James Orr, Sec. II.
    "Criticism" (The Graff-Wellhausen Hypothesis), by
    Burton Scott Easton.
    "Genesis," by Wilhelm Moller, Secs. II, IV, V.
    "Exodus, The Book of," by Wilhelm Moller, Secs. I, II.
    "Deuteronomy," by George L. Robinson, Secs. 6, 8, 9.
    Volume III
    "Leviticus," by Wilhelm Moller, Secs. II, III.
    Volume IV.
    "Pentateuch," by Harold M. Wiener, Secs. II, IV.
    "Pentateuch, Problem of," by M. G. Kyle.
Allis, *The Five Books of Moses*.
The Interpreter's Bible, Vol. I:
    "The Literature of the Old Testament," by William A. Irwin,
    pp. 175-84.
    "The Growth of the Hexateuch," by Cuthbert A. Simpson,
    pp. 185-200.

Davis-Gehman, *The Westminster Dictionary of the Bible*, "Pentateuch,"
pp. 465-70.
Douglas, *The New Bible Dictionary*, "Pentateuch," pp. 957-64.
Interpreter's Dictionary of the Bible (A-Do), pp. 418-37.

1. Of such importance are these definitive ideas relating to the nature of God's revelation that I am
appending a list of additional references which support and add to their significance: Gen. 12:1-3; 17:
1-8; Ex. 3:2-6; 6:2-4; Josh. 1:1-8; 8:30-35; Ps. 119; Is. 1:1; 6:1-5; Jer. 1:4-10; 31:31-34; 36:1-8; Mt. 5:
17-20; 26:54; Mk. 7:6, 10; 12:36, 37; Lk. 2:55; 16:16, 17; 18:31-33; 22:37; Jn. 1:1-18; 5:39; 12:37-50; Acts
3:17-26; 4:25; 28:23-25; Rom. 1:16, 17; 3:2, 4; 15:1-6; 16:25-27; 1 Cor. 10:1-11; 2 Cor. 3:4-18; Heb. 3:7;
4:1-13; 8:5-13; 10:15-18; 1 Pet. 1:10-12; Rev. 1:1-3.
2. Rev. J. H. Titcomb, *Revelation in Progress from Adam to Malachi, A Series in Bible Studies*
(London: The Religious Tract Society, 1871), p. 10.
3. Dr. Gustav Friedrich Oehler, *Theology of the Old Testament*, revised by George E. Day (New
York: Funk and Wagnalls Co., 1870), p. 5.
4. *Old Testament Theology* (Edinburgh: T. & T. Clark, 1892), Vol. I, pp. 1, 2.
5. Geerhardus Vos, *Biblical Theology, Old and New Testaments* (Grand Rapids: Wm. B. Eerdmans
Publishing Co., 1948), p. 13.
6. *Ibid.*, pp. 14-17.
7. J. Barton Payne, *The Theology of the Older Testament* (Grand Rapids: Zondervan Publishing
House, 1962), p. 17.
8. A. B. Davidson, *The Theology of the Old Testament* (Edinburgh: T. & T. Clark, 1904), p. 1.
9. *Ibid.*, pp. 2, 10.
10. Edmond Jacob, *Theology of the Old Testament*, translated by Arthur Heathcote and Phillip
Allcock (New York: Harper and Brothers, Publishers, 1958), p. 11.
11. *Ibid.*, p. 12.
12. *Ibid.*, pp. 12, 13.
13. George E. F. Knight, *A Christian Theology of the Old Testament* (Richmond: John Knox Press,
1959), p. 7.
14. *Ibid.*, p. 10.
15. For the distinctive viewpoints of other scholars in this class see: Baab, *The Theology of the Old
Testament*, pp. 7-9. Eichrodt, *Theology of the Old Testament*, Vol. I. pp. 13-16. Jacob, *Theology of the
Old Testament*, pp. 27-33. Vriezen, *An Outline of Old Testament Theology*, pp. 9, 10, 12-29.
16. For other presentations of the history of biblical theology as a theological discipline see: Oehler,
Old Testament Theology, pp. 22-41. Jacob, *Theology of the Old Testament*, pp. 11-26. Eichrodt, *Theology
of the Old Testament*. Vol. I, pp. 28-35. Payne, *The Theology of the Older Testament*, pp. 25-43.
Betz, *Interpreter's Dictionary of the Bible*, Vol. A-D, "History of Biblical Theology," pp. 432-37.
17. *Ibid.*, p. 17.
18. Oehler, *ibid.*, p. 33.
19. *Ibid.*, p. 18.
20. Oehler, *ibid.*, p. 37.
21. Quotation by J. L. Neve, *A History of Christian Thought* (Philadelphia: The Muhlenberg Press,
1946), Vol. II, p. 133.
22. *Theology of the Old Testament* (Philadelphia: The Westminster Press, 1961, translated by J. A.
Baker), Vol. I, p. 31.
23. *Op. cit.*, p. 175.
24. Able presentations of the traditional viewpoint are found in the I.S.B.E. See articles on the
Pentateuch by Harold M. Wiener and Melvin Grove Kyle. Dr. Oswald T. Allis, representing the old
Princeton Seminary viewpoint, has written an able volume, *The Five Books of Moses*. After studying
again the viewpoints expressed by these works and comparing them with those of modern scholars such
as Pfeiffer and the authors of articles in the *Interpreter's Bible* I feel that there is still a great deal
to be said in favor of the traditional viewpoint. I shall enlarge on what appears to be the abiding truth
in the traditional viewpoint in a later paragraph.
25. The modern viewpoint is expressed by Dr. Cuthbert A. Simpson in "The Growth of the
Hexateuch," in Volume I of the *Interpreter's Bible*.
26. See Josh. 1:7; 8:31; 1 Kings 2:3; 8:53; 2 Kings 14:6; 21:8; 23:25; 1 Chron. 6:49; 22:13; 2 Chron.
8:13; 23:18; 25:4; 30:16; 33:8; 34:14; 35:12; Ezra 6:18; 7:6; Neh. 1:7, 8; 3:1, 14; 9:13, 14; 10:29; 13:1;
Dan. 9:11, 13; Mal. 4:4; Mk. 12:19, 26; Lk. 20:28; 24:27, 44; Jn. 1:45; 5:46; 7:19, 22, 23; 8:5; Acts 3:22;
28:23; 1 Cor. 9:9; 2 Cor. 3:15; Heb. 9:19; 10:28.
27. See "Archaeology and Criticism" in I.S.B.E., Vol. I, pp. 226 ff.

28. This is the title of Studies in Biblical Theology No. 8 by G. Ernest Wright.
29. See Ex. 17:14; 24:4; 34:27; Num. 33:2; Deut. 31:9, 22.
30. *The Westminster Dictionary of the Bible*, "History" (Philadelphia: The Westminster Press), p. 248.
31. *Op. cit.*, p. 25.
32. The covenant made through Christ will be treated in my *Theology of the New Testament*.
33. *Op. cit.*, pp. 41, 42.
34. Other works which to a certain extent follow this pattern are those of Schultz, Heinisch-Heidt, Ludwig Köhler, Knight, Eichrodt, and von Rad.

CHAPTER II
GOD'S REVELATION IN THE CREATION AND IN THE FALL OF MAN

1. Introduction

Perhaps the first impression one receives in studying the biblical account of the Creation is that here is an exceedingly simple and at the same time a very profound and meaningful account of creation. One fairly staggers with amazement and awe at the unfathomable truths here recorded. And yet a child reads it with much profit.

The pure monotheism of the record is most significant. It has no background or source in Mesopotamian polytheistic creation stories. Close study of polytheistic creation stories should convince us that the biblical record is not a refinement or purification of these polytheistic accounts into one of monotheism, but rather that the Bible preserves the original and true tradition of creation and that all others are degenerate forms of this tradition.

The rich and concentrated doctrinal content of the first two chapters of Genesis requires special notice. As we shall note presently, unfathomable teachings meet us in almost every verse. Among these are the teachings concerning God, the Creation, light and darkness, the firmament, day, vegetation, animals, man in the likeness and image of God, male and female, God's rest, the tree of life, and the tree of the knowledge of good and evil.

We should note also that the Creation is perhaps the theme most frequently referred to in the entire Bible. It shall be my purpose at the proper place to examine some of these teachings as they explain further or throw light on the meaning of the Genesis account. Wherein biblical writers unfold this truth further than that found in the Genesis record, these teachings shall be reserved for study at the proper places throughout this work.

We need to observe that man did not witness God's creative activity but that in some way God revealed to man His work of creation. The viewpoint may be best described by the word "phenomenal," i.e., the account is given as it would appear to man who sees God performing His creative work. The problem of whether or not there is any figurative language in this record is a very real one. The terms "myth" and "parable" have been used to describe much of the language of these first two chapters. While these two terms (when properly defined) may express elements of truth, they possess the liability of discrediting the historical character of the creation account. At the same time we need to recognize an outstanding characteristic of the Hebrew language. It was pictorial. Almost all verbs of the Hebrew language are pictures of actions. On this account the interpreter needs to sense correctly the true meaning of the language. He needs to grasp the picture painted by the author. He must reproduce in his mind the thoughts which the writers intended to convey. He must seek to discern aright what is literal and what is presented in picture form. Only where this is done conscientiously and with an open mind can he gain confidence in having rightly divided the word of truth.

Many students of Genesis have come to the conclusion that chapters 1 and 2 present two accounts of creation, the first covering Genesis 1:1 — 2:3, and the second 2:4-25. The writer of Genesis gave no intimation of having done so. This viewpoint has its basis in a literary analysis of the Book of Genesis as a whole and of these two chapters in particular. If two documents are embedded in this account, the writer saw no contradiction between them but rather a grand unity. A clear monotheism is found in both parts. Both accounts describe the same creation. The creative activity of God is the same in both-parts of the narrative. This does not ignore some difficulties which arise in efforts to harmonize some of the details. For instance, the creative work of chapter 2 discloses a different purpose and follows a divergent pattern from that of chapter 1. This becomes evident as one lists the creative acts of chapter 2 alongside those of chapter 1. It is my conviction that these difficulties of harmonization have been overworked by many students. It would seem that a safer course to follow is to search for the grand harmony and unity which obtains in these two chapters. When this becomes clear, the details of harmonization dwindle in size proportionately.

2. God the Creator

The opening words of the Book of Genesis are exceedingly arresting. We read, "In the beginning God created the heavens and the earth." These words declare the theocentric character of the creation account. The author ascribed creative work to God alone. It is noteworthy that the writer always placed God as the subject of the verb "create" (*bara*). The work of creation is thus distinctly a work of God. In the two chapters on the Creation the author concentrated on what God did. There are fully fifty instances in these two chapters where God is the subject of verbs showing what He did in the way of creation. Thus God created, God said, God called, The Lord God made, God saw, He rested, God hallowed, The Lord God formed, The Lord God planted, The Lord God commanded, The Lord God called, and did much more.

In a very real way the God of Genesis 1 and 2 is the God who acts.

The author portrayed God as alone the uncreated being. His One-ness is self-evident and is everywhere apparent. There is no rival God. The account shows His absolute lordship and sovereignty.

Throughout the narrative a radical distinction is made between God and His creation. It is equally clear that the created universe is not an emanation from God. Very plainly He transcends His creation.

It is noteworthy to observe the frequency with which other bibli-cal writers refer to, add some comment on, draw some lesson from, or base a warning on the creation account. For these reasons I am giving a great deal of space to these creation references. The following in-stances are especially worthy of careful study.

Moses in the first of his closing messages to Israel (Deut. 4:32-35) raised some pertinent questions with regard to "the day that God created man upon the earth." He asked, "Did any people ever hear the voice of a god speaking out of the midst of a fire?" and again, "Has any god attempted to go and take a nation for himself from the midst of another nation by trials, by signs, by wonders, and by war, by a mighty hand and an outstretched arm, and by great terrors?" The obvious answer to these questions is, "To you it was shown that you might know that the Lord is God; there is no other beside him." In this way Moses affirmed the Oneness of God who without rival is the absolute Lord of the universe. The author of Job presented by dramatic references to God's creative power the Lord's answer to the perplexities of Job. God asked, "Where were you when I laid the foundation of the earth? . . . Who determined its measurements . . . or who stretched the line upon it? On what were its bases sunk, or who laid its cornerstone, when the morning stars sang together, and all the sons of God shouted for joy" (Job 38:4-7)? These and similar questions proved the glory and majesty of God, the Creator.

The psalmists in beautiful poetic language made reference to God's creative work. Here are a few choice allusions:

> "When I look at thy heavens, the work of thy fingers, the moon and the stars which thou hast established" (8:3); "The heavens are telling the glory of God; and the firmament proclaims his handiwork" (19:1); "By the word of the Lord the heavens were made, and all their host by the breath of his mouth. He gathered the waters of the sea as in a bottle; he put the deeps in store-houses" (33:6, 7).

This poetic description of God's work of Creation is prefaced in verse 5 by words which express very clearly the character of God as revealed in creation. It reads, "He loves righteousness and justice; the earth is full of the steadfast love of the Lord."

Similarly, in 89:2-18, where a poetic description of God's creation is given the psalmist referred to God's steadfast love, His faithfulness, His righteousness, His justice. In Psalm 104, the matchless hymn of Creation, the psalmist displayed the manifold works of God. He exclaimed, "In wisdom hast thou made them all" (v. 24b). He ascribed their creation to the Spirit, whom He sent forth (v. 30).

Psalm 136 drew attention to the character of God as displayed in the Creation as well as in other mighty works. The worshiper should give thanks to God, "for he is good," "for his steadfast love endures for ever" (v. 1). In verses 5-8 the psalmist gave details of God's creation which reflect the Genesis 1 account. The writer of Psalm 148 bids every part of God's creation, the sun, the moon, the shining stars, to praise the name of the Lord, "for he commanded and they were created." In this sublime way the psalmist leads us to see the worthiness of God to receive praise and glory for His creation.

When King Hezekiah was confronted with Sennacherib's defiance and threat, he appealed to God, enthroned above the cherubim, the One who as God alone "hast made heaven and earth" (Is. 37:13-16).

In the prophet's message of comfort to the people of God, he described God's might and power in cosmic operation. God can be likened to no one. He created the heavens. The highest reach of the prophet's eloquence found expression in the words, "The Lord is the everlasting God, the Creator of the ends of the earth." By reason of the power manifested in creation, "They who wait for the Lord shall renew their strength, they shall mount up with wings like eagles, they shall run and not be weary, they shall walk and not faint" (40:28, 31).

In the first of the great *Servant of the Lord* passages (42:1-9) God's predictions through the prophet were effectual because it was He "who created the heavens and stretched them out, who spread forth the earth and what comes from it, who gives breath to the people upon it and spirit to those who walk in it" (42:5). In His message through Isaiah to the heathen monarch, Cyrus, God declared His power as manifested in creation (Is. 45):

I am the Lord, and there is no other (v. 5),
I form light and create darkness (v. 7).
I made the earth,
 and created man upon it;
it was my hands that stretched out the heavens,
 and I commanded all their host (v. 12).
For thus says the Lord,
who created the heavens
 (he is God!),

who formed the earth and made it
  (he established it;
he did not create it a chaos,
  he formed it to be inhabited!) (v. 18).

The Lord directed Jeremiah to tell Zedekiah in his predicament: "It is I who by my great power and my outstretched arm have made the earth, with the men and animals that are on the earth, and I give it to whomever it seems right to me" (Jer. 27:5). In the promised new covenant context the most significant facts of astronomy stand out:

Thus says the Lord,
who gives the sun for light by day
  and the fixed order of the moon
    and the stars for light by night,
who stirs up the sea so that its waves roar —
  the Lord of hosts is his name:
"If this fixed order departs
  from before me, says the Lord,
then shall the descendants of Israel cease
  from being a nation before me for ever."
Thus says the Lord:
"If the heavens above can be measured,
  and the foundations of the earth below
    can be explored,
then I will cast off all the descendants of Israel
  for all that they have done, says the Lord." (Jer. 31:35-37)

The creative work of God served as the basis for warnings given by several of the minor prophets. Thus Amos forewarned sinners, "Prepare to meet your God, O Israel," on the basis of the greatness of God as Creator: "For lo, he who forms the mountains, and creates the wind, and declares to man what is his thought; who makes the morning darkness, and treads on the heights of the earth — the Lord, the God of hosts, is his name" (Amos 4:12, 13)! In a later exhortation Amos commanded the people to seek the Lord and live, declaring, "He who made the Pleiades and Orion, and turns deep darkness into the morning, and darkens the day into night, who calls for the waters of the sea, and pours them out upon the surface of the earth, the Lord is his name" (5:6-8).

In like manner Zechariah prefaced a message of warning with an echo of the Genesis account: "Thus says the Lord, who stretched out the heavens and founded the earth and formed the spirit of man within him" (12:1). As Malachi chided the people for their faithlessness one to another, he injected the pertinent question, "Has not one God created us" (2:10)? He exhorted God's people to be faithful one to another in view of God's having created them all. Hear Ezra speak: "Thou art the Lord, thou alone; thou hast made heaven, the heaven of heavens, with all their host, the earth and all that is on it, the seas and all that is in them; and thou preservest all of them; and the host of heaven worships thee" (Neh. 9:6). Note that Ezra injects the idea of God's preservation.

Turning to the New Testament, one is impressed with the frequency as well as the significance of the references to the Creation by Jesus and the apostles. Thus Jesus took His hearers back in time in such language as, "From the beginning of the creation which God created until now" (Mk. 13:19). Jesus based the indissolubility of marriage on words found in the creation account. He asked, "Have you not read that he who made them from the beginning made them male and female, and said, 'For this reason a man shall leave his father and mother and be joined to his wife, and the two shall become one'?" On the basis of their nature by creation Jesus observed, "So they are no longer two but one. What therefore God has joined together, let no man put asunder" (Mt. 19:4-6).

The Apostle John in a very significant reference to the Creation unfolded further what seems implicit in the Genesis account. His declaration, "In the beginning was the Word," suggests that some relation exists between the repeated expressions "God said" (Gen. 1) and "the Word," who was in the beginning. This thought gains greater weight when we read the psalmist's language, "By the word of the Lord the heavens were made, and all their host by the breath of his mouth" (Ps. 33:6-9). Moving with restraint in regard to the relation of the Genesis language, "God said," and John's language, "the Word," let us observe nevertheless the explicit language: "He was in the beginning with God; all things were made through him, and without him was not anything made that was made. In him was life, and the life was the light of men" (Jn. 1:1-4).

In like manner Paul ascribed the Creation to Jesus, "For in him all things were created, in heaven and on earth, visible and invisible, whether thrones or dominions or principalities or authorities — all things were created through him and for him" (Col. 1:16). Very significantly he added another truth in the words, "He is before all things, and in him all things hold together" (v. 17). In the way of pointing up the dignity of the Son the author of Hebrews wrote, "Through whom also he created the world" (Heb. 1:2). In the same context he ascribed to the Son the creative work described in Psalm 102:25-27, "Thou, Lord, didst found the earth in the beginning, and the heavens are the work of thy hands." It is very noteworthy that the author of Hebrews showed the place of faith with regard to our knowledge of the creation of the world, when he wrote, "By faith we understand that the world was created by the word of God, so that what is seen was made out of things which do not appear" (11:3). The author would have us understand that the act of creation involved one of the profoundest of mysteries, namely, that what is seen was made out of things which do not appear. By this he showed that belief in the creative work of God is not naive but has a firm assurance and conviction which rest securely on the Genesis account of what God said and accomplished. It remained for Christ Himself to give testimony to His work of creation as follows: "The words of the Amen, the faithful and true witness, the beginning of God's creation" (Rev. 3:14).

A unique way of referring to the Creation is found in the use of the word "foundation" (*katabole*). This conceives of the Creation as the laying down of a foundation to a house. Thus Christ spoke of the Father's love for Him "before the foundation of the world" (Jn. 17:24). In similar language Paul wrote how God chose us in Him before the foundation of the world. The writer of Hebrews gave a strong and forceful warning against those who refused to believe the Word of God when he wrote, " 'They shall never enter my rest,' although his works were finished from the foundation of the world." This warning is based on the fact that "God rested on the seventh day from all his works" (Heb. 4:3, 4). Perhaps the most significant use of the expression "the foundation of the world" occurs in the Revelation where reference is made to "every one whose name has not been written before the foundation of the world in the book of life of the Lamb that was slain" (13:8; see also 17:8).

3. God's Act of Creation

The definitive word used to describe God's acts of creation in Genesis 1 and 2 is *bara*.[1] This word possesses a breadth of meaning. It is used with reference to bringing all things into existence: the heaven, the earth, man (male and female), great sea monsters, every winged bird, etc. Its meaning is heightened by the fact that in all instances the word is used with reference to the origin of the world. God is its subject. From this we gather that the kind of activity expressed by *bara* is deity work. The Septuagint translators used the word *ktizo* (to create), as its nearest equivalent in the Greek language. The word *bara* is used as a parallel with *asah* (to make) (Gen. 1:26, 27; Is. 41:20; 45:18); with *yatsar* (to form) (Amos 4:13; Is. 43:1; 45:18); and with *kun* (to establish) (Is. 45:18; Ezek. 28:13). It is very instructive to observe that in Isaiah 45:18 four different verbs are used to describe God's acts of creation, "For thus says the Lord, who created [*bara*] the heavens (he is God!), who formed [*yatsar*] the earth and made [*asah*] it (he established [*kun*[it; he did not create [*bara*] it a chaos, he formed [*yatsar*] it to be inhabited!)" This shows that the verb "create" (*bara*) is similar in meaning to the words translated *formed, made, established.*

It is also profitable to observe the anthropomorphic language used in Genesis and elsewhere to describe God's creative work: *banah* (to build) Gen. 2:22; Amos 9:6); *yasad* (to found, to lay foundations)[2]; *qanah* (to make or to possess) (Gen. 14:19, 22; Deut. 32:6); and *kun* (to establish).[3] It should be observed that this anthropomorphic language does not destroy the idea of creation but rather enhances it. It is language that is entirely congruous with the most spiritual conception of God. It might yet be observed that the Septuagint translators used the verb *poieo* to translate *bara*[4] and *asah*.[5] The verb *poieo* used very frequently in the Septuagint and in the New Testament carries the meanings *make, produce, create,* and *cause.*

A concluding thought on the meaning of creation: prefacing every creative act in the Genesis 1 account, the words "God said" carry a very significant meaning. They suggest God's free and spontaneous action. God was not involved in a strenuous act of labor which would exhaust His powers; we see, rather, the ease of God's speaking the word and the creative act taking place. The Hebrew word *bara* (create), carries the same idea. Says von Rad, "Here is an idea of the absolute effortlessness of the divine creative action."[6] Very significantly, later writers used the same term, "and God said," to describe these acts.[7] They would have us note that at the word of God the universe came into being.

Throughout the Christian era Bible students have concerned themselves with the question whether or not God's creation was out of nothing (*creatio ex nihilo*). The author of Genesis did not concern himself with bringing this matter into sharp focus. True indeed, he used anthropomorphic language carrying the idea of making, building, laying foundations, forming, etc., but this language is not to be interpreted in a childish fashion. The verb *bara* (create) gives us the true lead as to the nature of the creative act. It is an act which God alone can perform. It stands in sharp contrast with the kinds of acts just named. God, the eternal God, the One who alone stands over against all finite existence, is the One who spoke the word and all things came into being. There is absolutely no sound exegetical basis for holding that the creation account merely presents God as fashioning the world out of already existing materials. The scholars who hold this idea are building an unwarranted structure on the word *void* (chaos). Verse 1 stands as a complete sentence. This statement declares that God brought into being the heavens and the earth which had not before existed even in a chaotic form. Verse 2 takes up the narrative which describes in detail God's creative work. It would seem that 1 Maccabees 7:28; Romans 4:17; and Hebrews 11:3 give clear support to this idea. It is the judgment of the author that those who interpret Genesis 1, 2 in the way of God's fashioning already existing materials out of a chaos are depending more upon pagan mythology than upon the ideas presented both in the Genesis account and in the later writings just mentioned.

The element of time involved in the creation account also requires study. At first thought the reader of Genesis 1 might conclude that we have here a record of six days of ordinary length involved in creation. Close study will show that an extremely literal view of the creation days presents some insurmountable problems. These problems center in the acts of creation on these several days. For instance, there are certain time involvements in such expressions as "Let the earth put forth vegetation" (v. 11), "the earth brought forth vegetation" (v. 12), "Let the waters bring forth swarms of living creatures" (v. 20), and "Let the earth bring forth living creatures according to their kinds" (v. 24). In addition to this the account of man's creation in chapter 2, as it stands in relation to the other parts of the creation narrative as well as its relation to the account in chapter 1, presents some real problems concerning the time elements in the Creation. We also need to be aware of the different senses given to the word "day" in these two chapters.[8] Another aspect of the time element is found in the manner in which the days are numbered. Thus we have: one day, a second day, a third day, a fourth day, a fifth day, and a sixth day. It should also be noted that this form of expression does not occur with the seventh day. With these considerations in mind we may be sensing the mind of the writer that he was not expressing precise twenty-four-hour days of creation as though his first concern was to present the time element but rather that he was using this form of expression to set forth the orderly method of creation as well as the greatness of the creative acts. There was an orderly progression in God's acts of creation.

We may be justified by bringing into the picture the time elements involved in geology and astronomy. These constitute God's world. We should expect that God's word and God's world do not stand in conflict but that a grand harmony exists between them. The rock strata and fossils both indicate great eras of time. In like manner we are told that it has required millions of years for light to travel from the most distant star to this planet. The bearing of all this upon our interpretation of the creation account is at once evident. There is need for giving as much recognition to what God's world reveals as to what God's word reveals. It is for these reasons that I have come to the conclusion that the author of Genesis did not intend the word "day" to be understood according to the usual meaning of this word. He would have us see the great creative acts of God standing out before us in all clearness, orderliness, and progress.

It should be noticed in passing that there is no sound exegetical basis for translating the verb *hayithah* (was) as *become* (Gen. 1:2). The verbs *to be* and *to become* stand out in Hebrew, Greek, and English as setting forth two distinct ideas. The verb *to be* points to persistence of being, while the verb *to become* has the idea of change from one thing to another. For this reason there is no justification for translating the verb *to be* as *to become*. No translation of this verb into any language gives any recognition for translating it otherwise. Those who have translated the verb *to become* have sought to find biblical evidence for the geological ages and on this account place a great gap between 1 and 2 of Genesis 1. The "gap" theory has no foundation either in this passage or anywhere else in the Scriptures. The Bible makes no reference to an earlier creation than what is recorded in chapters 1 and 2 of Genesis. Exodus 20:11 and 31:17 support this idea. We dare never make the Scriptures bend to help us out in an otherwise difficult problem. God's word properly interpreted and God's world properly understood do not stand in conflict even though we may not be able to explain all the problems to our complete satisfaction.

It lies beyond my purpose to enter into a detailed study of the acts of creation. In passing, a few perspectives might be noted. First, the initial statement that God created the heavens and the earth stands out with tremendous significance. We may conclude that the creation account is not geocentric. God created the heavens and the earth, the order of expression implying the subordinate position of the creation of the earth to that of the heavens. As we noted earlier, the creation account moves forward in an orderly fashion from vegetation to the lower animals, to the higher animals, and finally to man. The account very plainly depicts the high position of man in God's creation. All creation was made subject to man. Man exercises dominion over all the rest of creation. This position of man's dignity of his being created in the image of God, furnishes the true perspective in the interpretation of the creation account. We become aware also that certain fixed laws are found in the Creation, the most significant of which pertain to the heavenly bodies, through which we have the succession of seasons, days, and years. The biological factors bound up in the expression "according to its kind" also point to certain fixed laws instituted by God, the Creator.

4. Creation of Man

a. Man the Climax of Creation

The creation of man marks the climax of God's creative work. As von Rad says, "On the topmost step of this pyramid stands man, and there is nothing between him and God."[9] We begin to approach the reason for God's creating man when we observe that he was created in the image and likeness of God. It was given to him to have dominion over all the rest of God's creation. The reason for the creation of man becomes more evident when we observe that God breathed into his nostrils the breath of life and man became a living being. His life came from God. It was a life designed to be eternal in that by eating of the tree of life he would live forever. The dignity of man is further described in that he had a nature which, when he became morally mature, would enable him to know good from evil. Later revelation specifically states that God created man for His glory (Is. 43:7). It is for this reason that the psalmist could write, "Thou hast made him little less than God, and dost crown him with glory and honor. Thou hast given him dominion over the works of thy hands; thou hast put all things under his feet" (Ps. 8:5, 6).

b. Man's Unique Dignity

By reason of man's being made a little less than God, he possesses a unique dignity. The most expressive language setting forth this dignity is that he was created in the image and likeness of God. According to Ralph H. Elliott the word "image" (*tselem*) "implies a carved or hewn statue or 'copy' of something else, while 'likeness' (*demuth*) similarly means a facsimile. Thus, the words do not imply that man is divine. He is copied after a divine one with some of his attributes; he has functions which are like God's. Thus, God showed Himself to be the *prototype* and the *original* of man."[10]

New Testament Scriptures will lead us to a fuller understanding of the terms "image" and "likeness." Luke traced the genealogy of Jesus back to "Adam, the son of God." Paul confirmed the earlier teaching when he declared that "[man] is the image and glory of God" (1 Cor. 11:7). Paul most explicitly expressed man's being in the likeness and image of God in his letters to the Ephesians and Colossians. In Ephesians he wrote, "Put on the new nature, created after the likeness of God in true righteousness and holiness" (4:24). Similarly in Colossians he admonished believers to "put on the new nature, which is being renewed in knowledge after the image of its creator" (3:10). These aspects of the image of God, righteousness and holiness, were lost in the Fall but they belong to the new nature gained through the renewal in the spirit. It is a process of renewal, of becoming a new creation; its goal, the likeness of God. In this way God created man for personal relationship with Himself. It is the solid basis for the "I" and "Thou" relationship which is so essential to the Christian religion.

We have yet to note that God created man a sexual being. In Genesis 1 the writer made no distinction in time in the creation of man and woman. This suggests that whatever else chapter 2 adds to the creation of woman, we should regard man and woman as equal before God. God's blessing of the human pair included the command, "Be fruitful and multiply, and fill the earth" (1:28). In the chapter 2 account, the creation of woman is separated from that of man by God's creating all forms of animal life. Among these the man found no animal fit for him. On this account God made woman from a rib taken from the side of man. In her man found one who was bone of his bones, and flesh of his flesh, and he called her woman. Paul laid hold of the relative dignity of woman in relation to man when he wrote, "Woman is the glory of man" (1 Cor. 11:7). On this point Matthew Henry, writing more than two centuries ago, said, "If man is the head, she is the crown, a crown to her husband, the crown of the visible creation. The man was dust refined, but the woman was dust double refined, one remove further from the earth." Commenting on the woman's being made of a rib out of the side of Adam, Matthew Henry continued, "Not made out of his head to rule over him, nor out of his feet to be trampled upon by him, but out of his side to be equal with him, under his arm to be protected, and near his heart to be beloved."[11] According to Vriezen, "Love is the original relationship between man and woman according to God's intention; she was made for him and he will cleave to her."[12]

This account of creation comes to a climax in the author's words, "Therefore a man leaves his father and his mother and cleaves to his wife, and they become one flesh" (Gen. 2:24). Here the fundamental character of marriage stands forth. It is the forming of a new union of one man and one woman. His cleaving to his wife indicates the love relationship between the two. The words "one flesh" describe the nature of the union. They assert the indissolubility of the marriage relation. It is most noteworthy that this concept of marriage stands in the original account of creation.

It is a matter of some importance that man created in the image of God is alone a sexual being. God is not a sexual being. Herein is the radical difference between Israel's God and the Canaanite gods of ancient times. This fact lay at the basis of the condemnation of cultic prostitution at the sanctuaries of worship in Israel.[13]

As we leave the account of the creation of Adam and Eve, it remains to be said that the author of Genesis represented Adam and Eve as being historical persons. The genealogies begin with them. The authors of 1 Chronicles and the Gospel of Luke in recording the genealogies looked to them as the progenitors of the human race. Both Paul and Jude confirmed the historicity of Adam and Eve.[14]

c. Cessation of Creation

The closing words of the first account of creation (Gen. 2:1-3) arrest the reader's attention: "Thus the heavens and the earth were finished, and all the host of them. And on the seventh day God finished his work which he had done, and he rested on the seventh day from all his work which he had done. So God blessed the seventh day and hallowed it, because on it God rested from all his work which he had done in creation." Contrary to the usual interpretation, "God finished his work on the seventh day" rather than on the sixth day; but God also rested on the seventh day. This marked the cessation of creation. Accordingly, God blessed this seventh day and hallowed it. This setting apart of the seventh day had reference to God. No reference is made to the bearing of the Sabbath day on man. It is this fact that challenges us to discover, if possible, the meaning of God's resting on the seventh day. The interest in this inquiry becomes all the greater when we observe that there is no closing statement with reference to the seventh day as in the case of the six days. How are we to account for the absence of an expression such as "And there was evening and there was morning, a seventh day"? Does the absence of such an expression mean that in the mind of God the seventh day has not yet closed, that He continues to rest from His creative labor? Does it suggest that at some future time God will again perform a work of creation? This author believes that embedded in these verses is a profound implication that God at some future time will continue His work of creation. If this interprets the narrative correctly, we have here the first note of eschatology in the Bible. There is here a forward look to a new creation.

This interpretation of the seventh day language gains support when we read, "For behold, I create new heavens and a new earth; and the former things shall not be remembered or come into mind" (Is. 65:17). We do not know what lay in the prophet's mind when he wrote these words but very clearly he was predicting a new creation, one that by contrast stands over against the creation account in Genesis. The author of Hebrews voiced something of the same sort when he quoted Psalm 95:11 as pointing to a future rest for the people of God. He noted, however, that God had finished His works of creation from the foundation of the world and that God rested on the seventh day from all His work. By this he implied that the future rest referred to in this psalm will be one that will follow a future work of creation. Peter, with evident intention of quoting Isaiah, predicted the coming of the Day of God in which the present creation will be destroyed. He wrote, "But according to his promise we wait for new heavens and a new earth in which righteousness dwells" (2 Pet. 3:13). It remained for John to climax this idea by writing, "Then I saw a new heaven and a new earth; for the first heaven and the first earth had passed away" (Rev. 21:1). It would appear that these writers confirm the explicit eschatological note of Genesis 2:1-3.

This prepares us to understand that God will be acting to accomplish in history all that must take place to consummate all things in a new creation. This is perhaps the profoundest note of all divine revelation. It is this fact that will give meaning to the numerous instances of a forward look in the Bible. It becomes one of the major tasks of biblical theology to bring these eschatological notes into their true perspective. This conscious anticipation of the future became very distinctive in God's revelation to man. The ongoing disclosures of God's purposes in the world as found in all the Scriptures from Genesis to Revelation constitute one of the major proofs that God has spoken and that He is acting in history. It is these predictions of the world to come on which faith lays hold. The child of God believes what God has promised; he trusts that God will fulfill all His promises. He has the faith voiced by von Rad when he wrote, "Thus Genesis 2:1 ff. speaks about the preparation of an exalted saving good for the world and man, of a rest, 'before which millennia pass away as a thunderstorm' (Novalis). It is as tangibly 'existent' protologically as it is expected eschatologically in Hebrews (Heb. ch. 4)."[15]

d. Religious Aspect of Creation

One of the most significant purposes of the Creation was that of leading man into a spiritual relationship with God. Herein lies the essence of true religion. We shall examine this from three angles: first, the theocentric aspect of the relationship; second, the anthropocentric aspect; and third, these two aspects brought into focus as furnishing the essence of religion.

First, the theocentric aspect. Since God created man, the latter is subject to God. God possesses absolute supremacy over His creature man. The intimacy of this relationship is heightened all the more because of man's creation as a personal being. On this account man's subjection to God is a personal choice. As a creature, man is absolutely dependent on God. While God gave man dominion over all that He created, yet all things that man has under his care come from God.

This theocentric aspect, to use the words of Bernhard W. Anderson, "sets the stage for the unfolding of the divine purpose and inaugurates a historical drama within which first Israel and, in the fullness of time, the church were destined to play a key role. Thus the creation stands in an inseparable historical relation to the narratives that follow, particularly those that span the generations from Abraham to Joshua."[16] The idea that creation is inseparable from the history that follows becomes very clear in the frequent references to creation in the Bible. See again these references given in an earlier section, and note how the various writers linked a particular event in history or gave pertinent instruction on the basis of God's being the creator of the world.

This theocentric aspect becomes still clearer as we note the relation of this divine purpose to the theological concepts of preservation and providence. The author of Hebrews presented the idea of preservation when he referred to the Son, whom God appointed the heir of all things, "through whom also he created the world. He reflects the glory of God and bears the very stamp of his nature, upholding the universe by his word of power" (Heb. 1:1-3). The outworking of divine preservation comprehends the broad scope of divine providence. Throughout the history of the universe and continuing until the consummation, the hand of God is evident in leading the affairs of the world to its goal, the new creation. This has a vital bearing for man in relation to his creator. Man needs to be subject not only to the providential workings of God, but he needs also to strive, through loving obedience to God, to work together with Him to accomplish this goal. One of the saddest aspects of human history is man's failure to work with God in this ongoing divine providence.

Second, the anthropocentric aspect of God's purpose in creation. As noted above, man's creation in the image of God determined the level of God's dealings with him. The writer of Psalm 82 grasped the point of man's likeness to God when he wrote, "I say, 'You are gods, sons of the Most High, all of you' " (Ps. 82:6). This divine aspect of man's nature points to the character and pattern of man's approach to God. In the setting of the psalm just quoted, man is the son of God and hence he is divine, but not in the fullness of Christ's deity (Jn. 10:34).

There is another side to this anthropocentric aspect. It is the basic idea of the unity of the human race. All mankind are descendants of Adam. Herein we find the basis of the terrible fact of universal sinfulness of man. Paul wrote, "Therefore as sin came into the world through one man and death through sin, and so death spread to all men because all men sinned" (Rom. 5:12). In like manner there is a common need of redemption. God's redemptive provision is applicable to the entire human race. As Paul said, "Then as one man's trespass led to condemnation for all men, so one man's act of righteousness leads to acquittal and life for all men" (Rom. 5:18). To gain the full force of this anthropocentric aspect we might think of the difference it would have made if God had created many human beings without any relationship one to the other. In such a situation the sin of one man would not have affected all mankind leading to universal depravity. It would have affected only the descendants of the one who had sinned. In like manner the saving benefits of Christ's redemptive work would not reach to all who have sinned because He would not have borne a relationship as a human being to all mankind.

Third, the theocentric and the anthropocentric aspects held in focus. We gain the true concept of the essence of religion through a study of the relation of man, the creature, to God, the Creator. This relationship is experiential in character. The most potent expression of man's religion is found in worship. Space forbids a presentation of worship as found in the great book of Psalms but a casual reading of such familiar psalms as 8, 19, 23, 24, 32, 42, 51, 90, 91, 95, 104, 136 will show that central in worship are praise, prayer, communion, and fellowship, repentance, faith and commitment. Before worship can be real the worshiper needs to repent from sin and cry to God for forgiveness.

It is this convergence of the theocentric and anthropocentric aspects which leads to covenant relationship between God and man. It will become evident when we study God's approach to our first parents after they sinned. He initiated the reconciliation and restored them to fellowship with Him. It will become still clearer in the covenants made with Noah, Abraham, Israel, and the new covenant instituted by Christ. A study of these covenants will show how essential this relationship between God and man is to the whole idea of religion. In fact, we shall discover that the entire discipline of biblical theology centers in the covenant relationship between God and man. Among the students of biblical theology, Walther Eichrodt grasped most fully this covenant aspect of biblical theology. He says, "In the face of all objections, the 'covenant' has been retained as the central concept, by which to illuminate the structural unity and the unchanging basic tendency of the message of the Old Testament. For it is in this concept that Israel's fundamental conviction of its special relationship with God is concentrated. . . . Every expression of the Old Testament which is determinative for its faith rests on the explicit or implicit assumption that a free act of God, consummated in history, has raised Israel to the rank of the people of God, in whom the nature and will of God are to be revealed." [17]

5. God's First Revelation to Man

a. Interpreting the Garden of Eden Narrative

The Garden story offers many real problems for interpretation. Some of these problems have been noticed already in the discussion of the creation stories. It would seem that the principles of interpretation followed in those stories would obtain here. To begin, we need to exercise caution against an extreme literalism in determining the details of the Garden scene. Some students have carried the literalism of interpretation to the extent of regarding the fruit of the trees as possessing some magical powers. The biblical narrative rightly understood does not give this idea.

Some Bible students are content to trace elements of the Garden story to pagan myths. There is no proof for this procedure. This is the same situation that they find in comparing the creation account with similar stories found in ancient nations. It would appear that some students are content to trace these stories back to heathen nations rather than to believe that the heathen nations received them from the people to whom God revealed them. The absolute monotheism of the biblical narratives as compared with the polytheism of pagan myths should stand as adequate support of the authenticity and priority of the biblical narratives as over against the degenerate forms of these stories among pagan nations.

There are a number of elements in this story which support an actual event in the Garden. Further, there are evidences which point to a profound meaning lying back of the elements of the story. This would suggest that the historical narrative of the Garden scene possesses elements of symbolism or of a sacrament, as we shall note presently. The very names of the two trees give expression to this idea. This is the sort of thing found all through the Bible. A study of circumcision, offerings and sacrifices, and the Christian sacraments shows that an outward physical act was given a deep spiritual significance. This same principle obtains here as well. Let us proceed then to allow the narrative to stand in its own right and to speak for itself. Later biblical references to the Garden scene should give us a true understanding of the story. Seen in this light, a profound meaning attaches to the Garden of Eden incident. Any other kind of interpretation nullifies the intent of the narrative.

b. Meaning of the Garden of Eden Story

The narrative begins with the words, "And the Lord God planted a garden in Eden, in the east; and there he put the man whom he had formed" (Gen. 2:8). It is not naive to regard this statement as expressing the actual planting of a garden in Eden. It was an actual geographic locality in the east. It was entirely natural for later writers to refer to this as the Garden of the Lord.[18] On this account we should think of it as the dwelling place of God on this earth. God had planned that the Garden should be His meeting place with man. He received man into fellowship with Himself in a simple and expressive way. The Garden illustrated the God-centered character of religion. God designed that the human race should always dwell in this Garden where there would be full and free access to Him. This suggests the awfulness of the tragedy when our first parents were driven from the Garden and could no longer experience this free access to God.

After the sin of our first parents, God provided for man's access to Him outside of the Garden by way of personal appearances, as in the case of Abraham; by way of His providing a dwelling place among men, as in the tabernacle and temple; by way of the earthly ministry of the incarnate Son of God; by way of the indwelling Holy Spirit in man; and ultimately and gloriously in Paradise regained, when it will be said, "Behold, the dwelling of God is with men. He will dwell with them, and they shall be his people and God himself will be with them" (Rev. 21:3).

The tree of life stood in the midst of the Garden. God designed that after proper testing of our first parents they should eat of the tree of life and live forever (Gen. 3:22). By reason of their disobedience this privilege was denied to them. The story gives no indication that the tree of life possessed the dynamic of giving eternal life to those who ate of it. Consistency of interpretation would hold that the literal eating of the fruit of this tree was the symbol of God's giving to them eternal life.

Later references to the tree of life may help us to understand its meaning. By reason of their context the four references to the tree of life in the Book of Proverbs[19] give a little illumination on this point. Ezekiel's vision of the trees growing on both sides of the river may bear some relationship to the tree of life. In the vision the river flows from the sanctuary of God. The trees growing on both sides of the river draw their nourishment from the river so that they bear fruit, fresh fruit every month. Their fruit was to be for food and their leaves for healing. Since the sanctuary was the dwelling place of God we may properly conclude that Ezekiel was teaching that spiritual life, even eternal life, comes from God.

References to the tree of life in the Book of Revelation serve as the best commentary on the Genesis story. The church of Ephesus was told, "To him who conquers I will grant to eat of the tree of life, which is in the paradise of God" (Rev. 2:7). These words suggest that all Christians are in a conflict just as our first parents were in the Garden of Eden. Those who conquer will be allowed to eat of the tree of life. This is parallel to the scene in the Garden. If our first parents had been obedient in their test, they would have been granted the right to eat of the tree of life. Most expressive are the words from the last chapter of Revelation, "Then he showed me the river of the water of life, bright as crystal, flowing from the throne of God and of the Lamb through the middle of the street of the city; also, on either side of the river, the tree of life with its twelve kinds of fruit, yielding its fruit each month; and the leaves of the tree were for the healing of the nations" (Rev. 22:1, 2). These verses reflect both the Garden of Eden scene and Ezekiel's vision. The picture serves to confirm the idea that Ezekiel's vision expanded the truth of the Garden scene. The vision of John pointed clearly to the spiritual significance of the literal tree of life in Eden. This approach in interpretation is comparable to that applied to other biblical teaching. Circumcision was a literal act but in the days of Moses we read of uncircumcised lips and uncircumcised hearts.[20] In like manner Paul dealt with the Passover when he regarded Christ as our Passover.

c. Tree of Knowledge of Good and Evil

The starting point in the interpretation of the tree of the knowledge of good and evil is to be found in God's prohibition against the eating of the fruit of this tree. Here was a test, a proving, that turned solely on obedience. Adam and Eve, created in the image of God, were subject to God. God the Creator required absolute obedience of those who were created in His image. He would lead them to choose the good in the setting of a free and responsible decision between good and evil. The test turned entirely on the principle of obedience. Through obedience they would continue to have full fellowship with God. It would eventually lead them to eat of the tree of life, which was the symbol of their gaining eternal life. Without a doubt the fruit of this tree was most delicious. There was nothing sinful in the eating of this fruit apart from God's command. The name of the tree gives adequate grounds for believing that God designed that this test should lead our first parents from a state of moral innocence to that of moral maturity.

To gain a knowledge of good and evil meant to learn the ethical antagonism between right and wrong. The test of obedience to God in an area not ethically wrong in itself most clearly revealed this antagonism. As we shall observe presently, Satan used this test as the occasion for tempting them to disobey God. He deceived Adam and Eve by concealing the fact that by eating of the tree they would become guilty before God. By eating of the tree their eyes were opened and they came to know good and evil, but it was by the way of transgression. God had intended that they should come to know the difference between right and wrong through obedience to His command. He would lead them to moral maturity without the experience of sin. The experience of sin deprived them of eating of the tree of life. This interpretation has support in later biblical teaching which pointed to early manhood or womanhood as the age in which people come to know this ethical antagonism. Isaiah picked up this idea in his prediction of Immanuel. He pointed to the time in the life of Immanuel when He would know how to refuse the evil and choose the good.[21]

This study of the tree of life and of the tree of the knowledge of good and evil naturally leads us to inquire into the meaning of the words, "In the day that you eat of it you shall die" (Gen. 2:17). What is the concept of death given in Genesis 2, 3? To begin, the author of Genesis brought the idea of death into the narrative without defining it. This requires us to search for its meaning by a study of its usage in the context. The presence of the tree of life in the Garden suggested that man, according to God's plan, should eventually eat of this tree. By eating of the tree of life man would live forever (3:22). From this we may conclude that man by creation was mortal. Eternal life depended on eating of the tree of life. It would appear that God designed that after man showed obedience in the test he could then eat of the tree of life. God had not planned that man should die, even though by creation he was mortal. In the wisdom of God the way of being saved from dying would be by obedience to God in this test.

In the temptation scene Satan deceived Eve by combining the truth and a lie. The truth lay in this that by eating of the tree of the knowledge of good and evil they would not immediately experience physical death. The deception lay in the fact that there was an immediate experience of death of a different kind. The sequence of the narrative shows that this breaking of fellowship between them and God was death. On this account God would not allow them to eat of the tree of life in a state of broken fellowship. Only those in full fellowship with God could eat of this tree. The language, "You are dust and to dust you shall return" (3:19), applied to Adam and Eve as a result of their eating of the tree of the knowledge of good and evil. That is, the curse upon our first parents culminated in physical death. These words were spoken after their transgression. The entire context teaches that death involved both physical and spiritual aspects which were inseparable. Their transgression of God's command immediately broke their relation with God. It led to physical death, which in due time would take place. God's words to Ezekiel may shed some light on the spiritual aspect of death found in the Genesis narrative. God said, "The soul that sins shall die" (Ezek. 18:4).[22] In like manner the Apostle Paul intensified the spiritual aspect of death when he wrote, "Therefore as sin came into the world through one man and death through sin, and so death spread to all men because all men sinned" (Rom. 5:12).[23] That the physical aspect of death is closely associated with the spiritual became evident in the death of Adam (Gen. 5:5).

d. Serpent's Encounter with Eve

The initial problem that we face here is that of interpreting the serpent. Most modern scholars trace the idea of the serpent back to Babylonian myths. For this line of descent there is no proof. It is more in accord with the facts of the case to hold that the Babylonian myths are degenerate forms of the true tradition given in the Bible. An explanation of the serpent, nevertheless, does call for solution. The writer introduced the narrative without any explanation more than to note, "The serpent was more subtle than any other wild creature that the Lord God had made" (Gen. 3:1). So far as the narrative is concerned, we are not able to determine how the serpent could speak. One thing is very clear, the encounter with the woman involved the most subtle form of temptation. Human ingenuity could hardly make a temptation scene more real or graphic. Some students attempt to escape the problem by calling this a parable or myth. Whether or not it is proper thus to solve the problem of taking the language literally, sound interpretation points to a real experience of temptation coming into the lives of our first parents. Any view that denies the reality of a temptation encounter fails to interpret the intended meaning of the narrative. Furthermore the writer gave no idea of the serpent being Satan. The existence of a personal archenemy of mankind, Satan, was not revealed so early.

Later biblical writers did not explain the problem of a literal serpent being the agent of temptation. Their identification of Satan as the agent manifested in the serpent or working through the serpent is very clear. As early as the apocryphal Book of Wisdom we read, "By the envy of Satan death entered into the world" (II:20). In Jesus' explanation of the Weeds of the Field parable, He identified the enemy who sowed the weeds as the devil (Mt. 13:39). By this Jesus attributed the presence of sin in the world to the devil. On another occasion Jesus spoke of the devil as being a murderer from the beginning. He is a liar and the father of lies (Jn. 8:44). In similar language John wrote, "He who commits sin is of the devil; for the devil has sinned from the beginning" (1 Jn. 3:8). Paul made an evident allusion to the tempter in the Garden when he wrote, "The God of peace will soon crush Satan under your feet" (Rom. 16:20). Elsewhere Paul referred to the serpent as having deceived Eve by his cunning, but he identified Satan with the serpent in the same context (2 Cor. 11:3, 14). In the Revelation the clearest identification becomes evident. We read, "And the great dragon was thrown down, that ancient serpent, who is called the Devil and Satan, the deceiver of the whole world — he was thrown down to the earth" (Rev. 12:9; 20:2).

The serpent encountered the woman with a question which sounded very innocent. It had to do with a certainty of fact, "Did God say, 'You shall not eat of any tree of the garden' " (Gen. 3:1)? The question had in it the implication of a serious problem of doubt. It could easily lead her to distrust God's command. Her answer was such that the serpent could move forward in his design to deceive her. He said a half-truth in the words, "You will not die. For God knows that when you eat of it your eyes will be opened, and you will be like God, knowing good and evil" (Gen. 3:4, 5). The deception lay first in the meaning of the word "die." The serpent implied a physical death. Further, there was truth in the idea that her eyes would be opened and in that sense she would be like God, knowing good and evil. The deception lay in her coming to know good and evil by way of committing sin. This was not the intention of God. He purposed that they should come to know good and evil without the experience of sin. By their remaining true to God's command and by their being obedient to the test, in a state of pure innocence their eyes would have been opened to know good and evil. Herein lay the lie and the deception. By giving heed to the serpent's deceptive words, the woman yielded to the beauty of the fruit and to the desire to make herself wise, and ate of the fruit — together with her husband.

Since the temptation of Jesus, the second Adam, had much in common with the temptation of Eve, we may gain a fuller understanding of the

Garden scene by noting the similarity of Jesus' temptation with that of our first parents. There was purpose in Jesus' probation. The Spirit led Him into the wilderness to be tempted by Satan. Satan encountered Jesus specifically on the point of obedience during the probation. Jesus, the God-man, needed to prove Himself genuinely human through the fundamental aspect of humanity, that of obedience to God. To turn stones into bread and to eat was in itself nonmoral. But for Jesus to have done so would have violated the limitations of human nature. The temptation turned solely on the matter of obedience to God. Jesus' temptation was real. The test of obedience on the part of Jesus was identical in nature with that of our first parents. Satan's words of deception to Jesus in the second and third temptations were similar in character to the words he spoke to the woman.

The immediate effects of the sin of Adam and Eve are very noteworthy. Their eyes were opened and they knew that they were naked. They immediately sought to cover their nakedness. For them nakedness had become a shame. They had come to know good and evil but it was not experienced in the way God had intended. They came to know good and evil by the way of transgression and its accompanying guilt of sin. Their guilty consciences spoke in the sense of shame in being naked. Why their sense of guilt expressed itself in this way is not entirely clear. Perhaps the reason for the shame of nakedness experienced by mankind throughout human history may suggest the reason for their shame. This shame of bodily nakedness bears a close relation to the powers of procreation given to the human race. The sense of guilt manifested itself in this way in order to teach the most tragic lesson: the effects of sin in the way of guilt center in the powers of procreation because all mankind were then sinful in their very nature. The shame of bodily nakedness ever continues to reflect the guilt of our first parents' sin.

e. God's Encounter with Sinful Man and Woman

Because of the tragic event described above, the Lord God came on the scene, "walking in the garden in the cool of the day." This reflects one purpose of the Garden; namely, that in this environment the Lord God would fellowship with those who were created in His image. By reason of their guilt and shame the man and his wife hid themselves from the presence of the Lord God. The scene that follows is full of instruction as an account of God's self-revelation to man.[24]

Let us note first that in this situation God took the initiative. It was not a case of the man and woman seeking for God by reason of their guilt and shame, but rather that God sought them out. This divine initiative is but the beginning of uncounted approaches that God has made to man because of his sin. On this account God's coming on the scene obtains special significance in that it becomes the prototype of all future encounters of God with man. It suggests at once that sinful man is helpless and that God acts in man's behalf to restore broken fellowship. It anticipates the grandest divine initiative expressed in the words, "For God so loved the world that he gave his only Son, that whoever believes in him should not perish but have eternal life" (Jn. 3:16).

The Lord God's conversation with the sinful pair led at once to the prediction of a coming conflict. This conflict would center in what God does to put enmity between the serpent and the woman. What this means is that the newly established friendship of the man and the woman with the serpent would be broken. God would restore friendship and fellowship of the man and the woman with Himself. The breaking of the friendship with the serpent and the reestablishing of friendship with God would have a direct bearing on their affections. Change of affection results from acts of love and compassion on the part of the supposed enemy. By implication, God would restore the love relationship between Himself and sinful man through something that He would do.

God declared that the conflict would involve the seed of the woman and the seed of the serpent. It would not be the outcome of an immediate combat. The battle would continue. The language implies that the conflict would involve the entire human race. This suggests that the entire human race would ultimately be involved in a temptation experience similar to that of Adam and Eve. Human experience has confirmed this. The conflict between man and the serpent came to a climax in the temptation of the God-man, Jesus Christ. Very plainly, the temptations of Adam and Eve, of Jesus Christ, and of all mankind are essentially one in character. The difference lies in this that the disobedience of the man and the woman must be undone. This leads to the heart of the conflict predicted in Genesis 3:15.

The Lord God also pointed to the issue of the conflict. The seed of the woman would bruise the head of the serpent. The serpent would bruise the heel of the seed of the woman. We do not know how the man and the woman understood this language. It is possible that they realized that out of the race would come the fatal blow. Whatever meaning they took from these words, they had grounds for believing that God would destroy the serpent.

As God's conversation continued, the elements of justice and mercy in God's dealings with the man and the woman became apparent. Justice would manifest itself in the pain of childbearing, in the curse inflicted on the ground, in the toil of man for his food, and in physical death. Mingled with these acts of justice was the expression of grace. Even though childbearing would be painful, yet through it the race would be propagated. Even though the ground was cursed and man needed to toil for his food, yet through his toil he would acquire food.

The sequel to this encounter became evident in God's provision of garments of skins by which the Lord God clothed Adam and Eve. We naturally inquire whether or not there was any special significance to this act of God. Avoiding extremes of giving too little or too much meaning to this act of God's, one may make two observations on this provision of clothes for Adam and Eve. In the first place, the Lord God made the provision. He discarded the aprons of fig leaves and provided the garments of skins. Apparently Adam and Eve did not possess the knowledge of what kind of garments would cover their nakedness.

The initiative taken by God bears the same character as that found in the entire encounter. God needed to do what man was unable to do. In the second place, the provision of garments of skins may carry deeper meaning by reason of the shedding of blood required for providing them. A momentous fact soon rises before us. Beginning with Abel and continuing through Noah, Abraham, Moses, and throughout Israel's history we meet bloody sacrifices. How did these bloody sacrifices originate? There is no recorded command of God for His people to make such offerings. Is it going too far with this narrative to say that Abel gained the idea of a bloody sacrifice when he heard how God had clothed his parents with garments of skins? In my judgment this incident carries such potential meaning. [24]

A few concluding thoughts bring the study of this encounter to a close. The entire incident underscored the idea of eschatology in God's revelation. We will need to judge whether or not the account of the seventh day of creation and this story possess any eschatological significance. At some point along the way, whether in the time of Noah or of Abraham, this aspect of divine revelation does become entirely clear. At whatever time this characteristic of divine revelation does become evident, the fact is of highest importance. Divine revelation looked forward to what God would accomplish in the future. He was moving forward to a definite goal. The God who acts in history would magnify His glory in what He would ultimately accomplish in His mighty works. This aspect of eschatology marked the beginning and gave the ground of hope on the part of man in his relation to God. This hope has its basis, its foundation in man's faith-relation to God. It is the idea grasped, enlarged, and intensified by the author of the letter to the Hebrews when he wrote, "Now faith is the assurance of things hoped for, the conviction of things not seen. For by it the men of old received divine approval" (Heb. 11:1, 2). The author's message began with Abel and included men and women of faith throughout sacred history. He concluded with the words, "All these, though well attested by their faith, did not receive what was promised, since God had foreseen something better for us, that apart from us they should not be made perfect" (Heb. 11:39, 40).

For Additional Reading and Reference:

Baab, *The Theology of the Old Testament*, pp. 42-48, 81-83.
Bonhoeffer, *Creation and Fall*.
Davidson, *The Theology of the Old Testament*, pp. 30 ff.
Eichrodt, *Theology of the Old Testament*, Vol. I, pp. 230 ff.
Elliott, *The Message of Genesis*, pp. 22-51.
Heim, *The World: Its Creation and Consummation*, Part I.
Heinisch-Heidt, *Theology of the Old Testament*, pp. 146-77.
Interpreter's Bible, Vol. I, pp. 458-65.
Jacob, *Theology of the Old Testament*, pp. 136-49, 166-73.
Knight, *A Christian Theology of the Old Testament*, pp. 107-27.
Köhler, *Old Testament Theology*, pp. 85-88, 131-47.
Leupold, *Expositions of Genesis*, I, pp. 35-185.
Napier, *Songs of the Vineyard*, pp. 45-52.
Oehler, *Theology of Old Testament*, pp. 49-54.
Payne, *The Theology of the Old Testament*, pp. 132-40.
von Rad, *Old Testament Theology*, Vol. I, Genesis in loco, pp. 136-84.
Raven, *The History of the Religion of Israel*, pp. 11-24.
Robinson, *Inspiration and Revelation of the Old Testament*, pp. 17-33.
————, *Religious Ideas in the Old Testament*, pp. 70-76, 83-87.
Schultz, *Old Testament Theology*, Vol. II, pp. 180-213, 292-306.
Vischer, *The Witness of the Old Testament to Christ*, Vol. I, pp. 37-68.
Weidner, *Biblical Theology of the Old Testament*, pp. 37-40, 78-83.
Wingren, *Creation and Law*. See Index: Creation, Temptation.

See articles, "Creation" and "Fall," in the following:
Allmen, Ed., *A Companion to the Bible*.
Douglas, Ed., *The New Bible Dictionary*.
Harrison, Ed., *Baker's Dictionary of Theology*.
Interpreter's Dictionary of the Bible.
International Standard Bible Encyclopaedia.
Richardson, Ed., *A Theological Word Book of the Bible*.

1. Gen. 1:1, 21, 27; 2:3, 4; 5:1, 2; 6:7; Deut. 4:32.
2. Pss. 24:2; 78:69; 89:11; 102:25; 104:5; Prov. 3:19; Is. 48:13; 51:13, 16; Amos 9:6; and Zech. 12:1.
3. Pss. 8:3; 24:2; 65:6; 93:1; 96:10; 119:73, 90; Is. 45:18; Jer. 10:12; 51:15; Ezek. 28:13.
4. Gen. 1:21, 27; 5:1, 2; 6:7; Is. 42:5; 43:1; 45:7, 18.
5. Gen. 1:7, 11, 12, 16, 21, 25, 26, 31; 2:2-4; 3:1; 5:1; 6:6.
6. *O.T. Theology*, Vol. I, p. 142.
7. Ps. 33:9; 148:5; Is. 45:12; Heb. 11:3; 2 Pet. 3:5, 6.
8. 1:5, 14, 16; 2:4.
9. *Op. cit.*, p. 144.
10. *Message of Genesis*, Broadman Press, p. 36.
11. *An Exposition of the Old and New Testaments* (New York: Fleming H. Revell Company), Vol. I comments on 2:21-25.

12. *An Outline of Old Testament Theology* (Boston: Charles T. Branford Co., 1958), p. 206.

13. See Lev. 19:29; Deut. 23:18; 1 Sam. 2:22-25; 1 Kings 15:12; 22:46.

14. Rom. 5:14; 1 Cor. 15:22, 45; 2 Cor. 11:3; 1 Tim. 2:13, 14; Jude 14.

15. *Genesis, A Commentary*, by Gerhard von Rad (Philadelphia: The Westminster Press, 1961), p. 61.

16. *The Interpreter's Dictionary of the Bible*, "Creation" (New York: Abingdon Press, 1962), A-D, p. 727.

17. *Theology of the Old Testament* (Philadelphia: The Westminster Press, 1961), Vol. I, pp. 13, 14.

18. Gen. 13:10; Is. 51:3; Ezek. 28:13; 31:8, 9.

19. Prov. 3:18; 11:30; 13:12; 15:4.

20. Ex. 6:12, 30; Lev. 26:41; Ezek. 44:7, 9.

21. Is. 7:13-16. See also Deut. 1:39; Num. 14:29, 30.

22. See also vv. 19-32; 33:11-16.

23. See also 6:23; Eph. 2:1-6; Col. 2:13.

24. See Vos, *op. cit.*, pp. 52-55, for a significant discussion of God's encounter with Adam and Eve.

CHAPTER III
COURSE OF HISTORY TO
THE REVELATION THROUGH ABRAHAM

1. General Trend of the Narrative

A study of Genesis 4 — 6 shows two lines of descent which disclose two opposite trends in the human race. In the line of Cain there is pictured the downward plunge of humanity in sin and wickedness. Over against this is the godly line of Seth. It is our concern to learn what the writer sought to teach in this earliest period of human history. Again it is plain that the writer had a purpose and this purpose became evident as he unfolded the account. By way of anticipation, he would have us see that the sinful line of Cain worked deadly havoc in the human race, leading to the verdict: "The Lord saw that the wickedness of man was great in the earth, and that every imagination of the thoughts of his heart was only evil continually" (Gen. 6:5). Alongside of this the author showed that a godly line did continue through this era until it became evident that the growing forces of evil would finally overcome the faithful remnant unless God would intervene. Very clearly the writer had no intention of presenting a formal history of this era. His concern centered in a religious purpose based nevertheless on the course of history.

2. Offerings of Cain and Abel

This familiar story also requires close study in order to gain an understanding of the author's purpose. We need to observe that Cain and Abel followed two different modes of life: one tilled the ground and the other kept sheep. In their worship they brought two kinds of offerings; one offered of the fruit of the ground and the other of the firstlings of the flock and of their fat portions. We are confronted with the problem of understanding the reason for the rejection of Cain's offering and for the acceptance of Abel's. It would appear on the surface that each one brought an offering related to his vocation, in which case it would appear that both offerings should have been accepted by God. The narrative presents an explanation. To Cain God said, "If you do well, will you not be accepted? And if you do not do well, sin is couching at the door; its desire is for you, but you must master it" (Gen. 4:7). This explanation pointed to a spiritual lack in Cain. He was not doing well. Sin was couching at Cain's door. Like a ravenous beast, sin had the desire to devour Cain. God would lead Cain to recognize this foe and enter into combat with it. By implication, God accepted Abel's offering because Abel was doing well. He was recognizing sin as his foe and was mastering it.

The author of Hebrews gave an explanation of this incident in the words, "By faith Abel offered to God a more acceptable sacrifice than Cain, through which he received approval as righteous, God bearing witness by accepting his gifts; he died, but through his faith he is still speaking" (Heb. 11:4). This gave another reason for the rejection of Cain's offering and the acceptance of Abel's. It turns on the word "acceptable." This word carries the meanings *superior, more excellent, richer, greater,* and *better.* It pointed to a qualitative superiority of Abel's offering over that of Cain's. The nature of this superiority calls for study. To begin, Abel's superior sacrifice was an act of faith. Evidently Cain's offering was not by faith. The meaning of Abel's faith must be gained from the use of the word "faith" in this Hebrews 11 context. The author of Hebrews defined faith as "the assurance of things hoped for, the conviction of things not seen" (Heb. 11:1). Evidently Abel entertained a hope of God's fulfilling some promise. This hope was based on his faith and trust in God. The narrative, however, does not tell us the content of Abel's hope. Is it possible that the nature of Abel's sacrifice may tell us something of the content of Abel's hope? In the discussion of the Garden of Eden story we saw that some meaning may have attached to the shedding of blood necessary for the provision of the garments of skin for Adam and Eve. It is conceivable that when Abel learned of this he concluded that a bloody sacrifice was necessary to cover his sins. By this offering he would be showing his faith in God with respect to the hope bound up in God's promise to his parents (Gen. 3:15). Evidently Cain refused to recognize any guilt of sin and consequently had no confidence in this promise. In his mind all that was necessary was an offering of thanks to God. Abel, on the other hand, realized his sin and recognized God's provision for the covering of sin. Cain had no regard for this provision. If this interpretation is correct, the difficult problem of determining the origin of bloody sacrifices in biblical history finds a solution.

3. Author of Genesis Interprets Antediluvian History

Cain's murder of his brother set the stage for the course of history through his descendants. The Apostle John gave an analysis of Cain's character in the words, "Cain who was of the evil one and murdered his brother. And why did he murder him? Because his own deeds were evil and his brother's righteous" (1 Jn. 3:12). Cain's response to the Lord's punishment failed to show a spirit of penitence. He was more concerned about his own preservation than for the impact of his sin upon others. At least two things should become evident in tracing the descendants of Cain. First, the author showed the degrading effects of sin among those who departed from God. Lamech stood out as a typical example of the outworking of sin in this line. He not only broke God's law of monogamous marriage, a most grievous sin, but he also became a murderer like his ancestor, Cain.

The nature of this degradation became clear in the words already quoted (Gen. 6:5) which stated that the wickedness of man was great in the earth. The forcefulness of this language is very striking. The writer did not stop with the single statement with respect to the wickedness of man but he intensified the language, showing most vividly the inward nature of sin. Sin centered in the heart; human depravity had gone to the depths that "every imagination of the thoughts of his heart was only evil continually." What a terrible judgment on man's degradation in sin! The nature of sin also became clear in the life of Cain. It showed itself in the anger of jealousy toward his brother in his refusal to master sin, which led to murder as the outworking of his hatred. And sin's nature became still more evident in his lack of repentance and faith toward God. These same aspects characterized the sinfulness of Lamech. In him there was a total disregard for God's law of marriage. His acts of murder revealed the inner working of the spirit of vengeance. He would outdo Cain by a seventy-seven-fold act of vengeance. Thus sin was viewed not merely as outward acts but as something fundamentally inward. This statement of the inner nature of sin was underscored by Christ when He said, "For out of the heart come evil thoughts, murder, adultery, fornication, theft, false witness, slander" (Mt. 15:19).

The line of Seth shows an entirely different picture. The author of Genesis had an evident purpose in presenting an unbroken lineage from Seth to Noah. The Cain line was left incomplete for the possible reason that all of his descendants at the time of the Flood perished in the Flood. On the other hand, the line of Seth by reason of its godliness was preserved from destruction and continued beyond the Flood. In preserving this continuous genealogy the author was evidently giving expression to his forward look. It was the line of descent to Abraham, Isaac, and Jacob to whom the Lord gave the great promises. A comparison of this genealogy with that of 1 Chronicles and of Luke would seem to confirm the eschatological outlook of the author of Genesis. It would appear that he desired to trace the line of descent to that member of the seed of the woman who would deal the crushing blow on the head of the serpent.

In the narrative of this descent the author made a statement of considerable significance. He wrote, "At that time men began to call upon the name of the Lord" (Gen. 4:26). Students have wrestled with this statement for many years. The interpretation which seems to fit best into the meaning of the narrative is that with Seth there is the beginning of man's worship of the Lord. If this interprets correctly the meaning of this verse, we discover here one of the profound reasons for the perpetuation of the godly line. Among the descendants of Seth were those who called upon the name of the Lord. They involved themselves in the worship of their Creator. It would account for the faith and life of Enoch, who walked with God. His manner of life pleased the Lord. His walking with God was a continuation of the close fellowship found between man and God in the Garden of Eden. While the Garden was closed to man's access, yet this godly man experienced a similar fellowship in his walk with God. It was a walk that did not terminate, "for God took him." He did not experience physical death.[1]

Another evidence of the godliness and faith found in the line of Seth becomes evident in the naming of Noah. His father, Lamech, said, "Out of the ground which the Lord has cursed this one shall bring us relief from our work and from the toil of our hands" (Gen. 5:29). Back of these words lay a deep-seated realization of the effects of sin upon the human race. The nature of man's wickedness as described in Genesis 6:11, 12 gives additional insight as to the sinfulness of the world. It reads, "Now the earth was corrupt in God's sight, and the earth was filled with violence. And God saw the earth, and behold, it was corrupt; for all flesh had corrupted their way upon the earth." So unspeakably wicked had the human race become!

One more picture of the state of affairs calls for explanation. It is the commingling of the two lines, thus threatening the complete destruction of the godly line. It is this which led the J writer to announce the imminent judgment upon the world. Some formidable problems center in this brief paragraph (Gen. 6:1-4). It has to do with the interpretation of "sons of God," "the daughters of men," and the Nephilim. Since this brief paragraph carries significance for the study of the unfolding of divine revelation, I shall present my understanding of its meaning. To begin, we may expect that the author of the J document, together with that of the final recensionist, gives us an account free from pagan influences. The terms used are to be oriented to the thinking of God's people. They do not have their roots in paganism. This would suggest that the marriage of the sons of God with the daughters of men refers to the intermarriage between the godly line and the ungodly line. The manner in which the final writer of the Book of Genesis presents the lines of Cain and of Seth seems to prepare the reader for the possibility, even the probability, of their commingling. The words of the Lord, "My spirit shall not abide in man for ever, for he is flesh, but his days shall be a hundred and twenty years" (v. 3), stand as the result of the conduct described in verses 1, 2. In my judgment this fact completely nullifies the interpretation which would identify the sons of God with angels.

The meaning of Nephilim remains as a problem. It is usually taken to mean giants but it could carry the sense of extraordinary physical strength. It does not seem necessary to give it a meaning lying beyond natural biological laws of heredity.

The Lord, the righteous judge, condemned the world to destruction. The J writer expressed the Lord's words in this fashion: "I will blot out man whom I have created from the face of the ground, man and beast and creeping things and birds of the air, for I am sorry that I have made them" (Gen. 6:7). The P writer quoted God as saying to Noah, "I have determined to make an end of all flesh; for the earth is filled with violence through them; behold, I will destroy them with the earth" (Gen. 6:13). Both statements are very expressive. Only through divine judgment could God save the few remaining faithful ones from being engulfed in the stream of wickedness.

4. Revelation Given Through Noah

a. God, His Nature and Acts

This section of the Book of Genesis builds on the foundation laid in the creation account. We have seen God as the Creator of all things and observed how He dealt with Adam and Eve in justice, love, and mercy. In the crisis of extreme wickedness that resulted in mankind's bringing upon the world the just judgment of God, these attributes stand out in still bolder relief. The Lord showed Himself the God of righteousness in relation to man's sin; the God of justice in relation to the judgment of the Flood; the God of mercy in sparing Noah and his family; and the God of love in drawing Noah into covenant relationship with Himself. He is the God who acts in history, in the most remarkable way of destroying the world by the Deluge. God who created the world also destroyed this world.

We should observe further that God established a standard of living for His people. He declared the sacredness of human blood because He had made man in His own image.

The anthropomorphic language used in Genesis 6:6, 7 should be interpreted in the same manner that we understand figurative language. The only way in which man can grasp the nature of God is by the way of anthropomorphic language. This mode of expression shows to us the likeness of personality in man to that of God. When we lift this likeness to Deity level, we begin to understand the personality of God. There is the inner nature of God that finds true expression in the language of human emotions. To use the words of Elliott with reference to the Genesis writer's account of God's reaction to man's sin, "It grieved the Lord that man had behaved as he had. This is an expression of God's concern and compassion for man."[2] With these personality traits raised to divine level, it is entirely natural that the record should represent Noah as finding favor in the eyes of the Lord. The Lord communicated with Noah in the language of seeing, speaking, commanding, and the like. The intimacy of this relation of God to Noah in this anthropomorphic setting possesses great meaning. The narrative represented God as remembering Noah, blessing him, and, most significantly, establishing a covenant with him.

b. Life of the People of God

It is significant for our study that very early in human history attention is given to the life of the people of God. I have already noted the positive aspect of this in the instance of Abel and in the godly line from Seth to Noah. Abel's manner of life was such that God had regard for Abel and his offering. In the time of Seth men began to call upon the name of the Lord. Enoch walked with God. Noah stood forth as a man who also walked with God, for he "was a righteous man, blameless in his generation" (Gen. 6:9).

The words "righteous" and "blameless" are definitive as setting forth godliness in character. The Lord spared Noah and his family from destruction because he was righteous. This word stands over against the wickedness of men who were destroyed by the Flood. Appearing in an ethical setting, the word carries the idea of that which is conformed to a standard. This standard lies in the character of God. As we shall note later, Abraham was concerned that in the destruction of Sodom, the righteous would not be slain with the wicked. He raised the question, "Shall not the Judge of all the earth do right" (Gen. 18:25)? This God-centered trait of Noah's character was so outstanding that Peter called him a "herald of righteousness" (2 Pet. 2:5). Significant for our purpose here, Peter used an opposite term, "ungodly," to describe the people who were destroyed by the Flood. Thus ungodliness is the antonym of righteousness. The word translated "blameless" has the literal idea "without blemish," a term used regularly throughout the law to describe animals which were fit for sacrifice. In the ethical realm it carries the idea of perfect, undefiled, upright, sincere, and sound.[3] We should note that these two words, *righteous* and *blameless*, became the leading normative expressions used to describe men and women of God. As we would expect, the writer of Hebrews attributed Noah's building of the ark to his faith, and through this act he "became an heir of the righteousness which comes by faith" (Heb. 11:7). From this we should learn that righteousness and blamelessness are found alone in men of faith. This is a very significant aspect of the life of the people of God.

c. Noah's Worship of the Lord

Closely associated with the life and character of the man Noah was his worship of the Lord. On leaving the ark Noah built an altar to the Lord on which he offered burnt offerings of clean animals and birds. The meaning of these acts calls for study. To begin, there is entire absence of a recorded command from God for Noah to do this. The rise of sacrificial worship remains unexplained. As I noted earlier, we may find some suggestion in God's providing garments of skins for Adam and for Eve and also in the bloody offerings of Abel. The shedding of blood is common to both of these incidents. This fact may suggest some reason for Noah's bloody offering.

Looking into history, we may note the prominence of burnt offerings among the people of God. The large place devoted to these offerings in Israel's ceremonial worship would suggest their importance here and also give the reason for the writer's noting that they were "burnt offerings." In the Mosaic legislation we will discover the meaning of the details relating to this sacrifice. The altar was built to the Lord and represented the participation of God in the sacrifice. The offerings were placed on the altar to indicate their dedication to God. The slaying of the animals for the burnt offerings involved a shedding of blood, the forfeiture of life. In some way Noah recognized a relationship of his sin to the kind of offering he should bring. He had come to realize that by the offering of animals his own life would be spared by God. The distinctive aspect of the burnt offering, namely, that of burning the entire animal on the altar, had profound meaning for Noah, and would suggest that he realized by this act that he was setting apart himself unto God. It represented a complete surrender to his God.

The reader should recognize that the narrative in Genesis 8:20-22 says nothing about the meaning of this offering. I have pushed backward from the time of Moses the meaning and symbolism of the burnt offerings. If it did not carry for Noah the full significance which became clear in the time of Moses, it certainly possessed some such meaning for him. In passing we should note that the Lord had spoken to Noah before the Flood with reference to animals distinguished as clean and unclean. No word of explanation was given for this distinction. Nevertheless, in Noah's offering clean animals and birds were used. It is conceivable that there were unrecorded words of God to Noah in which this distinction was made, including the idea of clean animals being used in burnt offerings.

Noah's offering was acceptable to God and brought forth the promise, "I will never again curse the ground because of man, for the imagination of man's heart is evil from his youth; neither will I ever again destroy every living creature as I have done. While the earth remains, seedtime and harvest, cold and heat, summer and winter, day and night, shall not cease" (Gen. 8:21, 22). Here are words which also call for careful study. First, there is the Lord's promise never again to curse the ground because of man. This implied that the Lord would use positive measures of grace to deal with man's sinfulness. The description of man's sinful nature given here repeats the indictment given before the Flood which described the sinfulness of mankind outside of the godly line. Here the words are given as being true also of the righteous. The godly people were sinful by nature just as the Cain line. In the promise that followed, the temporal character of the earth stands out. The earth will not remain eternally, but while it does remain the course of nature will continue without interruption.

This suggests an eschatological aspect of the Deluge. It would appear that Peter saw in the Deluge a note of eschatology (1 Pet. 3:20, 21; 2 Pet. 2:5). While the first of these references by Peter presents some very difficult problems for interpretation, it is clear that Peter found some connection between Noah's being saved through building the ark and water baptism. The saving of Noah and his family through the ark possessed the eschatological note of salvation through water baptism. While the second statement by Peter lies in a different context, it reflects a similar idea. If this eschatological explanation interprets Peter's observation correctly, we may conclude that a profound lesson stands forth in the Flood: Just as the Flood brought judgment upon wicked men, and the few righteous were saved by means of the ark, so judgment will come upon all the ungodly, but those baptized into Christ will be saved.

It is significant also that Jesus compared His return with that of the days of Noah (Mt. 24:37-39). The Flood came suddenly upon the ungodly. In like manner His return will bring sudden judgment upon all the ungodly. From this point of view, the Deluge in the days of Noah prefigured the final judgment at the return of our Lord. The saving of the righteous Noah and his family anticipates the saving of the church of Jesus Christ at His return.

d. *God's Covenant with Noah*

This section (Gen. 9:1-7) shows that God's provision for mankind will continue in the world even though it is under a curse on account of sin. Life shall be propagated. God delivered all living things into the hand of man. Both animals and plants become the food of man. At this point an unexpected but significant prohibition is given. Man shall not eat flesh with its life, that is, its blood. In man's power over all living things he is forbidden to eat blood. By this restriction God would teach man the sacredness of life, but this command was not an end in itself. It would appear that the final author of the Pentateuch introduced these words here to prepare the reader for what God said in Lev. 17: 10, 11. This context repeats the idea of the relation of life and blood: "The life of the flesh is in the blood." To this God added, "I have given it for you upon the altar to make atonement for your souls; for it is the blood that makes atonement, by reason of the life." This Leviticus passage shows how God's unfolding revelation led man to a fuller understanding of the great message of the atonement. In this manner the whole sacrificial system instituted by Moses, as well as the the sacrifice of Christ, has its roots in this message of God to Noah.

The picture of animals' fear and dread of man would also seem to possess an eschatological note. This becomes clear in such passages as Isaiah 11:6-9; 65:25, and Habakkuk 2:14. These prophetic passages envision a time when there will no longer be animal fear and dread of man. They picture the restoration of the Edenic conditions before the Fall. Without attempting to interpret this prophetic language, it is sufficient for our present purpose to note God's plan to remove the curse which came upon man and beast by reason of the Fall and to restore the peaceful condition of Eden.

God's final instruction to Noah in this context has to do with the command, "Whoever sheds the blood of man, by man shall his blood be shed; for God made man in his own image." Students differ as to whether this statement is to be understood as a simple statement of a future condition or whether it is a command. The addition of the words, "God made man in his own image," seems to indicate that the words, "by man shall his blood be shed," are to be understood as an imperative. This means that God entrusted to mankind, living in that period, the responsibility of taking the life of the murderer. This appears to be the correct interpretation of these words. Although all through Old Testament times capital punishment was practiced, it is my belief that this command no longer obtains in this present age of grace because in Christ, love and mercy annul the law of vengeance.

Several New Testament Scriptures appear to have a bearing on God's command to Noah to avenge murder. In Romans 13:1-7 Paul wrote of the Christian's subjection to the governing authorities. He maintained that governments have been instituted by God. The government is the servant of God to execute His wrath on the evildoer. History tells us that outside of the theocracy of Israel no governments arose by direct institution of God. Peoples set up governments by their own initiative. But as in all human affairs, God uses human institutions to fulfill His purposes. In this sense existing governments have been instituted by God and fulfill His purposes. On this account, Daniel told the proud monarch Nebuchadnezzar that "the Most High rules the kingdom of men, and gives it to whom he will, and sets over it the lowliest of men" (Dan. 4:17). In the same strain Moses had spoken to Pharaoh the word of the Lord in the words, "For this purpose have I let you live, to show you my power, so that my name may be declared throughout all the earth" (Ex. 9:16). It belongs to New Testament theology to bring together the love and grace manifested in the kingdom of Christ and the authority to use force entrusted to the civil government.

This brings us to the covenant God established with Noah. God said to Noah, "Behold, I establish my covenant with you and your descendants after you." This word "covenant" (*berith*), we shall learn, is one of the most important in the whole study of theology. Since this is its first occurrence in the Old Testament, we do well to study its meaning here. Later we shall learn what meaning it carried when God made a covenant with Abraham and at a later time with Israel at Mt. Sinai. The new covenant made by Christ builds on the ideas in the Old Testament usage of this word and carries the covenant idea to its climax.

At least five aspects of the word "covenant" become apparent in its use here. First, God instituted the covenant. He took the initiative in establishing it. This shows the tremendous import which attaches to this word.

Second, it was an everlasting covenant. That is, it was not subject to change; it was unalterable; it possessed eternal validity. Thus Jeremiah, with possible conscious reference to this covenant, said, "Thus says the Lord: If I have not established my covenant with day and night and the ordinances of heaven and earth, then I will reject the descendants of Jacob and David my servant and will not choose one of his descendants to rule over the seed of Abraham, Isaac, and Jacob" (Jer. 33:25, 26).

Third, this was a universal covenant. It included the entire human race. It was not limited to one nation as was the covenant instituted at Mt. Sinai.

Fourth, in establishing this covenant God bound Himself by a solemn promise. Great importance attaches to the idea that God in His wisdom made such solemn commitment to Noah.

Fifth, God gave a token or sign of the covenant. Very significantly the sign was connected with "the ominous force of nature from which it pledges protection."[4] Some students see in this a symbol of God's tender mercy such as was expressed in Ezekiel's vision of God. He wrote, "Like the appearance of the bow that is in the cloud on the day of rain, so was the appearance of the brightness round about. Such was the appearance of the likeness of the glory of the Lord" (Ezek. 1: 28, 29).

Sixth, the covenant involved a clear note of eschatology. This was explicitly stated in Isaiah 54:9, 10: "For this is like the days of Noah to me: as I swore that the waters of Noah should no more go over the earth, so I have sworn that I will not be angry with you and will not rebuke you. For the mountains may depart and the hills be removed, but my steadfast love shall not depart from you, and my covenant of peace shall not be removed, says the Lord, who has compassion on you." This shows that the promise given to Noah pointed to God's steadfast love and His covenant of peace as eternally abiding with His people.

e. Noah's Prophetic Deliverance

The story of Noah's drunkenness, together with the conduct of his sons in relation to it, leads to a very significant prophetic utterance concerning his sons and their descendants (Gen. 9:20-27). With the exceptions of Enoch's predictions and the very brief statement of Noah's father concerning the relief which Noah would bring, these words mark the beginning of prophetic utterances by men of God. This is a very distinctive phenomenon in divine revelation. God chose certain servants of His, later called prophets, through whom He gave important predictions having to do with the affairs of men. In Noah's prophetic words we discern in greater detail God's direction of the course of history. The predictions had to do with the lives of men. They covered the gamut from the curse upon Canaan and his descendants to the blessings to be received by Shem and Japheth and their descendants.

This introduces a problem of how prophetic utterances dealing with the affairs of men should be interpreted. On the surface it would appear that Canaan by reason of his father's sin had become the victim of a curse from which he had no power to deliver himself. Along with this there appeared to be the inevitable blessings to Shem and Japheth without any apparent conditions. The problem centers in the bearing of divinely given predictions upon man's exercise of free will. Does God the creator of man prevent man from exercising the freedom belonging to human personality?

In the solution of this question let us note the following. First, we may safely assume that God the creator of man would always deal with him as a personal being with full powers and responsibility of moral choice. Man created in the image of God is held responsible to God for uncompromising obedience. When man chooses to disobey God, he brings upon himself just judgment for his sins. Second, prophetic utterances have their basis in God's omniscience. This omniscience on the part of God does not predetermine man's conduct. On this account predictions concerning the affairs of men do not as such predetermine the actions of men. Third, the biblical narratives up to this point have already shown a most significant characteristic of God's actions in the world. Theology has provided the term "divine providence" to describe this characteristic. This word "providence" has come into use in an effort to express a basic principle involved in a thoroughgoing theism. God is working in the affairs of men with the purpose of leading the world to the goal He has planned. In all these dealings with men God does not infringe upon man's freedom. Divine providence includes the direct guidance of men by God as well as His indirect guidance. Thus the stories of the line of Cain and of Seth, culminating in the Deluge with the saving of Noah and his family, can be understood only through the factor of divine providence. This will become increasingly apparent as we study the lives of Abraham, Jacob, Joseph, the children of Israel, and all other historic events of Old Testament history.

The curse upon Canaan was most severe. This curse becomes intelligible as we note the outworking of his father's sinful conduct among Canaan's descendants. The sins of the Canaanites partook of the same nature as that of Ham. It is very noteworthy that later Old Testament references bear out this fact.[5] The conditions of slavery to which the Canaanites became subject were the natural outworking of their sinfulness. That is, there was no direct intervention of God which brought the Canaanites into subjection to the descendants of the Shemites and of the Japhethites. Perhaps the most graphic biblical incident proving this is found in Israel's conquest of the land of Canaan. The overthrow of the Canaanites was God's judgment upon their sinfulness. In the actual outworking of this judgment Israel was the instrument of God in bringing it to pass.

Concerning Shem, Noah said, "Blessed be the Lord, the God of Shem and may Canaan be his servant" (Gen. 9:26).[6] The wording of this is unexpected. In contrast with what was said concerning Canaan we would expect the words, "Blessed be Shem." This form of language suggests the special blessing that will come to Shem by reason of the Lord being his God. The use of the word "Lord" thus far in the Book of Genesis leads us to believe that the writer was tracing events in the history of God's people which would bring to fulfillment the redemptive promise of Genesis 3:15. This implied that Noah recognized the distinctive character of the faith of Shem manifested in having the Lord as his God. To put it another way, since the Lord was his God, the distinctive blessings and grace of the Lord would be shared by Shem. There was nothing of merit in Shem for this blessing. Further, it appears to affirm that through Shem's descendants would come the knowledge of the true God.

Noah's last prophetic words were, "God enlarge Japheth, and let him dwell in the tents of Shem; and let Canaan be his slave." The interchange of divine names between this blessing and that of Shem is not without significance. If the J writer sought to dwell on those elements of early history which led to the choosing of a family and a nation in whom God would bring to fulfillment the redemption promise of Genesis 3:15, we may here find a close relation between the uses of God *(Elohim)* and the Lord *(Yahweh)* God. It was His desire to magnify God *(Elohim)* in relation to the universe as in Genesis 1 and also the Lord *(Yahweh)* God who brought on the Deluge and finally made a covenant with Noah with respect to the continuation of the world order. This is to say, *Elohim* is none other than *Yahweh Elohim.*

Two problems arise in the interpretation of this blessing: first the meaning of *enlarge* and second the antecedent of the word "him." It makes good sense to think of this enlarging as being territorial. It could well include the idea of prosperity. Certainly this has become literally true in that the Japhethites have become the dwellers of the largest land areas of the world. Included in the expansion of the Japhethites over the greatest portions of Asia, Europe, the Americas, and Australia, are the immeasurable resources found on these continents. Second, what is the antecedent of the pronoun "him" — Japheth or God? The thought of Japheth dwelling in the tents of Shem does carry great meaning; and, for this reason, may be the proper construction. If it is interpreted in this way, their dwelling as guests among the Shemites would lead to their sharing in the special blessings that would come to Shem. While it is true that the Greeks and Romans subjugated the Shemites politically, yet the identity of the Shemites was not destroyed. It was through this means that the blessings which belonged to the Shemites were appropriated by the Japhethites. Delitzsch made the striking comment, "We are all Japhethites dwelling in the tents of Shem."[7] On this point Driver wrote, "The words are a reflection of the more friendly regard with which religiously minded Israelites viewed the Japhethites, as compared with the Canaanites. They may also include perhaps in germ the thought (which is developed afterwards more fully by the great prophets, e.g., Is. 2:2-4) of the ultimate inclusion of the **peoples referred to Japheth as** their ᴵ **ancestor in the spiritual priv**ileges enjoyed by the descendants of Shem."⁸ In view of Driver's comment, is it too much to state that such passages as Genesis 12:3; 17:4; Isaiah 49:6; 60:3-5 reflect on this promise that God would give Japheth the promise that by right of descent belonged to Shem? It is certainly true that the note of universalism began as early as the promise to Abraham, developed throughout the Old Testament, and came to a climax in Isaiah's prophecies. Such is one of the greatest of wonders in the prophetic revelations of the Old Testament.

5. The Lord's Direction of History to the Call of Abraham

a. Table of Nations, Genesis 10

According to the testimony of archaeologists and historians this is the oldest recorded list of nations. Its structure at once arrests attention. Instead of the genealogy of Shem coming first by reason of his being the oldest son of Noah, it comes last. This suggests an evident purpose of the table. In the words of Richardson, "Here in Genesis 10 it is implied that God's purpose embraces all the nations, for all are in truth one big family, sprung from a common ancestor. An attempt is made to show the relationship of Israel to the other nations of the earth. After this has been done, the editor can devote his attention exclusively to the true line of development from Shem to Terah, the father of Abraham (11:10-26)."⁹ This purpose becomes still clearer in the light of the larger intent of the entire Book of Genesis. Of the fifty chapters in the book the author devoted eleven to an account of the acts of God which were necessary to the understanding of the call of Abraham, leading to the setting apart of the people of Israel to their great redemptive purpose in biblical history. The Shemites receive this special position of prominence because they constitute the race through whom the Lord provided redemption. At the same time other nations and races receive proportionate attention. They are not dropped from the realm of sacred history. They are also a part of the human race which God created. This table shows that all nations descended from a common stock. Before God they are all on a common level, men created in the image of God. This table is the necessary precedent to the genealogy of Shem leading to the patriarchs.

b. Tower of Babel and the Confusion of Tongues

Some students regard this story, Genesis 10, as a parable or myth. While the narrative presents some problems of interpretation, there appear to be no adequate reasons for rejecting its historical character. Practically all details of the narrative are in entire accord with what does take place in the affairs of men. The chief problem encountered in recognizing this as an actual historical event has to do with what appears to be an instantaneous confusion of languages. But nothing is given as to the time element involved in the confusion of tongues. The judgment of confusion of tongues does not lose its reality even if it did require years of time for it to be fulfilled.

The evident purposes for building a city and a tower lead to an understanding of the entire story. The builders said, "Let us make a name for ourselves, lest we be scattered abroad upon the face of the whole earth." The Lord interpreted their intention in the words, "This is only the beginning of what they will do; and nothing that they propose to do will now be impossible for them" (Gen. 11:4-6). Richardson finds in their motives an expression of pride. He says, "In the parable THE WHOLE EARTH desires to MAKE A NAME — and so it happens that man seeks to set up his name as a rival name to the *shem Jahweh,* to which alone praise and glory properly belong. (Cf. In the parable of the Fall the desire of Adam to be 'as God,' 3:5.) Man seeks by his own virtue and cleverness to BUILD A TOWER WHOSE TOP MAY REACH TO HEAVEN, to erect a civilization that recks little of God's grace and therefore of His law."[10]

Richardson also draws attention to the same spirit seen in Sodom and Gomorrah, Tyre, Babylon, and Rome. The wickedness of each is graphically portrayed in later Scriptures. It would almost seem that later writers reflected on the sins of the builders of Babel when they described the sins of these cities and countries. Richardson adds, "The author of the Apocalypse clearly has the parable of Genesis 11:1-9 in his mind when he writes: 'Thus with a mighty fall shall Babylon, the great City, be cast down, and shall be found no more at all' (Rev. 18:21)."[11] God's intervention had the evident design of checking sin's advance. It was a judgment upon the sinfulness of the world's civilization.

Less obvious is the fact that in this confusion of tongues the Lord took a further step toward the call of Abraham and the nation of Israel for their specialized task of carrying forward God's plan of salvation for all mankind. If the race had remained one, the separation of the family of Abraham evidently would have been impossible.

This incident possessed a clear note of eschatology. As Richardson puts it, "The story of Pentecost, with its miraculous reversal of the Babel confusion of languages, is itself a parable of the power of the divine love 'to bind together men from every nation under heaven' in the New Covenant of grace (Acts 2:5-11); the story of the Gift of Tongues at Pentecost is nothing other than the Babel story in reverse."[12]

It may be that Paul had in mind also the reversal of the confusion of tongues at Babel when he wrote, "There is neither Jew nor Greek, there is neither slave nor free, there is neither male nor female; for you are all one in Christ Jesus. And if you are Christ's then you are Abraham's offspring, heirs according to promise" (Gal. 3:28, 29). This is to say that oneness in the human race which is acceptable to God is possible alone through being one in Christ Jesus. The oneness of the race in building the Tower of Babel led to sinfulness because it was building up the power of sin. The oneness in Christ is that alone which gives honor and glory to God.

A similar picture of the reversal of the Babel confusion of languages has its glorious setting in heaven, where John beheld "a great multitude which no man could number, from every nation, from all tribes and peoples and tongues, standing before the throne and before the Lamb" (Rev. 7:9). This then is the eternal revocation of the Babel confusion of languages.

c. Election of the Shemites

The Lord chose the descendants of Shem to be the recipients of His revelation and witnesses to the world of His redemption (Gen. 11: 10-33). A very striking phenomenon characterizes the genealogy recorded in these verses. It gives the line of descent from Shem to Abraham. At once we ask, "What does this restricted line of descent mean?" for there is evident purpose in this genealogy. Here we meet the phenomenon of election: it is not the genealogy of Japheth nor of Ham but that of Shem which leads to Abraham. Naturally we wonder whether or not there was any peculiar fitness of the Shemitic line which lay at the basis of this election. Did individuals in the line of this descent show qualities of leadership which resulted in their being chosen? Varying answers have been given to these inquiries. Many students have sought to solve the problem on the basis of a natural development arising from some inherent fitness of the Shemites for religious leadership. None of these explanations satisfy the facts of the case.

We shall note presently that God encountered Abraham, calling him for his special task. There was no recorded qualification of Abraham for his special mission. Later Scriptures declare that this call manifested the grace of God toward him. While it is true that the Shemites possessed some traits which fitted them for receiving divine revelation, the call cannot be based on these traits. Vos noted that "The Shemites had a predominantly passive, receptive, rather than active or productive mentality."[13] Further, he observed that in the matter of religion the Shemites had departed the least from the true worship of God.

When every possible factor is considered, we must conclude that we have here one of the most staggering facts found in human history. It is this: The Shemites and not the Japhethites nor the Hamites were the people chosen by God for a special mission. The writer of Genesis was aware of this and consequently presented the line of descent from Shem to Abraham. The election of the Shemites grew out of God's fore-knowledge of their response and of how they would carry forward God's plan of salvation in the world.

Undoubtedly, God's election of these people for carrying out His purposes in the world went deeper than an act of grace. God surely bestowed upon His chosen servants the gifts needed for their tasks. But this brings in another consideration. It is the fact that "Israel was the elected nation, but as a nation it miserably failed in its vocation. . . . It would seem, then, as if, on the external side, election had failed of its result."[14] James Orr proceeded to show that even though Israel failed as a nation, there was, nevertheless, a remnant which was faithful to God in whom God fulfilled His purposes. A number of biblical passages give some light on the doctrine of election as shown in this narrative.[15] None of these, however, explain the mystery of election. The most staggering idea of human history, the election of the Shemites, remains.

For Additional Reading and Reference:

Napier, *Song of the Vineyard*, pp. 52-60.
Oehler, *Theology of the Old Testament*, pp. 54-57.
Payne, *The Theology of the Older Testament*, p. 96.
von Rad, *Old Testament Theology*, Vol. I, pp. 154-65.
Sauer, *The Dawn of World Redemption*, pp. 63-88.
Schultz, *Old Testament Theology*, Vol. I, pp. 86-125.
Thielicke, *How the World Began*, pp. 187-300.
Titcomb, *Revelation in Progress* (written in 1871), pp. 16-25.
Vischer, *The Witness of the Old Testament to Christ*, pp. 68-116.
Vos, *Biblical Theology — Old and New Testaments*, pp. 56-78.
Weidner, *Biblical Theology of the Old Testament*, pp. 40-46.

See Indexes for Gen. 4 — 11, Abel, Cain, Deluge, Flood, Babel, Semites, Noah, in the following references:
Baab, *Theology of the Old Testament.*
Burrows, *An Outline of Biblical Theology.*

Davidson, *The Theology of the Old Testament.*
Eichrodt, *The Theology of the Old Testament,* Vol. I.
Jacob, *Theology of the Old Testament.*
Kaufmann, *The Religion of Israel.*
Knight, *A Christian Theology of the Old Testament.*
Knudson, *The Religious Teaching of the Old Testament.*
Köhler, L., *Old Testament Theology.*
Pfeiffer, *Religion in the Old Testament.*
Robinson, *Inspiration and Revelation in the Old Testament.*
Rowley, *The Re-Discovery of the Old Testament.*
Vriezen, *An Outline of Old Testament Theology.*
Wahlstrom, *God Who Redeems.*
Wingren, *Creation and Law.*

Appended Note

Use of the Name *Lord* in Genesis

The name "Lord" poses a problem of considerable dimension. While its involvements become clear only after we have traced the biblical narrative to the time of Moses, there is need of giving it some attention here. God said to Moses, "I am the Lord. I appeared to Abraham, to Isaac, and to Jacob, as God Almighty, but by my name the Lord I did not make myself known to them" (Ex. 6:2, 3). It may be profitable to give an attempted solution at this point so that along the way we can check its accuracy as the elements of the problem become more apparent. In an earlier chapter I noted the interchange of divine names, which on the basis of literary criticism gives evidence of embedded documents in the Book of Genesis. Thus in Genesis 1:1 — 2:3 the word *Elohim* (God) is used, whereas in the second account of creation the name of *Yahweh Elohim* (Lord God) is used. This interchange of names for Deity continues throughout the Pentateuch. On this account the author's statement that men began to call upon the name of the Lord arrests our attention. According to literary criticism this statement belongs to the J Document, that in which the word for God is *Yahweh,* translated Lord. Throughout Genesis in these so-called J sections both the writer and the speakers used the word "Lord" in speaking of God. Thus Lamech the father of Noah, Noah, Abraham, and Jacob used the word "Lord" in their quoted words. Very striking in this respect are Jacob's words, "If God will be with me . . . then the Lord shall be my God" (Gen. 28:20, 21). Over against all this are the words of God to Moses in which God explicitly said that by His name, The Lord, He had not made Himself known to the patriarchs. He had appeared to them as God Almighty.

By way of an attempted solution, we might begin with the fact that the final author of the Pentateuch saw no need of explaining the problem. In making this final recension he allowed the use of the word "Lord" in the J Document to stand. Evidently the author of the J Document did not think it necessary to declare when the name "the Lord" was revealed to the people of God. He was content to use the name "the Lord" all through his narrative from the Creation onward. The original author of Exodus 6:3, 4 did have a concern to state when God had actually made known His name. For this reason all through the Genesis narrative the author of this Document used the word "God" for deity. Thus understood the problem of the use of the name, "the Lord" throughout the J Documents of Genesis does not conflict with the statement of P in Exodus 6:3. In this connection it may add to our discussion to note what appears to be the distinctive character of the J Document. For our purpose it would appear that the author of the J Document had a concern to present deity in relation to His covenant people. The Lord sought to restore the fellowship between Himself and man as found in the Garden of Eden. He would accomplish this by entering into covenant relationship with them.

1. See note appended at the end of the chapter.

2. Ralph H. Elliott, *The Message of Genesis* (Nashville: Broadman Press, 1961), p. 65.

3. See my work, *The Holy Spirit and the Holy Life* (Scottdale: Herald Press, 1959), pp. 12-14.

4. Vos, *op. cit.*, p. 67.

5. Gen. 15:16; 19:5; Lev. 18:3; 22:24; Deut. 9:4, 5; 12:29-32.

6. *The Berkeley Version in Modern English.*

7. Vos, *op. cit.*, p. 71.

8. *The Book of Genesis* (New York: Edwin S. Gorham, 1907), pp. 110 f.

9. *Gen. I-XI Introduction and Commentary* (London WCI: SCM Press, Ltd. 1954), p. 116.

10. *Op. cit.*, p. 124.

11. *Op. cit.*, p. 125.

12. *Op. cit.*, p. 126.

13. *Op. cit.*, p. 73.

14. *Dictionary of the Bible*, edited by James Hastings, revised edition by Frederick C. Grant and H. H. Rowley (New York: Charles Scribner's Sons, 1963), "Election," by James Orr, revised by Norman H. Snaith, p. 239. This is a brief but very instructive article on election.

15. See Josh. 24:1 ff.; Acts 7:1-5; 13:17; Gal. 3:6-18; Heb. 11:8.

CHAPTER IV
GOD'S REVELATION THROUGH
THE PATRIARCHS

1. Critical Views of the Historicity of the Patriarchs

Quite a number of modern works in the areas of biblical history, commentaries on Genesis, and of Old Testament theology raise serious questions on the historicity of the Bible characters, Abraham, Isaac, Jacob, and Joseph. Denials of their existence or of the historical character of the Genesis narratives are the result of the authors' views of the origin of the Pentateuch. In no case is any historical evidence given which denies or disproves the historicity of these characters. These views ignore the positive evidence found in the Book of Genesis together with numerous references given throughout the Old and New Testaments which add their witness to the lives of these patriarchs. Through whatever process the Pentateuch came into its present form, there is no escape from believing that the writers sought to represent these men as historical persons together with the family stories associated with each. The integrity of all those who shared in the writing of the Pentateuch is deeply involved at this point. The reader is invited to study the appended scriptural references in this footnote.[1] How some scholars can reject or ignore all this evidence is difficult to understand. Were the authors of the Pentateuch and such Bible characters as Moses, Joshua, Elijah, Hezekiah, Ezra, Isaiah, Micah, Matthew, Luke, Jesus, Peter, Stephen, Paul, the author of Hebrews, and James so uncritical as to interpret the Genesis stories as actual history? The characteristic which underlies all biblical history, whether of the Old Testament or the New, is that it "is the record of that series of events which form the basis for the religion of the Bible."[2]

It is essential that we become aware of the issues involved in the rejection of the historical character of the patriarchs. The definition of biblical history just given clearly points up the issue involved. In a word it is this: Is the religion of the Bible grounded in historical fact or in mere folklore or myth? Biblical history is unique in this that it presents the record of the supernatural, whether we are reading of the call of Abraham, the dividing of the Red Sea in the time of Moses, the falling of fire from heaven to consume Elijah's sacrifice, Daniel's interpretation of Nebuchadnezzar's dream, the virgin birth of Christ, the raising of Lazarus, or our Lord's resurrection.

In all of these we are dealing with supernatural events which occurred in history as recorded in several books of the Bible. The structure of the Bible is that of history and not of folklore. Biblical history arose in the same fashion as all other history arose. Added to this is the full recognition given to the characteristic that history includes the supernatural acts of God. The writers attested the historicity of these supernatural acts. The greatest of all history was the resurrection of our Lord. Paul put the evidence in this fashion: "He appeared to Cephas, then to the twelve. Then he appeared to more than five hundred brethren at one time, most of whom are still alive, though some have fallen asleep. Then he appeared to James, then to all the apostles. Last of all, as to one untimely born, he appeared also to me" (1 Cor. 15:5-8). This sort of approach to giving proof of an event of the past is absolutely trustworthy. Paul knew that he was giving attestation to the miracle of miracles of biblical history. This same viewpoint attaches to all biblical history. Justification for giving all this biblical data rests on the supreme importance of the fact under consideration. On this ground then I shall proceed, having full confidence in the historical character of the narratives dealing with the patriarchs.

2. God's Encounters with Abraham

a. The Call

The call of Abraham brings us again to the element of election. God manifested the election of Abraham by way of a direct call. The author of Genesis wrote, "Now the Lord said to Abram, 'Go from your country and your kindred and your father's house to the land that I will show you. And I will make of you a great nation, and I will bless you, and make your name great, so that you will be a blessing. I will bless those who bless you, and him who curses you I will curse; and by you all the families of the earth will bless themselves'" (Gen. 12:1-3). Both Stephen and the author of Hebrews gave their attestation to this direct call (Acts 7:2-4; Heb. 11:8). Stephen added the idea that the God of glory appeared to Abraham when he was in Mesopotamia before he lived in Haran. It was in this appearance that God gave the command to Abraham. The author of Hebrews noted the fact of Abraham's obedience on receiving the call. It involved a special mission of Abraham and his posterity in the world. The threefold promise made to Abraham included possession of the land of Canaan, numerous posterity, and through his descendants the blessing of all the families of the earth. Certainly this call led to a great promise in Abraham's life.

The author of Hebrews also pointed to the faith aspect of Abraham's call. Abraham believed God and on the basis of this faith, he obeyed. The faith aspect obtained larger significance in the fact that while Abraham was only a sojourner in the land of promise he looked forward "to the city which had foundations, whose builder and maker is God." In other words, Abraham's faith reached beyond the inheritance of the land of Canaan to that great spiritual possession of the city built by God.

God's call of Abraham anticipated election as a continuing operation among the chosen people of God. Paul touched on this point when he wrote of the great spiritual blessings which came to Israel (Rom. 9:4-13): "To them belong the sonship, the glory, the covenants, the giving of the law, the worship, and the promises; to them belong the patriarchs, and of their race, according to the flesh, is the Christ." He continued, "Not all who are descended from Israel belong to Israel, and not all are children of Abraham because they are his descendants; but 'Through Isaac shall your descendants be named.' " He showed that the promise was continued through Isaac and through Jacob. The principle that operated through all this was "that God's purpose of election might continue, not because of works but because of his call." Paul carried the thought a bit further with reference to the people of Israel by writing, "At the present time there is a remnant, chosen by grace. But if it is by grace, it is no longer on the basis of works; otherwise grace would no longer be grace" (Rom. 11:5, 6). By comparing these two quotations it becomes evident that there is a close relationship between election and grace. Thus while Paul unfolded the idea of election among the descendants of Abraham and by so doing showed that election was operating through patriarchal history, this election was not an evidence of unconditional predestination but rather of God's unlimited grace.

The election of Abraham emphasized another element, namely, universalism. All the families of the earth would be blessed through Abraham. God was separating Abraham from the rest of mankind in order that through his descendants blessings should come to all mankind. The incident of Melchizedek's blessing Abraham set forth this truth in a somewhat veiled form. This Melchizedek was the king of Salem and priest of God Most High. This great king-priest who did not belong to the chosen family but stood in the Genesis account as the last representative of mankind outside the Semitic line who still worshiped God Most High — this Melchizedek seemed to grasp the specialized mission of Abraham and his descendants. On this account he said, "Blessed be Abram by God Most High, maker of heaven and earth; and blessed be God Most High, who has delivered your enemies into your hand" (Gen. 14:19, 20). In recognition of Melchizedek's greatness Abraham gave him a tenth of everything.

Centuries later David gave profound meaning to this incident when with reference to the coming Messiah he wrote, "The Lord has sworn and will not change his mind, 'You are a priest for ever after the order of Melchizedek' " (Ps. 110:4). By this language he described the coming King-Priest, the Messiah, as being a Priest after the order of Melchizedek. From the standpoint of the Genesis narrative, no record appears of the beginning of his priestly service, nor of its termination. This became typical of the great King-Priest to come who would in all reality be a Priest forever. It would appear from this psalm that Melchizedek saw in one of Abraham's descendants the One who would be a Priest forever.

It remained for the author of Hebrews to confirm this idea. He showed that the Lord Jesus Christ is this Priest after the order of Melchizedek. We might have expected that Jesus would be a Priest after the order of Aaron. But a priesthood of a superior character was needed. Melchizedek, in type, represented a superior priesthood to that of Aaron's. Jesus, the Son of God, alone could qualify as an eternal Priest. On this account, just as Melchizedek ministered to mankind in general in his day, from Abraham's seed One should come who would minister to all mankind as an eternal Priest. The call of Abraham led to the universalism of Christ's eternal Priesthood (Heb. 5:6-10; 7:1-19).

b. The Promise

The threefold promise made to Abraham calls for additional attention. There was mounting significance to each promise. To receive the land of Canaan was indeed a great promise. History shows that this land was strategically located as the pathway of the nations from Asia to Africa. The people in controlling this narrow strip of land occupied a most strategic position. The promise of numerous posterity was still more significant in view of Abraham's having no prospect of any children. The fulfillment of this promise required a miracle. The third promise carried still greater significance. It was bound up with the idea of all families of the earth being blessed through his seed. God did not disclose the nature of this blessing but we would gather that it would come from the Lord and would be spiritual in character.

The precise meaning of the third promise presents a problem involving a point of Hebrew syntax. The verb translated *will bless themselves* (RSV) occurs five times in the Genesis narratives. In three of these (12:3; 18:18; 28:14) the Niphal stem occurs. This usually has a passive sense but it may also be reflexive. In the others (22:18; 26:4) the Hithpael stem is found. This carries a reflexive sense only. The Septuagint translated all of these cases as passive. The two New Testament quotations (Acts 3:25; Gal. 3:8) also give the passive form to this verb. Among the English translations the KJV and the ASV translate all five as passive. It would seem to me that since the Septuagint and the New Testament quotations translate the verb as passive, the sense of the verb is properly understood as passive. There is nevertheless no serious difference of meaning between the reflexive sense and the passive sense. Understood as the passive, the promise meant that God would bless all nations through Abraham. The reflexive sense would carry the idea that all nations would appropriate the blessings coming through Abraham. The passive idea came to fulfillment in all nations being blessed through Jesus Christ. There is also the reflexive sense shown in the need of all peoples receiving and appropriating by faith the salvation offered by Christ.

This third promise took on a distinctive meaning in the Lord's later disclosures to Abraham.[3] Most explicit are the words, "In thy seed shall all the nations of the earth be blessed" (22:18, ASV). Paul laid hold of this distinctive promise when he wrote, "Now the promises were made to Abraham and to his offspring. It does not say, 'And to offsprings,' referring to many; but, referring to one, 'And to your offspring,' which is Christ" (Gal. 3:16). This Messianic reference of the singular noun *zerah*, translated *seed, offspring,* or *descendant,* shows Paul's profound insight as to the meaning of Scripture. In the hands of some scholars this interpretation is merely a piece of "Rabbinical invention." But this is an unwarranted criticism; it lacks the spiritual insight possessed by Paul as to the meaning of the entire narrative. Frequently New Testament writers make clear hidden truths found in Old Testament predictions.

Careful study of the nature of the unfolding of divine revelation will show that Paul's interpretation is in harmony with the several narratives which refer to God's promise to Abraham. Romans 9:6-13 may be regarded as an enlargement of the truth given in Galatians 3:16. In the Romans context, *seed* had reference to Isaac alone and not to Ishmael, to Jacob and not to Jacob and Esau. Thus through the unfolding history as disclosed in the several genealogies of the Bible, the seed of Abraham definitely pointed to Christ. This became most explicitly clear in Matthew's genealogy. The seed of Abraham found its fulfillment in Christ, and through Him the blessing came to Abraham's true descendants, as expressed by Paul, "If you are Christ's, then you are Abraham's offspring, heirs according to promise" (Gal. 3:29).

c. The Covenant

God's covenant with Abraham disclosed a larger and more significant meaning than it possessed for Noah. This is entirely what we should expect. As the Lord instituted the covenant with Noah, so He also instituted the covenant with Abraham (Gen. 15:7-21). This gave the covenant-relation unique significance by establishing the Lord's authoritative relation with Abraham. The patriarch came to recognize that he was drawn into a most sacred relationship with God. The heart of the encounter of the Lord with Abraham became clear in the fellowship established between them. It had its foundation in the grace of God as manifested in the promise. Later writers expressed this relationship in terms of Abraham's being the "Friend of God."[4]

The covenant made with Abraham had its basis in a very significant sacrifice (Gen. 15:7-17). In comparison with the sacrifices instituted by Moses we gather that since it was a bloody sacrifice it involved the idea of expiation. It does not appear, however, that expiation lay at the center of this bloody sacrifice. Since no special use was made of the blood, we may conclude that the significance of the sacrifice lay in the other acts of the transaction. The cutting of the animals in two and of laying each half over against the other, followed by the smoking firepot and flaming torch passing between these pieces, would lead to the meaning of the sacrifice. From Jeremiah 34:18-20, as well as similar sacrifices of other peoples, we gather that both parties entering into a covenant relationship would pass between the divided pieces of the sacrifice. By so doing they were bringing upon themselves the curse of having their bodies divided if they broke the covenant. The unique difference found in this case lay in the fact that Abraham did not pass between the pieces. Only the smoking firepot and flaming torch which symbolized God's part in the covenant passed between the pieces. As in a later time, "The appearance of the glory of the Lord was like a devouring fire on the top of the mountain in the sight of the people of Israel" (Ex. 24:17).[5] It may be that the one-sidedness of this act of covenant institution shows that it was not a pact but a promise. God made the promise and bound Himself to keep it. While Abraham made the sacrifice, he did not as such become a party to the covenant. He was the receiver of the promise. When the Lord made the promise to Abraham that his descendants should be as numerous as the stars of the heavens, Abraham "believed the Lord; and he reckoned it to him as righteousness" (Gen. 15:6). This makes still clearer the "promise" nature of the covenant and of Abraham's faith relationship to it. The writer of Genesis had the insight to add that God reckoned this faith to

Abraham as righteousness. Paul picked up this statement and used it as the chief structural foundation for his letters to the Galatians and to the Romans.[6] In other words, Paul found in this whole transaction the heart of the gospel.

This covenant promise given to Abraham carried with it a strong ethical requirement. The Lord said, "I am God Almighty; walk before me, and be blameless" (Gen. 17:1). Through these words the patriarch learned that his manner of life would need to be conformed to God's nature. We observed that Noah was a righteous man and blameless in his generation. And now God commanded Abraham to walk before Him in the same manner of life. As Abraham looked about to other peoples of his time, he undoubtedly was aware of man's sinfulness. Now God bade him lead a blameless life, a life free from moral defect, a perfect life.

One more very significant part of the transaction calls for study. It was the institution of the rite of circumcision. In the record of its institution (17:9-14) circumcision became the sign of an individual's share in the covenant, as well as his obedience to it. This was not a new ceremony. It had been practiced by the people of Egypt, Ethiopia, Phoenicia, and Arabia. For reasons unknown to us it was not practiced by the people of Babylonia, Assyria, and Philistia. The absence of an account of the origin of circumcision presents some problems in our study. Some scholars conclude that the Lord instituted circumcision not as something new but as a ceremony already existing — but gave it a new significance. It is conceivable that at an earlier time God may have given some unrecorded commands with reference to circumcision as well as to sacrifices in general, which were perpetuated by the various peoples in more or less deteriorated forms. As I have already emphasized, instead of the people of God borrowing from other nations the various forms of polytheistic worship and of giving them a true monotheistic pattern, it is more in accord with the history of religion and with the Bible to believe that all religions outside of the religion of the Hebrew nation represent deteriorations and degradations of the true religion.

The Genesis record does not give any explanation of the meaning of circumcision. It seems evident that both in Israel and outside of Israel circumcision was an act designed for removing physical uncleanness and did not have a religious significance. We have here the instance of an act which in time obtained great spiritual significance. Moses felt himself unqualified to speak to Pharaoh because he regarded himself as a man of uncircumcised lips. The Lord speaking through Moses referred to the uncircumcised heart of Israel which required heart humbling and making of amends. Moses also spoke of the necessity of circumcising the heart and of no longer being stubborn. Looking to a future time Moses wrote, "The Lord your God will circumcise your heart and the heart of your offspring, so that you will love the Lord your God with all your heart and with all your soul, that you may live."

In these several cases[7] it becomes clear that circumcision symbolized the removal of moral uncleanness. It stood for a spiritual cleansing. Both Jeremiah and Ezekiel attached the same spiritual meaning to this rite.[8] Paul brought circumcision into clear focus when he concluded a discussion with the words, "real circumcision is a matter of the heart, spiritual and not literal" (Rom. 2:25-29). In speaking of Abraham he placed circumcision in relation to Abraham's faith and to his being accounted righteous. Paul wrote, "He received circumcision as a sign or seal of the righteousness which he had by faith while he was still uncircumcised. The purpose was to make him the father of all who believe without being circumcised and who thus have righteousness reckoned to them, and likewise the father of the circumcised who are not merely circumcised but also follow the example of the faith which our father Abraham had before he was circumcised" (Rom. 4:11, 12).[9]

With this spiritual significance of circumcision understood it is proper to inquire what significance attaches to its being performed on male infants on the eighth day. Since it was required and not optional, we may gather that whatever significance attached to the act had to do with all mankind. Since the act was performed so early in infancy it would suggest that spiritual uncleanness traces back to earliest infancy. Since circumcision had to do with the male organ of generation, we may have here the suggestion that man in his very nature is sinful. He does not become sinful in the process of development. Rather, it is the case of the uncleanness and sinfulness of the whole human race. It is a truth developed by Paul in Romans 5:12-21, where he said, "Death spread to all men."

d. The Tests

According to Hebrews 11:17 the Lord tested Abraham on a number of occasions. Always the faith of the patriarch shone forth in all clearness. The recorded instances of these tests had their beginning already in Ur of the Chaldeans. Stephen gave witness to this when he said, "The God of glory appeared to our father Abraham, when he was in Mesopotamia, before he lived in Haran, and said to him, 'Depart from your land and from your kindred and go into the land which I

will show you' " (Acts 7:2, 3). For Abraham to leave the fertile land
of Ur and to go into a land which God would show him was an exceedingly severe test of faith. Whether or not God had given the threefold promise to Abraham in Ur, had little bearing on the severity of
the test, which centered in leaving his fatherland, being completely detached from his kindred, and going to a land unknown to him. The
famine in the land of Canaan which made it necessary for Abraham to
go to Egypt intensified this test of faith. He may have thought, "Of
what value is a land in which famines occur?"

The test took on new dimensions when Abraham and Sarah were
kept childless beyond the time of natural childbirth. Yet the promise
centered in a child to be born to them. While Sarah's suggestion that
Abraham take Hagar as a wife and in this way become the father of
a child has the appearance of a lack of faith on the part of Sarah and
Abraham, it may be that Abraham did not have a full comprehension of
the specific nature of the promise. At any rate there is no recorded rebuke to Abraham for taking this step. The entire incident serves to
show the severity of the test.

God's tests of Abraham reached their climax in the command to offer Isaac as a burnt offering. The fervent trust of Abraham in God
stands forth in the entire narrative, especially so at the point where
Isaac made inquiry about the lamb for the burnt offering. Abraham
proceeded to carry out God's command literally to the moment when he
took the knife to slay Isaac. At this point the angel of the Lord intervened and spared Abraham from slaying his own son for a burnt offering.

We are not aware of how Abraham understood the idea of a burnt
offering. If we may again project backward from the time of Moses the
significance of a burnt offering, we may conclude that it symbolized for
Abraham the consecration, the setting apart of Isaac wholly unto the
Lord. The command was of such a character that Abraham would
no longer have Isaac with him as a son. On this point the author of
Hebrews expressed the clear meaning of this entire incident when he
wrote, "He considered that God was able to raise men even from the
dead; hence, figuratively speaking, he did receive him back" (Heb.
11:19). Such a test is unparalleled in human history.

All these tests served to show that Abraham's life was a school of
faith. Through these tests his faith became stronger, was deeply enriched, and revealed for all time the real character of a godly man's
trust in God. In a word, his faith in God was a trust in God's omnipotence. Let us take a closer look at this omnipotence of God and
Abraham's response of faith.

3. Supernatural Power of God and Abraham's Response of Faith

a. *The Lord Revealed as God Almighty*

"The Lord appeared to Abram, and said to him, 'I am God Almighty; walk before me, and be blameless' " (Gen. 17:1). With these words the Lord revealed to Abraham a most significant aspect of His nature, The Lord is God Almighty. The meaning of the Hebrew expression *El Shaddai* (God Almighty) presents some problems. The trend of thinking among scholars leads to the explanation of *Shaddai* as, "The Mountain One." Edmond Jacob, following Albright, feels that this explanation may be regarded as established.[10] On the other hand, von Rad says, "The meaning of the name *El Shaddai* has not yet been explained satisfactorily."[11] On this point Vriezen says, "The use of *El* to denote God is a feature of the patriarchal period; it emphasizes the greatness and sublimity of God, which emphasis is found even more strongly in *El Shaddai*. . . . Sometimes God is referred to by *periphrasis;* as such may be regarded the names: . . . *Shaddai* (perhaps 'the Mountain,' a widespread Semitic word for God, denoting the stability of the Divine; cf. the image of God as a *Rock* in the Old Testament)."[12]

The Septuagint translators varied in the translation of *El Shaddai.* Throughout the Pentateuch the Greek word *Theos* (God) is used to translate *Shaddai.* This suggests that the translators looked at the word *Shaddai* as an intensifier of the word "God." Throughout the Book of Job the Greek word *Pantokrator* (Almighty) is used to translate *Shaddai.* From this it appears that the English translation, God Almighty, expresses accurately the thought of the Hebrew. If this conclusion is correct, we may then say that God by this statement made the claim that He was omnipotent. The gods of the people of the land of Canaan were speechless and accordingly could make no such claim. Abraham's God revealed Himself by way of an appearance or manifestation and spoke to him the words, "I am God Almighty." The frequent use of this expression for "God" throughout the Bible indicates the profound meaning which the people of God attached to it.

b. *Abraham's Response of Faith*

At the close of one of the incidents in which the Lord spoke to Abraham, He gave the promise that the patriarch's descendants would be as numerous as the stars of the heavens. The writer concluded, "And he believed the Lord; and he reckoned it to him as righteousness" (Gen. 15:6). This statement in its setting at once arrests the reader's attention. It expressed Abraham's response of faith to God's most extraordinary promise. In the first place, this statement placed the matter of faith in a religious context. It indicated that when Abraham believed the Lord, He accounted Abraham as righteous. Abraham stood before God as a righteous man not on the basis of his own good works but on the gracious acceptance of Abraham by reason of his faith. In a very striking manner Paul picked up the same words and used them to show how all believers gain right standing with God. This faith relationship of Abraham to the Lord lay at the very center of Abraham's religious experience. It showed that the promise rested on the grace of God.[13]

In the second place, this statement contains in a nutshell the ingredients of Abraham's faith.[14] First, Abraham's faith was a belief in the trustworthiness of God. Through the several revelations of the Lord, Abraham had come to realize that God was worthy of his trust. Through these several encounters with God the relationship of Abraham and God had become an intimate, personal one. Second, Abraham's believing the Lord was an act of trust. The literal rendering of *heemin* (believed) as it is connected with *be* (in) construed with *Yahweh* (Lord) carries the idea of Abraham's developing confidence in the Lord. He proved constant in his faith. He was relying upon the Lord as the One who is true and stable or as von Rad put it, "as fixing oneself on *Yahweh*."[15]

Third, Abraham's believing the Lord was distinctive in that it was a trust in the omnipotent One. Paul gave a measure of this kind of trust when he wrote concerning Abraham, "In hope he believed against hope" (Rom. 4:18) and a bit farther on, "No distrust made him waver concerning the promise of God, but he grew strong in his faith as he gave glory to God, fully convinced that God was able to do what he had promised" (vv. 20, 21). The author of Hebrews pointed up this matter still more sharply when he wrote, "He considered that God was able to raise men even from the dead; hence, figuratively speaking, he did receive him back" (Heb. 11:19). This aspect of faith in God occurs repeatedly in biblical history. Reflect on Moses' words to the people of Israel at the Red Sea wher. he said, "Fear not, stand firm, and see the salvation of the Lord" (Ex. 14:13). Or witness Elijah on Mt. Carmel in the presence of all the prophets of Baal when in response to his prayer to God the fire of the Lord fell and consumed the burnt offering. Then again listen to Daniel as he related to Nebuchadnezzar his dream and expounded it or as he interpreted to Belshazzar the handwriting upon the wall. All these reveal God as the Omnipotent One.

Fourth, this faith had its counterpart in Abraham's submission, humility, and obedience in the presence of the Lord. This became apparent on occasions when God was speaking to Abraham that he fell on his face (Gen. 17:3). The same spirit is apparent in Abraham's conversation with the three men who came to his tent door to reassure him of his having a son. Also witness the intercession of Abraham for Sodom. This incident revealed the genuine humility of being able to trust that the Judge of all the earth would do right (Gen. 18:22-33). James grasped the obedience counterpart to trust when he wrote, "You see that faith was active along with his works, and faith was completed by works" (Jas. 2:22).

Fifth, the faith of Abraham involved a friendship such as is possible alone through absolute trust in God. Three times in Holy Writ Abraham was called the friend of God.[16] The title, "Friend of God," expressed in most meaningful language the experiential relationship between Abraham and the Lord. As a case in point, when God was entering into a covenant relationship with Abraham as recorded in Genesis 15, "The dividing of the animals and the walking of God (alone) between the pieces literally signifies that God invokes upon Himself the fate of dismemberment in case He should not keep faith with Abraham."[17] For some reason the English rendering *friend* does not give the literal translation of either the Hebrew (*ahab*) or the Septuagint (*agapao*). In the Old Testament occurrences of *friend* Abraham was God's beloved one. As some scholars point out, the idea of reciprocity found in the word *friend* is not contained in the word *beloved*, yet uniformly English translations use the word *friend*. Probing into this matter a bit we may conclude that for Abraham to be God's *beloved* involved the reciprocal response on the part of Abraham. Thus to be the Friend of God Abraham regarded the Lord as his Beloved. This is the nature of Abraham's friendship as giving meaning to his trust in God.

Sixth, Abraham's faith laid hold of the spiritual nature of the Lord's promises. Jesus spoke of this ingredient when He said, "Your father Abraham rejoiced that he was to see my day; he saw it and was glad" (Jn. 8:56). The author of the Hebrews described Abraham's leaving his own land and sojourning in the land of promise as in a foreign land and living in tents, "For he looked forward to the city which has foundations, whose builder and maker is God" (Heb. 11:8-10). These words tell us not only that Abraham's faith laid hold of the idea of a permanent dwelling in Canaan, but also that his faith grasped the ultimate realization of this promise of his future eternal abode in heaven.

Seventh, Abraham's faith rose above a belief in the existence of many gods. His trust in God excluded the existence of other gods; it possessed the unique character of a trust which is possible alone in a thoroughgoing monotheism. This characteristic of his faith becomes all the more apparent as it stands in contrast with the polytheistic concept held by other peoples in his time.[18] The experiential relations of Abraham to the Lord have meaning alone in his belief that the Lord was the one and only true God.

In the third place, note the ethical aspect of Abraham's faith in God. The manner of life of the people of God as it stood in contrast with the wickedness of mankind became evident in the lives of Enoch and Noah. Both of these men "walked with God." It was said of Noah that he "was a righteous man, blameless in his generation." Now the Lord encountered Abraham and said, "Walk before me, and be blameless" (Gen. 17:1). Moffatt gives the sense very effectively in his translation, "Live ever mindful of my presence, and so be blameless." With this command the Lord made clear to Abraham that to be a sharer in a covenant relationship with Him made specific requirements upon the patriarch's manner of life. He should seek to satisfy a righteous and holy God by a life that bore likeness to his God. This likeness was expressed in the word "blameless." The Hebrew word *tamim*, translated blameless, was the word commonly used to describe the physical perfection required in animals for sacrifice. They were to be without blemish. This was a very fitting word to be given a moral connotation as was frequently done in the Old Testament. Note the instance of Moses speaking to Israel, "You shall be blameless before the Lord your God" (Deut. 18:13). This word carries the sense of perfect, faultless, undefiled, upright, sincere, and sound. It was a very appropriate word for capturing a total view of a godly man's manner of life.

Having already given attention to the meaning of circumcision, we may note here only that this rite also contributed to Abraham's grasp of the ethical character of his faith in God. His comprehension of a blameless walk before God may have led him to see in the rite of circumcision a symbol of the inner cleansing of the heart. The Lord knew the inner nature of Abraham's life according to which he would charge his children "to keep the way of the Lord by doing righteousness and justice" (Gen. 18:19). The ethical character of Abraham's faith in God comes vividly to the forefront in his intercession for Sodom. Abraham's faith could accept only an affirmative reply to his question, "Shall not the Judge of all the earth do right" (Gen. 18:22-33)?

4. Forms of Revelation During the Patriarchal Period

The author of Hebrews grasped the significance of the fact that God spoke to the fathers "in many and various ways." It is this phenomenon that became evident in God's revelation to Abraham. The different forms or modes of revelation became increasingly important, especially as they related both to the fact of divine revelation and to its content.

Varying modes of revelation do not point to different levels in the fact of divine revelation. The different modes of revelation, as Dr. Warfield wrote, "occur side by side, God is speaking, on the same level. No discrimination is drawn between them in point of worthiness as modes of revelation, and much less in point of purity in the revelations communicated through them." After commenting on the different forms of revelation Warfield continued, "The fundamental fact in all revelation is that it is from God. This is what gives unity to the whole process of revelation, given though it may be in divers portions and in divers manners and distributed though it may be through the ages in accordance with the mere will of God, or as it may have suited His developing purpose." [19]

a. Spoken Words of the Lord [20]

Speaking is the most direct form of divine revelation. Presumably the spoken word was audible. We need not attempt to say, however, whether or not God's words were always audible. It is essential, nevertheless, to hold that the Lord's speech to man was objective and intelligible, just as we think of human speech between persons. The intimacy of this form of revelation becomes very apparent in the Lord's conversation with Aaron and Miriam in regard to their complaint against Moses. The Lord said, "Hear my words: If there is a prophet among you, I the Lord make myself known to him in a vision, I speak with him in a dream. Not so with my servant Moses; he is entrusted with all my house. With him I speak mouth to mouth, clearly, and not in dark speech; and he beholds the form of the Lord" (Num. 12:6-8).

b. Appearance of the Lord [21]

The passive form (*Piel*) of the verb translated *appear*, gives the sense, *lets himself be seen*. This is the beginning of the Lord's manifestations to man, often called *theophanies*. Through these appearances of the Lord the word spoken obtained greater effectiveness. It resembled very closely the speech of man to man. It would seem that the appearances of the Lord possessed another significance. They who experienced these manifestations of the Lord may have seen in them a reflection of God's dwelling with man in the Garden of Eden. Their transient nature may have reminded them of man's sin, which brought to a close the glorious Edenic experiences. Further, these epiphanies may have led these Old Testament saints to look forward and to anticipate the restoration of God's permanent dwelling with man. This possible hope brings into proper perspective the abiding glory of the Lord which filled the tabernacle.

Observe also that in response to an appearance of the Lord the witness of the appearance built an altar.[22] This indicated "a consciousness that the place had in some sense become the seat of God's presence. The patriarchs returned to these places, to call upon the name of God."[23] Witness the cases of Abraham and of Jacob, both of whom returned to Bethel where each had built an altar to the Lord.[24] We gain the impression that these appearances of the Lord were confined to definite places and, with the exception of the altar built by Noah, they were all located in the land of promise.

c. Visions[25]

The Hebrew words *chazon* and *marah*, including their derivatives, lie back of the biblical word "vision," the former carrying the sense of seeing a vision and the latter the idea of seeing or observing. The noun forms found in these passages as well as in later Old Testament Scriptures are uniformly translated vision. As used in the Old Testament, "vision means an ecstatic experience in which new knowledge is revealed through something seen."[26] In the incidents before us, especially in that one involving Abram, the vision was given for the purpose of guiding him in an immediate situation. While the details of the vision (Gen. 15) present some real problems for explanation, it may be most consistent with the narrative to interpret the entire scene as one vision. For my present purpose it suffices to say that Abram had an ecstatic experience in which he saw the Lord and the Lord spoke to him. The word spoken had to do with the future of Abraham and his descendants. A four-hundred-year oppression at the hands of another nation lay before them but God would fulfill His covenant of giving to his descendants the land of Canaan. It is clear that the vision form of revelation was well adapted to God's communications with His people. The Lord revealed Himself clearly and effectively through visions and speech.

d. Dreams[27]

This form of revelation calls for special attention in view of certain circumstances or spiritual standing of the people who received it. On one side were individuals who did not belong to the people of God, such as Abimelech, Laban, the butler, the baker, Pharaoh, and in later times Nebuchadnezzar, while on the other side were those who were spiritually immature such as Joseph and those who were out of touch with God such as Jacob. In contrast with the preceding forms of revelation, the dream is an experience in which the consciousness of the individual is more or less detached from his personality.

The individual does not share in the revelation. His mind is only the receptacle of the message. God is in direct encounter with the individual and has complete control of all that takes place. This fact does not lower in any way the revelation character of the dream, but serves to show that the revealing God chooses the mode of revelation best fitted for the occasion.

e. The Angel of the Lord[28]

The most significant form of divine revelation in the Old Testament was that through the angel of the Lord. This angel was carefully distinguished from other angels. This is not to ignore a question of philology in which the Septuagint, following the Hebrew, does not use the article with the word "angel" in most of these references. A careful study of all of these references will show that a translation, "an angel of the Lord," to use the words of J. N. Schofield, is grammatically inadmissible."[29] In all these instances reference was made to a particular angel, who sustained an extraordinary relationship to God.

The angel of the Lord was a visible manifestation of God. While he acted and talked as the Lord, yet he was clearly distinguished from the Lord. Herein is a profound mystery but the frequency and clarity of the language identifying the angel as God and yet as being distinct from God is beyond all question. In the presence of this profound truth there are reasons for believing that in the angel of the Lord we have the beginning of the unfolding of the profoundest mystery of all Holy Writ. It is the disclosure of the truth that the one and only God is so constituted that while He dwells in the heavens above He is able to manifest Himself in person to His people. It would be going too far to say that the witnesses to the appearances of the angel of the Lord understood them to be what later revelation made clear in the incarnation and in the triune existence of God. A real purpose of this form of disclosure is to be found in God's desire to come close to His people in a definitely personal encounter for the purpose of giving assurance to His people of His concern for and His presence with them. While the angel acted and talked as the Lord, they understood that above and distinct from the angel of the Lord was the invisible God. It is important to note that this form of divine revelation obtained still greater significance in the time of Moses.

5. Revelation in the Era of Jacob

a. Continuing Principle of Election

At the very beginning of the life of Jacob the principle of election arose in very clear perspective. The Lord told Rebecca that she would become the mother of twins and that the elder would serve the younger. No reason was given for this prediction. It remained for the outworking of this prediction to disclose its meaning. The first step toward its fulfillment took place when Esau sold his birthright to Jacob. It is difficult for us to understand the reckless disposal of the birthright by Esau. Perhaps Esau had little confidence in the promises given to his grandfather and repeated to his father. Jacob, on the other hand, appears to have believed in these promises and sought the opportunity of bargaining for the birthright. When Esau showed no confidence in its meaning, Jacob cruelly supplanted his brother. This act cast the die and paved the way for Jacob's obtaining Isaac's blessing at the suggestion and trickery of his mother. Thus the covenant blessing came to Jacob even through the deception and dishonesty of both Rebecca and Jacob.

At first thought a difficult ethical problem centers in these two transactions. Briefly stated, the question arises, How could the holy and righteous God bestow His covenant blessing upon one who so ruthlessly and dishonestly robbed his brother? I believe that the remainder of Jacob's life gives the answer to this problem. On one hand Jacob suffered bitter remorse when he received at the hands of his father-in-law, Laban, the same kind of treatment he himself had given to Esau. As we shall note presently, Jacob's experiences at Bethel and Peniel revealed very clearly a genuine spiritual change and renewal on the part of Jacob. Truly his life history is the story of a transformed life. He had seen God face to face and through the mercy of God his life was preserved.

Returning to the principle of election as it continued to operate in the life of Jacob, let us probe again into Paul's profound exposition of this principle as found in Romans 9. In the history of the patriarchs God's purpose of election was a continuing experience. It was "not because of works but because of his call" (v. 11). This principle lay back of the Lord's words to Rebecca, "the elder will serve the younger." On the surface Paul appears to complicate the problem by basing the principle involved on the words, "Jacob I loved, but Esau I hated." The problem is resolved when we understand more clearly the meaning of the words "love" and "hate." God's love for Jacob was the covenant love expressed in the promise to Abraham. So great, so distinctive, was this covenant love that God's relation to Esau, who had rejected this covenant relationship, appeared as an attitude of hatred. Let us note again that Paul placed the idea of grace as the equivalent of election. God's election is the expression of God's love.

b. Elements of Revelation in the Life of Jacob

Three closely interwoven aspects present themselves in a study of
the life of this patriarch. First is the spiritual experience of Jacob manifested in the transformation in his life from that of a supplanter (Jacob)
to that of one who lets God rule (Israel). Second is the element of
divine providence working in Jacob's life. Third is the element of
divine revelation given during his life.

Isaac's parting words to Jacob as he left for Paddan-aram are quite
significant. Said the patriarch, "God Almighty bless you and make you
fruitful and multiply you, that you may become a company of peoples.
May he give the blessing of Abraham to you and to your descendants
with you, that you may take possession of the land on your sojournings
which God gave to Abraham" (Gen. 28:3, 4)! This parting blessing undoubtedly served as a tremendous challenge to Jacob's faith. He could
look to his grandfather's God, God Almighty, for blessings comparable
to those received by his grandfather. He could anticipate his
descendants becoming a company of peoples. The land of his sojournings
would become the land of his possession. In brief, Jacob and his
descendants had become heirs of the threefold promise given to
Abraham.

On the way to Haran, as he lay down for sleep, he experienced
a dream-vision of utmost significance. The ladder set up on the earth and
reaching to heaven with angels of God ascending and descending upon
it undoubtedly possessed great meaning for Jacob. Was he to understand by this dream that the messengers of God were carrying his in-
most soul needs to the very presence of God and were returning to
earth with the gracious response of God to his spiritual needs? At
least Jacob could see that there was a bridge of communication between
earth and heaven. Wherever he would go the God of heaven was near
at hand. God was attending to his needs. Very significantly the words
from heaven took the form, "I am the Lord, the God of Abraham your
father and the God of Isaac" (Gen. 28:13). The use of the word "Lord"
suggested the overwhelming meaning attached to the God who made the
covenant with Abraham. The Lord, the God Almighty, who made the
covenant promise was now addressing Jacob. The promises given to
Abraham were now bestowed on Jacob. In addition the Lord assured
Jacob that He would be with him and in due time bring him back to
the land of promise.

The words of Jesus to Nathanael may help us to understand
better the meaning of Jacob's experience of wonder and amazement.
When Nathanael marveled at Jesus' supernatural knowledge, Jesus replied,

"You shall see greater things than these. . . . You will see heaven opened, and the angels of God ascending and descending upon the Son of man" (Jn. 1:50, 51). With these words Jesus was saying that He Himself is the ladder extending from earth to heaven and that the angels, messengers of God, would through our Lord be carrying man's needs and burdens to God and returning to man with the blessings made possible through the Son of man. For Jacob as well, there was a mediator between man and God. Through this revelation the Lord sought to show Jacob that the spiritual needs of his life could be supplied through the ascending and descending angels of God. Implicit in Jacob's experience was an inner consciousness of his having wronged his brother. This experience gave evidence of an intense conflict in his soul, a conflict which was bound to increase and would not be resolved until he would be reconciled with his brother Esau.

Jacob's response to this revelation voiced something of a God-consciousness on the part of Jacob but his words still seemed to be cast in the mold of a bargainer. Whether or not Jacob was still showing a bargainer's attitude, he was making a deep commitment to God. In effect it was this: If God would fulfill all of His promises and bring him again to his father's house in peace, then the Lord would be his God. He would then place his trust in all the promises bound up in the covenant made by the Lord with Abraham (Gen. 28:20, 21).

Jacob's years at Haran were filled with experiences that showed the grace of God working to lead him to a full consciousness of his own sinfulness. He found in Laban his double as a cheater. While there was little outward response of a change in Jacob's heart, it would appear that Jacob was coming to realize that his sin was finding him out. Evidence of an awakening consciousness of spiritual need stands out in Jacob's words, "I am not worthy of the least of all the steadfast love and all the faithfulness which thou hast shown to thy servant" (Gen. 32:10). Jacob knew only too well that this return to his father's house according to the Lord's command would bring him face to face with Esau. On learning that Esau was coming to meet him, Jacob did not know what this would involve. Perhaps Esau could be appeased but perhaps not. The inner struggle took the form of an outward encounter with a man who wrestled with him the entire night. Not until the man touched the hollow of Jacob's thigh and put it out of joint was he able to overcome him. At daybreak the man sought to leave Jacob but the latter replied, "I will not let you go, unless you bless me." The meaning of this struggle becomes clearer when we observe that the man blessed Jacob and changed his name to Israel, a name which carried the meaning, "You have striven with God and with men, and have prevailed." The impact of this incident upon Jacob found expression in his calling the place Peniel. By this name he indicated its meaning for him, as he further said, "For I have seen God face to face, and yet my life is preserved" (Gen. 32:24-30).

A number of problems arise at this point. The first has to do with the question whether this was an external experience for Jacob, or whether it is a "myth." If it is to be regarded as a "myth," the story would indicate only an inner struggle on the part of Jacob. Some students would reduce it to a mere story which possesses no spiritual meaning. I believe that the manner in which this incident is presented shows that the author of Genesis sought to present a very significant objective experience for Jacob. If we accept the historical character of the story, another problem arises: Was this all night wrestling an evidence of Jacob's continued struggle against God or does the entire incident show the intense inward struggle of Jacob to gain peace with God? The latter view seems to be the more consistent of the two. If this is correct, we would interpret the outward wrestling as symbolic of the inward struggle through which Jacob, like the prodigal son, finally came to himself. The change of name from Jacob to Israel would be evidence of the spiritual transformation of Jacob through the power of God which occurred when Jacob sought the blessing from the Lord. It is this element that makes the story of Jacob so significant as a type of the spiritual transformation which takes place in the lives of all Christians in the conversion experience. Hosea's meditation on this incident is most instructive. "In the womb he took his brother by the heel, and in his manhood he strove with God. He strove with the angel and prevailed, he wept and sought his favor. He met God at Bethel, and there God spoke with him — the Lord the God of hosts, the Lord is his name: So you, by the help of your God, return, hold fast to love and justice, and wait continually for your God" (Hos. 12:3-6). Hosea saw in the life experience of Jacob, a picture of man returning to God, of holding fast to love and justice, and of waiting continually for God.

On Jacob's return to Bethel at the command of God he built an altar and called the place El-bethel. On this occasion God appeared to Jacob again, which appearance may well serve as the climax of Jacob's experiences with God. In this appearance God repeated His announcement of the change of Jacob's name to that of Israel. God also reaffirmed the promises to Jacob, first given to Abraham and later to Isaac. It was God Almighty who spoke thus to Israel. In response to this revelation Jacob set up a pillar of stone and poured out a drink offering on it and poured oil on it. This was an act of consecration of the altar to God, of setting it apart as being most holy (Ex. 30:22-29).

In this manner he expressed the fullness and completeness of his devotion to God Almighty. It was very fitting for the author of Hebrews to place Jacob's name among the heroes of faith, saying, "By faith Jacob, when dying, blessed each of the sons of Joseph, bowing in worship over the head of his staff" (Heb. 11:21).

c. Joseph, a Model of Moral Integrity and an Agent of Divine Providence

For the purposes of biblical theology the life of Joseph presents two very closely entwined topics for study: first, that of Joseph's nobility of character, and second, the workings of God's providence in his life. The manner of life of the people of God in this early period of biblical history has already been observed. Thus Abel, Enoch, Noah, and Abraham exhibited righteousness, blamelessness, and faith of the highest order. The life of Jacob revealed the saving grace of God which ultimately changed his life. The life of the people of God, what it should be and how it should be achieved, very naturally becomes a major inquiry in a study of the unfolding revelation of God. On this account the "Princely character of Joseph"[30] stands out as one of the noblest recorded in all biblical history.

To begin, the simple boyhood faith of Joseph, the dreamer, stood in sharp contrast to the hatred and jealousy of his brothers. After being sold to Potiphar, an officer of Pharaoh, it was not long until his master "saw that the Lord was with him, and that the Lord caused all that he did to prosper in his hands" (Gen. 39:3). Tempted by Potiphar's wife to commit grievous sin, Joseph showed his consciousness of the wickedness of this sin and also his integrity of character by refusing to yield to it. He answered Potiphar's wife, "How then can I do this great wickedness, and sin against God" (Gen. 39:9)? When Potiphar put Joseph in prison, "The Lord was with Joseph and showed him steadfast love, and gave him favor in the sight of the keeper of the prison" (Gen. 39:21). This uprightness of character was such that God could entrust to him the interpretation of the dreams of the butler, the baker, and Pharaoh. In a humble manner Joseph told Pharaoh that it is God who shows the meaning of dreams. After he had interpreted Pharaoh's dreams Joseph showed his understanding of the purposes of God by telling Pharaoh, "The thing is fixed by God, and God will shortly bring it to pass" (Gen. 41:32).

Joseph's treatment of his brothers when they came to Egypt for food does not cast a shadow over his integrity. He was putting his brothers under test in order to ascertain their attitude toward their great sin committed against him. If he had yielded to a spirit of vengeance, he would never have supplied them food. His forgiving spirit is unquestionably shown when he said, "God sent me before you to preserve for you a remnant on earth, and to keep alive for you many survivors. So it was not you who sent me here, but God" (Gen. 45:7, 8). Commenting on the life of Joseph, Melvin Grove Kyle wrote, "His nobility of character, his purity of heart and life, his magnanimity as a ruler and brother make him, more than any other of the Old Testament characters, an illustration of that type of man which Christ was to give to the world in perfection. Joseph is not in the list of persons distinctly referred to in Scripture as types of Christ . . . but none more fully illustrates the life and work of the Saviour: He wrought salvation for those who betrayed and rejected him, he went down into humiliation as the way to his exaltation, he forgave those who, at least in spirit, put him to death, and to him as to the Saviour, all must come for relief or perish."[31]

Commenting on the significant details of Joseph's life, Kyle drew attention to their meaning when he wrote, "All these constitute one of the most majestic, God-like movements of Providence revealed to us in the Word of God, or evident anywhere in history. The same Providence that presided over the boy-prince in his father's house came again to the slave-prince in the Egyptian prison. The interpretation of the dreams of the chief butler and the chief baker of Pharaoh (Gen. 40: 1 — 41:24) brought him at last through much delay and selfish forgetfulness to the notice of the king, and another dream in which the same cunning hand of Providence is plainly seen (Chap. 41) is the means of bringing Joseph to stand in the royal presence. The stuff that dreams are made of interests scarcely less than the Providence that was superintending over them. . . . The Providence that had shaped and guided the whole course of Joseph from the Palestinian home was consummated when, with the words, 'Inasmuch as thou art a man in whom is the spirit of God,' Pharaoh lifted up the Bedouin slave to be again the Bedouin prince and made him the prime minister."[32]

For Additional Reading and Reference:

Heinisch-Heidt, *Theology of the Old Testament*, pp. 8-12.
Jacob, *Theology of the Old Testament*, pp. 73-85.
Kaufmann, *The Religion of Israel*, pp. 216-23.
Napier, *Song of the Vineyard*, pp. 61-71.
Oehler, *Theology of the Old Testament*, pp. 60-67.
Payne, *The Theology of the Older Testament*, pp. 97-99, 246 f.
Pfeiffer, *Religion in the Old Testament*, pp. 12-44.
von Rad, *Old Testament Theology*, Vol. I, pp. 165-75.
Raven, *The History of the Religion of Israel*, pp. 11-41.
Ringgren, *Israelite Religion*, pp. 17-27.

Rowley, *The Biblical Doctrine of Election*, pp. 15-36.
Sauer, *The Dawn of World Redemption*, pp. 89-107.
Schultz, *Old Testament Theology*, Vol. I, pp. 86-125.
Titcomb, *Revelation in Progress*, pp. 26-40.
Vischer, *The Witness of the Old Testament to Christ*, pp. 117-65.
Vos, *Biblical Theology — Old and New Testaments*, pp. 79-114.
Vriezen, *An Outline of Old Testament Theology*, pp. 243-49.

See Indexes for Gen. 12 — 50, Covenant, Abraham, Isaac, Jacob, and
    Monotheism, in the following references:
Baab, *Theology of the Old Testament*.
Burrows, *An Outline of Biblical Theology*.
Davidson, *The Theology of the Old Testament*.
Eichrodt, *The Theology of the Old Testament*, Vol. I.
Jacob, *Theology of the Old Testament*.
Knight, *A Christian Theology of the Old Testament*.
Köhler, L., *Old Testament Theology*.
Robinson, *Inspiration and Revelation in the Old Testament*.
Vriezen, *An Outline of Old Testament Theology*.
Wahlstrom, *God Who Redeems*.

See commentaries on Genesis 12 — 50.

See articles in Bible dictionaries and encyclopedias.

1. Ex. 3:6, 15, 16; 6:2-4; Deut. 6:10; Josh. 24:2-4; 1 Kings 18:36; 2 Kings 13:23; 2 Chron. 30:6; Neh. 9:7; Ps. 105:6-9; Is. 29:22, 23; 51:2; Jer. 33:26; Ezek. 33:24; Mic. 7:20; Mt. 1:1, 2; 8:11; Lk. 3:34; Jn. 8:33-58; Acts 3:13, 25; 7:2-10; 13:26; Rom. 4; Heb. 6:13-18; Jas. 2:21-23; and 1 Pet. 3:6.
2. *The Westminster Dictionary of the Bible*, "History," p. 248 (Philadelphia: The Westminster Press, 1944).
3. Gen. 12:7; 13:15; 17:7; 22:18; 24:7.
4. 2 Chron. 20:7; Is. 41:8; Jas. 2:23.
5. See also Ps. 18:8.
6. Rom. 4:1-12; Gal. 3:6-8.
7. Ex. 6:12, 30; Lev. 26:41; Deut. 10:16; 30:6.
8. Jer. 4:4; 6:10; 9:25, 26; Ezek. 44:7.
9. See also Eph. 2:11; Phil. 3:3; Col. 2:11-13.
10. *Theology of the Old Testament* (New York: Harper and Brothers, Publishers, 1958), p. 46.
11. *Genesis, A Commentary* (Philadelphia: The Westminster Press, 1961), p. 193.
12. *An Outline of Old Testament Theology* (Boston: Charles T. Branford Company, 1958), pp. 196 f.
13. Rom. 4:1-21; Gal. 3:6-14.
14. For the following discussion of the ingredients of Abraham's faith the author is deeply indebted to Vos's searching analysis of this statement. See his *Biblical Theology*, pp. 98-102.
15. *Op. cit.*, p. 180.
16. 2 Chron. 20:7; Is. 41:8; Jas. 2:23.
17. Vos, *op. cit.*, p. 100.
18. See Josh. 24:2, 3; Gen. 31:19; 35:2.
19. *The International Standard Bible Encyclopaedia*, James Orr, General Editor (Chicago: The Howard-Severence Company, 1930), Vol. IV, "Revelation," by Dr. B.B. Warfield, pp. 25-77.
20. Gen. 12:1, 4; 13:14; 15:1; Num. 12:8; Ps. 147:19.
21. Gen. 12:7; 17:1; 18:1; 26:2-5, 24.
22. Gen. 12:7; 35:1, 7, 9-15.
23. Vos, *op. cit.*, p. 83.
24. Gen. 13:4; 35:1-7.
25. Gen. 15:1; 46:2; Num. 12:6; 24:4, 16.

26. *A Theological Word Book of the Bible*, edited by Allan Richardson (New York: The Macmillan Company, 1955), "Vision," by E. C. Blackman, p. 277.

27. Gen. 20:3; 31:10, 11, 24; 37:5-20; 40:5-16; 41:7-32.

28. Gen. 16:7 ff.; 21:17 ff.; 22:11 ff.; 24:7, 40; 31:11, 13; 32:24-30; 48:15, 16.

29. Richardson, Ed., *op. cit.*, "Angel," p. 18.

30. James Orr, *op. cit.*, Vol. III; "Joseph," by Melvin Grove Kyle, p. 1739.

31. *Ibid.*, p. 1740.

32. *Ibid.*, p. 1739.

CHAPTER V
REVELATION IN THE ERA
OF MOSES

1. Place of Moses in God's Revelation

The opening chapters in the Book of Exodus make it evident that a towering figure is before us in the person of Moses. To begin, there are the unusual providential circumstances which led to his being taken into the home of Pharaoh. Becoming a son of Pharaoh's daughter, Moses was in all probability heir to the throne of Egypt. This accounts for Stephen's comments that "Moses was instructed in all the wisdom of the Egyptians," and that "he was mighty in his words and deeds" (Acts 7:22). A similar estimate of Moses was already given in the Book of Exodus where the writer said, "The man Moses was very great in the land of Egypt, in the sight of Pharaoh's servants and in the sight of the people" (Ex. 11:3).

Walther Eichrodt laid hold of Moses' greatness in his discussion of the founder of Israel's religion, in which he described the extraordinary charismatic gifts of Moses.[1] In his enlightening discussion Eichrodt observed: "It is characteristic of Moses that it should be impossible to classify him in any of the ordinary categories applicable to the leader of a nation; he is neither a king, nor a commander of an army, nor a tribal chieftain, nor a priest, nor an inspired seer and medicine man. To some extent he belongs to all these categories; but none of them adequately explains his position."[2] He then proceeded to show how Moses exercised varied responsibilities such as kingly authority, serving as mediator between God and His people, and being God's seer and prophet. Moses became "the messenger who should proclaim God's will for social, political, and cultic life." He was an organizer, the national leader, the man who directed the worship of God. He was a wonderworker.

Looking more closely into the Bible's presentation of Moses' greatness let us note those aspects of his work which may be compared with that of Christ's. First, Moses was called the servant of the Lord.[3] God's own words lead us into the meaning of this expression. He said, "Not so with my servant Moses; he is entrusted with all my house" (Num. 12:7). What greater responsibility could be expressed than by the language of being entrusted with all God's house! This was the servant Moses' responsibility.

Second, Moses exercised a priestly work that climaxed in the service of intercession.[4] This priestly work came to a focus in Moses' responsibility for mediating the covenant at Mt. Sinai. It was he who wrote all the words of the Lord, who built an altar and twelve pillars on which to offer the covenant sacrifice. It was he who sprinkled the blood of the sacrifice both upon the altar and upon the people. His intercessory work became most evident when he interceded for Israel at the time of the making of the golden calf.

Third, Moses performed kingly functions in giving to Israel the laws which were to guide them in daily living. These laws were both civil and religious. While Israel was under the rule of God, Moses acted in behalf of God when he brought to Israel all the laws based on the Sinaitic covenant.

Fourth, Moses was a prophet.[5] He was God's spokesman to Pharaoh and to Israel. Even a casual reading of the books from Exodus through Deuteronomy shows the extent to which Moses was God's mouthpiece.

Fifth, Moses was a man of the spirit (Num. 11:17-29; 12:9). Though an explicit statement of the Spirit of God coming upon Moses is lacking, the fact that the Holy Spirit worked through him is everywhere clearly implicit. A case in point is that of the Lord's directing Moses to choose seventy men of the elders of Israel to assist him in fulfilling his many duties. The Lord said that He would take some of the Spirit which was upon Moses and put it upon these seventy elders. When the Lord did this, they prophesied, thus showing that the Spirit rested upon them (Num. 11:16, 17). When Eldad and Medad continued to prophesy, Joshua asked Moses to forbid them as though he was jealous for Moses' sake. To this Moses exclaimed, "Would that all the Lord's people were prophets, that the Lord would put his spirit upon them" (vv. 26-29)! Since Moses was a prophet, the Spirit of God plainly rested upon him. It is entirely in order to say that in all the responsibilities of Moses as servant of the Lord, as priestly mediator, as performer of kingly functions, and as prophet, the Holy Spirit empowered him for this work.

Sixth, later writers and speakers in both the Old and New Testaments placed Moses in a position of greatness comparable to that of Christ. He was excelled alone by the Lord Jesus. Repeatedly throughout the Former and Latter Prophets, the writers made reference to the authoritative Book of the Law of Moses as the record of what God commanded His servant Moses. Several of the psalms — such as 103, 105, and 106 — magnify Moses as the recipient of God's revelation. The appearance of Moses and Elijah at the transfiguration of Jesus also attested to Moses' greatness. While John's words, "The law was given through Moses; grace and truth came through Jesus Christ" (Jn. 1:17) magnify the superior position of the revelation through Christ over that of Moses, it should be observed that the law, the high-water mark of Old Testament revelation, was given through Moses.

Perhaps the greatest tributes given to Moses in the New Testament are given by the author of Hebrews in the words, "Consider Jesus, the apostle and high priest of our confession. He was faithful to him who appointed him, just as Moses also was faithful in God's house. . . . Now Moses was faithful in all God's house as a servant, to testify to the things that were to be spoken later" (Heb. 3:1-5). The greatness of Moses undergirded God's revelation through him. Truly Eichrodt and von Rad point the way for the student of biblical theology to take a new look at Moses' greatness and to make a fresh appraisal of this servant of God.[6]

2. Redemption of Israel from Egypt

a. Deliverance Wrought Through the Mighty Acts of God

The Exodus account of Israel's deliverance from Egypt gave special emphasis to the supernatural workings of God. A casual study of these references[7] reveals a vocabulary which unequivocally asserts the demonstration of miraculous power. This vocabulary includes such words as *wonders, signs, miracles, mighty acts,* and *powers.* These words most aptly describe the ten plagues, the dividing of the Red Sea, the giving of manna, and the supplying to them water from the rock.

This leads us to observe that the Lord manifested an adequate purpose in performing these miracles. He would lead Pharaoh to believe in His almighty power. The expressed purpose for these mighty acts was to deliver Israel from the Egyptian bondage so that they would know that He was their God (Ex. 6:7). It is inevitable that a far greater purpose lay back of this. God would lead the polytheistic Egyptians to forsake their gods and worship the true God, the Lord of the enslaved Israelites. The heart hardening of Pharaoh showed his unwillingness to believe the adequate evidences for the omnipotence, righteousness, and holiness of the Lord. Very meaningful are the words of the Lord spoken to Pharaoh, "For this purpose have I let you live, to show you my power, so that my name may be declared throughout all the earth" (Ex. 9:16).

It is essential at this point to note the real character and significance of these events. Some scholars either reject them entirely or reduce them to commonplace happenings which were heightened by tradition to being supernatural in character. Either of these ways of interpreting the plagues fails to do justice to the intent of the author of Exodus, who represented them as supernatural occurrences. The whole matter of the reality of the miraculous confronts us at this point. For our purposes the following definition expresses the main elements contemplated in the word "miracles": "In the narrowest biblical sense, miracles are events in the external world wrought by the immediate power of God and intended as a sign or attestation. They are possible because God sustains, controls, and guides all things, and is personal and omnipotent."[8] This definition of miracles captures the intended sense of the words "wonders," "miracles," "signs," "mighty acts," "power," and other descriptions of what took place.

With regard to the occurrence of miracles in biblical history let us observe also that the biblical record is very emphatically not a meaningless conglomeration of fantastic stories coming from Israel's folklore but rather that a profound purpose attaches to their occurrence. In the article cited above the authors Davis and Gehman elaborate thus, "The miracles of the Bible are confined almost exclusively to four periods, separated from each other by centuries. The time of: (1) The redemption of God's people from Egypt and their establishment in Canaan under Moses and Joshua. (2) The life and death struggle of the true religion with heathenism under Elijah and Elisha. (3) The Exile, when Jehovah afforded proof of His power and supremacy before the gods of the heathen, although His people were in captivity (Daniel and his companions). (4) The introduction of Christianity, when miracles attested the person of Christ and His doctrine. Outside these periods miracles are rare indeed (Gen. 5:24). They were almost totally unknown during the many centuries from the Creation to the exodus."[9] In the light of this view of miracles as having spiritual purpose, the marvelous acts of God wrought in the deliverance of Israel from Egypt naturally prepare us to anticipate very meaningful spiritual aspects of the deliverance.[10]

b. Spiritual Aspects of the Deliverance from Egypt

(1) A Manifestation of Israel's Election Through the Grace of God. This became evident in God's message to Pharaoh: "Thus says the Lord, Israel is my first-born son" (Ex. 4:22). This language indicates that Israel's relation to God was unique. Concerning no other people of the world had it been said that they bore the relationship of son to the Lord. Forty years later Moses told Israel, "You are the sons of the Lord your God. . . . You are a people holy to the Lord your God, and the Lord has chosen you to be a people for his own possession, out of all the peoples that are on the face of the earth" (Deut. 14:1, 2). These words unfold more fully the idea of election. They suggest that God's choice of Israel was not on the basis of any merit on their part but solely as an act of God's grace. Moses spoke more specifically to this

point.[11] Their election was not due to their great numbers or uprightness of heart but it was because of the Lord's love for them. He was
keeping the oath which He had spoken to their fathers. Through their
election God showed Israel that their God is "the faithful God who keeps
covenant and steadfast love with those who love him and keep his
commandments, to a thousand generations" (Deut. 7:9). In the same context Moses spoke of the judgment that God would bring upon Israel if
they refused to obey His commandments.

(2) A Deliverance from Sin's Dominion. Egypt was a land of idolatry.
A careful study of the ten plagues will show that through them God
was bringing judgment upon this form of wickedness in Egypt. At a
later date Ezekiel likened the sins of Judah and Israel to the lewdness,
whether literal or figurative, of the Egyptians (Ezek. 23:19, 21, 27). It
may have been the imagery of Egyptian bondage which underlay the
teaching of Jesus and of Paul that sinners are in a state of bondage to
sin.[12]

(3) A Redemption from Sin. Closely related to the foregoing point
is the redemption aspect of this deliverance.[13] The verbs, *gaal* (claim
for one's own, redeemed by paying value for), *padah* (to free, to redeem,
to ransom), and *qanah* (to purchase, procure, acquire), express the
nature of the deliverance. It was the kind of act that sprang from God's
love. It was a purchase, a redemption by paying a value to give Israel
their freedom. It is noteworthy that this language of redemption constitutes the coining of the terminology used to describe the meaning of
the Lord's suffering and death. Jesus said, "The Son of man came . . .
to give his life as a ransom for many" (Mt. 20:28). In similar vein Paul
wrote, "Christ redeemed us from the curse of the law" (Gal. 3:13). The
author of Hebrews wrote of Christ as "securing an eternal redemption
[for us]" (Heb. 9:12, 15). It should be noted that the Greek vocabulary
used in the New Testament for describing Christ's redemptive work is
that employed in the Septuagint to translate the Hebrew words used
in connection with Israel's redemption from Egypt.

(4) Israel's Redemption Symbolized by the Passover.[14] In biblical
history the Passover occupied the highest place among Israel's holy
occasions. It symbolized God's greatest act in their redemption from
Egypt. Bound up with it were a number of details which added depth
of meaning to this sacrifice. We should observe that this Passover
sacrifice possessed elements of great significance in the sacrificial system
soon to be established at Mt. Sinai. First was the substitutional aspect
of the Passover lamb. The lamb was offered instead of the firstborn
son. Second was the expiatory aspect. A very significant use was
made of the blood; it was put on the two doorposts and the lintels of

the houses. In this respect the Passover sacrifice resembled the sin offering. Third was the purification aspect. The bunch of hyssop used to
smear the blood on the lintel and the two doorposts carried this significance. Hyssop is aromatic and was used in later times for ceremonial
purification (Lev. 14:4, 6, 49-52). David expressed this purification aspect
in his prayer, "Purge me with hyssop, and I shall be clean; wash me, and
I shall be whiter than snow" (Ps. 51:7).

Fourth was the consecration characteristic. Another class of bloody
offerings instituted later by Moses was that of the burnt offering. The
significant act of this offering was the burning of the entire animal
on the altar. It symbolized consecration or self-dedication of the one
who offered the sacrifice to the Lord. In the case of the Passover Lamb
not a bone of the animal was to be broken. All that remained of
the animal after the eating of the Passover was burned. This
similarity between the Passover sacrifice and that of the burnt offering suggests that the burning of what remained of the animal
symbolized the consecration of the firstborn son to the Lord.

Fifth was the fellowship characteristic. The eating of the Passover
lamb bore a close similarity to the peace offering later instituted.
Being the last in sequential order of the bloody offerings, the peace
offering symbolized covenant fellowship with God. On this account the
eating of the Passover lamb would appear to yield the same symbolism.
Through this Passover sacrifice the fellowship of Israel with the Lord,
their Deliverer, found expression.

Sixth, God gave an unusual command concerning the Passover lamb
in these words, "You shall not break a bone of it" (Ex. 12:46; Num. 9:12).
John's quotation of this command in his account of the crucifixion gave
grounds for believing that the command in Exodus possessed the potential
of a prediction. For this reason John wrote, "These things took place
that the scripture might be fulfilled" (Jn. 19:36). This is the ground for
believing that the Passover lamb typified the Lamb of God slain on
Calvary. Paul confirmed this in his words, "For Christ, our paschal
lamb, has been sacrificed" (1 Cor. 5:7).

Seventh, God commanded Israel to eat the Passover lamb with unleavened bread (Ex. 12:8). This is yet another similarity between the
Passover and some of the later instituted sacrifices. Paul grasped its
symbolism when he wrote, "Cleanse out the old leaven that you may be
fresh dough, as you really are unleavened" (1 Cor. 5:7). Regarding
Christ as our paschal Lamb, he bade the Corinthians to "celebrate
the festival, not with the old leaven, the leaven of malice and evil,
but with the unleavened bread of sincerity and truth" (v. 8). The conclusion follows that the unleavened bread used in the Passover meal

symbolized the absence of corrupting influences as it did in later sacrifices and typified the Christian graces of sincerity and truth.

Eighth, God commanded Israel to observe the Passover as an ordinance forever (Ex. 12:14). Israel's redemption from Egypt was a once for all experience. It did not need to be repeated periodically. Thus the Passover feast, observed annually, brought to mind the finality of God's great saving act. Through it Israel became God's purchased possession. In this also is a rich typical meaning looking forward to the sacrifice of Christ. Because of the efficacy of His sacrifice, "there is no longer any offering for sin" (Heb. 10:18). In conclusion, these eight aspects or characteristics of the Passover become cumulative and give both height and depth to the meaning of the Passover. This justifies the recognition of the Lord's Supper as bearing the same relation to the sacrifice of Christ as the Passover observance bore to the Lord's passing over Israel.

3. Israel Drawn into Covenant Relationship with the Lord

a. Historical Character of the Covenant

Since Walther Eichrodt's *Theology of the Old Testament* has appeared on the scene, modern scholars are again coming to realize that the Sinaitic covenant had its origin in historical fact. The controlling idea of this scholarly work is the covenant relationship between God and Israel. With utmost skill, Eichrodt structured Old Testament theology on this covenant relationship. He saw the author of Exodus as presenting the account of the institution of the covenant at Mt. Sinai as an authentic event in Israel's history. The frequent references to this covenant throughout the Old Testament and the New confirm this conclusion. Most assuredly the name given to the first part of the Bible, the Old Testament, has its sure foundation in the institution of the old covenant.

b. The Covenant Concept

Since the word "covenant" is so foundational to understanding the Scriptures I shall give further attention to its meaning. I noted in an earlier chapter of Genesis the nature of God's relation to Adam and Eve in the Garden of Eden. While this did not bear the name of covenant, the words of God bound Adam and Eve to obedience. God's covenant with Noah had its leading characteristic in the form of an unchanging promise of God to Noah. God also bound Noah to obedience. We observed in God's covenant with Abraham the special emphasis upon God's faithful promise. God used bloody sacrifices to seal the covenants with both Noah and Abraham. In the covenant with Abraham we discovered also an ethical aspect in that God imposed on Abraham the command to be blameless. From these instances we learned that God sought to draw sinful man into deep and meaningful covenant relationship with Himself. He initiated the covenants and bound Himself to keep them. This prepared the way for God's drawing not just individuals but His people into a similar covenant relation. For Israel this involved a commitment of obedience to God.

The opening verses of Exodus 19 record God's proposal to Israel of entering into covenant relationship. Again God took the initiative for its institution. Likely the people of Israel did not take the initiative in making a covenant with God because of their sinfulness. Israel had not come to realize their need of searching out God for covenant fellowship. The Lord assured Israel of His choice of them to become His people in the words, "I bore you on eagles' wings and brought you to myself" (Ex. 19:4). Herein is the element of election. God had chosen Israel to become His own possession from among all peoples. This fact further teaches that the idea of election is cumulative. We gain its full meaning by considering it in relation to the election of the Shemites, to the call of Abraham, to the choice of Isaac and of Jacob, and now to the choosing of Israel to become His people. The elements of love and grace have become increasingly evident. What greater expression of love can be found than that of the Lord when He said, "I bore you on eagles' wings and brought you to myself"!

The Lord used the most expressive language to describe the position of Israel under the proposed covenant. Israel would be the Lord's own possession among all peoples. The Hebrew word *segullah* (special possession) is a word used of a private treasure.[15] The KJV rendering, "a peculiar treasure," carried a rich connotation, namely, specially one's own. Later writers picked up this expression and used it as the basis for earnest exhortation. The note of praise in Psalm 135 grew out of the realization that "The Lord has chosen Jacob for himself, Israel as his own possession."

Peter reached the peak of his exhortations in the words, "You are a chosen race, a royal priesthood, a holy nation, God's own people, that you may declare the wonderful deeds of him who called you out of darkness into his marvelous light" (1 Pet. 2:9). Peter also laid hold of the key expressions which described Israel's position under their covenant. The expression "kingdom of priests" gave the idea of "a kingdom whose citizens are all priests, living wholly in God's service, and ever enjoying the right of access to Him."[16] Peter would have us understand that the church of Jesus Christ is now all that Israel was under the earlier covenant. The expression "holy nation" has in it the idea of being separate from other nations and of being set apart to the Lord. The literal idea of separate and aloof leads to the ethical concept of being pure and godlike. Peter enlarged on the implicit purpose of Israel's position in the world when he said, "that you may declare the wonderful deeds of him who called you out of darkness into his marvelous light" (1 Pet. 2:9).

God made clear, nevertheless, that this covenant relation into which Israel was now being drawn involved uncompromising obedience to Him. It is noteworthy that three times during the arranging of this covenant Moses spoke the words which made up the covenant, to which the people replied, "All that the Lord has spoken we will do, and we will be obedient" (Ex. 19:7, 8; 24:3, 7). In this covenant proposal two important ideas attach themselves to the concept of covenant. The first was that of Israel's unique position as God's own possession, and the second was Israel's commitment to obedience. From this point onward the two-sided nature of the covenant received special recognition. It was this idea that Jeremiah brought home to his people in most forceful manner at the time of Israel's impending judgment when he said, "But this command I gave them, 'Obey my voice, and I will be your God, and you shall be my people; and walk in all the way that I command you, that it may be well with you.' But they did not obey or incline their ear, but walked in their own counsels and the stubbornness of their evil hearts, and went backward and not forward" (Jer. 7:23, 24).

c. Making of the Covenant

The portion of Exodus lying between God's proposal of entering into covenant relationship and the account of its institution constitutes the Book of the Covenant. Central to the Book of the Covenant are the Ten Commandments. We shall first study the enactment of the covenant and then examine the contents of the Book of the Covenant.

The covenant agreement had its basis in the written document known as the Book of the Covenant. The manner in which this document came to serve as the basis of Israel's commitment to God was through two bloody offerings: burnt offerings and peace offerings (Ex. 24:1-10). The building of the altar symbolized God's participation in the covenant agreement, and the twelve pillars, Israel's share in the transaction. The two kinds of offerings made in this transaction call for close study. Noah, Abraham, and Jacob had offered burnt offerings but in none of these occasions did the writer give the meaning of the sacrifice. On this occasion of Israel's accepting the covenant this writer also left the meaning of these sacrifices unexplained. Its symbolism becomes clearer, however, as we study all these occasions.

In the foregoing instances the meaning that this sacrifice possessed, according to the ceremonial laws given after this, was projected backward to the earlier occasions. We shall do the same here. On this occasion God's chosen people were being drawn into this covenant relationship. The symbolism suggested in the other instances, that of consecration and self-dedication to God, best describes its meaning here. They were in the act of committing themselves to absolute obedience to the Lord. It involved a setting apart of themselves for God's holy purposes. Since the people of Israel were corporately entering into this relationship, the burnt offerings most fittingly expressed this consecration. In the instance of the peace offerings we follow the same procedure. The ceremonial law recognized the peace offerings as the climax of all bloody offerings. It symbolized the resulting fellowship between man and God after having offered the appropriate sin, trespass, and burnt offerings beforehand. On this occasion these offerings symbolized for Israel the resulting fellowship which they were beginning to experience with God. It was the fellowship symbolized in the eating of the sacrifice in which the Lord was the Host and Israel the guests. In Oriental fashion this was the most significant way of picturing fellowship.

This brings us to the official enactment of the covenant. Moses took half of the blood and threw it against the altar; then after reading the Book of the Covenant and receiving the people's commitment to obedience, Moses used the other half of the blood to throw upon the people. The enacting words follow, "Behold the blood of the covenant which the Lord has made with you in accordance with all these words" (Ex. 24:8). This most remarkable use of the blood suggests its relationship to the later instituted sin offering, whose symbolism was expiation through the sprinkling of the blood gotten from a sin offering.

The climax to the whole transaction occurred when Moses and his companions, including seventy of the elders, went up to the mountain where they saw the God of Israel. The grand climax of the entire occasion became evident in the words, "They beheld God, and ate and drank" (v. 11). This is the sublime picture of the covenant fellowship experienced by the people of God's own possession and the Lord Himself. Forty years later Moses explained this experience to Israel with the view of safeguarding them against possible misinterpretation of Israel's having seen God. He said, "The Lord spoke to you out of the midst of the fire; you heard the sound of words, but saw no form; there was only a voice" (Deut. 4:12). This explanation served two purposes.

First, Moses showed the people that human beings are not able to behold God in all of His glory. Second, this denial of seeing the form of God served as a warning against their making a graven image of God (v. 16).

Through the institution of this covenant the Lord established His rule over Israel. Moses anticipated this great fact when he sang, "Thou wilt bring them in, and plant them on thy own mountain, the place, O Lord, which thou hast made for thy abode, the sanctuary, O Lord, which thy hands have established. The Lord will reign for ever and ever" (Ex. 15:17, 18). The Lord's proposal for establishing a covenant with His people took on a theocratic character when He regarded Israel as His possession and their being to Him "a kingdom of priests and a holy nation" (Ex. 19:6). Israel's promise of absolute obedience to God was thus an acknowledgment of His absolute authority, kingly in every respect. Balaam's prophecy concerning Israel also took the form of kingly rule when he said, "The Lord their God is with them, and the shout of a king is among them" (Num. 23:21). In Moses' final blessing of the people of Israel he spoke of the Lord as having come from Sinai: "He came from the ten thousands of holy ones, with flaming fire at his right hand. Yea, he loved his people; all those consecrated to him were in his hand; so they followed in thy steps, receiving direction from thee, when Moses commanded us a law, as a possession for the assembly of Jacob. Thus the Lord became king in Jeshurun, when the heads of the people were gathered, all the tribes of Israel together" (Deut. 33:2-5). This made it clear that Moses regarded the establishment of the covenant at Sinai as the setting up of God's kingdom.

It was on this account that Gideon refused to be made king over Israel. He said, "The Lord will rule over you" (Judg. 8:22, 23). The rule of God came into still clearer focus when Israel requested of Samuel that he appoint a king for them. When Samuel prayed to the Lord about this request, he received the reply, "They have not rejected you, but they have rejected me from being king over them" (1 Sam. 8:5-7; cf. 12:12). It is quite evident that Josephus coined the word "theocracy" to express God's covenant relation to Israel. This rule of God brought the entire life of an individual under God's jurisdiction. To use modern terminology, it included the social, economic, civil, and religious aspects of life. No distinction existed between the so-called church and state. As we shall note a bit later, the Ten Commandments brought all these aspects under God's rule.

At this point three fundamental concepts come into close and vital relationship. They are bound up in the words "covenant" (*berith*), "theocracy" (God's rule), and "congregation" (*qahal*). Their interrelation becomes evident when we observe that through the covenant God established His rule, and the people of God who were obedient to this rule composed the congregation. This relationship prepares us to understand the new order of things when Christ through the new covenant established the Christocracy under which His people are the church. This profound relationship among covenant, kingdom, congregation (church) unfolds a basic truth underlying both the Old and New Testaments.

The account in Exodus 24 does not define the official position of Moses in the institution of the covenant at Sinai. From one point of view he performed a prophetic function through his writing all the words of the Lord and his bringing Israel to the commitment of obedience to these words. From another point of view he performed a priestly function through the offering of the sacrifices. Plainly Moses stood between the Lord and Israel. His was the work of a mediator. This title comes from the letter to the Hebrews, where the author used this term to define Jesus' relationship to the making of the new covenant (8:6; 9:15; 12:24). Just as our Lord was the mediator of the new covenant, so Moses was the mediator of the old covenant. Just as Christ brought the church into covenant relationship with the Lord through the new covenant, so Moses brought Israel into this fellowship through the old covenant.

4. Function of the Law Under God's Rule

Since Moses was the mediator of the covenant, it was entirely natural that he would expound the function of the law under this covenant. Perhaps the most compact statement of the law's function is found in God's words, "You shall therefore keep my statutes and my ordinances, by doing which a man shall live: I am the Lord" (Lev. 18:5). In a number of Moses' Deuteronomic discourses he enlarged on the purpose of the law. In 4:1-8 he established the rule that obedience to the statutes and ordinances would be the condition under which Israel could take possession of Canaan. God designed that the peoples of Canaan would see Israel's wisdom and understanding and come to recognize the Lord, their God. In the 6:1-15 portion Moses pointed up the love relationship with their God when he said, "The Lord our God is one Lord; and you shall love the Lord your God with all your heart, and with all your soul, and with all your might." On this account people should teach their children diligently all the words of God's law. In the 8:1-10 section Moses explained the meaning of their experiences in the wilderness. God sought to test them and to prove what was in their hearts, whether they would keep His commandments or not. The 10:12-22 paragraph gives what may well be called the theme of Deuteronomy. Moses said, "And now, Israel, what does the Lord your

God require of you, but to fear the Lord your God, to walk in all his ways, to love him, to serve the Lord your God with all your heart and with all your soul, and to keep the commandments and statutes of the Lord, which I command you this day for your good?" For the foundation for such exhortation Moses pointed to the dignity of the Lord their God as Creator. In Deut. 28:1-19 Moses recounted the blessings that would come upon Israel if they obeyed, and also the curses if they would not obey the voice of the Lord. Moses brought these several messages to a climax in the words, "See, I have set before you this day life and good, death and evil. . . . I call heaven and earth to witness against you this day, that I have set before you life and death, blessing and curse; therefore choose life, that you and your descendants may live, loving the Lord your God, obeying his voice, and cleaving to him; . . . that you may dwell in the land which the Lord swore to your fathers, to Abraham, to Isaac, and to Jacob, to give them" (30:15-20).

As we move from the Old Testament into the New, we discover that the law possessed a larger purpose than that actually expressed in the Old Testament. In several contexts Paul showed that one function of the law was to make known to man his own sinfulness of nature.[17] Man is a slave to sin. On this account man cannot depend upon the law for salvation. "For Christ is the end of the law, that every one who has faith may be justified" (Rom. 10:4). In slightly different language Paul said, "The law was our custodian until Christ came, that we might be justified by faith" (Gal. 3:24). Thus while from the Old Testament point of view people would live through keeping the law, the New Testament advanced to the truth that the law possessed no merit for salvation. It possessed no power to save. The penitent sinner can be accounted righteous before God only on the basis of faith in Jesus Christ.

5. The Decalogue

Before entering upon a discussion of the Ten Commandments it appears necessary to recognize that some serious critical problems with reference to the origin of these commandments confront the student of biblical theology. Very few scholars recognize these commandments as having their origin in the Book of the Covenant. My approach here is similar to that followed in other instances where literary criticism holds to different conclusions from those based on internal evidence. How some scholars fail to recognize the subjective character of literary criticism and at the same time give no recognition to the internal claims of authorship is very difficult to understand. This is not to ignore the valid inquiries of literary criticism. In this situation I am seeking to recognize the validity and authenticity of what the final author or authors of the Book of Exodus represented as the source of a given portion. Here the narrator said, "And God spoke all these words, saying." A sound approach to this claim recognizes its authenticity until *evidence* is forthcoming to the contrary. Add to this the internal claim that "Moses wrote all the words of the Lord" (Ex. 24:4), a statement which refers to the Book of the Covenant (Ex. 20 — 23).

Let us now give consideration to the place of the Decalogue as it relates to the Mosaic covenant. We noted above that the Book of the Covenant was that in which the covenant centered. It was the written document to which Israel promised obedience. On the basis of this commitment Moses mediated the covenant between God and Israel. This leads us to believe that the Book of the Covenant, the Ten Commandments in particular, was to function as the fundamental law for God's people. From one point of view, it stands as an advance resume of all the laws given later. In the words of Vos, "It not so much anticipates as condenses, and in condensing eliminates and idealizes. It joins together the beginning and the end of the entire theocratic movement, the redeeming act of God, and the resultant state of holiness and conformity to the nature and will of God into which the theocracy is designed to issue. At the same time it gives these elements in a form that is adjusted to the practical needs and limitations of the people."[18]

More specifically, in the words of John R. Sampey, "It was to Israel that the Decalogue was primarily addressed, and not to all mankind. Thus the reason assigned for keeping the 5th Commandment applies to the people who were on their way to the land which had been given to Abraham and his descendants (Ex. 20:12); and the 4th Commandment is enforced by reference to the servitude in Egypt (Deut. 5:15). It is possible, then, that even in the Ten Commandments there are elements peculiar to the Mosaic system and which our Lord and His apostles may not make a part of faith and duty for Christians."[19] Sampey's closing statement possesses great significance as it has to do with another facet of biblical theology, namely, the relation of Old Testament ethics to New Testament ethics. While it belongs to the discipline of Old Testament theology to evaluate Old Testament codes of ethics in the light of the final revelation in the New Testament, it suffices to say here that Sampey's observation should alert us to examine with scrutiny the ethical teachings of the Old Testament as they confront us. The same is true with reference to the problem as to how long Old Testament institutions possess authority.

The Decalogue presents itself as a direct revelation of God and as such possesses absolute divine authority. In this set of laws God relates all human conduct and behavior directly to Himself. The entire gamut of human conduct thus bears a deeply religious character. Fundamental to the Decalogue is the basic oneness of the ideas of redemption and the resultant life of holiness and conformity to the nature and will of God. The precedent for this approach to human conduct was already set in God's words to Abraham when He said, "I am God Almighty; walk before me, and be blameless" (Gen. 17:1).

A few students have had some difficulty in understanding the negative character of most of the commandments. They feel that a positive approach to setting forth the fundamental laws of conduct would be more fitting for a set of commandments purporting to come directly from God. But this is to misinterpret the stress of these commandments. Moses himself supplied the true viewpoint. In the closing discourse in which he repeated the Ten Commandments he gave this positive approach, "Hear, O Israel: The Lord our God is one Lord; and you shall love the Lord your God with all your heart, and with all your soul, and with all your might" (Deut. 6:4). This shows conclusively that the apparent negative approach to human conduct found its true expression in the love relation of God to His covenant people and of their love response to the Lord their God. There is hardly to be found in all the New Testament a statement of a love relationship as emphatic and explicit as these words of Moses, especially when considered in the light of God's taking Israel to be His own possession (Ex. 19: 4, 5). Jesus emphasized the primacy of this love relationship between man and God when He quoted to the lawyer the great commandment in the law. Thus Christ gave witness to the fact that Moses' command was the great and first commandment. He then quoted Leviticus 19:18, giving it the second place among the commandments: "You shall love your neighbor as yourself" (Mt. 22:36-40). Jesus added one more essential point when He said, "On these two commandments depend all the law and the prophets." We may conclude that most profoundly the Ten Commandments found their fundamental expression in these two positive commandments.

The Ten Commandments have as their preamble or introduction, "I am the Lord your God, who brought you out of the land of Egypt, out of the house of bondage." These words served as a fitting introduction to the Decalogue. God's commandments had their basis in His redemptive acts. We may have expected God to introduce the Decalogue with words such as "I am the Lord your God, who created the heavens and the earth." Instead, He built the commandments on His great act of redemption. The Lord God acted in history and directed its course.

Since He, the Lord God of the Israelites, had brought them out of the house of bondage, He possessed the authority to direct their manner of life. The special connotation belonging to the name "Lord," the covenant name of God, made it clear that it was the God of Abraham, of Isaac, and of Jacob who was giving these commandments.

The first commandment reads, "You shall have no other gods before me." The expression *al-panaa* presents some problems of meaning. The RSV margin has *besides me*. Other versions vary among *except me, but me*. and *before my face*. The last appears to be a literal rendering of the phrase. The Septuagint rendering is *plenemou* which has the sense, *except* or *save me*. W. J. Harrelson suggested that it "might better be rendered 'in opposition to me.' *Yahweh* will tolerate no rivals to His authority."[20] While this commandment does not give an explicit denial of the existence of other gods, it plainly prohibits the worship of any other god. To this Sampey added, "If it be said that this precept inculcates monolatry and not monotheism, the reply is ready to hand that a consistent worship of only one God is, for people surrounded by idolatry, the best possible approach to the conclusion that there is only one true God. The organs of revelation, whatever may have been the notions and practices of the mass of the Israelitish people, always speak in words that harmonize with a strict monotheism."[21] For those who might feel that this first commandment should be worded differently to express monotheism, Sampey's explanation is very much to the point.

The second commandment (vv. 4-6) prohibits the making of a graven image or any likeness of God. This was a prohibition against making images for worship. All efforts to make an image of the Lord God are strictly prohibited. The details of this prohibition, together with Moses' rehearsal of it (Deut. 4:15-24), reflected plainly the efforts of their neighboring idolatrous peoples to make graven images in the forms of all kinds of beasts, birds, and fish. The command also prohibits the worship of the sun, moon, and the stars. The Lord their God was a jealous God. He would not tolerate divided affections among His people. Their love for Him must be like a wife's exclusive love for her husband. Unfaithfulness to this love would bring judgment upon idolaters. But to those who are faithful in their love He would show steadfast love.

The third commandment prohibits the taking of the name of the Lord in vain. It is the common notion among idolatrous peoples that man can control the power of the gods and use this power for his own service. God will not permit His people to use His name for their own purposes as the heathen do in their magic or divination. To use God's name in this way is to take His name in vain. This is the sin of false swearing and cursing, which was frequently condemned in the Old Testament.[22] Harrelson says, "The command is, accordingly, a prohibition of the use of the divine name to invoke curses or blessings or to reinforce one's own false oaths by the invoking of the divine name. God's name is not to be placed, by man, into man's service and control."[23]

The kernel of the fourth commandment is, "Remember the sabbath day, to keep it holy." The full statement of this commandment, together with Moses' version of it (Deut. 5:12-15), presents a remarkable perspective of man's relation to time under the direction of the Lord God. The word "remember" suggests that a law of the Sabbath already existed. In Exodus 16:22-30 we have evidence of its existence before Israel came to Mt. Sinai. Concerning the seventh day, God had said, "Tomorrow is a day of solemn rest, a holy Sabbath to the Lord." This is the first clear reference to Sabbath observance.

A close study of the account of the flood leads to the impression that time was being marked by seven-day periods. This may lead to the conclusion that some concept of the Sabbath existed in the time of Noah. This allows us to push the inquiry back to the creation week to search a second time for possible evidence relating to the Sabbath. An eschatological difference was suggested, namely, that God's resting on the seventh day anticipated another era of creation. We noted that in the second part of Isaiah, God spoke of creating new heavens and a new earth (Is. 65:17), and that this prophetic strand was repeated by Peter and John.[24] If an eschatological note does shine forth from this creation account we may have some reasons for concluding that man consciously interpreted the creation week as laying the pattern for his own life; six days of work followed by a hallowed day of rest. Whether or not this interprets correctly God's seven-day creation week, as it related to man's work and rest, the word "remember" still remains.

The six days of labor followed by the seventh day of rest showed that God designed that man should copy God's way in His work of creation. The intent of remembering the Sabbath day was compactly stated in the words, "to keep it holy." It was to be a Sabbath to the Lord, a day of holy rest. This God-centered meaning of the Sabbath says a great deal. Since it is to be a day set apart to the Lord, the command suggests that it is not to be merely a day of idleness but rather one of devotion to the Lord. It gave birth to the idea of man's worship of God on this day. The appended reason for this day of rest lay in God's resting on the seventh day from all His work of creation.

God's pattern of six days' labor before His day of rest provided purpose for man's working six days before resting. Our finite minds are not able to probe into the mind of God as it found expression in the creation week, but we may be able to discover in a small way God's wisdom in establishing a plan for man's week. God designed that man shall involve himself in creative work. He also ordained that man shall spend the seventh day as a day of holy rest to the Lord. When Moses recounted the giving of the Ten Commandments (Deut. 5:1-21), he linked the Sabbath observance to Israel's deliverance from the bondage of Egypt. Their six days of work should remind them of their life of slavery in Egypt and their seventh day of rest should remind them of their deliverance from this servitude by the mighty hand of the Lord their God.

In the later legislation given by the Lord through Moses we discover a notable extension of the Sabbath concept into the sabbatical years and the seven weeks of years which culminated in the fiftieth year, the Year of Jubilee. The sabbatical year was a year of rest for their land. The Year of Jubilee marked the return of property to the original owner, the release of debts, as well as the freeing of those who had been sold for their indebtedness. A most remarkable buildup of the sabbatical concept! So evident was the prophetic potential of this arrangement that it became the foundation for God's later revelation in the words, "In a time of favor I have answered you, in a day of salvation I have helped you" (Is. 49:8). Paul grasped this eschatological significance when he declared, "Now is the acceptable time; behold, now is the day of salvation" (2 Cor. 6:2).

But this does not exhaust the eschatological content of the Sabbath. The psalmist saw in the land of Canaan the promised rest for Israel (Ps. 95:11). By reason of Israel's unbelief they could not enter into Canaan rest. The author of Hebrews saw in this psalm a prediction of a sabbath rest for the people of God yet to be realized (Heb. 3:4). This sabbath rest is the rest of heaven. This passing from sabbath rest to Canaan rest and finally to heaven rest is most sublime. It is another sample of the potential truths inherent in the Old Testament Scriptures. We may conclude that the ultimate purpose of the fourth commandment was to prepare the people of God for the realization of heaven rest, of which the Sabbath day was a type. This typical aspect of the Sabbath became clearer in Paul's language when he said with reference to Old Testament festivals, including the Sabbath, "These are only a shadow of what is to come; but the substance belongs to Christ" (Col. 2:17).

The fifth commandment, the statute to honor father and mother, turns to human relationships. Very naturally if man obeys the first four commandments, his attitude in all human relations will be vitally affected. This commandment has to do with fostering the unit of society, the family. Children in their immaturity need parental training and discipline to guide them to maturity. This commandment instills the proper attitude of children to parents. It is one of honor and respect. Moses gave some pointed, detailed instruction on this command.[25] These laws specified some acts of grievous dishonor, such as striking and cursing father and mother. The stubborn and rebellious son who did not obey his parents, even though they chastised him, should be stoned to death. A familiar proverb laid hold of this commandment in reverse. It read, "Train up a child in the way he should go, and when he is old he will not depart from it" (Prov. 22:6). The fifth commandment together with this proverb embodied the principle which would perpetuate the covenant relation between Israel and God as each succeeding generation was trained to love God and so insured the attached promise, "that your days may be long in the land which the Lord your God gives you."

The sixth commandment, "You shall not kill," sets forth the sacredness of human life. The creation of man in the image of God had already placed supreme dignity on the nature of man as compared with all other living creatures. Cain had failed to grasp this truth and became the first murderer. After the Flood, God laid down this principle, "Whoever sheds the blood of man, by man shall his blood be shed; for God made man in his own image" (Gen. 9:6). And now God wrote this principle into the fundamental law, the Decalogue. Later the Lord proclaimed through Moses a fuller statement of this sixth commandment. It reads, "You shall not hate your brother in your heart, but you shall reason with your neighbor, lest you bear sin because of him. You shall not take vengeance or bear any grudge against the sons of your own people, but you shall love your neighbor as yourself: I am the Lord" (Lev. 19:17, 18). As noted earlier, Jesus raised this last statement to the position of being the second great commandment. This helps us to understand the comprehensive implication bound up with the simple statement, "Thou shalt not kill."

The seventh commandment, "You shall not commit adultery," has its foundation in the creation of man and woman and of their relation as husband and wife. God early established the fundamental law of marriage in the words, "Therefore a man leaves his father and his mother and cleaves to his wife, and they become one flesh" (Gen. 2: 24). The act of adultery is a defiance of "the one flesh" nature of marriage. By creation God entrusted the powers of procreation to be exercised alone in marriage. The act of adultery constitutes an irreparable breach of the marriage covenant and of marriage love. Another facet of this commandment has to do with a child's inalienable right to be born in a family with a father and a mother. Adultery robs a child of this right.

The eighth commandment, "You shall not steal," voices man's right
to the ownership of property. Through this God declares the responsibility
of man to perform the necessary work to secure food, clothing, and shelter, which are necessary to preserve life. It instills the principle of
personal responsibility to do these things, and thus establishes the
individual's right to possess the things necessary for life. We noted in the
discussion of the Sabbath that God had made provision in the Sabbatical Year and in the Year of Jubilee for taking care of human needs
when individuals in the various experiences of life had suffered losses.
This eighth law affirmed man's right to what is his in the normal circumstances of life.

The ninth commandment, "You shall not bear false witness against
your neighbor," protects another very sacred right of man. The dignity
of man's creation in the image of God secures for him the right to
honor, respect, and a good name. The bearing of false witness robs a
neighbor of this right. So flagrant is this sin that the author of
Proverbs expressed it in popular form, "A faithful witness does not
lie, but a false witness breathes out lies" (Prov. 14:5; 19:5). Very bluntly
he wrote, "A man who bears false witness against his neighbor is like
a war club, or a sword, or a sharp arrow" (Prov. 25:18). Jesus voiced
the same principle when He declared, "Judge not, that you be not
judged" (Mt. 7:1). In the same vein James wrote, "Do not speak evil
against one another, brethren. He that speaks evil against a brother or
judges his brother, speaks evil against the law and judges the law"
(Jas. 4:11). Observe that James associated this admonition with the law,
evidently referring to this ninth commandment.

The tenth commandment. Here the sin of coveting is prohibited.
This commandment touches another aspect of stealing but it goes deeper
than the outward act. It condemns the unlawful desire for what belongs
to another, for inevitably the unlawful desire will spring forth in actual
seizure. This commandment probes deeper than the acts of sin. It condemns the evil which flows forth from the heart. To quote Christ's
words, "For from within, out of the heart of man, come evil thoughts
. . . coveting" (Mk. 7:21, 22). This commandment leads us to recognize
that the Decalogue probes into the sinfulness of wrong thoughts, as well
as of wrong acts.

This commandment brought home to Paul the consciousness of sin.
Seeing the purpose of the law in the light of Christian experience Paul
wrote, "If it had not been for the law, I should not have known sin.
I should not have known what it is to covet if the law had not said,
'You shall not covet.' But sin, finding opportunity in the commandment,
wrought in me all kinds of covetousness. Apart from the law sin lies

dead. I was once alive apart from the law, but when the commandment came, sin revived and I died; the very commandment which promised life proved to be death to me" (Rom. 7:7b-10).

For Additional Reading and Reference:

Baab, *Theology of the Old Testament,* pp. 136-38.
Buber, *The Revelation and the Covenant,* pp. 39-55, 69-79, 110-46.
Davidson, *The Theology of the Old Testament,* pp. 38-73, 235-59, 289-300.
Eichrodt, *Theology of the Old Testament,* Vol. I, pp. 36-48, 289-96.
Heinisch-Heidt, *Theology of the Old Testament,* pp. 12-18.
Jacob, *Theology of the Old Testament,* pp. 209-17.
Kaufmann, *The Religion of Israel,* pp. 223-43, 317-22.
Knight, *A Christian Theology of the Old Testament,*   pp. 149-66.
     (Presents a typical case of applying literary criticism to the Pentateuch.)
Köhler, L., *Old Testament Theology,* pp. 59-71.
Napier, *Songs of the Vineyard,* pp. 71-100, 109-17.
Oehler, *Old Testament Theology,* pp. 68-245.
Payne, *The Theology of the Older Testament,* Consult Index.
von Rad, *Old Testament Theology,* Vol. I, pp. 175-219, 280-305.
Raven, *The History of the Religion of Israel,* pp. 42-72.
Ringgren, *Israelite Religion,* pp. 28-40.
Robinson, *Inspiration and Revelation in the Old Testament,* pp. 148-59.
─────, *The Religious Ideas of the Old Testament,* pp. 186-90.
Rowley, *The Re-Discovery of the Old Testament,* pp. 114-25.
─────, *The Biblical Doctrine of Election,* pp. 36-68.
Schultz, *Old Testament Theology,* Vol. I, pp. 125-39.
Titcomb, *Revelation in Progress,* pp. 52-59.
Vischer, *The Witness of the Old Testament to Christ,* pp. 166-212.
Vos, *Biblical Theology — Old and New Testaments,* pp. 115-59.
Vriezen, *An Outline of Old Testament Theology,* pp. 253-56.
Weidner, *Biblical Theology of the Old Testament,* pp. 53-61, 117-20.

Consult commentaries on Exodus.

See "Covenant" in:
Allmen, Ed., *A Companion to the Bible.*
Davis-Gehman, *The Westminster Dictionary of the Bible.*
Douglas, Ed., *The New Bible Dictionary.*
Harrison, Ed., *Baker's Dictionary of Theology.*
Hastings, Ed., *Dictionary of the Bible.* Frederick C. Grant and H. H.
     Rowley, Ed., Revised Edition.
Interpreter's Dictionary of the Bible.
International Standard Bible Encyclopaedia.
Richardson, Ed., *A Theological Word Book of the Bible.*

---

1. *Theology of the Old Testament,* Vol. I (Philadelphia: The Westminster Press, 1961), pp. 289-96.
2. *Ibid.,* p. 289.
3. Ex. 4:10; 14:31; Num. 11:11; 12:7; Deut. 3:24; 34:5.
4. Ex. 24; 32:11-14; 33:12-16; 34:1-9; Deut. 9:13-21; 10:10, 11.

5. Ex. 5:5, 23; 6:6-9; Deut. 4:10; 18:15.

6. Eichrodt, *op. cit.*, I, pp. 289 ff. Gerhard von Rad, *Old Testament Theology*. Vol. I (New York: Harper Brothers, 1962), pp. 289 ff.

7. Ex. 3:20; 4:2-9, 21; 6:6, 7; 7:3, 9-12; 8:19; 9:15, 16; 14:22, 31; 15:8, 11; 34:10; Ps. 78:42-51.

8. Davis-Gehman, *The Westminster Dictionary of the Bible* (Philadelphia: The Westminster Press, 1944), "Miracle," p. 399.

9. *Ibid.*, p. 399.

10. Ex. 34:10; Josh. 24:4-7; Ps. 105:23-42; 106:7-33; 136:10-16.

11. Mic. 6:4; Acts 7:20-44; 13:17, 18; Rom. 9:17; Deut. 7:6-10; 9:4-6; 10:15; 32:6.

12. Jn. 8:33; Rom. 8:20, 21.

13. Ex. 6:6; 15:13; Deut. 7:8; 9:26; 13:5; 15:15; 21:8; 24:18.

14. Ex. 12:1-13, 16; Deut. 16:1-8.

15. 1 Chron. 29:3; Eccles. 2:8.

16. *The Cambridge Bible for Schools and Colleges*, A. F. Kirkpatrick, General Editor (Cambridge: The University Press, 1911), "The Book of Exodus," by S. R. Driver, p. 171.

17. Rom. 7:7-20; 10:1-5; Gal. 3:12-24.

18. *Op. cit.*, p. 145.

19. James Orr, *op. cit.*, Vol. V, "The Ten Commandments," by John R. Sampey, p. 2944B.

20. George Arthur Buttrick, *op. cit.*, R-Z, "The Ten Commandments," p. 570.

21. *Op. cit.*, p. 2946.

22. Ex. 23:1; Lev. 19:12; Ps. 12:2; 15:3; 24:4; 41:6; Jer. 5:2; 7:9; Zech. 5:4; Mal. 3:5.

23. *Op. cit.*, p. 571.

24. 2 Pet. 3:13; Rev. 21:1.

25. Ex. 21:15-17; Lev. 20:9; Deut. 21:18, 21; 27:16.

CHAPTER VI
WORSHIP IN THE ERA OF MOSES

1. Introduction

Worship in Israel tied in very closely with the tabernacle. On this account the historicity of the tabernacle — together with the pattern of worship centering in the tabernacle — constitutes a matter of greatest concern. From the days of Wellhausen to the present many scholars have rejected the historicity of the tabernacle. Since this is a problem involving biblical criticism, its full treatment lies outside of the study of biblical theology. However, the impact of this type of biblical criticism upon our study is so great that it requires some attention.[1] In view of the strong biblical and archaeological evidence for the historicity of the Mosaic tabernacle I shall proceed to discuss the subject with full confidence that Moses constructed the tabernacle according to the pattern which God revealed to him in the mountain (Ex. 25 — 31, 35   40).

2. Structure of the Tabernacle: Its Symbolism and Typical Significance

a. Pattern of the Tabernacle

To begin, it is of exceeding importance to observe that God commanded Moses to build the tabernacle. This sanctuary did not have its origin with Moses or the people of Israel. This fact stands in direct contrast to the sacred buildings associated with other religions. The fundamental significance of this sanctuary is also of highest importance. God said, "Let them make me a sanctuary, that I may dwell in their midst" (Ex. 25:8). Since God planned to dwell with His people, it was entirely natural that He should design its structure. Hence God revealed to Moses the pattern for this building, as well as its furniture.

So detailed were the directions for the construction of the tabernacle and its furniture that biblical scholars have been able to construct models of this building.[2] The plan of the tabernacle is unique. Its central feature was the ark of the covenant located in the holy of holies. A veil separated this part of the tabernacle from the rest of the sanctuary, where were located the altar of incense, the golden candlestick, and the table of showbread. In the courtyard outside the tabernacle were the laver and the altar of burnt offering. Since God patterned the tabernacle as His dwelling place among His people, the total structure and its furnishings naturally possessed profound meaning. It possessed a symbolism of rich significance which leads directly to the nature of Israel's worship.

b. Symbolism of the Tabernacle Structure and Furnishings

Man's worship of God from the Garden of Eden to Mt. Sinai laid hold of what we may properly call symbolism. A symbol is an act, an object, or something in the external world which gives an expression of something spiritual. Vos says, "A symbol is in its religious significance something that profoundly portrays a certain fact or principle or relationship of a spiritual nature in visible form."[3] The etymology of symbol suggests the idea of laying one thing alongside another in order that the first may lead to an understanding of the second.

We have already learned that the trees in the Garden of Eden had symbolic significance. The altar built by Noah together with the burnt offerings which he made possessed spiritual meaning. Abraham's offering of Isaac and the substitution of the ram in his place were meaningful acts of worship, spiritual in nature. In like manner the Passover lamb taught the spiritual lesson of a substitute dying in the place of the firstborn. In the institution of the covenant at Mt. Sinai the altar represented God's part in the transaction, and the twelve pillars, that of the twelve tribes of Israel. These antecedents prepare us to understand the still greater symbolism found in Israel's worship.

God's statement that He was going to reveal the pattern of the tabernacle and its furniture leads us to anticipate the rich symbolism found in its structure. It was to be a sanctuary in which He would dwell. The division between the holy of holies and the holy place suggested that the former centered in God and the latter in the people's approach to God. The only piece of furniture in the holy of holies was the ark of the covenant with its mercy seat and the cherubim with outstretched wings. Whatever else we may associate with this piece of furniture, we may conclude that the Lord was showing His people that His relationship to them centered in their covenant relationship. Israel met their Lord at the mercy seat. Grace and mercy lay at the very heart of God's dealings with His people. The veil closed direct access of the people into His dwelling place.

The furniture of the holy place carried meaning as to how the people of God would gain entrance into His very presence. Just outside the veil was the altar of incense. The burning of incense gave a pleasing odor which spread into the holy of holies. Then there was the bread of the presence which was set on the table, and last was the lampstand with its seven lamps. In the court to the east of the tabernacle were the laver and the altar of burnt offering. God designed all these to symbolize something essential in man's approach to Him in worship. Each of these objects and arrangements portrays a certain fact, principle, or picture of a present spiritual reality. A physical object taught a spiritual lesson.

c. Typical Element of the Tabernacle and Its Furniture

The devout Israelite who had laid hold of God's promises to Adam and Eve, Noah, Abraham, Isaac, and Jacob may have sensed that the Lord's provision for worship in the tabernacle did not in itself fulfill the promises. The deep prophetic content of God's revelation built up an eschatological viewpoint on the part of His people. In a word, God's dwelling with Israel in the tabernacle did not exhaust the profound content of the promises. On this account the spiritual-minded Israelite may have anticipated something greater, richer, and more meaningful to be revealed by God in the future. Even Moses prepared the people to expect God to raise up a prophet like himself, one to whom God would speak face to face. In this respect Moses could be thought of as a type of Christ.

While there is no explicit evidence in support of symbols having typical meaning, it is conceivable that the Israelites may have seen in these symbols that which prefigured something far richer to be revealed in God's own time. Because the New Testament laid hold of the prefiguring aspect of the Old Testament symbols, it is proper for us to study how these New Testament writers interpreted this aspect of Old Testament worship. In this sort of context Paul used the word "type" to express this prefiguring aspect of something in the Old Testament (Rom. 5:12-14). In his exposition of how sin came into the world, Paul called Adam a type of Christ. Something about Adam prefigured Christ, our Lord.

The author of Hebrews elaborated this idea very explicitly (Heb. 8 — 10). He brought into the picture a sizable number of words which show how tabernacle worship prefigured the new worship through the great High Priest, Jesus the Son of God. The author demonstrated the superiority of the new covenant over the old (chap. 8). To begin, the Christian's High Priest "is seated at the right hand of the throne of the Majesty in heaven, a minister in the sanctuary and the true tent which is set up not by man but by the Lord" (v. 1). The word "true" (*alethinos*) conveys the idea of *real, ideal,* and *genuine.* The old tent prepared the mind of Israel for the genuine Tent.

Speaking concerning the offerings and sacrifices under the law, the writer said, "They serve a copy and shadow of the heavenly sanctuary; for when Moses was about to erect the tent, he was instructed by God, saying, 'See that you make everything according to the pattern which was shown you on the mountain'" (v. 5). The words "copy," "shadow," and "pattern" call for study. The Greek word *hupodeigma* translated "copy" carries the meaning *figure, representation,* or a *sign* suggestive of something. The Greek word *skia* translated "shadow" has the idea of the *image* or *outline* cast by an object. Both of these words show how in the plan of God the tabernacle prefigured the heavenly sanctuary. The Greek word *tupos* translated "pattern" carries the meaning of *type, model, example.* It bears the technical sense of the thing to be made conforming to the pattern. God had commanded Moses to make the tabernacle according to the pattern shown to him on the mountain. It is conceivable that what Moses saw on the mountain was not a mere model of the tabernacle but rather the indescribable glory of God's dwelling place in heaven. This suggests that the earthly tabernacle built by Moses bore the pattern of the eternal dwelling place of God. This is certainly what the writer is saying when he pictured Christ as seated at the right hand of the throne of the Majesty in heaven and as His being a minister in the sanctuary and the true tent. Obviously, the true tent is heaven itself. The Mosaic tabernacle was a type of this true tent.

In chapter 9 the author also pictured the furnishings of the old tent. As he described the high priest's duties in the tabernacle, he added the following significant comment: "By this the Holy Spirit indicates that the way into the sanctuary is not yet opened as long as the outer tent is still standing (which is symbolic for the present age). According to this arrangement, gifts and sacrifices are offered which cannot perfect the conscience of the worshiper, but deal only with food and drink and various ablutions, regulations for the body imposed until the time of reformation" (Heb. 9:8-10). The word "symbolic" (*parabole*) is quite expressive. This is the word Christ used frequently in His teachings. It carries the idea of *comparison, figure, illustration, analogy.* By this language the author was showing that the old system of worship in the tabernacle stood as a parable or illustration of worship in the present age. The old form of worship was a symbol of the vastly superior worship through Christ. Christ introduced the time of reformation. The Greek word *diorthosis* (making straight, a reforming, a new order) is most expressive in describing the present time as compared to that of Moses.

Later in the chapter the author gave a summary of the comparison between the New and Old by saying, "Thus it was necessary for the copies [*hupodeigma*] of the heavenly things to be purified with these rites, but the heavenly things themselves with better sacrifices than these. For Christ has entered, not into a sanctuary made with hands, a copy of the true one, but into heaven itself, now to appear in the presence of God on our behalf" (Heb. 9:23, 24). The word "copy"

(v. 24) which translates the Greek word *antitupos*, stands in opposition to the word "type" (*tupos*) (8:5). Even though the words "type" and 'antitype" present some ambiguity in meaning, it seems clear that here the word *antitupos* carries the idea that the old sanctuary was a copy, a representation of the true tabernacle, the archetype in heaven. The writer makes still another significant statement in the words, "For since the law has but a shadow of the good things to come instead of the true form of these realities, it can never, by the same sacrifices which are continually offered year after year, make perfect those who draw near" (Heb. 10:1). The word "shadow" (*skia*) stands in opposition to the word *eikon* (image, likeness, copy). The author is saying that the law has but a shadow of the good things to come. This shadow standing as the opposite of the reality which now exists, shows that the present fulfillment constitutes the true nature of these realities. How profoundly the writer of the Hebrews laid hold of the typical and eschatological aspects of the worship in the Mosaic tabernacle!

3. The Tabernacle, Dwelling Place of God

a. Purpose of the Tabernacle Symbolism

(1) To Develop Covenant Fellowship. God would have Israel know that He was their friend. He provided the tabernacle with the design of developing this friendship through covenant fellowship. The Lord would bring to full realization what He had said earlier in the words, "You have seen . . . how I bore you on eagles' wings and brought you to myself. Now therefore, if you will obey my voice and keep my covenant, you shall be my own possession among all peoples; . . . and you shall be to me a kingdom of priests and a holy nation" (Ex. 19:4-6). The very names used for the tabernacle suggest this purpose. For example, *mishkan*, the usual word for tabernacle, means *dwelling place* (Ex. 25:9; 26:1, etc.). For the Lord to dwell among His people is to assert His fellowship with them. The idea of conscious intercourse found expression in the name *ohel moed* (tent of meeting). It signified the meeting of the Lord with His people. The Lord said, "[I shall be] . . . at the door of the tent of meeting before the Lord, where I will meet with you, to speak there to you. . . . And I will dwell among the people of Israel, and will be their God. And they shall know that I am the Lord their God, who brought them forth out of the land of Egypt that I might dwell among them; I am the Lord their God."[4] The expression *ohel ha'eduth* (tent of testimony) stresses the great redemptive nature of God's revelation to Israel. While references to the tent of testimony are found chiefly in the Pentateuch (Num. 1:50, 53; 9:15, etc.),

the psalmists also laid hold of its precious spiritual content.[5] Observe a few very familiar examples: "The law of the Lord is perfect, reviving the soul; the testimony of the Lord is sure, making wise the simple" (19:7). "In the way of thy testimonies I delight as much as in all riches" (119:14). "In thy steadfast love spare my life, that I may keep the testimonies of thy mouth" (119:88). "Thy testimonies are wonderful; therefore my soul keeps them" (119:129). "Thy testimonies are righteous for ever; give me understanding that I may live" (119:144). These precious meditations on the testimonies arose out of the spiritual experiences which the people of Israel received through the tent of testimony.

(2) To Teach the Holiness of God. The very name "sanctuary" (*miqdash*) applied to the tabernacle leads us to the heart of the tabernacle's symbolism. The word *miqdash* carries the idea of *a sacred place, a place consecrated,* and is usually translated *sanctuary.* The Septuagint translators used the word *hagiasma* which carries the sense of *sanctuary.* It is the place where people are being sanctified and consecrated to God. It is the idea which ties in with the words, "I am the Lord your God; consecrate yourselves therefore, and be holy, for I am holy" (Lev. 11:44, 45; 19:2; 20:7, 26). We should observe that these four occurrences of this statement in the Book of Leviticus serve very explicitly to set forth the meaning of Israel's worship in the tabernacle.

In the main, Leviticus served as God's book of directions to the priests for conducting the tabernacle worship. It is here that we meet the word "holy" as it sets forth the central aspect of God's nature, as well as that to which man should attain. We should observe that the word *qadosh* (holy) has the same root as *miqdash* (sanctuary). It is in the *miqdash,* the dwelling place of God, that His people become *qadosh.* The literal idea of *qodesh* (holiness) is separateness or aloofness, and this easily leads to the idea of majesty.

A double thought emerges from a careful study of Israel's access to God by way of the tabernacle. On one hand, it was a most glorious truth that God had come to dwell among His people. But we need also to observe that God did not fellowship with His people openly and freely. The Lord dwelt in the holy of holies between the cherubim on the ark of the covenant. The people of Israel could not come into the holy of holies. Three severe but meaningful limitations prevented this. Only the high priest could enter the holy of holies. He could enter this place only once a year on the Day of Atonement. He could come into God's presence only after offering sin and burnt offerings and sprinkling the blood of the sin offering on the corners of the mercy seat. The reason for this lay in God's separateness. God kept somewhat aloof because of Israel's sinfulness. Both expiation for sin and consecration were necessary in order that the high priest might enter the holy of holies. After making this expiation and consecration for himself, he made similar offerings for the people. Only a holy person could come into God's presence. The tabernacle worship taught Israel the real meaning of God's holiness.

The Lord did not separate Himself from His people merely to keep aloof from them. The ethical quality of purity in His very nature was the real cause for His separation from them. For this reason the word "holiness" in common biblical usage looks to God's purity, His perfection of character, His goodness, His freedom from sin. Peter had grasped this idea when he wrote, "As obedient children, do not be conformed to the passions of your former ignorance, but as he who called you is holy, be holy yourselves in all your conduct; since it is written, 'You shall be holy, for I am holy' " (1 Pet. 1:14-16). Isaiah's vision of the Lord sitting upon His throne also magnifies the idea. He heard the seraphim calling to one another saying, "Holy, holy, holy is the Lord of hosts; the whole earth is full of his glory" (Is. 6:3). On seeing this, Isaiah cried, "Woe is me! For I am lost; for I am a man of unclean lips, and I dwell in the midst of a people of unclean lips; for my eyes have seen the King, the Lord of hosts" (Is. 6:1-5)! Having been granted this vision of the holy Lord, the godly prophet Isaiah could do nothing else than to look at his own lost condition and his unclean lips.

(3) To Show the Meaning of Worship. The two aspects of the tabernacle symbolism just noticed lead very naturally to the third, that of the worship of the Lord. As Vos put it, "It is the palace of the King in which the people render Him homage."[6] The symbolism studied above related quite directly to the holy of holies. Let us now look at the holy place with its altar of incense, the table of the lamp of the Presence, and the lampstand. The altar of incense stood nearest to the curtain. The burning of the incense produced a sweet odor which entered the holy of holies. We might interpret this sweet smelling odor as symbolic of man's approach to God. We may gain the most accurate interpretation of this altar of incense from the Lord's revelation to John of worship in heaven. He saw golden bowls full of incense which he learned were the prayers of the saints. We may conclude that the burning of incense in the holy place symbolized the prayers of God's people. The people of Israel could know that their prayers were as sweet and acceptable to the Lord as the pleasant odor from the burning incense is to one who inhales this sweet odor.

The bread of the Presence which was set on the table in the holy place added to the meaning of worship (Ex. 25:30; Lev. 24:5-9).

Certain details attract attention and may suggest the meaning of the bread of the Presence. First, the stress on the twelve loaves evidently made reference to the twelve tribes. Second, the bread was continually kept on this table and changed every seven days. Third, special holiness attached to the bread. While it is very clear that the bread of the Presence had symbolic significance, Bible students have some difficulty in laying hold of its specific meaning.[7] From the standpoint that the loaves represented the labors of the people in the growing of grain and the making of bread, some scholars feel that the bread of the Presence symbolized the consecration of all the activities of life to God. Other scholars stress the idea that the Lord is the source of all material blessings. The presentation of the loaves would represent Israel's response in worship and in recognition that all the bounties of the earth come from God. They would see here the elements of thanksgiving and consecration to God. The loaves would stand as a symbol of man's continued and unbroken dependence on God. While these statements present some variety in viewpoint, they all agree that man's worship of God finds expression in recognizing God as the source of all material blessings and in giving thanks for these blessings. Worship will culminate in the consecration of these material things to God.

The third piece of furniture in the holy place, the lampstand, suggests a rich symbolism even though we may not be able to explain it to our satisfaction. The lampstand had seven lamps arranged so as to give light in the holy place. The receptacle of oil transformed the oil into light. We may anticipate that the lampstand, like the other articles of furniture in the holy place, expressed some symbolism having to do with worship. It is our privilege to look elsewhere in the Bible for teaching which may reflect the symbolism of the lamp holder. One such passage is Zechariah 4:1-6. While this vision of Zechariah is quite complex, we discover the common element of the lampstand of gold with seven lamps. The Lord revealed the meaning of this vision in the words, "Not by might, nor by power, but by my Spirit, says the Lord of hosts." This may suggest that the oil symbolized the Spirit of God and the holders the recipients of the Spirit. If this senses the basic meaning of the symbolism, we may interpret the lamp holders as follows: Just as the receptacle of oil transforms the oil into light, so the people of God should transform the Spirit into such forms of light as will induce others to praise God. Through this means God was teaching Israel that they should serve as a light to the peoples of the world. God had entrusted the Holy Spirit to His people. Through His power and influence they should be a light to the world.

This leads me to believe that Jesus made specific reference to the symbolism of the lampstand when He said, "You are the light of the world. A city set on a hill cannot be hid. Nor do men light a lamp and put it under a bushel, but on a stand, and it gives light to all in the house. Let your light so shine before men, that they may see your good works and give glory to your Father who is in heaven" (Mt. 5: 14-16). It may be true also that in Christ's revelation to John of the seven golden lampstands, with Christ standing in the midst of them, we may have another clear reflection of the tabernacle lampstand. Our Lord's explanation of this vision would seem to confirm the interpretation suggested above: "As for the mystery of the seven stars which you saw in my right hand, and the seven golden lampstands, the seven stars are the angels of the seven churches and the seven lampstands are the seven churches" (Rev. 1:12-20).

In conclusion, we have seen that the three pieces of furniture in the holy place took hold respectively of three important aspects of worship: prayer, thanksgiving for and consecration to God of all His bounties, and the transformation of the Spirit into light which will lead all mankind to praise God.

b. Problems Concerning the Interpretation of Symbolism

First, shall we regard symbolism as being an end in itself or shall we recognize in it a certain actuality of spiritual meaning? This question recognizes the tension between an actuality lying back of the symbol and a purely spiritual concept not possessing any reality. In answer to this question I have sought to show that lying back of the symbols were spiritual realities in which the symbols represent so many bridges between the natural and these spiritual realities. From a certain point of view, spiritual reality is intangible. It belongs to the part of our being related to God, who is Spirit. The tabernacle and the sacrifices which led to covenant fellowship were the symbols. The covenant fellowship was the spiritual reality that described the mutual relation of God to man. The symbolism which expressed the holiness of God led to man's understanding of the most profound aspect of the nature of God, namely, His holiness. Since holiness belongs to God's nature, it is real. The symbolism which showed the meaning of worship described man's approach to God in worship. It had to do with his own most spiritual experience. Nothing can be more spiritual or more real than man's worship of God.

The second question sharpens the problem of the interpretation of symbols. How shall we conceive of the divine presence, the Shekinah glory, as it appeared in the tabernacle? Specifically, what is the proper interpretation of the following statement? "Then the cloud covered the tent of meeting, and the glory of the Lord filled the tabernacle" (Ex. 40:34). This problem arises also in the following quotation: "And the Lord said to Moses, 'Tell Aaron your brother not to come at all times into the holy place within the veil, before the mercy seat which is upon the ark, lest he die; for I will appear in the cloud upon the mercy seat' " (Lev. 16:2). Was this presence of God tangible or was it a purely spiritual reality? Here we have to do with one of the major problems of divine revelation. Obviously, the passages quoted assert the manifestation of God in the tabernacle. If these were the only Scriptures setting forth the revelation of God, the problem would have larger dimensions. But He revealed Himself in other ways. We might bring into the picture God's speaking to Abraham, to Moses, and to the prophets. We might examine John's words when he said, "And the Word became flesh and dwelt among us, full of grace and truth; we have beheld his glory, glory as of the only Son from the Father" (Jn. 1:14). We might also listen to Paul in his reference to the appearances of the risen Lord (1 Cor. 15:5-8). With these illustrations in mind plus many others, we come to realize the impact of the inquiry as to the reality of the glory of the Lord filling the tabernacle or whether it was without any foundation in reality. Faithfulness to the fact of divine revelation leads me to accept these statements in Exodus and Leviticus as descriptive of the Shekinah glory of God actually filling the tabernacle. Certainly God did not dwell in the tabernacle in the fullness of His glory. It is proper to state that the tabernacle with its accompanying glory of God was a symbol of the heavenly habitation of God where He dwells in the fullness of His glory. This fact does not impose any metaphysical problem as to how God could at one and the same time dwell in the tabernacle and also dwell in the heavens. We are dealing with spiritual realities and not with metaphysical problems.

Very interestingly the same names are given to the earthly dwelling place of God as to His heavenly habitation. Thus *ma'on* (dwelling, dwelling place, habitation),[8] *hekal* (palace, house, temple),[9] and *zebul* (dwelling, habitation)[10] refer to the earthly tabernacle and also to God's heavenly habitation or palace. From this point of view the tabernacle served as a symbol of God's heavenly habitation. Since we may properly understand God's dwelling in the tabernacle as real and actual, we come to realize the pertinent fact that biblical piety is God-centered.

c. Typical Significance of the Tabernacle

The typical significance has its basis in the symbolism just considered. We observed earlier that an eschatological, forward-looking characteristic was already apparent in God's earliest revelation to His people. There appears to be no evidence, however, that the tabernacle structure and worship really prefigured Christian worship or the perfected worship in heaven. The New Testament unfolded the concept of the type and became the safe guide to discovering this element in the Old Testament. From one point of view a study of the New Testament basis for Old Testament types belongs to New Testament theology. From another point of view it is entirely justifiable to give it consideration at this place because the New Testament interpreted the Old Testament. Further it is our purpose to understand correctly all that God revealed in the Old Testament. There is no desire nor justification for going beyond the New Testament interpretation of the Old. Very explicitly these New Testament contexts unfold great bodies of truth which lie beyond the scope of the Old Testament. They constitute the full and complete revelation of God to man. In this presentation we shall seek to discover the close dependence of the typical on the symbolic elements of the tabernacle. Briefly stated, the inquiry here seeks to answer the question, Where do these religious principles and realities as found in the symbolism of the tabernacle reappear in the subsequent history of redemption centering in the Lord Jesus Christ? Three separate but closely related themes appear in the language of type: first, those elements which typify the Lord Jesus Christ and His work; second, those elements that typify the church, which is the body of Christ and the "house of God"; and third, those elements which typify the eternal eschatological stage which is heaven itself. Let us examine briefly the biblical presentation of these three groups of types.

(1) Types Fulfilled in the Lord Jesus Christ and His Redemptive Work. John presented this truth in these words, "The Word became flesh and dwelt among us, full of grace and truth; we have beheld his glory, glory as of the only Son from the Father" (Jn. 1:14). In this language the apostle reflected on the Shekinah glory manifested in the tabernacle. God had dwelt among Israel and they beheld the glory of the Lord. This close similarity in language and in thought gives us ground for believing that John chose this manner of expression because the Lord's dwelling among His people in the tabernacle prefigured Christ's dwelling among men during His earthly ministry.

Jesus spoke in similar language in the words, "You will see heaven opened, and the angels of God ascending and descending upon the Son of man" (Jn. 1:51). With equal clearness Jesus showed how the ladder of Jacob prefigured Himself. The word "type" is not used in either of these illustrations, but the references to the Old Testament incidents are clear beyond question. Another statement of Jesus may show the language of type. In answer to the Jews, Jesus said, "Destroy this temple, and in three days I will raise it up" (Jn. 2:19). John explained that Jesus was speaking of the temple of His body. The temple which succeeded the tabernacle and possessed the same symbolism of God's dwelling with His people suggests that He, the Son of man, would be dwelling in the temple of His body in the same fashion that the Lord dwelt in the temple. We may believe that Paul used the same figure when he wrote concerning Christ, "For in him the whole fulness of deity dwells bodily" (Col. 2:9).

The author of Hebrews picked up another strand of teaching which had to do with Christ as our high priest. He showed in several contexts how our Lord fulfilled the Old Testament type of the high priest (Heb. 8:1-4). In this context the writer pictured the vastly superior glory of Jesus, our high priest, as compared to the high priest of the tabernacle. As noted in an earlier context, Jesus our Lord is "a minister in the sanctuary and the true tent which is set up not by man but by the Lord" (Heb. 8:2). Very naturally the true tent in which our Lord ministers is as superior to the old tabernacle in glory as Christ the great high priest is superior to the tabernacle high priest. In this same context the author brought in the third stage, according to which the earthly sanctuary, the tabernacle, was but a copy and shadow of the heavenly sanctuary. He probed deeper into this mystery when he drew attention to the purifying quality of Christ's blood as over against that of goats and calves. He based his thought on the ideas of the blood atonement accomplished through the Old Testament sacrifices. Devout Christian Jews, as well as other Christians, could easily pass in thought from the redemptive privileges of Old Testament sacrifices to the once-for-all sacrifice of Jesus, our great high priest. It is in this context (9:23-28) that the author used the significant words *hupodeigma* (figure, copy) and *antitupos* (seal, copy) with the purpose of showing the inferior value of tabernacle purification as compared with the truly efficacious purification wrought by our great high priest, the Lord Jesus Christ.

(2) The Tabernacle as a Type of the Church. Paul makes us conscious of this typical relationship in his great epistle on the church, the letter to the Ephesians. He wrote: "You are no longer strangers and sojourners, but you are fellow citizens with the saints and members of the household of God, built upon the foundation of the apostles and prophets, Christ Jesus himself being the chief cornerstone, in whom the whole structure is joined together and grows into a holy temple in the Lord; in whom you also are built into it for a dwelling place of God in the Spirit" (Eph. 2:19-22). The idea of type becomes clear in Paul's

language, which reflected the building of the temple. Paul saw the church being built in like manner, but of course it was a spiritual temple. God indwells the church as He dwelt in the temple. The special point of superiority of the fulfillment over against the type is the fact that the church is a spiritual dwelling in which God in the Spirit dwells. Paul again laid hold of the structural terms of the temple or even of the tabernacle, when he called the household of God "the church of the living God, the pillar and bulwark of the truth" (1 Tim. 3:15).

In the letter to the Hebrews (3:1-6) we see a notable comparison between Moses and Christ. Both served in the house of God, Moses as a servant, and Christ as a Son. In this fashion the author spoke of Moses as being the type of Christ. We as the church of Jesus Christ belong to the house of God in the same way that Israel belonged to God's house in the time of Moses. This way of presenting the type in contrast with its fulfillment shows again the indescribable superiority of the latter over the former. In a later chapter (10:19-25) the worship aspect of the two houses comes into view. We who belong to Christ's church "enter the sanctuary by the blood of Jesus, by the new and living way which he opened for us through the curtain, that is, through his flesh, and since we have a great high priest over the house of God, let us draw near with a true heart in full assurance of faith, with our hearts sprinkled clean from an evil conscience and our bodies washed with pure water." By this language the author portrayed most vividly the typical aspect of tabernacle worship, and all the more so because it lies in the context of its unsurpassed fulfillment in Christ. Let us yet observe how Peter made the comparison when he said, "Come to him, to that living stone, rejected by men but in God's sight chosen and precious; and like living stones be yourselves built into a spiritual house, to be a holy priesthood, to offer spiritual sacrifices acceptable to God through Jesus Christ" (1 Pet. 2:4, 5). While he did not use the word "type," he certainly presented his thought in this framework. Peter's quotations show how appropriately he could speak in the language of type.[11] It is noteworthy that Peter closed this line of thought with words first spoken concerning Israel but now applying with still greater richness to the church. He wrote, "You are a chosen race, a royal priesthood, a holy nation, God's own people" (1 Pet. 2:9).

(3) The Tabernacle a Type of God's Eternal Dwelling Place. John heard a voice from the throne saying, "Behold, the dwelling of God is with men. He will dwell with them, and they shall be his people, and God himself will be with them" (Rev. 21:3). "And I saw no temple in the city, for its temple is the Lord God the Almighty and the Lamb" (v. 22). This is the apocalyptic manner of describing the truth already

noted in Hebrews 8:5, where we read of the tabernacle serving as a "copy and shadow of the heavenly sanctuary." This apocalyptic view of the dwelling of God with men is the *summum bonum* of typology.

Two concluding observations may be in order. In the first place, the New Testament witness to the typical elements of the tabernacle symbols increases our understanding of these symbols. In the large, this culminating New Testament revelation has made clear the potential meaning of primitive revelation. In the second place, the relation of symbol and type gives a new and sound basis for believing in the grand unity of God's revelation in the Scriptures.

4. Sacrificial System in Israel's Worship

a. Background of Pre-Mosaic Sacrifices

In the foregoing chapters I paid attention to sacrifices and offerings recorded in the Book of Genesis. A few observations on these sacrifices may serve to introduce us to the sacrificial system instituted by Moses. First, there are no recorded sacrifices before the fall of Adam and Eve. All sacrifices belong to man's state in sin. Second, this fact may establish a connection between man's sinfulness and the origin of sacrifices. Third, Genesis gives no account of the origin of sacrifices. Fourth, the question remains: Did God institute sacrifices or did man originate them? Fifth, on several occasions the offering made was called a burnt offering but on no occasion did the author give an explanation of this kind of offering.

b. Ends or Purposes Served by Sacrifice

Perhaps the best starting point in a study of the Mosaic sacrificial system is a consideration of the ends or purposes served by sacrifices. An effort to classify these sacrifices seems to lead directly to the ends or purposes which they served. In the first place, God's words point to a fundamental differentiation among sacrifices. He said, "For the life of the flesh is in the blood; and I have given it for you upon the altar to make atonement for your souls; for it is the blood that makes atonement, by reason of the life" (Lev. 17:11). This leads us to observe that when a man's spiritual state required atonement, he needed to bring a bloody offering. This draws a line between the bloody and the nonbloody sacrifices. This would lead us to understand that when man's relation to God did not require atonement he was permitted to bring offerings of a nonbloody sort. In the second place, the varying uses of the blood, as well as the differing elements of spiritual significance, would lead to a classification of the bloody sacrifices. This in turn should bring into clear view the ends or purposes served by these respective sacrifices. To this end the following outline of bloody sacrifices may prove helpful.

The Bloody Sacrifices

Name	Distinctive Act	Point of Significance
Sin and Guilt Offerings	Use of the Blood	Expiation
Burnt Offering	Burning of the Sacrifice	Consecration
Peace Offering	Eating of the Sacrifice	Fellowship

This table shows a definite progress in the distinctive acts relating to each sacrifice. With respect to the sin and guilt offerings the blood is used in the ritual of the sacrifice, whereas in the burnt and peace offerings the blood is allowed to flow out unused. According to the verse quoted (Lev. 17:11) the offerer places the blood upon the altar, where it makes atonement (literally, *a covering*) for "your souls." Explicitly, the significance of the sin and guilt offerings has to do with making atonement. The literal meaning of the Hebrew verb *kapar* is *to cover*. The Septuagint translators used the verb *hilaskomai* to express the idea of covering. This verb means to *conciliate, appease, propitiate, expiate*, etc. Briefly, the first end or purpose of sacrifice is that of expiation or propitiation. These two words are almost synonymous; the former directs attention to the covering for sin while the latter looks at the sacrifice from the angle of satisfying divine justice and effecting reconciliation between God and man. The forfeited life of the animal spared the man from losing his life as a punishment for sin.

In the burnt offering the burning of the sacrifice was the distinctive act. It was significant in this class of offerings that the entire animal was burned completely on the altar. The Bible has not given in specific language the purpose or point of significance of this offering, although in a number of places its implicit meaning becomes evident. As explained by J. J. Reeve,[12] "This was perhaps the most solemn of the sacrifices, and symbolized worship in the full sense, i.e., adoration, devotion, dedication, supplication, and at times expiation." Perhaps Paul reflected on the symbolism of burnt offerings when he wrote, "Present your bodies as a living sacrifice, holy and acceptable to God, which is your spiritual worship" (Rom. 12:1). Consecration lies at the heart of this exhortation. If this interprets Paul correctly, we may gather that when the people of Israel looked at the burning of the entire animal on the altar and saw the smoke ascending to heaven, they saw in this offering the symbol of their complete dedication to God and consecration to His service.

The peace offering revealed the third purpose served by sacrifice. The eating of the sacrifice suggested that they were at the table of the Lord where He was the Host and they were the guests. In Oriental fashion this eating together symbolized fellowship. It was an occasion of great joy, because, as Reeve says, "These were sacrifices of friendship expressing or promoting relations with the Deity."[13] These purposes served by the several kinds of sacrifices reveal the profound nature of the entire sacrificial system. They make clear the real nature of Israel's worship. It began with expiation, continued with consecration, and culminated in fellowship with God.

c. *Category of Sacrifice Expressed by* Corban[14]

While the word *corban* occurs very infrequently in the Old Testament, it carries, nevertheless, the general idea of sacrifice. Its root meaning signifies a gift, something brought near. Its use in the Bible always relates to a gift to God. A similar expression is *mattenoth kodhesh.*[15] It carries the meaning *holy gifts.* The usage of these two expressions shows that they cover much more than sacrifices proper. All things devoted to God may properly bear either of these names. The distinguishing aspect of a sacrifice is that a whole or a part of the animal comes upon the altar. The placing of the sacrifice upon the altar and its being consumed by fire may carry the symbolism of its being food for God. But this does not mean that Israel thought of God as needing food.[16] The holy character of these offerings led to the prohibition that no man "who has a blemish shall come near to offer the Lord's offerings by fire. . . . he shall not come near to offer the bread of his God. He may eat the bread of his God, both of the most holy and of the holy things, but he shall not come near the veil or approach the altar, because he has a blemish, that he may not profane my sanctuaries; for I am the Lord who sanctify them" (Lev. 21:17-23). This requirement concerning one who came near the veil or approached the altar showed again that Israel's God was holy. Even physical defects disqualified one for service in offering the Lord's offering by fire. To ignore this prohibition would profane His sanctuary.

d. *Materials for Sacrifice*

The materials for sacrifice pointed also to the holy nature of the sacrificial system. Only clean animals and birds, such as bullocks, goats, sheep, doves, and pigeons, qualified, but camels or asses were not acceptable. Fish and wild animals could not be used even though they were available for food. Cereals, flour, oil, and wine, which were the chief constituents of man's daily food, could be used for sacrifice. Among animals which could be used, males were preferred to females. Mature animals were more acceptable than young animals. All needed to be physically perfect. The attempt to discover the principle underlying this division between acceptable offerings and those unacceptable creates some problems. Some students have felt that the acceptable animals and vegetables could be used for sacrifice, because they were the products of men's labors. With these offerings man learned that such products rather than fish and wild animals had far greater meaning to him and would more fully give expression to the symbolism of the several offerings. We may conclude that, whatever may have been the real point of distinction between acceptable and unacceptable materials for sacrifice, this factor added to the spiritual meaning of their worship.

e. Relation Between the Offerer and His Sacrifice

The people of Israel encamped at Mt. Sinai possessed a rich spiritual heritage of worship. Because of their special relation to the Lord as His chosen people, they preserved the traditions of God's meeting with their spiritual forefathers and of the worship experiences which followed. They treasured the approaches made to God by such God-fearing men as Enoch, Noah, Abraham, Isaac, Jacob, and Joseph, so that the provision of the tabernacle for worship had its foundations in this spiritual heritage. It was not a mere story that Enoch had walked with God. Israel could recognize in Enoch's experience the reality of a personal and friendly relationship between man and God. Their God had acted throughout their history. It would seem that as Noah contemplated his having been saved from the Flood through the providence of God and as he and his family began life anew on the earth, he felt the urge to completely devote himself to God. Since God had preserved his life, he therefore owed to God his entire life. The unexplained burnt offerings brought by Noah become intelligible as we see in them a symbol of the giving of himself to God in obedience and consecration. He could see in the consuming of the entire animal on the altar an expression of his yielding himself to God in order to fulfill God's purposes in him. This point became still clearer in Abraham's sacrifice of Isaac. In the substitution of the ram for Isaac, Abraham saw vividly the idea of substitution or vicariousness. In implicit obedience, he had already in his heart offered Isaac as a burnt offering. This complete dedication of Isaac to the Lord was an actual experience and illustrates most intimately Abraham's relation to his sacrifice.

With this background of sacrifice in Israel's spiritual history we are in a position to anticipate the relation of the offerer to his offering in the Mosaic system. The structure of the tabernacle and the provision for Israel's approach to God through the bloody and nonbloody sacrifices showed them most clearly the idea of a meaningful symbolism in their worship. As we have already noted, the bloody and nonbloody offerings by the distinctive act in each, symbolized expiation, consecration, fellowship, thanksgiving, and praise to God. This symbolism covered the whole gamut of worship. By means of the external aspects of their worship the people of Israel who were not spiritually mature came to realize the spiritual character of their worship. It was most natural that they entered experientially into the meaning of their sacrifices. They saw in their system of worship God's provision for them to enter into fellowship with Him as well as to regain this fellowship when they sinned. We have adequate reasons for believing that when an individual brought a sin or guilt offering, he did so not merely on the grounds of external laws of sacrifice, but because of a changed attitude toward his sin, namely, penitence and repentance. This also involved faith in God's provision for him to enter again into fellowship with the Lord. While this discussion does not have its basis in explicit declarations with reference to the relation of the offerer to the offering, I have attempted to express the meaning which the authors of the Pentateuch sought to express. The explanation given is implicit rather than explicit.

We are not left alone to the Pentateuchal presentation of Israel's worship. It is our privilege to examine the assumptions and declarations of later Scriptures which should confirm the conclusions suggested above. Most significant in the Old Testament is the great Servant of the Lord passage in Isaiah 53. Almost the entire chapter looks at the suffering Servant; and in doing this, the prophet gave repeated implications of the relation of the offerer to his offering. His message accorded with the form and pattern of Mosaic worship. The Servant of the Lord did not merely present a symbolism of suffering and death, but He also experienced this awful reality.

As the devout Israelite looked to this Servant of the Lord, he entered into the worship of the Lord by way of a most significant spiritual involvement. He believed that the Servant "was wounded for our transgressions, he was bruised for our iniquities; upon him was the chastisement that made us whole, and with his stripes we are healed. All we like sheep have gone astray; we have turned every one to his own way; and the Lord has laid on him the iniquity of us all. . . . Yet it was the will of the Lord to bruise him; he has put him to grief; when he makes himself an offering for sin, he shall see his offspring, he shall prolong his days; . . . by his knowledge shall the righteous one, my servant, make many to be accounted righteous; and he shall bear their iniquities. . . .

He poured out his soul to death, and was numbered with the transgressors; yet he bore the sin of many, and made intercession for the
transgressors" (Is. 53:4-12). The devout Israelite who read this message interpreted it in terms of his concept of worship as developed by
Moses.

Paul made repeated references to Israel's worship under the law,
usually in a context in which he showed the vastly superior character
of Christian worship through the finished work of the Lord Jesus
Christ. Among these references we find a number of expressions which
show that the Israelite in his worship knew that the sacrifices went far
beyond a meaningless symbolism. He shared in the spiritual experiences
which those sacrifices symbolized. In line with this Paul based his entire
letter to the Romans on an Old Testament quotation, "He who through
faith is righteous shall live" (Hab. 2:4). His development of the nature
of saving faith had its basis in the familiar words, "Abraham believed
God, and it was reckoned to him as righteousness" (Rom. 4:3). These
quotations, drawn from pre-Mosaic times to the period near the close
of Old Testament history, give clear evidence of the experiential side
of Israel's worship.

Observe how Paul developed this theme, using the thought, forms,
and structure drawn from Moses' system of worship. Paul's words
descriptive of Christ follow: "But now the righteousness of God has been
manifested apart from law, . . . the righteousness of God through
faith in Jesus Christ for all who believe. . . . They are justified by his
grace as a gift, through the redemption which is in Christ Jesus, whom
God put forward as an expiation by his blood, to be received by
faith" (Rom. 3:21-25). Without question the worship of Israel reflected
in this passage showed that with them there was the element of
faith. Israel trusted in the redemption wrought by God. Their sin and
guilt offerings symbolized this commitment of faith. They could see
that the righteousness of God lay back of all of His provision for their
entering into fellowship with Himself. The same implication becomes
clear in another of Paul's statements concerning Christ. Paul wrote,
"For our sake he made him to be sin who knew no sin, so that in
him we might become the righteousness of God" (2 Cor. 5:21). These
words gain great meaning when examined in the thought forms of the
Mosaic sacrifices. Israel's ritual of sin and guilt offerings symbolized
the disposal of their sins. The animals' being without blemish and clean
reflect a symbolism that is very apparent. It was through their
trusting in the expiation wrought by these sacrifices that they became the righteousness of God. While faithful Israelites were spiritual
children of God, they did not realize the fullness of Christ's redemptive

work. The elements of Christian faith together with the associated elements of Christian worship had, nevertheless, a real expression among the God-fearing Israelites.

It is in the letter to the Hebrews that we learn most fully of the relation of the offerer to his sacrifice in the Old Testament worship. Like Paul, the author of Hebrews was showing the superior character of Christ's sacrifice and of His high priestly work. But in all these contexts the relation of the offerer to his sacrifice was as experiential as the Christian's relation to the sacrifice of Christ — in a word, it was a faith relationship. The author wrote concerning Christ, "He had to be made like his brethren in every respect, so that he might become a merciful and faithful high priest in the service of God, to make expiation for the sins of the people" (Heb. 2:17). The Israelites knew very well what it meant to have a merciful and faithful high priest, one who would make expiation for their sins. Again the author wrote, "For every high priest chosen from among men is appointed to act on behalf of men in relation to God, to offer gifts and sacrifices for sins. He can deal gently with the ignorant and wayward, since he himself is beset with weakness. Because of this he is bound to offer sacrifice for his own sins as well as for those of the people" (Heb. 5:1-3). Undoubtedly the author of Hebrews was reflecting on the worship experiences of Israel. They expected their high priest to act on their behalf in relation to God. They were aware that their high priests needed to offer sacrifice for their own sins as well as for those of the people. This reflected on Israel's dependence upon their sacrifices as the way of gaining access to God. In chapter 9:1-22 the author went to greater lengths, first of all to present a picture of the tabernacle and its furnishings and then to explain more fully the work of the high priest — all this to show how the Mosaic worship stood as a type for the present age. Since the purifying of the conscience in order to serve the living God is the direct result of a definite act of faith, we may also conclude that the purification of the flesh from uncleanness through a bloody sacrifice was also an act of faith on the part of the offerer.

The relation between the offerer and his sacrifice should now be transparently clear. Each part of the tabernacle possessed a symbolism and each step in the ritual of sacrificial offerings possessed a symbolism in line with that of the tabernacle structure. The specific point of symbolism of each kind of sacrifice found realization in the several acts of worship, which began with making expiation for sin, advanced to the offerer's giving himself to God in consecration, and culminated in fellowship with God. While the modes of worship were adapted to a people who were children in faith, the actual participation of the individual in his offering obtained meaning just as real as that experienced by mature Christians in the worship of God through the Lord Jesus Christ. This is another essential link in the continuity of the idea of worship of the people of God from the earliest times on to the revelation of Jesus Christ. To deny that the offerer shared experientially in his sacrifices is virtually to deny the genuineness of Israel's worship of God and ultimately to deny the Christian's worship through our great high priest, the Lord Jesus Christ.

f. Steps or Stages in the Ritual of Sacrifice

A study of the steps in the ritual of sacrifice leads to a clearer understanding of Israel's worship. The first step was the selection of the particular animal for sacrifice. Only a perfect specimen, an animal without any physical defects, could be chosen. Only a clean animal qualified. These requirements certainly had meaning. Since the offerer needed to make expiation for sin, we may conclude that the perfect and clean animal for sacrifice symbolized a spiritual reality. The offerer realized that through the provision of God his sins could be covered by the blood of such an animal. There is nothing inconsistent in recognizing the physical perfection of a clean animal, a nonmoral creature, as symbolizing the ethical perfection of a personal being. In fact, we may discover here a characteristic of divine revelation according to which God used such natural means of leading His people to understand the real nature of spiritual truth — in this case the spiritual concept of redemption.

That this element of divine revelation appeared in the choice of an animal for sacrifice becomes apparent in the Servant of the Lord passage (Is. 53) referred to earlier. While the author did not explicitly ascribe ethical perfection to the Servant of the Lord, this trait is certainly implicit. Only a sinless One could be wounded for the transgressions of others and bruised for their iniquities. Only the chastisement of such a One could make a sinner whole. Only by His stripes could sinners be healed. Only upon a sinless person could the Lord lay the iniquity of us all. All these statements reflected the symbolism of the sin offering. The Servant of the Lord in order to be an offering for sin needed to be morally perfect and clean. Only on the merits of the righteous Servant could many be accounted righteous.

The author of Hebrews also caught this principle when he wrote of Christ as having offered Himself without blemish to God (Heb. 9:14). This language shows how the physically perfect, clean animal used in sacrifice was the type of Christ, the perfect sacrifice. Peter expressed the same truth in the words, "You know that you were ransomed from the futile ways inherited from your fathers, not with perishable things such as silver or gold, but with the precious blood of Christ, like that of a lamb without blemish or spot" (1 Pet. 1:18, 19). These biblical references show conclusively that a profound spiritual symbolism lay in the choice of physically perfect, clean animals for sacrifice. So clearly had this truth gripped the hearts of the people of God that later writers, especially those of the New Testament, could easily find in this principle a type of Christ.

The second step in the ritual was the laying on of hands (Lev. 1:4; 3:2, 8, 12, etc.). This step had various purposes but in each sacrifice a common point of significance is apparent: The act symbolized the transfer of something from one person to another. In bestowing blessing on Joseph's sons, Jacob placed his right hand on the head of Ephraim and his left hand on the head of Manasseh. This fact was the symbol of blessing bestowed upon these boys. In the ceremony of setting apart the Levites for their priestly service, the people of Israel laid their hands upon them and Aaron offered the Levites before the Lord as a wave offering for the people of Israel. Their specialized task was to do the service of the Lord (Num. 8:10, 11). In this same ceremony the Levites laid their hands upon the heads of the bulls which were offered, the one for a sin offering, and the other for a burnt offering to the Lord. They did this to make atonement for the Levites. It seems clear that in these two instances there was a common symbolism, something transferred from one to the other. The point of special value is that the former instance leads to an understanding of the latter. Laying hands on the heads of the bulls symbolized the transfer of sin from the Levites to the animals; the people's laying hands on the Levites symbolized the transfer of the Levites in complete dedication to God and to His service through the burnt offering.

Two other illustrations of the laying on of hands outside the category of sacrifice are found in the commissioning of Joshua to serve as Moses' assistant, and again in his appointment as Moses' successor (Num. 27:18-20; Deut. 34:9). The most explicit example of the laying on of hands in the ritual of worship was that having to do with the dismissal of the scapegoat on the Day of Atonement. Concerning this we read, "Aaron shall lay both his hands upon the head of the live goat, and confess over him all the iniquities of the people of Israel, and all their transgressions, all their sins; and he shall put them upon the head of the goat, and send him away into the wilderness by the hand of a man who is in readiness. The goat shall bear all their iniquities upon him to a solitary land; and he shall let the goat go in the wilderness" (Lev. 16:21, 22). This act possessed great realism for Israel. They heard Aaron confess over the scapegoat all their iniquities, transgressions, and sins. Aaron put them upon the head of the goat and the goat bore all their iniquities upon him out into the wilderness. It was this symbolism that the author of Isaiah 53 used concerning the Servant of the Lord in the words, "The Lord has laid on him the iniquity of us all." Peter also appropriated this symbolism when he wrote concerning Christ, "He himself bore our sins in his body on the tree" (1 Pet. 2:24).

The third step in the ritual was the slaying of the animal. The offerer killed the animal for his sacrifice. The law specified the place for the slaying of the animal as the north side of the altar. This suggested a specific meaning in the death of the animal which becomes evident in the study of the several contexts in Leviticus where the slaying of the animal comes into view. It is noteworthy also that a number of significant Scriptures cast light on the meaning of this step in the ritual. To begin, the key passage, "For the life of the flesh is in the blood" (Lev. 17:11), makes it clear that the death of the animal was the most significant act in the ritual of sacrifice. It significantly sets forth the forfeiture of life as the price of expiation. The death of the suffering Servant in Isaiah 53 built directly on this fact. Paul voiced the same idea in a context dealing with the meaning of Christ's death when he wrote, "And you, who once were estranged and hostile in mind, doing evil deeds, he has now reconciled in his body of flesh by his death, in order to present you holy and blameless and irreproachable before him" (Col. 1:21, 22).

Since the author of the letter to the Hebrews gave such a matchless exposition of Christ's sacrificial work in the language of the Mosaic sacrificial system, we see still more clearly the meaning attached to the slaying of the animal. He wrote, "We see Jesus, who for a little while was made lower than the angels, crowned with glory and honor because of the suffering of death, so that by the grace of God he might taste death for every one. . . . Since therefore the children share in flesh and blood, he himself likewise partook of the same nature, that through death he might destroy him who has the power of death, that is, the devil, and deliver all those who through fear of death were subject to lifelong bondage" (Heb. 2:9, 14, 15). In the heart of his discussion on the meaning of Christ's work he wrote further, "Therefore he is the mediator of a new covenant, so that those who are called may receive the promised eternal inheritance, since a death has occurred which redeems them from the transgressions under the first covenant. For where a will is involved, the death of the one who made it must be established. For a will takes effect only at death, since it is not in force as long as the one who made it is alive" (Heb. 9:15-17).

The fourth step in the ritual was the manipulation of the blood. We have already observed that varying uses of the blood are found in the several sacrifices. In the burnt offerings and peace offerings no special use was made of the blood. But in the sin and guilt offerings the blood was sprinkled on the altar. This suggested a special meaning attached to the use of the blood. We should note, however, that all bloody sacrifices possessed an element of expiation even though as in the instances of the burnt and peace offerings no significant use was made of the blood. To be more specific in the instances of the burnt and peace offerings, the direction was given that "the priests shall present the blood, and throw the blood round about against the altar that is at the door of the tent of meeting" (Lev. 1:5-15; 3:2-13).

In the sin offering the following ritual was observed: "And the anointed priest shall take some of the blood of the bull and bring it to the tent of meeting; and the priest shall dip his finger in the blood and sprinkle part of the blood seven times before the Lord in front of the veil of the sanctuary. And the priest shall put some of the blood on the horns of the altar of fragrant incense before the Lord which is in the tent of meeting, and the rest of the blood of the bull he shall pour out at the base of the altar of burnt offering which is at the door of the tent of meeting.[17]

As we shall note in a discussion of the ritual of the Day of Atonement, the use of the blood in the sin offerings was still more significant (Lev. 16:14, 15). In this type of offering the high priest entered the holy of holies and sprinkled blood with his finger on the front of the mercy seat and seven times before the mercy seat. The explanation of this act was, "Thus he shall make atonement for the holy place, because of the uncleannesses of the people of Israel, and because of their transgressions, all their sins" (Lev. 16:16). This description lays special stress on the expiatory aspect of the sacrifices on the Day of Atonement.

This leads us to consider the meaning of this use of the blood. Returning to the key passage on this theme (Lev. 17:11), we gain, perhaps, the clearest idea of the meaning given to the blood. Since the life of the flesh is in the blood, and since the sprinkling of the blood upon the altar made atonement for the souls of the people, we may gather these ideas: first, that the shed blood stood for death; second, that the death of the animal was the substitute for a person; and third, that when the substitute died and its blood was offered on the altar, the sinner was free from all guilt. He stood before God in full covenant relationship. The entire transaction led to the unexplainable mystery of divine redemption.

Later biblical language used with reference to the meaning of

Christ's death obtained its form and structure of thought from the sacrificial system under study. Several of Paul's expressions help us to understand the vicarious nature of these bloody sacrifices. Most briefly, Paul expressed it thus, "I live by faith in the Son of God, who loved me and gave himself for me" (Gal. 2:20). Note also his succinct statement: "Christ redeemed us from the curse of the law, having become a curse for us" (3:13). In another context he wrote, "In him we have redemption through his blood, the forgiveness of our trespasses, according to the riches of his grace which he lavished upon us" (Eph. 1:7). Through these and other pointed statements Paul made it clear that the sacrificial animal through its death took the place of the offerer to whom death was due. It was the forfeiture of life for life. The author of Hebrews described the vicariousness in still more picturesque language (Heb. 9:6-14). Speaking of the entrance of the high priest into the holy of holies, he commented, "The high priest goes . . . not without taking blood which he offers for himself and for the errors of the people." The language "for himself" (*huper heautou*) looks to an act performed in behalf of himself, so intimate that it is visualized as being done vicariously. In verse 12 the writer again reflected on the work of the high priest, in which the taking of the blood of goats and calves secured a redemption which prefigured that wrought by the blood of Christ.

Some students have pressed the question as to whether the expiation, the covering for sin, was obliterative or protective. It would seem that since the whole sacrificial provision expressed the mercy and grace of God, the concept of obliteration expresses the thought more accurately. The bloody sacrifice covered man's sin. It was not an act of placating Deity as the Greek word *hilaskomai* or the Latin *propitic* might connote. It is rather unfortunate that the KJV translated *hilasmos* "propitiation" (1 Jn. 2:2; 4:10) and *hilasterion* "propitiation" (Rom. 3:25). For this reason the literal rendering of the Hebrew verb *kaphar* (cover) should guide us in understanding the symbolism embodied in the use of the blood as a covering for sin.[18] In all these instances the atoning work has its bearing on man's sin and not in appeasing, propitiating, or placating God. It is extremely gratifying that the RSV corrected this error of the KJV translation.

The fifth step in the ritual was the burning of certain parts of the animal on the altar. The verb used here for burning is *qatar* (to burn as incense or to cause the smoke to ascend). This is the verb used to describe the burning of offerings on the altar and stands in contrast to such verbs as *saraph*, which is used with reference to the burning of parts of the animal outside the camp for the purpose of completely consuming it. This leads us to expect a certain symbolism in this step of the ritual. The burning of incense on the altar yielded a sweet odor recognized as being pleasing to the Lord. Reflecting on this step in the ritual, Paul wrote concerning Christ, "[He] loved us and gave himself up for us, a fragrant offering and sacrifice to God" (Eph. 5:2). Thus Paul declared that the burning of parts of the animal on the altar typified Christ's offering of Himself as a burnt sacrifice to God!

The sixth and last step in the ritual, which was peculiar to the peace offerings, was the sacrificial meal. On two significant occasions before this time, the eating of the sacrifices stood out with strong symbolism. These occasions were the Passover and the making of the covenant at Mt. Sinai. Both times the element of fellowship between Israel and the Lord became very apparent through the eating of the sacrifice. God was their host and they were guests at the table of the Lord. Paul comes to our aid again in clarifying the symbolism of this sacrificial meal. In a context in which he gave an exposition of the Lord's Supper, he observed, "Consider the practice of Israel; are not those who eat the sacrifices partners in the altar" (1 Cor. 10:14-22)? Paul here made explicit the truth that those who ate the sacrifices became sharers in the altar. It was a fellowship experience. Again we may exclaim how grandly the sacrificial meal typified the Lord's Supper!

g. Day of Atonement

The sacrificial system as instituted by the Lord came to a fitting climax in the annual Day of Atonement.[19] We gain a perspective of the entire sacrificial system of worship as presented in Leviticus when we see that it converged in the Day of Atonement. This was an annual day of worship in which the people ate no food and did no work. It was 'a sabbath of solemn rest" (Lev. 16:29-31). The worship of this day centered in the work of the high priest who, on this day, and this day alone, entered into the holy of holies three times. His first entrance into this most sacred place was for the purpose of preparing the way for his presenting a sin offering for himself and for his house. On entering the holy of holies he took a censer full of coals of fire from the altar before the Lord and two handfuls of sweet incense beaten small and brought it within the veil. He then put the incense on the fire before the Lord, so that the cloud of the incense would cover the mercy seat. The burning of the incense may have been the symbol of their seeking to gain the favor of God toward his sin offering. Then leaving the holy of holies, he entered the second time with some of the blood of the bull. He sprinkled it with his finger on the front of the mercy seat, and before the mercy seat he sprinkled the blood with his finger seven times. On his third entrance to the holy of holies he brought the blood of the goat as a sin offering for the people and administered it in the same way as he had done for himself. Through this act the high priest made atonement for "the holy place, because of the un- cleannesses of the people of Israel, and because of their transgressions, all their sins." The high priest then went out to the altar and made atonement for it, using the blood of the goat and putting it on the horns of the altar. He sprinkled blood upon it with his finger seven times. By so doing he cleansed it and hallowed it from the uncleannesses of the people of Israel.

The next significant step had to do with the live goat. The high priest presented the live goat, laid both his hands upon its head, and confessed over it all the iniquities, transgressions, and sins of Israel. He put them upon the head of the goat and sent it away into the wilder- ness by a man assigned to this responsibility. With these tasks completed the high priest removed his linen garments, bathed his body in water, and put on his high-priestly garments. Then he offered burnt of- ferings for himself and for the people — in this way making atonement. He burned the fat of the sin offering upon the altar. Aaron was the first to serve in this high-priestly function on the Day of Atonement. Undoubtedly, through his service on this annual occasion during the years of his high priesthood, the Day of Atonement gained its promi- nence as the crown of the sacrificial worship instituted through Moses.

For the purposes of this study a few points call for comment and thought. First, we need to observe the heightened significance of the high priest's entrances into the holy of holies. It would be natural to inquire why such entrances could not be made frequently. This ques- tion finds possible answer in the fact that Israel's God was holy. He would have Israel learn that only a holy people could share in this privilege, and even they could come into the presence of God only representatively in the person of the high priest. Israel needed to learn that by reason of their sins direct access to God was impossible. Only through God's gracious provision, symbolized by the burning of in- cense in the holy of holies and by the offering of sin offerings ap- plied by the sprinkling of blood on the mercy seat, could God permit even the high priest to come into His presence. Through this means the Lord led His children to spiritual maturity. Looking backward from the completed revelation through the Lord Jesus Christ, we are able to see the profoundness of spiritual truth into which God was leading His people. God was directing them through these external means of wor- ship to the spiritual realities beyond the symbols as well as to their typical significance.

Second, the worship on the Day of Atonement leads us to the clearest understanding of the act of making atonement. The blood served as a covering for sin. The blood of the animal given as a sin offering indicated the forfeiture of its life in order to give life to the offerer. Thus the people of Israel learned the meaning of sin and God's provision for atonement.

Third, the sending away of the other goat to Azazel taught a different lesson, yet the truth gained was fundamentally the same as that taught by the sacrifice of the first goat. The high priest's laying hands upon the head of the live goat and confessing over it the sins of the people symbolized the laying of their sins upon the animal and the animal's bearing all their iniquities out of their sight. This act stood as an emblem of one of the profoundest truths of salvation, namely, what happens when God forgives sin. The live goat symbolically bore them on himself out into the wilderness.

Associated with this problem is that the goat is being let go to Azazel. We may safely assume that this act possessed real meaning, even though with our present knowledge, we are not able to determine it. At this stage of Israel's religious development we can hardly assume that they knew of a personal devil. If the people of Israel knew the tradition of the temptation of Adam and Eve, they were in a position to make some association between the enemy of our first parents and Azazel. It is possible to believe that just as other elements in Israel's spiritual heritage, such as God's revelation through the patriarchs, were known to them, so the record of the temptation could contribute to their spiritual heritage. I tend to believe that this association is both possible and probable. Azazel, symbolizing the accuser of man to God, suffered defeat in his accusations when the scapegoat bore to him the sins of the people for which atonement had been made.

Fourth, the worship on the Day of Atonement furnished the most explicit evidence in support of the typical character of Israel's worship, as it pointed to the finished work of the Lord Jesus Christ. It is these typical elements that lend such richness to the whole sacrificial system of Israel's worship.

5. Meaning of Uncleanness and Purification

The Lord gave a command to Israel which calls for careful study. He said, "You are to distinguish between the holy and the common, and between the unclean and the clean" (Lev. 10:10). The Lord amplified this command a bit when He said, "You shall not make yourselves abominable with any swarming thing that swarms; and you shall not defile yourselves with them, lest you become unclean. For I am the

Lord your God; consecrate yourselves therefore, and be holy, for I am holy" (11:43, 44). He was teaching Israel "to make a distinction between the unclean and the clean and between the living creature that may be eaten and the living creature that may not be eaten" (v. 47). Another command expressing ceremonial distinctions reads, "For the life of every creature is the blood of it; therefore I have said to the people of Israel, You shall not eat the blood of any creature, for the life of every creature is its blood; whoever eats it shall be cut off. And every person that eats what dies of itself . . . shall wash his clothes, and bathe himself in water, and be unclean until the evening; then he shall be clean. But if he does not wash them or bathe his flesh, he shall bear his iniquity" (Lev. 17:14-16).

The Lord enlarged on these commands of what might be eaten and what was forbidden in definitive language which set forth two closely related distinctions (Deut. 14:1-21). The first is the difference between the clean and the unclean; and the second, between the holy (sacred) and common (unholy). These terms call for definition and explanation. One of the first observations which we should note is that they refer to qualifications for worship. The terms "clean" and "unclean" do not refer to physical or even moral conditions. They have to do with fitness or unfitness for ceremonial use. An unclean person was excluded from the sanctuary, but contrary to what we might then conclude, it did not exclude him from fellow Israelites. In order to approach God a man needed to put away uncleanness. Having become clean, he could then become holy. At any moment a person knew whether he was clean or unclean. If he was unclean, he had to follow the procedure which would remove the uncleanness; when this was done he was holy, and so qualified for worship. The act of removing uncleanness bore the name "purification." Through guilt and sin offerings an unclean person became pure. These offerings made atonement for him.

Having noted that the terms "clean" and "unclean" have no reference to physical cleanness or its opposite, we need to observe, nevertheless, how the washing of the body and the garments being worn became closely associated with the ceremonial act of cleansing.[20] Frequently people who were unclean needed to wash their clothes and be unclean until the evening. The washing of the clothes did not make the person ceremonially clean but it would appear that this washing was a necessary requirement to becoming ceremonially clean. Under certain circumstances the individual washed his clothes and also bathed his body in water. These requirements suggest that bodily cleanliness did have a relation to ceremonial cleanness. While the connection between the two is not specifically stated, the uniform sequence of washing the clothes and bathing the body followed by the ceremony of purification would seem to point to a vital connection between the two.

This leads to a more difficult problem, the solution of which prepares us to understand the profound spiritual symbolism expressed by the terms "clean," "unclean," and "purification." A number of circumstances or conditions in life rendered the individual unclean, and the requirement for removing the ceremonial defilement involved bloody sacrifices such as the sin, guilt, and burnt offerings. Among these conditions were leprosy, bloody discharges of both men and women, childbirth, and touching a human corpse. The symbolism involved in these bloody offerings indicated the individual's need of expiation for sin. But in none of these instances of ceremonial uncleanness had the individual sinned. It is apparent that these several conditions rendering an individual unclean are the result of the curse which came upon the human race after Adam and Eve had sinned. It is conceivable that this fact may have a bearing upon the requirement of a bloody offering. It is certainly true, in the light of God's entire revelation, that the Lord unfolded to mankind through biblical history the meaning of the curse and its outworking in human depravity. The description of man's utter sinfulness as found in Isaiah 53:5, 6 may serve as a proof of the above explanation. Paul's exposition of human depravity (Rom. 5:12-21) is the classic passage on this subject.

This requirement of bloody offerings for the removal of the several kinds of uncleanness leads to the idea that ceremonial uncleanness was a symbol of ethical impurity and of sin. This becomes evident throughout the rest of the Bible.[21] Note the words of the psalmist: "Who shall ascend the hill of the Lord? And who shall stand in his holy place? He who has clean hands and a pure heart, who does not lift up his soul to what is false, and does not swear deceitfully" (Ps. 24:3, 4). The psalmist used the words "holy," "clean," and "pure" with the spiritual implications of ceremonial purity and holiness as well as with ethical content. When Isaiah heard the seraphim calling to one another with the words, "Holy, holy, holy is the Lord of hosts," he used language of ceremonial significance when he said, "Woe is me! For I am lost; for I am a man of unclean lips, and I dwell in the midst of a people of unclean lips" (Is. 6:3, 5). What more fitting language could he have used to express his own sinfulness! When the Pharisees and scribes found fault with the disciples of Jesus when they did not wash their hands before eating, Jesus replied with language which showed emphatically the spiritual symbolism found in the ceremonial laws. He showed that it is not "whatever goes into the mouth [that defiles a man]. But what comes out of the mouth [that] proceeds from the heart, and . . . [that] defiles a man. For out of the heart come evil thoughts, murder, adultery, fornication, theft, false witness, slander. These are what defile a man; but to eat with unwashed hands does not defile a man" (Mt. 15:17-20). The Pharisees prevented the disciples from grasping the real symbolism of their ceremonial law.

6. Life of the People of God

Essentially related to genuine worship is the manner of life which issues from it. Along with the detailed instructions with regard to offerings and sacrifices, the Book of Leviticus gave sundry instructions as to how the people of God should live. These instructions showed them the vital connection between worship and ethics. The fundamental starting point of these instructions found expression in the words, "You shall be holy; for I the Lord your God am holy" (Lev. 19:2). In similar strain was the injunction, "Consecrate yourselves therefore, and be holy; for I am the Lord your God. Keep my statutes, and do them; I am the Lord who sanctify you." Yet once again God commanded, "You shall be holy to me; for I the Lord am holy, and have separated you from the peoples, that you should be mine" (20:7, 8, 26). From these three commands we may discover at least three distinct emphases. First, holiness, which is central in God's nature, should also be found in His people. Second, keeping God's statutes and doing them is inseparable from consecration to God. Third, being holy is the inevitable requirement of being God's special possession.

Among the first of these instructions were those pertaining to marriage, chief among which was the forbidding of incest. The nations of Canaan, whom God was driving out from their land, had defiled themselves with such abominations. Here then was a fundamental law of human relations which God required of His people.

Among other sundry regulations the Lord provided for the poor and the sojourner. These needy folks could follow the harvesters and grape gatherers to pick up what was purposely left for them. The Lord forbade stealing, dealing falsely, and lying to each other. Employers had to pay wages promptly. The Lord prohibited injustice to the poor and partiality to the rich. The standard of righteousness was the guide in judging one's neighbor. Here we find the second great commandment in the words, "You shall not take vengeance or bear any grudge against the sons of your own people, but you shall love your neighbor as yourself" (Lev. 19:18). This nullified a criticism sometimes launched against the regulations of the law to the effect that the commands were chiefly negative and legalistic. Christ's verdict that the love of neighbor stands second among the commandments clearly shows that fundamentally the commands were positive and not mere prohibitions; and further, that all these commandments centered in a love relationship between man and his neighbor. From these laws, then, we discover two central principles of biblical ethics: likeness to God in holiness, and love for one's neighbor.

The Lord upheld fair business practices as indicated by commands such as, "You shall have just balances, just weights, a just ephah, and a just hin" (Lev. 19:36). He condemned the various abominable sexual practices, including adultery and fornication. Instructions such as these prepared Israel for their contacts with people who indulged in all kinds of sexual irregularities.

Special arrangements for the poor were found also in the laws pertaining to the Sabbatical Year and Year of Jubilee. On the seventh year, the year of solemn rest for the land, there was no sowing or reaping of crops. The poor were allowed to gather for themselves what they needed. In the Year of Jubilee a man was freed from his debts and those who had been sold for their debts were released from their slavery. God commanded the people to help the man who had become poor. The charging of interest and the giving of food for profit were prohibited. Herein God instituted a great economic law. It prevented the rich from becoming richer at the expense of the poor. Even in Israelite society sound and just economic practices were essential for the well-being of all people. As an incentive to obedience as well as a warning to disobedience, the Lord led the people to an understanding of the high ethical character bound up in their laws.

7. Concluding Observation

First, the elaborate ritual of worship was deeply religious in character. We dare not conclude that the detailed regulations were indications of legalism but rather that through this elaborate ritual, the Lord led His people to genuine spiritual worship. Second, the worship revealed in this legislation is the same in nature as that revealed under the new covenant. The New Testament patterns of man's approach to God show the same kind of progress made possible through the Lord Jesus Christ and the outpoured Holy Spirit. Third, the tabernacle worship required personal involvement just as significant as that under the new covenant. Fourth, redemption and atonement bore as close a relation to worship under the old covenant as they do under the new.

There is need for allowing these Pentateuchal Scriptures to speak for themselves rather than to judge these laws on the basis of the Pharisaical perversions of them. By lifting the tabernacle worship to its true position we not only gain a new view of its spiritual character but we also rise to far greater heights in our comprehension of New Testament worship.

For Additional Reading and Reference:

Davidson, *The Theology of the Old Testament,* pp. 306-38, 352-62.
Eichrodt, *The Theology of the Old Testament,* Vol. I, pp. 70-177.
Heinisch-Heidt, *Theology of the Old Testament,* pp. 223-36.
Jacob, *Theology of Old Testament,* pp. 246-50, 254-59.
Kaufmann, *The Religion of Israel,* pp. 110-21, 180-84.
Knight, *A Christian Theology of the Old Testament,* pp. 242-45, 282-86.
Köhler, *Old Testament Theology,* pp. 119-26.
Napier, *Song of the Vineyard,* pp. 100-7.
Oehler, *Theology of the Old Testament,* pp. 246-352.
Payne, *The Theology of the Older Testament,* 247-52; (scattered
    portions) pp. 350-400.
von Rad, *Old Testament Theology,* Vol. I, pp. 232-79.
Raven, *The History of the Religion of Israel,* pp. 73-155.
Robinson, *Inspiration and Revelation in the Old Testament,* pp. 130-48.
Titcomb, *Revelation in Progress,* pp. 59-80.
Vos, *Biblical Theology — Old and New Testament,* pp. 159-200.
Vriezen, *An Outline of Old Testament Theology,* pp. 263-69, 276-92.
Weidner, *Biblical Theology of the Old Testament,* pp. 154-208.

See articles: "Clean (O.T.)," "Sacrifices (O.T.)," "Tabernacle" in Bible dictionaries, encyclopedias, and word books.

Consult commentaries on Exodus and Leviticus.

Appended Note

**An Examination of Critical Opinions Concerning the
Historicity of the Tabernacle**

It is at once apparent that if Moses did not construct a tabernacle according to Exodus 25 — 40 we have little knowledge of Israel's worship from the time of their deliverance from Egypt to that of the building of the temple by Solomon. It is equally evident that a full consideration of the historicity of the tabernacle lies beyond the study of biblical theology. However, since the acceptance or rejection of the historicity of the tabernacle has such great bearings on the study of Israel's worship, it seems necessary to give a brief review of the usual viewpoint together with what appears to be the correct understanding of the Pentateuchal records. The rejection of the historicity of the tabernacle was an outcome of Wellhausen's reconstruction of Israel's religious history and his view of its bearings upon the origin of the Pentateuch. According to Wellhausen no tabernacle was built by Moses, but rather the account of the building of the tabernacle arose after the

exile of Israel. The so-called Priestly Code arose as an effort to perpetuate temple worship. One device used by the priestly writers was that
of projecting back to the time of Moses an imaginary structure, the
tabernacle, which was fashioned after the pattern of the temple. But
for Wellhausen no tabernacle according to the Exodus description ever
existed. He said that it was a product of pure imagination. Although no
historical evidence exists for Wellhausen's theory, he presented arguments in support of his views. In view of his radical conclusions on
this matter, it seems necessary to give consideration to his arguments.

Since the time of Wellhausen, critical scholars have made a careful
study of his views. Many have found his arguments fallacious and have
proceeded to present modified views of Israel's early worship and of the
tabernacle. One trend of thought identifies the tabernacle with the tent
of meeting but it regards *P's* presentation of the tabernacle as a gross
overstatement of what actually did exist in the wilderness. This group of
scholars give some validity to Israel's worship of the Lord through the
medium of a simple tent of meeting. I present this critical viewpoint
briefly, and along the way I attempt to give a consistent interpretation
of the Scriptures involved.

1. Some scholars hold that the tent of meeting according to the JE
document and the tabernacle of the P document are identical. According to this view the priestly writers greatly exaggerated the structure
of the tent of meeting and the worship associated with it. This embel-
lishment of the tabernacle structure together with its worship is regarded
simply as a copy of the structure and worship of Solomon's temple and
had no basis in actual history.

By way of reply, according to the biblical record in Exodus the
tabernacle had not yet been built when the tent of meeting of Exodus
33:7 was pitched outside the camp of Israel. Chapters 35 — 39 describe
the making of the tabernacle with all its furniture. Chapter 40 records
the erection of the tabernacle. It is impossible to gainsay this internal
evidence from the Exodus narrative.

2. It is held that the biblical account of the Mosaic tabernacle bears
internal marks of its being completely unhistorical in character. This
criticism has its basis in some of the elaborate details of the tabernacle
structure, which in the minds of many scholars could not be found in a
structure erected in the wilderness.

It is certainly true that problems such as this do arise, but then we
need to observe that the argument is entirely subjective. Because of its
length and nature the Exodus account possesses such characteristics that
its historical character cannot be rejected. Among other things let us note
first, that God revealed to Moses the plan for the tabernacle. This build-

ing would possess profound symbolism. God said, "Let them make me a sanctuary, that I may dwell in their midst" (Ex. 25:8). In a very marvelous way the tabernacle expresses this symbolism. Second, the detailed instructions for the building of the tabernacle and for the making of the furniture are entirely natural and not overdrawn. We do not expect a blueprint according to modern methods nor does the lack of details weaken the historical character of what is given. Third, the narrative mentions the skilled workmen, among whom was Bezalel, a man concerning whom God said, "I have filled him with the Spirit of God, with ability and intelligence, with knowledge and all craftsmanship to devise artistic designs, to work in gold, silver, and bronze, in cutting stones for setting, and in carving wood, for work in every craft" (Ex. 31:3-5). The Lord also appointed Oholiab together with other able men to whom God gave the ability to make all furniture. True indeed, the people of Israel were slaves in Egypt, but this fact does not exclude the idea that certain of their men were involved in similar tasks in the land of Egypt and there learned such skills. Fourth, the narrative speaks of the erection of the tabernacle including the date of its being built. It was "In the first month in the second year, on the first day of the month" (Ex. 40:17). Fifth, we learn that "the cloud covered the tent of meeting, and the glory of the Lord filled the tabernacle. And Moses was not able to enter the tent of meeting, because the cloud abode upon it, and the glory of the Lord filled the tabernacle" (Ex. 40:34, 35). Sixth, the writer described the pattern of movement of the people of Israel: "Whenever the cloud was taken up from over the tabernacle, the people of Israel would go onward; but if the cloud was not taken up, then they did not go onward until the day that it was taken up. For throughout all their journeys the cloud of the Lord was upon the tabernacle by day, and fire was in it by night, in the sight of all the house of Israel" (Ex. 40: 36-38). We may most certainly conclude that this entire narrative purports to be historical. No evidence exists for rejecting this internal character of the narrative.

3. Critics have held that the people of Israel during their desert experience were not in a position to erect such a sanctuary. They lacked the materials for building such an elaborate structure. It would seem evident that even in the wilderness acacia wood would be available. The people were not necessarily poor and without silver and gold. In this connection we need to recognize how the Egyptians were urgent to have Israel leave their land after the slaying of the firstborn and gave to Israel jewelry of silver and of gold and clothing to the extent that they despoiled the Egyptians (Ex. 12:33-36).

4. Critics maintain that there is a virtual silence in the biblical

narrative concerning the tabernacle from the time of the settlement in Canaan to the building of the temple. Some go to the extreme of saying that there is no trace of the Mosaic tabernacle to be found in the pre-Solomonic period.

This is true only if we accept the views of certain textual critics pertaining to these narratives. It appears that these critics have very skillfully ruled out certain details presumably based on the lack of textual support. At this point the subjectiveness of the critics again appears evident. Space forbids a detailed study of the later Pentateuchal references to the tabernacle.[22] It would appear that the Mosaic tabernacle was built at Shiloh,[23] and was later moved to Nob[24] and still later to Gibeon.[25] In all these instances the authors were referring to the Mosaic tabernacle and not to the tent of meeting.

5. Critics hold that the Scriptures have nowhere stated that Solomon's temple was constructed after the pattern of the Mosaic tabernacle.

While it is true that there is no specific reference made to the temple being built after the pattern of the Mosaic tabernacle, it needs to be observed that the temple became the permanent dwelling place of God among His people and that the furniture of the tabernacle was permanently located in the temple. The temple displaced the tabernacle, and by so much its structure was similar to the tabernacle.

6. Many scholars hold that the preexilic prophets did not know anything of the Levitical ceremonial system of which the Mosaic tabernacle was the center. Against such a claim, the words of Amos stand as positive evidence: "I hate, I despise your feasts, and I take no delight in your solemn assemblies. Even though you offer me your burnt offerings and cereal offerings, I will not accept them, and the peace offerings of your fatted beasts I will not look upon. . . . Did you bring to me sacrifices and offerings the forty years in the wilderness, O house of Israel" (Amos 5:21, 22, 25)? The words of the Lord to Isaiah confirm this conclusion. "What to me is the multitude of your sacrifices? says the Lord; I have had enough of burnt offerings of rams and the fat of fed beasts; I do not delight in the blood of bulls, or of lambs, or of he-goats. . . . Bring no more vain offerings; incense is an abomination to me. New moon and sabbath and the calling of assemblies — I cannot endure iniquity and solemn assembly. Your new moons and your appointed feasts my soul hates; they have become a burden to me, I am weary of bearing them" (Is. 1:11, 13, 14). The prophet Jeremiah gave further confirmation to the historicity of the Mosaic tabernacle (Jer. 7:21-26). Through Jeremiah the Lord directed Israel's thought to the vast importance of obedience over that of the literal sacrifices, thus showing

the spiritual accompaniment of the outward sacrifices. The Lord dated this worship as having its beginning when Israel came out of Egypt. This possessed meaning only on the basis of an actual tabernacle as described in Exodus.

7. The New Testament made clear references to the tabernacle. Stephen specifically spoke of the tabernacle in the words, "Our fathers had the tent of witness in the wilderness, even as he who spoke to Moses directed him to make it, according to the pattern that he had seen. Our fathers in turn brought it in with Joshua when they dispossessed the nations which God thrust out before our fathers. So it was until the days of David, who found favor in the sight of God and asked leave to find a habitation for the God of Jacob. But it was Solomon who built a house for him" (Acts 7:44-47). In this language Stephen confirmed the Exodus narrative concerning the building of the tabernacle. It is unthinkable to surmise that he did not know the facts. He made it clear also that the temple of Solomon succeeded the Mosaic tabernacle. The author of Hebrews also made specific reference to the tabernacle. Notice the details which he gave: "For a tent was prepared, the outer one, in which were the lampstand and the table and the bread of the Presence; it is called the Holy Place. Behind the second curtain stood a tent called the Holy of Holies, having the golden altar of incense and the ark of the covenant covered on all sides with gold, which contained a golden urn holding the manna, and Aaron's rod that budded, and the tables of the covenant; above it were the cherubim of glory overshadowing the mercy seat. Of these things we cannot now speak in detail" (Heb. 9:2-5). It is entirely proper to believe that both Stephen and the author of Hebrews were giving authentic witness to the historicity of the Mosaic tabernacle.

In conclusion, we may properly note the cumulative strength of all this biblical evidence. The great New Testament Greek scholar, Brooke Foss Westcott, made this comment on the matter just considered: "It seems to be an incredible inversion of history to suppose the tabernacle was an imaginary ideal constructed either from the temple of the monarchy or from the temple of the return."[26] William Foxwell Albright, the greatest living archaeologist, presented the evidence of archaeology for the antiquity of the kind of worship associated with the tabernacle. He said, "The archaeologist no longer has any difficulty in proving antiquity of any details in the description which is given in the Priestly Code. The uniform testimony of our sources with respect to the existence of some kind of sacrificial ritual in earliest Israel can hardly be erroneous, though the constant reaction of the prophets against the formalism and externality of sacrificial cult hardly suggests that undue emphasis was laid upon it in the Mosaic system."[27] J. A. Thompson gave a similar evaluation of the historicity of the tabernacle from the angle of archaeology: "The shape and structure of the tabernacle were both familiar to other peoples at the time, particularly to the Canaanites. The materials used were all such as could be obtained in the areas where the Israelites were wandering. Recent discussion has inclined scholars in general to take the biblical accounts of the tabernacle in the wilderness more seriously than they have for the past century."[28]

1. See Appended Note at the end of chapter.
2. A full-size model of the tabernacle with all of its furnishings has been built and can be seen at the Mennonite Information Center, Lincoln Highway, East, Lancaster, Pa., and is open to tourists. This model is most serviceable in helping one to visualize the ancient Mosaic tabernacle.
3. Vos, *op. cit.*, p. 161.
4. Ex. 29:42-45. See also Ex. 33:7 ff.; 39:32, 33.
5. Ps. 19:7; 78:5; 119:14, 31, 36, 88, 99, 111, 129, 144, 157.
6. Vos, *op. cit.*, p. 168.
7. See Bible dictionaries, Bible encyclopedias, Old Testament biblical theologies, and commentaries.
8. 1 Sam. 2:29, 32; Ps. 26:8; Deut. 26:15; 2 Chron. 30:27.
9. 1 Sam. 1:9; 3:3; Ps. 5:7; 11:4; Is. 6:1.
10. 1 Kings 8:13; 2 Chron. 6:2; Is. 63:15.
11. Is. 8:14, 15; 28:16; Ps. 118:22.
12. *The International Standard Bible Encyclopaedia*, Vol. IV, "Sacrifice in the Old Testament," p. 2638.
13. *Ibid.*, p. 2638.
14. Lev. 1:2, 3; 2:1; 3:1; Num. 7:12-17; Mk. 7:11.
15. Ex. 28:38. The noun occurs alone in Lev. 23:38; Num. 18:6, 29; Ezek. 20:26, 31.
16. Lev. 3:11, 16; 21:6, 8, 17, 21, 22; 22:25; Num. 28:2; Ezek. 44:7; Mal. 1:7, 12; 1 Cor. 10:21; Rev. 3:20.
17. Lev. 4:5-7, 16-19, 25, 29, 30, 34; 5:9.
18. See the strategic uses of *kaphar* in Leviticus, especially 4:20, 26, 31, 35; 5:6, 10, 13, 18; 16: 6, 11, 16, 18, 24, 32; 17:11, etc.
19. Ex. 30:10; Num. 23:26-32; 29:7-11; Lev. 16.
20. Ex. 19:10-14; Lev. 6:27; 11:25, 28, 40; 13:6, 34, 54, 55, 58; 14:8, 9, 47; 15:5, 8, 10, 11, 13, 21, 22, 27; 16:26, 28; 17:15, 16; Num. 8:7, 21; 19:7, 8, 10, 19, 21, 22; 31:21-24.
21. Ps. 19:9; 24:3, 4; 51:2, 7, 10; Is. 6:5; Jer. 2:22; 4:14; 13:27; Mic. 2:10; Hab. 1:13; Mt. 15:3-20; Mk. 7:6-23; Acts 21:20-26; Rom. 14:14-23.
22. See Lev. 8:10, 11; 15:31; Num. 1:50-53; 3:7, 8, 21-40; 4:16, 24-33; 7:1-11; 9:15-23; 10:11-21; 16:1-28; Deut. 12:5-14.
23. 1 Sam. 1:3, 9, 19, 24; 2:11, 12; 3:3.
24. 1 Sam. 21:1-6.
25. 1 Kings 3:4; 2 Chron. 1:3, 13.
26. *The Epistle to the Hebrews* (London: Macmillan and Co., 1892), p. 233.
27. *From the Stone Age to Christianity* (Baltimore: The Johns Hopkins Press, 1957), p. 266.
28. *The Bible and Archaeology* (Grand Rapids: Wm. B. Eerdmans Publishing Co., 1962), p. 72.

CHAPTER VII
MOSES' FINAL EXPOSITION
OF THE LAW

1. Introduction

The Book of Deuteronomy stands as a fitting climax to the Mosaic era of revelation. Given at the close of the wilderness wanderings, this "second law" constituted Moses' final exposition of God's revealing work. At once it is a monumental presentation of (1) the theology of the inheritance of Canaan, (2) the uniqueness of Israel's God, (3) God's direction of history, (4) the distinctiveness of Israel as God's peculiar possession, (5) the nature of Israel's worship, (6) obedience to God as the special characteristic of the life of the people of God, and (7) the eschatological aspect of revelation.

The bearing of literary criticism on the interpretation of this book is very obvious. Most critical scholars regard the Book of Deuteronomy as the product of the reforms of Josiah, a book written with the view of leading Israel back to the worship of the Lord. Some scholars maintain that this book is a seventh-century compromise between the priests and the prophets. Neither of these views has any evidence for its support. Both views are products of literary criticism. While literary criticism is a legitimate mode of inquiry, the critic needs to exercise great vigilance so that he does not allow subjective considerations to form the basis for the conclusions reached.

For instance, in the narratives concerning the book of the law (2 Kings 22:8 — 23:3; 2 Chron. 34:14-33) the narrator does not give the name of the book which Hilkiah found. From the nature of the reforms instituted by Josiah it is conceivable that this was the Book of Deuteronomy. Further, the narrator represents the book as having been found in the house of the Lord. Josiah recognized it as the book of the covenant. There is absolutely no hint of anyone having secretly written the book, of having hidden it in the temple with the view of its passing for a book of Moses, and of its having the design of being used by the king to bring Israel back to the covenant worship of the Lord. The nature of the narratives in 2 Kings and 2 Chronicles simply refutes the idea that this book was a forgery. It is very easy to believe that the book of the law could have been lost during the reign of the wicked king, Manasseh. It is entirely natural that the godly high priest, Hilkiah, who ministered during the reign of King Josiah, should find a lost copy of the law in the temple and deliver it to the godly king.

I am venturing a positive approach to the origin of this book. In the first place, there is complete absence of any external evidence for the origin of the book, either as to date or author. Some scholars believe that in the later books of the Old Testament more or less clear references were made to the Book of Deuteronomy.[1] In the second place, the only evidence of its origin is internal. This evidence must be accepted until external evidence is presented to disprove the internal evidence. Throughout the book it is clear that a narrator is presenting an account made up almost entirely of direct quotations from Moses' words and also from what the Lord said to Moses. Samples of the narrator's words are 1:1-5; 4:4; 15:5; 32:44-46; 34:1-12. In a number of instances a brief introduction on the part of the narrator stands apart from the quoted language of Moses or of the Lord to Moses. In the third place, there is a total absence of any historical data beyond the death of Moses. There is absolutely no hint of its being produced later than the time of Moses.

For these reasons I accept the Book of Deuteronomy as giving an authentic record of Moses' discourses, together with the words of the Lord to Moses. There is absolutely no evidence of the book's being written to meet a crisis such as occurred in the days of Josiah. There are no grounds for a form criticism approach to the writing of this book. No evidence exists for the backward projection of any priestly or prophetic viewpoint from the days of Josiah. The book's declared purpose (Deut. 10:12-22) was to lead Israel on the eve of their entrance into Canaan to a life of implicit obedience to their Lord. The narrator definitely dated the words of Moses and gave the geographical location of the people of Israel. Moses and the Lord were speaking in anticipation of Israel's entrance into the land of Canaan and were conditioning them for the problems which they would encounter in the settlement of this new land. There is plainly a forty-year interval between the Mt. Sinai experiences and the giving of these closing messages of Moses. Whatever period of time elapsed between the death of Moses and the writing of this book is of little consequence so long as we recognize its historical authenticity and accuracy. Whether or not there were any redactions made after the first edition is of little consequence so long as we accept the words of Moses and of the Lord through Moses as being genuine. I accept the claim made in 31:24-26 to the effect that Moses wrote the words of this law in a book to the very end and that he gave commandment to place the book of the law by the side of the ark of the covenant of the Lord. This recorded claim of Moses obviously refers to all of his quoted messages throughout the entire book of Deuteronomy.

2. God's Direction of the Course of Israel's History

Perhaps the leading impact that a reader of the book receives is that of God's directing the affairs of the people of Israel throughout their history. This was not merely an everyday guidance of the people, but it had eschatological bearings. In the large, God's direction of Israel had in view the ultimate purposes of this nation to be worked out in due time.

a. The Conquest Understood in the Light of God's Promises to Abraham

As the Lord was preparing Israel for their conquest of Canaan, He repeatedly referred to the promises made to Abraham.[2] Repeatedly, throughout the Book of Genesis we have observed God's prophetic words as to what He would accomplish in the affairs of men. The most conspicuous of these predictions were the promises given to Abraham. This eschatological note came repeatedly into view in the intervening history of the chosen people. On this account it was entirely natural that the Lord should remind Israel of the imminent fulfillment of these promises as they had to do with their gaining possession of the land of Canaan, especially since they were established by covenant agreement. Moses sought to build up Israel's trust in these promises by reminding them of their deliverance from the land of Egypt by His mighty power. Moses assured the people with the words, "Know therefore that the Lord your God is God, the faithful God who keeps covenant and steadfast love with those who love him and keep his commandments, to a thousand generations" (Deut. 7:9). Moses would have Israel realize that their gaining possession of the land of Canaan would require the same measure of faith as the fathers showed in their being delivered from Egypt. He even referred to the extent of the land that would be theirs according to the promise given to Abraham (Deut. 11:24; Gen. 15:18-21). In order to involve the people of Israel more directly in these covenant promises Moses expressed the purpose in the words, "That he may establish you this day as his people, and that he may be your God, as he promised you, and as he swore to your fathers, to Abraham, to Isaac, and to Jacob" (Deut. 29:13).

b. Theology of the Inheritance of Canaan

On the eve of Israel's entrance to the land of Canaan the Lord imposed several restrictions and limitations which suggest that some significant reasons lay in God's direction of the conquest.[3] The land given to Israel was a well-defined area. Certain sections were denied to them. We soon observe that this apportioning of land to Israel was not arbitrary. God had given Mt. Seir to Esau and Ar to the sons of Lot. God remained faithful to this apportioning of the land. Since Sihon, king of Heshbon, and Og, king of Bashan, had not allowed Israel to pass through their land but had attacked them, God gave these peoples and their land to Israel. He would do likewise with the seven nations of Canaan.

The Lord began to disclose the reasons for Israel's gaining the land of Canaan for their possession. He said, "You are a people holy to the Lord your God; the Lord your God has chosen you to be a people for his own possession, out of all the peoples that are on the face of the earth" (Deut. 7:6). These words built directly on what God had told Israel forty years earlier when He was about to make a covenant with them at Mt. Sinai (Ex. 19:5, 6). We may gather that the Lord was calling Israel to a special mission in the world, namely, to the service of being a kingdom of priests and a holy nation. God was directing the affairs of Israel to the accomplishment of this eschatological mission. The Lord made it clear, nevertheless, that the giving of the land of Canaan to Israel was not a result of their goodness. He said specifically, "Do not say in your heart, after the Lord your God has thrust them out before you, 'It is because of my righteousness that the Lord has brought me in to possess this land'; whereas it is because of the wickedness of these nations that the Lord is driving them out before you. Not because of your righteousness or the uprightness of your heart are you going in to possess their land; but because of the wickedness of these nations the Lord your God is driving them out from before you, that he may confirm the word which the Lord swore to your fathers, to Abraham, to Isaac, and to Jacob" (Deut. 9:4, 5). The Lord added a severe note of warning by calling them a stubborn people, and by reminding them of their corruption when Moses was in the mountain to receive the tables of the covenant. Also the Lord reminded them of other instances when they had provoked Him to wrath. They had been rebellious against Him from the first.

Why then did the Lord use such a people to be His own possession? The first reason had to do with the magnifying of His grace, mercy, and love through Israel's mission to the world to the end that all the nations of the world would be blessed through them. Having experienced the immeasurable outpouring of the grace of God, they were in a position to herald a message of His saving grace to the world. The second reason was that Israel's gaining possession of Canaan gave them the most strategic geographical location for worldwide evangelism. Jerusalem was the point from which evangelists could most easily reach

every part of the then known world. The third reason was that the
land of Canaan lay at the center of surrounding nations which would be
the most susceptible to the message which Israel would give to the world.
This point becomes more evident when we note the success of such
servants of the Lord to other peoples as Solomon, Jonah, Daniel,
Philip, Peter, and Paul. The fourth reason may be that the geographical
location of Israel aided the development of a people of great strength.
In what other land appeared as many prophets, priests, and kings of
the stature of those in Israel?

c. Ethical Aspects of the Conquest

Throughout the Book of Deuteronomy we read of God's commands
to kill men, women, and children in their conquest of Canaan.[4] In the
light of the full revelation in later Scriptures, these commands present
some difficult ethical problems. We dare not evade these questions. If the
Bible is truly the revealed Word of God, we need to find a consistent
answer to them. First, the destruction of the Canaanites came expressly as a judgment for their sins. All through history God has
brought judgment upon wicked nations. Second, the unfolding of divine
revelation lays hold of the real problem involved. The people of Israel
were in their earliest stages of spiritual development. God in His
wisdom brought to them divine truth as they were in position to
receive and understand it. It was a long way from their understanding
of love of neighbors and the Christian comprehension of this teaching.
God used Israel as His agents for this destruction because they had
not advanced sufficiently to grasp the meaning of Jesus' words, "Love
your enemies," or of Paul's exhortation, "Beloved, never avenge
yourselves, but leave it to the wrath of God; for it is written, 'Vengeance
is mine, I will repay, says the Lord' " (Mt. 5:44; Rom. 12:19). Israel
needed to advance in spiritual understanding from sharing in the
execution of vengeance to leaving it to the wrath of God. Because of
human carnality, men are disqualified to share in the execution of
judgment upon their fellowmen. God alone is able to execute vengeance without committing sin. This is impossible to us as sinful
human beings.

3. The God of Israel

The Book of Deuteronomy advanced far beyond the other books of
the Pentateuch in its unfolding of God's nature and of His workings in
the world. Evidence of this has just been presented as God's direction
of Israel's history came into view. By reason of this involvement of

God in the affairs of men, we anticipate the unfolding of His person and work.

a. The Lord Revealed as the Only True God

As Moses looked backward to God's leading through the wilderness, he said, "O Lord God, thou hast only begun to show thy servant thy greatness and thy mighty hand; for what god is there in heaven or on earth who can do such works and mighty acts as thine" (Deut. 3: 24)? This omnipotent God manifested Himself in many significant ways. Looking at Deuteronomy 4:15-40 we have a sample of this self-revelation of God. Moses drew attention to the fact that Israel saw no form of God when He spoke to them at Mt. Horeb out of the midst of the fire. This served as a warning against their making graven images of God. Their God was a spiritual being and consequently He possessed no form. Nevertheless the Lord had brought them forth out of the iron furnace, out of Egypt, and He was about to give them an inheritance in the land of Canaan. It was this God who had made a covenant with His people at Mt. Sinai; hence to make a graven image of God would bring upon them His wrath. The Lord their God was a devouring fire, a jealous God. Through the mighty works of their God, Israel had abundant evidence that "there is no other beside him."

Moses looked down through history and predicted Israel's apostasy and the judgment of their being scattered by God among other nations. He assured them that if they would then seek their God, search after Him with all their heart and soul and return to Him in obedience, He would be merciful to them. Their God was supremely the God of love. It was He who had created man upon the earth. He was "God in heaven above and on the earth beneath; there is no other." This is a clear declaration of monotheism. It stands in the Book of Deuteronomy, not as a newly discovered truth, but rather as the reaffirmation of the belief of the people of God dating back to the Creation. The polytheism and idolatries of the Canaanites represented departure from this true faith.

b. The Lord, the God Who Speaks to His People

This central thought stands as another characteristic of true deity as found in the God of Israel (chap. 5). The Lord had spoken to Israel face to face at the mountain out of the midst of the fire. For the benefit of this new generation Moses repeated these Ten Commandments and stressed the importance of obedience to them and to other statutes and ordinances by which God had amplified the commandments.

So important were God's spoken words that He commanded that they be written. The Ten Commandments as recorded in Exodus and

Deuteronomy, together with all the laws recorded in Exodus, Leviticus, and Numbers, stand as the result of this command. What makes the entire book of Deuteronomy so important is the fact that this book constitutes the written record of what God spoke through Moses.

Since one of the fundamental doctrines of the Christian faith had to do with the character of the written Word, it is essential that we understand correctly the nature and authority of this written Word. Among other things, we should note the human side of the written Word, the divine side, and also the special regard with which the people of God recognized this body of writings. Here is a sample of how the Lord would have Israel regard these written words: "And these words which I command you this day shall be upon your hearts; and you shall teach them diligently to your children, and shall talk of them when you sit in your house, and when you walk by the way, and when you lie down, and when you rise. And you shall bind them as a sign upon your hand, and they shall be as frontlets between your eyes. And you shall write them on the doorposts of your house and on your gates" (Deut. 6:6-9). A final note on the importance of the written Word becomes clear in their placing the book of the law by the side of the ark of the covenant in the tabernacle. This indicated that the written law was held with the same holy regard as the ark of the covenant.

c. The Faithful God Who Keeps Covenant and Steadfast Love

This point bears repetition in view of its taking us closest to the heart of God. By means of covenant relation the Lord taught Israel through His own faithfulness how they also should be faithful to Him. The word *chesed* (steadfast love, RSV) is most expressive. No English word does justice to its meaning. The ASV translated it, *loving kindness,* and the KJV, *mercy.* We should lay hold of the culmulative meaning of these three translations.

4. Deuteronomy, a Gospel of God's Redeeming Love

In the most appropriate manner conceivable we think of the glad tidings of salvation through Jesus Christ as the gospel. It is consistent, though, to use this meaningful word with reference to other glad tidings found in the Bible. The Book of Deuteronomy is a case in point, for it certainly reveals a gospel of God's redeeming love. It will be very profitable to observe the common ground of "good news" in this book and that of the gospel of Jesus Christ.

a. Israel, the Elect of God

Moses stated this most explicitly in the words, "For you are a people holy to the Lord your God, and the Lord has chosen you to be a people for his own possession, out of all the peoples that are on the face of the earth."[5] We noted earlier that this statement reflects the thought of Exodus 19:5, 6. The words "holy," "chosen," and "his own possession" carry great meaning. The Lord had set Israel apart unto Himself. Israel had separated and consecrated themselves to their Lord. From among all the nations of the world the Lord had elected Israel to be His own special possession. Note the closeness of this relation to God. God had taken the initiative in choosing Israel for this high position. We need not concern ourselves at this point with reference to the relationship which all the other nations bore to God. This problem has its solution in God's provision for the salvation of all mankind through Jesus Christ. The tremendous meaning attached to the idea of Israel's election prepared the way for the still greater dimensions of election found in the gospel of Jesus Christ. Peter saw fit to apply these words to the position of Christians under the new covenant when he wrote, "You are a chosen race, a royal priesthood, a holy nation, God's own people" (1 Pet. 2:9). Paul devoted an entire section of his letter to the Romans (8:28 — 11:36) to explain this doctrine of election. Thus the New Testament confirmed the large place given to election in the Old Testament, particularly in Deuteronomy.

b. A Faith Requiring Obedience, Trust, and Patience

At this point two contexts come into the picture, chiefly because our Lord quoted from them in His replies to Satan in the temptation.[6] Deuteronomy 8:1-10 furnishes a profound insight into the meaning of Israel's experiences in the wilderness. The trials which Israel experienced were not merely happenings by chance or accident. Moses explained their meaning as follows: God designed all these experiences "that he might humble you, testing you to know what was in your heart, whether you would keep his commandments, or not. And he humbled you and let you hunger and fed you with manna, . . . that he might make you know that man does not live by bread alone, but that man lives by everything that proceeds out of the mouth of the Lord. . . . Know then in your heart that, as a man disciplines his son, the Lord your God disciplines you. So you shall keep the commandments of the Lord your God, by walking in his ways and by fearing him" (Deut. 8:2-6). Very clearly God was testing Israel during these forty years. Through tests He humbled His people to bring their inner motivation clearly into view. Were they following God out of a genuine spirit of obedience or was it solely to gain the land of Canaan? Through hunger and utter dependence upon Him for their food, the Lord was disciplining His people. God was showing them that faith in Him required obedience on their part.

This is the meaning that Jesus attached to His temptation when Satan would have Him turn stones into bread. In reply Jesus was saying that He as the God-man owed implicit obedience to God. True indeed Jesus had the power to turn stones into bread, but the exercise of this power would have been a violation of His human nature. Thus in the experiences of Israel and of Jesus, we come to see the real nature of obedience. The intimate personal exercise of faith in God involves uncompromising obedience to Him.

Moses gave a strong warning to Israel that they should not put the Lord to test as they did at Massah.[7] Israel's experience at Rephidim was indeed a trying one. Lately come out of Egypt they had not yet learned the privations that would accompany their experiences in the wilderness. God had supplied their needs through the giving of the manna. By means of this daily miracle Israel had seen the glory of God (Ex. 16:7, 10). Now that they had come to thirst for water, how should they have reacted to this need? Should they not have trusted God to give them water to drink, as they looked back over the experiences of their deliverance from the land of Egypt and recalled that God supplied their needs?

In such circumstances as these, what should have been the true response of faith in God? Was it conceivable that the Lord have some reasons for allowing them to be without water? Moses interpreted Israel's faultfinding and murmuring as putting the Lord to proof. The Lord had a very positive purpose in allowing His people to become thirsty. By this means He would teach them that faith in God involved absolute trust. Only by experiencing this need, could Israel actually learn that trust involves absolute commitment to God and complete dependence upon Him. God was showing Israel that genuine faith means trust in Him to the extent of absolute self-surrender.

This is what Jesus was saying to Satan in answer to the second temptation. Jesus had just experienced the most wonderful revelation of God to Him at the time of His baptism. The heavens were opened and Jesus had seen the Spirit of God descending like a dove and lighting on Him and then there had been the witness of the voice from heaven, "This is my beloved Son, with whom I am well pleased" (Mt. 3:16, 17). With such extraordinary experience within the recent past, did Jesus need repeated spectacular manifestations of God to assure Him that He was God's beloved Son? For Jesus to have thrown Himself down from the pinnacle of the temple with the anticipation of being borne up by the angels, would have demonstrated His lack of trust in God. The experience of Jesus was similar to that of Israel at Rephidim in that both experiences called for implicit trust in God. All through these wilderness experiences God was leading Israel to understand that the deliverance from Egypt, in which they saw the salvation of the Lord, was an act of God's redeeming love. Faith in such a God called for implicit trust.

A third strong exhortation of God to Israel came in the anticipation of their entrance into a land flowing with milk and honey. Since the Canaanites worshiped other gods, a severe temptation faced Israel. Looking at the abundance of natural food, Israel may have concluded that the gods of the Canaanites had given them these things. As for Israel, they had been suffering privation for forty years. Israel may have concluded that they should also worship the gods of the Canaanites in order to secure similar blessings from them as the Canaanites did. Herein was the basis for the third real test. Would Israel have the patience to wait until God's own good time to give them such great material blessings? Could Israel see that the Lord had permitted them to suffer such great privations in order to determine whether or not their faith would support them in patient endurance?

Again we turn to Jesus' temptation, where we hear the devil's offer to give all the kingdoms of the world and their glory to Jesus on condition that He fall down and worship him. Jesus found in Israel's experience the answer to Satan's temptation. Jesus had caught the meaning of His humiliation and was willing, patiently, to suffer death and to be exalted to kingship in God's own time. Had Jesus fallen down and worshiped Satan He would have showed the same lack of patience as Israel showed in their worship of the gods of the Canaanites. God's ways are oftentimes beyond human comprehension, but genuine faith in Him will enable His people to wait in patience until He fulfills His promises.

In summary, Moses was showing Israel that faith in God's saving work involved implicit obedience, absolute trust, and enduring patience.

c. Love to God Manifested in Obedience

The Lord taught Israel that He shows "steadfast love to thousands of those who love . . . [him] and keep . . . [his] commandments" (Deut. 5:10). In this expression love and obedience are brought close together. It implies that obedience grows out of love. The full scope of love becomes clear in the command, "You shall love the Lord your God with all your heart, and with all your soul, and with all your might" (Deut. 6:5). This shows that genuine love to God involves one's entire being. Love to God is not merely a psychological experience; it is supremely spiritual in character. In language specifically denoting obedience Moses added, "And now, Israel, what does the Lord your God require of you, but to fear the Lord your God, to walk in all his ways, to love him, to serve the Lord your God with all your heart and with all your soul, and to keep the commandments and statutes of the Lord, which I command you this day for your good" (Deut. 10:12)?

Let us observe again the wide gamut of meaning expressed in the verbs, *fear, walk, love, serve,* and *keep the commandments.* This shows again that love and obedience are inseparable. God warned the people of a possible test to their loving obedience when a prophet or dreamer of dreams would advise them to go after other gods and serve them. God made clear the meaning of this kind of experience in the words, "For the Lord your God is testing you, to know whether you love the Lord your God with all your heart and with all your soul. You shall walk after the Lord your God and fear him, and keep his commandments and obey his voice, and you shall serve him and cleave to him" (Deut. 13:3, 4).

d. Ethical Aspects of Obedience

Repeatedly the Lord warned the people of Israel against the abominable practices of the Canaanite nations. God's holy people would need to keep aloof from these sinful ways. Deuteronomy 18:9-14 makes clear the ethical aspect of obedience. Israel needed to learn that the reason for these prohibitions lay in the sinfulness of the things prohibited. These were not mere arbitrary commands given by God but they stood alongside a great positive spiritual command, namely, "You shall be blameless before the Lord your God" (Deut. 18:13). In this manner God led Israel to an understanding of the ethical principles involved in their religion. Their faith led to a manner of life different from that of the heathen nations.

e. Eschatological Aspect of Israel's Faith

Moses made yet another kind of approach to lead Israel to an unfailing faith in God. He disclosed to them their future if they would not be obedient. This was to serve in the most powerful manner conceivable as a restraint to apostasy. He predicted that if they acted corruptly and did what was evil, they would soon utterly perish from the land and be destroyed. God would scatter them among the other nations, and there they would serve gods of wood and stone. What an awful future lay before Israel! This prediction should have pierced their hearts and led them to ask the Lord for grace to be faithful to Him.

Moses did add the gracious note when he said, "From there you will seek the Lord your God, and you will find him, if you search after him with all your heart and with all your soul. When you are in tribulation, and all these things come upon you in the latter days, you will return to the Lord your God and obey his voice, for the Lord your God is a merciful God; he will not fail you or destroy you or forget the covenant with your fathers which he swore with them" (Deut. 4:29-31). Through these predictions of coming dispersion and return to the Lord, Israel learned that their God explained the meaning of present events in the light of the future. The reverse of this statement was also true. The Lord explained the future in the light of the present.

We meet here a new expression, "latter days," which was destined to become the leading eschatological term applied to a future age. Balaam had already used this expression in his discourse concerning Israel (Num. 24:14-20). Very significantly Balaam's words described One to come: "I see him, but not now; I behold him, but not nigh: a star shall come forth out of Jacob, and a scepter shall rise out of Israel." In the unfolding of the prophetic Scriptures this prediction was soon interpreted as referring to the Messiah. These two references soon occupied an important place in the continuous forward look of divine revelation. The era held in view was plainly in the far distant future. In the Deuteronomy passage (4:29-31) together with its parallel (chap. 28), we gain a view of Israel's future described in terms of two general periods: the first, that in which through their faithfulness to God they would experience great blessings; the second, that in which they would suffer the curses of God's judgment that would culminate in their captivity by other nations. This foreview also included their ultimate return to the Lord. The future repentance of Israel marked the era of the latter days.

Students of the prophetic Word have delved into these predictions and have discovered their literal fulfillment in such great events of history as the fall of Samaria, the overthrow of Jerusalem (587 B.C.) and the total destruction of Jerusalem at the hands of the Romans. Even the gruesome prediction of Israel's eating their own offspring (28:53) had a literal fulfillment in the siege of Jerusalem by the Romans in A.D. 70. In these judgments, as the Lord predicted, He brought on the people of Israel "extraordinary afflictions, afflictions severe and lasting, and sicknesses grievous and lasting" (Deut. 28:59). These awful future judgments stood as a solemn warning to the people of Israel. These coming judgments heightened the eschatological aspect of divine revelation. Clearly God designed that this prophetic side of revelation should lead Israel to an unwavering faith in their Lord.

f. Israel's Faith Strengthened by a Central Place of Worship

Repeatedly, [8]Moses told the people that the Lord would choose a place in the land of Canaan in which to make His name dwell. To this central place of worship Israel would bring burnt offerings and sacrifices, tithes and votive offerings in their worship. Here they would keep all of their feasts. Three times a year all the males would appear before the Lord. While no specific reasons were given for setting up a central place of worship, the following may lead us to the true answer. First, a central place of worship would help Israel to understand that the Lord their God was one Lord. It is conceivable that many places of worship would lead the people to the worship of many gods. Second, the central place of worship would provide a place for a common fellowship among all the people. Third, it would give to the people a unified body of teaching. It would prevent a disparity in instruction which could happen if the important religious teachings were given in different places. Fourth, the central place of worship could become prophetic of "the Deliverer" coming from Zion (Rom. 11:26) and of the outpouring of the Holy Spirit, both of which did occur in the same city.

To conclude this chapter, we may say that the Book of Deuteronomy is a fitting climax to the work of Moses. While most of the doctrines of the book appear elsewhere in the Pentateuch, they become most explicit in this book. It is here that the journeys of the children of Israel in the wilderness find their true meaning. The imminent conquest of Canaan stands out in its true perspective. The doctrinal truths which shine forth in the treatment of these great events reveal God as the one and only true God who manifested Himself to His people by showing His love, mercy, grace, and redemption. Such a God as He was the One who was directing Israel's history and would continue to do so. Such messages inspired faith and gave Israel the courage to launch forward in the conquest of Canaan.

For Additional Reading and Reference:

International Dictionary of the Bible (A-D), pp. 837 f.
International Standard Bible Encyclopaedia, Vol. II, p. 836.
Interpreter's Bible. Vol. II, pp. 326-29.
Interpretation, July 1952, pp. 325-39.
The International Critical Commentary, Deut. pp. XIX-XXXIV.
Pfeiffer, *Religion in the Old Testament*, pp. 161-74.
von Rad, *Old Testament Theology*, Vol. I, pp. 219-31.
————, *Studies in Deuteronomy* (Studies in Biblical Theology, No. 9).
Titcomb, *Revelation in Progress*, pp. 97-111.
Vischer, *The Witness of the Old Testament to Christ*, pp. 241-52.
Consult indexes of other biblical theologies for articles on Deuteronomy.

1. See *The International Standard Bible Encyclopaedia*, Vol. II, "Deuteronomy" by George L. Robinson. Under arabic 8 he gave the following references: Deut. 13:15 ff. (Josh. 6:17, 18; 10:40); Deut. 7:2; 20:16, 17 (Josh. 11:12, 15); Deut. 13:10; 17:5 (Josh. 7:25); Deut. 20:14 (Josh. 8:27); Deut. 21:23 (Josh. 8:29; 10:26, 27); Deut. 27:4-6 (Josh. 8:31); Deut. 27:3, 8 (Josh. 8:32); Deut. 11:29; 27:12, 13 (Josh. 8:33); Deut. 31:11, 12 (Josh. 8:34, 35); Deut. 12:5 (Josh. 22:29), etc.

2. Deut. 1:8; 4:31; 6:10, 23; 7:8, 12; 8:18; 11:8, 9; 29:13; 34:4.

3. Deut. 1:8, 21; 2:3, 8, 9, 19, 22, 37; 3:2, 3, 18-21; 4:3, 20; 7:1, 2, 16-26.

4. Deut. 2:36; 3:6; 7:2, 16, 22, 23; 9:4-6; 20:1-4; cf. Num. 21:1-3; 25:16-18.

5. Deut. 14:2. *See also* 4:37; 7:6, 7; 10:15.

6. Deut. 6:10-19; 8:1-20; cf. Mt. 4:1-11.

7. Ex. 17:7; Deut. 6:16-19; 9:22-24; 33:8.

8. Deut. 12:11-21; 14:23-25; 16:2-16; 26:1-15.

CHAPTER VIII
SIN AND SALVATION AS REVEALED IN THE PENTATEUCH

1. Introduction

Several doctrines in the Pentateuch still deserve study. The structural unity of this group of books calls for discussion of these doctrines at one point rather than division of the subject into smaller units based on the several periods of history already considered. This approach attempts to capture the Mosaic elements of the Pentateuch irrespective of the critical views pertaining to the time of the writing of these books. The gap of time lying between the historical events recorded in the Pentateuch and the writing of these books does not affect in any vital way their unity of thought.

In the preceding chapters we noted the life of the people of God. Incidentally the failures of God's people to achieve holy living came into view. In these contexts the subject of sin and the nature of man's spiritual needs became evident. The purpose of this chapter, then, is to make a study of sin, man's sinful nature, and the way of being saved from sin. Here we shall lay hold of the earliest teaching on the broad subject of salvation. The birth of the idea of God's saving work is paramount to the whole concept of biblical revelation.

2. Tragic Course of Sin

The reader of the Pentateuch might first be struck with the numerous incidents having to do with the sinful acts of men and women. The narration of these stories of sin reveals a profound purpose in these books. Among other things we notice the disobedience of Adam and Eve; Cain and Lamech, the murderers; the intermarriage of the godly and the wicked; the pride and arrogance of those who built the Tower of Babel; Jacob stealing his brother's birthright and blessing; the wickedness of Joseph's brothers; Egypt's enslaving of Israel; the deceptive work of Pharaoh's magicians; Israel's murmurings against God; the golden calf episode; Israel proving themselves to be a stiff-necked people; Israel's contentions with Moses and their complaints against God; and Balaam's subtle disobedience of God's commands. Among other lessons which these accounts of sin disclose we should note first that man's sin is against God. All disobedience to God, lack of faith and trust in Him, hardening of heart, and pride and revolt against God are most grievous sins. The God-related aspect of sin is most distinctive in these narratives of sin. These records also disclose the sinfulness which may center in human relations. Most tragic is that of murder and very close to it is human hatred. Then there are the sins of dishonesty, deception, theft, and failure to recognize the fair and equal rights of all mankind. Wrong acts against one's self also belong to the category of sin.

3. Vocabulary for Sin

A study of the vocabulary used for sin leads to the most accurate and comprehensive understanding of its nature. The author or authors of the Pentateuch used no less than fifteen different words for sin. This fact is of great significance in leading us to understand the earliest concepts of sin as disclosed in these records of biblical history extending from the Creation to the time of Moses. The definitions for these words are drawn from several Hebrew lexicons.[1] The order of these words depends somewhat on their first occurrences in these books. This may have some significance in showing when and how the several words for sin came into use. The English translation will show whether a given word is a verb, noun, or adjective. No effort will be made to distinguish among the grammatical forms in the several illustrations.

a. *Ra* (bad, evil, wicked). This word and its derivatives occur about ninety-five times in the Pentateuch. It is significant that the adjective form occurs in the Garden scene as the designation of one of the trees, the tree of the knowledge of good and evil (Gen. 2:9, 17; 3:5, 22). It stands as the opposite of *tob* used in its ethical sense of good and right. Thus at the very beginning of the Bible, the antagonism between right and wrong becomes clear, and the wrong is defined as that which is evil. Turning attention to the time of the Flood, we read, "The Lord saw that the wickedness of man was great in the earth, and that every imagination of the thoughts of his heart was only evil continually" (Gen. 6:5). The word occurs twice in this verdict on man's sinfulness. This underscores the emphatic ethical connotation of the word. When Potiphar's wife tempted Joseph to commit adultery, he called this sin wickedness (Gen. 39:9). The brothers of Joseph described their treatment of him as being evil and Joseph himself spoke of it as being evil (Gen. 50:15, 17, 20). Moses in a closing message to Israel gave specific instructions as to how they should purge evil from their midst (Deut. 17: 7, 12; 19:19; 21:21).

b. *Chata* (missed the mark or way, go wrong, sin). This word and its several derivatives, not including *chattath*, occur about one hundred and fifteen times in the Pentateuch. The noun from *chattath* is used to designate the most important bloody offering, known as the sin offering. The Lord used this word in warning Cain when He said, "If you do not do well, sin is couching at the door" (Gen. 4:7). The sin of Sodom and Gomorrah as indicated by the use of this word to describe their sin, was very grave (Gen. 18:20). Even Pharaoh knew this word and acknowledged that he had sinned against the Lord (Ex. 9:27; 10:16). With reference to Israel's worship of the golden calf, Moses used this word when he said, "[You] have sinned a great sin" (Ex. 32:30-34; Num. 32:23). The impact of this word increases when used in close connection with other words for sin. Observe its connection with *pesha* (trespass, offense) (Gen. 31:36; 50:17), *qesheh* (stiff-necked), and *avon* (iniquity) (Ex. 34:9); with *rasha* (wicked) (Num. 16:26); with *ra* (evil) (Deut. 9:18); with *qeshi* (stubbornness) and *resha* (wickedness) (Deut. 9:27). A word is known by the company it keeps.

c. *Chamas* (violence, wrongdoing, cruelty, ruthless outrage). This word looks at sin from the angle of its cruel and outrageous physical effects upon others. The author of Genesis used the word along with *shachath* (corrupt) to describe the condition of the earth before the Flood. "The earth was corrupt in God's sight, and the earth was filled with violence" (Gen. 6:11). Coming nearer to the idea of cruelty are the words spoken of Levi and Simeon: "Weapons of violence are their swords" (Gen. 49:5). A law in the Book of the Covenant reads, "You shall not join hands with a wicked man, to be a malicious witness" (Ex. 23:1). Here the author linked the word with *rasha* (wicked). More literally he is a witness of violence, thus showing more clearly the reason for its association with the word "wicked."

d. *Avon* (iniquity, perversity, guilt, punishment of iniquity). The use of this word by Cain presents a real problem of interpretation. The accepted translation is *punishment*, but the margins of KJV and of ASV have *iniquity*, and the Holy Bible from the Peshitta has *transgression* (Gen. 4:13). The words of the angels to Lot offer a similar problem (Gen. 19:15). There the KJV and the ASV translate the word "iniquity" with *punishment* in the margin; the RSV has *punishment* in the text, and the Holy Bible from the Peshitta has *sin*. I believe that *iniquity* expresses Cain's thought and that the angel's warning to Lot spoke of *punishment*. The idea of *guilt* or *iniquity* seems to be entirely clear in Judah's words to Joseph when he said, "God has found out the guilt of your servants" (Gen. 44:16). The same is true in the second commandment, where God spoke of visiting the iniquity of the fathers upon the children" (Ex. 20:5). This word comes in close relation with *pesha* (transgression) and *chattaah* (sin) in Exodus 34:7, where the mention of these classes of sins appears to cover the entire gamut of sin. There are a number of cases where the Scriptures speak of a man bearing his iniquities.[2] Very significant in this connection is the scapegoat, which bore all the iniquities of Israel out into the wilderness. This suggests an important aspect of the Day of Atonement in which the scapegoat symbolically removed Israel's iniquities out of their sight. The important lesson to gain here is that iniquities required atoning work for their removal. Observe that Aaron confessed over the scapegoat iniquities, transgressions, and sins, the same as those listed above.

e. *Rasha* (wicked, criminal). Used as a substantive it may refer to a person guilty of a crime or of hostility or of sin. This word and its several derivatives occur about one hundred and twenty times in the Pentateuch. In the study of this word one gets the impression that it is used in contrast with its opposite *tsaddiq* (righteous) (Gen. 18:23, 25; Deut. 25:1). Since *tsaddiq* carries the meaning *just* and *righteous* and is the word most descriptive of God's inner nature, the antonym *rasha* points to the entire absence or lack of righteousness. For this reason the use of this word to describe the godlessness of the nations of Canaan becomes very significant (Deut. 9:4, 5).

f. *Pesha* (transgression). While the usual meaning of this word is *transgression,* there are a few instances where it seems to carry the sense of *trespass, rebellion, offense,* or the general term *sin.* When Jacob upbraided Laban, he asked, "What is my offense? What is my sin" (Gen. 31:36)? In these two questions Jacob used the two words *pesha* and *chattath* (sin) which show close identity in their meaning. Note again the bringing together of the three words *iniquity, transgression,* and *sin* (Ex. 34:7) where the word *pesha* carries its usual meaning.

g. *Marah* (be contentious, refractory, rebellious). Though this word and its noun form occur only ten times, their use was very descriptive of Israel's attitude toward God. Typical cases were the rebellion against God's command at the waters of Meribah and the rebellion at Kadeshbarnea.[3] This distinctive meaning becomes still clearer when we observe its being coupled with *sarar* (stubborn, rebellious) and with *qasheh* (stiff-necked, stubborn, hard, severe) (Deut. 21:18, 20; 31:27).

h. *Asham* (offense, trespass, fault, guilt). The noun form of this word is used to designate the trespass offering found frequently in Leviticus and Numbers. Abimelech used this word when he reproved Isaac for his dishonesty. One of Abimelech's people could have brought guilt upon himself (Gen. 26:10). Joseph's brothers confessed that they were guilty concerning him (Gen. 42:21).

i. *Ma'al* (unfaithful, treacherous act). The KJV and the ASV usually translate this word *trespass* or *commit a trespass.* It would seem that the RSV comes nearer to the real meaning of the word by translating it *commit a breach of faith, act unfaithfully* or *break faith* (Lev. 6:2; 26:40; Deut. 32:51). This word certainly points up the sinfulness of a lack of integrity of character. In men's relations to one another and to God they need to prove themselves worthy of confidence and trust.

j. *Qashah* (be hard, severe, fierce). When Joseph's brothers came to Egypt for grain he spoke roughly to them (Gen. 42:7, 30). The Egyptians made the lives of the people of Israel bitter with hard service (Ex. 1:14). Frequently the adjective is construed so as to give the meaning *defect* (Ex. 32:9; 33:3, 5; 34:9; Deut. 9:6, 13). The adjective is brought into parallel relationship with *az* (strong, mighty, fierce). Jacob said, "Cursed be their anger, for it is fierce (*az*); and their wrath, for it is cruel *(qashah)*" (Gen. 49:7).

k. *Chalal* (pollute, defile, profane). The Lord sought to lead His people to a comprehension of His holy nature. This was the purpose of the elaborate ceremonial worship which centered in the tabernacle. In view of this purpose, places and things obtained sacred meaning. Thus the holy place and the holy of holies were the most sacred places. The altar and the various utensils used in the sacrifice were also sacred. Times and seasons, notably the Sabbath, were regarded holy. To disregard the detailed regulations concerning these holy places, things, and times, was to pollute, defile, or profane them. Such acts were not ethically wrong in themselves but they were sinful if done without regard to the restrictions imposed by God. The acts of defilement thus profaned the name of God. In reality he who committed sins of defilement did not reverence the holy name of God. Herein lay the sinfulness of *chalal.*[4] Marital infidelity and other irregularities also polluted and defiled the guilty parties.[5] It is noteworthy that this form of sin bore the name of pollution and defilement. Thus man's violation of the sacred institution of marriage was at heart a rejection of God's holiness. Sexual purity belongs to holy living. For one to disregard sexual purity is to bring upon himself defilement.

l. Less frequently used words. The noun *sarah* (turning aside, defection, apostasy, withdrawal) had a strong ethical connotation when used in reference to Israel's leaving the way in which the Lord had commanded them to walk (Deut. 13:5). The very frequently used verb form *sur*, usually carrying a nonmoral connotation, has several meaningful uses of ethical significance.[6] The sin lay in turning away from the commandments of God, in a word, in disobedience. The verb *shagah* (go astray, err, commit sin of ignorance) referred to sins committed unwittingly, or to failures to observe all of God's commands. This taught Israel that sinful acts were sin even though committed in ignorance. It showed the people that sin attaches to the very nature of wrong acts. The verb *shagag* (go astray, commit sin or error, sin ignorantly or inadvertently, was very similar in meaning to *shagah* and was used in the same contexts as this word.[7] In a time when laws were known only through oral communication, sins committed unwittingly were undoubtedly far more prevalent than in an age of written laws. The verb *marad* (be bold and audacious in acts of rebellion) looks at sin from the angle of the inner spirit of rebellion. This was all the more serious when man rebelled against God, the creature against his creator (Num. 14:9). The verb *ma'en* (refuse to obey, to disobey) came very forcibly into use in two questions asked by the Lord. "How long will you refuse to humble yourself before me?" "How long do you refuse to keep my commandments and my laws" (Ex. 10:3; 16:28)? The verb *ma'as* (reject, despise, refuse) looks at the sin of disobedience from the angle of rejecting and despising the Lord and His ordinances (Lev. 26:15, 43; Num. 11:20). This is again the sin of lowering God to a human level and by so doing despising one's Maker. The verb *rum* (be high, be exalted, be uplifted) is used a number of times to express the idea of self-exaltation and of haughtiness. Thus the person who did anything with a high hand (*rum*) reviled the Lord. A more serious form of this sin existed when the heart was lifted up and the people forgot the Lord their God (Num. 15:30; Deut. 8:14). The noun *avel* (injustice, unrighteousness) occurs in the command, "You shall do no injustice in judgment; you shall not be partial to the poor or defer to the great, but in righteousness shall you judge your neighbor" (Lev. 19:15). Thus in civil judgments, injustices stood opposed to righteous judgments with regard to weights and measurements. Those who violate in these matters were acting dishonestly (*avel*) and were an abomination to the Lord (Deut. 25:15).

By way of summary, this vocabulary for sin confirms the ideas gained from the narratives of sin in the books of Genesis, Exodus, and Numbers. The several words for sin are so woven into the narratives that we see sin in action. The extent of this vocabulary and the concepts it expresses reveal a deep understanding of the idea of sin. It is upon these concepts of wrongdoing that the prophets built their messages, and sought to lead apostate Israel back to the way of righteousness and holiness. We should note further that it was a purpose of divine revelation to disclose the nature of sin so as to give adequate reasons for the institution of the sacrificial system. Because of this disclosure, the several bloody offerings — the sin, trespass, burnt, and peace offerings — obtained real meaning. There would have been no need for bloody offerings if man had not sinned. This becomes evident in the Book of Leviticus and in the tabernacle worship.

Still further, this unfolding of sin gives the setting for the ethical teachings found in the Pentateuch. In the large, this disclosure of sin had its beginning in the Lord's solemn charge to Abraham in the words,

"Walk before me, and be blameless" (Gen. 17:1). God unfolded the nature
of this blameless life in the Book of the Covenant, in which the Ten
Commandments form the core of ethical teaching (Ex. 20 — 23). The
very center of ethics stands forth in the Lord's command, "You shall be
holy; for I the Lord your God am holy" (Lev. 19:2b). This ethical teaching reached its highest level in the Book of Deuteronomy when the
Lord said, "You shall love the Lord your God with all your heart, and
with all your soul, and with all your might" (Deut. 6:5). Equally significant are Moses' words by which he reminded Israel that they were a
people holy to the Lord, chosen by God for His own possession. He
stressed the principle of implicit obedience to God (Deut. 7:6, 11).

Finally, this study of sin shows more fully the reason for God's
drawing His people into covenant relationship. Since man was sinful, the
only way of salvation was through God's drawing him into the binding
relationship of a covenant. This covenant relationship involved the
most compelling commitment of both God and man. On the part of man
it involved love, faithfulness, and implicit obedience to God. Thus the
Ten Commandments, together with all the other ethical laws given by
the Lord, possessed the most binding authority. It was this that underlay Israel's commitment in the words, "All that the Lord has spoken we
will do, and we will be obedient" (Ex. 24:7). Moses' final service to
Israel as their leader was the institution of another covenant in Moab
(Deut. 29). In it the Lord spoke of the blessings that would come to
Israel if they obeyed, and of the curses that would come if they refused
to obey. Their conduct had a direct bearing on their covenant relationship. God said, "Be careful to do the words of this covenant, that you may
prosper in all that you do." Obedience was its keynote (Deut. 29:9, 29).

4. Birth of the Idea of Salvation

In the midst of Jacob's prophecy concerning his sons, he expressed
an extraordinary hope in the words, "I wait for thy salvation, O Lord"
(Gen. 49:18). He coined a word *(yeshuah)* which was destined to become
one of the most important words in all Holy Writ. In a nonreligious
sense this word had the meaning, *welfare, prosperity,* and *deliverance.*
The earliest uses of this word[8] look at salvation as being wrought by
God. In Israel's most serious crisis, Moses said, "See the salvation of
the Lord" (Ex. 14:13). After crossing the Red Sea he sang sublimely,
"The Lord is my strength and my song, and he has become my salvation" (Ex. 15:2). At the close of his life Moses gave testimony to the people of God's great salvation to them when he said, "Who is like you, a
people saved by the Lord" (Deut. 33:29). This aspect of salvation became
dominant in the history of Israel.

The Exodus account does not tell what the people of Israel associated with this salvation. Since it was the salvation by the Lord, they may have thought of it in relation to some of their experiences. First, this deliverance from Egypt immediately followed the Passover sacrifice. This may have led the people to see some relationship between the two. Through a bloody sacrifice the firstborn sons of Israel were saved. In the crossing of the Red Sea all Israel were saved. Again, the people may have associated their salvation with the efficacy of the Passover sacrifice. Second, through this deliverance the Israelites were saved from slavery and separated from the idolatries of Egypt. This may have led Israel to see that their slavery was more than merely political or social. It centered in a religious bondage. It required God's divine power to save them from this kind of bondage.

Third, the people came to realize that their being saved from Egypt was the initiatory event and prerequisite for experiencing covenant relationship and fellowship. Through this covenant Israel became God's special possession, "a kingdom of priests and a holy nation" (Ex. 19:4, 5). In a word, the salvation of the Lord led to Israel's becoming God's covenant people. Fourth, the system of worship instituted at Mt. Sinai and centering in the tabernacle was possible alone for people being saved. The sacrifices provided for expiation of sin, consecration to God, and for fellowship with Him. The tabernacle worship reached its climax in the high priest's entrance into the holy of holies, into the very presence of the Lord. It would seem that the people of Israel would soon associate this sublime experience of having God dwell in their midst with His great saving act at the Red Sea. Fifth, the Lord soon confronted Israel with His commandments dealing with their manner of life. Undoubtedly, the people of Israel saw how these great ethical standards condemned the Egyptians' way of life. To be saved from Egypt meant to be delivered from the sinful way of life. The salvation of the Lord led to holy living. As God said, "You shall be holy; for I the Lord your God am holy" (Lev. 19:2).

To what extent the people of Israel related these several ideas and experiences to their salvation we have no information. Again, by inquiring what light God's later revelation shed on the matter, we may observe that the Psalms, the prophetical books, and the New Testament unfolded very clearly their profound interrelation. The good tidings of salvation predicted in Isaiah 52 — 55 showed the heights reached in the Old Testament. The words of the angel to Mary, referred to the Old Testament concept of salvation: "You shall call his name Jesus, for he will save his people from their sins" (Mt. 1:21). Concerning the gospel Paul wrote. "It is the power of God for salvation" (Rom. 1:16).

5. Repentance and Confession of Sin

The verb *shub* (turn back, return), occurring over a thousand times in the Old Testament, has about four distinctive uses in a religious sense. In a setting where Moses was both warning the people of Israel against apostasy and in fact predicting it, he went further and said, "From there you will seek the Lord your God, and you will find him, if you search after him with all your heart and with all your soul. When you are in tribulation, and all these things come upon you in the latter days, you will return to the Lord your God and obey his voice" (Deut. 4:29, 30). Moses pictured Israel's return to God in language very clearly asserting the inner change of turning away from sin and of returning to God. Their search for God with all their heart and soul indicated the inner character of the experience and one which would be followed by their obedience to Him. Later in the book Moses used almost identical language to describe Israel's return to God after a future apostasy (Deut. 30:2, 8, 10). This idea of turning to God is almost identical in meaning with the idea of repentance expressed in two Greek verbs, *metanoeo* (to change one's mind or purpose, hence, to repent) and *epistrepho* (to turn about, to return to God). The second verb is used very frequently in the Septuagint to translate the Hebrew verb *shub*. It is very important then for us to observe that this spiritual experience of repentance found such clear expression as early as the time of Moses.

Closely related to the idea of returning to God is that of confession of sin. The Lord told the people of Israel that when anyone committed sins, which in other words was a breaking of faith with the Lord, "he shall confess his sin which he has committed; and he shall make full restitution for his wrong" (Num. 5:5-7). The confession of sin served the purpose of showing the genuineness of the wrongdoer's return to God.

6. Awakening of a Faith Relationship with God

Yet another aspect of man's involvement in his relationship to God was that of belief, expressed by the Hebrew word *aman*. This word rose to a position of highest importance in view of God's making promises to His people which required His supernatural working in history to effect their accomplishment. The first example of this kind occurred when the Lord made His threefold promise to Abraham. We read, "He believed the Lord; and he reckoned it to him as righteousness" (Gen. 15:6). This illustrated most vividly the personal aspect of trust in God. Centuries later when Moses faced the problem of having Israel believe that the Lord had appeared to him, the Lord gave him a sign, that of turning Aaron's rod into a serpent. This miracle was designed to lead Israel to believe that the Lord had appeared to Moses. Along with this sign was another, that of Moses' hand becoming leprous and of its being healed (Ex. 4:2-8). These and other signs (Num. 14:11; 20:12; Deut. 1:32; 9:23) showed how God would build up firmness of faith on the part of Israel. Belief in God involved a trust in His supernatural power such as God alone can exercise.

To summarize the entire chapter I would point up the interrelation of the several topics treated — sin, salvation, repentance, confession of sin, and finally faith. It may be said, first, that the Lord's bringing conviction of sin to His people had the potentiality of leading them to see the need of being saved from sin. The consciousness of this need could lead to repentance and confession of sin. God's part in the entire work of salvation led Israel to believe that He would fulfill His promises. Latent in the promises given to Abraham was the life that God would bestow upon His people. Tracing out these doctrines pertaining to personal salvation supplements the study of worship centering in the tabernacle. The New Testament makes entirely plain the interrelation of these topics. In the final analysis, the chief justification for bringing them together, so far as the Pentateuch is concerned, lies in the New Testament presentation of these truths.

For Additional Reading and Reference:

Baab, *Theology of the Old Testament*, pp. 84-155.
Jacob, *Theology of the Old Testament*, pp. 281-98.
Oehler, *Theology of the Old Testament*, pp. 158-166.
Schultz, *Old Testament Theology*, pp. 281-313.
Baker's Dictionary of Theology, "Sin," pp. 486 f.
Hastings, *Dictionary of the Bible*, "Sin." pp. 916 f.
Interpreter's Dictionary of the Bible, R-Z, "Sin," pp. 361-63.
Richardson, *Theological Word Book of the Bible*, "Sin," pp. 226-28.

---

1. *A Hebrew and English Lexicon of the Old Testament*, edited by Francis Brown, S. R. Driver, and Charles A. Briggs (Oxford: At the Clarendon Press, 1962). *Lexicon In Veteris Testamentis Libros* by Koehler and Baumgartner, Vols. I, II (Grand Rapids: Eerdmans, 1951).
   2. Lev. 5:17; 7:18; 10:17; 16:22.
   3. Num. 20:24; 27:14; Deut. 1:26, 43; 9:23; 31:27.
   4. Ex. 20:25; 31:14; Lev. 19:8, 12; 20:3; 21:6, 12, 23; 22:2, etc.
   5. Gen. 49:4; Lev. 18:23; 19:29; 21:14, 15, etc.
   6. Ex. 32:8; Deut. 9:12, 16; 11:16, 28; 17:20; 31:29.
   7. Lev. 4:2, 13, 22, 27; 5:15, 18; 22:14; Num. 15:22, 24, 25-29; 35:11, 15.
   8. Gen. 49:18; Ex. 14:13, 30; 15:2; Deut. 32:15; 33:29.

The next major portion of the Old Testament carries the technical title, The Prophets. The first part of this division, often called The Historical Books, is more properly titled The Former Prophets. The books of the writing prophets, excluding Daniel, are called The Latter Prophets. Since the historical books bear the name "The Former Prophets," it is natural to include their theological content in this major part of Old Testament theology. We have very little grounds for knowing why the usual label for these books is The Former Prophets. Most scholars believe that they received this name because they were written by prophets and by so much represent a prophetic viewpoint. In fact, as indicated above, the name "Former Prophets" is more fitting and consistent than the name "Historical Books." While it is true that the books, Joshua, Judges, 1 and 2 Samuel, and 1 and 2 Kings, contain much historical material, closer study will show that the purpose of these books was prophetic rather than historical. For the purposes of this work I shall consider 1 and 2 Chronicles along with The Former Prophets, and the Book of Daniel along with The Latter Prophets.

CHAPTER I
THE RISE OF PROPHETISM

From the earliest Old Testament times, certain men of God possessed the gift of prophecy or bore the name "prophet." The meaning of this fact should be held in view as we study the rise of prophetism. To anticipate some of the conclusions we may reach, I am suggesting the following. First, the possession of the prophetic gift, or of people bearing the name of prophet, makes us aware that almost from the beginning of human history, God was revealing Himself to mankind. Second, these divine revelations through the prophets gave a distinctive character to biblical history. They draw a sharp line of demarcation between biblical history and secular history. Third, this fact has a definite bearing on the origin and distinctive character of the Scriptures.

1. Prophetism Before the Era of Moses

The predictive elements found in the word of the Lord to Adam and Eve after they had sinned show that God knows the future as well as the present. It leads us to anticipate that He will continue to make Himself known to man. To Enoch was ascribed the first prophetic message, preserved for us by Jude (vv. 14, 15). The content of Enoch's words strikes us with unusual force. This becomes clear when we observe that to Jude this first prophetic message centered in the Lord Jesus Christ. We should note also that this prediction looked forward to what, in the light of completed revelation, we call end-time events or the consummation.

In Noah we have "a herald of righteousness" (2 Pet. 2:5). The Greek word *keruka* (herald) suggests that Noah was God's spokesman to the world. That is, the Lord was using Noah to proclaim His message to mankind. The record does not call Noah a prophet but he possessed the gift of prophecy. Noah's blessing of his sons contained predictive elements. Having already considered the content of these predictions, it suffices to state here that the blessing of Shem pointed to a special relationship between the Lord and Shem's descendants. As later history showed, the Lord separated the Hebrews and later the descendants of Jacob as recipients of His revelation and bearers of His redemptive purposes.

In speaking to Abimelech, God called Abraham a prophet, *nabi*. As we shall note later, *nabi* carried the idea of one being a spokesman for another. Abraham, a friend of God, had such an intimate fellowship with God that God spoke through him. In several contexts (Gen. 15:1-8; 18:17-32; Heb. 11:8-18) we gain some idea as to the ways in which Abraham was a prophet. The Lord had direct personal intercourse with Abraham. He revealed Himself and His purposes to him. Abraham believed the promises of God, which means that he put full trust in what the Lord would accomplish through his descendants. God had chosen Abraham, knowing that he would have a great influence upon his descendants, "to keep the way of the Lord by doing righteousness and justice" (Gen. 18:19). Outstanding in Abraham's prayer ministry was his intercession for the righteous people in Sodom. These and other aspects of Abraham's life give the picture of a prophet and his work.

Both Isaac and Jacob exercised prophetic gifts when they blessed their sons.[1] Likewise Joseph spoke to his brothers prophetically when he promised their exodus from Egypt and associated this event with God's promise to the patriarchs (Gen. 50:24; Heb. 11:22). These manifestations of the prophetic gift by Isaac, Jacob, and Joseph, given at the close of their lives, were unique. From the narratives which record these blessings, we may conclude that these prophetic words came through the revelation of God.

2. Manifestations of the Prophetic Gift from Moses to Samuel

Moses stands out as the prophet of prophets, second only to Jesus Christ. We gain a clear picture of Moses' prophetic office in the account of his call (Ex. 4:10-16). When he pleaded that he was slow of speech and of tongue, God replied, "I will be with your mouth and teach you what you shall speak." When Moses continued to refuse this responsibility, God chose Aaron to be Moses' spokesman. God said, "You shall speak to him and put the words in his mouth; and I will be with your mouth and with his mouth, and will teach you what you shall do. He shall speak for you to the people; and he shall be a mouth for you, and you shall be to him as God." This detailed conversation presents an accurate picture of how a prophet is the mouthpiece of God to the people. When the prophet spoke it was God who was speaking. The narrative does not suggest that the Lord would give Moses certain ideas which he would express in his own words to Aaron. The human element involved in ordinary conversation such as thought formation and verbal expression is entirely lacking. This problem will receive more consideration in the following chapter.

The service that Moses performed in the institution of the covenant at Mt. Sinai supplies valuable insights into his prophetic office (Ex. 19 — 24). We note that the Lord gave Moses a specific message to tell to the people of Israel. This had to do with the covenant which the Lord proposed to make with Israel. Moses was God's spokesman who mediated this covenant. In the act of instituting the covenant Moses performed both prophetic and priestly functions, according to which he served as mediator between God and man. On a number of occasions (Ex. 18:19; 32:11-13; Num. 12:11, etc.) Moses performed the work of a mediator and interceded with God in behalf of the people. This service was both prophetic and priestly.

The nature of the prophet's work was clarified when Moses predicted that God would raise up a prophet like unto himself (Deut. 18: 15-20; Acts 3:22, 23; 7:37). A prophet was a man chosen from his fellowmen. This placed him on the same level as the people whom he served. Concerning Moses, God said, "I will put my words in his mouth, and he shall speak to them all that I command him. And whoever will not give heed to my words which he shall speak in my name, I myself will require it of him. But the prophet who presumes to speak a word in my name which I have not commanded him to speak, or who speaks in the name of other gods, that same prophet shall die." This shows again that the words spoken by the prophet were the very words of God. The accompanying warning stated this truth in a negative way. A prophet might yield to the temptation of palming off his own words as the words of God and by so doing be worthy of death.

Stephen described Moses' work in the words, "He received living oracles (*logia zonta*) to give to us" (Acts 7:38). This is very apt language to describe the nature of a prophet's words. His words were not his own but were the living messages from God. We might say that the prophet quoted the Lord so that what the prophet spoke could very properly be enclosed in quotation marks and be footnoted as the words of God. The closing words of Deuteronomy gave some additional details of Moses' prophetic office. We read, "The Lord knew Moses face to face." He performed signs and wonders in the land of Egypt and showed mighty power in working great and terrible deeds in the sight of all Israel. This reflected an earlier incident when the Lord spoke concerning Moses, "With him I speak mouth to mouth, clearly, and not in dark speech; and he beholds the form of the Lord" (Num. 12:8).

Some less honored persons such as Miriam, Aaron, and the seventy elders, and Balaam deserve mention.[2] The possession of the prophetic gift by Balaam is of considerable importance and presents some problems centering in his being a soothsayer. It is sufficient to say that the Lord overpowered Balak by leading Balaam to speak true prophetic words. The Lord turned the intended curse into a blessing for the sake of Israel (Deut. 23:5).

While Joshua was not called a prophet, he exercised the prophetic gift. At the command of God, Moses invested Joshua with some of his authority. Moses laid hands upon Joshua and by this act Joshua was filled with the spirit of wisdom (Num. 27:18-20; Deut. 34:9). Joshua 23 and 24 give inspiring examples of his prophetic gift as a true spokesman of God. He spoke God's words and exhorted Israel through a covenant-agreement to serve the Lord and to obey His voice. Later Deborah, a prophetess, came on the scene and composed a wonderful song (Judg. 4:5). When the Midianites were troubling Israel, the Lord sent a prophet to His people who introduced his message with the words, "Thus says the Lord" (Judg. 6:7-10). Observe that he was a *prophet* (*nabi*), thus showing that God used only chosen men, prophets, through whom He would speak to the people. In the days of Eli "a man of God" came to the old priest introducing his message with the words, "Thus the Lord has said" (1 Sam. 2:27-36). Here we have a new title for one who spoke the word of the Lord. His message to Eli was genuinely prophetic in that it rebuked the old priest for his failure to discipline his sons for their evil living and predicted the punishment that God would bring on Eli's house. This title, "man of God," will receive further consideration in a later chapter. Here it stands as a practical equivalent of the word "prophet." The author of 1 Samuel gave no explanation for this title even though he noted that Samuel was established as a prophet of the Lord.

3. Prophetic Office from Samuel to Elisha

a. Samuel

The prophet Samuel marked the beginning of a new era in prophetism. This becomes evident when we follow the course of events in Israel's history from the period of the judges to that of the kingdom and observe the part that Samuel had in this change. The details relating to the birth of Samuel and to his call to the prophetic office support this conclusion. As a boy he received a prophetic message to give to the aged priest, Eli. The author of 1 Samuel confirmed this in the words, "And Samuel grew, and the Lord was with him and let none of his words fall to the ground. And all Israel from Dan to Beersheba knew that Samuel was established as a prophet of the Lord. And the Lord appeared again at Shiloh, for the Lord revealed himself to Samuel at Shiloh by the word of the Lord" (1 Sam. 3:19-21). From this sketch we should observe the nationwide knowledge of Samuel's mission and the descriptive language relating to his office as prophet.

Saul's first meeting with Samuel displayed the prophet in the exercise of his prophetic work. We should observe that among the people, Samuel was known as a *man of God*. Its occurrence here confirms the practical identification of the expressions "man of God," and "prophet" with each other (1 Sam. 9:6). The author added an important parenthetic note when he said, "Formerly in Israel, when a man went to inquire of God, he said, 'Come, let us go to the seer'; for he who is now called a prophet was formerly called a seer" (1 Sam. 9:9). From this we learn that the title "seer" (*roeh*) was an earlier name which had given way to the new title "prophet" (*nabi*). It had the meaning: *one who sees, perceives, looks at, observes, etc.* All three of these expressions "man of God," "seer," and "prophet" built up the concept of the prophetic office. We might observe that the terms "prophet" and "seer" were applied also to Gad (2 Sam. 24:11). The author of 1 Chronicles (29:29) called Samuel and Gad *seers* but applied the term "prophet" to Nathan. (For a fuller discussion of these titles see the next chapter.)

In Samuel's old age the elders of Israel came to him with the request that he appoint a king to govern them as the other nations had. Samuel was greatly distressed over this request but the Lord told him its real meaning. Israel had not rejected Samuel but they had rejected the Lord Himself from reigning over them. This shows that a distinction existed between the office of king and that of prophet. It is essential that this distinction become clear and that the relationship among the offices of *prophet, priest,* and *king* also be understood. The Lord authorized Samuel to make them a king. A bit later when Saul came to Samuel to make inquiry about his father's asses, Samuel secretly took the vial of oil and anointed him to be king over Israel. This belonged to Samuel's work as a prophet and not as a priest. We may interpret this distinction as meaning that Samuel, who was God's spokesman to Israel, was the proper official to set apart a king for his work. We should note also that Samuel's anointing Saul as king had the result of giving Saul another heart and that the "spirit of God came mightily upon him" (1 Sam. 10:10). Through this gift Saul also prophesied.

In this connection we should observe the existence of a band of prophets, with whom Saul then identified himself. From this point onward we become aware of a continuing company of prophets. They formed an association, wandering about from town to town and exercising the prophetic gift on various occasions. Many of the later prophets belonged to this band. Whether or not the prophetic company, with whom Elijah associated, was a continuation of the one established by Samuel, is not entirely clear. Our interest in these prophetic associations lies in the continuing prophetic witness throughout this era as over against the intermittent prophets living between the time of Moses and Samuel.

From this time onward Samuel became the guardian of the kingdom of Israel. He rebuked Saul for offering burnt and peace offerings, a responsibility which belonged to the priest. Because of this sin, Samuel told Saul that the Lord would choose another to be king in his place. Through Samuel the Lord commanded Saul to completely destroy the Amalekites, and when Saul failed to do so, Samuel rebuked him for not carrying out the Lord's command. With God's authorization Samuel anointed David to be king in place of Saul. Note that while the king ruled in God's place, the prophet was, nevertheless, still God's spokesman to His people. He continued to counsel, exhort, and rebuke both king and people. Thus in the setting up of the modified theocracy, God did not cease to witness to His people through the prophet.

b. Nathan, Gad, Ahijah, Shemaiah, and Others

Nathan followed the same pattern of relationship to the king as did Samuel. When King David counseled with Nathan about building a temple, the latter encouraged him to build one. The Lord intervened however and instructed Nathan to tell David that the building of a temple would belong to his son. Observe that the word of the Lord came to Nathan at night, and the form of revelation was a vision. On a later occasion the Lord sent Nathan to rebuke David for his sin with Bath-sheba.

The interrelationship of prophet, priest, and king comes into view again at the close of David's life. He called Zadok, the priest; Nathan, the prophet; and Benaiah, the Levite; and asked them to anoint Solomon to be king over Israel. While Zadok appears to be the one who actually anointed Solomon, Nathan was also involved in the ceremony (1 Kings 32:40). Note also that the Apostle Peter referred to David as a prophet and quoted three of his psalms which predicted the coming Messiah.[3] David made a prophetic claim himself in the words, "The Spirit of the Lord speaks by me, his word is upon my tongue. The God of Israel has spoken, the Rock of Israel has said to me" (2 Sam. 23:2, 3).

The author of 2 Samuel referred to Gad as a *prophet* and also as David's seer (2 Sam. 24:11). From this it appears that Gad served in a special way as David's counselor and spiritual adviser. Later we read that Hezekiah "stationed the Levites in the house of the Lord with cymbals, harps, and lyres, according to the commandment of David and of Gad the king's seer and of Nathan the prophet; for the commandment was from the Lord through his prophets" (2 Chron. 29:25). We should note, first, that this provision for the promotion of music in worship came from both king and prophets, giving the idea that there was a sharing of kingly and prophetic responsibility in this provision. Second, the seer stood in a more personal relation to the king than the prophet and yet the author apparently identified the two. Third, the prophet was God's spokesman in making this provision for the development of music in worship.

During the reign of Solomon God sent Ahijah to the king to advise him that because of his departure from God, the Lord would give ten tribes to Jeroboam. Ahijah introduced his message with the words, "For thus says the Lord, the God of Israel" (1 Kings 11:29-39). Shemaiah came on the scene in the reign of Rehoboam, giving him a command from the Lord not to fight against the new nation of Israel (1 Kings 12: 24). After Jeroboam had established places of worship at Bethel and Dan, a man of God came out of Judah to Bethel by the word of the Lord and condemned the worship he had set up. Why the writer chose the expression "man of God" and in the same context spoke of an old *prophet* in Bethel, thus making an apparent distinction between the two, is not clear. Certainly the man of God was carrying out the word of the Lord, and the old prophet was also speaking the word of the Lord, when he condemned the man of God for not carrying out fully the Lord's commands. Further, the man of God was not entirely faithful to the Lord's directions when he yielded to the temptation of the old prophet. The Lord, nevertheless, fulfilled the prediction of the man of God. All of these incidents serve to show how vitally the prophets were involved in giving counsel and warning to the kings. These mouthpieces of God served to guide the altered theocracy into the ways of God's rule. This became especially evident when kings such as Solomon and Jeroboam failed so badly in view of their ruling by divine right.

c. Elijah, Micaiah, Elisha, and the Unnamed Prophets

As conditions were becoming worse, especially in the Northern Kingdom, prophets became deeply involved in the several crises which arose. The most spectacular was the work of Elijah in confronting the evil king Ahab, and in bringing the conflict between the true and false worship to the crucial test at Mt. Carmel. In Elijah's dramatic encounter with Ahab in which he predicted that there would not be dew or rain except by his word, the distinctive responsibilities of prophet and king became clear. Since this was a spiritual crisis it was the prophet's responsibility to deal with it. The test on Mt. Carmel proved conclusively that the Lord was God. The Lord responded to the prayer of the prophet by sending fire to consume his offering. Thus Ahab and all the prophets of Baal knew that the Lord was God, and that Elijah's words were the words of the Lord. The story concludes with the coming of rain in answer to Elijah's prayer. When Ahab returned to Jezreel, Elijah paid due respect to him as king by running before him to the entrance of the city. In this act Elijah, the prophet, paid proper respect to the king who was ruling in the place of God. Elijah's final responsibility as prophet appears in his anointing Hazael to be king over Syria, Jehu to be king over Israel, and Elisha to be prophet in his place. Through the anointings of these kings by the prophet, the Lord made clear to them that they would be ruling by divine right. It remained for Elijah to give stern rebukes to Ahab and Ahaziah. Both had sinned grievously, the former in killing Naboth, and the latter in seeking help of Baalzebub when he had fallen through the lattice from his upper chamber. Elijah made it clear that there was a God in Israel, and that His prophet spoke the word of the Lord to the effect that Ahaziah would not recover from his illness (1 Kings 17 — 2 Kings 2).

It is natural to expect that because of the extraordinary gifts of the prophets some men would falsely claim to give the words of God.

Jehoshaphat faced this problem when he desired to know whether or not he should go to battle against Ramoth-gilead. Four hundred prophets, through their representative, Zedekiah, urged Jehoshaphat and his ally to go up and triumph. The two kings staged a spectacular scene as they sat on their thrones arrayed in their robes. Ahab accepted the words of Zedekiah but Jehoshaphat insisted that they inquire of the Lord through the prophet Micaiah. Zedekiah ridiculed Micaiah, and Ahab ordered the prophet to be put into prison until the king returned in peace. To this Micaiah replied, "If you return in peace, the Lord has not spoken by me" (1 Kings 22:5-28). The prediction of Micaiah refuted the advice of the false prophets and proved that the Lord had spoken by Micaiah. Other unnamed prophets (1 Kings 20:13, 22, 28, 35) appeared on the scene at different times, each giving a significant word from the Lord.

The prophetic labors of Elisha covered a wide range of activities, all of which were very important in setting forth the office and work of the prophet. Especially significant were his miracles of increasing food, healing Naaman the leper, striking men with blindness and later opening their eyes, and raising the son of the Shunammite woman. When Ben-hadad sent Hazael to inquire of Elisha about his possible recovery, Elisha spoke forthrightly to Hazael, exposing the treachery which he had planned against the king. Elisha also served in the anointing of Jehu to be king. The last recorded service of Elisha was the predictive message he gave to Joash, king of Israel, with regard to his war with Syria. He rebuked the king for not having faith to believe that he would be able to completely overcome the king of Syria.

The author of 2 Kings gave a fitting conclusion to this entire discussion concerning the rise of prophetism, when he wrote a summary of Israel's history after the capture of Samaria by Assyria. He noted that the fall of Samaria resulted from Israel's sin against the Lord. He described their apostasy in the light of their deliverance from Egypt by their God. They had sinned grievously against the Lord in their idol worship. Then he wrote, "Yet the Lord warned Israel and Judah by every prophet and every seer, saying, 'Turn from your evil ways and keep my commandments and my statutes, in accordance with all the law which I commanded your fathers, and which I sent to you by my servants the prophets.' But they would not listen, but were stubborn, as their fathers had been, who did not believe in the Lord their God. They despised his statutes and his covenant that he made with their fathers, and the warnings which he gave them" (2 Kings 17:7-18.)

For Additional Reading and Reference:

Davidson, *Old Testament Prophecy,* pp. 16-74.
Dictionary of the Bible, Hastings, Vol. IV, pp. 106-12.
Lindblom, *Prophecy in Ancient Israel,* pp. 47-104.
von Rad, *Old Testament Theology,* Vol. II, pp. 6-32.
Sampey, *Syllabus for Old Testament,* pp. 151-56, 260-76.
The Interpreter's Dictionary of the Bible, K-Q, pp. 905-10.
Vos, *Biblical Theology — Old and New Testament,* pp. 203-8.

1. Gen. 27:27-29, 39, 40; 28:3, 4; 49; Heb. 11:20, 21.
2. Ex. 15:20, 21; Num. 12:2, 6; Ex. 7:1; 4:14-16; Num. 11:24, 29, 22 — 24.
3. Acts 2:30, 31; Ps. 132:11; 16:10; 110:1.

CHAPTER II
PLACE OF PROPHETISM IN THE OLD TESTAMENT

1. Introduction

The survey of the rise of prophetism has shown how large a place it occupied in Israel's history. This would become still clearer if this survey included a preview of prophetism during the time of the writing prophets, when it formed an integral part of the Old Testament revelation. We now turn our attention to this later period as preparation for a study of the theology of the prophets.

2. Concept of Prophetism

The various titles or names applied to those who possessed the gift of prophecy lead directly to the true concept of prophetism. In most cases the titles speak for themselves. We gain additional help in understanding them by studying the contexts in which they were used. This gives us a pattern of approach to the concept of prophetism.

a. Man of God[1]

This title gives the most general idea of the prophet. It suggests his close relation to God. Since it was more intimate than that of other men, he was in position to say, "Thus the Lord has said." The widow of Zarephath came to think of Elijah as a man of God because of his miraculous power and because the word of the Lord in his mouth was truth. The Shunammite woman called Elisha a holy man of God. As such God had set apart Elisha for the special work as a prophet, and Elisha had consecrated himself to this task. It is possible that Peter reflected this idea of a prophet when he wrote, "No prophecy ever came by the impulse of man, but men moved by the Holy Spirit spoke from God" (2 Pet. 1:21).

b. Servant of the Lord[2]

This title first appeared with reference to Moses. It gained prophetic meaning when the Lord rebuked Miriam and Aaron with the words, "With him I speak mouth to mouth, clearly, and not in dark speech; and he beholds the form of the Lord. Why then were you not afraid to speak against my servant Moses" (Num. 12:8)? This description of the Lord's communication to Moses created the title "servant of the Lord" as a connotation of prophet. The writer of Deuteronomy 34 applied both titles to Moses. A number of times the authors made

double reference, using the expression, "his servants, the prophets."
This title gained great significance through its application to Moses. As
Israel's leader and founder of the theocracy, Moses as the servant of
the Lord was performing a public service with its accompanying authority. The author of Hebrews wrote, "Now Moses was faithful in all
God's house as a servant, to testify to the things that were to be
spoken later" (Heb. 3:5). It was very natural then that prophets
such as Ahijah, Jonah, Isaiah, and Zechariah should bear this title
"servant of the Lord." With all this background of meaning, the servant of the Lord passages of the Book of Isaiah most fittingly described
the coming Messiah. It led the people of God to attach the responsibilities
of the prophet to the coming servant of the Lord.

c. Messenger of the Lord[3]

In early Hebrew history a frequent mode of God's revelation was
through an angel of the Lord. The biblical records would give the impression that these angels of the Lord were actual angels coming to men
in human form. This may be the source of the title "messenger or
angel of the Lord" as applied to the prophets. Its late appearance in
human history would suggest that after so long a time, the people of
God discovered a unique likeness of function between their prophets
and the actual angels of the Lord. At any rate the prophets were messengers of the Lord giving God's messages to His people. In a special
way the use of this title may show that it had a close relation to the
distinctive authority exercised by the angels of the Lord; and as a result,
it came to be associated with the prophets.

d. Mediator (luts-teacher, interpreter)

The Lord said, "Your first father sinned, and your mediators transgressed against me" (Is. 43:27). Some Bible students hold that the word
"mediator" refers to Moses and the prophets. If this is the correct interpretation, this word gives a valuable insight into the work of a
prophet. Perhaps the word "interpreter" expresses most accurately the
sense of the Hebrew word. If this is correct, the Lord was referring to
those who interpreted to Israel the ways of God. As Davidson said,
"This name is exceedingly descriptive of the whole attitude of the
prophet: he interpreted God's doings to men; he realized the meaning
of Israelitish history, and expressed it to the people. No name is more
apt. The history reflected itself in the prophet's mind as a mirror, and
through him the nation read the meaning of God's procedure with it.
As this truth reflected itself in the prophet's mind, it awoke in himself
also the sense of his people's sin and imperfection. He is, so to speak,
their conscience."[4]

e. Seer (roeh)[5]; (chozeh)[6]

These two Hebrew words are almost indistinguishable in meaning. Their uses in the Old Testament suggest the ideas, *insight* or *discernment*. It intimates a seeing that goes beyond natural eyesight, a seeing that was spiritual in nature. The Lord was describing the apostate Israelites as those "who say to the seers, 'See not'; and to the prophets, 'Prophesy not to us what is right; speak to us smooth things, prophesy illusions, leave the way, turn aside from the path, let us hear no more of the Holy One of Israel' " (Is. 30:10, 11). According to this the people of Israel did not want their seers and prophets to see or tell them what was right. They wanted smooth speech and prophetic illusions. Equally elucidating are the words, "For the Lord has poured out upon you a spirit of deep sleep, and has closed your eyes, the prophets, and covered your heads, the seers" (Is. 29:10). Observe again that the titles "seer" and "prophet" are brought together practically as synonyms and that here both prophets and seers were lacking in spiritual discernment.

f. Watchman (tsaphah)[7]; (shamar)[8]

The former of these two words carried the idea of one who spies, one who is on the lookout, or one who watches. The second of these words had the idea of watchman, one who observes. Davidson said, "These are words that describe not so much the actual mode of reaching truth as the kind of effort put forth by the prophet to reach it. He looked out, he watched for God's revelation."[9] Habakkuk brought these two words together when he said, "I will take my stand to watch, and station myself on the tower, and look forth to see what he will say to me, and what I will answer concerning my complaint. And the Lord answered me: 'Write the vision; make it plain upon tablets, so he may run who reads it' " (Hab. 2:1, 2). The verb *shamar* occurs in the first line and the verb *tsaphah*, translated *look forth to see*, in the second. The answer came in vision form *(chazon)* and Habakkuk made this plain upon his tablets. Another significant illustration occurs in Ezekiel, "[The Lord said] 'Son of man, I have made you a watchman for the house of Israel; whenever you hear a word from my mouth, you shall give them warning from me' " (Ezek. 3:17).

g. Prophet (nabi)

This is the most frequently used word for prophet. Most scholars believe that its root meaning has the idea of one who announces. It may carry the connotation of an excited, impassioned speaker.[10] According to biblical usage the *nabi* "was a person qualified by God to be His spokesman to men."[11] The Lord told Israel that He would raise up a prophet like Moses and described his prophetic activity in the words, "I will put my words in his mouth, and he shall speak to them all that I command him" (Deut. 18:18). From this we may gather that the fullest concept of *nabi* is found in Christ. He, above all other prophets, gave the words of God. He was God's official spokesman to men. To a certain degree we may conclude that *nabi* carried the combined meaning of all the foregoing words. He was a holy man of God, a servant of the Lord, a messenger of the Lord, an interpreter of God, a seer of the things of God, and speaker of the things of God to men. The Septuagint translators used *prophetes* to translate *nabi* and its cognate forms. This word carries the idea of one who acts as an interpreter or forthteller of the divine will. We may observe also that *prophetes* was used to translate *roeh* four times, and *chozeh* four times, thus showing that the Septuagint translators brought these several Hebrew words close together in meaning.

3. Influence of the Prophetic Concept on Old Testament Canon

We cannot discover much about the reason for the order and arrangement of books in the Hebrew Old Testament. Our task is chiefly that of interpreting the facts of their order and arrangement without any historical data to guide us. The first division of the Hebrew Bible was the Pentateuch. This constituted the so-called Five Books of Moses. The Jews regarded these books as prophetic in nature because they regarded Moses as prophet second to none. The second main division had the title "The Prophets," with the subdivisions, "The Former Prophets" and "The Latter Prophets." The books making up The Former Prophets were Joshua, Judges, 1 and 2 Samuel, and 1 and 2 Kings. The most evident reason for the heading "Former Prophets" appears to be that these books were written by prophets, and they revealed a prophetic viewpoint. While these books contained much historical material, the purpose of the writers went far beyond this. The writers sought to give a prophetic view of Israel's history. This purpose begins to become clear when we observe the frequent reference to the work of the prophets during Israel's history. The summary for the downfall of the Northern Kingdom as described in 2 Kings 17:7-18 spoke to the point very definitely. It is most evidently the words of an inspired prophet who was able to give a true interpretation of events.

The division, "The Latter Prophets," contains all the prophetical books of our English Bible except Daniel. This heading presents no problem. The next division bears the name "The Holy Writings."

This contains all the remaining books of the Old Testament plus the books of Chronicles. This division presents more difficult problems for explanation. The major one has to do with the interpretation of the canon formation of the Old Testament. The traditional view held that the process of canonization took place after all the books were written and that this last group was called The Holy Writings because it was thought that their authors were not officially prophets.

Most scholars now hold that the three divisions of the canon represent three stages in its formation. One argument advanced in favor of this is that this view accounts best for the position of the books of Chronicles which would more naturally appear among The Former Prophets. Likewise the Book of Daniel belongs more naturally to The Latter Prophets. No evidence exists either for or against the idea of there being three stages in the forming of the canon. For the purpose of this study the chief point to be recognized in the arrangement of the books in the Old Testament canon has to do with the prophetic character of The Former Prophets. It is noteworthy also to observe that the last division bears the name "The Holy Writings," which would give to them unique significance even though the authors of these books were not officially known as prophets.

4. Place of Prophetism in Biblical Revelation

Foundational to the entire idea of biblical revelation is the fact that the Lord spoke through the prophets. It is highly essential that this fact be recognized. Inquiry into this subject involves the most fundamental truth, namely, that the Lord has revealed Himself to mankind.

a. The Prophet, God's Spokesman to His People

The unquestioned conclusion to the discussion of the concept of prophetism is the fact that the Lord called men to whom He revealed Himself and that these men spoke His words to mankind. These chosen men were the prophets. This distinctive office stands over against the office of the king and the priest, held by men who were also chosen to serve the Lord in their respective offices. When the people of Israel rejected the theocracy, God set apart kings to rule in His place. God provided priests who would represent the people before Him. The priest stood between man and God. Since the Lord spoke through the prophets and the prophets spoke the word of the Lord, theirs was also a mediatorial task. They became the agents of divine revelation. This fact gives a sure and firm basis for our entire concept of divine revelation.

b. The Prophetic Order and the Theocratic Kingdom

In the survey of the rise of prophetism we noted the official responsibility of the prophets in the setting up of the theocratic kingdom, of defining the mediatorial character of this kingdom, and of giving direction and guidance to it. Merely to mention the names of such prophets — Moses, Samuel, Nathan, Gad, Elijah, Elisha, Isaiah, Jeremiah, and Daniel — is to assert the great function of the prophets in giving guidance to the kings. Since the kings were ruling in the place of God, spokesmen for God were necessary to give the kings counsel and guidance. We noted that God instituted the theocracy through the prophet Moses. He became the interpreter of the rule of God. We noted also that the Lord used the prophet Samuel to establish the kingdom of Israel and to anoint David as king. The importance of the prophetic office is shown by the fact that Samuel took part in establishing the Davidic kingdom, which became the pattern and type of the Messianic kingdom which God in His own time would establish. This fact stresses still more strongly the eschatological aspect of the prophet's work and shows how vitally it related itself to God's unfolding revelation.

It is this truth which lay at the basis of the prophet's responsibility of giving guidance to the kingdom. History has shown that the kingdom tended to degenerate to the level of other nations, and by so much, lost the standards and patterns which were to be prophetic of the Messiah's kingdom. The prophets supported the authority which the Lord gave to the kings. It was prophetic of the "all authority" to be given to the Messiah. The prophets also fostered the highest standards of holy living and of worship. This explains Elijah's challenge to the prophets of Baal on Mt. Carmel. It gives meaning to the high ethical standards maintained by the writing prophets. Outstanding were the exhortations which the prophets gave to Israel on the futility of the offerings and sacrifices when the lives of the people did not conform to the spiritual meaning of the sacrifices (Is. 1:2-17; Jer. 7:21-26).

It was the writing prophets' severe task to warn the people of God's coming judgment on the kingdom which would lead to the captivities — all centering in the Day of the Lord. In this way the prophets shared in making known to Israel the sinfulness of sin and the inevitable judgment. This was an important part of God's revelation to men. God also used the prophets to give predictions concerning the kingdom of the Messiah and the eternal rule of God. These marvelous unfoldings of the future challenged the faith of God's people and led them to see the grandeur of the Latter Days, to which the unfolding revelation of God was pointing.

c. The Prophet, the Agent of Divine Revelation

In word and act, as Vos suggested, the Lord's approach to Israel was eminently the approach of speech.[12] The content of these words formed the body of truth underlying the religion of the Old Testament. Not until we give careful study to the books of the prophets, even those of The Former Prophets, do we gain a comprehension of the vast body of truth revealed through the prophets. This will become more evident when we note the major doctrinal themes set forth by the prophets. The prophets wrote, among other topics, of the God of Israel, the election of Israel, the Messiah and the Messianic kingdom, the Day of the Lord, the Latter Days, and the life of the people of God. When we assemble the teachings in these and other areas, we stand in wonder at the wealth of spiritual truth found in these books.

Hardly less significant are the insights gained as to God's acts in history. The survey of the rise of prophetism gave incidental attention to what God did in biblical history. Every step of biblical history showed God's direction of the affairs of men. While the writers of The Former Prophets gave special attention to the activity of God in history, The Latter Prophets were almost equally incisive on this point. In most of the prophetic references to God's activity in history we gain an understanding of the meaning of events. For instance, almost the entire book of Hosea deals with the imminent judgment coming upon the Northern Kingdom. The prophet Amos depicted judgments which were soon to come upon the nations surrounding Judah and Israel, as well as upon these two nations themselves. In the mode of dreams and visions the Lord revealed to Daniel the rise and fall of nations until the setting up of the Messiah's kingdom, which would not be destroyed.

d. Relation of God's Revelation to Biblical Inspiration

Beyond all question, the Bible is unique among all books of literature. This fact is evident in its contents and in the manner in which it came to be written. In view of these facts we should seek to discover the bearing of this revelation of God to the prophets upon the nature and content of the written Word. When we observe the specific claims of the prophets that they were speaking the Word of God, we naturally consider the record of these messages to be unique. This consideration of the relation between the spoken words of the prophets and their writings becomes all the more significant when we keep in mind that prophets were the authors of most, if not all, of the Old Testament Scriptures. It is this fact which lay at the basis of Jesus' words when He said, "And scripture cannot be broken" (Jn. 10:35). Paul gave this body of writings the distinctive name "the holy scriptures" (Rom. 1:2). On this account he called this body of writings "the sacred writings" and added, "All scripture is inspired by God" (2 Tim. 3:15, 16). Still more explicitly Peter wrote concerning the Old Testament, "No prophecy of scripture is a matter of one's own interpretation, because no prophecy ever came by the impulse of man, but men moved by the Holy Spirit spoke from God" (2 Pet. 1:21). These commonly quoted proof texts of inspiration dare never lose their message for us. We need to capture again the full significance that Christ, Paul, and Peter attached to the nature of the Old Testament Scriptures.

e. Prophetic Periods

For the purpose of biblical theology the line of cleavage between the non-writing prophets, extending from Moses to Elijah and Elisha, and the writing prophets, beginning with Hosea or perhaps Joel and extending to Malachi, is most significant. The former prophets sought to lead the people of Israel back to the true faith. They preached repentance and confession. They encountered the sinful trends as though the true faith were still salvable. Even Elijah and Elisha preached as though a return to the faith of their fathers were possible.

On the other hand, the earliest of the writing prophets suddenly struck the new note of imminent judgment. The Day of the Lord was near at hand. The wickedness of Israel had gone beyond the point of return. While the date of the Book of Joel is a matter of dispute, I believe that the position of his book near the beginning of The Minor Prophets is strong evidence of his being a contemporary or near-contemporary of Hosea and Amos. This prophet Joel cried out vehemently that the Day of the Lord was near. His severe note of coming judgment needs to be viewed, however, along with a call to repentance in which he says, " 'Yet even now,' says the Lord, 'return to me with all your heart, with fasting, with weeping, and with mourning; and rend your hearts and not your garments.' Return to the Lord, your God, for he is gracious and merciful, slow to anger, and abounding in steadfast love, and repents of evil" (Joel 2:12, 13). In a context of imminent judgment and of promised mercy, Joel struck a new prophetic note of hope. He looked beyond the imminent Day of the Lord to an era in the future in which the Lord would restore the people of Israel to covenant fellowship and would pour out His Spirit on all flesh. The prophet Joel in these ways illustrated the fundamental approach of the writing prophets. The message was threefold: first, imminent judgment; second, a call to repentance; third, the forward look to the Messiah.

This prophetic message established the line of cleavage between the non-writing prophets and the writing prophets and determined still more clearly the place of prophetism in biblical revelation. The rising great eastern powers bent on world conquest became the instrument of God's judgment. The nations of Israel and Judah lay in the path of these conquests. From a political point of view their overthrow was inevitable, especially if they resisted the invading powers. These pagan nations did not know that they were God's tools to inflict judgment upon His people. From the angle of divine providence God raised up these foreign powers to bring judgment upon His people at the very time in which their apostasy had gone beyond the point of return. It was the writing prophets who interpreted the Lord's acts throughout this period.

For Additional Reading and Reference:

Davidson, *Old Testament Prophecy*, pp. 1-29, 75-114.
Heinisch-Heidt, *Theology of the Old Testament*, pp. 18-22.
Henshaw, *The Latter Prophets*, pp. 59-71.
Jacob, *Theology of the Old Testament*, pp. 239-46.
Kirkpatrick, *The Doctrine of the Prophets*, pp. 3-30.
Payne, *The Theology of the Older Testament*, pp. 47-63.
von Rad, *Old Testament Theology*, Vol. II, pp. 96-102.
Rowley, *Re-Discovery of the Old Testament*, pp. 133-60.
Sampey, *Syllabus for Old Testament Study*, pp. 151-56.
Vos, *Biblical Theology — Old and New Testament*, pp. 203-215.
Vriezen, *An Outline of Old Testament Theology*, pp. 55-71, 256-63.
Young, *My Servants the Prophets*. pp. 13-94.

See articles "Prophets" and "Prophecy" in Bible dictionaries and in Bible encyclopedias.

---

1. 1 Sam. 2:27; 1 Kings 13:1; 17:18, 24; 20:28; 2 Kings 4:9, 16, 22, 25, 40, 42; 5:20; 6:9, 10, 15; 7:17-19.

2. Ex. 14:31; Num. 12:7, 8; Deut. 34:5; Josh. 1:2, 7, 13, 15; 24:29; 1 Kings 14:18; 2 Kings 9:7, 36; 14:25; Is. 20:3; Dan. 9:10, 11; Amos 3:7; Zech. 1:6; 3:8.

3. 2 Chron. 36:15; Is. 42:19; 44:26; Hag. 1:13; Mal. 3:1.

4. *Old Testament Prophecy*, by the late A. B. Davidson, edited by J. A. Patterson (Edinburgh: T. & T. Clark, 1912), pp. 80 f. See Chapter VII of this work for a very helpful discussion on "Prophet: Names and Definitions." I want to recognize help received from this chapter for the entire discussion.

5. 1 Sam. 9:9, 11, 18, 19; 2 Sam. 15:27; 1 Chron. 9:22; 26:28; 29:29; 2 Chron. 16:7, 10; Is. 30:10.

6. 2 Sam. 24:11; 2 Kings 17:13; 1 Chron. 21:9; 25:5; 29:29; 2 Chron. 9:29; 12:15; 19:2; 29:25, 30; 33:18, 19; 35:15; Is. 20:10; Amos 7:12; Mic. 3:7.

7. Is. 21:6, 8; 52:8; 56:10; Jer. 6:17; Ezek. 3:17; 33:7.

8. Is. 21:11, 12; 62:6.

9. Davidson, *op. cit.*, p. 8.

10. *Ibid.*, p. 86.

11. *The Westminster Dictionary of the Bible*, by the late John B. Davis, revised and rewritten by Henry Snyder Gehman (Philadelphia: The Westminster Press, 1944), "Prophet," p. 493.

12. Vos, *op. cit.*, p. 205.

CHAPTER III
NATURE OF THE PROPHETIC GIFT

1. Call to the Prophetic Office

The call of Moses and of Samuel to the prophetic office has already been observed. For both their being set apart for this special work was explicitly an act of God. For both the call came by an audible voice from the Lord. There is little or nothing given as to how the other non-writing prophets were set apart by God.

As we turn to the writing prophets we observe that they referred explicitly to the call of the Lord. Amos gave a brief account of his call: "I am no prophet, nor a prophet's son; but I am a herdsman, and a dresser of sycamore trees, and the Lord took me from following the flock, and the Lord said to me, 'Go, prophesy to my people Israel'" (Amos 7:14). The Lord had called Amos from an ordinary vocation with no apparent preparation for his prophetic work. Isaiah's call to the prophetic office was extraordinary (Is. 6:1-13). Evidently he received it when he was in the temple. He saw the Lord sitting upon His throne and heard the seraphim calling to one another, "Holy, holy, holy is the Lord of hosts." With this view of the Lord, Isaiah at once turned his thought inward in self-condemnation. In the presence of the Lord of hosts he was a man of unclean lips. The Lord removed his guilt and forgave his sin. In response to God's call, Isaiah answered, "Here I am! Send me." The Lord then gave him his commission. His message for Israel was most pointed. In brief, it was a condemnation of spiritual blindness on the part of Israel for their refusal to heed the words of the Lord through His prophets. Isaiah's task was to preach this message until the cities would be laid waste, the land would be utterly desolate, and the people removed to a foreign land. This account of Isaiah's call illustrates the objectivity of the Lord's communication to him.

Jeremiah's account of his call is also brimming with interest (Jer. 1:1-12). The word of the Lord came to Jeremiah as follows: "Before I formed you in the womb I knew you, and before you were born I consecrated you; I appointed you a prophet to the nations." Through this message Jeremiah learned that even before his birth, the Lord had set him apart for the prophetic office. Being yet a youth, when God spoke to him, Jeremiah had not become engaged in any vocation. His lifework was that of being a prophet to the nations. When Jeremiah answered that he did not know how to speak, the Lord replied, "Behold, I have put my words in your mouth." This significant statement indicated the manner in which God's words became the words of the prophet. Then the Lord told Jeremiah his mission in the words, "See, I have set you this day over nations and over kingdoms, to pluck up and to break down, to destroy and to overthrow, to build and to plant." The nature of Jeremiah's task was staggering. Jeremiah's words would possess divine power. They would build or destroy nations and kingdoms. In other words, Jeremiah's call to the prophetic office involved him in implementing the declarations of God which would affect the kingdoms of the world. These declarations stand in sharp contrast to the literal destroying or setting up of nations by other world powers, usually accomplished by wars and conquests.

The Lord gave Ezekiel a vision of the likeness of the glory of the Lord (Ezek. 1, 2). In this vision Ezekiel also heard the Lord's voice. He told Ezekiel how rebellious, impudent, and stubborn the people of Israel were. To such a people Ezekiel was sent to give a prophetic witness by which they would know that a prophet had been among them. This vision was external and objective. By this means Ezekiel knew that the Lord was speaking to them. In addition, the spirit of God, through whom he received his commission, entered into him. Other writing prophets followed almost a common pattern of announcing their prophetic call; a sample of it is found in the statement, "The word of the Lord that came to Hosea" (Hos. 1:1).[1] A slight variation occurs in Amos: "The words of Amos . . . which he saw concerning Israel" (Amos 1:1; Mic. 1:1).

2. Affirmations of Real Communications from God

The exercise of the prophetic gift by the prophets leads to the very heart of divine revelation. Considerations such as the following call for study. Was the communication by God to the prophets, whether by word, vision, or dream, objectively real? Did it become a part of the prophet's actual experience? What likeness, if any, existed between the alleged revelation of God to the prophets and the heathen divinations found among other nations? Were the words of the prophets genuinely human? Were their insights entirely on a human level? These questions arise out of a denial by some theologians of actual revelations of God to the prophets. Some scholars would grant some general revelation by way of heightened human insights or through certain ecstatic experiences, but they would deny a supernatural communication objectively given to man.

For this reason it is necessary to examine and evaluate carefully the forms of expression used by the prophets to express the nature and character of God's revelation to them. I am moving forward with the settled conviction that the prophets were men of moral integrity. They spoke the truth and did not misrepresent the source and origin of their words. This does not deny the existence of certain problems which will receive due consideration. For instance, were the words of the Lord audible? Were the visions seen with the natural eye? What human relation did exist between the revelation given to the prophets and the actual words of the prophets? These questions and others require a forthright examination. With these things in mind let us survey the various forms of expression used by the prophets to introduce their messages:

a. To Moses God said, "I will be with your mouth and teach you what you shall speak" (Ex. 4:12, 15, 16).

b. "The vision of . . . which he saw" (Is. 1:1; 2:1; Obad. 1; Ezek. 1: 1; Nahum 1:1).

c. "The Lord said to . . ." (Is. 7:3; 8:1, 5, 11; Hos. 1:2, 4; 3:1; Ezek. 2:1; 3:1, 4).

d. "The oracle concerning . . ." (Is. 13:1; 15:1; 17:1, etc.).

e. "Thus says the Lord" (Amos 1:3; Mic. 3:5; Zeph. 1:10; Jer. 7:21; Ezek. 6:11; Hag. 1:2; Zech. 11:4).

f. "Hear this word that the Lord has spoken" (Amos 3:1).

g. "Thus the Lord God showed me" (Amos 7:1).

h. "I saw the Lord . . . and he said" (Amos 9:1).

i. "The oracle of God which . . . saw" (Hab. 1:1; Zech. 12:1; Mal. 1:1).

j. "The words of Jeremiah . . . to whom the word of the Lord came" (Jer. 1:1, 2).

Besides these statements there are many references to the work of the Holy Spirit in the prophets.[2]

3. Analysis of the Prophetic Claims

The preceding data present two general patterns of divine revelation: first, that of God's speaking accompanied by man's hearing the voice of God; and second, that of God's showing through visions and dreams, accompanied by man's seeing what God has shown. We should observe that God's speaking also accompanied a vision or dream.

a. God's Speaking and Man's Hearing

The frequency and variety of expression to the effect that the prophets were speaking the words of God should be interpreted in the manner in which they expected their words to be understood. In all these forms of speech, the commonly accepted language of communication was used. Throughout the prophetic writings there were instances where a prophet repeated the words of his fellowmen.[3] If we accept these conversations between man and man at their face value, consistency requires that we also accept the recorded words of God to the prophets at their face value. There is no occasion or need for thinking that the prophets were mere machines mechanically reporting God's word; yet at the same time, the forms of expression used, taken at their face value, aim to assert the accuracy of the prophets' disclosure of God's revelation. There is no occasion for asserting the verbal identity of the words spoken to the prophets, by the Lord, with the words that the prophets spoke to the people. At the same time the prophets left no room for a distinction between what the Lord said to them and what they said to the people. There is little to be gained by attempting to decide whether the words of the Lord were heard audibly by the prophets or whether the words of the Lord entered the minds of the prophets through the power of the Holy Spirit and the prophets spoke accordingly. The point at issue is this: was there an objective communication between the Lord and the prophets with the result that the prophets spoke the words revealed to them by the Lord? Habakkuk spoke directly to this issue when he wrote, "What profit is an idol when its maker has shaped it, a metal image, a teacher of lies? For the workman trusts in his own creation when he makes dumb idols! Woe to him who says to a wooden thing, Awake; to a dumb stone, Arise! Can this give revelation? Behold, it is overlaid with gold and silver, and there is no breath at all in it. But the Lord is in his holy temple; let all the earth keep silence before him" (Hab. 2:18-20).

There remains, nevertheless, an unexplainable mystery, that of accounting for the divine and the human elements of the words spoken by the prophets. Very clearly, there was the divine side in which the Lord spoke to the prophets. There was also the human side in which the prophets spoke the words of the Lord. Certainly the prophets were not mere record players, mechanically playing off a divine record. Just as there is the unexplainable mystery of accounting for both the divine and human sides of the written Word of God, known as *inspiration*, or of accounting for the divine-human Jesus, so we have a similar mystery in the divine and human aspects of the words of the prophets. Faith moves forward to believe these mysteries because no human explanation can account for the amazing nature and content of the prophetic Scriptures, the character of the written Word, and the divine-human Jesus. There is no need to present a theory which attempts to explain how the prophets spoke the very words of God.

b. God's Showing and Man's Seeing

Visions and dreams give the pattern of God's showing and man's seeing. There appears to be no sharp distinction between visions and dreams; one shades off into the other. The Hebrew words for vision also present a wide range of meaning, varying from that which is almost equivalent to the disclosure of the word of the Lord as we find in Amos 1:1; Isaiah 1:1, and elsewhere to that which the prophets saw. Ezekiel illustrated the more technical meaning of the vision when he said, "The heavens were opened, and I saw visions of God" (Ezek. 1:1). What Ezekiel saw in the vision becomes clear in the words, "Such was the appearance of the likeness of the glory of the Lord. And when I saw it, I fell upon my face, and I heard the voice of one speaking" (Ezek. 1: 28). This is the use of *vision* in which we are presently concerned. Much of the prophetic material of Ezekiel and Daniel came in vision form. For Daniel visions and dreams had, at times, a very close relationship.

The interpretation of visions and dreams presents more difficult problems than does the speaking and hearing form of expression. An approach to the interpretations of visions and dreams follows. First, some of the visions and dreams have an accompanying explanation or interpretation of their meaning. This is true of the dreams of Pharaoh and of Nebuchadnezzar, as well as of Daniel's vision (Gen. 41:2, 4, 7, etc.). The interpretation of these dreams and visions gives helpful insights for interpreting other revelations given in this form. Second, the context of a given vision or dream may suggest its meaning. This becomes evident in Isaiah's vision of the Lord in His temple. It led Isaiah to recognize the holiness of the Lord. The same is true of Ezekiel's vision of the Lord in which the closing verse of this scene, quoted above, gives the great and sublime truth pictured in this vision. Third, in a few instances, later biblical references may give a lead as to the meaning of a given vision.[4] Fourth, art pictures and visions have much in common. There are great works of art, such as "The Last Supper," which yield great meaning through careful study of the picture. Guides to picking up the thought which the artist sought to convey apply almost as well to the interpretation of visions and dreams. Let us bear in mind that the vision or dream form of divine revelation lent itself to clear understanding of its meaning in the same way as pictures do in the field of art.

4. Modes of Communication Used by the Prophets

The first and most significant mode of communication used by the prophets was that of speech. Here we meet the phenomenon of divine speech passing over into human language. The great body of prophetic truth came to the prophets through the word of the Lord. Almost uniformly, the prophets claimed that their words were the words of the Lord. From the point of view of interpretation no gap exists between the words of the Lord and the words of the prophets. There is little occasion to differentiate between the meaning of the prophets' words and the meaning of the words of the Lord spoken to the prophets.

A somewhat different problem confronts us as we attempt to interpret the prophets' verbal delivery of their visions. They had the task of expressing an optical experience in words. This is a process almost identical to that of a student of art explaining in words the message of a great painting. There are a number of instances where a prophet did a strange act which bore a symbolic meaning or portrayed a lesson.[5]

A third means of communication by prophets was that of miracles, specifically miracles of prediction. Thus in the prophetical books a great body of predictions served as a mode of communication to the people. Most of these foretold the imminent Day of the Lord and the Latter Days in which the Messiah would appear. These predictions also present problems of interpretation, but it is highly gratifying that the New Testament recognized the fulfillment of many of them or gave some word of explanation about those yet to be fulfilled. Hence a study of the New Testament references to the fulfillment of the predictions serves as an invaluable guide to the interpretation of the prophetic Scriptures. It is our privilege to recognize New Testament allusions to Old Testament predictions, as given through the Holy Spirit, and to these authoritative interpretations of the predictions.

For Additional Reading and Reference:

Davidson, *The Theology of the Old Testament*, pp. 115-223.
Douglas, Ed., *The New Bible Dictionary*, pp. 1039 f.
Lindblom, *Prophecy in Ancient Israel*, pp. 105-219.
Vos, *Biblical Theology — Old and New Testament*, pp. 230-52.
Warfield, *International Standard Bible Encyclopaedia*, Vol. IV, p. 2573, "Revelation."

1. Joel 1:1; Jon. 1:1; Zeph. 1:1; etc.
2. Num. 24:2; 1 Kings 22:24; 1 Chron. 12:18; 2 Chron. 15:1; 20:14; 24:20; Neh. 9:20, 30; Is. 48:16; Hos. 9:7; Mic. 3:8; Zech. 7:12. Observe also the New Testament witness to the work of the Holy Spirit in the prophets. Acts 28:25; 1 Pet. 1:10-12; 2 Pet. 1:19, 21.
3. Is. 7:2-17; 36; 39; Jer. 20:3-6; 21:2, 3; 28:5-11; 29:1-9; 36:11-19; 38:4-28, etc.
4. Dan. 4:12, 21 (Mt. 13:32); Dan. 7:13, 14 (Mt. 24:30; 26:64).
5. Is. 20; Jer. 13:1-7; 19; Ezek. 3:26; 4:1-3; 12:1 ff.; 24:15; Hos. 1:3.

CHAPTER IV
THEOLOGY OF THE FORMER
PROPHETS

1. Introduction

In Chapter II the evident influence of prophetism on the arrangement of the Old Testament books came into view. The group of books known as The Former Prophets very likely received this label because they gave a prophetic view of Israel's history. They showed very definitely God's leading in this period of history. In view of this dominant note it becomes necessary to study the theology of this group of books.

2. God's Revelation from Joshua to Samuel

a. Fulfillment of the Promises

In the study of the theological unfolding recorded in the Book of Deuteronomy we observed how frequently the Lord referred to the promises made to Abraham which were about to be fulfilled in the inheritance of Canaan.[1] Some students feel that the author of Joshua built on this basic idea also by referring to the fulfillment of these promises.[2] Joshua in his last message to Israel recounted in considerable detail the history of the chosen people from the time of Abraham onward (Josh. 24:3-13). The Lord was the speaker in most of this narrative, as we may note in these statements: "I took your father Abraham. . . . I gave him Isaac, . . . I sent Moses and Aaron, . . . I plagued Egypt. . . . I brought your fathers out of Egypt. . . . I brought you to the land of the Amorites, . . . I gave them into your hand, . . . I would not listen to Balaam. . . . I sent the hornet before you. . . . I gave you a land on which you had not labored," etc. In this manner the Lord led Israel to see all that He had done up to that time in a step-by-step fulfillment of the promises given to Abraham. This fulfillment of God's promises had become a reality in Israel's experience. They were beginning to realize that the fulfillment of these promises in their generation was only a part, significant as it was, of a continuous unfolding of all that God had foretold. The note of eschatology was becoming clearer and stronger. Through all these experiences Israel was learning more of their God. He was a God of purpose, who made promises and fulfilled them. The fulfillment of the promises required great power, not only to overthrow their enemies, but also to bring the plagues upon the Egyptians, divide the Red Sea, give manna in the wilderness, supply water out of the rock, stop the flow of the Jordan

River, and bring down the walls of Jericho. The people of that generation were witnesses to all these manifestations of divine power. Joshua also reminded the people of the central truth taught by Moses concerning their God, namely, that "He is a holy God; he is a jealous God" (Josh. 24:19). On account of this, Joshua stressed again the need for implicit obedience to their Lord and for serving Him faithfully. Joshua drew the people into a covenant promise, binding them to fulfill their words, "The Lord our God we will serve, and his voice we will obey" (v. 24).

b. God's Continued Action in History

We have noted Joshua's rehearsal of God's activity throughout their history. The books of Joshua and Judges gave repeated witness to the victories gained through the power of God in the conquest of Canaan. Through these many extraordinary events Israel was learning the meaning of the providence of God. Their Lord not only foresaw coming events but He predetermined them so that His purposes would be fulfilled. This truth is pertinent in all of God's actions in history.

One aspect of this verity was the purpose of the disciplinary judgments which God brought upon His people because of their sins. Joshua warned them, "Therefore be very steadfast to keep and do all that is written in the book of the law of Moses. . . . If you turn back, and join the remnant of these nations left here among you . . . know assuredly that the Lord your God will not continue to drive out these nations before you; but they shall be a snare and a trap for you, a scourge on your sides, and thorns in your eyes, till you perish from off this good land which the Lord your God has given you" (Josh. 23: 6-13). The people of Israel failed to follow these stern warnings. Repeatedly in the Book of Judges we have the statement, "And the people of Israel did what was evil in the sight of the Lord. . . . So the anger of the Lord was kindled against Israel, and he gave them over to plunderers."[3] It is conceivable that the author of Judges, living possibly during the days of the declining kingdom of Judah, wrote this book to show the people of his time the kind of disciplinary judgments which the Lord brings upon His people because of their sins and apostasy.

c. Worship of Israel During This Period

The biblical record includes a few significant incidents related to Israel's worship during this period. As Joshua was about to lead the people in the conquest of Canaan, the Lord commanded him to administer the rite of circumcision, which had been neglected throughout the wilderness wanderings. The reason for this neglect was that "they did not hearken to the voice of the Lord" (Josh. 5:6). We do not know why Moses had not kept up this ritual during the forty years of their wilderness experience, but the writer of Joshua gives the impression that the people of Israel consciously neglected God's command. When Joshua fulfilled this responsibility, the Lord said, "This day I have rolled away the reproach of Egypt from you." (Josh. 5:9). Through this rite the people of Israel preserved a distinction required of God to be maintained between them and the nations of Canaan. Circumcision carried the meaning of purification and of being set apart for God. With this command fulfilled, Israel kept the Passover.

Israel took another significant step in worship when Joshua built an altar to the Lord in Mt. Ebal (Josh. 8:30-35). This fulfilled Moses' commandment (Deut. 27:2-8) which Joshua referred to as having been written in the book of the law of Moses. The narrative affirms that this book of the law of Moses was then in Joshua's possession. (Aside from our present discussion, note the references to an authoritative body of writings which forged the idea expressed in the terms "Holy Scriptures" and "Sacred Writings."[4]) They offered on this altar burnt offerings to the Lord and sacrificed peace offerings. We get the impression that these two bloody offerings were most frequently made by the people of Israel. Undoubtedly their symbolism was the same as when Moses instituted them. Now in the midst of their conquest of Canaan they had gained the vantage point of Mt. Ebal, they were renewing their consecration to God, and they were experiencing fellowship with their Lord.

After the conquest of Canaan had been completed, the whole congregation assembled at Shiloh and set up the tent of meeting there (Josh. 18:1). This was the first step toward maintaining a single place of worship in the land of promise. God had given commandments before the conquest that Israel should have such a central place of worship. The Lord knew what divisive effects many places of worship could have, even causing a breakdown in the worship of one God. A sample of such departure is found in the case of Micah and the Danites, who set up a graven image for themselves in the city of Dan.

There is no further record of the observance of the Passover throughout Joshua and Judges, in fact, not until the time of Josiah (2 Kings 23:21-23). Second Chronicles does refer, nevertheless, to a keeping of the Passover during the reign of Hezekiah (2 Chron. 30). The apparent conflict between the two references presents a problem of harmonization. One solution of the problem, which has some points in its favor, is that no such great observance of the Passover had occurred between the time of the judges and Josiah. The disparity between the records would likely disappear if we knew all the facts. It seems almost inconceivable that in view of the central place of worship, first at Shiloh and later at Nob and in Gibeon, superseded then by Solomon's temple, there should not have been any Passovers held until the days of Hezekiah or Josiah. In view of the nature of the narratives in these historical books we may safely conclude that the Passover was kept throughout this era but not with the publicity or magnitude connected with Josiah's reforms.

Returning to the matter of Israel's worship during this period, we need to evaluate properly the meaning of the worship experiences of Deborah, as she sang her song of triumph; of Gideon, as he prepared for delivering Israel from the Midianites; even of Jephthah; of Samson, during his better moments; of Naomi and Ruth, in their return to the land of Israel; and finally of Boaz, who could say to his reapers, "The Lord be with you," and they would respond, "The Lord bless you" (Ruth 2:4).

d. Disclosure of God and His Nature

Note again Joshua's words, "He is a holy God; he is a jealous God; he will not forgive your transgressions or your sins. If you forsake the Lord and serve foreign gods, then he will turn and do you harm, and consume you, after having done you good" (Josh. 24:19, 20). This statement reflected the ideas presented in the second commandment. Its significance at this point is that Joshua picked up this definitive expression of God's nature and laid the message on the hearts of Israel. We have already observed the frequency of the words, "The Lord said," which indicated His closeness to His people. The Lord revealed His holy nature through the numérous warnings against their falling into the ways of the Canaanite nations. While the ideas of love, mercy, and forgiveness found meager expression in these books, we need to recognize that the general thought content of these books did not center in these ideas. However, among Joshua's final exhortations he did indicate how the Lord their God had given rest to the people of Israel. On the basis of this he could tell the tribesmen who lived east of the Jordan, "Take good care to observe the commandment and the law which Moses the servant of the Lord commanded you, to love the Lord your God, and to walk in all his ways, and to keep his commandments, and to cleave to him, and to serve him with all your heart and with all your soul" (Josh. 22:5). Without any question Israel's God, who required such love and obedience from His people, was Himself the God of love. Though Israel broke her covenant with the Lord, yet He declared, "I will never break my covenant with you" (Judg. 2:1). When the people would have made Gideon king, he recognized that the Lord was their ruler. Through all of these experiences, when "every man did what was right in his own eyes" (Judg. 17:6; 21:25), the Lord displayed His righteousness, justice, love, and mercy. He was long-suffering with His people. "When the people of Israel cried to the Lord, the Lord raised up for them a deliverer" (Judg. 3:15).

It is instructive to note the frequency of the references to the "Spirit of the Lord" in the Book of Judges.[5] As part of the revelation of the nature of God, these references possess great value. Note the several expressions, "The Spirit of the Lord came upon him"; "The Spirit of the Lord came mightily upon him"; and "The Spirit of the Lord began to stir him." These statements follow the same pattern as those in the Pentateuch.[6] The first thing to be observed is the personal distinction made between the Lord Himself and the Spirit of the Lord. To interpret the spirit of the Lord as being merely an outflow of God's power upon these judges is to reject their real import. Certainly when the Spirit of God came upon these men, they received unusual power; but we need to go further than this, and to recognize that an important distinction does exist between the Lord and the Spirit of the Lord. In the light of the New Testament unfolding of the doctrine of God these references give a foreshadowing of the distinction between the Lord and the outpoured Holy Spirit. On one hand, care should be taken not to project backward into the Old Testament the fully revealed truth of the New Testament; on the other, there is equal need to recognize that the fully revealed truths of the New Testament had their roots in the Old.

The nature of the relationship expressed in the language, "The Spirit of the Lord came upon him," leads us to anticipate a similar connection in the New Testament expressed in the language of a person's being filled with the Spirit. It carried the germinal idea that man possesses a spiritual nature through which the Spirit of the Lord operates, and gives him the kind of power needed whether of physical strength or of prophetic speech.

e. Life of the People of God

The most heartening aspect pertaining to the life of the people of God as manifested during this period, comes from the Book of Hebrews. It is the element of faith. In spite of the fact that this era of Israel's history sometimes goes by the name of the "Dark Ages," the author of Hebrews referred to more individuals by name from this period than from any other period of Old Testament history. Note as well the acts of faith during this age: "By faith the people crossed the Red Sea as if on dry land. . . . By faith the walls of Jericho fell down. . . . By faith Rahab the harlot did not perish. . . . For time would fail me to tell of Gideon, Barak, Samson, Jephthah, of David and Samuel and the prophets" (Heb. 11:29-32). We could wish that time had not failed the author of Hebrews to tell of the faith that these heroes manifested. This would have given us rich instruction in the nature of faith.

Achan, who represents the many who failed to live by faith and by God's standard of righteousness, confessed to the outworking of sin in his life when he said, "Of a truth I have sinned against the Lord God of Israel, and this is what I did: . . . I saw . . . I coveted . . . and took them" (Josh. 7:20, 21). On the other hand, Joshua stands out as a man of extraordinary character. He was in position to admonish Israel to be "very steadfast to keep and do all that is written in the book of the law of Moses, turning aside from it neither to the right hand nor to the left," and to say further, "Fear the Lord, and serve him in sincerity and in faithfulness" (Josh. 23:6; 24:14). The Book of Judges served to show how God's people should *not* live. Repeatedly we read, "The people of Israel did what was evil in the sight of the Lord, forgetting the Lord their God." The final verdict on their manner of life stands: "Every man did what was right in his own eyes."[7]

An evaluation of the life of the people of God during the time of the judges must observe the God-fearing lives of such people as Naomi, Ruth, and Boaz. Such examples of uprightness should lead us to conclude that even though the Book of Judges gives dark pictures of Israel's sinfulness there were, nevertheless, God-fearing men and women during this period. The author of Judges fulfilled his prophetic mission by picturing the outworking of sin in the lives of God's people together with the resulting judgments that came because of sin. It becomes more evident that he wrote this book to serve as a warning to Israel when the overthrow of Jerusalem by the Babylonians was imminent. The judgments of God upon Israel's sinfulness in this early history would be repeated unless the nation repented.

3. God's Revelation During the Period of the Monarchy

The prophetic note observable in the books of Joshua and Judges became more obvious in the books of Samuel, Kings, and Chronicles. In the period of time covered by the latter group of books the establishment of the kingdom, the building of the temple, the division of the kingdom, the crisis of Baal worship, and the downward plunge of the kingdoms to the captivities, all called for prophetic interpretation. Chronologically this period included most of the writing prophets. As we shall observe later, the writing prophets set forth explicitly the meaning of the downward plunge of the kingdoms to their respective captivities. While the authors of the books now under consideration did not deal with the issues in the same manner as the writing prophets did, they wrote, nevertheless, from the viewpoint of prophets and interpreted this period of history in the light of God's revelation to them.

a. God and His Revelation

The first words about the Lord in the books of Samuel, those of Hannah's prayer, come to us from a beautiful setting. Having been given a son in answer to prayer, Hannah brought him to the house of the Lord and said, "As long as he lives, he is lent to the Lord" (1 Sam. 1:28). On this occasion she uttered a prayer which stands as a sublime witness to her understanding of the Lord. She prayed, "There is none holy like the Lord there is none besides thee; there is no rock like our God" (1 Sam. 2:1-10). She spoke of the Lord as being the God of knowledge. She saw Him as being active in the affairs of men, bringing blessings to the poor and humble; as guarding the feet of His faithful ones but cutting off the wicked in darkness. She bore witness to God's work of creation in the poetic words, "For the pillars of the earth are the Lord's, and on them he has set the world." She closed her prayer with the words, "The Lord will judge the ends of the earth; he will give strength to his king, and exalt the power of his anointed." Such a presentation of the Lord hardly finds a parallel in the entire Old Testament.

Some students have labored over the problem centering in God's words, "I repent that I have made Saul king" (1 Sam. 15:10). It would seem that if we as human beings would lift the idea, *change of mind,* to the divine level, these words would no longer cause difficulty. It is the nature of a personal being to take a different course of action under given circumstances. In this specific case Saul had turned back from following the Lord and was no longer worthy of being king. In human experience a change of mind often occurs on account of limited knowledge. With Deity there is omniscience. Even so, *repent* is the only word that conveys to human thinking God's attitude toward unfaithfulness such as that found in King Saul.

In David's prayer for Solomon, we find another statement filled with meaning, pertaining to the nature and work of God. He said, "Thine, O Lord, is the greatness, and the power, and the glory, and the victory, and the majesty; for all that is in the heavens and in the earth is thine; thine is the kingdom, O Lord, and thou art exalted as head above all" (1 Chron. 29:11). He prayed further in the words, "I

know, my God, that thou triest the heart, and hast pleasure in uprightness" (v. 17). It would be in order to draw from David's psalms similar
statements setting forth the majesty of the Lord.[8] A study of these
psalms shows how fully David had comprehended the doctrine of God.
He did not speak of God as though he presented ideas gained through
his own thinking, but rather as the unfolding of what the Holy Spirit
had revealed to him.

David noted also that God tries the heart. He himself had experienced this when he wrote, "Prove me, O Lord, and try me; test my
heart and my mind. For thy steadfast love is before my eyes, and I walk
in faithfulness to thee."[9] At a later time when the Lord had blessed
Hezekiah with great wealth and envoys of the princes of Babylon came
to see him, we read, "God left him to himself, in order to try him and
to know all that was in his heart" (2 Chron. 32:27-31). God's trying of
the heart presents an important aspect of God's relation to man,
especially to His own people. God would lead them to implicit obedience
in all things. Accordingly, the Lord has often placed His people under unusual circumstances whereby men would reveal their inner
heart conditions. Thus the God of Israel would draw His people to a life
of commitment even in the face of severe tests. Only on the basis of
being proved by the Lord could they appropriate the distinctive blessings
which God had in store for them.

In these books a new title for God arises. He is the Lord of hosts.[10]
The meaning of this name of God calls for study. Already in the time
of Moses we have the expression, "All the hosts of the Lord," which,
evidently, referred to all the people of Israel. When Israel was about
to attack Jericho a man encountered Joshua, perhaps in vision form,
and declared himself as being the "commander of the army of the
Lord" (Josh. 5:14, 15). This suggested a heavenly army as distinguished
from Israel's army. This explanation may express the meaning of this
name but some of its later uses may suggest a grander meaning implied
in a number of the psalms, as for instance in the words, "By the word
of the Lord the heavens were made, and all their host by the breath
of his mouth" (Ps. 33:6). According to this explanation the name "the
Lord of hosts" is practically equivalent to the Lord of heaven and earth.
It was a simple but meaningful way of ascribing absolute supremacy
and sovereignty to God. This is certainly what David expressed when he
wrote, "Who is this King of glory? The Lord of hosts, he is the King
of glory" (Ps. 24:10).

An important prophetic note should be observed in the expression, "Thus says the Lord of hosts." This is the language Samuel
used at the anointing of Saul and Nathan in speaking to David.[11] While

these are the only uses of this expression in The Former Prophets, it became the usual pattern for introducing the word of the Lord by five of the writing prophets.[12] This detail possesses a number of points of interest for our study. First, there was significance in the communication of God through the prophets Samuel, Nathan, and in a modified form through Elijah. Second, this language lends significance to this group of books being called The Former Prophets. That is, the writer of the books of Samuel and Kings (including Chronicles) used the same mode of expression that a number of the prophets used (2 Sam. 7:8; 1 Chron. 17:7). Apparently the authors of Samuel and Chronicles consciously chose the same formula of expression as these writing prophets used.

We should not bypass the opening words of David's song when he was delivered from the hand of Saul: "The Lord is my rock, and my fortress, and my deliverer, my God, my rock, in whom I take refuge, my shield and the horn of my salvation, my stronghold and my refuge, my savior; thou savest me from violence" (2 Sam. 22:2, 3). Through these words and others equally precious we learn that the Lord entered into very close relationship with David.

b. God's Revelation Through the Davidic Kingdom

The authors of the books of Samuel, Kings, and Chronicles gave a prophetic view of the kingdom of David. The Lord explained to Samuel the real meaning of Israel's request for a king. From the point of view of history, this step marked the close of the era of the judges and the beginning of the era of kings. This change, however, involved a deeper meaning. As the Lord explained to Samuel, Israel had rejected God from being their king. God's rule established at Mt. Sinai had given way to the rule of earthly kings. God permitted the change and through the change He began to work out larger purposes which became quite clear in these writings. The Lord provided a king to rule in His place and by divine right. The Lord gave the extraordinary authority displayed by the kings of Judah and Israel.

Another word which points very aptly to the nature of this rule is *mediator*. This descriptive title gained supreme significance in the New Testament.[13] Thus the term "mediator" held in view the total work of Christ as Prophet, Priest, and King. New Testament writers projected the idea of mediatorial kingship backward to the time of David in order to give clearer meaning to the nature of his rule. All the kings of Judah and of Israel may be properly regarded as mediatorial kings. The Lord had said to David, "You shall be shepherd of my people Israel, and you shall be prince over Israel" (2 Sam. 5:2).

The Lord began to unfold His larger purpose, eschatological in nature through the prophet Nathan. The Lord promised David a son through whom He would establish His kingdom (2 Sam. 7:4-17). While this prediction had immediate reference to the birth of Solomon, the language possessed a potential that might reach to the One greater than Solomon. The Lord said, "I will establish the throne of his kingdom for ever. I will be his father, and he shall be my son." It is possible that Jesus Himself was reflecting on these words when He said, "Something greater than Solomon is here" (Mt. 12:42). The author of Hebrews quoted these words as an explicit prediction of Christ (Heb. 1:5). Here then the larger meaning of the Davidic kingdom became evident. We may believe that the people of God had some understanding of its meaning, especially at a later time, when the writing prophets unfolded the nature of the Messianic kingdom. If we are correct in understanding that David wrote Psalms 2 and 110, we may believe that he had grasped the Messianic import of the Lord's words. In these two psalms he referred definitely to the Lord's Anointed and to the One who would sit at the right hand of God, exercising unlimited power and authority. The Lord raised up prophets in order to give guidance to the kings of Israel so that the people of Israel, and especially the kingly line, would remain faithful to God. Only through a godly line could the Lord work out His purposes in establishing the kingship of the Anointed One, the Messiah.

c. God's Actions in History

Almost every page of The Former Prophets, including Chronicles, shows God's working in history, not only among His own people but also among other nations. The Lord withheld and also gave children (1 Sam. 1:5, 19, 20). The Lord slew the men of Bethshemesh because they looked into the ark of the Lord (1 Sam. 6:19, 20). This act of God led the people of Bethshemesh to say, "Who is able to stand before the Lord, this holy God?" Through this judgment the people of Bethshemesh came to recognize the holiness of God. Samuel saw fit to rehearse to the people of Israel all that the Lord had wrought among them since the days of Moses and Aaron (1 Sam. 12:6-18). He brought into the picture the saving deeds of the Lord which He had performed for their fathers since the time of Jacob's going down into Egypt. In order to demonstrate the Lord's continued workings among them, Samuel told the people to stand still and see what the Lord would do before their eyes. It was the time of wheat harvest, when thunder and rain were most unlikely. They heard Samuel pray to the Lord and the Lord answered with thunder and rain that day.

From these relatively minor incidents of God's actions, we move to Ahijah's prophetic word to Jeroboam in which Ahijah told him that the Lord was about to make him, Jeroboam, king over the northern tribes (1 Kings 11:26-40). In the outworking of this prediction we gain the detail, "So the king did not hearken to the people; for it was a turn of affairs brought about by the Lord that he might fulfil his word, which the Lord spoke by Ahijah the Shilonite to Jeroboam the son of Nebat" (1 Kings 12:15). Of still greater moment was Assyria's conquest of Samaria, resulting in Israel's being carried captive to Assyria. The explanation of this event appears in the words, "And this was so, because the people of Israel had sinned against the Lord their God," followed by a detailed account of Israel's departure from the Lord (2 Kings 17:7-18). Nebuchadnezzar's conquest of Judah in the days of Jehoiakim was also brought on by the Lord. We read, "And the Lord sent against him bands of the Chaldeans . . . and sent them against Judah to destroy it, according to the word of the Lord which he spoke by his servants the prophets. Surely this came upon Judah at the command of the Lord, to remove them out of his sight, for the sins of Manasseh, according to all that he had done" (2 Kings 24:1-7).

It is highly gratifying that many students of theology are accepting this aspect of biblical history. It gives new meaning to the Scriptures. The God of Israel was He who guided all the affairs of Israel to the outworking of His ultimate purposes. It is this profound truth which helps us to believe that God worked most marvelously in history through the sending of His Son into the world, to be born of a woman, to suffer, die, and be raised to life and to be seated at the right hand of the Father, "far above all rule and authority and power and dominion" (Eph. 1:21).

d. The Temple, the House of the Lord

The building of the temple by Solomon was an epochal step in the development of Israel's worship. The grandeur of this building was unsurpassed in its day. Built after the pattern of the tabernacle, the temple symbolized the dwelling of God in the midst of His people. Very appropriately it bore the name "the house of the Lord." It stood as the central place of worship for the people of God. It was a bulwark against any other worship. This shows the heinousness of Jeroboam's sin in setting up rival altars for calf worship at Bethel and at Dan. The house of the Lord stood as the emblem of the Lord's being the one and only true God. In Solomon's prayer of dedication he expressed this truth very forcibly in the words, "O Lord, God of Israel, there is no God like thee, in heaven or on earth, keeping covenant and showing steadfast love to thy servants who walk before thee with all their heart" (2 Chron. 6:14).

From the standpoint of God's unfolding revelation, the house of the Lord not only bore the symbolism of God's dwelling with His people but it foreshadowed or typified the more spiritual indwelling of God within His church, as well as in the hearts of His people. This is the truth to which the New Testament writers gave their attestations.[14] In this new temple, the bodies of Christian believers, the Holy Spirit dwells. It is this overwhelming spiritual truth which accounts for the temple structure. Through its magnificence the Lord sought to show His people that His glory required the most costly and elaborate building to symbolize His dwelling place, and to foreshadow the sanctity of the individual Christian and the church as being the dwelling place of the Holy Spirit. We believe that the unusual amount of space devoted to describing the erection of the temple and to its dedication led the people of Israel to look forward to the vastly more spiritual dwelling of God in His people.

e. The Lord's Judgment on Israel

The authors of Kings and of Chronicles sought to depict the downfall of Israel and Judah as the outcome of their apostasy. The accounts are not mere recitals of historical events. The writers showed evident purpose when they described the captivities as the result of the people's worship of Baal. As we noted in an earlier chapter, the Lord used the prophets to bring appropriate warning to Israel and to Judah. The crisis of Baal worship became very clear in the contest on Mt. Carmel. In spite of the miraculous demonstration of God's power on this occasion, the people of Israel continued on their downward plunge. They had reached the point of no return. As we shall note in the next chapter, the first of the writing prophets not only preached repentance but added a new note of imminent judgment. On their failure to repent, both Israel and Judah suffered overthrow and were carried into captivity. The Former Prophets thus gave through their historical narratives the truth which the writing prophets elaborated theologically, namely, the meaning of apostasy and God's judgment upon sin.

f. The Spirit of the Lord

The descriptions of the work of the Spirit of the Lord are similar to those noted in Joshua and Judges. After Samuel anointed Saul to be king, he told Saul of a meeting he would have with a band of prophets through which the Spirit of the Lord would come mightily upon him. As a result of this experience, Saul would prophesy with these prophets and be turned into another man (1 Sam. 10:1-13). Samuel's prediction came to fulfillment, and as a result the people inquired, "Is Saul also among the prophets?" We should observe that the gift of prophecy was the outcome of the Spirit's work in him. This operation of the Spirit worked a complete change in Saul comparable to the New Testament experience of the new birth. As Saul faced the crisis concerning the men of Jabesh, the Spirit of God again came mightily upon him. Being empowered by the Holy Spirit he met the crisis. When David was anointed king, he also had the experience of the Spirit of the Lord coming mightily upon him (1 Sam. 16:13).

Since the coming of the Spirit upon David accompanied his being anointed with oil, this act would appear to be the symbol of his receiving the Holy Spirit. Peter made a significant statement which may confirm this interpretation, when he said, "God anointed Jesus of Nazareth with the Holy Spirit and with power" (Acts 10:38). This coming of the Spirit upon David enabled him to write, "The Spirit of the Lord speaks by me, his word is upon my tongue" (2 Sam. 23:2). By reason of Saul's unfaithfulness we learn that "the Spirit of the Lord departed from Saul, and an evil spirit from the Lord tormented him" (1 Sam. 16:14). These words give grounds for believing that so long as the Spirit of the Lord abode in Saul, the evil spirit was not able to trouble him. The Spirit of the Lord enabled Saul to overpower the evil spirit. This statement is almost identical in meaning with New Testament language which shows how the Holy Spirit empowers the Christian to overcome sin (Rom. 8:13; Col. 3:5).

The Spirit of the Lord came upon Jahaziel the son of Zechariah, empowering him to speak the words of the Lord (2 Chron. 20:13-17). Years later Ezra spoke of the work of the Holy Spirit in language which very fittingly serves as the conclusion of this section. Speaking of Israel, Ezra said, "Many years thou didst bear with them, and didst warn them by thy Spirit through thy prophets; yet they would not give ear" (Neh. 9:30). By this language Ezra was asserting that the prophets received their messages from the Lord through the Holy Spirit. Peter expressed this truth in almost identical language when he wrote, "No prophecy ever came by the impulse of man, but men moved by the Holy Spirit spoke from God" (2 Pet. 1:21). We need to observe again how Old Testament accounts of the person and work of the Holy Spirit follow so closely similar reports in the New Testament.

g. Life of the People of God

This theme gains increasing significance as we proceed in the development of biblical theology. From the angle of discovering the extent to which the people of God achieved the manner of life and the ethical standards which the Lord upheld for His people, this period presents some severe contrasts in character and conduct. At the same time the life of many an individual discloses disparities almost as great. Inspiring nobility of character was found in Hannah, Samuel, David, Asa, Elijah, Elisha, Hezekiah, and Josiah. Note a few character traits of some of these godly people. Hannah's prayer and her dedication of Samuel to the service of the Lord marked her as a woman of exceptional devotion to God. The friendship of David and Jonathan is almost beyond parallel in history. The heart-rending experiences through which David passed speak to us through the psalms which reflect these experiences.[15] Many psalms reflect the character of him who was a man after God's own heart (1 Sam. 13:14). Solomon paid a fitting tribute to his father's character in the words, "He walked before thee in faithfulness, in righteousness, and in uprightness of heart toward thee" (1 Kings 3:6). These tributes to David's character do not relieve us from examining forthrightly the seriousness of his sins.[16] Heinous as they were, David sincerely repented and confessed his guilt by saying, "I have sinned against the Lord." On another occasion he said, "I have sinned greatly in that I have done this thing. But now, I pray thee, take away the iniquity of thy servant; for I have done very foolishly" (2 Sam. 12:13; 1 Chron. 21:8). Psalms 32 and 51 reveal a spirit of genuine repentance and confession of sin.

The spiritual insights reflected in these two psalms possess great value for our instruction. Among other sacred truths we learn the experiential aspect of forgiveness in the words, "Blessed is he whose transgression is forgiven, who sin is covered. Blessed is the man to whom the Lord imputes no iniquity, and in whose spirit there is no deceit" (32:1, 2). David gave witness to a smiting conscience on account of unconfessed sin. In the second great penitential psalm David acknowledged the steadfast love of God shown in the mercy poured out upon him (Ps. 51:1). He had come to realize that his sin was covered. A thorough washing from his iniquities and a cleansing from his sins were necessary. Only through a spiritual purging could he be clean and again be filled with joy and gladness. He described the inner change necessary by the words, "Create in me a clean heart, O God, and put a new and right spirit within me." This redemptive language is about as explicit as anything found in the New Testament. David realized that the Holy Spirit could be taken from him if he continued to sin. He knew that the only sacrifice acceptable to God was "a broken spirit; a broken and contrite heart."

Nobility of character and faithfulness to God were shown by kings such as Asa, Hezekiah, Josiah, and others as they sought to counteract the sins of the people and to bring about reforms. Most courageous was Elijah, who could stand against Ahab, Jezebel, and all the prophets of Baal. In contrast with all this, the sins of Israel and Judah which led to their captivities revealed the deep-seatedness of their departure from God, as well as the real nature of sin both as evil acts and as wickedness of character.

For Additional Reading and Reference:

A. General Treatments:
Kaufmann, *The Religion of Israel,* pp. 245-90.
Oehler, *Theology of the Old Testament,* pp. 353-436.
Pfeiffer, *Religion in the Old Testament,* pp. 58-116.
von Rad, *Old Testament Theology,* Vol. II, pp. 6-32.
Raven, *The History of the Religion of Israel,* pp. 156-297.
Ringgren, *The Messiah in the Old Testament,* pp. 41-65.
Rowley, *The Re-Discovery of the Old Testament,* pp. 83-132.
Schultz, *Old Testament Theology,* Vol. I, pp. 139-74.
Titcomb, *Revelation in Progress,* pp. 112-235.

B. Theological Contents of the Former Prophets:
The Anchor Bible, 1 Chronicles, pp. LXIV-LXXXV.
The Interpreter's Bible, Vol. 2.
    "Joshua," pp. 548 f.
    "Judges," pp. 684-86.
    "1 and 2 Samuel," pp. 868-75.
The Interpreter's Bible, Vol. 3.
    "1 and 2 Kings," pp. 15 f.
    "1 and 2 Chronicles," pp. 342-45.
    "Ezra and Nehemiah," pp. 566 f.
The Interpreter's Dictionary of the Bible, A-D
    "Chronicles 1 and 2," pp. 573-75.
The Interpreter's Dictionary of the Bible, E-J.
    "Joshua," p. 995.
    "Judges," pp. 1022 f.
The New Bible Dictionary.
    "Joshua," pp. 663 f.
    "Judges," p. 679.
    "Kings, Books of," p. 698.

1. Deut. 1:8; 4:31; 6:10, 23; 7:8, 12; 8:18; 11:8-12, 22-32; 29:13; 34:4.
2. Josh. 1:3; 22:4; 23:5, 14, 15; 24:2-13.
3. Judg. 2:11-15, 16-23; 3:7-9, 12-15; 4:1-3; 6:1, 2; 9:56, 57; 10:6-16.
4. Josh. 1:8; 8:31; 23:6; 24:26.
5. Judg. 3:10; 6:34; 11:29; 13:25; 14:6, 19; 15:14.
6. Ex. 31:3; 35:31; Num. 11:20; 24:2; 27:18; Deut. 34:9.
7. Judg. 3:7, 12; 10:6; 17:6; 21:25, etc.
8. Pss. 8, 19, 24, 29, 33, 47, 74, 89, 93, 95, 96, 99, 104. See Part III, I, 3, a.
9. Ps. 26:2, 3. *See also* 17:3; 66:10; and 105:19.

10. 1 Sam. 1:3, 11; 4:4; 15:2; 17:45; 2 Sam. 6:2, 18; 1 Kings 19:14; Ps. 24:10; 46:7, 10.

11. 1 Sam. 15:2; 2 Sam. 7:8; 1 Chron. 17:7.

12. Is. 3:15; Jer. 6:9; Hag. 1:5, 7; Zech. 1:3, 4; Mal. 1:4, etc.

13. Gal. 3:19, 20; 1 Tim. 2:5; Heb. 8:6; 9:15; 12:24.

14. 1 Cor. 3:9, 16, 17; 6:19, 20; 2 Cor. 6:14 — 7:1; Eph. 2:19-22; Heb. 3:1-6; 8:5; 9:23-28; 1 Pet. 2: 4-10; Rev. 3:12; 7:15; 11:1-19; 21:22.

15. 1 Sam. 19:11, 12 (Ps. 59); 22:1 (Ps. 34); 23:14 (Ps. 63); 24:5 (Pss. 57, 142).

16. 2 Sam. 11:2-27; 24:1-9; 1 Chron. 21:1-17.

CHAPTER V
GOD'S REVELATION THROUGH THE PROPHETS OF THE ASSYRIAN PERIOD, 746-625 B.C.

1. Introduction

a. Problems Centering in Literary Criticism

We are able to give only passing notice to problems of literary criticism, leaving it to the reader to consult appropriate discussions in Bible dictionaries, introductions to commentaries, and works in the field of biblical criticism. The date of the prophet Joel is pertinent for our studies. Two extremes in scholarly opinions find expression here. The traditional view places Joel among the earliest of the writing prophets, in what may be called the pre-Assyrian period. Other scholars date his work among the last, in the time of the Babylonian exile or even the Persian period. Since evidence is lacking for determining this question, I am presenting two considerations which may lead to an early date for the writing of the book. The first is that of the position of Joel among the Minor Prophets. All scholars recognize a general chronological scheme in the order of these books. Since this obtains with regard to the other books in this group, it is natural to conclude that it applies also to Joel. In the second place, the nature of the contents would also place it among the earlier of the Minor Prophets. Joel's great burden has to do with the Day of the Lord, which for him was just about to be ushered in. This great prophetic theme belongs to the time of Hosea, Isaiah, Amos, and Micah, because these prophets were expounding imminent judgment, framed in the language of the Day of the Lord. To place this prophetic work late makes it an anachronism.

The problem of the unity of the Book of Isaiah also confronts us. While the bulk of modern scholars hold to a second and a third Isaiah, the case is not closed against a single author of the book. One's judgment is placed under severest test in attempting to decide this question. I am inclined to believe that there are two sides to the question, so that the solution to the problem is not entirely an either-or as to the unity of the book. There are elements of unity which still remain. At the same time it seems irrefutable that some of the sublimest truths and profoundest revelation may have had a later origin than the time of the prophet Isaiah, the son of Amoz.[1] By reason of the distinctive nature of chapters 40 — 66 I am giving a special treatment of this portion in the following chapter. I see no need for giving attention to other critical problems having to do with the books of the prophets, the most acute being that centering in the date of the Book of Daniel. For the purposes of biblical theology, inquiry concerning the date of the writing of this book has little bearing on the question, so long as we recognize its contents as presenting the prophetic messages of the prophet Daniel.

b. Method of Approach to Prophetic Revelation

Since the genius of biblical theology study centers in the chronological unfolding of divine revelation, it seems appropriate to divide the writing prophets into four groups according to the respective periods in which they lived. First, the Assyrian period, *c.*746 B.C. to 625 B.C. Here I shall include the prophets Obadiah, Joel, Jonah, Hosea, Amos, Isaiah, and Micah. Second, the Chaldean period, *c.*625 B.C. to 585 B.C., in which the prophets Nahum, Zephaniah, Habakkuk, and Jeremiah lived. Third, the period of the Babylonian exile, c. 602 B.C. to 534 B.C. This is the time of Ezekiel and Daniel. Fourth, the Persian period, *c.* 520 B.C. to 430 B.C. Here we find the prophets Haggai, Zechariah, and Malachi.

I shall present the material according to major doctrines based upon the theological ideas apparent in the prophetic messages. The treatment will proceed according to the following outline, with variations according to subject material.

1. The God of Israel.
2. The Spoken and Written Word of God.
3. Israel's Election Actualized by Covenant Relation with God.
4. The Day of the Lord — Judgment.
5. The Messiah and the Messianic Kingdom.
6. The Latter Days — Prophetic Eschatology.
   (a) Restoration of Israel.
   (b) God's Redemption and Salvation.
   (c) Outpouring of the Holy Spirit.
   (d) God's Servant Given as a Light to the Nation.
7. Life of the People of God.
8. Nature of Sin — Man's Sinfulness.
9. Repentance, Faith, and Regeneration.
10. Death and Sheol.
11. Satan.

A little study will show that the first six topics, excluding number 2, lay at the very heart of the prophetic messages. Naturally we begin with what is written concerning the God of Israel. This leads to the covenant relation established between God and His people. Because of Israel's apostasy the prophets, especially the earlier ones, had much to say concerning the coming judgment which would take place in the Day of the Lord. In view of this imminent judgment, the prophets sought to challenge faith by looking to the coming One, the Messiah, and to the Messiah's kingdom. This would inaugurate a new era lying beyond the Day of the Lord called the Latter Days. In connection with this coming age, the prophets unfold their eschatology. They see the restoration of Israel. They depict this restoration as centering in God's redemption and salvation. In the coming era God will pour out His Spirit upon all mankind. It is the time in which God's Servant will be given as a light to the nations.

The remaining topics are also very essential, even though they do not fit into the development of thought just presented. I consider it essential to observe along the way what the Scriptures tell about the life of the people of God. The prophets also spoke significantly of the nature of sin and of man's sinfulness. We gain some basic ideas as to the nature of repentance, faith, and regeneration. There are a few notes concerning man's life beyond the grave. Significantly the prophets spoke of Satan. Incidentally we learn a few things concerning man's nature involving body, soul, and spirit.

My method will be to present the teachings of the prophets according to these twelve topics in each of the four periods of prophets. This will make it possible to grasp the unfolding divine revelation according to the periods. By this method we may achieve a proper perspective of each prophet's message as it stands in the period in which he lived. I have no interest in stressing details of the unfolding revelation, but I do firmly believe that the messages of the prophets had a distinctive thrust.

2. The God of Israel: His Nature and Manifestations

Before viewing the prophetic revelation given by the God of Israel we need to examine a very important critical problem. Briefly, it is this: were the prophets guardians of monotheism or did they lead Israel from a polytheism up to monotheism? The latter view is advocated by those who apply the theory of evolution to the development of religion from animism through various forms of polytheism to monotheism. As applied to the history of Israel, these scholars hold that the prophets were agents for leading Israel to monotheism. It seems very evident that this group of scholars have been guided more by their philosophy than by the Bible's own presentation of its religious history. In earlier chapters I noted that the monotheism of the patriarchs and of Moses was very clear, provided we accept the Bible's own presentation of its religious history. The rewriting of Israel's religious history, in order to make it agree with the evolutionary philosophy of religion, is utterly unscientific. Historical data show the deterioration of religion from monotheism to all the other degraded forms. It is a clear case of distorting these well-authenticated historical data in order to make history agree with these scholars' philosophical prepossessions. On this account I shall not introduce a formal discussion of monotheism as found among the prophets. The reader may investigate this problem for himself.

a. Joel

Joel's great burden was to warn Israel that the Day of the Lord was near (1:15). But he had a still greater concern that Israel should return to the Lord their God, "for he is gracious and merciful, slow to anger, and abounding in steadfast love, and repents of evil" (2:13). Looking to the future, Joel predicted a restoration of the fortunes of Judah and Jerusalem upon their repentance. He continued his message by showing all that God would do in behalf of His people. He would remove their enemies; He would restore the early and the latter rain; He would again make it possible for them to enjoy an abundance of food. Certainly the Lord had dealt wondrously with His people. Joel concluded his message, "You shall know that I am in the midst of Israel, and that I, the Lord, am your God and there is none else. And my people shall never again be put to shame." This brief declaration showed that God even determined weather conditions, and that He was actually in their midst. He possessed the majesty of being the one and only God.

The Lord gave a prediction through which He revealed the nature of His being: "I will pour out my spirit on all flesh" (2:28). This led Israel to grasp the truth that the Lord was by nature a being so constituted that He could come upon all mankind in the person of His Spirit. The fulfillment of this prediction on the day of Pentecost led Peter to say by way of explanation that God the Father through the enthroned Christ had sent the Holy Spirit (Acts 2:1-36). The prediction given through Joel possessed the potential meaning of the triune being of God.

b. Jonah

Jonah gave a brief but comprehensive confession of faith in the words, "I fear the Lord, the God of heaven, who made the sea and the dry land" (1:9). Referring to God as Creator became the usual way of expressing the distinctive nature of Israel's God. When God saw that the people of Nineveh repented at the preaching of Jonah, He spared the city. This mercy of God angered Jonah but at the same time he acknowledged, "Thou art a gracious God and merciful, slow to anger, and abounding in steadfast love, and repentest of evil" (4:2). Both Jonah and Joel built up a clear image of the Lord, who shows love and mercy in the presence of penitent sinners.

Bound up in Jonah's story are God's unique and varied workings in history. The Lord hurled the great wind upon the sea. He appointed a great fish to swallow Jonah and later to vomit him out. He threatened the overthrow of Nineveh within forty days. He caused a plant to come up to be a shade for Jonah. He prepared a worm to attack the plant. Finally He had a sultry east wind blow on Jonah. All these acts of God reveal His nature and power. While many scholars regard the Book of Jonah as an allegory or parable, the interpretation of the book as a historical document follows the obvious sense of language. Jonah was a prophet, tied in with Israel's genealogy as the son of Amittai.

c. Hosea

Against the background of Israel's spiritual harlotry, the prophet Hosea spoke God's words of love and mercy: "I will betroth you to me in righteousness and in justice, in steadfast love, and in mercy" (2:19). Later we have God's words, "When Israel was a child, I loved him, and out of Egypt I called my son" (11:1). Like a heartbroken father, the Lord exclaimed, "How can I give you up, O Ephraim! How can I hand you over, O Israel! . . . My heart recoils within me, my compassion grows warm and tender" (11:8). The Lord commanded Israel to return to Him, adding the promise, "I will heal their faithlessness; I will love them freely, for my anger has turned from them" (14:1, 4). Such words of love and mercy, expressed to a people who were unfaithful to their bond of spiritual marriage, revealed the very heart of God.

Along with this message of steadfast love and mercy, God spoke words of judgment: "I will put an end to the kingdom of the house of Israel." Israel had become "Not pitied" and "Not my people" (1:4-8). This requires us to think of God who is at once a God of pity and a God without pity. It involves the reconciliation of justice and mercy in His nature. Such a being is "the Lord the God of hosts, The Lord is his name" (12:5).

d. Amos

Amos's prophetic work opened with the stern words that for the transgressions of Damascus, Gaza, Tyre, Edom, Ammon, Moab, Judah, and Israel, the Lord would not revoke the punishments due to them (1:2). He pronounced woe to those at ease in Zion and to those living in luxury (6:1-8). He was calling for a judgment by fire, and only through the prophet's intercession was the judgment stayed (7:4-6). Because of His holiness (4:2) He commanded, "Let justice roll down like waters, and righteousness like an ever-flowing stream" (5:24).

The prophet added God's note of love and mercy in the words, "Hate evil, and love good, and establish justice in the gate; it may be that the Lord, the God of hosts, will be gracious to the remnant of Joseph" (5:15). When the Lord gave Amos the vision of locusts by which He disclosed the impending crisis of judgment, the prophet interceded in Israel's behalf. In response to this plea, the Lord repented concerning the sending of a judgment by fire. But by reason of Israel's continued sin God did bring judgment upon the nation. The book closes, nevertheless, with the most gracious prediction of a coming era in which the Lord would bless His people (9:11-15). The nature of God, revealed in this book, confronts us again with the problem of holding in proper focus God's justice and His steadfast love.

The bringing of judgment upon the several nations involved God's intervention in history. Secular historians who wrote the history of these nations were likely unaware of these predicted judgments. Accordingly their accounts of the overthrow of these nations gave no recognition to God's part in their overthrow. This fact makes these two chapters of Amos quite vivid in showing God's work in history. The people of Israel, on the other hand, had a long history in which they knew what God had done for them (2:10, 11; 3:1; 9:7). Throughout the Book of Amos, the Lord showed to Israel that His actions in the affairs of men during the preceding ages provided grounds for believing that He would continue to work on their behalf in the future. The Lord had predicted not only His bringing of judgment upon Israel, but also the restoration of David's kingdom, including the rejuvenating of Israel's land (9:14, 15).

The Lord used yet another way of bringing home His message of judgment to Israel. His withholding of rain, smiting with blight and mildew, sending of pestilence, and overthrowing of some of them with fiery judgments, all showed that He was the God of creation, and, therefore, that all countermanding change came through His intervention. On this account the Lord said, "Prepare to meet your God, O Israel!" The prophet supported that command with the language: "For lo, he who forms the mountains, and creates the wind, and declares to man what is his thought; who makes the morning darkness, and treads on the heights of the earth — the Lord, the God of hosts, is his name" (4:12, 13)! The prophet carried this point further in the words, "He who made the Pleiades and Orion, and turns deep darkness into the morning, and darkens the day into night, who calls for the waters of the sea, and pours them out upon the surface of the earth, the Lord is his name, who makes destruction flash forth against the strong, so that destruction comes upon the fortress" (5:8, 9). Amos further exalts God as Creator in these words: "The Lord, God of hosts, he who touches the earth and it melts, and all who dwell in it mourn, and all of it rises like the Nile, and sinks again, like the Nile of Egypt; who builds his upper chambers in the heavens, and founds his vault upon the earth; who calls for the waters of the sea, and pours them out upon the surface of the earth — the Lord is his name" (9:5, 6). Aside from the distinctive purpose of noting this prophet's view of God these quotations describing God's creative activity are brimming with interest. Amos covered the activities of God all the way from regulation of weather conditions and control of cosmic changes of the earth on up to the creation of the heavenly bodies. Amos magnifies the wonders of God's creative work in superb poetry. Undoubtedly the prophet sought to lay hold of the cumulative value of all of these creative acts and to present the lesson to be gained in crying out, "The Lord, the God of hosts, is his name!" This prepares us to gain the true perspective of the prophetic presentations given by the God of creation. We observe this already in the Pentateuch and we should continue to note the frequency with which the prophets spoke concerning the Lord as the Creator and the content of their messages.

e. Isaiah (1 — 39)

(1) The Sovereign Majesty of God. In the mind of Isaiah the sovereign majesty of God lay at the very center of his concept of the Lord (Is. 2:10-21; 24:14; 26:10). He presented this sovereign majesty as it affects the ungodly in the words, "Enter into the rock, and hide in the dust from before the terror of the Lord, and from the glory of his majesty." Again he commented in the same vein, "And men shall enter the caves of the rocks and the holes of the ground, from before the terror of the Lord, and from the glory of his majesty, when he rises to terrify the earth." These passages emphasize the idea that God's majesty confronted the ungodly to cause them to realize that the terror of the Lord would be manifested in His acts of judgment. As for the righteous, Isaiah said, "They lift up their voices, they sing for joy; over the majesty of the Lord they shout from the west. Therefore in the east give glory to the Lord. . . . From the ends of the earth we hear songs of praise, of glory to the Righteous One." The idea of God's sovereign majesty became apparent already in chapter 1, where Isaiah presented in legal terms the case of the Lord against Judah.

The Lord charged Judah with rebellion against Him. Their sinfulness involved their entire being. Their sacrifices no longer expressed the true spirit of worship. The only cure would be an inner cleansing. The Lord of hosts, the Mighty One of Israel, brought the charge. The Lord had granted Isaiah a vision of Himself in which Isaiah "saw the Lord sitting upon a throne, high and lifted up; and his train filled the temple." The seraphim were calling one to another and saying, "Holy, holy, holy is the Lord of hosts; the whole earth is full of his glory" (6:1-3). As Isaiah looked forward to the coming days of the Messiah, he declared that the people would see "the glory of the Lord, the majesty of our God" (35:1, 2). Glory and majesty belonged to Israel's Lord and God. Further study of God's attributes will show how Isaiah brought them to a focus in God's sovereign majesty.

(2) The Holiness and Righteousness of God. Isaiah spoke of God's holiness and righteousness in significant language: "They have forsaken the Lord, they have despised the Holy One of Israel, they are utterly estranged" (1:4). In his love song concerning the Lord's vineyard, Isaiah wrote, "But the Lord of hosts is exalted in justice, and the Holy God shows himself holy in righteousness" (5:16). Thus he described the justice and the righteousness of God as revealing His holy nature. He showed how fundamentally justice, righteousness, and holiness are one and how they set forth the nature of the Lord. In Isaiah's vision, the call of the seraphim one to another intensifies the meaning bound up in the word "holy." Isaiah led the people of Judah to see the tension that exists between destruction and righteousness. The remnant of Israel "will lean upon the Lord, the Holy One of Israel, in truth. . . . Destruction is decreed, overflowing with righteousness" (10:20-22). Finally the decreed destruction will come by righteousness. This characterized the judgment of the Holy One of Israel.

Isaiah in his "apocalypse" (24 — 27) describes the awfulness of the coming destruction upon Judah but then pictures singing for joy and hearing songs of praise (24:14-16). Here the majesty of the Lord and His righteousness are brought together. Thus Isaiah made it clear that even though the judgments of God would be just and terrible, the righteous would still be able to sing songs of praise and of glory to the Righteous One. In the predictions of Israel's glorious future the Lord said, "Behold, I am laying in Zion for a foundation a stone, a tested stone, a precious cornerstone, of a sure foundation: 'He who believes will not be in haste.' And I will make justice the line, and righteousness the plummet" (28:16, 17). Both Paul and Peter caught the Messianic significance of these words.[2] The Lord made it clear to His people that the spiritual temple which He would build would be characterized by righteousness. What a marvelous picture of the Messiah's spiritual temple! This language which vividly describes God's holiness and righteousness also intensifies the meaning of these attributes as they pertain to the Lord. Holiness sets forth that which is central in the nature of God, that which is pure and separate from sin. Righteousness takes on added meaning when Isaiah shows how the holy God of Israel deals with His people. The conformity of God's acts with His own holy nature stresses the nature of His righteousness.

(3) The God of Love and Mercy. Perhaps the most graphic picture of God's love and mercy shines forth from the "love song concerning his vineyard." The positive aspects of God's love for His people find poetic description in what the owner does for his vineyard. Just as the grower of grapes does all in his power to produce an abundance of grapes, in the same manner the Lord cared for Israel so that they would produce the spiritual fruit that He desired. All this care and attention manifested God's love and mercy. But they produced wild grapes. They were shedding blood and dealing unrighteously with one another. They lived luxuriously. They drank strong drink; drew iniquity with cords of falsehood; called evil good and good evil; were wise in their own eyes, shrewd in their own sight. In spite of the Lord's manifestation of love for His people, they persisted in their evil ways. "They do not regard the deeds of the Lord, or see the work of his hands" (5:12). As God dealt with His people in love and mercy, it could most truthfully be said, "The Lord of hosts is exalted in justice, and the Holy God shows himself holy in righteousness" (5:16). This paragraph makes it entirely clear that God's exercise of love and mercy did not exclude His justice.

Isaiah displayed God's love and mercy also in the song of thanksgiving (12). Looking forward to a future day of repentance Isaiah quoted Israel in the language, "I will give thanks to thee, O Lord, for though thou wast angry with me, thy anger turned away, and thou didst comfort me. Behold, God is my salvation; I will trust, and will not be afraid; for the Lord God is my strength and my song, and he has become my salvation." Isaiah showed Israel that God became the salvation of those who repented of their sins, and enabled them with joy to draw water from the wells of salvation.

Later Isaiah said, "The Lord will have compassion on Jacob and will again choose Israel, and will set them in their own land, and aliens will join them and will cleave to the house of Jacob" (14:1). Isaiah again voiced this note of salvation which magnifies God's love and mercy in the words, "He will swallow up death for ever, and the Lord God will wipe away tears from all faces, and the reproach of his people he will take away from all the earth; for the Lord has spoken. It will be said on that day, 'Lo, this is our God; we have waited for him, that he might save us. This is the Lord; we have waited for him; let us be glad and rejoice in his salvation'" (25:8, 9). In a setting where the Lord pronounced woe upon rebellious children, the note of love again became evident in the words, "Therefore the Lord waits to be gracious to you; therefore he exalts himself to show mercy to you. For the Lord is a God of justice; blessed are all those who wait for him. Yea, O people in Zion who dwell at Jerusalem; you shall weep no more. He will surely be gracious to you at the sound of your cry; when he hears it, he will answer you" (30:18, 19).

These passages which proclaim the love and mercy of God become all the more meaningful when we examine them against the background of God's judgments upon the ungodly. These contexts prepare us for the great outpouring of God's love when He gave His Son to suffer and die that we might be saved.

(4) The God of Judgment. In some of the portions just reviewed the God of love and mercy also stands forth as the God of judgment. These two attributes do not need to be reconciled. A human approach to this study may create such a problem, but Isaiah recognized no conflict here. He could write or speak with entire freedom on these two attributes. In the same contexts in which Isaiah presented the case of the Lord against Judah, and spoke very forcibly of imminent judgment, he quoted God's invitation to Judah, "Come now, let us reason together." God promised to cleanse them if they repented, adding, nevertheless, "But if you refuse and rebel, you shall be devoured by the sword; for the mouth of the Lord has spoken" (1:18-20). A section such as 2:6 — 4:1 gives a graphic picture of the Lord's judgment. He gave stern warning, "Enter into the rock, and hide in the dust from before the terror of the Lord, and from the glory of his majesty. . . . And men shall enter the caves of the rocks and the holes of the ground, from before the terror of the Lord, and from the glory of his majesty, when he rises to terrify the earth."

Later in this section Isaiah added, "The Lord has taken his place to contend, he stands to judge his people. The Lord enters into judgment with the elders and princes of his people" (3:13, 14). In such language the Lord revealed His own nature as the God of judgment. Looking again at the parable of the vineyard, we see that the repeated woes pronounced upon ungodly Judah show how "the anger of the Lord was kindled against his people, [and] . . . for all this his anger is not turned away and his hand is stretched out still" (5:25). Isaiah repeated this expression at least four times ; each time it was the concluding word of judgment upon Judah.

In another message Isaiah wrote, "Behold, the Lord is coming forth out of his place to punish the inhabitants of the earth for their iniquity, and the earth will disclose the blood shed upon her, and will no more cover her slain" (26:21). In the same strain he said, "For the Lord has a day of vengeance, a year of recompense for the cause of Zion" (34:8). In these passages and others Isaiah made it clear that God's people brought these judgments upon themselves by their continued sinning. It belonged to the very nature of God to judge sin. To summarize, we note that the Lord revealed Himself in majestic sovereignty, in holiness and in righteousness, in love and mercy, and in judgment. A profound unity exists among these attributes. These constitute the high peak of God's revelation of Himself in the Old Testament.

(5) The God of Creation. References to the God of creation in Isaiah 1 — 39 are rare as compared to those in chapters 40 — 66. This fact may have a bearing on the problem of a first and a second Isaiah. The first reference to creation occurs in the remarkable Messianic portion in 4:2-6. It is plainly eschatological in character but it points up the Lord's creativity in the Messianic age. After referring to the branch of the Lord and to the Lord's cleansing work among the people of Israel, Isaiah wrote, "Then the Lord will create over the whole site of Mount Zion and over her assemblies a cloud by day, and smoke and the shining of a flaming fire by night; for over all the glory there will be a canopy and a pavilion." Isaiah used the common verb *bara* (create), which predicts a definite creative work by God, which He will perform in the Messianic age. Leaving for later consideration the predicted creation of the new heavens and a new earth as described in chapters 65 and 66, we may gather that there is a vital connection between the predictions in chapter 4 and those in chapters 65 and 66.

When Isaiah described the coming Day of the Lord, he used the language which plainly reflected God's creative work: "For the stars of the heavens and their constellations will not give their light; the sun will be dark at its rising and the moon will not shed its light" (13:10). Since the Day of the Lord will manifest God's judgment, the implication of this language is that only God the Creator could effect these changes with reference to the stars, sun, and moon.

In a later setting Isaiah wrote, "In that day men will regard their Maker, and their eyes will look to the Holy One of Israel" (17:7). Isaiah recorded the prayer of Hezekiah in which he set forth the glory of the Lord, when he prayed, "O Lord of hosts, God of Israel, who art enthroned above the cherubim, thou art the God, thou alone, of all the kingdoms of the earth; thou hast made heaven and earth" (37:16). Certainly Isaiah had a clear concept of God as Creator, but we are caused to wonder why he made so few references to Him as such. I shall reserve for later consideration the bearing of this fact on the unity of Isaiah.

(6) The God Who Acts in History. Our studies thus far deepen the realization that the Lord of Israel acted in history. God's arraignment of Israel (chap. 1) concludes with the predictions of what He would do in view of Judah's apostasy. He would involve Himself in the affairs of Judah, giving vent to His wrath and avenging Himself on His foes. Words of hope and also of judgment follow: "Zion shall be redeemed by justice, and those in her who repent, by righteousness. But rebels and sinners shall be destroyed together, and those who forsake the Lord shall be consumed" (1:27, 28). The entire book of Isaiah demonstrated how God accomplished these ends among the people of Judah. The love song concerning His vineyard most vividly predicts the God who acts: "He will raise a signal for a nation afar off, and whistle for it from the ends of the earth; and lo, swiftly, speedily it comes" (5:26)! The nation which came from afar was, clearly, Babylon. From a secular historian's point of view, Babylon's attack on Judah gave no evidence of what God did to bring it about. The king of Babylon was not consciously fulfilling God's command. The nation of Judah lay in the pathway of the two great world powers of the time. These kingdoms were in continual warfare, and the overthrow of Judah was a relatively small detail in this conflict. Nevertheless, the Lord whistled for it from the ends of the earth, and speedily the nation of Babylon came on the scene. God was acting in history.

When King Ahaz came into conflict with Rezin and Pekah, he was greatly disturbed. The Lord sent Isaiah to Ahaz to give him advice in this crisis. Isaiah quoted the Lord as saying that Syria and Israel would not conquer Judah. Their plans would not come to pass. Within sixty-five years Ephraim would be broken to pieces so that it would no longer be a people. This promise to Ahaz made a tremendous demand on his faith, as became evident in the Lord's words, "If you will not believe, surely you shall not be established" (7:9). Syria and Israel knew nothing of this communication. God intervened and fulfilled this prediction. The Lord challenged the faith of Ahaz by giving him the most extraordinary sign as proof that the plans of Rezin and Pekah would not be carried out. It involved the most wonderful miracle of human history: A virgin, especially designated the virgin,[4] "shall conceive and bear a son, and shall call his name Immanuel" (7:14). The infancy narratives of Matthew and Luke describe in detail and with precision the manner in which the Lord fulfilled this prediction.

Isaiah continued with this eschatological aspect of God's acting in history in the two predictions of the coming Messiah (9:11). For our present purpose observe that Isaiah dated this future act as coming to pass "in the latter time." He continued, "He will make glorious the way of the sea, the land beyond the Jordan, Galilee of the nations" (9:1). Farther on he said, "For to us a child is born, to us a son is given; and the government will be upon his shoulder. . . . Of the increase of his government and of peace there will be no end, upon the throne of David. . . . The zeal of the Lord of hosts will do this" (vv. 6, 7). The fulfillment of this became all the more humanly impossible when the Davidic kingdom was overthrown, but the birth of Christ showed how marvelously God directed the course of history in bringing it to pass. Add to this, "In that day the root of Jesse shall stand as an ensign to the peoples" (11:10, 11). These and other Messianic predictions which involved God's direction of the course of history for their fulfillment, served as challenges to the faith of God's people. No less marvelous were the predictions concerning Babylon, Moab, Damascus, Egypt, and other nations (12 — 23), all of which required God's direction of human affairs for their fulfillment.

This discussion of the God of Israel could well include another sub-heading, "The God of Redemption," but since this is almost entirely eschatological in nature, I shall give it consideration in the section, "The Latter Days." Isaiah's presentation of the God of Israel was full and complete. Although he did not present any distinctively new ideas concerning God, the entire revelation of God's nature, attributes, manifestations, and acts, stands as a landmark of revealed truth.

f. Micah

Micah's presentation of the God of Israel bears great similarity to that of Isaiah's. He launched his prophetic message with a forthright presentation of the Lord God as a witness against Judah and Israel. From His holy temple the Lord went forth to tread upon the high places of the earth and to destroy it with a mighty earthquake and violent storm. This language, whether to be understood as literal or figurative, was very forceful. Micah explained, "All this is for the transgression of Jacob and for the sins of the house of Israel" (1:2-9). This came as God's judgment upon all forms of wickedness and sin found among His people. They coveted fields and seized them. They oppressed a man and his house. They hated good and loved evil. They abhorred justice and perverted all equity. For all this Micah declared, "Zion shall be plowed as a field; Jerusalem shall become a heap of ruins, and the mountain of the house a wooded height" (3:12). Thus Micah led his people to see that their God was a God of judgment. His nature required Him to bring punishment for sin.

Micah turned abruptly from this message to that of future blessing. He described in language identical with that of Isaiah,[5] what the Lord had in store for His people. A restoration would take place because their God was loving and kind and merciful. Micah closed his prophetic message with words hardly matched anywhere in all the Bible: "Who is a God like thee, pardoning iniquity and passing over transgression for the remnant of his inheritance? . . . He will again have compassion upon us, he will tread our iniquities under foot. Thou wilt cast all our sins into the depths of the sea. Thou wilt show faithfulness to Jacob and steadfast love to Abraham, as thou hast sworn to our fathers from the days of old" (7:18-20).

The judgments God brought upon Judah and Samaria manifested His acts in history. Micah predicted succinctly, "Zion shall be plowed as a field; Jerusalem shall become a heap of ruins" (3:12). History records that God used Babylon as a tool to bring this destruction.

3. The Spoken and Written Word of God

When the nature of the prophetic gift was presented (Chap. III), I was concerned to establish the historicity of God's revelation through the prophets. We observed the various forms of expression by which they introduced their messages. Let us now examine these claims made by the prophets with respect to God's having spoken through them. This study demonstrates how the distinctive nature of the prophetic messages undergirded and determined the concept of the written word of God expressed in the terms *Holy Scriptures* and *Sacred Writings*. Incidentally, let us observe any evidence which gives support to the concept of an already existing body of written materials which are now a part of the Bible. The question is this: Did the prophets have access to the Pentateuch as a whole or to any part of it? And further, did the writing prophets give any expression as to the unique character of such writing that would supply to us basic ideas underlying the whole concept of biblical inspiration?

a. Obadiah, Joel, and Jonah

The brief message of Obadiah contains at least two statements which definitely set forth the authority of God's spoken word. Verse 1 reads, "Thus says the Lord God concerning Edom: We have heard tidings from the Lord, and a messenger has been sent among the nations." In his enlargement of the great prophetic theme, the Day of the Lord, Obadiah closed with the authoritative note, "for the Lord has spoken" (v. 18), an expression that certainly gave emphasis to his message.

Joel and Jonah add very little to the subject under consideration. The simple pronouncement, "The word of the Lord that came to Joel," introduced God's message of the awful judgment to be brought upon the people in the imminent Day of the Lord. He was speaking words of divine authority from which Israel could not escape. The prophet Jonah learned through a most harrowing experience that he could not afford to disobey the word of God. After the Lord had delivered Jonah from the belly of the whale, He repeated the command to go to Nineveh with the message of its coming overthrow. This time Jonah obeyed and so recognized the Lord's absolute authority.

b. Hosea

The prophet Hosea gave repeated witness to the Lord's speaking to him. The frequency intensified the impact of his message. The prophet appears to have made a number of references to the Ten Commandments and to the Mosaic covenant.[6] Israel had forgotten the law of their God and had broken their covenant with Him. The manner in which he made the references to the Ten Commandments and to the law of God does not determine whether this was a written body of law or only what had been preserved through oral tradition. Neither does it become clear whether the scope of this body of written material or oral tradition includes the entire Pentateuch or only Deuteronomy. It is evident that the Lord made definite reference to the Sinaitic covenant and to a body of written law based upon this covenant. These references do, however, not give conclusive evidence for the existence of the Pentateuch as it now appears in the Bible. In passing we should note in Hosea's book some definitive statements concerning the office of the prophet. God said, "I spoke to the prophets; it was I who multiplied visions, and through the prophets gave parables. . . . By a prophet the Lord brought Israel up from Egypt, and by a prophet he was preserved" (12:10-13). According to this language the prophets were the official spokesmen of the Lord. Their words possessed divine authority.

c. Amos

The prophet Amos supported his words of judgment with repeated uses of the expressions, "Thus says the Lord" and "Thus the Lord God showed me." This was not a mere literary device but rather a most effective means of presenting the authoritative word of the Lord. Amos also referred to the line of prophets from Moses onward, through whom the Lord revealed His secrets (2:11; 3:7). He gave witness to the law of the Lord (2:4). The language implies a written body of statutes *(torah)* given when Israel entered into covenant relationship with God. Amos gave his final thrust with regard to the word of the Lord when he wrote, " 'Behold, the days are coming,' says the Lord God, 'when I will send a famine on the land; . . . of hearing the words of the Lord. . . . They shall run to and fro, to seek the word of the Lord, but they shall not find it' " (8:11, 12). Undoubtedly the people of God inwardly recognized the authority of His words, and when He sent this famine they became greatly concerned to find them.

d. Isaiah (1 — 39)

Isaiah introduced his prophetic message with the words, "Hear, O heavens, and give ear, O earth; for the Lord has spoken" (1:2). This introduction to the Lord's arraignment of Judah and Israel assumed the absolute authority of the Lord who spoke. The Lord's plea with the people took the form of a plea: "Come now, let us reason together, says the Lord: though your sins are like scarlet, they shall be as white as snow; though they are red like crimson, they shall become like wool. If you are willing and obedient, you shall eat the good of the land; but if you refuse and rebel, you shall be devoured by the sword; for the mouth of the Lord has spoken" (1:18-20). The authority of these words is at once apparent. The closing statement stands as a forceful climax to the Lord's appeal to His people. Isaiah intensified this emphatic statement when he introduced a message of warning by applying the titles, "the Lord of hosts" and "the Mighty One of Israel" (1:24, 26). This emphatic way of introducing words of the Lord continues throughout the book and supports the unique character of the prophet's messages.

Isaiah also gave more or less explicit references to the law of Moses, for example, in this address: "Hear the word of the Lord, you rulers of Sodom! Give ear to the teaching *(torah)* of our God, you people of Gomorrah" (1:10)! The use of the word *torah* in this connection has great significance because it is the word applied to the Mosaic law. It possesses a broader connotation, however, and could refer to specific teachings of God given at that time. The reference to the law of the Lord as found in 5:24 appears to concern quite definitely the law given at Mt. Sinai. It does not appear to refer to teachings recently given, but rather to the long existing body of Mosaic law. The expression, "To the teaching *(torah)* and to the testimony" (8:20), would seem to carry the same meaning. The clearest reference to the Mosaic law occurs in the charge, "They have transgressed the laws, violated the statutes, broken the everlasting covenant" (24:5). Here the law and the covenant stand in close relationship. The covenant instituted at Sinai was an ever-lasting covenant that served as the authoritative basis of the law. The expression, "the book of the Lord" (34:16), had baffled interpreters. To whatever body of writing Isaiah referred, whether to the law of Moses, to his own writing, or to some other book, a special significance attached to this book. It relates to the unique character of the written word of God.

4. Israel's Election Actualized by Covenant Relation with God

a. Obadiah

Obadiah's burden had to do with Edom, which had done great violence to Israel. His condemnation of Edom had a broader aspect than merely a brother's rejoicing at the ruin of a people with whom there had been many conflicts. The Day of the Lord was near. Since the people of Edom had polluted the holy mountain, they themselves would suffer judgment. The holy mountain with its center, Jerusalem, was a symbol of Israel's special relation to the Lord. God had chosen Israel to be His own people. He had promised them the land of Canaan. Through their nation all the peoples of the world would be blessed. This blessing would go forth from the holy city, Mt. Zion. Since Israel was the chosen people of God, "the kingdom shall be the Lord's" (v. 21).

b. Hosea

Hosea stands first among the prophets in the presentation of Israel's election which was actualized by covenant relation with the Lord. In spite of certain difficult interpretational problems the teachings of the Book of Hosea stand forth with great clarity. The message of the book takes its beginning with the marriage of Hosea to Gomer and with the birth of three children. The name of each was symbolic. The firstborn son was Jezreel, whose name was prophetic of Israel's downfall as a nation. The Lord commanded that the second child, a daughter, should be called, Not pitied, because He would "no more have pity on the house of Israel, to forgive them at all." The Lord commanded that the third child, a son, should receive the name, Not my people, signifying "you are not my people and I am not your God" (1:4-9). The prophet struck a prophetic note in the words, "Yet the number of the people of Israel shall be like the sand of the sea, which can be neither measured nor numbered; and in the place where it was said to them, 'You are not my people,' it shall be said to them, 'Son of the living God.' . . . Say to your brother, 'My people,' and to your sister, 'She has obtained pity' " (1:10 — 2:1). This leads us into the heart of the message of the book, which described God's relation to His people, under the figure of a spiritual marriage bond. The prophet wove into his book a number of the significant uses of the word "covenant" (*berith*),[7] which show that the marriage bond stood as the symbol of the covenant relation between God and Israel. This covenant was specifically the one made by the Lord with Israel at Mt. Sinai. Let us study Hosea's exposition of the covenant built on the analogy of his marriage experience.

(1) Marriage, a Symbol of a Covenant Relation. As suggested above, the names, Not pitied (*Loruhamah*) and Not my people (*Loammi*), yield meaning when understood as symbols of God's covenant relation with Israel. This thought becomes clearer when we observe the language of God's wooing of Israel (2:14). This interpretation gains richness from references to the wilderness wanderings, and to Israel's coming out of the land of Egypt, and from their use of the expression, "My husband." Only in a covenant relation do verses 19, 20 gain full meaning: "And I will betroth you to me for ever; I will betroth you to me in righteousness and in justice, in steadfast love, and in mercy. I will betroth you to me in faithfulness; and you shall know the Lord." This vocabulary which includes words such as righteousness, justice, steadfast love, mercy, and faithfulness, is most descriptive of God's relation to Israel. By reflecting on the institution of the covenant at Mt. Sinai (Ex. 19 — 24) we discover that these words explain most clearly every aspect of the agreement. For Israel the burnt and peace offerings gave support to the concepts of consecration and fellowship. God manifested His righteousness and justice in accepting Israel's commitment through these offerings. The word *chesed* (steadfast love) describes most aptly the manifestation of God's love and mercy in delivering Israel out of Egypt. The institution of the covenant looked to the faithfulness of both God and Israel in the agreement sealed by the covenant sacrifice.

(2) Development of the Covenant Idea in Hosea. First, this was a national covenant.[8] The unfaithful wife was the nation of Israel.[9] God said, "They have broken my covenant, and transgressed my law." Here covenant and law stand in the same close relationship as existed between the Sinaitic covenant and the law. Second, the *berith* (covenant) centered in a spiritual relation. This becomes evident in practically every expression referring to this husband-wife relationship. The physical adultery described in chapter 2 is clearly symbolic of spiritual unfaithfulness. Marriage love is the most fitting symbol of covenant love. The spiritual betrothal language of 2:19, 20 is unexcelled in spiritual significance. In this relationship God desired "steadfast love and not sacrifice, the knowledge of God, rather than burnt offering" (6:6). While God had commanded Israel to bring their sacrifices, He indicated

by this language the supreme spiritual response of steadfast love and knowledge of Him which He desired of Israel. Israel had turned to Baal worship and had multiplied altars for sinning (7:16; 8:11). Hosea made an appeal for a new kind of sowing in the words, "Sow for yourselves righteousness, reap the fruit of steadfast love; break up your fallow ground, for it is the time to seek the Lord, that he may come and rain salvation upon you" (10:12). The Lord's closing appeal gave final support to the spiritual relationship expressed in the covenant when He said, "I will heal their faithlessness; I will love them freely, for my anger has turned from them" (14:4). Hosea could finally conclude, "The ways of the Lord are right, and the upright walk in them, but transgressors stumble in them" (14:9). These and other statements greatly enriched the concept of the spiritual character of Israel's relation to God through the covenant.

Third, the *berith* was accompanied by a law regulating the manner of life. This becomes evident in 4:2-6, where the sins being condemned follow the pattern of the Ten Commandments. Hosea needed to repeat these commandments since Israel had forgotten the law of their God. Fourth, a covenant was initiated by God and thus had a definite historical beginning. The Lord's institution of covenant relationship with Israel lies back of the expressions, "My people" *(Ammi)* and "She has obtained pity" *(Ruhamah)*. Israel did not seek to enter into covenant relationship with God; rather, the Lord, through His righteousness, justice, steadfast love, and mercy, had drawn Israel into this relationship. The words, "They have broken my covenant, and transgressed my law," assert the same truth (8:1).

The Lord gave further confirmation of His acts of drawing Israel into covenant relationship in the words, "When Israel was a child, I loved him, and out of Egypt I called my son" (11:1). This verse testified also to the election aspect of Israel's relation to God. The making of the covenant at Mt. Sinai actualized this election. Perhaps the strongest language supporting this idea appears in the words, "I am the Lord your God from the land of Egypt; you know no God but me, and besides me there is no savior. It was I who knew you in the wilderness" (13:4, 5). The use of the word "know" pointed to the intimacy of this relationship symbolized by marriage love.

Fifth, the covenant possessed binding quality. At the very basis of the covenant agreement lay the requirement that a covenant dare never be broken. This pointed up the seriousness of Israel's sin as expressed in the words, "But at [marg. *like*] Adam they transgressed the covenant; there they dealt faithlessly with me" (6:7). The Lord repeated this charge, saying, "They have broken my covenant, and transgressed my law" (8:1). Just as the marriage bond presupposes life-long faithfulness between husband and wife, so the covenant relationship allowed no breach. The marriage bond was the most fitting symbol from human experience which could set forth the unbreakable spiritual relationship between man and his God. Sixth, the covenant expressed a love relationship. Repeatedly God set forth the love which underlay the covenant.[10] It involved God's love for Israel and also Israel's love for God.

Seventh, God was willing to restore the covenant bond. This theme takes its beginning from the names, "My people" and "She has obtained pity" (2:1), and continues on to the words, "I will heal their faithlessness; I will love them freely, for my anger has turned from them" (14:4). The Lord's willingness to restore the broken bond gives the measure of His steadfast love and mercy. Both Paul and Peter picked up this restoration strand and applied it to both Jews and Gentiles. Paul wrote, "What if God . . . in order to make known the riches of his glory for the vessels of mercy, which he has prepared beforehand for glory, even us whom he has called, not from the Jews only but also from the Gentiles? As indeed he says in Hosea, 'Those who were not my people I will call "my people," and her who was not beloved I will call "my beloved." ' And in the very place where it was said to them, 'You are not my people,' they will be called 'sons of the living God' " (Rom. 9:22-26). Peter set forth the favored position enjoyed by the church in the words, "Once you were no people but now you are God's people; once you had not received mercy but now you have received mercy" (1 Pet. 2:10). These quotations constitute two great links between the Old Testament prediction and New Testament fulfillment, and in this way prove the unity of the Scriptures. It is noteworthy that the point of unity stressed here centers in the renewal of the covenant bond which Israel broke by their sins.

c. Amos

While the prophet Amos made no specific reference to the Mosaic covenant, he spoke, nevertheless, very pointedly on Israel's special relation to the Lord: "They have rejected the law of the Lord, and have not kept his statutes" (2:4). The nature of this reference to the law of the Lord clearly identifies it with the body of the Mosaic law which was based on the Sinaitic covenant. This conclusion finds support in the frequent references to Israel as a people in specific relationship with the Lord. Such expressions as "My people, Israel," "House of Israel," and "Zion"[11] intensify Amos's witness to Israel's covenant relation with the Lord. The Lord's closing message to Israel anticipated raising up the booth of David and restoring the fortunes of His people Israel (9:11-15). Most interpreters understand the expression "the booth of David" to refer to the Davidic kingdom. If this is correct, we have here final confirmation of Amos's witness to covenant relationship. The kingdom of David had its foundation in the rule of God established in the Sinaitic covenant.

The prophetic viewpoint of this portion looks forward to the far greater glory of God's people in the Messianic kingdom. James gave witness to this view when he interpreted the ministry of Barnabas and Paul among the Gentiles as being the fulfillment of this prediction. He was speaking of the universal nature of the gospel as based on the new covenant (Acts 15:12-18). Hence it is proper to conclude that this eschatological portion of Amos had its basis in the Mosaic covenant.

d. Isaiah (1 — 39)

There appears to be only one clear reference to the Mosaic covenant found in this part of Isaiah. It reads: "They have transgressed the laws, violated the statutes, broken the everlasting covenant" (Is. 24:5). The transgression of the laws was also the breaking of the covenant. Occurring in Isaiah's apocalypse, this statement shows how deeply rooted the covenant lay in the mind of Isaiah. In the opening verses of the book the Lord referred to His people as sons. Israel's sins were in reality the rebellion of sons against a father. This was the basis for Isaiah's call to Israel to repent and to lead a life befitting the people of God. Repeatedly he or the Lord made references to Israel's being significant as a people in special relation to God.[12] Such expressions as Zion, Judah and Jerusalem, House of Jacob, and Israel gave a definitive meaning to Israel's relation to their God. The great prophetic pictures of the Messianic kingdom show that the relation of the people to their Lord during the days of the Messiah would take the same pattern as that of Israel under the Mosaic covenant.[13] While there is no prediction of the making of a new covenant, the qualitative superiority of the glories of the Messianic age implies the existence of a covenant which would be truly everlasting.

e. Micah

The prophet Micah made no specific reference to Israel's covenant with God. But his prophetic work was very similar to that of Isaiah's, especially as he described Israel's relation to God. The names he ascribed to God's people (Jacob, Israel, Judah, Zion, and Jerusalem) all point to a nation who bore a distinct relation to the Lord. Micah referred to

Israel's redemption from Egypt in such a way as to show that the Lord required of them "to do justice, and to love kindness, and to walk humbly with . . . [their] God" (6:4-8). This was the distinctive manner of life required of people who were in covenant relationship with their Lord. Micah also predicted the glorious relation which the people of God would sustain in their covenant relation with the Messiah. Descriptive of this glory are these words: "The mountain of the house of the Lord shall be established as the highest of the mountains, and shall be raised up above the hills; and peoples shall flow to it, and many nations shall come, and say: 'Come, let us go up to the mountain of the Lord, to the house of the God of Jacob; that he may teach us his ways and we may walk in his paths.' For out of Zion shall go forth the law, and the word of the Lord from Jerusalem" (4:1, 2). Just as from Mt. Sinai went forth the Mosaic covenant and its laws, so out of Zion would go forth the higher law of the new covenant.

In conclusion, let us observe how deeply Israel's election became engraved in the hearts of the people. The prophets of this era showed most conclusively that the Lord had actualized this election by the establishment of the covenant at Mt. Sinai. This relationship would continue until Israel's relation to the Lord would be enriched far more exceedingly through the Messianic institution of the new covenant.

5. The Day of the Lord — Judgment

This theme came from the pens of the earliest writing prophets, unannounced and unexplained. This fact presents an unusual task for the student of biblical theology. What is the Day of the Lord? What did the prophets declare concerning it? When was this Day of the Lord to be fulfilled? We do not go very far until we observe that this is one of the most dominant themes of the writing prophets. Incidentally, the chief reason for my believing that the prophet Joel was among the first of the writing prophets lies in the dominance of this theme in his book. We should note also by way of introduction that both Paul and Peter laid hold of this theme and that Christ, Jude, and John developed the idea in a somewhat modified form.

a. Obadiah and Joel

Obadiah's prophecy centered in the punishment of Edom on account of the violence done to Israel. After condemning the Edomites for all they had done against God's people, Obadiah added, "For the day of the Lord is near upon all the nations. As you have done, it shall be done to you, your deeds shall return on your own head" (v. 15). Obadiah's vision went beyond the Day of the Lord as he pictured a future time, when "Saviors shall go up to Mount Zion to rule Mount Esau; and the kingdom shall be the Lord's" (v. 21). Here we discover a pattern followed repeatedly by the prophets. They spoke of the coming Day of the Lord, stressing its imminence, and then they looked beyond this imminent judgment to the time when the kingdom would be the Lord's. They label this grand new era "the Last Days" or "the Latter Days." This theme of the Last Days will receive some consideration later, but in the study of the Day of the Lord we should anticipate whatever relationship exists between them. Neither theme can be fully understood without a clear perception of the other.

Joel opened his book with a graphic comparison between a pestilence of locusts and a coming destruction of Judah at the hands of an invading nation. This became the setting for Joel's words, "Alas for the day! For the day of the Lord is near, and as destruction from the Almighty it comes" (1:15). He continued his description in the language of an imminent famine. He added the words, "Blow the trumpet in Zion; sound the alarm on my holy mountain! Let all the inhabitants of the land tremble, for the day of the Lord is coming, it is near, a day of darkness and gloom, a day of clouds and thick darkness" (2:1, 2)! Israel's land, likened to the Garden of Eden, would become a desolate wilderness. He intensified the coming destruction by describing further a devastation caused by locusts. He gave the destruction the dimensions of a cosmical disturbance: "The earth quakes before them, the heavens tremble. The sun and the moon are darkened, and the stars withdraw their shining. The Lord utters his voice before his army, for his host is exceedingly great; he that executes his word is powerful. For the day of the Lord is great and very terrible; who can endure it" (2:2-11)? While some students see here only the prediction of an awful devastation by locusts, others interpret it as a most graphic picture of a destruction caused by foreign nations. The enemy appears to come from the north. Perhaps Joel referred to Tyre, Sidon, and Philistia. Even Egypt and Edom may also be in view (2:20; 3:4, 19). Whether or not Joel is naming these nations, the coming judgment is near and is very terrible.

The idea of judgment becomes closely bound up with the Day of the Lord. Joel used this prediction as a call to repentance. When he quoted the words of the Lord, "Return to the Lord, your God, for he is gracious and merciful, slow to anger, and abounding in steadfast love, and repents of evil" (2:13), he was drawing attention to the conditional element of his prediction. This Day of the Lord which was near would not come to fulfillment if Israel would return to the Lord with all their heart. This conditional element became an essential part of the predictions of the prophets. For Joel a coming judgment could be forestalled because Israel's Lord was gracious and merciful.

Joel's prediction extended beyond the immediate future to an era in which the Lord would pour out His Spirit on all flesh. This era would come to an end through what we may call a culminating aspect of the Day of the Lord described in the words, "I will give portents in the heavens and on the earth, blood and fire and columns of smoke. The sun shall be turned to darkness, and the moon to blood, before the great and terrible day of the Lord comes. And it shall come to pass that all who call upon the name of the Lord shall be delivered; for in Mount Zion and in Jerusalem there shall be those who escape, as the Lord has said, and among the survivors shall be those whom the Lord calls" (2:30-32). A comparison of this prediction of the Day of the Lord with that given early in the book leads to some very difficult problems of interpretation. On the basis of the Book of Joel alone it would appear that a sequence of events may be the meaning which we should gain from these predictions. Accordingly, there was to be an imminent judgment to be known as the Day of the Lord. Then there would follow an era lying beyond this Day of the Lord in which God would pour out His Spirit upon all flesh. This would culminate in a consummating Day of the Lord far in the future.

It is very gratifying that Peter gave an authoritative interpretation of Joel's language on the day of Pentecost. He introduced his explanation of Pentecost with the words, "This is what was spoken by the prophet Joel," and then he followed with the quotation from Joel 2:28-32. Peter saw in the cosmic effects which accompanied the crucifixion of Christ, together with the supernatural manifestations which attended the outpouring of the Holy Spirit, the fulfillment of Joel's prediction of wonders in the heaven above and signs in the earth beneath. The coming of the Holy Spirit introduced the era when "Whoever calls on the name of the Lord shall be saved." This is the age in which God made Jesus both Lord and Christ. It will terminate with a consummating Day of the Lord which is yet future. Peter wrote of this coming day in the language, "The day of the Lord will come like a thief, and then the heavens will pass away with a loud noise, and the elements will be dissolved with fire, and the earth and the works that are upon it will be burned up" (2 Pet. 3:10). With these words Peter identified the still future aspect of the Day of the Lord with the final consummation. Paul also associated the Day of the Lord with the return of Christ.[14]

Yet a third time Joel spoke of the Day of the Lord (3:9-15). Here in warlike terms the Lord commanded, "Beat your plowshares into swords, and your pruning hooks into spears. . . . Let the nations bestir themselves, and come up to the valley of Jehoshaphat; for there I will sit to judge all the nations round about. . . . Multitudes, multitudes, in the valley of decision! For the day of the Lord is near in the valley of decision. The sun and the moon are darkened, and the stars withdraw their shining." On a first reading, this section would appear to predict an unprecedented battle among the nations of the world as marking the chief event of the Day of the Lord. The quotation of this passage in Revelation 14:14-20 may throw some light on its meaning. Since the context in Revelation evidently describes the consummation, the passage in Joel becomes descriptive, not of a massive war, but rather of the consummation. Hence it parallels in meaning the references made by Paul and Peter to the coming Day of the Lord as being the time of final judgment (2 Thess. 2:2-12; 2 Pet. 3:10-13). From this we may conclude that Joel laid the groundwork for understanding the nearer fulfillment of the Day of the Lord as an imminent crisis of judgment and the far-distant culminating aspect of the Day of the Lord as the final judgment taking place at the consummation of all things.

b. Amos

The prophet Amos devoted almost half of his book to recording God's judgment upon the nations, including Damascus, Gaza, Tyre, Edom, Ammon, Moab, Judah, and Israel. His approach took the form, "For three transgressions . . . and for four, I will not revoke the punishment" (1:3). Then he enlarged on the specific transgressions of each of these nations. He proceeded to show how the Lord had already brought upon them various forms of judgment and he led to the command, "Prepare to meet your God, O Israel" (4:12)! He advised further, "Seek good, and not evil, that you may live; and so the Lord, the God of hosts, will be with you, as you have said. Hate evil, and love good, and establish justice in the gate; it may be that the Lord, the God of hosts, will be gracious to the remnant of Joseph" (5:14, 15).

It would appear that some of the people in Israel thought that the Day of the Lord would be a time of receiving blessings from the Lord. He answered them by saying, "Woe to you who desire the day of the Lord! Why would you have the day of the Lord? It is darkness, and not light; as if a man fled from a lion, and a bear met him; or went into the house and leaned with his hand against the wall, and a serpent bit him. Is not the day of the Lord darkness, and not light, and gloom with no brightness in it" (5:18-20)? It would appear that the people of Israel were slowly grasping the element of judgment belonging to the Day of the Lord. They were escaping, as it were, from one calamity only to be confronted with another. The expected light was darkening. Israel's lack of genuine piety, even though they observed feasts and offered sacrifices, their being at ease in Zion, and their indulging in the luxuries of life, called for God's judgment. He was about to bring a judgment of fire, but at the intercession of Amos He repented from bringing immediate judgment. Because of Israel's continued sinning, the Lord said, "The end has come upon my people Israel; I will never again pass by them" (8:2). He continued His words of judgment, " 'And on that day,' says the Lord God, 'I will make the sun go down at noon, and darken the earth in broad daylight. I will turn your feasts into mourning, and all your songs into lamentations; I will bring sackcloth upon all loins, and baldness on every head; I will make it like the mourning for an only son, and the end of it like a bitter day' " (8:9, 10). With these and similar statements Amos confronted the nation with oncoming judgments that would characterize the Day of the Lord.

We should yet observe that Amos closed his book with the note of future blessing that God offered those who would repent. As compared with Joel, Amos developed more fully his messages of coming judgment but at the same time he showed greater concern to lead Israel to repentance. The Lord who would bring judgment upon Israel in the Day of the Lord said nevertheless, "Seek me and live" (5:4).

c. Isaiah (1 — 39)

The prophet Isaiah had much to say about coming judgment both upon the kingdom of Judah and upon foreign nations, Babylon in particular. In the first chapter, where the Lord presented His case against His people, He said, "Your country lies desolate, your cities are burned with fire; in your very presence aliens devour your land; it is desolate, as overthrown by aliens. And the daughter of Zion is left like a booth in a vineyard, like a lodge in a cucumber field, like a besieged city. If the Lord of hosts had not left us a few survivors, we should have been like Sodom, and become like Gomorrah" (1:7-9). Later in the chapter we have the words, "Ah, I will vent my wrath on my enemies, and avenge myself on my foes. I will turn my hand against you and will smelt away your dross as with lye and remove all your alloy" (1:24, 25). These first references to the coming judgment predicted the destruction of Judah at the hands of an alien power. God's design was to cleanse His people from their besmirching sins and impurities. Those who repent will be redeemed, "But rebels and sinners shall be destroyed together, and those who forsake the Lord shall be consumed" (1:27, 28). This arraignment of Judah gave the pattern for Isaiah's messages throughout the book. He gave these warnings of imminent judgment in the framework of the Day of the Lord: "For the Lord of hosts has a day against all that is proud and lofty, against all that is lifted up and high. . . .

And the haughtiness of man shall be humbled, and the pride of men shall be brought low. . . . And men shall enter the caves of the rocks and the holes of the ground, from before the terror of the Lord, and from the glory of his majesty, when he rises to terrify the earth" (2:12-22). Coming judgment was certain and imminent. Isaiah picked up the theme again in the parable of the vineyard when he wrote, "And now I will tell you what I will do to my vineyard. I will remove its hedge, and it shall be devoured; I will break down its wall, and it shall be trampled down. I will make it a waste; it shall not be pruned or hoed, and briers and thorns shall grow up; I will also command the clouds that they rain no rain upon it" (5:5, 6).

Then follow the six woes by which Isaiah laid the sins of the people upon their hearts (5:8-23). Isaiah predicted that his people would go into exile. When the Lord gave the charge to Isaiah, the prophet asked, "How long, O Lord?" The Lord replied, "Until the cities lie waste without inhabitant, and houses without men, and the land is utterly desolate, and the Lord removes men far away, and the forsaken places are many in the midst of the land" (6:11-13). This again describes the desolation that would come through invasion by foreign nations. To Ahaz, who was weak in faith, Isaiah gave the warning, "The Lord will bring upon you and upon your people and upon your father's house such days as have not come since the day that Ephraim departed from Judah — the king of Assyria" (7:17). In a fourfold use of the phrase "In that day" Isaiah enlarged upon the nature of the coming destruction (7:18-25).

The oracle concerning Babylon read, "Hark, a tumult on the mountains as of a great multitude! Hark, an uproar of kingdoms, of nations gathering together! The Lord of hosts is mustering a host for battle. They come from a distant land, from the end of the heavens, the Lord and the weapons of his indignation, to destroy the whole earth" (13:4, 5). As he enlarged on this message of doom, Isaiah used the formula, "the day of the Lord," stating that it was near. It would come as a destruction from the Almighty. It would come with wrath and fierce anger to make the earth a desolation. It would even have its effect upon the heavenly bodies: "For the stars of the heavens and their constellations will not give their light; the sun will be dark at its rising and the moon will not shed its light" (13:10).

As we search for the meaning of this language, we may observe that Christ quoted these words in His Olivet discourse when He spoke of His return (Mt. 24:29-31). John also quoted it when he spoke of the opening of the sixth seal (Rev. 6:12-17). This use by John gave further confirmation of the potential meaning in Isaiah's use of "the day of the Lord." This corresponds to the apparent double reference in the expression "the day of the Lord" made by Joel. It shows again the large dimensions given to this idea by the prophets. Isaiah very emphatically ascribed the judgments of the Day of the Lord to the wrath and the fierce anger of the Lord (13:9, 13).

In chapters 13 — 23 Isaiah pronounced judgments upon the nations surrounding Israel. In his apocalypse (24 — 27) the prophet combined messages of judgment with words of hope, hardly paralleled by anything else in the Old Testament. He spoke again of how the Lord would lay waste the earth and make it desolate. These judgments lay in the fact that "they have transgressed the laws, violated the statutes, broken the everlasting covenant" (24:5). This shows the grievousness of Israel's sin. Isaiah's warning of coming judgment had to do not only with the wicked of this earth but also with the host of heaven. It included not only earthly calamities but also that of the heavenly bodies. Most strikingly he said, "On that day the Lord will punish the host of heaven, in heaven, and the kings of the earth, on the earth. . . . Then the moon will be confounded, and the sun ashamed; for the Lord of hosts will reign on Mount Zion and in Jerusalem and before his elders he will manifest his glory" (24:17-23).

These quotations bring together God's judgment in relation to His reign. We would gather that the reign of the Lord of hosts assumed the overthrow and punishment of God's enemies. This became the theme of the Book of Revelation, where we learn that after all the foes of Christ have been overthrown He will reign forever (Rev. 11:15). Chapter 34 gives Isaiah's final message concerning the Day of the Lord. He stated, "The Lord is enraged against all the nations," and he brought his message to a focus in the words, "For the Lord has a day of vengeance, a year of recompense for the cause of Zion" (34:2, 8).

In conclusion, we should observe that God's judgment, centering in the Day of the Lord, would come upon all the wicked, whether of Israel or of the nations of the world. Isaiah enlarged on these judgments in great detail. He showed that there were cosmic implications to the Day of the Lord. This should lead us to realize that sin reaches beyond man. There is the implication of a great enemy of man in the spiritual world, who will ultimately be overthrown in the culmination of this Day at the coming of the Lord. Isaiah stressed the anger and wrath aspect of God's judgments. Finally, he made it clear that for the wicked this would be a day of vengeance, but for the righteous a year of recompense for the cause of Zion. Indeed, not only to Isaiah but also to the other prophets there was in addition to the judgment aspect of the Day of the Lord the implicit idea that for the righteous, the Day of the Lord would bring joy and happiness. The New Testament confirmed this idea, for, as Paul says, "God has not destined us for wrath, but to obtain salvation through our Lord Jesus Christ" (1 Thess. 5:9). In like manner Peter, after he had noted that the Day of the Lord would come like a thief, added the word, "But according to his promise we wait for new heavens and a new earth in which righteousness dwells" (2 Pet. 3:11-13).

d. Micah

The prophet Micah developed the theme of the Day of the Lord in a fashion similar to that of Isaiah. He opened his message by calling on the Lord God to be a witness against God's people. He pictured the Lord as coming out of His place to bring judgment upon the transgression and sin of His people. They were aware that evil had come down from the Lord to the gate of Jerusalem. The Lord's people abhorred justice and perverted all equity. They built Zion with blood and Jerusalem with wrong. On this account, "Zion shall be plowed as a field; Jerusalem shall become a heap of ruins, and the mountain of the house a wooded height" (3:9-12).

Micah did not use the expression "the day of the Lord" but simply "that day," from which it is evident that his hearers understood these words. Concerning that Day, Micah said, "In anger and wrath I will execute vengeance upon the nations that did not obey" (5:10-15). Another prediction of judgment by God reads, "Therefore I have begun to smite you, making you desolate because of your sins. You shall eat, but not be satisfied, and there shall be hunger in your inward parts; you shall put away, but not save, and what you save I will give to the sword. You shall sow, but not reap; you shall tread olives, but not anoint yourselves with oil; you shall tread grapes, but not drink wine" (6:13-15). Like the other prophets Micah wove into his message a reference to the Latter Days. The imminent Day of the Lord would be followed by a new era lying far in the future. In these Latter Days, "The mountain of the house of the Lord shall be established as the highest of the mountains. . . . For out of Zion shall go forth the law, and the word of the Lord from Jerusalem" (4:1-7). This was the age in which the Lord would reign in Mt. Zion, "from this time forth and forevermore."

Again we see that this pattern of the Day of the Lord being followed in some future time by the Latter Days in which the Messiah would reign, stands forth as a fundamental concept in the theology of the prophets. The Day of the Lord assumed such great importance because of the imminent overthrow of Israel and Judah. These prophets who predicted the judgments of the Day of the Lord gave the faithful remnant a basis on which their faith could rest. In genuine humility they should place their trust in the Lord, who would bring to fulfillment the glorious future during the age of the Messiah.

6. The Messiah and the Messianic Kingdom

a. Obadiah and Joel — The Dawn of Messianic Understanding

Only by implication may we conclude that Obadiah gave any prediction of the Messiah and His kingdom. Verses 17-21 look to the future. Judah and Israel appear to be living again in their own lands. The kingdom shall be the Lord's. In this last statement the prophet may be forecasting the reign of the Messiah. It would appear that if the stream of Messianic prediction as given in the Davidic psalms and earlier writings had been available to Obadiah, he would have stated more explicitly the rule of the Messiah. Hence the question remains whether he had in view the Messianic kingdom.

The Book of Joel offers a similar problem. While Joel looked beyond the Day of the Lord and predicted the outpouring of the Holy Spirit, he made no reference to the Messiah or to His kingdom. Certainly the prediction that "all who call upon the name of the Lord shall be delivered" would obtain meaning through the Messiah's work (Joel 2:32). The same is true of Joel's words, "And in that day the mountains shall drip sweet wine, and the hills shall flow with milk, and all the stream beds of Judah shall flow with water; and a fountain shall come forth from the house of the Lord and water the valley of Shittim. . . But Judah shall be inhabited for ever, . . . for the Lord dwells in Zion" (3:18-21). This pictorial language certainly depicted the Messianic era, even though the prophet Joel did not identify it as such.

b. Hosea's Messianic Understanding

The Messianic picture becomes clearer in Hosea. He noted that "the people of Judah and the people of Israel shall be gathered together, and they shall appoint for themselves one head" (Hos. 1:11). Given in a context of prediction, this statement is quite explicit in its reference to the Messiah, even though the name "Messiah" does not occur here. In 3:5 the Messianic reference becomes clearer. Note the words, "Afterward the children of Israel shall return and seek the Lord their God, and David their king; and they shall come in fear to the Lord and to his goodness in the latter days." From the standpoint of time this prediction would find fulfillment in a new age, the Latter Days.

The meaning of this era becomes clearer through a careful study of its occurrences in the prophetic books. There is here the clear prediction of a successor to the throne of David. The words, "When Israel was a child, I loved him, and out of Egypt I called my son" (11:1), offer a real problem of interpretation. Is this only a historical reference or is it a prediction? It does not appear to be a prediction, and yet Matthew regarded Jesus' coming out of Egypt as the fulfillment of Hosea's words (Mt. 2:15). If Matthew inferred that Hosea's words were a prediction, then it is proper to regard it as Messianic. The word "fulfill" (*pleroo*) has a much wider meaning than *bring to pass*. God's promise to heal Israel's faithlessness and to love them freely stands in a context which seems to confirm its Messianic import (Hos. 14:4-7).

c. Amos — Messianism

The only portion of Amos that appears to possess Messianic import is 9:11-15. The Lord predicted the restoration of David's kingdom in a future era. He foretold also the fruitful conditions of the earth which would characterize this coming age, and promised to restore the fortunes of His people Israel. Plainly, this future period lay beyond the imminent Day of the Lord, described elsewhere in this book. For this reason the restoration of the kingdom possessed Messianic import. While the Lord did not call the king of the restored kingdom the Messiah, the implication of the language supports the idea. The Lord would have His people lay hold of this prediction with the faith and confidence that He would bring it to pass.

d. Isaiah (1 — 39) — The Messiah and His Kingship

The prophet Isaiah foretold most fully the coming of the Messiah and the nature of His kingdom. His first prophetic announcement appeared in the words, "In that day the branch of the Lord shall be beautiful and glorious." This context (4:2-6) looks plainly to the future. Most Bible students recognize Isaiah's words as the source of the Messianic prophecies involving a "branch." While there is a problem to relate verses 2a and 2b, we may bypass it in view of the generally accepted Messianic interpretation given to "the branch of the Lord." Since the prophets Jeremiah and Zechariah enlarged so grandly on its Messianic meaning,[15] we may with confidence attach this expression to all the other Messianic references in the Book of Isaiah.

The Lord challenged the faith of Ahaz in the words, "Behold, a young woman shall conceive and bear a son, and shall call his name Immanuel" (7:14-17). A biblical theology approach to the meaning of this verse leads to the following observations: First, there may be a clear reference to a young woman of that time who had already conceived and was about to bear a son. Her naming him Immanuel would be her personal response to Ahaz's victory over Syria and Ephraim. Second, Matthew quoted this verse to show that the virgin birth of Jesus fulfilled the prediction made by the Lord to Ahaz. Matthew's statement, "All this took place to fulfil what the Lord had spoken by the prophet" (Mt. 1:22), is clear and to the point. Third, Matthew definitely gave the connotation "virgin" to the Hebrew word *almah*. While he was undoubtedly quoting the Septuagint, he clearly affirmed that the virgin birth fulfilled the prediction of Isaiah. Fourth, this interpretation poses a problem of reconciling the meaning of *almah* as it referred to the mother of a child born in the time of Ahaz and its meaning with the restricted sense of "virgin" as found in the instance of Mary, the mother of Jesus. Since Matthew did not take note of any such problem, we may safely let it pass.

One thing of which we become aware in the study of predictive prophecy is double or multiple fulfillment. Sometimes we discover quite a wide disparity between the near and the more distant fulfillment. A case in point is the promise of Nathan to David concerning the birth of a son. Solomon fulfilled this promise, but the author of Hebrews (Heb. 1:5) definitely ascribed this prediction to Christ. While a father-son relationship existed between God and Solomon, a qualitative, infinitely superior father-son relationship existed between God and Jesus Christ. If this fact does not stagger us in our thinking, there appears to be no need for letting the problem of a double fulfillment of the Isaiah 7:14 passage trouble us.

Fifth, the name "Immanuel" specifically connotes the deity of the One to be born. This affirmation had its proof in the fact that at His birth the angel declared Him to be Christ the Lord. Certainly the baby born at the time of Ahaz was not divine. But the name gained its immeasurably heightened sense in the naming of the baby born to Mary. Sixth, verses 15-17 declared that when the baby about to be born would be old enough to refuse the evil and choose the good, the land before whose two kings Ahaz was in dread would be deserted. The added prediction given in 8:5-10 appears to confirm a fulfillment of the Immanuel prediction in the time of Ahaz. When the problems of Ahaz became still greater, Isaiah wrote, "Be broken, you peoples, and be dismayed. . . . Take counsel together, but it will come to nought; speak a word, but it will not stand, for God is with us."[16]

Isaiah buttressed God's message by telling the people that they should not be troubled by what some people called conspiracy. He exhorted them to regard the Lord of hosts as holy. He then added words which Paul and Peter interpreted as referring to Christ: "He will become a sanctuary, and a stone of offence, and a rock of stumbling to both houses of Israel, a trap and a snare to the inhabitants of Jerusalem. And many shall stumble thereon; they shall fall and be broken; they shall be snared and taken" (8:14, 15). Paul used this passage to clinch his argument that the Jews in his time had not pursued righteousness through faith. They stumbled over the "stone" whom Paul identified as Christ (Rom. 9:30-33). Peter wrote, "Come to him, to that living stone, rejected by men but in God's sight chosen and precious. . . . For it stands in scripture: 'Behold, I am laying in Zion a stone, a cornerstone chosen and precious, and he who believes in him will not be put to shame'" (1 Pet. 2:4-6). Again New Testament writers aid in the interpretation of the Old Testament.

The very familiar prediction of the birth and reign of the Prince of Peace (9:1-7) now challenges our study. To begin, Isaiah spoke of the future era known as the Latter Time. It lay beyond the imminent Day of the Lord. He framed his prediction in the language of the Lord's making Galilee glorious. The people who walked in darkness had seen a great light. In such a setting he could predict, "For to us a child is born, to us a son is given; and the government will be upon his shoulder, and his name will be called 'Wonderful Counselor, Mighty God, Everlasting Father, Prince of Peace.' Of the increase of his government and of peace there will be no end, upon the throne of David, and over his kingdom, to establish it, and to uphold it with justice and with righteousness from this time forth and for evermore. The zeal of the Lord of hosts will do this." This prediction plainly asserted that the child to be born would have the name which expresses Deity. It also harmonizes with the prediction of Immanuel's birth. Herein was the profound mystery but the birth of Jesus confirmed it. Born of a virgin, Jesus showed Himself to be at once divine and human. He was God manifest in the flesh. The New Testament interpreted and confirmed the predictions of Isaiah, who had written of a child to be born who should be called Wonderful Counselor, Mighty God, Everlasting Father, Prince of Peace.

A few meditations on these names may be appropriate. The name "Wonderful Counselor" may have the meaning, "wonderful in counsel, and excellent in wisdom" (Is. 28:29). The name "Mighty God" leads us to think of the Lord who appeared to Abraham saying, "I am God Almighty." Jesus certainly manifested this power in performing miracles, wonders, and signs. The name "Everlasting Father" points to Christ's eternal existence as Father. We do well to explore what wealth of meaning attaches to Jesus as being the everlasting Father; we may conclude that what is spoken of the Lord of hosts would also be true of the child to be born. Jesus' claim to divine Sonship, and to being the

Good Shepherd fulfilled this prediction, even though He did not bear the title "Father."

The name "Prince of Peace" suggests that He is ruler of the world. He not only makes wars to cease but positively He supplies all the blessings of peace. Isaiah expanded this theme in 2:2-5; 11:3-10, where he predicted a rule of righteousness that would result in beating swords into plowshares, and the wolf dwelling with the lamb. Most glorious was the prediction, "The earth shall be full of the knowledge of the Lord as the waters cover the sea." The dimensions of this peace have become greatly enlarged in the New Testament since Christ stands as the mediator between God and man, and through this mediatorial authority establishes peace between them.

The kingship of the child to be born would be exercised on the throne of David. The Lord, who is king of Israel by covenant right, would give His Son kingly authority to rule in His stead. The throne of David thus became the type of the Messiah's throne. All governmental authority would rest upon Him. His government would extend through the entire universe and would accomplish peace in the world. He would establish and uphold His kingdom with justice and righteousness, which alone would lead to peace.

In chapter 11 Isaiah presented an equally sublime picture of the Messiah and His kingdom. In language implying the downfall of the kingly line of David, Isaiah presented the idea of a new branch springing from the stump of Jesse. This becomes significant when we observe the course of history in which the kingdom of Judah ceased to exist, and for centuries there was no king in Israel. This fact makes the genealogy given by Matthew all the more significant, because it shows conclusively that Jesus was the rightful heir to David's throne.

Isaiah proceeded to show the spiritual power of this Branch. The Spirit of the Lord, the Holy Spirit, would rest upon Him. It would appear that the Gospel writers in describing the coming of the Holy Spirit upon Jesus at His baptism were conscious that this descent fulfilled Isaiah's prediction.[17] This dwelling of the Spirit in the Messiah would possess the dynamic to give Him wisdom, understanding, counsel, might, knowledge, and fear of the Lord. With this spiritual equipment the Messiah would exercise His rule. The strength of His rule would lie in His righteousness and faithfulness. Accordingly, peaceful conditions would exist on the earth.

While some students interpret verses 6-9 as being literal language, to be fulfilled in a restoration of Edenic conditions, others hold that the peaceful conditions predicted here are spiritual. Christ's rule would bring about conditions of peace among mankind and between man and

God. Note the language: "They shall not hurt or destroy in all my holy mountain; for the earth shall be full of the knowledge of the Lord as the waters cover the sea. In that day the root of Jesse shall stand as an ensign to the peoples; him shall the nations seek, and his dwellings shall be glorious" (vv. 9, 10). While a literal fulfillment of a restoration of Edenic conditions carries considerable significance, the spiritual import of the passage is far greater than this. The root of Jesse, the standard bearer to the peoples, would effect peace of the highest order. Because of this the nations shall seek Him and His dwellings shall be glorious.

Paul confirmed this understanding of the root of Jesse when he wrote, "For I tell you that Christ became a servant to the circumcised to show God's truthfulness, . . . in order that the Gentiles might glorify God for his mercy. . . . Isaiah says, 'The root of Jesse shall come, he who rises to rule the Gentiles; in him shall the Gentiles hope.' May the God of hope fill you with all joy and peace in believing, so that by the power of the Holy Spirit you may abound in hope" (Rom. 15:8-13). From this we see that Paul spoke of this entire section as now being fulfilled by the enthroned Lord Jesus Christ.

Throughout the remaining chapters of 1 — 39 Isaiah gave a number of additional predictions concerning the Messiah and His kingdom.[18] In the imagery of building the temple the Lord said, "Behold, I am laying in Zion for a foundation a stone, a tested stone, a precious cornerstone, of a sure foundation: 'He who believes will not be in haste.' And I will make justice the line, and righteousness the plummet" (28:16, 17). Paul used this statement to show how the rejection of Christ by the Jews had been predicted by Isaiah. He showed that Isaiah was laying stress on the faith aspect of the coming kingdom (Rom. 9:33). In a different kind of context Peter stressed the same truth. He invited his readers to come to Christ, "to that living stone, rejected by men but in God's sight chosen and precious; and like living stones be yourselves built into a spiritual house, to be a holy priesthood, to offer spiritual sacrifices acceptable to God through Jesus Christ." He based his exhortation on this passage from Isaiah, adding the obvious conclusion, "To you therefore who believe, he is precious, but for those who do not believe, 'The very stone which the builders rejected has become the head of the corner' " (1 Pet. 2:4-8). These emphases on the faith element of the gospel message had their foundation in Isaiah's understanding that even though the Messiah would be established in His kingdom, it was necessary for all to believe this fact.

Isaiah drew attention to the supernatural credentials by which people would know that the predicted One had come. He wrote, "The eyes of the blind shall be opened, and the ears of the deaf unstopped; then shall the lame man leap like a hart, and the tongue of the dumb sing for joy" (35:5, 6). Jesus used this Scripture to bolster the faith of the Baptist (Mt. 11:5, 6). Close study of such portions from Isaiah gives us reason to believe that he predicted not merely miracles such as sight to the blind and hearing to the deaf, but that the blind, the deaf, and the lame also received spiritual sight, hearing, and healing. The physical healing was the forerunner of spiritual healing. Throughout the Gospels we receive repeated confirmation that Jesus' saving acts of healing symbolized His saving acts of spiritual healing (Mt. 9:21, 22).

Isaiah also used the language of the highway to describe a spiritual road. On this Holy Way the redeemed shall walk. They shall "come to Zion with singing, with everlasting joy upon their heads; they shall obtain joy and gladness, and sorrow and sighing shall flee away" (Is. 35: 8-10). The expression "the Holy Way" has the imagery of a road leading to Zion. Only the redeemed travel this way. What a sublime picture of the Christian life! It is remarkable that Isaiah laid hold of this note of joy and gladness which belong to the people of God. John had this in mind when he pictured the New Jerusalem and quoted the angelic message, "Behold, the dwelling of God is with men. He will dwell with them, and they shall be his people, and God himself will be with them; he will wipe away every tear from their eyes, and death shall be no more, neither shall there be mourning nor crying nor pain any more, for the former things have passed away" (Rev. 21:2-4). This forward look of Isaiah's predictions not only comprehended the glories of the present life experienced by the citizens of Christ's kingdom, but also the far greater glories of the heavenly Jerusalem.

e. Micah — Messianism

In language almost as grand as that of Isaiah, Micah also depicted the glory of the coming Messiah and of His kingdom. The Lord promised to gather Judah and Israel from their captivities and to lead them again to their own land (Mic. 2:12, 13). He depicted the events of the Latter Days, when the law and the Word of the Lord would go forth from Jerusalem. The peaceful world conditions described would become possible through this Word of the Lord. It would come to pass when the Lord would reign in Mt. Zion, "from this time forth and for evermore" (4:7). Micah also predicted the birth of the One who would be ruler in Israel (5:2-4). This One would come from the city of Bethlehem, the land of David. In this way Micah shared with Isaiah the idea of the restoration of the Davidic kingdom. This ruler would be one "whose origin is from of old, from ancient days." The language expressed an existence prior to the time in which He would become ruler in Israel. This idea supported what Isaiah had predicted concerning the person of the Messiah. At the time of the birth of Jesus, the scribes and the chief priests interpreted this passage as predicting the birth of the Messiah in Bethlehem (Mt. 2:1-6). The Jews also interpreted these Scriptures as predicting the descent of the Christ from David and His coming from Bethlehem. Concerning this coming ruler Micah added, "And he shall stand and feed his flock in the strength of the Lord, in the majesty of the name of the Lord his God. And they shall dwell secure, for now he shall be great to the ends of the earth" (5:4). This is one of the predictions which undoubtedly supported Jesus' significant claim, "I am the good shepherd" (Jn. 10:1-18).

This survey of these early prophetic messages concerning the Messiah highlights the remarkably clear image which these prophets gave of this coming One. The time of His coming would be in the Latter Days. He would spring from the line of David. The Spirit of the Lord would rest upon Him. Hence His reign as Messiah would be characterized by justice, righteousness, and faithfulness. It would be an eternal reign and would accomplish peace in the world. As a result the meek would obtain fresh joy in the Lord. The ruling Messiah would save His people and the redeemed would walk on the Holy Way. Herein is the essence of the gospel.

7. The Latter Days –– Prophetic Eschatology

The preceding study serves as an orientation to the present theme, the Latter Days. The relationship is so close that it becomes quite difficult to avoid duplication of subject matter pertinent to both. The presentation of this topic is very essential to the theology of the prophets. We noted in the preceding discussion that the prophets looked beyond the Day of the Lord to a far distant era which they called the Latter Days. We have seen the Messianic age in the perspective of these Latter Days. The present aim is to analyze prophetic eschatology as it relates to the restoration of Israel, God's redemption and salvation, and the outpouring of the Holy Spirit.

a. Restoration of Israel

(1) Obadiah and Joel. Obadiah appeared to look beyond the Day of the Lord to a time when the house of Jacob would possess their own possessions. It would be a time in which all the tribes would again live in their own country. While the chronological sequence is not entirely clear, the restoration of Israel to their own land and the re-

newal of their relation to their Lord are evident from the closing sentence, "The kingdom shall be the Lord's." The prophet Joel made clearer reference to this restoration. He spoke specifically of the Lord's restoring the fortunes of Judah and Jerusalem. He closed his book with the words, "But Judah shall be inhabited for ever, and Jerusalem to all generations" (Joel 3:20). This would be possible because "the Lord dwells in Zion."

In this study of Israel's restoration, it is important to observe carefully Israel's spiritual condition. Implicit in the idea of this restoration was Israel's repentance and their turning back to God. I shall try to lay hold of clear declarations of this spiritual change. Also involved is the question whether Israel's restoration would be limited to a return to their own country or whether the prophets' thought centers on its spiritual aspect. This question carries larger implications in view of Israel's history after their return from the captivities. When Israel did return to their land, they remained under foreign control until A.D. 70, when they were again scattered over the Roman Empire. Throughout this period Israel's spiritual condition was at a low state. The promised glories of the restoration, from a spiritual point of view, had not been fulfilled. Only in the spiritual Israel did this restoration come to realization. These considerations bring into sharper focus the meaning of Joel's words in 3:16-21. These verses lead us to believe that while Joel predicted a national restoration of Israel to their own land, the burden lay chiefly in a spiritual restoration.

(2) Hosea and Amos. The prophet Hosea said little or nothing about Israel's being carried into captivity. He did say this: "The people of Judah and the people of Israel shall be gathered together, and they shall appoint for themselves one head" (Hos. 1:11). This statement points to a regathering of Israel to their own land. Hosea's burden lay, nevertheless, with Israel's spiritual restoration. Very plainly Israel would again become "Sons of the living God," which indicated a genuine spiritual restoration. The time for the fulfillment of this promise would be in that Day, which as we noted earlier is equivalent to the Latter Days.

Although the prophet Amos said little about the coming captivities, his warning to Israel stressed coming judgment. With reference to Israel's restoration, Amos quoted God as saying, "I will restore the fortunes of my people Israel, and they shall rebuild the ruined cities and inhabit them. . . . I will plant them upon their land, and they shall never again be plucked up out of the land which I have given them" (Amos 9:14, 15). God's raising up the booth of David implied a spiritual restoration.

(3) Isaiah. Isaiah spoke more clearly of Israel's restoration. He clearly placed it in the Latter Days (Is. 2:2). It centered in a spiritual

restoration. However, he introduced a new word "remnant." Note his words, "In that day the remnant of Israel and the survivors of the house of Jacob will no more lean upon him that smote them, but will lean upon the Lord, the Holy One of Israel, in truth. A remnant will return, the remnant of Jacob, to the mighty God. For though your people Israel be as the sand of the sea, only a remnant of them will return" (10:20-23). Observe also his further words: "In that day the Lord will extend his hand yet a second time to recover the remnant which is left of his people, from Assyria, from Egypt, from Pathros, from Ethiopia, from Elam, from Shinar, from Hamath, and from the coastlands of the sea" (11:11).

These passages indicated that the remnant would constitute a small body of the people of Israel, those who remained true to the Lord. Undoubtedly they had a large influence upon apostate Israel, but history showed that relatively only a small portion of those carried into captivity returned to their own land. We gather that many of those who did not return had become prosperous in these foreign lands. The opportunity for their return to their own land involved an act of faith. Even the promise made in 14:1, 2 required faith on the part of captive Israel: "The Lord will have compassion on Jacob and will again choose Israel, and will set them in their own land, and aliens will join them and will cleave to the house of Jacob." The faith requirement became evident again in 27:6: "In days to come Jacob shall take root, Israel shall blossom and put forth shoots, and fill the whole world with fruit."

Before Israel's captivity this prediction may not have had much meaning, but in a foreign land such a promise challenged their trust in the Lord. This test of the faith of the remnant appeared again in this prediction: "In that day from the river Euphrates to the Brook of Egypt the Lord will thresh out the grain, and you will be gathered one by one, O people of Israel. And in that day a great trumpet will be blown, and those who were lost in the land of Assyria and those who were driven out to the land of Egypt will come and worship the Lord on the holy mountain at Jerusalem" (27:12, 13). These words gave strong witness to a spiritual restoration of Israel.

Isaiah's development of this remnant idea had its origin in his call to the prophetic office. The Lord had commissioned Isaiah to bring a message of warning to His people and to continue his preaching until the Lord would remove men far away. The Lord stressed the idea of the remnant when He declared: "And though a tenth remain in it, it will be burned again, like a terebinth or an oak, whose stump remains standing when it is felled." Isaiah added, "The holy seed is its stump" (6:13). This teaching on the remnant leads us to see that the restoration of Israel would have been impossible if there were no holy seed.

(4) Micah. The prophet Micah spoke of God's restoration of His people in close connection with the woes He was pronouncing on them because of their sin. He said, "I will surely gather all of you, O Jacob, I will gather the remnant of Israel; I will set them together like sheep in a fold, like a flock in its pasture, a noisy multitude of men." As a bellwether sheep places himself at the head of the flock and then breaks through the enclosure and leads them out to pasture, so the Lord also would open the breach made by Israel's captors and would lead His people out of their captivity (Mic. 2:12, 13). This description of Israel's restoration to their own land was certainly a challenge to their faith. In their captivities they keenly realized the obstacle to their return. There had to be a breakthrough of the enclosure built up by the nations which had led them captive.

As Micah directed his attention to the Latter Days and spoke of the law going out of Zion and the word of the Lord from Jerusalem, he was presupposing Israel's spiritual restoration to God. As he continued his warning he said, "Writhe and groan, O daughter of Zion, like a woman in travail; for now you shall go forth from the city and dwell in the open country; you shall go to Babylon. There you shall be rescued, there the Lord will redeem you from the hand of your enemies" (Mic. 4:10). Thus in the same verse Micah predicted both the captivity and also the restoration of Israel; he used the language both of rescuing and of redeeming to describe Israel's restoration. Thus the restoration would be a work of the Lord and it would bear the nature of a saving act through His power. This adds a new dimension to the idea of Israel's restoration. Micah's words receive still deeper meaning in the light of the closing verses of his book. Israel could be restored and would be restored only through God, who pardons iniquity and shows steadfast love.

In brief summary, we should observe how prominently God's restoration of Israel stands out in the theme of the Latter Days. The prophets looked to a restoration of Israel to their land but more especially to a spiritual restoration to God. It was the Lord who restored the people to Himself. The elements of repentance and faith were the conditions of their restoration. Not all of Israel had become apostate. There was a remnant, a holy seed, who remained true to God. Without this faithful remnant there would have been no restoration. God's compassion upon His people and His willingness to pardon iniquity and to show His steadfast love to them made restoration possible. It became a reality through Israel's response of repentance and faith.

b. God's Redemption and Salvation

The prophets' presentation of God's redemption and salvation had its foundation in the Mosaic sacrificial system. The magnificent temple of Solomon fostered Israel's worship. To what extent and degree the people of Israel perpetuated the Mosaic ceremonies and sacrifices is not clearly known. In an earlier chapter we noted the references which the Former Prophets made to the observance of the Passover and to other sacrifices. The sparsity of references to the observance of these sacrifices does not constitute evidence against their performance. We shall observe the rebukes given by the Lord through the prophets to Israel for their lack of a genuine spirit of worship and for their failure to bring sacrifices to the Lord. With this background we should learn that the references to God's redemption and salvation were focused on the era of the Latter Days. We note that the prophets were not giving further expositions of their offerings and sacrifices, but were giving forecasts of what the Lord would accomplish in the future for man's redemption and salvation.

(1) Joel, Hosea, and Amos. When the prophet Joel foretold the outpouring of the Holy Spirit, he concluded his message with the words, "And it shall come to pass that all who call upon the name of the Lord shall be delivered" (Joel 2:28-32). The meaning of the verb "shall be delivered" (*malat*) is not too clear. It could point to merely a physical deliverance but the context would suggest that it was spiritual in nature. Again Peter and Paul gave its clear meaning. At Pentecost Peter (following the LXX) quoted this passage: "And it shall be that whoever calls on the name of the Lord shall be saved" (Acts 2:21; cf. Rom. 10:13). His sermon made it clear that Joel was predicting a spiritual deliverance. The verb *sozo* is the usual word used in the New Testament to express deliverance from sin and the giving of eternal life through Jesus Christ. Joel did not say how this deliverance would be accomplished, but the language suggests that it would be through the power of the Lord. Joel did not suggest any redemptive basis for this salvation. Since the sacrificial worship was conducted in the temple, the prophet may have implied a redemption through bloody sacrifice.

The redemption significance of Hosea 13:14 is quite puzzling. A careful study of the context seems to show that God is not giving a promise to ransom Ephraim from the power of the grave or to redeem them from death as the KJV suggests. Ephraim had gone beyond the point of return in his sin and for this reason compassion was hid from the eyes of the Lord. The RSV gives the correct sense: "Shall I ransom them from the power of Sheol? Shall I redeem them from Death?

O Death, where are your plagues? O Sheol, where is your destruction? Compassion is hid from my eyes."[19] The old commentator, Huxtable, gave the following explanation which anticipated the RSV translation: "In the present instance, the full import of the terms is satisfied by our taking the entire verses as a commination. Both the prophet and Saint Paul summon Death and Hell to come forth and do their worst: the prophet, in solemn earnest, because they were still terrible Powers, and had then a work of divine vengeance to execute; the Apostle, in derisive irony because at the time he refers to, Death and Hell shall be brought utterly to naught."[20]

This verse is certainly in harmony with what Hosea writes elsewhere in his book with regard to redemption. Let us note in passing, the two Hebrew verbs *padah* (ransom) and *gaal* (redeem). The Septuagint used the verb *rhuomai* (rescue, deliver) to translate the former and *lutroo* (to release by paying ransom, to redeem) to translate the latter. Both of these Greek verbs carry great significance in the New Testament as they give the meaning to Jesus' redemptive work. It would seem that in what Hosea has to say throughout his book with reference to the restoration of the covenant bond between God and Israel, he was thinking in terms of ransom and redemption.[21] Most pertinent to these ideas are the words describing the manner in which the Lord would deal with their sinful condition: "I will heal their faithlessness; I will love them freely, for my anger has turned from them."

The words of Amos (9:11, 12) came nearest to expressing the idea of God's redemption and salvation. He predicted the raising up of the booth of David which, according to the New Testament, referred to the exaltation and enthronement of Jesus as Lord and Christ. The meaning of verse 12 offers a problem especially when the Hebrew text is compared with the Septuagint translation. At the Jerusalem council James quoted this passage, following, in the main, the Septuagint translation. God would rebuild the ruins of David's dwelling, "that the rest of men may seek the Lord, and all the Gentiles who are called by my name, says the Lord, who has made these things known from of old" (Acts 15: 16-18). The Septuagint did not follow the Hebrew text and there is no evidence for the existence of a variant reading in the Hebrew.

Some scholars feel that the Septuagint laid hold of the latent meaning of Amos's words. If this gives us a proper lead, and this is what James interpreted it to mean, Amos was foretelling the enthronement of Christ which would result in all men, Jews and Gentiles, seeking the Lord. According to New Testament fulfillment, this involved the redemptive work of Christ and the salvation made possible for all mankind. This is a striking example of the New Testament interpreting Old

Testament language, imbuing it with far greater spiritual meaning than appears on the surface of the Old. We should observe that these earliest writing prophets were expressing formative ideas concerning the redemption and salvation which the Lord would accomplish through the Messiah. He who would rebuild the dwelling of David would make it possible for all men to call upon the Lord and be saved. Basic words such as *deliver, ransom,* and *redeem* furnished the vocabulary used in the New Testament to describe the meaning of Christ's redemptive work.

(2) Isaiah. As the Lord brought His charges against Israel, He described their sinfulness in most forceful language (1:4-6). He commanded them to cleanse themselves from all their wickedness, and assured them that even though their sins were like scarlet they would become like wool (1:16-18). Isaiah proceeded to build up grounds for hope that a spiritual cleansing could and would take place (4:2-6). In a future day there would be left in Zion those who would be called holy, those who had been "recorded for life in Jerusalem, when the Lord shall have washed away the filth of the daughters of Zion and cleansed the bloodstains of Jerusalem from its midst by a spirit of judgment and by a spirit of burning" (4:3, 4). The word "holy" had a background of meaning extending as far back as Moses when through the institution of sacrificial worship, the people of Israel learned that they should be holy even as the Lord their God was holy (Lev. 19:2).

Isaiah presented the idea of a book in which were the names of those who had been recorded for life in Jerusalem. This reflected the practice of cities having a register of all their inhabitants. At once we think of the New Jerusalem where dwell "those who are written in the Lamb's book of life" (Rev. 21:27). This gives us ground for believing that the word "life" as used in Isaiah (4:3) foreshadows eternal life. The Lord will have washed away their filth and cleansed their bloodstains. This language of redemption occurs in a setting where such an idea is pertinent. It is definitely descriptive of a spiritual experience involving not only the removal of sinful acts but also the inward cleansing of the heart. God would accomplish this "by a spirit of judgment and by a spirit of burning." These details, cumulatively significant, present in somewhat veiled language a description of the Messiah's redemptive work.

Isaiah's call to the prophetic office (Is. 6) unfolded further the theme of God's redemption and salvation. Note first the sense of uncleanness which he experienced after having seen "the King, the Lord of hosts." The description of his cleansing confirmed the spiritual nature of his uncleanness. The burning coal taken from the altar and touching his mouth removed his guilt and sin and indicated an inner spiritual change. In New Testament language this was Isaiah's conversion. While the prophet made no reference to the aspects of redemption and salvation, these are implicit in the narrative. God's words, "Lest they see with their eyes, and hear with their ears, and understand with their hearts, and turn and be healed," suggested more clearly the redemptive aspect of Isaiah's ministry and also of his own experience. It involved the inner *seeing, hearing,* and *understanding;* accompanied by their *turning* and *being healed.* On three occasions the New Testament quoted this passage, and each time the message of salvation received special stress.[22] Underlying this salvation message was the implicit truth of God's redemption.

It was entirely natural that Isaiah should use the words *yeshuah, yasha* (salvation, save) which gained great significance at the time of the exodus (Ex. 14:13, 30). Moses said, "Stand firm, and see the salvation of the Lord." After reciting the wonderful experience of Israel's deliverance the writer concluded, "Thus the Lord saved Israel that day from the hand of the Egyptians." These words soon gained great spiritual significance. Isaiah's use of them appears in statements like the following: "God is my salvation"; "With joy you will draw water from the wells of salvation" (12:2, 3); "He will swallow up death for ever. . . . It will be said on that day, 'Lo, this is our God; we have waited for him, that he might save us. . . . Let us be glad and rejoice in his salvation' " (25: 8, 9). In this context Isaiah caught the basic idea of God's swallowing up death with that of salvation. In this lay the idea of eternal life. Paul interpreted this verse as a prediction of the resurrection, and John referred to it in his description of the eternal state of the righteous (1 Cor. 15:54; Rev. 7:17; 21:4). In Isaiah's song of trust we have the words, "We have a strong city; he sets up salvation as walls and bulwarks. Open the gates, that the righteous nation which keeps faith may enter in. Thou dost keep him in perfect peace, whose mind is stayed on thee, because he trusts in thee. Trust in the Lord for ever, for the Lord God is an everlasting rock" (26:1-4). This exquisite song pictured the salvation of the righteous in the language of a walled city into which the righteous could enter. Such are kept in perfect peace because of their trust in the Lord, who is the everlasting rock.

A few concluding thoughts drawn from the message of these prophets are in order. The idea of redemption was beginning to find expression. These prophets, especially Isaiah, grasped the meaning of the spiritual cleansing involved in God's salvation. This idea of God's salvation became one of Isaiah's great contributions to the unfolding divine revelation of God. He thought of salvation both as a present spiritual experience and also as belonging to the future eternal life.

c. Outpouring of the Holy Spirit

Several matters of special importance call for intensive study as we examine the references to the Spirit. These include: first, the work of the Holy Spirit in the prophets; second, the Spirit's relation to the coming Messiah; third, the work of the Spirit in relation to man's salvation; and fourth, the nature and personality of the Holy Spirit.

(1) Joel. The first prophet to predict the outpouring of the Holy Spirit was Joel. Quoting the Lord, Joel wrote, "And it shall come to pass afterward, that I will pour out my spirit on all flesh; your sons and your daughters shall prophesy, your old men shall dream dreams, and your young men shall see visions. Even upon the menservants and maidservants in those days, I will pour out my spirit" (2:28, 29). The time of the outpouring of God's Spirit would be in the era beyond the Day of the Lord, denoted by the expression "afterward." Peter recast this expression, using the more familiar words, "the last days." This dating of the prediction placed the event during the days of the coming Messiah. The special significance of this prediction lay in the idea that God would pour out His Spirit on all flesh. The manifestation of the Spirit of God had been restricted to prophets, priests, kings, and others to whom God had entrusted special responsibilities. The prediction did not express any difference between the manner of the Spirit's coming upon the people in the future and that already manifested among God's servants. The supreme significance of the future outpouring lay in the fact that the Spirit would come upon all of God's people. Prophesying, dreaming dreams, seeing visions, would no longer be limited to chosen servants of the Lord.

It is important to observe that Peter included verses 30-32 in his quotation from Joel. In doing this he drew attention to the supernatural manifestation which would accompany the outpouring of the Holy Spirit to serve as proofs of the fulfillment of the predictions. It would appear that Peter interpreted the darkness and the earthquakes occurring at the time of Jesus' death on the cross, along with the rush of the mighty wind at Pentecost, as being the fulfillment of Joel's prophecy. From this we should gather that God provided the necessary credentials in the outpouring of the Holy Spirit so that all those present at Pentecost would have grounds for believing in the fulfillment of God's prediction.

(2) Isaiah. We do not know whether Isaiah had access to Joel's prediction. If Joel was among the earliest of the writing prophets, it is possible that Isaiah knew of his prophecy. At any rate his words (32: 15, 16) are quite similar to those of Joel and would indicate that he was

already aware of this prediction. Isaiah's reference to the coming of the Spirit is in a Messianic context in which he declared, "Behold, a king will reign in righteousness, and princes will rule in justice." He gave appropriate warning to sinful people of his time and then he disclosed the blessings of the Messianic age. It would be marked by the Spirit being poured upon them from on high.

A debatable reference to the Holy Spirit is found in the words, "Seek and read from the book of the Lord: Not one of these shall be missing; none shall be without her mate. For the mouth of the Lord has commanded, and his Spirit has gathered them" (Is. 34:16). If the RSV translation is correct, we have here an interesting and instructive parallelism. In the context God is pronouncing His wrath against the nations. Support for the prediction was found in the book of the Lord. "The mouth of the Lord" is structurally parallel to "his Spirit." In this manner Isaiah was identifying the *mouth of the Lord* and *his Spirit*. This idea is certainly evident elsewhere in the Scripture. Nearest like this are the words of Peter, "Men moved by the Holy Spirit spoke from God" (2 Pet. 1:21).

(3) Micah. Two references to the Spirit of the Lord come from the pen of Micah: "Is the Spirit of the Lord impatient?" and also "But as for me, I am filled with power, with the Spirit of the Lord, and with justice and might" (Mic. 2:7; 3:8). In the former passage Micah noted that just as the Spirit of the Lord displayed patience in the presence of Israel's sin, so the Lord's words do good to him who walks uprightly. The second reference contrasted the false prophets and seers, who made a profession of speaking from God, with Micah, the true prophet, who was actually filled with power and with the Spirit of the Lord. Micah's testimony was identical with the New Testament description of the indwelling Holy Spirit, who gives power to those in whom He dwells.

This survey of the outpouring of the Holy Spirit gives a significant perspective to the Latter Days. The Spirit was already significantly present in the prophet Micah, but it was Joel who forecast the outpouring of the Holy Spirit upon all flesh. He did not predict a different manner of the Spirit's work in God's people; but rather, that all of God's servants would experience the Spirit's indwelling as did the prophets, priests, and kings in Old Testament times. Isaiah indicated that through the Spirit's power, the Messiah would perform mighty works. These descriptions and predictions of the Holy Spirit presented the idea of His being a person. Further, the Spirit of the Lord stands forth as being distinct from the Lord Himself, but yet as true Deity. These prophets did not seek to explain the unfathomable mysteries involved in the personality and deity of the Spirit of the Lord.

8. Life of the People of God

The prophets of this period had a great deal to say concerning the life of the people of God. Usually the occasion for their writing lay in the people's sinfulness. This led the prophets to rebuke them for their sins and to set forth the standard of living required by God. In such contexts we see graphic pictures of the nature of sin and of man's sinfulness. The prophets pointed the way of return to God through repentance and faith. This led naturally to the setting up of ethical standards of life. The prophets made clear the nature of the godly life; they described the way of holiness.

a. Joel — Call to Godly Living

Against a background of imminent judgment Joel called the people of God to repentance in view of the coming terrible Day of the Lord. God said, "Return to me with all your heart, with fasting, with weeping, and with mourning; and rend your hearts and not your garments" (Joel 2:12, 13). The change which was required was the inner experience of returning to the Lord. There would be the outer manifestation of fasting, weeping, and mourning and not mere tearing of one's clothes. The tearing of the heart is most descriptive of repentance. Only upon such people would the Lord pour out His Spirit. The manner of life required of God's people stands forth in this book more by implication than by direct command. Joel must have been successfully upholding God's words to Israel, for the people knew that the Lord was dwelling in their midst and that He alone was God. He most naturally called Israel to obedience to the commandments and statutes in the books of Moses.

b. Jonah — Living in the Fear of the Lord

Even the Book of Jonah gives some valuable truths concerning the life of the people of God. He could testify, "I fear the Lord, the God of heaven, who made the sea and the dry land" (Jon. 1:9). Jonah's attempted flight to Tarshish was interpreted as a "fleeing from the presence of the Lord." Jonah was a man of prayer. He believed that God heard and answered prayer. From the belly of the whale he longed to look again upon God's holy temple. With the voice of thanksgiving he would sacrifice to the Lord and pay his vows. He recognized that "Deliverance belongs to the Lord" (2:9). Yet Jonah had not grasped the implication of the Lord's being "a gracious God and merciful, slow to anger, and abounding in steadfast love" (4:2).

c. *Hosea — Holy Living in Reverse*

Hosea dwelt at great length on Israel's sinfulness. What he wrote showed how the people of God should not live. The starting point of his treatment was Israel's spiritual adultery. Their sin was first of all and fundamentally unfaithfulness to their God (Hos. 2:2). Israel showed no knowledge of God. Specifically the Lord said, "There is swearing, lying, killing, stealing, and committing adultery; they break all bounds and murder follows murder" (4:1, 2). God had specified these forms of sin to show Israel the heinousness of these acts also as they destroyed the peaceful relations between man and man. God would have love to reign in human relationships. The Lord showed that Israel's sin was not a mere lapse into wrongdoing but that at heart they were rejecting knowledge, forgetting the law of God, and forsaking the Lord (4:12-19). Israel's unfaithfulness to God was at the center the breaking of their covenant relation with Him. "They, like Adam, transgressed the covenant; there they broke faith with me" (Hos. 6:7, RSV m., Berkeley). Israel's multiplying of altars for sacrifice was a most defiant way of breaking this fellowship (8:11-14). They did this because their hearts were false (10:2).

The flagrancy of Israel's sin becomes still clearer when we observe what needed to be done to renew their covenant relationship with the Lord. God desired steadfast love and the knowledge of Himself (6:6). These two expressions lead to the very heart of the spiritual relation that should exist between man and God. In language familiar to people of the soil the Lord said, "Sow for yourselves righteousness, reap the fruit of steadfast love; break up your fallow ground, for it is the time to seek the Lord, that he may come and rain salvation upon you" (10:12). Righteousness is the most descriptive word used to express the life of the people of God. It becomes the key word to describe the nature of a God-fearing life. The Lord expressed the way in which Israel could again enter into relationship with Him in the words, "So you, by the help of your God, return, hold fast to love and justice, and wait continually for your God" (12:6). This return would be possible alone by His help. Herein is a new dimension in Hosea's ethics: man does not possess the inner power to live a godly life. Love and justice constitute the pattern for this kind of life. For power to live in love and righteousness His people need to wait continually for their God. In the words of Harper they need to "cultivate absolute faithfulness."[23] Hosea's closing admonition reads, "The ways of the Lord are right, and the upright walk in them" (14:9). Hosea was explicit in his description of man's sinfulness, but he held forth the true way of life in most expressive language.

d. Amos — Unholy Living Condemned

Amos's presentation of the life of the people of God also took its beginning with a forthright condemnation of the sins of the nation. For each nation his attack took the form of "Thus says the Lord: 'For three transgressions . . . and for four, I will not revoke the punishment' " (Amos 1:3). These condemnations had to do largely with the inter-relations of these nations as they lived in the land of Canaan. They were always at war with one another and were constantly retaliating for the injuries received from their neighbors. The Lord condemned Judah because they had rejected His law and had not kept His statutes. He rebuked Israel for various injuries committed against the righteous and against the poor and needy. Their acts of adultery and other degrading practices in worship also came under censure. In view of these various forms of sin and corruption, the Lord declared, "Prepare to meet your God, O Israel" (4:12, 13)! He sought to lead them back to a godly pattern of life because He was the God of creation. He admonished them: "Seek me and live." Israel needed to be aware that God knew their many transgressions and great sins. For this reason the Lord said, "Seek good, and not evil, that you may live. . . . Hate evil, and love good, and establish justice in the gate" (5:14, 15).

Since many of Israel's sins centered in afflicting the righteous and obstructing justice, the Lord added, "Let justice roll down like waters, and righteousness like an everflowing stream" (5:24). With their increased wealth, Israel was living in luxury. This brought upon them pronouncements such as "Woe to those who are at ease in Zion, and to those who feel secure on the mountain of Samaria. . . . Woe to those who lie upon beds of ivory, and stretch themselves upon their couches, and eat lambs from the flock, and calves from the midst of the stall; who sing idle songs to the sound of the harp, and like David invent for themselves instruments of music; who drink wine in bowls, and anoint themselves with the finest oils, but are not grieved over the ruin of Joseph" (6:1-7)! Thus the Lord showed Israel the sins which were being committed in their selfish ease and luxury. The messages of Amos show that Judah and Israel knew the standard of living which the Lord required of His people: uprightness, holiness, righteousness, and justice.

e. Isaiah (1 — 39) — Holy Living: Positive and Negative

Like the other prophets, Isaiah portrayed the life of the people of God against the background of Israel's sinfulness. These portrayals very significantly show the nature of sin, and make clear the kind of remedy necessary. Isaiah described the nation's sins in terms of a rebellion against God: "Ah, sinful nation, a people laden with iniquity, offspring of evildoers, sons who deal corruptly! They have forsaken the Lord, they have despised the Holy One of Israel, they are utterly estranged" (1:4). This language presents sin in its worst form. As conscious rebellion against God and as utter estrangement from Him.

Using the metaphor of physical infection, Isaiah wrote, "The whole head is sick, and the whole heart faint. From the sole of the foot even to the head, there is no soundness in it, but bruises and sores and bleeding wounds; they are not pressed out, or bound up, or softened with oil" (1:5, 6). What a graphic picture of the spiritual infection of sin! The cure for this kind of spiritual ailment came in these words, "Wash yourselves; make yourselves clean; remove the evil of your doings from before my eyes; cease to do evil, learn to do good; seek justice, correct oppression; defend the fatherless, plead for the widow" (1:16, 17). The remedy for sinfulness lay in a spiritual washing and cleansing, a definite turning from sin and learning again the righteous way of life. The Lord assured them, nevertheless, in the words, "Come now, let us reason together, says the Lord: though your sins are like scarlet, they shall be as white as snow; though they are red like crimson, they shall become like wool." This is perhaps the most graphic picture of the sinfulness of sin found in the Old Testament. At the same time it is most vivid in its promise of complete removal of sin and its effects by the grace of God.

Implicit throughout this arraignment is the standard of holy living to which the Lord would lead His people. The words "good, "justice," "obedient," "faithful," and "righteousness" reflect this ethical ideal. Even when Isaiah, in the presence of the Lord, judged himself to be a man of unclean lips, the Lord removed his guilt and forgave his sin, showing again that by the grace of God man's sins can be removed. This is a model of how a man of God responds when he becomes aware of his sin. This became the bulwark of Isaiah's strength of character.

Another aspect of sin becomes apparent in the message God gave to Isaiah for Israel: " 'Hear and hear, but do not understand; see and see, but do not perceive.' Make the heart of this people fat, and their ears heavy, and shut their eyes; lest they see with their eyes, and hear with their ears, and understand with their hearts, and turn and be healed" (6:9, 10). This message presented the spiritual outcome of refusing to obey God's commands, a hardening of heart. When people knowingly and consciously refuse to be obedient to the Lord, they lose their spiritual perception of right and wrong. True people of God will eschew this attitude. Very significantly, this teaching was used three times in the New Testament to describe a similar state of affairs.[24] When Ahaz stood at the brink of overthrow at the hands of Rezin and Pekah, the Lord spoke through Isaiah, challenging him to faith in the words, "If you will not believe, surely you shall not be established" (7:1-9). As king of Judah, Ahaz should have responded with simple faith but he had forgotten the faith aspect of his religion. As Isaiah predicted the imminent Day of the Lord which would come upon the nation of Babylon, he quoted the Lord's words, " 'I will punish the world for its evil, and the wicked for their iniquity; I will put an end to the pride of the arrogant, and lay low the haughtiness of the ruthless' " (13:1-11). This direct judgment showed sin as manifesting itself in pride and haughtiness. Babylon through its worldwide conquests had become truly proud. In a word, Babylon was saying, " 'I will make myself like the Most High' " (14:1-14). It is clear that when sin reaches its climax, man foolishly exalts himself as God.

Isaiah related Israel's sin to their covenant relation with God in the words, "They have transgressed the laws, violated the statutes, broken the everlasting covenant" (24:5). This was the most serious aspect of Israel's sin. God had drawn them into covenant relationship with Himself but they did not have the integrity to remain obedient to their covenant commitment. Equally expressive was the language, "This people draw near with their mouth and honor me with their lips, while their hearts are far from me, and their fear of me is a commandment of men learned by rote. . . . Woe to those who hide deep from the Lord their counsel, whose deeds are in the dark, and who say, 'Who sees us? Who knows us' " (29:13-15)? In this indictment the Lord exposed the sinfulness manifested in the disparity of lip profession and heart attitude. This is the heinousness of hypocrisy.

Isaiah predicted a future era in which God's people would demonstrate the manner of life which befits His chosen people: "We have a strong city; he sets up salvation as walls and bulwarks. Open the gates, that the righteous nation which keeps faith may enter in. Thou dost keep him in perfect peace, whose mind is stayed on thee, because he trusts in thee. Trust in the Lord for ever, for the Lord God is an everlasting rock. . . . The way of the righteous is level; thou dost make smooth the path of the righteous. In the path of thy judgments, O Lord, we wait for thee; thy memorial name is the desire of our soul. My soul yearns for thee in the night, my spirit within me earnestly seeks thee" (26:1-9). Thus Isaiah declares that graces of godliness such as righteousness, faithfulness, and trust lead to perfect peace.

f. Micah — Godly Living in All Areas of Life

Micah presented a pattern of life for God's people similar to the one given by Isaiah. He began by exhorting the people of Israel and Judah to let the Lord God be a witness against them. The transgressions and sins centered in Samaria and Jerusalem. Samaria had given up the true worship for that of idols. She had become a city of immorality. Their sinfulness had become incurable and had begun to infect the people of Jerusalem. Throughout the book Micah exposed the sins of these nations in all their atrociousness. Their manifold character showed the many areas in life in which holiness and righteousness needed to become dynamic and real in order to effect the cure (2:1, 2; 3:2, 3; 6:10-12, etc.).

Micah made it clear that when the sacrifices were not accompanied by the experience of worship which they symbolized, they were futile. He said, "He has showed you, O man, what is good; and what does the Lord require of you but to do justice, and to love kindness, and to walk humbly with your God" (6:8)? Here in brief the prophet presented truly holy living.

9. Nature of Sin and Man's Sinfulness

The preceding discussion has already laid bare the prophets' view of sin as understood in the setting of the people's departure from the standard of holy living. As directed by the Lord, the prophets denounced these sins through which Israel had degraded themselves. In these arraignments the prophets disclosed a large vocabulary relating to the nature of sin, comparable to that used in the Pentateuch. The prophets enlarged, developed, and intensified the concepts expressed by the words in the Pentateuch. The present approach to our subject will be to show how each prophet dealt with the sin question in his own writings. The vocabulary for sin will receive only secondary attention. The reader may wish to review Part I, Chapter VIII, before reading this section.

a. Obadiah and Joel

The prophet Obadiah predicted the imminent Day of the Lord in which God would punish Edom for his violence (*hamas*) done to Israel (v. 10). Joel exhorted the people of Judah to turn to the Lord with all their heart because their wickedness (*ra*) was great. God would also bring judgment upon Egypt and Edom for the violence (*hamas*) done to the people of Judah (Joel 3:13, 19). The prophet Jonah went to Nineveh to cry against the inhabitants because of their wickedness (*ra*). His message proved to be very effective because the king gave a decree that his people should cry mightily to God, and that "everyone turn from his evil way (*ra*) and from the violence (*hamas*) which . . . [was] in his hands" (Jon. 1:2; 3:8).

b. Hosea and Amos

The prophet Hosea laid bare the sins of Judah and Israel in the language of spiritual harlotry. The marital unfaithfulness of Hosea's wife became the symbol of the nation's spiritual unfaithfulness to God, centering in their covenant relationship with Him. This comparison of natural marriage with covenant relationship taught the high spiritual quality of this relationship. On this account Israel's infidelity to God was shown to be most grievous. Thus the essence of sin is infidelity to God. Hosea used no less than fifteen different words to state the nature of Israel's sin.

Hosea began his exposure of Israel's sin by noting that God's people were being destroyed for lack of knowledge. They rejected (*ma'as*) knowledge (4:6). Here was the conscious rejection of God's law. Hosea proceeded to declare how Israel sinned (*hata*) against the Lord and fed on, were even greedy for, their iniquity (4:7, 8). Hosea repeated this verb in noting that Ephraim had multiplied altars for sinning. Rather than show steadfast love for God and experience knowledge of Him Israel transgressed (*abar*) the covenant and dealt faithlessly (*bagad*) with Him (6:6, 7). The high places of Aven were the sin of Israel. Israel sinned more and more through their worship of Baal (8:8; 10:8; 13:2).

The prophet intensified the meaning of *hata* by combining it with *avon*. Twice he used the identical expression, "He will remember their iniquity (*avon*), he will punish their sins (*hata*)" (8:13; 9:9. *See also* 13:12). Hosea used another parallel in a statement of burning irony when he said, "The prophet is a fool, the man of the spirit is mad, because of your great iniquity (*avon*) and great hatred (*mastemah*)" (9:7). Speaking for the Lord, Hosea used the word *ra* when he exposed the *wicked* deeds of Samaria, their *evil* works, their wickedness, and their evil devisings.[25] Hosea pointed up the offense or guilt aspect of sin (*asham*) when he declared that Ephraim had incurred *guilt* through Baal (Hos. 13:1. *See also* 4:13; 5:15; 10:2). He used the verb *sarah* (7:14) and *sarar* (4:16; 9:15) to set forth Ephraim's sin as rebellion and stubbornness. Because Ephraim plowed iniquity (*rasha*) they reaped injustice (*avel*) (10:13). Israel's apostasy was a refusal (*ma'an*) to return to the Lord. Because of Israel's prosperity their hearts were lifted up (*rum*) and they rebelled (*marah*) against their God (13:6, 16). Hosea's last word with regard to sin found expression in his closing sentence: "The ways of the Lord are right, and the upright walk in them, but transgressors (*pesha*) stumble in them" (14:9). This use of *pesha* is most climactic in view of its having been used earlier (6:7; 8:1) with reference to Israel's most grievous sin in transgressing God's law and in breaking their covenant with the Lord.

The prophet Amos was equally severe in denouncing the sins of the people of God. By means of a most vigorous literary device, "For three transgressions (*pesha*) . . . and for four," he exposed the sinfulness of the nations, including Judah and Israel.[26] It would appear that in Amos's mind the word *pesha* expressed most accurately the sin common to all these nations. Acts of afflicting the righteous, taking bribes, and turning aside the needy he called transgressions (*pesha*) and sins (*hata*) (5:12). In a positive way he exhorted the people to "Seek good, and not evil (*ra*), that you may live. . . . Hate evil (*ra*), and love good, and establish justice in the gate" (5:14, 15). Many of his denunciations had to do with the luxurious living of the people of Judah and Israel. God abhorred the exaltation, the pride (*gaon*) of Jacob. Only in the last five verses of his book did Amos give a brighter picture, which shone forth from the era lying beyond the judgment of the imminent Day of the Lord.

c. Isaiah and Micah

The prophet Isaiah introduced his messages with a blunt confrontation and arraignment of Judah concerning their sins. The Lord had brought up His people as sons but they rebelled (*pasha*) against Him. This word became the most descriptive of all expressions relating to the sins (about fifteen in number) mentioned in the book. The Lord added, "The ox knows his owner, and the ass its master's crib; but Israel does not know, my people does not understand" (Is. 1:3). With this simple metaphor God would lead His people to the real nature of their spiritual lack of knowledge. Isaiah then gave his own analysis in the words, "Ah, sinful (*hata*) nation, a people laden with iniquity (*avon*), offspring of evildoers (*raa*), sons who deal corruptly (*shachath*)! They have forsaken the Lord, they have despised the Holy One of Israel, they are utterly estranged" (1:4; 5:18; 6:7; 27:9). Note the inner nature of sin expressed in this indictment. Isaiah showed still more vividly this inner nature by comparing it with bodily ailments especially grievous for not having been treated. Sin-sickness, especially rebellion (*sarah*), could scarcely have a more forceful parallel (1:5, 6).

Because of this sinful condition Israel's sacrifices and offerings had no meaning. Isaiah gave the remedy in the words, "Wash yourselves; make yourselves clean; remove the evil (*ra*) of your doings from before my eyes; cease to do evil, learn to do good; seek justice, correct oppression; defend the fatherless, plead for the widow" (1:16, 17). Here the word for evil stands in contrast with its opposite, good, thus sharpening their ethical antagonism. The Lord began the confrontation with the frank description of sin (*hata*). It had the redness of scarlet cloth but this could be changed to the whiteness of snow. This cleaning could be made effective if they were willing and obedient. At once Isaiah injected the awful outcome if they should refuse (*ma'an*) and rebel (*sarah*) — they would be devoured by the sword. He placed the virtues — faithfulness, justice, and righteousness — in opposition to the several forms of sinfulness, such as harlotry, murder, rebellion (*sarar*), thievery, etc. (1:21-23).

With Isaiah this line of demarcation between the good and the evil was very sharp (1:27, 28). He labeled two additional grievous sins: haughtiness (*gaavah*) and pride (*rum*) (2:11, 12, 17). Both of these words stand opposed to humility; they do not exalt God. The six "woes" of Chapter V are declared against so many kinds of sin among God's people. These pronouncements included extravagance, intemperance, and ignoring the antagonism of good and evil. There were those who drew iniquity (*avon*) as with cords of falsehood and sin (*chattaah*) as with cart ropes. To be guilty of all these sins was very clearly to reject the law of the Lord. In the setting of the coming judgments of the Day of the Lord we face perhaps the darkest picture of sin in the entire book of Isaiah. God said, "I will punish the world for its evil, and the wicked for their iniquity; I will put an end to the pride of the arrogant, and lay low the haughtiness of the ruthless" (13:9-11). Observe the vocabulary for sin in this verse: evil (*ra*), wicked (*rasha*), iniquity (*avon*), pride (*gaon*), arrogant (*zed*), haughtiness (*gaavah*), and ruthless (*arits*). As we would expect, Isaiah stated the involvement of sin in relation to their covenant with God. He wrote, "They have transgressed the laws, violated the statutes, broken the everlasting covenant" (24:5). A second time Isaiah gave a fivefold pronouncement of woe against so many classes of sinners:[27] drunkards, those who hid their sins, the rebellious, those who looked to Egypt for help, and those who were destroying others and acting treacherously (*bagad*).

The prophet Micah opened his book with a severe indictment in the words, "Let the Lord God be a witness against you" (Mic. 1:2). His judgment was imminent because of the transgressions (*pesha*) and the sins (*hata*) of his people (1:5, 13; 3:8; 6:7). The prophet brought another charge expressed in a "woe" pronounced upon those who devised wickedness (*aven*) and worked evil (*ra*) upon their beds. They coveted fields and seized them and oppressed a man by robbing him of his house and his inheritance. God's people were walking haughtily (*romah*) (2:1-3). A similar rebuke came: "Is it not for you to know justice? — you who hate the good and love the evil (*ra*)" (3:2). The prophet enlarged on this condemnation by using extremely brutal terms, such as tearing the skin off the people, and the flesh from their bones. He continued his attack by charging the rulers with abhorring justice and perverting all equity (3:9). Because of all this wickedness Zion would be plowed as a field and Jerusalem would become a heap of ruins. Even in the sublime section (chapters 4, 5), in which he predicted the glorious times of Israel in the Latter Days, the prophet spoke of the Lord's executing vengeance upon the sorcerers, the soothsayers, and those who were bowing down to Asherim (5:10-15). The Lord asked, "Can I forget the treasures of wickedness (*resha*) in the house of the wicked (*rasha*), and the scant measure that is accursed (*zaam*)? Shall I acquit the man with wicked (*resha*) scales and with a bag of deceitful weights (*mirmah*)? Your rich men are full of violence (*chamas*); your inhabitants speak lies, and their tongue is deceitful (*remiyyah*) in their mouth" (6:10-12). They perpetuated the wickedness of Omri and of Ahab. In the midst of all this wickedness the prophet Micah sensed his loneliness because "The godly man has perished from the earth, and there is none upright among men; they all lie in wait for blood, and each hunts his brother with a net" (7:2).

The prophet continued with this language and exposed still further the deep-seated wickedness of God's people. All of these most severe condemnations of Israel's sin served, nevertheless, to magnify God's steadfast love expressed in the words, "Who is a God like thee, pardoning iniquity and passing over transgression for the remnant of his inheritance? . . . Thou wilt cast all our sins into the depths of the sea. Thou wilt show faithfulness to Jacob and steadfast love to Abraham" (7:18-20). To summarize, Micah's vocabulary for sin was wide and comprehensive. His charges against God's people covered the range from idolatrous practices to the grievous social sins prevalent in a society given over to lawlessness and violence.

10. Repentance, Faith, and Regeneration

The unfolding of these concepts ties in very closely with the preceding section. As these early writing prophets disclosed the nature of sin, the nature of the remedy for sin — repentance, faith, and regeneration — became evident. The specific and clear-cut exhortations as to how Israel could be saved from their sins had their bases in the prophets' detailed and accurate knowledge of their sins.

a. Joel's Call to Repentance

After Joel had warned Judah of the "great and terrible" Day of the Lord, he added some consoling words, " 'Yet even now,' says the Lord, 'return to me with all your heart, with fasting, with weeping, and with mourning; and rend your hearts and not your garments.' Return to the Lord, your God, for he is gracious and merciful, slow to anger, and abounding in steadfast love, and repents of evil" (Joel 2:12, 13). The Hebrew verb translated "return" is *shub*. The Septuagint used the word *epistrepho* to express this idea in the Greek language. Both of these words are commonly used in a nonmoral sense, but it is this usage which furnished the mold for its spiritual application of turning to God. It was the returning to God with all the heart, man's innermost being, involving his affections, purposes, and intentions. If Joel was one of the earliest of the writing prophets, it becomes very significant that this deep insight into the nature of repentance appeared so early in Hebrew thought.

b. Hosea's Teaching on Repentance, Faith, and Regeneration

We observed in our earlier discussions that the prophet Hosea involved himself very deeply in the spiritual condition of Judah and Israel. This became increasingly evident in the repeated statements of what God required of His people to restore them to covenant relationship. The eschatological setting of the great body of his teachings makes this prerequisite all the more imperative. It took its beginning in the prophetic disclosure of Israel's future name. They were to be called Ammi (*My people*) and also Ruhamah (*She has obtained pity*) (Hos. 2:1). Obviously a great inner change would be involved in Israel's turning from Lo-ammi (Not my people) to that of being "Sons of the living God." Hosea's first condition for this spiritual change appears in the words, "Afterward the children of Israel shall return and seek the Lord their God, . . . and they shall come in fear to the Lord and to his goodness" (3:5). The constituent elements of this change give the formative idea of repentance.

Hosea rebuked a halfhearted return on the part of Israel and Judah. When he noted their pride and guilt, he said that they would seek the Lord but would not find Him. The Lord had withdrawn from them because they had dealt faithlessly with Him (5:6, 7). The kind of spiritual experience which should lie back of a real return to the Lord was steadfast love and the knowledge of God. God's people needed to learn again the binding commitment of covenant relation with Him (6:6, 7). Ephraim's unrestrained mingling with idolatrous people stood in antithesis to their return to the Lord and their seeking Him. Genuine repentance required uncompromising separation from the world (7:8-10). Hosea showed the real nature of repentance in the words, "Sow for yourselves righteousness, reap the fruit of steadfast love; break up your fallow ground, for it is the time to seek the Lord, that he may come and rain salvation upon you" (10:12). Thus in pastoral terms Hosea commanded his people to turn away from plowing iniquity, reaping injustice, and eating the fruit of lies. In similar vein he said, "So you, by the help of your God, return, hold fast to love and justice, and wait continually for your God" (12:6). Herein are two aspects of salvation: the power of God which makes return possible, and the love of God which bestows the enabling grace.

It is noteworthy that this truth found such clear expression in this stage of divine revelation. It is clear that Ephraim was responsible to return to God, but involved in this return was the necessity of God's help. Herein are the two aspects of salvation, the human and the divine. Yet once more Hosea commanded Israel to return to the Lord. On their obedience, God would heal their faithlessness and would love them freely (14:1-4). This repeated the idea of God's part in salvation. It is a healing work, a familiar but meaningful figure. Just as physical healing requires the power of God, so spiritual healing is supremely a divine work.

c. Amos's Call to Repentance

The prophet Amos brought his people to the sad truth that in spite of all the judgments which God brought upon them, they would not return. Hence God gave the stern warning, "Prepare to meet your God, O Israel" (4:12)! But this was not God's last word to them. Repeatedly He said, "Seek the Lord and live. . . . Seek good, and not evil, that you may live. . . . Hate evil, and love good, and establish justice in the gate" (Amos 5:4, 6, 14, 15). Only in seeking Him would they live. God was calling for the spiritual responses expressed in the words, "Let justice roll down like waters, and righteousness like an ever-flowing stream" (5:24). Thus while Amos called for an inner spiritual change on the part of Israel, there was little evidence of response.

d. Jonah's Witness to Repentance

Moved by Jonah's prediction concerning Nineveh's overthrow the king of Nineveh gave the command, "Let man and beast be covered with sackcloth, and let them cry mightily to God; yea, let everyone turn from his evil way and from the violence which is in his hands" (3:8). Thus the king of Nineveh understood the spiritual aspect of repentance. He was conscious of the antagonism between good and evil. He saw clearly that their sinfulness had brought upon them the fierce anger of the Lord. The sad part of the story is that while Jonah was aware that God was gracious and merciful and abounding in steadfast love, he himself was unable to show the same forgiving spirit as God showed. The chief lesson remains, nevertheless, that imminent judgment awakened the king's consciousness of sin and led him, as well as his people, to turn from their evil way; and finally, that penitent sinners have to do with a gracious and merciful God who abounds in steadfast love and forgives penitent sinners.

e. Isaiah's Teaching (1 — 39) on Repentance, Faith, and Regeneration

Isaiah began his prophetic message by bringing a severe indictment against Judah. He described her ailment as a deep-seated spiritual affliction, the remedy for which would need to be spiritual. The elements of faith and spiritual renewal became evident when he told them that their sins, which were red like crimson, could be transformed so that they would be as white as snow and wool. The change wrought here is not a mere cessation from acts of evil, but looks to a work wrought in the heart by the power of God. It is a work of God which Israel could refuse, thus showing man's responsibility for receiving the gracious inner working of the Holy Spirit. Isaiah repeated this idea in a context having an eschatological slant when he said, "The Lord shall have washed away the filth of the daughters of Zion and cleansed the bloodstains of Jerusalem from its midst by a spirit of judgment and by a spirit of burning" (4:4).

This is a work impossible to man, and for this reason the experiences described here prepare us for the full unfolding of spiritual renewal depicted in the New Testament.[28] Isaiah's encounter with the Lord presents this truth in terms of personal experience. In the presence of the Lord he expressed his undone condition in the words, "I am lost; for I am a man of unclean lips, and I dwell in the midst of a people of unclean lips." His inner change of heart found expression in the figurative language of a burning coal touching his mouth to take away his guilt and forgive his sin (6:5-7). This supernatural act of God brought about the spiritual transformation of the prophet.

In an entirely different setting the Lord challenged Ahaz not to fear the nearby kings, assuring him that these kingdoms would soon be overthrown. Then He added, "If you will not believe, surely you shall not be established" (7:1-9). The Lord confirmed His promise by giving Ahaz a sign relating to the birth of Immanuel. From a human viewpoint Ahaz's overthrow was imminent, but God's words became a challenge to his faith. Again from a human point of view the impossible would take place if Ahaz would believe God's promise. In this idea is the essential element of faith. In another context the spiritual requirement for faith in God again emerged. The Lord was giving counsel to Isaiah in his position as mediator between God and Israel. He warned Isaiah not to walk in the way of the people of Israel, but to fear the Lord. He should regard God as holy, and let Him be his fear and dread (8: 11-15). This command required of Isaiah a holiness in conformity with that of the Lord his God. Only such a person could experience genuine worship.

The sinfulness of Israel had become so great that the Lord hid His face from the house of Jacob. Isaiah maintained his obedience to the Lord and said, "I will wait for the Lord, who is hiding his face from the house of Jacob, and I will hope in him. Behold, I and the children whom the Lord has given me are signs and portents in Israel from the Lord of hosts, who dwells on Mount Zion" (8:17, 18). In the face of the people's consulting mediums and wizards, Isaiah asked pointedly, "Should not a people consult their God? Should they consult the dead on behalf of the living? To the teaching and to the testimony" (8:19, 20)!

This spiritual crisis magnified the utter folly of Israel's apostasy and also the dynamics of Isaiah's faith in God. In the setting of the great Messianic prediction (9:1-7) Isaiah spoke forcefully against Israel's wickedness, and when they failed to respond he referred four times to God's anger in the words, "For all this his anger is not turned away and his hand is stretched out still."[29] Even such forceful language failed to lead Israel back to their God in repentance; God's gracious love and mercy could not compel the people of Israel to repent. In a grand eschatological context Isaiah foretold the day when Israel would turn to God in loving recognition of His willingness to forgive. At that time Israel would say, "Behold, God is my salvation; I will trust, and will not be afraid; for the Lord God is my strength and my song, and he has become my salvation" (12:1, 2). Thus Isaiah challenged his people to make this promise come true in his own time. God's anger would be turned away. With joy they could draw water from the wells of salvation. Here is a picture of a vital personal relationship which could be realized if they would return to God. Isaiah gave to the word "salvation" (*Yeshuah*) a new dimension of meaning. He identified God and salvation. A similar note of salvation comes in the words, "Lo, this is our God; we have waited for him, that he might save us. This is the Lord; we have waited for him; let us be glad and rejoice in his salvation" (25:9). This passage and other similar ones describe the saving work of God as being accomplished alone by His power.

The eschatological becomes increasingly dominant in Isaiah's thought. He sought to lead his people back to God by these glorious prophetic pictures, which could be realized in their own time if they would commit themselves in faith to God. Note, for example, these words: "We have a strong city; ne sets up salvation as walls and bulwarks. Open the gates, that the righteous nation which keeps faith may enter in. Thou dost keep him in perfect peace, whose mind is stayed on thee, because he trusts in thee. Trust in the Lord for ever, for the Lord God is an everlasting rock" (26:1-4). Add the picture in these great words: "Behold, I am laying in Zion for a foundation a stone, a tested stone, a precious cornerstone, of a sure foundation:'He who believes will not be in haste' " (28:16). What a marvelous inscription for a foundation stone to be laid in Zion! The inscription of the stone becomes more intelligible in the translation, "The believer is not anxious" or "alarmed."[30] These passages speak directly on salvation, trust in God, and the resulting peace in the believer's personal experience.

Yet two more pictures of the Messianic era (32, 35) draw our attention. In the first we see the blessed conditions that result from the outpouring of the Spirit upon the world. As a result, "Justice will dwell in the wilderness, and righteousness abide in the fruitful field. And the effect of righteousness will be peace, and the result of righteousness, quietness and trust for ever" (32:15-17). These words confirm earlier teaching that the outpouring of the Holy Spirit would lead men to repentance and faith, and would effect their spiritual transformation. In this great Messianic era, "The eyes of the blind shall be opened, and the ears of the deaf unstopped; then shall the lame man leap like a hart, and the tongue of the dumb sing for joy. . . . And a highway shall be there, and it shall be called the Holy Way. . . . And the ransomed of the Lord shall return, and come to Zion with singing, with everlasting joy upon their heads; they shall obtain joy and gladness, and sorrow and sighing shall flee away" (35:5-10). What a marvelous way to end these disclosures of the Messianic kingdom! How wonderfully these verses illuminate the themes of repentance, faith, and regeneration!

f. Micah's Message of Repentance, Faith, and Regeneration

As already noted, the message of Micah had to do chiefly with the condemnation of Israel's sins. Very forcibly he pronounced woe on those who devised wickedness. Alongside his predictions of coming judgment, Micah gave some very significant predictions of the coming Messiah. He sensed vividly how he should come before the Lord. It should not be with sacrificial offerings but with a life which harmonized with what the Lord required of His people. In a word it was, "to do justice, and to love kindness, and to walk humbly with God" (Mic. 6:8). Here the idea of turning away from sin to God was implicit. Micah's fellowmen were perishing from the earth, but he was looking to the Lord and waiting for the God of his salvation (7:1-7). Micah's closing words strongly implied repentance and faith as well as change of heart among his people. God pardons iniquity and passes over transgression. He does not retain His anger forever because He delights in steadfast love. He will again have compassion upon His people and will tread all their iniquities underfoot. He will cast all their sins into the depths of the sea. He will show faithfulness to Jacob and steadfast love to Abraham. All this is the Lord's response to a penitent people.

To conclude, let us note that this group of prophets remarkably unfolded the ideas of repentance, faith, and regeneration. Joel, Hosea, and Amos laid the chief stress on repentance. The ideas of faith and spiritual renewal receive less attention but some teachings on these experiences are quite explicit. It remained for Isaiah to give the fullest teachings in all these areas. He intensified the unfolding of these doctrines by presenting them in their eschatological settings. Isaiah made the strongest appeal for Israel to return in repentance and faith, and stressed the need of spiritual renewal — all in contexts which forecast the glory of the Messianic age. By this type of appeal he sought to lead his people back to God. It is very remarkable how the New Testament built on these spiritual concepts as disclosed by this group of prophets.

11. Death and Sheol

Hosea and Isaiah were the only prophets of this period who spoke concerning man's state after death. The words of Hosea (13:14) present a number of difficult problems centering in translation and interpretation. Following the Hebrew as it stands the verse would read, "Out of the hand of hell will I redeem them; from death will I set them free! Where are thy plagues, O death? Where thy destruction, O hell! Repentance is hidden from mine eyes."[31] According to this translation the first half of the verse is a promise, while the second half expresses a triumphant note in question form. Many biblical students hold that since the second half of the verse is in question form, the first half should be also. It is possible that Paul gave us a clue as to its meaning by quoting Isaiah's triumphant note, "Death is swallowed up in victory." He had discovered in these two verses the common note of victory. This would lead to the conclusion that verse 14a gives a promise of triumph and does not constitute a threat.[32] If this senses properly the meaning of Hosea's words, we find in this verse one of the earliest references to man's state after death.

The Hebrew word *Sheol* denotes the abode of the soul after death. The KJV varied in its translation using the words "grave," "pit," and "hell." Because of uncertainty of meaning, most modern versions leave this word untranslated. At times it is necessary to distinguish between the lexicographical meaning of a word and that which is strictly its biblical connotation. Hosea's words suggest that *Sheol* does not express a state of unconsciousness or that the individual is removed from God's power. If we accept the Hebrew as it stands in verse 14a, we have here God's promise of ransoming His people from the power of Sheol and of redeeming them from Death. Hosea did not explain the power of Sheol or of Death's ownership of the departed. Certainly Hosea's view of God would exclude any power or ownership exercised by Sheol or Death, which was not ultimately under God's control. God will pay the ransom and redeem His people. By implication this redemption is unto a new life.

As we shall note presently, Isaiah may have picked up Hosea's teaching when he wrote, "He will swallow up death for ever, and the Lord God will wipe away tears from all faces, and the reproach of his people he will take away from all the earth; for the Lord has spoken" (Is. 25:8). The Apostle Paul very definitely confirmed the interpretation given here when he wrote concerning the return of Christ and of the resurrection: "Then shall come to pass the saying that is written: 'Death is swallowed up in victory.' 'O death, where is thy victory? O death, where is thy sting'" (1 Cor. 15:54, 55)? Here then is the dawn of a new hope for the people of God when they come under the power of Sheol and Death. Implicit in Hosea's words is the idea of the resurrection, when death will be swallowed up in victory. Triumphantly Hosea then could ask, "O Death, where are your plagues? O Sheol, where is your destruction?"

Isaiah made references to Sheol in which he unfolded further the abode of the soul. Among the woes pronounced against God's people (Is. 5:13, 14) Isaiah predicted that when Judah would go into exile many would die and then he added, "Therefore Sheol has enlarged its appetite and opened its mouth beyond measure, and the nobility of Jerusalem and her multitude go down." This is a grim picture of death but it does not tell us anything of the state of those who die. On a later occasion Isaiah spoke of his children as being signs and portents in Israel from the Lord of hosts and he gave them this counsel: "And when they say to you, 'Consult the mediums and the wizards who chirp and mutter,' should not a people consult their God? Should they consult the dead on behalf of the living" (Is. 8:18, 19)? This would indicate that many people of Judah believed that mediums and wizards were acquainted with the secrets of the unseen world. In rebuttal of such a view Isaiah upheld the grander truth that Judah should consult God. He asked ironically, "Should they consult the dead on behalf of the living?" This passage adds very little to Isaiah's concept of Sheol. It would appear that he assumed the conscious existence of those who had died. He gave no room for any communication between the dead and the living.

When the king of Babylon was at the height of his power, Isaiah spoke of his overthrow in terms that throw additional light on the meaning of Sheol (Is. 14:3-20). Isaiah spoke of how Sheol was stirred up to meet the king of Babylon when he would meet death. In taunting language he wrote, "Your pomp is brought down to Sheol, . . . maggots are the bed beneath you, and worms are your covering. . . . You are brought down to Sheol, to the depths of the Pit. Those who see you will stare at you, and ponder over you. . . . All the kings of the nations lie in glory, each in his own tomb; but you are cast out, away from your sepulchre, . . . clothed with the slain, . . . pierced by the sword, who go down to the stones of the Pit, like a dead body trodden under foot. You will not be joined with them in burial." Here is strange language from which we may gather that the wicked dead are in Sheol in a state of consciousness. No distinction seems to be made between the state of the righteous dead and the wicked dead. Isaiah also quoted some scoffers in Jerusalem who said, "We have made a covenant with death, and with Sheol we have an agreement; when the overwhelming scourge passes through it will not come to us" (Is. 28:14, 15). Against such reckless talk the Lord spoke of a foundation to be laid in Zion for which He would make justice the line and righteousness the plummet. In view of this Isaiah added, "Then your covenant with death will be annulled, and your agreement with Sheol will not stand; when the overwhelming scourge passes through you will be beaten down by it" (Is. 28:18). These statements about Sheol expose the utter folly of the wild boasts of the scoffers.

In sharp contrast with this, Hezekiah spoke of his remarkable recovery from his illness in the words, "It was for my welfare that I had great bitterness; but thou hast held back my life from the pit of destruction, for thou hast cast all my sins behind thy back. For Sheol cannot thank thee, death cannot praise thee; those who go down to the pit cannot hope for thy faithfulness. The living, the living, he thanks thee" (Is. 38:17-19). In this way Hezekiah realized that his life was in the hands of God. God had forgiven his sins, and thus had held back his life from the pit of destruction. This suggests that for the wicked, death leads to punishment. Through his recovery Hezekiah saw that those who go down to the pit cannot hope for God's faithfulness. Only the living can give thanks to the Lord. We might expect Hezekiah to have made some distinction between the state of the righteous dead and of the wicked dead, but on this point he was silent.

The most significant words of Isaiah concerning the state of man after death are the following: "Thy dead shall live, their bodies shall rise. O dwellers in the dust, awake and sing for joy! For thy dew is a dew of light, and on the land of the shades thou wilt let it fall" (Is. 26:19). These magnificent words appear to stand in direct contrast with what the prophet spoke concerning the wicked. "They are dead, they will not live; they are shades, they will not arise; to that end thou hast visited them with destruction and wiped out all remembrance of them" (Is. 26:14). What Isaiah appears to be saying is that the wicked dead will not experience a resurrection such as that to be shared in by the righteous. While there may be implied a resurrection of the wicked dead, there is not the clear distinction which Daniel made when he wrote, "And many of those who sleep in the dust of the earth shall awake, some to everlasting life, and some to shame and everlasting contempt" (Dan. 12:2). It is conceivable that Isaiah implied a resurrection of the wicked in verse 14, but since the resurrection would differ so radically from that of the righteous, he simply wrote that the wicked would not live, they would not arise. On the other hand, the righteous dead shall live. Their bodies shall arise. He could say, "O dwellers in the dust, awake and sing for joy!" And then in the imagery of the dew or the night mist, as it brings forth the life of vegetation in the dry land of Palestine, Isaiah could add, "For dew of dawn is thy dew, and the earth shall bring to life the dead."[33] This climactic passage on the resurrection constitutes a very significant unfolding of divine revelation of this great biblical truth. Central to the idea that the dead are in a state of consciousness is the sublime truth that the righteous shall rise, presumably in bodies that shall live eternally.

For Additional Reading and Reference:

The Interpreter's Bible:
  Vol. 5, "Isaiah," pp. 163 f.
  Vol. 6:
    "Hosea," pp. 554-63.
    "Joel," pp. 734 f.
    "Amos," pp. 767-70.
    "Obadiah," p. 859.
    "Jonah," pp. 871-74.
Kaufmann, *The Religion of Israel*, pp. 363-400.
Oehler, *Theology of the Old Testament*, pp. 437-536. A general treatment of all the prophets.
Pfeiffer, *Religion in the Old Testament*, pp. 117-58. A doctrinal approach to all the prophets.
von Rad, *Old Testament Theology*, Vol. II, pp. 129-87.

Raven, *The History of the Religion of Israel,* pp. 298-513. (A separate
chapter on each prophet.)
Ringgren, *The Messiah in the Old Testament,* pp. 25-38. Studies in
Biblical Theology, No. 18.
Schultz, *Old Testament Theology,* Vol. I, pp. 220-300; Vol. II. See
Index of Subjects.
Titcomb, *Revelation in Progress,* pp. 235-337.
Vos, *Biblical Theology,* pp. 253-318.

Interpreter's Dictionary of the Bible, E-J, pp. 126-30.
See articles on the individual prophets.

1. As samples of recent treatments which still recognize two sides to the argument (see "Isaiah" in
the *Westminster Dictionary of the Bible,* and also *The New Bible Dictionary.*
2. Rom. 9:33; 10:11; 1 Pet. 2:4-6.
3. 9:12, 17, 21; 10:4.
4. The word "the" occurs in the Hebrew, Septuagint, and in the Gospel of Matthew.
5. Is. 2:2-4. Scholars differ as to whether Micah quotes Isaiah or vice versa.
6. Hos. 4:2, 6; 8:1, 12; 13:2, 4.
7. Hos. 2:18; 6:7; 8:1; 10:4; 12:1.
8. Hos. 1:10, 11; 2:7, 15, 16, 23.
9. Hos. 6:1-3; 8:1-10; 14:1-7.
10. Hos. 2:1, 19, 20; 6:6; 11:1-9; 13:4, 5; 14:4-7.
11. Amos 3:1-3; 4:12; 5:1, 4, 25; 6:1; 7:8, 15; 8:2; 9:14.
12. Is. 1:1; 2:1, 5; 3:1; 5:1-30; 9:8 — 10:27; 14:1, 32; 16:5; 17:4-8; 18:7; 29:22-24.
13. Is. 2:1-4; 4:2-6; 7:14; 9:1-7; 11:1-10; 14:1, 2; 16:1-5; 24:23; 28:16; 35:8-10.
14. 1 Thess. 4:13 — 5:11. *See also* Rom. 2:5-16; 1 Cor. 3:13-15; 2 Cor. 1:14; Phil. 1:6-11, etc.
15. Jer. 23:5; 33:15; Zech. 3:8; 6:12.
16. Boslooper, *The Virgin Birth;* Machen, *The Virgin Birth of Christ;* Mowinckel, *He That Cometh;*
Orr, *The Virgin Birth of Christ;* articles on "Immanuel" in Bible dictionaries, encyclopedias, and
word books; commentaries on Is. 7:14. Biblical theologies: Oehler, pp. 527-29; Knight, pp. 321 f.; Payne,
pp. 266-69; von Rad, II, pp. 173 f.; Ringgren, pp. 271 f.; Raven, pp. 389-96; Rowley, *Re-Discovery of
the O.T.,* pp. 292-94; Schultz, II, pp. 408-14.
17. Mt. 3:13-17; Mk. 1:9-11; Lk. 3:21, 22.
18. Is. 16:5; 24:23; 28:16, 17; 29:18, 19; 32:1-5, 15-20; 33:5, 6, 17, 20-22; 35.
19. See also Berkeley and Moffatt translations. Most commentaries favor this translation as over
against KJV.
20. *The Holy Bible Commentary* (London: John Murray, Albemarle St., 1876), Vol. VI, p. 487.
21. See 1:10 f.; 2:15 f.; 3:5; 14:4-8.
22. Mt. 13:14, 15; Jn. 12:39-41; Acts 28:26, 27.
23. *The International Critical Commentary* (Edinburgh: T. & T. Clark, 1910) "Amos" and "Hosea,"
p. 383.
24. Mt. 13:14, 15; Jn. 12:39-41; Acts 28:26, 27.
25. Hos. 7:1, 2, 3, 15. *See also* 9:15, where both the adjective and the noun forms occur.
26. Amos 1:3, 6, 9, 11, 13; 2:1, 3, 6.
27. Is. 28:1; 29:15; 30:1; 31:1; 33:1. *See also* 21:2; 24:16.
28. Jn. 3:3-8; Rom. 8:1-17; Eph. 2:1-10, etc.
29. Is. 9:12, 17, 21; 10:4.
30. *The Interpreter's Bible* (New York: Abingdon Press), Vol. V, The Book of Isaiah, Introduction
and Exegesis, by R. B. Y. Scott, p. 318.
31. *Biblical Commentary on the O. T.,* by Keil and Delitzsch. "The Twelve Minor Prophets," Vol. I
(Edinburgh: T. & T. Clark), p. 159.
32. See a discussion by Harper in his commentary on "Amos" and "Hosea," *The International
Critical Commentary* (Edinburgh: T. & T. Clark), pp. 404 f.
33. Is. 26:19b. Translation by Elmer A. Leslie, *Isaiah* (New York: Abingdon Press, 1963), p. 270.

CHAPTER VI
THEOLOGY OF ISAIAH (40 — 66)

1. Introduction

In the introduction to Chapter V I noted that many modern scholars think of a second Isaiah who wrote chapters 40 — 66, and that most scholars hold to both a Deutero-Isaiah (40 — 55), and a Trito-Isaiah (56 — 66). This is a question for literary criticism to settle, but the student of biblical theology can hardly ignore the problem. One thing is clear: Chapters 40 — 66 are quite different in structure and content from chapters 1 — 39. This will become more apparent as we lay hold of the theology in chapters 40 — 66. The following observations may have some bearing on this matter. First, the location of chapters 40 — 66 after the historical portion of chapters 36 — 39 may have some significance. We may well ask, Why did not chapters 40 — 66 follow chapter 35? Second, the time element of chapters 40 — 66 appears to be later than Isaiah's time. The judgment of Jerusalem is not something future but is in the past. Jerusalem's warfare is ended and she had received from the Lord's hand double for all her sins. Third, the writer referred to Cyrus as a contemporary. The language is historical, not predictive in form. Fourth, the judgment on Babylon (47) is described as a past event. The statement of verse 6 is not predictive; rather, it is descriptive of what had come upon God's people. The same is true of 52:1-10; 54:7-10. Fifth, the word "Redeemer" (*gaal*) and its derivatives occur twenty-one times in 40 — 66, and only once (35:9) in 1 — 39. Sixth, assuming the unity of the Book of Isaiah, it is almost unexplainable why the Servant of the Lord, found in 40 — 66, is not identified with the Immanuel of the first part of the book. Seventh, the setting of the prophetic materials and doctrinal content of 40 — 66 seems to be different from that of 1 — 39. These considerations have led me to give a separate treatment of chapters 40 — 66.

2. The God of Israel: His Nature

a. The Sovereign Majesty of God

Isaiah 40:5-31 is one of the grandest portions of the Bible setting forth God's sovereign majesty. Here we learn that the word of God will stand forever. The Lord God manifests power and might, and at the same time shows the tenderness of a shepherd toward the lambs of his flock. So great in majesty is He that the waters of the sea, the heavens and the mountains, are measured by Him as a human being uses weights and measures. Unlike finite beings the Lord is far above all need of counseling, being taught, and being shown the way of understanding. According to His measurements all the nations are like a drop of water or a speck of dust. There is no likeness with which to compare Him. It is He who sits above the circle of the earth, and stretches out the heavens like a curtain. In a word, "The Lord is the everlasting God, the Creator of the ends of the earth" (40:28). Most soul satisfying is the idea that this sovereign majesty of God does not remove Him from the most intimate relationship to mankind. In very truth "they who wait for the Lord shall renew their strength, they shall mount up with wings like eagles, they shall run and not be weary, they shall walk and not faint."[1] Thus God manifested His majesty as Israel's Creator, King, and Father.

b. God, the Holy One and Redeemer of Israel[2]

This title carries the same meaning as it possessed in 1 — 39. Three times (40:25; 43:15; 49:7) Holy One stands alone. This usage gives it an absolute sense and expresses God's transcendence and separateness above all other beings. The Holy One distinguishes Him from all other gods.[3] Thus the Holy One (*qadosh*) ranks with God (*Elohim*) and Lord (*Yahweh*) as personal names of Deity. In a very special way the Holy One is Israel's God and this gives special meaning to the expression "the Holy One of Israel." The idea of separateness as found in *qadosh* leads to that which is supremely the very center of God's nature. God is separate from all sin and ungodliness. In a positive way the Holy One is pure and righteous. The word "righteous" comes the nearest to expressing the positive moral quality of God's nature. The writer repeatedly identified the Holy One of Israel as their Redeemer and Savior. He had given Egypt as their ransom (43:3). In the same context God said, "I am the Lord, your Holy One, the Creator of Israel, your King" (43:15). "The high and lofty One who inhabits eternity, whose name is Holy," dwells "in the high and holy place" (57:15). In this same context we read that God also dwells with him that is of a contrite and humble spirit. Note the spiritual qualifications of one in whom God dwells.

The Hebrew word for Redeemer (*gaal*) and its derivatives occur twenty-one times in chapters 40 — 66. The word *gaal* carries the meaning, to redeem, to act as a kinsman. A personal relationship exists between an individual and his kinsman. When the prophet refers to God as Israel's Redeemer, this personal element obtains special significance. The uses of redemption as an external act furnish the image

of its spiritual connotation. This becomes all the more evident in the
eight or more instances in which Redeemer is associated with the Holy
One. This idea suggests itself when the Lord said, "Your redeemer is
the Holy One of Israel" (41:14). As Israel's redeemer the Lord was the
nearest spiritual relative to this nation. The Lord had manifested His
holiness in all the mighty works and wonders wrought from the time of
Israel's redemption from Egypt onward. Now that they were in exile,
their Redeemer and Holy One would break down the power of Babylon and make possible the return of Israel to their own land.[4] The
great Servant of the Lord passage (49:1-13) brings the Lord, the redeemer of Israel, and His Holy One into the close relationship of being
the Lord's Servant. God gave Israel as a covenant to the people so
that through them He might bring blessings to all nations. The day of
salvation for Israel was the dawn of the day of salvation for all mankind. The Lord also referred to Himself as Israel's Maker and husband. For a brief moment He had forsaken His people but with everlasting love He would have compassion on them. His steadfast love
and covenant of peace would not be removed (54:5-10). It became very
fitting then that Israel should be called the holy people, the redeemed
of the Lord (62:12). We may conclude that the bringing together of the
titles "the Holy One" and "Redeemer" showed that the Lord's redemption of Israel would result in their becoming the holy people.

c. The God of Righteousness and Salvation

The author of this part of Isaiah brought together the concepts of
the God of righteousness and the God of salvation in about ten contexts.[5] The word *tsadaq* and its derivatives carried the meaning of being
straight or right. It signified fidelity to a standard. When used with
reference to God, it referred to His being faithful to His own nature. He
who is holy acted in harmony with the perfection of His innermost being.
God manifested His righteousness in being true to His covenant promise.
This became evident in the words, "I am the Lord, I have called you
in righteousness, . . . I have given you as a covenant to the people, a
light to the nations" (42:6, 7). By this God was saying that His servant,
the people Israel, represented His unfailing promise to bestow the
blessings of salvation upon all mankind. The author enlarged on the
covenant idea in two other contexts (54:10; 55:3). Here the Lord declared that His steadfast love and His covenant of peace should ever
continue. He promised to make with Israel an everlasting covenant having
its foundation in His steadfast love for David. To what extent, if any,
the use of the word "covenant" in these passages reflected the Sinaitic
covenant is difficult to state. Certainly by reason of the covenants made

by God with His people from the time of Abraham onward, this word gained profoundest significance. The Lord used this word with all its accumulated meaning to magnify the outworking of His righteousness in the salvation of His people. Note several variations in the sense of *tsadaq* from the common meaning of *righteousness* to that of victory (41: 2), deliverance (46:12; 51:1, 5, 6, 8), and vindication (62:1, 2). The RSV recognized these adaptations. Other translations add *integrity* and *justice* to the list.

The Hebrew word *yesha* and its derivatives carry the meaning *deliverance, rescue, salvation.* The word's frequent use to denote physical deliverance furnishes the mold for a profound spiritual meaning. The saving act, whether physical or spiritual, is one which the individual is totally unable to accomplish for himself. Just as the people of Israel learned the meaning of salvation in a physical sense at the dividing of the Red Sea, so through the following centuries they came to realize its spiritual meaning which their deliverance from the spiritual domination of the Egyptians symbolized.

The first instance where righteousness and salvation are brought together occurs in the Lord's message to Cyrus. In a setting where the Lord spoke of His work as Creator, He said, "Let the skies rain down righteousness; let the earth open, that salvation may spout forth, and let it cause righteousness to spring up also; I the Lord have created it" (45:8). Later the author spoke of God as Savior and noted that "Israel is saved by the Lord with everlasting salvation" (45:15-17). Hence the Lord presented Himself as a righteous God and Savior. He invited all men to turn to Him and be saved, for only in Him are righteousness and strength. In the presence of Israel's wickedness God found no one to intervene. "Then his own arm brought him victory, and his righteousness upheld him. He put on righteousness as a breastplate, and a helmet of salvation upon his head" (59:16, 17).

Looking back to this message, Paul would tell us that just as God entered the battle against man's wickedness, His righteousness and salvation served the respective functions of breastplate and helmet. In like manner the Christian must protect himself through his own spiritual integrity manifested in righteousness and salvation. As the author pictured the future glory of Zion, he used the vivid language of a building of most durable quality and added, "I will make your overseers peace and your taskmasters righteousness. . . . You shall call your walls Salvation, and your gates Praise" (60:17, 18). It is possible that it was the Servant of the Lord who said, "I will greatly rejoice in the Lord, my soul shall exult in my God; for he has clothed me with the garments of salvation, he has covered me with the robe of righteousness" (61:10).

The foregoing uses of righteousness and salvation have shown that they are almost synonymous in meaning. God manifests His righteousness in the salvation of man.[6]

d. The God of Love and Mercy

The very close relationship of this theme to the two preceding ones shows that the author had interwoven his strands of thought so closely that a breakdown of subject matter under several headings may not be best. Both procedures have their merits. This part of the Book of Isaiah opens with a special message of comfort to Jerusalem. The Hebrew verb *naham* (40:1) has a variety of meanings in its several stems. It may mean, *be sorry, have compassion, suffer grief, comfort, console,* etc. The consolation which the Lord would bring to His people was that their warfare was ended and their iniquity pardoned. Jerusalem had received double from the Lord's hand for all their sins. This then was certainly a message of love and mercy to the apostate nation in their Babylonian captivity. These words of hope soon take on an eschatological note, looking forward to the coming Messiah whose forerunner was John the Baptist.

Leaving this point for later study, let us observe that the prophet was predicting the revelation of the glory of the Lord which would be a herald of good tidings. Because the Lord had created and redeemed Israel, He said, "You are precious in my eyes, and honored, and I love you" (43:1-4). This context shows that God's love and mercy was grounded in man's being created by the Lord. Very truly the Lord could say, "You are mine." Among the richest declarations of God's love and mercy are the words, "For a brief moment I forsook you, but with great compassion I will gather you. In overflowing wrath for a moment I hid my face from you, but with everlasting love I will have compassion on you. . . . My steadfast love shall not depart from you, and my covenant of peace shall not be removed, says the Lord, who has compassion on you" (54:7-10). Here the expressions, *great compassion, everlasting love, steadfast love,* and *covenant of peace,* carry great cumulative meaning. Peace between the Lord and His people was bound up in an unbreakable covenant. Chapter 55, rich in its gospel message, gives these appealing words: "I will make with you an everlasting covenant, my steadfast, sure love for David. . . . Seek the Lord while he may be found, call upon him while he is near; let the wicked forsake his way, and the unrighteous man his thoughts; let him return to the Lord, that he may have mercy on him, and to our God, for he will abundantly pardon" (vv. 3-7). Here is the promise that the love covenant with David would become everlasting. On this account all the wicked might return to the Lord, who would be merciful to them, and they would be forgiven. The prophet said, "I will recount the steadfast love of the Lord, the praises of the Lord, according to all that the Lord has granted us, and the great goodness to the house of Israel which he has granted them according to his mercy, according to the abundance of his steadfast love. For he said, Surely they are my people, sons who will not deal falsely; and he became their Savior. In all their affliction he was afflicted, and the angel of his presence saved them; in his love and in his pity he redeemed them; he lifted them up and carried them all the days of old" (63:7-9). Nowhere else in the Old Testament do we find so many rich teachings setting forth the love and mercy of God. These words give distinctive character to Deutero-Isaiah, and become dominant in all of its doctrinal content.

e. The God of Judgment

There are definite values in considering God's judgment of sin in close connection with His love and mercy. When God addressed Israel as His servant (43:8-28), He rebuked them severely for their faithlessness. The people whom He had formed for Himself did not call upon the Lord. They no longer brought sheep for burnt offering. They had burdened the Lord with their sins and iniquities. At the same time the Lord made it clear that He blots out transgressions and does not remember sins. Their first father, likely Jacob, and their mediators, the prophets, transgressed against the Lord. This brought upon them God's judgments, expressed in the words, "I profaned the princes of the sanctuary, I delivered Jacob to utter destruction and Israel to reviling " (43:28). This was a prophetic interpretation of God's judgments upon Israel through the overthrow of their nation. But the God who brought judgment upon the wicked was also the God who forgave.

The same thought occurs in connection with the description of Cyrus. The Lord had raised up this world ruler to punish the sinful Babylonians for carrying Israel into captivity (44:28; 45:1 ff.). In the midst of a description of God's majestic handling of the nations Isaiah proclaims the Lord's invitation, "Turn to me and be saved, all the ends of the earth! . . . From my mouth has gone forth in righteousness a word that shall not return: 'To me every knee shall bow, every tongue shall swear' " (45:22, 23). Paul's interpretation of these words is the safest guide (Rom. 14:10-12; Phil. 2:9-11). He explained that God exalted Jesus so that every knee would bow and every tongue confess that Jesus Christ is Lord. This was the note of salvation in the prophet's message, but Paul found here a larger eschatological note when he wrote, "We shall all stand before the judgment seat of God" and concluded, "So each of

us shall give account of himself to God." Here then was a very significant prediction of final judgment. We are not able to conclude that
the prophet was consciously foretelling final judgment but it is clear
that he was probing into the future, foretelling God's acts of mercy as
well as of judgment.

The Lord also pronounced judgment upon Babylon for all her pride
and sinfulness. He said, "I will take vengeance, and I will spare no
man" (47:3). The Lord made it clear that while Israel's overthrow was
a judgment from God, yet the nation of Babylon would be judged for
their own sinfulness. These judgments upon Israel and Babylon show
that God, the Judge, is the Holy One of Israel, their Redeemer. In
chapter 48, where God rebuked Israel's unfaithfulness, His work as
judge became still clearer. Note the words, "For my name's sake I
defer my anger, for the sake of my praise I restrain it for you, that I
may not cut you off. Behold, I have refined you, but not like silver; I
have tried you in the furnace of affliction. For my own sake, for my
own sake, I do it, for how should my name be profaned? My glory
I will not give to another" (48:9-11). God declared that His judgments
were in harmony with His righteousness. The prophet spoke of a
double task he had to perform. First, he was to bring good tidings to the
afflicted and liberty to the captive, that is, to proclaim the year of the
Lord's favor; and second, he had also to proclaim the day of God's
vengeance. Here again in one view we have both the gospel of salvation and the day of vengeance. The writer would have his readers
understand that God's nature includes at once love and justice. (See 63:
1-6 and 64:8-12, where the same truth recurs most dramatically.) These
repeated instances of bringing together in one view God's mercy and
justice are distinctive of chapters 40 — 66. This definite unfolding of
God's nature constitutes the highest peak of Old Testament revelation.

f. The God of History

Many of the contexts which set forth the God of judgment also
reveal Him as the God of history. A number of references give a general
view of God's activity in history while a few others are quite specific.
A sample of the former appears in the words, "Behold, the nations
are like a drop from a bucket, and are accounted as the dust on the
scales; behold, he takes up the isles like fine dust. . . . All the nations
are as nothing before him, they are accounted by him as less than nothing
and emptiness" (40:15, 17). Another such reference reads, "Who stirred
up one from the east whom victory meets at every step? He gives up
nations before him, so that he tramples kings under foot; he makes them
like dust with his sword, like driven stubble with his bow. He pursues

them and passes on safely, by paths his feet have not trod. Who has performed and done this, calling the generations from the beginning? I, the Lord, the first, and with the last; I am He" (41:2-4). Implicit in these statements is the truth that God acts in history and brings things to pass according to His will.

Another context becomes more specific in its historical references. Observe the words, "I give Egypt as your ransom, Ethiopia and Seba in exchange for you." But then the Lord continued, "Because you are precious in my eyes, and honored, and I love you, I give men in return for you, peoples in exchange for your life. Fear not, for I am with you; I will bring your offspring from the east, and from the west I will gather you; I will say to the north, Give up, and to the south, Do not withhold; bring my sons from afar and my daughters from the end of the earth, every one who is called by my name, whom I created for my glory, whom I formed and made." Still more specific are the words, "For your sake I will send to Babylon and break down all the bars, and the shouting of the Chaldeans will be turned to lamentations" (43:3-14). Most specific is the reference to Cyrus, whom God used to bring judgment upon Babylon, to free Israel from their captivity, and to open a way for their return to their holy land (44:24 — 45:8). Cyrus did not know that the Lord had anointed him for the special responsibility of returning Israel to their native land. Concerning his mission the Lord said, "I have aroused him in righteousness, and I will make straight all his ways; he shall build my city and set my exiles free, not for price or reward" (45:13).

The Lord gave a severe rebuke to Babylon, even though He had used this nation to bring judgment upon His people. Back of the historical events of Babylon's leading Israel into captivity lay the work of the God who acts in history. In most pointed words God said, "Sit in silence, and go into darkness, O daughter of the Chaldeans; for you shall no more be called the mistress of kingdoms. I was angry with my people, I profaned my heritage; I gave them into your hand, you showed them no mercy; on the aged you made your yoke exceedingly heavy. You said, 'I shall be mistress for ever,' so that you did not lay these things to heart or remember their end. . . . These two things shall come to you in a moment, in one day; the loss of children and widowhood shall come upon you in full measure, in spite of your many sorceries and the great power of your enchantments" (47:5-9). The prophet continued to quote the words of the Lord, the most significant of which were these: "But evil shall come upon you, for which you cannot atone; disaster shall fall upon you, which you will not be able to expiate; and ruin shall come on you suddenly, of which you know nothing." All these predictions came to fulfillment in Cyrus's overthrow of Babylon.

This entire section (Is. 40 — 66) not only revealed the God of history but it also gave what is called in modern terminology a philosophy of history. There is still another pattern of God's acting in history expressed in the words, "It is too light a thing that you should be my servant to raise up the tribes of Jacob and to restore the preserved of Israel; I will give you as a light to the nations, that my salvation may reach to the end of the earth" (49:6). These words, supplemented with the great climactic Servant of the Lord prediction of 52:13 — 53:12, foretold how God would work in history to bring salvation to all mankind.

g. The God of Creation

Very impressive in the preceding discussion is the fact that the author built his idea of the God of history upon the truth that He is the Creator. It soon became obvious that the God of history could be none other than the God of creation. After the prophet depicted the wonders of this world and of the nations dwelling in it, he could ask, "Lift up your eyes on high and see: who created these?" and he could answer, "The Lord is the everlasting God, the Creator of the ends of the earth" (40:12-28). God through the prophet asserted that His care for the poor and needy was possible because He, the Holy One of Israel, had created the world (41:17-20). When the Lord chose His Servant for the great task of bringing justice to the nations, He referred to Himself as "the Lord, who created the heavens and stretched them out, who spread forth the earth and what comes from it, who gives breath to the people upon it and spirit to those who walk in it" (42:1-5). Only such a God could give His servant as a covenant to the people and as a light to the nations. The Lord spoke of Israel as the people whom He created for His glory (43:7). He emphasized this creative act by adding verbs *formed* and *made*. This language was intensified still further by the Lord's adding the titles, "Redeemer," "the Holy One of Israel," "the Creator of Israel," and their "King" (43:14, 15).

The vocabulary for creation mounts to four different terms in the statement, "For thus says the Lord, who *created (bara)* the heavens (he is God!), who *formed (yatsar)* the earth and *made (asah)* it (he *established [kun]* it; he did not create it a chaos, he formed it to be inhabited!): 'I am the Lord, and there is no other'" (45:18). All this leads to the incontrovertible conclusion that the Lord is the one and only God. This verse also gives the reason for God's creative work:

He formed the earth to be inhabited. The entire creation has the purpose of providing a dwelling place for man. This reflects the meaningful thought given in the Genesis creation accounts that man was the crowning work of God's creation, and thus all that God made had the design of serving man's needs and of making life meaningful to him. When the Lord bade the descendants of Jacob hearken to Him, He added the words, "I am he, I am the first, and I am the last. My hand laid the foundation of the earth, and my right hand spread out the heavens; when I call to them, they stand forth together" (48:12, 13). Israel was bound to heed this call because the Lord spoke of Himself by His authority as Creator. These and other references to God as the Creator made it plain that His creative work lay at the foundation of the eschatological character of His revelation and of history. Only the Creator could lead the course of history to its intended goal.

In concluding this study of God as revealed in Isaiah 40 — 66, let us observe some of His distinctive characteristics. First is the outstanding use of such titles as "the Holy One," "the Redeemer," and "the Creator." Second is the prominence given to the Lord as the God of righteousness and salvation. Third is the judgment aspect, in which such a close relationship obtains between God's acts of judgment and of His love and mercy. The Lord brought judgment on His people in order that they might turn from their sins and thus be redeemed and saved.

3. The Spoken and Written Word of God

A real value obtains in moving from a study of the God of Israel to that of His spoken word. Our concern continues to lay hold of the connection between the spoken word and the written word. Only through a search for this relationship can we gain a true comprehension of the New Testament formula, "It is written."

To begin, let us observe the connection between God's revelation and His spoken word as expressed in 40:5, "And the glory of the Lord shall be revealed, and all flesh shall see it together, for the mouth of the Lord has spoken." The Hebrew verb *galah* has the literal meaning of *uncover, display,* and naturally moves to the sense of *reveal* or *disclose.* The verb refers in a special way to what God makes known to man, either by word or by spiritual manifestation. In the verse just quoted, the ground for believing that the glory of the Lord shall be revealed, is the fact that the Lord has spoken it. This is the thought of 53:1, which reads, "Who has believed what we have heard? And to whom has the arm of the Lord been revealed?" Note also 56:1, "Thus says the Lord: 'Keep justice, and do righteousness, for soon my salvation will come, and my deliverance be revealed.' "

This close relationship between God's revealing activity and His spoken word obtains highest significance when we observe the more than forty occurrences of the expression, *says the Lord,* together with other modes of expression such as *hear this, hearken to me, listen to me,* and such verbs as *proclaim, declare, cry, shout, tell, speak, say, call, rebuke,* and other closely related expressions. Thus there are some seventy-five instances where the prophet referred to the spoken word of God. This phenomenon is unique in this part of the Bible. The multiplicity of expressions declares plainly that the writer was recording what the Lord had said and was not simply giving expression to his own thoughts.

Many of these instances of God speaking have a very definite eschatological setting.[7] The eschatological framework becomes evident in chapter 40. The Lord said to the prophet that he should speak tenderly to Jerusalem because the purposes of her affliction had been satisfied. God, the speaker, pointed to a new era whose chief characteristic would be that the glory of the Lord would be revealed and all mankind would see it (40:3-8). Luke captured this note when he quoted from this Scripture and sensed that the preaching of John the Baptist fulfilled this prediction (Lk. 3:4-6). Peter also found in these verses a foregleam of the spiritual new birth and called it the good news as predicted by the prophet Isaiah (1 Pet. 1:24, 25). The glorious scene of our Lord's return (Rev. 22:7, 12) serves as the climax to the eschatological unfolding in 40:10.

Closely related to this example is that of 44:6, 7, where the Lord says,"I am the first and I am the last; besides me there is no god. . . . Who has announced from of old the things to come? Let them tell us what is yet to be." He who is the first and the last involved Himself in determining things to come. This theme also appears in the Book of Revelation (1:17; 2:8; 23:13). Following a statement with reference to His return, the Lord quoted these words, thus showing their most comprehensive forward look. Then there are the Servant of the Lord passages, which also have a perspective on things of the future. The words spoken by the Lord to the servant in 49:6, 7 led Simeon to announce the mission of Jesus in the world as being "a light for revelation to the Gentiles, and for glory to thy people Israel" (Lk. 2: 32). This quotation is far more significant than being a mere fulfillment of the prediction. It recognized the work of the Servant in its eschatological dimension. In similar fashion, Paul laid hold of this prediction to undergird his own preaching to the Gentiles (Acts 13: 47). From the same context he picked up another statement (49:8) on which he based his teaching that now is the day of salvation (2 Cor.

6:1, 2). Paul would have the church at Corinth know that their time of acceptance and salvation was definitely predicted by the writer of the Servant of the Lord passages. Two other contexts, 52:13 — 53:12 and 61:1-4, are being reserved for study in a later division. These are the most precious among the eschatologically oriented passages.

By way of conclusion, let us observe that the spoken word of God, so prophetic in character, which permeates chapters 40 — 66 gives us a true perspective for understanding the nature of the written word of God. These records were written by "men moved by the Holy Spirit." While the author made no mention of his writing the words of God, it is evident that the written record of God's words is authentic. Other summary ideas have been so well expressed by Dr. Muilenburg that I shall quote at some length from his scholarly discussion.[8]

> The word of God fills all time and space, fulfills God's purpose from creation to redemption, and addresses itself to Israel, to the nations, to heaven and earth, and to the whole complex of events which constitute the eschatological drama. Thus the whole of nature and history come under the reign of God's speaking, and to it they respond with joy and praise. The word of God assumes numerous literary forms such as the words of judgment in the judicial scenes, words of promise and comfort in the oracles of salvation, and words of prediction which give meaning to history. Especially powerful and moving are the direct and intimate words of address to Israel, whom God calls by name and to whom He proclaims His name.

4. Israel the Chosen People and Servant of the Lord

a. Problem of Interpreting the Servant of the Lord

This is one of the most difficult problems of Old Testament study. Delitzsch attempted to cut the Gordian knot by saying that the figure, "Servant of the Lord," was designed to represent to the senses a pyramid. Its lowest base is collective Israel; its middle part, Israel according to the Spirit; and its apex, the person of the Redeemer. He maintained that the figure carries one and the same idea which when concentrated becomes personal and when extended is again national.[9] While few scholars accept Delitzsch's interpretation, there is a spiritual insight evident which should not be ignored. He saw a grand unity in all the Servant of the Lord passages. Difficulties arise, nevertheless, when an effort is made to apply this general interpretation to the numerous references to the Servant of the Lord. In working on this problem I have made two observations which may serve as a clue to a consistent interpretation of these Scriptures. First, these Servant of the

Lord passages divide themselves into two groups: a group which speaks of Israel as being God's Servant, and a group which makes no reference to Israel.[10] Second, the New Testament made no reference to the former group. All but one of the second group were quoted in the New Testament as referring to Christ. The fact that the former group were not quoted in the New Testament would suggest that they made no reference to Christ. I shall proceed to examine the former group as applying to Israel excepting, of course, the Cyrus passage, and will consider the second group under the heading of the Servant of the Lord.

b. The Servant Concept in Israel's Early History

The word "servant" (*Ebed*) in its noun and verb forms occurs more than a thousand times in the Old Testament. Its common meaning is *slave* or *servant*. More specialized meanings of the word are *subject, servant,* or *worshiper of God,* as used of the Levitical singers and of the prophets. But the word received a still more specialized sense with reference to the people of Israel as the servant of the Lord.

In Part I, Chapter V, I drew attention to Moses as God's servant. After the Lord had delivered Israel at the Red Sea, "the people . . . believed in the Lord and in his servant Moses" (Ex. 14:31). The heightening of Moses' responsibility as servant of the Lord became still clearer when the Lord spoke of him in these words, "He is entrusted with all my house. With him I speak mouth to mouth, clearly, and not in dark speech; and he beholds the form of the Lord" (Num. 12: 7, 8). This disclosed a special significance to Moses' responsibility as God's servant. God had entrusted him with all His house, the people of Israel. To Moses, and Moses alone, God had given this responsibility. In view of this calling, God's communication to Moses was especially intimate. It was "mouth to mouth," very like the manner in which God spoke through the prophets at a later time. On this account Moses' leadership as God's servant bore a close relationship to the prophetic office. Most significant was the fact that Moses beheld the form of God. This was an exceedingly rare privilege experienced by very few of God's servants. We should note again Moses' still greater prominence as mediator of the covenant at Mt. Sinai, performing in a priestly manner in behalf of Israel. Moses' tasks of giving to Israel God's law and of serving as their leader were kingly responsibilities. This meaning of servant gave form to later uses of this word, especially to the Servant of the Lord passages now under consideration.

We should observe that God had already spoken to Abraham as being His servant (Gen. 26:24) and that Moses spoke of Abraham,

Isaac, and Jacob as servants of the Lord (Ex. 32:13; Deut. 9:27). Other outstanding leaders spoken of as servants of the Lord included Caleb, Joshua, David, Elijah, Amos, and Isaiah. As early as the time of Moses, God regarded all Israel as His servants (Lev. 25:42, 55). Thus when the author of the second part of Isaiah wrote of all Israel as being servants of the Lord, he was recapturing an idea known by the people of Israel since the time of Moses.

c. The Servant Passages Not Quoted in the New Testament

In the first reference (41:8 ff.) God addressed Israel as His servant and chosen one, the offspring of Abraham, His friend. This suggests that the promise given to Abraham began to find fulfillment in the people of Israel, chosen for the special responsibility of being the servant of the Lord. Even though Israel was in captivity, God had not cast them off. In words of strongest encouragement, God said, "Fear not, for I am with you, be not dismayed, for I am your God; I will strengthen you, I will help you, I will uphold you with my victorious right hand." But Israel as God's chosen servant had proved unfaithful to God." Very tragically, Israel had become deaf and blind, and because they had sinned, the Lord gave them up to spoilers and robbers. But God would not forget Israel, His servant. In utmost love He said, "I have swept away your transgressions like a cloud, and your sins like mist; return to me, for I have redeemed you" (44:22).

The Lord assured His people of their return to their own land to build the cities which had been destroyed. Their temple would be rebuilt. The Lord would do all this so that all mankind would know that there was none like Himself. He is the Lord and there is no other. The Lord disclosed their sinfulness in the words, "I know that you are obstinate, and your neck is an iron sinew and your forehead brass" (48:4). The Lord knew that they would deal very treacherously and that from birth they would be called a rebel. On this account He added, "For my name's sake I defer my anger, for the sake of my praise I restrain it for you, that I may not cut you off. Behold, I have refined you, but not like silver; I have tried you in the furnace of affliction" (48:9, 10).

At least two things become evident in these Servant of the Lord passages: first, the Lord regarded all Israel as His servant; second, by unfaithfulness the people of Israel were disqualified to fulfill the responsibility committed to them. The promise made to Israel that the Lord would restore them to their native land and that the temple would be rebuilt suggested the future reinstating of Israel as the servant of the Lord (49:6).

d. The Servant Who Shall Bear the Sin of Many

One characteristic which distinguishes the Servant passages which are quoted in the New Testament is the focusing of the Servant idea to one person.[12] The character of this servant, most properly known as the Servant of the Lord, together with his most significant work, calls for serious study. It is aspects which the writers or speakers of the New Testament lay hold of when they show how Jesus Christ is unquestionably the Servant of the Lord.

The first idea which arrests our attention (42:1-4) is that the servant is one person. God's Spirit is upon him; his major task is to bring forth justice to the nations. The gentleness of his nature finds most vivid expression in such words as, "A bruised reed he will not break, and a dimly burning wick he will not quench." His mission of establishing justice is not merely to God's chosen people but to the entire world (Mt. 12:18-21).

The 49:1-6 passage quotes the Servant's claim that his call to be God's Servant had its beginning at his birth. He expressed an unusual endowment in the words, "He made my mouth like a sharp sword, in the shadow of his hand he hid me; he made me a polished arrow, in his quiver he hid me away." A suggestion of the people's rejection of the servant meets us in the words, "I have labored in vain, I have spent my strength for nothing and vanity." In spite of this he could continue with full assurance as indicated by this statement: "Yet surely my right is with the Lord, and my recompense with my God." The supreme task that the Lord committed to the servant was "to raise up the tribes of Jacob and to restore the preserved of Israel." But the Lord would have the servant's work extend far beyond the people of Israel. He said, "I will give you as a light to the nations, that my salvation may reach to the end of the earth." Thus the worldwide mission of the Servant found explicit expression. It was this worldwide mission upon which Paul laid hold in his message to the Jews at Antioch when they rejected the gospel, and also in his defense before King Agrippa (Acts 13:45-49; 26:22, 23).

In the 50:4-9 passage, the Servant is the speaker. He declared how the Lord God had given him the tongue of those who are taught, and had awakened his ear to hear as those who are taught. To this he was not rebellious nor did he turn backward. Then follow words which, though they are not quoted with reference to Christ, describe very accurately how Jesus acted in the presence of His enemies: "I gave my back to the smiters, and my cheeks to those who pulled out the beard; I hid not my face from shame and spitting." Matthew seems to have reflected these words when he wrote, "Then they spat in his face, and struck him; and some slapped him," and in similar language, "They spat upon him, and took the reed and struck him on the head" (Mt. 26: 67; 27:30). Through the help of the Lord, Christ was not confounded and was able to set His face like a flint. He recognized that God who would vindicate Him was near. He could have said, "The Lord God helps me; who shall declare me guilty?"

Without question the 52:13 — 53:12 poem presents the profoundest picture of the Servant of the Lord. The thirty or more quotations from this passage in the New Testament stand as so many witnesses to its importance. The writer vividly presented the humanity of the Servant in terms which described His humiliation and suffering. In explicit language he set forth the meaning of His death. He died on account of man's sins, and on Him were laid man's iniquities. But it was the will of the Lord that He should be an offering for sin. Through His death many should be accounted righteous. The Servant should be exalted and become man's mediator before God, interceding for man's transgressions. This Servant poem gives the fullest disclosure of Christ's suffering and death found in the Old Testament. It gives the doctrinal foundation for understanding His work as Savior and Lord, expressed in the terms, *substitute, expiation, mediator, justification, atonement,* and *salvation.*

Looking now to the 61:1-4 passage, I have no interest in attempting to prove that this has a Servant of the Lord context. However, since Jesus quoted part of this portion (Lk. 4:16-21) and also claimed to be the Servant of the Lord (Mt. 12:15-21; Lk. 22:37), it seems proper to consider this portion along with the recognized Servant of the Lord passages.

The writer presented the Servant of the Lord as He proclaimed His mission to the people of Zion. First, He laid claim to the gift of the Holy Spirit. Through this endowment the Lord had anointed Him with power to perform the extraordinary tasks as God's Servant. Thus the Servant of the Lord was the Messiah. The Servant-Messiah stated His mission as that of bringing good tidings and of proclaiming liberty to those in bondage. He would proclaim the year of the Lord's favor. These truths found expression in our most treasured message, the gospel. How wonderful it was for the people of Nazareth to hear Jesus read this message and to learn of its fulfillment in Him (Lk. 4:16-21)! The Servant, nevertheless, needed to proclaim a future day of vengeance which would always be imminent. Just as Israel's captivity was a day of vengeance, so there would be a future final day of reckoning of all mankind in judgment. The New Testament gave confirmation to the latent truth bound up in the expression "the day of vengeance" (2 Thess. 1:8).

5. The Messiah and the Messianic Kingdom

a. Relating the Servant of the Lord Passages to the Messianic Idea

We note first that the author of Isaiah 40 — 66 did not relate the Servant of the Lord to the Messianic predictions of Isaiah 7, 9, or 11, an identification which would seem almost inevitable if the writer of this part of Isaiah had identified the two in his own thinking. Neither did the writer associate the Servant of the Lord with the Davidic line of kings. He placed no link of descent, we may note, in the promise made to David by the prophet Nathan (2 Sam. 7:16) and the Servant of the Lord. If the writer had access to any of the Messianic Psalms (2, 45, 72, and 110), he would most likely have identified the Servant with the Lord's Anointed. Furthermore the writer did not associate the time of the coming of the Servant of the Lord with the age to come as did the prophets Hosea, Joel, Amos, and Isaiah (1 — 35) in their predictions of the Messiah. While this is an argument from silence, we cannot escape from the problem which it presents. This fact does not in the least lower the rich and distinctive character of the Servant of the Lord teachings. They stand in their own right as the most profound teachings found in the Old Testament.

Another aspect of the problem becomes evident when we observe that the Servant of the Lord does not stand forth with the distinctive character of a Prophet, Priest, or King and yet the Servant of the Lord carried prophetic, priestly, and kingly responsibilities in much the same way as did Moses.

b. New Testament Guidelines for Determining the Messianic Reference to the Servant of the Lord

Let us observe the manner in which the New Testament identified Jesus as the fulfillment of the Servant of the Lord predictions. For the purpose of clarity let us examine the Servant of the Lord passages in the order of their occurrences, noting also the New Testament witnesses to the identification of Jesus as being this One.

Simeon in his prophetic song of praise identified the baby Jesus as the "light for revelation to the Gentiles, and for glory to thy people Israel" (Is. 42:6; 49:6; Lk. 2:32). When Jesus healed the man with the withered hand, Matthew declared that this fulfilled the Isaiah 42:1-4 Servant passage (Mt. 12:17-21). He interpreted this miracle as a kingly work of the Servant. To the Jews who were rejecting Paul's preaching of the gospel, the apostle quoted 49:6, and by so doing showed that Jesus was given as "a light for the Gentiles" in order that He might "bring salvation to the uttermost parts of the earth" (Acts 13:47). Paul made it clear that Jesus was a descendant of David and that God had brought to Israel a Savior in the person of Jesus. In this way he identified the Servant of the Lord with the Messiah. He also made an allusion to a Servant passage (49:8) when he declared, "Behold, now is the acceptable time; behold, now is the day of salvation" (2 Cor. 6:1, 2). God manifested in Jesus ushered in this day of salvation.

As we move forward to the 52:13 — 53:12 Servant psalm we may observe the context in which it appears (52:7-12). We hear the messenger who is bringing good tidings of peace and salvation. Peter grasped the meaning of this when he declared that the good news of peace came through Jesus Christ (Acts 10:36). Paul had also identified Jesus as the One in whom the good tidings centered (Rom. 10:15, 16; Eph. 6:15). To Simeon we are indebted for declaring the newborn Babe as God's salvation (Lk. 2:30). Luke quoted from Isaiah 40:3-5, but followed the Septuagint in the last verse, where it says, "All flesh shall see the salvation of God" (Lk. 3:4-6). This helps us to understand the full meaning of salvation as presented in Isaiah 40 — 66 and confirms still more completely the New Testament identification of Jesus and the salvation of God.

Very naturally the 52:13 — 53:12 Servant song served as the foundation for the largest number of New Testament references which identify Jesus, the Messiah, with the Servant of the Lord. Paul wrote that he had preached the gospel of Christ in new areas and in so doing had fulfilled 52:15: "They shall see who have never been told of him, and they shall understand who have never heard of him" (Rom. 15:21). Thus Paul consciously identified Christ as the Servant of the Lord. John gave his witness by showing that the rejection of Jesus as the Christ fulfilled 53:1 (Jn. 12:36-38). Matthew accounted for Jesus' ministry of casting out spirits and of healing the sick by drawing attention to the fulfillment of 53:4 (Mt. 8:17). It was the Servant, Jesus, who "took our infirmities and bore our diseases." Peter wrote of the sufferings of Christ, using the descriptive language of 53:5, 6, 9 which so fittingly depicted these sufferings (1 Pet. 2:22-25). When Philip joined the Ethiopian eunuch while he was reading 53:7, 8, the evangelist began with this Scripture to tell him the good news of Jesus (Acts 8:28-35). From this it is obvious that Philip regarded Christ as the oppressed and stricken Servant of the Lord.

The climax to these several witnesses to Christ's being the suffering Servant comes from the lips of Jesus Himself. When He was speaking to the disciples of His imminent arrest and condemnation,

He said, "For I tell you that this scripture must be fulfilled in me, 'And he was reckoned with transgressors'; for what is written about me has its fulfilment" (Lk. 22:37). Through this quotation Jesus Himself most clearly claimed to be the Servant of the Lord. Here then is a sixfold witness from such qualified men as Paul, John, Matthew, Peter, and Philip, and last of all Christ Himself — all giving unequivocal testimony that Christ was the Servant of the Lord.

It is noteworthy that when Jesus entered the synagogue at Nazareth He chose 61:1, 2 for His Scripture reading and then He made the assertion, "Today this scripture has been fulfilled in your hearing" (Lk. 4:16-21). This was a most momentous scene. Jesus Himself, the reader, standing before these eagerly listening people, humbly but assuredly claimed to be this Anointed One to whom God had committed the great task mentioned in these verses. This 61:1-4 Scripture thus stands as the climax of all the Servant of the Lord passages, and Jesus' claim to be the fulfillment of this Scripture, becomes then the most authentic witness that He, the Christ, was the Servant of the Lord.

In conclusion let us observe: first, the absence of Messianic elements in chapters 40 — 66 such as characterize chapters 2, 9, 11, and 32 of this book; second, the plain declarations that the Lord God is Israel's king (43:15; 44:6); and third, the kingly traits of the Servant of the Lord (42:1-7; 49:6-9; 52:15; 53:12). The most significant traits become evident where it is noted that the Servant will establish justice in the earth, that the kings and princes will prostrate themselves before Him, that kings will shut their mouths because of Him, and that God will divide Him a portion with the great.

The reasons for going to this length to identify the Servant of the Lord with the Messiah have their bases in the following: first, Isaiah 40 — 66 did not identify the Servant with the Messianic predictions of 1 — 39; second, the New Testament identification of the Servant with the Messiah greatly enriched the Old Testament predictions relating to the person and work of the promised descendant of Abraham; third, Jesus' ministry as the Servant-Messiah gained immeasurable depth of meaning as witnessed by the New Testament;[13] fourth, this identification established the surest foundation for believing that Jesus is at once Prophet, Priest, and King.

6. Eschatological Viewpoint of Isaiah 40 — 66

a. Introduction

The glorious message of comfort which God commanded the prophet to give to His people had its basis in eschatology. God's people should place full confidence in what the Lord will accomplish among them during the unfolding ages of history.

One of the first impressions of this forward look in Israel's history is the almost total absence of a political framework. In the main, this eschatology centers in the salvation which God will bring to His people (45:17; 52:7). While there are some difficulties as to whether the language should be taken literally or figuratively, the message is inward and spiritual. Without a doubt chapters 40 — 66 are the most profound of any portion of the Old Testament.

Since this part of the book deals with the unfolding of Israel's history, it is quite significant that the expression "The Last Days" or "The Latter Days" is absent. Yet the content of these chapters is clearly prophetic in nature. This aspect of chapters 40 — 66 follows a different framework of thought from that of chapters 1 — 39.

b. "The Former Things" and "The Things to Come"

The eschatological perspective becomes apparent in the repeated expression, "The Lord, the first and the last" (41:4; 44:6; 48:12). The contexts of these expressions set forth the Lord as the One who is the Creator of all things and who is determining the course of history onward to the consummation of all things. He, the eternal God, will achieve His purposes throughout the course of history. This, indeed, is the basic idea of the whole concept of eschatology.

This perspective becomes clear also in a number of other references.[14] By having Israel look back to the former things, the Lord would lead them to anticipate the things to come. The former things served as a model of how God would unfold the future. The Lord sought to show the people that the things to come would be distinctively new. Most outstanding in this perspective of new things is the foreview of God's new creation, indicated by God's promise: "For behold, I create new heavens and a new earth; and the former things shall not be remembered or come into mind" (65:17). *New* carries the idea of *renew* or *making anew*. It will not be simply a repairing of the old universe, but it will involve an act of creation, resulting in a new universe immeasurably more glorious than the old. The glorified Lord Jesus revealed this new creation to John (Rev. 21:1 — 22:5), and thus corroborated God's promise (Is. 65:17-25; 66:22, 23). This is the grand climax of the eschatological perspective.

One of the ideas found in this forward look centered in the salvation which will reach to the ends of the earth.[15] God would have Israel know that the supreme blessings which will come to them will be shared by all mankind. Certainly, the nation of Israel were the called of the Lord, but God would have them know that He had chosen them to bring salvation to the entire human race. In that special way God gave Israel to the nations. Israel's mission was not merely to give physical sight to the blind or to release prisoners from their jails, but rather, as Paul interpreted the language, "to open their eyes, that they may turn from darkness to light and from the power of Satan to God, that they may receive forgiveness of sins and a place among those who are sanctified by faith in me" (Acts 26:18).

We should observe the vast buildup of meaning in this word "salvation" (*yeshuah*) in the Old Testament.[16] Throughout these Scriptures, salvation is of the Lord. Beginning with Israel's physical deliverance from Egypt the word "salvation" gained the distinctively spiritual meaning of being delivered from sin through the redemptive acts of God. Paul captured its full meaning when he defined the gospel as "the power of God for salvation to every one who has faith" (Rom. 1:16).

James Muilenburg laid hold of these ideas when he wrote: "The prophet sees all things from the point of view of the divine initiative and fulfillment. His prophecy is an Oriental drama of beginning and end, of former things and latter things, of memories and expectations."[17] Thus the poor and needy had painful memories of their lack of water in the wilderness and desert country, but God would supply an abundance of rain so that these lands would again be fruitful. The people would come to see that the Lord had done all this (41:17-20). The Lord would comfort Zion by making the wilderness like Eden. Joy and gladness would be found in Zion (51:2, 3). A literal fulfillment of such promises is sadly inadequate. God would have His people anticipate far richer spiritual blessings, of which these temporal blessings were mere symbols. The people of Israel had pleasant memories of God's former covenants. But now He assures them, "I will make with you an everlasting covenant, my steadfast, sure love for David" (55:3). Because of Israel's Lord, nations would come to His people in order to share in these covenant blessings (55:5).

c. The New Exodus: Israel's Restoration to Their Land

In thought forms reflecting Israel's exodus from Egypt the Lord brought to His people the promise of a new exodus.[18] The Lord would again make a way in the sea and a path in the mighty waters. Chariots, horses, and warriors would be extinguished. He would make a way in the wilderness, and rivers in the desert. Such promises given to a people in captivity under the world's strongest nation certainly challenged the faith of Israel. But added to this was the overwhelming promise that

Jerusalem, the temple, and the cities of Judah would again be built. To this joyous expectation were directed the words, "And the ransomed of the Lord shall return, and come with singing to Zion; everlasting joy shall be upon their heads; they shall obtain joy and gladness, and sorrow and sighing shall flee away" (51:11). This second exodus would require, however, an inner cleansing on the part of God's people. Israel's being carried captive to Babylon involved a defilement such as they had experienced in Egypt. Those who bore the vessels of the Lord would need to purify themselves unto the Lord. But the Lord promised, "You shall go out in joy, and be led forth in peace; the mountains and the hills before you shall break forth into singing, and all the trees of the field shall clap their hands" (55:12). The foreigners who had joined themselves to the Lord would also share in these blessings and would be allowed to offer burnt offerings and sacrifices in the restored temple; for, as God said, "My house shall be called a house of prayer for all peoples" (56:7). The Lord Himself "will come to Zion as Redeemer, to those in Jacob who turn from transgression, says the Lord." This last promise lays stress on the necessity of a spiritual change on the part of Israel; it meant a turning from their transgressions. In fulfillment of this spiritual requirement the Lord said, "My spirit which is upon you, and my words which I have put in your mouth, shall not depart out of your mouth, . . . from this time forth and for evermore" (59:20, 21). Most certainly these promises anticipated a literal return of Israel to their land, but the language possesses a spiritual potential which far surpassed a literal fulfillment.[19]

d. Future Glory of Zion

The three poems formed by chapters 60, 61, 62 form a trilogy which presents significantly the future glory of Zion. The first poem (60) intensifies the problem of interpretation, especially as to whether it should be regarded as literal prophecy or whether it is apocalyptic.[20] Ezra 3:7 supports a literal fulfillment of the prediction, while Revelation 3:9; 21:25, 26 suggests an apocalyptic meaning. It may be sound exegesis to conclude that both senses obtain meaning here. The literal fulfillment possessed meaning, but it belongs to the very nature of unfolding revelation that a spiritual significance also obtains. Thus it seems entirely consistent to conclude that since John quoted this language in his description of the New Jerusalem, this apocalyptic meaning is latent in Isaiah 60.

The second poem (61) contains the very familiar and rich portion read by Jesus in the synagogue at Nazareth (Lk. 4:16-21). Very pertinently, Jesus added that this Scripture was then being fulfilled. This fact furnishes a sure guide to its meaning. The earthly ministry of Jesus was fulfilling the glorious future of Zion predicted by the prophet. Thus Jesus claimed to be the Anointed One bringing good tidings to God's people. God had set apart Jesus through Holy Spirit anointing to bring about the full realization of Israel's predicted glory. As I indicated in the section, "The Servant of the Lord," Jesus' quotation of these words provides evidence for believing that this portion of Isaiah is also a Servant of the Lord context. Whether or not this is the correct understanding of this portion, Jesus identified Himself as being the Anointed One, the Messiah. He, the Messiah, was bringing good tidings. He was proclaiming the year of the Lord's favor. In Israel's history this was the Year of Jubilee. But in this prophetic setting Jesus gave this Year of Jubilee its true eschatological meaning, as referring to His own ministry as the Messiah. We should note that closely bound up with this year of the Lord's favor was also the prediction of the day of vengeance. Israel's position in this grand era of the Lord's favor was that of being priests of the Lord, a truth captured by Peter when he referred to all believers as a holy priesthood (1 Pet. 2:5, 9). The repeated reference to the Lord's making an everlasting covenant with His people underscores yet again what the Lord would accomplish in the eschatological Year of Jubilee. Most assuredly all spiritual Israel would be the "people whom the Lord has blessed" (61:9). Note also, "The Lord God will cause righteousness and praise to spring forth before all the nations" (61:11).

The speaker of chapter 62, whether the Servant of the Lord — as in 61 — or the prophet, maintained that he would continue to speak until Jerusalem's "vindication goes forth as brightness, and her salvation as a burning torch" (62:1). Jerusalem shall be called by a new name. No longer will it be Forsaken or Desolate but Hephzibah (My delight is in her) and Beulah (Married). In this way God's people will be a crown of beauty in a land of the Lord. In order to preserve and perpetuate this special favor with God, watchmen would be set upon the walls of Jerusalem. They would be constantly involved in prayer, reminding the Lord of fulfilling His promise in establishing Jerusalem and making it a praise in the earth. This apt figure of watchmen praying on the walls of Jerusalem represented all the prophets of the Lord. Using the pictorial language of building a highway, the prophets were preparing the people for the realization of the promise embodied in the words, " 'Behold, your salvation comes; behold, his reward is with him, and his recompense before him.' And they shall be called, The holy people, The redeemed of the Lord; and you shall be called Sought out, a city not forsaken" (62:11, 12). What a glorious future for Zion!

The prophet's prediction of the future glory of Zion reached its unmeasured height in the contexts of 65:17-25 and 66:10-23. The glory of the New Jerusalem finds expression in God's creation of new heavens and a new earth. So unexcelled will be their glory that the former things shall no longer be remembered. God said, "Behold, I create Jerusalem a rejoicing, and her people a joy" (65:18). Both Peter and John saw in this language the prediction of the world to come. Said Peter, "According to his promise we wait for new heavens and a new earth in which righteousness dwells" (2 Pet. 3:13). In language of inexpressible grandeur John wrote, "I saw a new heaven and a new earth; for the first heaven and the first earth had passed away, and the sea was no more. And I saw the holy city, new Jerusalem, coming down out of heaven from God, prepared as a bride adorned for her husband; and I heard a great voice from the throne saying, 'Behold, the dwelling of God is with men. He will dwell with them, and they shall be his people, and God himself will be with them; he will wipe away every tear from their eyes, and death shall be no more, neither shall there be mourning nor crying nor pain any more, for the former things have passed away' " (Rev. 21:1-4).

For Additional Reading and Reference:

The Interpreter's Bible, Vol. 5, pp. 398-414.
North, *The Second Isaiah*, pp. 12-22.
Oehler, *Theology of the Old Testament*, pp. 437-536 — a general treatment of all the prophets.
Pfeiffer, *Religion in the Old Testament*, pp. 117-58 — a doctrinal approach to all the prophets.
von Rad, *Old Testament Theology*, Vol. II, pp. 238-62.
Ringgren, *The Messiah in the Old Testament* (Studies in Biblical Theology, No. 18), pp. 39-53, 65-67.
Robinson, *The Cross in the Old Testament*, pp. 61-114.
Schultz, *Old Testament Theology*, Vol. I, pp. 310-20.
Wright, *The Rule of God*. pp. 1-19.
Zimmerli and Jeremias, *The Servant of the Lord* (Studies in Biblical Theology, No. 20).

1. Is. 40:31. *See also* 43:15-21; 44:6-17; 46:5-11; 57:15; 63:15, 16, etc.
2. This title occurs thirty-two times in the entire book of Isaiah, almost equally divided between the two parts of the book.
3. *The International Standard Bible Encyclopaedia* (Chicago: The Howard Severance Co., 1930), Vol. II, "God, Names of," by Edward Mack, p. 1266.
4. Is. 43:14. *See also* 44:24-28; 48:17-20.
5. This number compared with the two instances in the first part of the book (Is. 26:1-8; 33:5, 6, 22) may also have a bearing on the unity of Isaiah.
6. For other significant examples of these combined expressions, see 46:12, 13; 51:1-6; 62:1.
7. James Muilenburg, "Introduction," Chapters 40 — 66, *The Interpreter's Bible* (New York: Abingdon Press, 1952), Vol. V, p. 404. For an outstanding presentation of the theology of Isaiah 40 — 66, see pp. 398-414 of this volume.

8. *Op. cit.*, p. 404.

9. Oehler, *Theology of the Old Testament* (New York: Funk and Wagnall's Co., 1870), p. 533.

10. To the former group belong 41:8-29; 42:18-25; 43:8-13; 43:14 — 44:5; 44:6-8, 21-23; 44:24 — 45:13; 48. To the second group belong 42:1-4; 49:1-6; 50:4-9; 52:13 — 53:12; 61:1-4. Many students do not recognize the last reference as belonging to the Servant of the Lord passages. In my judgment, Christ's quotation of this passage confirms it as being a Servant of the Lord passage.

11. Is. 42:18-25; 43:8 ff., 44:21 ff.; 48:1 ff.

12. Is. 42:1-4; 49:1-6; 50:4-9; 52:13 — 53:12; 61:1-4.

13. Mt. 4:23, 24; 11:27-30; 12:15-21; 16:24; 26:26-29; Lk. 9:20-23; 22:37, 69; 24:46, 47; Jn. 1:29; 1 Cor. 15:3; 1 Tim. 2:5, 6; 1 Pet. 2:21-25.

14. Is. 41:22, 23; 42:9; 43:18, 19; 48:3-7; 65:17 ff.; 66:22.

15. Is. 42:1-7; 46:9-13; 49:6; 52:9, 10.

16. Gen. 49:18; Ex. 14:13; Deut. 32:15; Ps. 3:8; 62:2; 68:19; Is. 12:2; 33:2; 49:6, 8; 51:6, 8; 52:7, 10, etc.

17. *Op. cit.*, p. 400.

18. Is. 43:14-21; 44:26-28; 48:20, 21; 51:10, 11; 52:11, 12; 54:7, 8; 55:12, 13; 56:6-8; 58:12-14; 59:20, 21.

19. Jn. 10:16; Rom. 11:26, 27; 2 Cor. 5:17; 6:17; 1 Pet. 2:9; Rev. 18:4.

20. Alleman and Flack, *Old Testament Commentary* (Philadelphia: Muhlenberg Press, 1951), pp. 693 f.

CHAPTER VII
THEOLOGY OF THE PROPHETS OF THE CHALDEAN PERIOD 625-586 B.C.

The prophetic messages of these prophets differed widely from the others because of diverse situations which each had to meet. Nahum's oracle concerned Nineveh. The imminent overthrow of Judah was Zephaniah's burden. Habakkuk was greatly troubled about God's allowing the wicked Chaldeans to overthrow the more righteous Israel. Jeremiah, who suffered in the overthrow of the nation along with his fellow countrymen, continued to warn, rebuke, exhort, and counsel his people. While he is remembered as the weeping prophet, his message built up continued trust and hope in God. Let us note the distinctive teachings of each prophet in the light of his respective mission.

1. The God of Israel

a. Nahum

The opening verses of this book give quite a fundamental view of God. Since Nahum's message had to do primarily with the coming judgment of Nineveh, the nature of God as manifested toward her wickedness is very apparent. The Lord is a jealous God, One who takes vengeance and is wrathful but yet is slow to anger and of great might. He will by no means clear the guilty. No one can stand before His indignation or endure the heat of His anger. Nevertheless, says Nahum, "The Lord is good, a stronghold in the day of trouble; he knows those who take refuge in him" (Nahum 1:7). But the Lord will make a full end of His adversaries.

b. Zephaniah

Along with the other prophets Zephaniah referred to God by the title "Lord of hosts" and by so doing expressed proper reverence for God as He who rejoices over us with gladness and renews us in His love (3:17). He is righteous and shares justice (3:5). To the remnant of Judah the Lord will be mindful and restore their fortunes (2:7). He will manifest His judgment in the day of wrath (1:15-18; 2:11). To Zephaniah these divine attributes displayed a grand harmony.

c. Habakkuk

The imminent attack of the Chaldeans on Judah became a great

problem to Habakkuk. To begin, it was the Lord who was rousing the
Chaldeans to bring judgment upon Judah. How could the righteous
and holy God be "silent when the wicked swallows up the man more
righteous than he" (1:13)? Habakkuk's predicament centered in what was
ethical, namely, God's using a wicked nation to punish a righteous
people. In brief, the Lord's answer was, "He whose soul is not upright in him shall fail, but the righteous shall live by his faith" (2:4).
The Lord, accordingly, pronounced woes upon the Chaldeans, the
most significant of which was the condemnation of their idolatry:
"Woe to him who says to a wooden thing, Awake; to a dumb stone,
Arise! Can this give revelation? Behold, it is overlaid with gold and
silver, and there is no breath at all in it." In sharp contrast with im-
potent Chaldean gods, Habakkuk was aware that "the Lord is in his
holy temple; let all the earth keep silence before him" (2:19, 20).
Only the living God, to whom all nations of the world are subject,
could fulfill these woes. It was natural then for Habakkuk to exclaim,
"His glory covered the heavens, and the earth was full of his praise.
His brightness was like the light, rays flashed from his hand; and there
he veiled his power. Before him went pestilence, and plague followed
close behind. He stood and measured the earth; he looked and shook
the nations; then the eternal mountains were scattered, the ever-
lasting hills sank low. His ways were as of old (3:3b-6). This view of
God is especially significant in view of the mounting world power of
Chaldea and of the imminent overthrow of Judah, the people of the
Lord.

d. Jeremiah

Jeremiah's prophetic message concerning the Lord was most instructive and distinctive. At no time did he attempt to prove monotheism
but this concept of God was implicit in every statement he made
concerning the divine Being. In the prophet's references to creation
the personal attributes of God are exceedingly rich and point to the intimate relation between the Lord and His people. He is the God of love
and mercy, the God of righteousness and justice, the God who knows all
things, especially with reference to the affairs of men. It is He who tries
the hearts. His power and might are everywhere present. This becomes
especially apparent when he notes how God acts in history and directs
the affairs of men. With a Lord such as this, history is but the outworking of eschatology. The Lord is the God of salvation, Israel's
savior and redeemer. Let us examine in greater detail Jeremiah's
prophetic message of God.

(1) Implicit Monotheism. The title "Lord of hosts," occurring forty

times in this book, possesses its usual significance in support of monotheism. The frequency of the expression, "the word of the Lord came
to me saying," intensifies the idea that it was one and the same Being
who was speaking to the prophet.[1] This excluded any possibility of
there being many gods. In a context such as 2:5-32 Jeremiah quoted
a number of questions with which the Lord would confront His people.
These questions centered in the reality of God's deliverance of His people from the land of Egypt and of leading them to the promised land.
With this confrontation Israel could give no answer to the Lord when He
said, "For my people have committed two evils: they have forsaken me,
the fountain of living waters, and hewed out cisterns for themselves,
broken cisterns that can hold no water" (2:13). Thus the fact of God's
deliverance of Israel from Egypt constituted irrefutable evidence that
the Lord their God was one Lord (Deut. 6:4). With such a great historic
fact brought to the minds of apostate Israel, the Lord could chide them
with the question, "But where are your gods that you made for yourself? Let them arise, if they can save you, in your time of trouble; for
as many as your cities are your gods, O Judah" (2:28). In another response to God's warning, Jeremiah said, "There is none like thee, O
Lord; thou art great, and thy name is great in might. Who would not
fear thee, O King of the nations? For this is thy due; for among all the
wise ones of the nations and in all their kingdoms there is none like
thee" (10:6, 7). Jeremiah further asserted, "But the Lord is the true
God; he is the living God and the everlasting King. At his wrath the
earth quakes, and the nations cannot endure his indignation" (10:10).
Jeremiah buttressed this strong claim when he forthrightly declared,
"The gods who did not make the heavens and the earth shall perish
from the earth and from under the heavens" (10:11). He then made a
sublime statement of God's creative work: "It is he who made the earth
by his power, who established the world by his wisdom, and by his
understanding stretched out the heavens" (10:12). Implicit in God's great
work of creation was the fact that there is only one true and living God.
After still another rebuke to Israel the Lord said, "Am I a God at
hand, . . . and not a God afar off? Can a man hide himself in secret
places so that I cannot see him? . . . Do I not fill heaven and earth"
(23:23, 24)? Questions such as these are valid only on the basis of a
rigid monotheism. Another monument to Jeremiah's belief in the oneness of God appears when he combines God's work of creation with
that of His deliverance of the children of Israel from the land of Egypt,
and by this shows that there is nothing too hard for the Lord. Such a
one Jeremiah addresses, "O great and mighty God whose name is the
Lord of hosts, great in counsel and mighty in deed; whose eyes are

open to all the ways of men, rewarding every man according to his ways and according to the fruit of his doings" (32:17-25).[2]

(2) God the Creator. We noted above the very pertinent passage (10:12, 13) which describes God's work as Creator. Its implications are quite obvious: the earth had its beginning in time, it came into existence through the power of God, and God's wisdom and understanding account for the wonders of the world and of the heavenly bodies. Elsewhere Jeremiah repeated these ideas and expanded some of the details.[3] From these we learn that the Lord gives the rain in its season and keeps for us the weeks appointed for the harvest. He established the habits of the stork, the turtledove, swallow, and crane. He gives the earth to whomsoever He wills. He established the orderly movements of the sun, moon, and stars. "When he utters his voice there is a tumult of waters in the heavens, and he makes the mist rise from the ends of the earth. He makes lightnings for the rain, and he brings forth the wind from his storehouses." The scope and nature of these works Jeremiah understood and interpreted as God's acts of creation.

(3) The God of Love and Mercy. The Lord gave the command, "Return, faithless Israel. . . . I will not look on you in anger, for I am merciful. . . . I will not be angry for ever. Only acknowledge your guilt, that you rebelled against the Lord your God" (3:12, 13). These words revealed the inner nature of God as the merciful One. In a rebuke to the wise men who gloried in their wisdom and might, the Lord said, "I am the Lord who practice kindness, justice, and righteousness in the earth; for in these things I delight, says the Lord" (9:23, 24). This buildup of vocabulary showed that love and kindness do not exist as isolated graces in the nature of God but rather form one grand unity of His Being. Add to this the words, "I have loved you with an everlasting love; therefore I have continued my faithfulness to you" (31:3). In one of his prayers Jeremiah brought together God's steadfast love and His "requit[ing] the guilt of fathers to their children" (32:18). Jeremiah could write out of rich personal experience: "The steadfast love of the Lord never ceases, his mercies never come to an end; they are new every morning; great is thy faithfulness" (Lam. 3:22, 23).

(4) The God of Righteousness and Justice. Since the Lord is He who practices "kindness, justice, and righteousness in the earth," it was entirely natural for Jeremiah to declare, "Righteous art thou, O Lord" (9:24; 12:1). It was fitting that the predictions of the coming Messiah should also involve these ideas, as God asserted in this promise through Jeremiah: "I will raise up for David a righteous Branch, and he shall reign as King and deal wisely, and shall execute justice and righteousness in the land" (23:5; 33:15).

(5) The God Who Knows All Things. The Lord's opening message to Jeremiah (1:5) revealed His omniscience. God knew the unborn child, Jeremiah, and had set him apart to be a prophet to the nations. This was not a generalized statement of omniscience but it had to do with the life and calling of a person. This is characteristic of almost all of Jeremiah's references to God's omniscience. Jeremiah was fully aware that the Lord knew of his persecutions and would give him the grace and strength to endure them.[4] In support of His omniscience the Lord asked, "Am I a God at hand, . . . and not a God afar off? Can a man hide himself in secret places so that I cannot see him? . . . Do I not fill heaven and earth" (23:23, 24)? The sins of Israel were not hidden from God. "I am the one who knows, and I am witness, says the Lord" (29:23).

(6) The God of Power and Might. Conscious that the Lord was his strength and stronghold, Jeremiah poured out his heart against Israel's idolatry. To this effort the Lord replied, "Therefore, behold, I will make them know, this once I will make them know my power and my might, and they shall know that my name is the Lord" (16:21). As the Lord sought to bolster Jeremiah's courage, He asked, "Is not my word like fire, . . . and like a hammer which breaks the rock in pieces" (23:29)? This stood in sharp contrast to the impotence of Israel's gods and the deceitfulness of their prophets. Jeremiah's greatest witness to God's omnipotence shone forth in the words, "Ah Lord God! It is thou who hast made the heavens and the earth by thy great power and by thy outstretched arm! Nothing is too hard for thee, who showest steadfast love to thousands, . . . O great and mighty God whose name is the Lord of hosts, great in counsel and mighty in deed; . . . who hast shown signs and wonders in the land of Egypt, and to this day in Israel and among all mankind, and hast made thee a name, as at this day" (32:17-20). The prophet enlarged on the power of God manifested in the wilderness wanderings and the conquest of Canaan. In this context the Lord said, "Behold, I am the Lord, the God of all flesh; is anything too hard for me" (32:27)? In such settings Jeremiah spoke of God's omnipotence. He did not formally explicate God's power but gave praise to God for His almighty works.

(7) The God Who Tries the Hearts. Jeremiah's close association with God led him to realize a very meaningful aspect of His nature. He expressed this truth in these words: "The heart is deceitful above all things, and desperately corrupt; who can understand it? 'I the Lord search the mind and try the heart, to give to every man according to his ways, according to the fruit of his doings.' "[5] Thus Jeremiah came to realize that God tests the motives and thoughts of man's heart and

judges him accordingly. It is man's responsibility to love and obey God from his innermost being. This is one way of expressing the fundamental principle of ethics. Man in his entire being is first of all and supremely responsible to God.

(8) The God Who Acts in History. Jeremiah devoted much of his message to the Lord's activity in the affairs of His people and of other nations as well. This furnishes a profound philosophy of history, or better, a theology of history. He noted why God was active in history and showed how He accomplished His purposes. A secular history would likely be unaware of God's having had anything to do with the rise and fall of nations. But the Lord's revealing to Jeremiah what would take place showed that He determined the course of history. The Lord demonstrated this to Jeremiah most vividly when He sent him to the potter's house to observe the potter working at his wheel. He noticed that the vessel the potter was making was spoiled in the potter's hands; so he reworked the clay into another vessel. Then the Lord said, "O house of Israel, can I not do with you as this potter has done? . . . Behold, like the clay in the potter's hand, so are you in my hand, O house of Israel. If at any time I declare concerning a nation or a kingdom, that I will pluck up and break down and destroy it, and if that nation, concerning which I have spoken, turns from its evil, I will repent of the evil that I intended to do to it. . . . 'Behold, I am shaping evil against you and devising a plan against you. Return, every one from his evil way, and amend your ways and your doings' " (18: 5-11). The Lord was making clear His judgment of sin and His blessing for uprightness. In another context (21:4-10) the Lord showed how He would use the king of Babylon to overthrow Israel, but the door of mercy would still be left open. He said, "Behold, I set before you the way of life and the way of death." During the twenty-three-year period from the beginning of Nebuchadrezzar's reign, the Lord spoke through Jeremiah but the people of Judah would not listen. The Lord declared that He would send Nebuchadrezzar His servant to destroy the land of Judah. It would become a ruin and a waste during Judah's seventy years' captivity in Babylon. The Lord told Jeremiah, "Take from my hand this cup of the wine of wrath, and make all the nations to whom I send you drink it." Jeremiah obeyed God's command and listed all the nations, including those between Babylon and Egypt, and then concluded, "And after them the king of Babylon shall drink" (25:15-26).

During Zedekiah's reign the Lord gave Jeremiah an extraordinary message for the kings of the nations around Judah. It was that the Lord had given all those nations which were refusing to serve the king of Babylon into the hand of Nebuchadnezzar. He would punish them with the sword or with famine or with pestilence. He warned these nations not to listen to their prophets, diviners, soothsayers, dreamers, or sorcerers, because they would lie in their predictions (Jer. 27). The Lord fulfilled His command to Jeremiah. Later Jeremiah sent a unique letter to the exiles in Babylon (29:1-9). Voicing God's words he wrote, "Build houses and live in them; plant gardens and eat their produce. . . . Seek the welfare of the city where I have sent you into exile, and pray to the Lord on its behalf, for in its welfare you will find your welfare." This was a real test for the exiles because it sounded as though they would never again return to their native land. Jeremiah warned them not to permit their prophets and diviners to deceive them. Undoubtedly they were predicting an early return to Jerusalem. The prophet, moreover, repeated God's promise that after seventy years He would bring them back to their home country: "For I know the plans I have for you, says the Lord, plans for welfare and not for evil, to give you a future and a hope" (29:10-14). The Lord did not say how He would accomplish their return, but He would so direct the affairs of nations that Israel would be gathered from all the nations where they had been driven.

In grand poetic form, the Lord enlarged on His promise in which we have the precious words, "I have loved you with an everlasting love; therefore I have continued my faithfulness to you." And again, he affirmed, "He who scattered Israel will gather him, and will keep him as a shepherd keeps his flock" (31:3, 10). During Zedekiah's reign the Lord through Jeremiah gave a similar prediction of Jerusalem's overthrow by Nebuchadnezzar. He concluded His message, "For thus says the Lord: Just as I have brought all this great evil upon this people, so I will bring upon them all the good that I promise them" (32:42). We should observe that just as the Lord had brought judgment upon His people because of their many sins, so He would destroy Babylon because of their wickedness. Because of this Israel was commanded to flee from Babylon when the Medes would attack the nation. As evidence that the Lord would use the kings of the Medes as His agent in destroying Babylon, the Lord said, "You are my hammer and weapon of war: with you I break nations to pieces; with you I destroy kingdoms" (51:20). Babylon would become a heap of ruins (51).

This sampling of Jeremiah's predictions furnishes conclusive data of God's activities in history. In view of the improbability of any of these details being fulfilled as mere events of history, greater validity attaches to them as evidence of the Lord's directing the affairs of men. Hence God's activity in history becomes a fundamental aspect of Christian theism. World events do not just happen. God declares: "It is I who by my great power and my outstretched arm have made the earth, with the men and animals that are on the earth, and I give it to whomever it seems right to me" (27:5).

(9) The God of Salvation. Since Jeremiah revealed the Lord of Israel as the God of love, mercy, righteousness, and justice, it is very natural to expect that the prophet would reveal the Lord as the God of salvation. In view of Israel's captivity a problem arises as to whether Jeremiah's references to the saving acts of God refer to a literal restoration of Israel to their own land, or whether he is referring to a spiritual restoration. A careful study of these references would seem to show that some of them focus attention on the return from Babylon,[6] while other references speak of certain spiritual aspects which characterize New Testament references of salvation.[7] Certainly the former group has rich connotations which lay the foundation for the spiritual concept. Obviously, the vocabulary of saving and delivering by the hand of God may easily extend to a spiritual experience. The predictions which suggest spiritual implications of salvation are those connoting repentance, such as, "I will heal your faithlessness," "Our backslidings are many, we have sinned against thee," "If you will return, I will restore you," and "Heal me, . . . save me, . . . for thou art my praise." To summarize, Jeremiah's contribution to the unfolding revelation of salvation includes these truths: God is the Savior and Deliverer. The prerequisite to God's saving act is repentance and turning away from sin. Living in sin is spiritual bondage.

2. The Spoken and Written Word of God

a. Nahum, Zephaniah, and Habakkuk

The opening words of these three books state very briefly but significantly their prophetic messages. The first two of these prophets used the technical term "burden" or "oracle" to describe the contents of their books. This term carried the technical sense of prophecy. Nahum used the additional term "vision," which suggests the contents of the book as things being seen through his spiritual insight. The prophet Habakkuk saw what he spoke. In both instances the language indicated the revelation of God to the prophet. The same is true of Zephaniah's formula, "The word of the Lord." Their writings were not a product of their own thinking. All three of these prophets gave testimony to the distinctive character of their writing, which leads us a step further in understanding the nature of the written word.

b. Jeremiah

Frequent in the Book of Jeremiah are the expressions: "The word of the Lord came to me," and "Hear the word of the Lord."[8] Jeremiah disclosed how the Lord had set him apart for his special work as prophet: "Before I formed you in the womb I knew you, and before you were born I consecrated you; I appointed you a prophet to the nations." When Jeremiah responded that he did not know how to speak, the Lord put forth His hand and touched his mouth and said to him, "Behold, I have put my words in your mouth" (1:5-10). This disclosure affirms very clearly that the messages with a heading such as, "The word of the Lord came to me," were not the result of Jeremiah's own thinking, nor framed in his own language, but were the very words of God. I have no interest in overliteralizing these expressions, but it is my deep intention not to lower in any way the meaning of the language just quoted. Jeremiah gave no evidence of seeking to convey the thoughts and expressions of his own mind. From a certain point of view, the words of the Lord bypassed the mind of Jeremiah. In condemnation of the people's speaking falsely of the Lord, God said, "Because they have spoken this word, behold, I am making my words in your mouth a fire, and this people wood, and the fire shall devour them" (5:12-14). There could be hardly a more expressive way for the Lord to show the divine origin of Jeremiah's words, over against the false claims of God's people. In another context where the Lord was refuting the words of the false prophets, the Lord authenticated His words as spoken by Jeremiah with these questions: "Is not my word like fire, . . . and like a hammer which breaks the rock in pieces" (23:23-32)?

We also meet the phenomenon of written prophecy and its unique character. God spoke thus of Jeremiah's writings: "I will bring upon that land all the words which I have uttered against it, everything written in this book, which Jeremiah prophesied against all the nations" (25:13). Here we pass from the authority of the Lord's spoken words over to the written words, which possess identical authority. Bound up in this phenomenon is the basic nature of biblical inspiration. The spoken and written words of God as given by Jeremiah stand in the front rank of the Bible's unfolding of the divine character of the written word.

3. Israel's Election Actualized by Covenant Relation with God

The prophets Zephaniah and Habakkuk added nothing to the idea of Israel's covenant relation with God. On the other hand, the Lord gave through Jeremiah some very significant teaching dealing with Israel's unfaithfulness to God as His covenant people. The Lord began by noting Israel's love to Him as that of a bride. Israel was holy to the Lord. But the priests, who were responsible for the law, departed from the Lord. In the large, Israel was an example of marital unfaithfulness.

Repeatedly the Lord used the expression "faithless Israel." Israel was guilty, rebellious, and disobedient in relation to their covenant with the Lord. The nation had forgotten the ark of the covenant of the Lord. In view of this the Lord called for a spiritual circumcision (Jer. 2 — 4). In later contexts (6, 7) the Lord drew attention to Israel's disobedience in their rejection of the law. Their outward ceremonies and sacrifices were not acceptable to God. In the most emphatic language the Lord called for obedience. Bringing burnt offerings and sacrifices without the spiritual accompaniment of repentance from sin and consecration to God was valueless and hypocritical. Israel persisted in walking in their own counsels and in the stubbornness of their evil hearts. By this manner of life they had broken their covenant relation with the Lord.

In very direct language the Lord declared that Israel was not faithful to their covenant made with Him at Sinai (11:1-10). He regarded the relation with His people as being most intimate. The making of this covenant lay in His love for them. Their redemption from Egypt and God's giving them the land of Canaan were still the greatest events of Israel's history. The Lord spoke of Israel as "my people," "my beloved," "my heritage," "his vineyard," and "the Lord's flock." Such were the rich connotations of this old covenant.

With these reflections on the Sinaitic covenant we may ask how the people of Israel received the Lord's promise of making a new covenant.[9] They may have thought of their old covenant as continuing forever. The Lord's promise to make a new covenant with them may have suggested that something immeasurably superior to the old would characterize the new. Further, since the nations of Israel and Judah had been divided for centuries and had been so widely scattered through their captivities, the making of this covenant with both Israel and Judah might have seemed to the participants to be beyond all possibility. The content of this new covenant looked to the exceedingly rich spiritual relationship to be experienced by Israel with their Lord. The words, "I will put my law within them, and I will write it upon their hearts," showed that the new covenant would be inwardly received and obeyed, rather than externally inscribed on two tables of stone. All the people of God, under the new covenant, would know the Lord, as compared with the few spiritual leaders of Israel who had had this privilege. Finally, everyone under this new covenant would experience forgiveness of sins. The author of Hebrews built a most formidable argument on this Scripture to show that the old covenant was then obsolete and that the new was everlasting (Heb. 8:1 — 10:18).

In conclusion, both the house of Israel and the house of Judah received new grounds for believing that their election was actualized by covenant relation. Through the making of an everlasting covenant all Israel would share in this covenant relation with the Lord forever.

4. The Messiah and the Messianic Kingdom

By reason of the similarity of Nahum 1:15 with Isaiah 40:9 and 52: 7 the words of Nahum carry Messianic significance. I believe that Nahum did attach Messianic significance to his words. If this is correct, he has given a very remarkable prediction which underlies the gospel of Christ. Zephaniah struck a Messianic note (3:14-20) when he invited Israel to sing, shout, rejoice, and exult because the Lord had taken away the judgments against them and also because the King of Israel, the Lord, was in their midst. The future events, described as though they were already realized, became a strong challenge to Israel's faith. While Habakkuk did not give any explicit Messianic prediction, the Messiah's work was implicit in the words, "The righteous shall live by his faith" (Hab. 2:4). This should be interpreted in the light of the prophet's testimony, "I will joy in the God of my salvation" (3:18).

There are two closely interwoven strands of Messianic prediction given by the Lord through Jeremiah. The former of these (23:5, 6; 33: 14-16) gives the Lord's promise to "raise up for David a righteous Branch, . . . [who] shall reign as king and deal wisely, and shall execute justice and righteousness in the land. . . . He will be called: 'The Lord is our righteousness.' " This prediction built on earlier ones which speak of a descendant of David, the Anointed One, whose reign will be characterized by justice and righteousness (Is. 9, 11). Some Bible students suggest that Jesus identified Himself with this righteous Branch when He said, "I am the true vine" (Jn. 15:1). When we associate these Jeremiah passages on the righteous Branch with similar references (Is. 4:2; Zech. 3:8; 6:12), we have grounds for believing that these predictions are clearly Messianic, even though the New Testament does not confirm it. The Lord assured Jeremiah that David should never lack a man to sit on the throne of Israel, and also that the Levitical priests should never lack a man to offer sacrifices (Jer. 33:17, 18). The context of these verses indicates their Messianic content. They forecast both the kingly and the priestly work of the Messiah. Obviously, the language of this prediction is cast in the form of Israel's kingly and priestly offices. Looking back from New Testament times, it becomes clear that these predictions had their fulfillment in Christ, who has sat down on the throne of David and has become a Priest forever. This explanation may seem to go beyond the explicit meaning of this passage, but it gains validity when it is associated with the "righteous Branch" prediction immediately preceding it, together with the actualizing of Christ's kingly and priestly work as recorded in the New Testament.

5. The Day of the Lord -- Judgment

Zephaniah, who prophesied during the reign of Josiah, wrote very forcefully concerning the Day of the Lord: "I will utterly sweep away everything from the face of the earth. . . . I will overthrow the wicked; I will cut off mankind from the face of the earth, . . . I will stretch out my hand against Judah, and against all the inhabitants of Jerusalem; and I will cut off from this place the remnant of Baal and the name of the idolatrous priests . . . those who have turned back from following the Lord, who do not seek the Lord or inquire of him" (1:1-6). He then declared that the Day of the Lord was at hand and proceeded to describe in vivid detail the nature of the coming judgment: "A day of wrath is that day, a day of distress and anguish, a day of ruin and devastation, a day of darkness and gloom." He concluded with the words, "In the fire of his jealous wrath, all the earth shall be consumed; for a full, yea, sudden end he will make of all the inhabitants of the earth" (1:14-18). The prophet looked beyond the Day of the Lord to a new era of rejoicing and wrote, "The Lord has taken away the judgments against you, he has cast out your enemies. The King of Israel, the Lord, is in your midst; you shall fear evil no more" (3:8-20). Here is a sequence in which the eschatological pattern becomes increasingly evident. The Day of the Lord is the time of judgment. It is imminent, but beyond the Day of the Lord is a new era, one in which God's people could sing aloud, rejoice and exult with all their heart. It bears repeating that this prophetic structure of the Day of the Lord to be followed by a new era of salvation is built on the messages of Joel, Hosea, Amos, and Isaiah. From the standpoint of unfolding revelation these messages possess deepest meaning.

Habakkuk's message concerning coming judgment was quite different from that of Zephaniah's. The Lord disclosed to him that He was arousing the Chaldeans to bring judgment upon the people of Israel. This prediction became a severe problem for the prophet. He could not understand how the Lord could allow the wicked Chaldeans to swallow up the people of Israel, who were more righteous than they. In answer the Lord assured Habakkuk that "he whose soul is not upright in him shall fail, but the righteous shall live by his faith" (2:4). The prophet proceeded to show the treachery of wine and the doom of the arrogant man. Following this, Habakkuk uttered five woes against the Chaldeans. There is some lack of clarity in the prophet's language, which has led some students to suggest that these woes were pronounced against the people of Israel rather than against the Chaldeans. There are some grounds for believing that 2:4, 5, referred to above, are expanded in the five woes of verses 6-19. Even though there is a problem of interpretation, practically all scholars interpret these five woes as being directed against the Chaldeans. Though there is no reference to the Day of the Lord, these woes are quite comparable to the judgments predicted in such contexts. Among the judgments that would come upon the Chaldeans, Habakkuk predicted that the remnant of the nations would plunder them. Since the Chaldeans had cut off many nations, their own lives would be forfeited. Their idols of wood and of stone would not give them a revelation. In response to this Habakkuk could write, "But the Lord is in his holy temple; let all the earth keep silence before him" (Hab. 2:20).

Much of what Jeremiah had to say concerning the coming judgment upon the people of Judah is very similar to that spoken by earlier prophets with reference to the Day of the Lord. Note a few examples of predictive judgment or punishment: "Your wickedness will chasten you, and your apostasy will reprove you" (Jer. 2:19). "Besiegers come from a distant land; they shout against the cities of Judah. . . . Your ways and your doings have brought this upon you. This is your doom, and it is bitter; it has reached your very heart. . . . The whole land shall be a desolation; yet I will not make a full end" (4:16-27). "Therefore, behold, the days are coming, . . . when it will . . . be called . . . the valley of Slaughter. . . . And the dead bodies of this people will be food for the birds of the air, and for the beasts of the earth; . . . for the land shall become a waste" (7:32-34). "Death shall be preferred to life by all the remnant that remains of this evil family in all the places where I have driven them, says the Lord of hosts" (8:3). "I will appoint over them four kinds of destroyers. . . . the sword to slay, the dogs to tear, and the birds of the air and the beasts of the earth to devour and destroy. And I will make them a horror to all the kingdoms of the earth because of what Manasseh . . . did in Jerusalem" (15:3, 4). A study of these contexts supplies many details. The prophet Jeremiah was witnessing the fulfillment of most of these predictions. In fact, he shared in the suffering and destruction that had come upon the nation of Judah. This may account for the absence of the expression "the Day of the Lord" in these contexts. They were descriptions of the outpouring of God's wrath rather than predictions of the Day of the Lord.

Jeremiah did use the expression "the Day of the Lord" in his prophecy against the nation of Egypt and concerning Nebuchadrezzar's defeat of Pharaoh Neco's army by the river Euphrates. The Lord spoke concerning this defeat, "That day is the day of the Lord God of hosts, a day of vengeance, to avenge himself on his foes. The sword shall devour and be sated, and drink its fill of their blood." Later He said, "The day of their calamity has come upon them, the time of their punishment" (46:10, 21). The Lord brought similar words against Babylon: "Because of the wrath of the Lord she shall not be inhabited, but shall be an utter desolation." Yet again, "Woe to them, for their day has come, the time of their punishment" (50:13, 27). These and many other similar statements comprise chapters 50, 51. Jeremiah was showing that the Day of the Lord was confronting heathen nations as well as Israel and Judah. While there is little teaching on the Day of the Lord to be found in this group of prophets, these references stress again the importance of this prophetic message. All that Jeremiah had to say about coming judgments upon Judah, as well as upon the surrounding nations, included the common redemptive note expressed in the words, "It may be that the house of Judah will hear all the evil which I intend to do to them, so that everyone may turn from his evil way, and that I may forgive their iniquity and their sin" (36:3).

6. The Latter Days –– Prophetic Eschatology

Pointed as were Zephaniah's predictions of the Day of the Lord with its attending judgment, he believed that there was an age beyond this Day when the Lord would restore His people to their land and bring them again into His favor. The prophet may have been looking to a coming age when he wrote, "The Lord will . . . famish all the gods of the earth, and to him shall bow down, each in its place, all the lands of the nations" (Zeph. 2:11). This thought became plainer when the Lord said, "At that time I will change the speech of the peoples to a pure speech, that all of them may call on the name of the Lord and serve him with one accord" (Zeph. 3:9). These verses laid alongside the universalistic statements of earlier prophets may be sufficient to show that Zephaniah envisioned the worldwide mission of the gospel "at that time." As I noted earlier, he encouraged his people to sing aloud, shout, rejoice and exult with all their hearts. He added, "The Lord has taken away the judgments against you, he has cast out your enemies. The King of Israel, the Lord, is in your midst; you shall fear evil no more. . . . He will renew you in his love." The Lord concluded His message, "At that time I will bring you home, at the time when I gather you together; yea, I will make you renowned and praised among all the peoples of the earth, when I restore your fortunes before your eyes" (3:9, 14, 15, 17, 20). A message of this kind given before the overthrow of Judah certainly had the purpose of inspiring faith on the part of God's people, so that when they would experience their captivity, they would have grounds for believing that the Lord would bring them home again.

When the prophet Habakkuk was perplexed because of the imminent invasion by the Chaldeans, the Lord gave him the great promise, the realization of which looked to an era beyond the Chaldean invasion. It read, "The righteous shall live by his faith" (2:4). This gave the Apostle Paul the theme underlying the gospel as expressed in two of his great letters (Rom. 1:17; Gal. 3:11). The author of Hebrews also laid hold of these words, which in turn furnished the key to his great message on faith (Heb. 10:37-39; 11). This message given to Habakkuk was not predictive in essence but yet its full realization became possible through the gospel. It was this gospel which so clearly and climactically determined the era, the Latter Days. This accounts for its use by Paul and by the author of Hebrews.

In further support of the eschatological implications of the words quoted above, we should note a later statement, "For the earth will be filled with the knowledge of the glory of the Lord, as the waters cover the sea" (2:14). Add to this the words from Habakkuk's poetic prayer, "Thou wentest forth for the salvation of thy people, for the salvation of thy anointed" (3:13). On this account the prophet concluded, "I will rejoice in the Lord, I will joy in the God of my salvation. God, the Lord, is my strength; he makes my feet like hinds' feet, he makes me tread upon my high places" (Hab. 3:18, 19). While the predictive nature of these quotations is not quite clear, I believe that the salvation theme possesses the potential for the meaning later realized in the New Testament, and on this account gives justification for ascribing eschatological meaning to them.

The eschatological viewpoint of Jeremiah is very evident in his recognition of both the Day of the Lord and the Latter Days.[10] To Jeremiah the Latter Days was a well-defined period of time lying beyond the Day of the Lord. The judgments of the Lord would be past and those faithful to God would experience great blessings. The special blessings of the Lord would extend beyond God's chosen people and would include the people of Moab and of Elam. Jerusalem would be called the throne of the Lord and all nations would gather to it (3:17-19). This promise came in the wake of repeated statements that the Lord would not make a full end of His people. In such settings He said, "I will again have compassion on them, and I will bring them again each to his heritage and each to his land." This promise came to both Israel and their neighbors who had been carried into captivity. To their evil neighbors its fulfillment was conditioned on their learning the ways of

God's people and on swearing by His name (12:15-17).

This return to the land of Canaan would be an exodus similar to that of Israel's coming out of the land of Egypt in the days of Moses. Then the people would say, "As the Lord lives who brought up and led the descendants of the house of Israel out of the north country and out of all the countries where he had driven them" (16:14, 15; 23:7, 8). In realizing this promise God said, "I will give them a heart to know that I am the Lord; and they shall be my people and I will be their God, for they shall return to me with their whole heart." Thus the Lord demonstrated the real meaning of His words, "I have loved you with an everlasting love; therefore I have continued my faithfulness to you." What the Lord did for Israel finds most significant meaning in the words, "For the Lord has ransomed Jacob, and has redeemed him from hands too strong for him."[11] These promises certainly bolstered the hope of captive Judah and the Canaanite nations.

It is in these contexts that the Lord spoke of making a new covenant with the house of Israel and the house of Judah. In an earlier context we noted the significance of this promise to Israel. It was this promised new covenant which became the most dominant characteristic of the predicted Latter Days. The disciples of Jesus realized this fact when they heard their Lord say, "This is my blood of the covenant, which is poured out for many for the forgiveness of sins" (Mt. 26:28). The writer of Hebrews confirmed this evaluation when he quoted these words from Jeremiah at the climax of his presentation of the new covenant (Heb. 10:16-18). Finally in order to give His people the firmest foundation for their faith, the Lord added, "If you can break my covenant with the day and my covenant with the night, so that day and night will not come at their appointed time, then also my covenant with David my servant may be broken, so that he shall not have a son to reign on his throne, and my covenant with the Levitical priests my ministers. As the host of heaven cannot be numbered and the sands of the sea cannot be measured, so I will multiply the descendants of David my servant, and the Levitical priests who minister to me" (Jer. 33:20-22).

7. Life of the People of God

Like the prophets of the Assyrian period, the prophets Zephaniah, Habakkuk, and Jeremiah present the life of the people of God in a negative rather than in a positive manner. This disclosed Israel's failure to measure up to the standard of living appropriate to the people of God. In the midst of Zephaniah's prediction of the coming Day of the Lord he implored the people in the language, "Seek the Lord, all you humble of the land, who do his commands; seek righteousness, seek humility." Later he added, "A people humble and lowly . . . they shall do no wrong and utter no lies, nor shall there be found in their mouth a deceitful tongue" (Zeph. 2:3; 3:12, 13). In giving this counsel Zephaniah stressed the godly graces familiar to the people of Israel throughout their history. The Lord, speaking through Habakkuk, expressed both the negative and the positive aspects of holy living in the words, "Behold, he whose soul is not upright in him shall fail, but the righteous shall live by his faith" (2:4). The five woes which follow condemn the sins of the Chaldeans. Thus, stealing, plundering, shedding of blood, causing drunkenness, worshiping idols, and the like, all represent grievous violations of God's standard of righteousness.

The Lord speaking through Jeremiah referred to Israel's early history when His covenant people were holy to the Lord, the firstfruits of His harvest (2:3). This became the basis for the Lord's bringing strong indictments against His people and presented their sinful way of living as it stood opposed to the holy living which the Lord had planned for His people. The Lord was not merely asking for an empty ritual of offerings and sacrifices,[12] but He commanded, "Obey my voice, and I will be your God, and you shall be my people; and walk in all the way that I command you, that it may be well with you" (7:23). From the time of Israel's entrance into covenant relation with the Lord, He was seeking to lead His people into a fuller and richer expression of holy living. This was the immeasurable task of the prophets from the time of Moses on. Jeremiah's version of this prophetic guidance found expression in the Lord's word to him, "I will give them a heart to know that I am the Lord; and they shall be my people and I will be their God, for they shall return to me with their whole heart" (24:7). Jeremiah's paucity of positive direction placed his warnings, rebukes, and condemnations in most emphatic position as depicting what the manner of life of the people of God should not be.

8. Nature of Sin and Man's Sinfulness

a. Nahum

Nahum gave a woeful picture of Nineveh's sins. It was a bloody city, full of lies and booty. There was no end to the plunder. The cruelties shown in their wars resulted in hosts being slain — "all for the countless harlotries of the harlot, graceful and of deadly charms" (3:1-4). Such were the sins of this heathen nation. It was an extreme instance of the wickedness of uncontrolled lust.

b. Zephaniah

In the contexts of the judgments that would be brought upon Judah in the Day of the Lord, Zephaniah spoke repeatedly of the nature of man's sin and of his sinfulness. The Lord spoke of overthrowing the wicked (*rasha*). This general term included all forms of sin, such as the sinfulness of idol worship manifested by the people's swearing to the Lord by Milcom, and their turning back from following the Lord. They did not seek the Lord or inquire of Him (1:2-6). The next reference to sin also denounced idol worship and those who filled their master's house with violence (*hamas*) and fraud (*mirmah*). The Lord represented Himself as searching Jerusalem with lamps, and as finding those who thought they were hidden away, concealed from all discovery. Just as wine needs to be stirred and poured from vat to vat so that it gains strength, these wicked men were thickening upon their lees; that is, they were satisfied in their complacency and in absolute indifference to God. They could say, "The Lord will not do good, nor will he do ill." These were people who lived at ease and had sunk into spiritual indifference, thinking that the Lord would not interfere in human affairs. This vivid figure gave insight into a most grievous characteristic of sin (Zeph. 1: 9-13). The Lord then foretold the bringing of distress upon men because they had sinned (*hata*) against the Lord (1:14, 18). The nation did not turn pale. They were shameless. The antidote to sin was to seek the Lord, to seek righteousness and humility (2:1-3). The sins of Moab called for rebuke. They had taunted and reviled God's people. In this they showed their pride in scoffing and boasting against the people of the Lord (2:8-11). Finally the Lord rebuked the rebellious, defiled, and oppressing city: "She listens to no voice, she accepts no correction. She does not trust in the Lord, she does not draw near to her God. Her officials within her are roaring lions; her judges are evening wolves that leave nothing till the morning. Her prophets are wanton, faithless men; her priests profane what is sacred, they do violence to the law" (3:2-4). These unjust people knew no shame. Even though the Lord was bringing judgment upon His people, "all the more they were eager to make all their deeds corrupt" (3:5-7). As the Lord looked forward to a future time, He predicted a change of conditions in which He saw Israel as a humble and lowly people: "They shall do no wrong and utter no lies, nor shall there be found in their mouth a deceitful tongue" (3: 9-13). From this we should gather that the judgments of the imminent Day of the Lord would lead to a new age in which God's people will have turned away from all their grievous sins. This book has gone to greatest depths in its exposure of sin and man's sinfulness.

c. Habakkuk

The prophet Habakkuk was greatly troubled by the wrongs and trouble, destruction and violence, strife and contention evidently characteristic of the internal havoc taking place in Judah. Law and justice were perverted and the wicked were surrounding the righteous (1:2-4). When the Lord disclosed to Habakkuk that He was bringing judgment on Judah by the Chaldeans, the prophet faced a very severe ethical problem. He could not understand why God would use such a wicked nation to swallow up the more righteous nation of Judah. In response to Habakkuk's problem the Lord made it clear that those who are not upright shall fail. "The arrogant man shall not abide. His greed is as wide as Sheol; like death he has never enough" (2:4, 5). The five woes uttered by the Lord exposed the real nature of the sins of the Chaldeans: their evil gains by violence, the building of towns with bloodshed and iniquity, the sin of leading others to drunkenness so as to expose their shame, and last, the folly of idol worship. Thus while Habakkuk did not directly address himself to the task of exposing the nature of sin and man's sinfulness, what he did present harmonized with and gave adequate grounds for God's bringing judgment upon both Judah and the Chaldeans.

d. Jeremiah

Jeremiah laid bare the nature of Israel's sinfulness in most searching, analytical, and penetrating language. His vocabulary is perhaps more extensive and forceful than that of Isaiah. He seems to involve the reader in a very intimate and experiential relation to the nature of sin. A biblical theology approach to the prophet's exposure of sin presents a real problem with respect to organization of subject matter. I desire to present the material in such a manner as to make clear the prophet's deep insight into the nature of sin.

First and foremost, Jeremiah desired to lead Judah to a consciousness of their sins. The Lord began His indictment with the words, "Israel was holy to the Lord, the first fruits of his harvest. All who ate of it became guilty; evil came upon them, says the Lord" (2:3). This confronted Israel with the fact that the Lord had set them apart unto Himself. The Lord then interrogated His people to give their reasons for forsaking Him. It was the case of rejecting the fountains of living waters and of hewing out cisterns, broken cisterns, that could hold no water. Their wickedness would chasten them and their apostasy would reprove them. Through their sinfulness they were manifesting a rebellious attitude toward God, and were virtually breaking off their covenant relationship with Him. They had turned degenerate and their sin was of such a nature that they could not remove the stain of their guilt. They had gone after the Baals as an animal in heat sniffs the wind. A more vivid rebuke of sin than this was hardly possible (2:4-25).

Second, the prophet sought to show the many aspects of sin. This becomes evident in the extensive vocabulary for sin which he used. He brought these manifold aspects into focus in the use of such common words for sin as evil (ra), contrariness (hephek), iniquity (avon), wicked (rasha), and others of less frequency. Occasionally there is a buildup of words in a single sentence, such as, "We have heard of the pride of Moab — he is very proud — of his loftiness, his pride, and his arrogance, and the haughtiness of his heart. I know his insolence, . . . his boasts are false, his deeds are false" (48:29, 30). Some other sins named by the prophet follow: holding fast to deceit (ramah, 5:27; 8:5); perversion (avah, haphak, 3:21; 23:36); refuse (maan, 3:3; 5:3; 8:5; 9:6; 11:10); to commit adultery (naaph, 3:8, 9; 5:7; 7:9; 9:2); to be faithless, to deal treacherously (bagad, 3:7, 8, 10, 11, 20; 5:11; 9:2); to play the harlot (zanah, 2:20, 25; 3:1, 6-8; 5:7); to do violence (chamas, 6:7; 20:8; 22:3, 17; 51:35, 46); to be rebellious (sur, 2:21; 5:23; 17:5, 13; 28:16; 29:32); to rebel, to transgress (pasha, 2:8, 29; 3:13; 5:6; 33:8); to transgress (avar, 2:20; 34:18); stiffen the neck (qashah, 7:26; 17:23; 19:15); loftiness, be proud (gabah, 13:15; 48:29); pride (gaon, 13:9; 48:29); lie (bad, 48:30); pride, insolence (zadon, 43:2; 46:16; 50:31, 32); faithless, backsliding (meshubah, 2:19; 3:6-12; 5:6; 8:5; 14:7); haughtiness (rum, 48:29).

Third, the prophet disclosed the deep-rooted nature of sin. Briefly stated:

(1) Sin is against the Lord God (2:5, 17-19; 3:13-20; 16:10-13; 25:8; 32:32-35; 34:13-18).

(2) Sin centers in the heart (5:23; 7:24; 11:18; 13:10; 17:1, 9; 18:12; 23:17).

(3) Sin is ineradicable (2:22; 10:23; 13:23).

(4) Sin reveals excessive self-confidence (8:8 ff.; 18:18).

(5) Sin is obduracy (5:3, 19; 7:28; 13:22; 16:10).

(6) Sin manifests itself in stubbornness of the heart (3:10, 17; 4:14; 5:23; 7:24; 9:14, 26; 11:8; 16:12; 18:12; 48:29).

(7) Sin exposes itself in unrestrained sexual lust (2:20-25; 3:1-10; 5:7, 8; 13:26, 27).

(8) Sin manifests itself in profligacy (5:30, 31; 6:13-15; 14:14).

(9) Sin is faithlessness, apostasy, and backsliding (2:19; 3:6-12; 5:6; 8:5).

9. Repentance, Faith, and Regeneration

a. Zephaniah

Zephaniah called Judah to repentance in the words, "Seek the Lord, all you humble of the land, who do his commands; seek righteousness, seek humility; perhaps you may be hidden on the day of the wrath of the Lord" (2:3). The Lord promised: "At that time I will change the speech of the peoples to a pure speech, that all of them may call on the name of the Lord and serve him with one accord" (3:9). This language suggests God's word of regeneration involving repentance. The Lord promised to remove the rebellious and the proud so that only the humble and lowly would dwell in the land. They would live in a manner that befits God's people, for He would renew them in His love (3: 11-13, 17). All these references to godly living concerned repentance and faith which led to a spiritual renewal, and became the basis for hope in the future.

b. Habakkuk

Habakkuk gave nothing on the theme of repentance, even though he disclosed some of the profoundest teachings on faith and salvation. The Lord assured him that when the Chaldeans would attack Judah, "He whose soul is not upright in him shall fail, but the righteous shall live by his faith" (2:4). In this promise the moral quality of faith is very apparent. Life issues from faith. These concepts lie at the very foundation of regeneration. In addition they became prophetic of the time when "the earth will be filled with the knowledge of the glory of the Lord" (v. 14). They also led to the thought content of *salvation* (3:13, 14). Just as Israel had stood firm to see the salvation of the Lord, now in the Chaldean crisis they could believe that the Lord had gone forth for the salvation of His anointed people. Habakkuk could say, "I will joy in the God of my salvation" (3:18). Through these significant uses of the word "salvation" the prophet added meaning and content to the word destined to become the key word of the Bible.

c. Jeremiah

The weeping prophet stressed the call to repentance because of the exceeding sinfulness of Israel.[13] The Lord was inviting faithless Israel to return and He would be merciful to them. He pleaded, "Break up your fallow ground, and sow not among thorns." He said also, "O Jerusalem, wash your heart from wickedness, that you may be saved." Later the Lord said, "Amend your ways and your doings, and I will let you dwell in this place." The word "amend" has a forceful ethical sense in its use here. They were to execute justice one with the other and not to oppress the alien nor shed innocent blood. In their going after other gods they were making it appear that the altars to these gods were the temple of the Lord. The Lord had sent out the prophets, giving them the urgent command to say, "Turn now every one of you from his evil way, and amend your doings, and do not go after other gods to serve them."

Those who responded to these calls, confessed, "We have sinned against the Lord our God, we and our fathers, from our youth even to this day; and we have not obeyed the voice of the Lord our God" (3: 25). Judah also confessed: "Our backslidings are many, we have sinned against thee" (14:7). They said: "We acknowledge our wickedness, O Lord, and the iniquity of our fathers, for we have sinned against thee" (14:20). The prophet then besought the Lord not to spurn them nor to dishonor God's glorious throne but to remember and not to break His covenant with them. He concluded this general confession with the words, "We set our hope on thee, for thou doest all these things." These statements enlighten us on the meaning of confession. Lying back of an honest confession is a genuine change of mind and attitude toward sin. Israel's appeal to God based on His covenant with them shows again the importance of the covenant relationship in Israel's religion. It intensified the spiritual relation between the people and their God. This was the basis of Israel's faith and hope in God. Herein are manifested the personal and experiential elements of Israel's religion.

Although the prophet had much to say about the need of Israel's repentance, the sparsity of statements dealing with repentance and returning to God is very apparent. In addition to the confessions referred to above, there is another statement which shows the shallowness of their penitence. The Lord reminded Israel of the covenant at Sinai in which there was a regulation requiring them to release fellow Hebrews who had served six years as slaves. The Lord testified that Israel had recently repented of breaking this commandment, but that they were again bringing these liberated slaves into subjection. This shallow repentance stood in sharp contrast with the genuine experience which would take place at a future time (29:10-14).

The Lord promised His people that at the end of seventy years He would fulfill His promise to bring them to their own land. He sought to give them a future and a hope, but an inner change would have taken place. They would call upon the Lord in prayer and seek Him with all their heart. He emphasized that real repentance is an inner experience which involves one's entire being. In the great new covenant context (31:31-34) we gain the clearest idea of repentance found in Jeremiah. The new law will be written upon the heart and will manifest itself in an inner response of turning away from sin, so that the Lord will forgive Israel's iniquity and will remember their sin no more. This tie-in of genuine repentance and forgiveness with the new covenant is most distinctive. It sets forth man's repentance in relation to God, with whom he is bound by covenant agreement. Another forecast of future repentance and forgiveness reads, "I will cleanse them from all the guilt of their sin against me" (33:8). This reaffirms the close relationship of repentance, cleansing from guilt, and forgiveness.[14]

Jeremiah also drew attention to the faith aspect of repentance and forgiveness of sins. First of all, he showed the utter fallacy of trusting in human power.[15] Thus the fortified cities to which Judah looked for protection would be destroyed. They were placing confidence in deceptive words. Even the temple of the Lord, in which these deceivers would have Judah put her trust, would be destroyed. No longer could they place confidence in the common human relationships of brother and neighbor. Among these were found supplanters, slanderers, deceivers, and liars. A pitiful picture, indeed! On this account the Lord said, "Cursed is the man who trusts in man and makes flesh his arm, whose heart turns away from the Lord" (17:5). In sharp contrast with man's untrustworthy nature the Lord said, "Blessed is the man who trusts in the Lord, whose trust is the Lord. He is like a tree planted by water, that sends out its roots by the stream, and does not fear when heat comes, for its leaves remain green, and is not anxious in the year of drought, for it does not cease to bear fruit" (17:6-8). This sublime picture of trust in God becomes the capsheaf of repentance and faith.

By reason of the climactic nature of the new birth and regeneration as taught in the New Testament, it is consistent for us to search for foreshadowings of this experience in this book, especially since the prophet had spoken so forcefully on repentance and faith. A number of his utterances would seem to anticipate the New Testament teaching on the new birth.[16] Thus the remedy for defilement would seem to require an inner spiritual cleansing. The rite of circumcision had come to mean a spiritual cleansing of the heart. On this account the washing of the heart from wickedness was necessary for one to be saved. Just as access to supernatural power would be necessary for an Ethiopian to change his skin or the leopard his spots, so the change from doing evil to doing good would also require the inner working of divine power. Perhaps most expressive are the words, "I will give them a heart to know that I am the Lord; and they shall be my people and I will be their God, for they shall return to me with their whole heart." The Lord alone can change the heart. Writing the law upon the heart is a spiritual renewal wrought by the power of God.

For Additional Reading and Reference:

The Interpreter's Bible.
>   Vol. 5, pp. 784-87, "Jeremiah."
>   Vol. 6, p. 954, "Nahum."
>   Vol. 6, pp. 977 f., "Habakkuk."
>   Vol. 6, pp. 1012 f., "Zephaniah."

Oehler, *The Theology of the Old Testament,* pp. 437-536. A general treatment of all the prophets.

Pfeiffer, *Religion in the Old Testament,* pp. 117-58. A doctrinal approach to all the prophets.

von Rad, *Old Testament Theology,* Vol. II, pp. 188-219. (Jeremiah, Nahum, Habakkuk, Zephaniah)

Robinson, *The Cross in the Old Testament,* pp. 119-92. (Jeremiah)

Titcomb, *Revelation in Progress,* pp. 337-375.

Wright, *The Rule of God,* pp. 77-92.

1. Jer. 1:4, 7, 9, 11, 13; 2:1, 4; 3:6, 11, etc.
2. Jer. 14:22; 16:21; 17:13; 18:5-11; 33:19-22; 51:15, 16, etc.
3. Jer. 5:22, 24; 8:7; 14:22; 27:5; 31:35-37; 32:17; 51:15, 16.
4. Jer. 11:18; 12:3, 4; 15:15; 17:16; 18:23; 29:23.
5. Jer. 17:9, 10. *See also* 11:20; 12:3; 16:17; 20:12.
6. Jer. 2:27, 28; 30:10, 11; 31:7-9; 42:11.
7. Jer. 3:22, 23; 14:8, 9; 15:19, 20; 17:13, 14; 50:34.
8. Jer. 1:2, 4, 11, 13, 14; 2:1, 4; 3:6, 11, etc.
9. Jer. 31:31-34; 32:37-41; 33:20-22; 50:5.
10. Jer. 23:20; 30:24; 48:47; 49:39.
11. Jer. 24:4-7; 30:3-24; 31:1-25.
12. Jer. 6:20; 7:21-26; 11:15.
13. Jer. 3:12-14, 22, 23; 4:1-4, 14; 7:3-7; 26:13; 35:15.
14. Jer. 36:3; 50:20; Lam. 3:40-42.
15. Jer. 5:17; 7:4, 8, 14; 9:4, 5; 13:25; 17:5.
16. Jer. 2:22; 4:3, 4, 14; 9:26; 13:23; 24:7; 31:33, 34.

CHAPTER VIII
THEOLOGY OF THE PROPHETS
OF THE BABYLONIAN EXILE,
602-534 B.C.

1. Introduction

Since literary criticism has probed deeply into questions of authorship, date, historical accuracy, and prophetic viewpoint of the books Ezekiel and Daniel, a few observations as to their bearing on our study are pertinent. Unlike the other writing prophets, Ezekiel did not claim to be the author of the book bearing his name. Most critical scholars hold that an editor or biographer wrote the book. In applying this viewpoint some scholars maintain that certain parts of the book do not belong to the message of Ezekiel. My studies of this problem lead me to conclude that there is no internal claim or external evidence that an editor or biographer wrote the book. Ezekiel was the speaker, or the one to whom the Lord spoke. Throughout the book we observe the frequent and uniform use of the grammatical first person pronoun. This suggests that the writer was the prophet himself or one who wrote the oral messages for him. I believe that the entire book is an authentic record of Ezekiel's oral messages.

The Book of Daniel presents some of the most difficult problems in the field of biblical criticism. When the late Robert Dick Wilson introduced his discussion of the genuineness of the Book of Daniel, he wrote, "With the exception of the neo-Platonist Porphyry, a Greek non-Christian philosopher of the third century A.D., the genuineness of the Book of Daniel was denied by no one until the rise of the deistic movement of the seventeenth century. The attacks upon the genuineness of the book have been based upon (1) the predictions, (2) the miracles, (3) the text, (4) the language, (5) the historical statements."[1] At the present time almost all scholars reject the historicity of the person Daniel and also the contents of the book bearing his name. These scholars date the book in the time of Antiochus Epiphanes of the second century B.C. Their arguments are based: first, on the alleged inaccuracy of the historical data found in the book; second, on linguistic problems with regard to vocabulary allegedly unknown in the time of Nebuchadnezzar; and third, on a viewpoint which rejects predictive prophecy and miracles.

I shall give a brief presentation of my view. First, Christ, Paul, John, and Josephus gave their respective witness to Daniel as a man of God who lived in the time of Nebuchadnezzar. Second, the scholars John

D. Davis and Henry S. Gehman wrote, "The asserted historical inaccuracies in Daniel are not statements which are disproved by history but only statements which have seemed difficult to harmonize with the meager accounts of secular historians. The asserted historical inaccuracies have, moreover, been steadily diminishing before the increasing knowledge of the times of Cyrus. The existence of King Belshazzar was scouted; but now the records contemporary with the capture of Babylon have made him a well-known historical character; they have explained why he raised Daniel to the third place of power in the kingdom instead of the second, for his father and he already occupied the two higher places of authority; and they have made clear why he, and not Nabonidus, is mentioned as king of Babylon on the night of the capture of the city. They do not yet clear up the reference to Darius, the Mede's receiving the kingdom, but they show that the appointment of a regent for Babylonia by Cyrus was in accord with his policy. The allusions to Belshazzar as a descendant of Nebuchadnezzar agree with a custom of the time. The growth of our knowledge of this period shows how cautious one should be in doubting the historical accuracy of the biblical records."[2]

Third, the Book of Daniel represents Daniel and his companions as historical persons who lived during the reigns of Nebuchadnezzar, Belshazzar, and Darius. The many purportedly historical details fit very naturally into the Babylonian setting of 600 B.C. Fourth, the historical data presented need to be interpreted in the light of the prophetic and apocalyptic character of the book. This imposes a very difficult but not impossible task. Fifth, supreme value must be given to the internal evidences for what the book purports to be and to say. Every book stands in its own right until evidence is forthcoming which proves the internal claims to be erroneous. Being fully aware that my conclusions are not in accord with the bulk of modern scholarship, I am venturing to move forward nevertheless on the premise that the Book of Daniel accurately depicts the prophetic activity of the Daniel who lived in Babylon 600 B.C.

2. The God of Israel

a. The Sovereign and Glorious Majesty of God

The prophet Ezekiel said a great deal about the Lord God, especially concerning His sovereign and glorious majesty.[3] Almost the entire book was given in vision form. This mode of divine revelation stands in contrast to the usual pattern of God's speaking and man's hearing. In the vision, God shows and man sees His revelation. Ezekiel

1 shows how exceedingly effective the vision form of revelation was for disclosing the glory of the Lord. Ezekiel saw the appearance of God as the Almighty One. He closed the scene with the words, "Such was the appearance of the likeness of the glory of the Lord. And when I saw it, I fell upon my face, and I heard the voice of one speaking" (1:28). Throughout the book the glory of the Lord became the symbol of God's presence. Ezekiel recaptured the idea of God's glory which had been revealed in Israel's tabernacle. He magnified this idea of God's presence, shall we say, to an infinite degree in order to disclose the glory of the Lord as will be manifested in the new temple which shall stand in the center of the new promised land. The name of the city in which this heavenly temple will be found is "The Lord is there" (48:35).

The Book of Daniel also presented God in His sovereign majesty. On three occasions the heathen monarchs of Babylon expressed their understanding of God, especially in view of Daniel's interpreting their dream-visions.[4] Thus Nebuchadnezzar could say, "Your God is God of gods and Lord of kings, and a revealer of mysteries." Darius could testify, "He is the living God, enduring for ever; his kingdom shall never be destroyed, and his dominion shall be to the end. He delivers and rescues, he works signs and wonders in heaven and on earth, he who has saved Daniel from the power of the lions." Daniel described the sovereign majesty of God in the words, "Blessed be the name of God for ever and ever, to whom belong wisdom and might. He changes times and seasons; he removes kings and sets up kings; he gives wisdom to the wise and knowledge to those who have understanding; he reveals deep and mysterious things; he knows what is in the darkness, and the light dwells with him" (2:20-23). To Belshazzar Daniel said, "The Most High God rules the kingdom of men, and sets over it whom he will. . . . You have lifted up yourself against the Lord of heaven; . . . but the God in whose hand is your breath, and whose are all your ways, you have not honored" (5:21-23). These statements, directed to or coming from those who had experienced dreams and visions which Daniel interpreted, present an exalted concept of God who possesses sovereignty and glorious majesty.

b. The Living God

The statement, "as I live, says the Lord God," occurring fifteen times in the Book of Ezekiel, certainly possesses distinctive significance.[5] As Cooke says, "This solemn asseveration in the mouth of Jahveh Himself occurs . . . far more frequently than in any other prophet; it is in accordance with his austere conception of the reality of the divine

Being and the divine resentment against sin.''[6] The Lord God would have His people, Israel, know that He differed radically from the gods of the Babylonians in that He was the living God. The repeated use of this expression simply intensified the fact to captive Israel. This emphasis becomes all the more striking when each occurrence is studied in its context.

The Book of Daniel gives strong witness to the living God. Both Nebuchadnezzar and Darius testified that the God of Israel is the living God. We should note this clear-cut statement of the pagan monarch Darius, who said: "For he is the living God, enduring for ever; his kingdom shall never be destroyed, and his dominion shall be to the end" (6:26). Daniel said, "I heard him swear by him who lives for ever" (Dan. 12:7). Thus the words of the archangel were vouchsafed to Daniel through his solemn testimony, authenticated by Him who lives forever.

c. God, the Holy One of Israel

We naturally expect that Ezekiel, the priest, would magnify the holiness of God.[7] When the Lord promised Israel's return to their land, He spoke of their worshiping Him on His holy mountain. Concerning the restoration of worship in Jerusalem, God said, "I will manifest my holiness among you in the sight of the nations." His people should no more profane His holy name. The Lord noted all of Jerusalem's abominable deeds before her downfall. They had despised God's holy things and profaned His sabbaths. The priests had done violence to God's law, and had made no distinction between the holy and the common, neither did they teach the difference between the clean and the unclean. All this was a most serious breach of their worship established through the covenant made at Mt. Sinai. The Lord declared that Israel had defiled their land. Their conduct was like the uncleanness of a woman in her impurity. Hence they were scattered among the nations; and wherever they went, they profaned God's holy name. God determined to vindicate the holiness of His name. To accomplish this He would bring Israel into their own land, give them a new heart and a new spirit within them, and cause them to walk in His statutes. Through all these saving acts the nations would come to know that the Lord is the Holy One of Israel.

Chapters 40 — 48 tell how the hand of the Lord was upon Ezekiel and through the medium of visions brought him into the land of Israel. The Lord showed him the temple built on the same pattern as that of Solomon, but immeasurably more glorious. There the prophet witnessed the glory of God coming from the east, causing the earth to shine with His glory. It was similar to the vision he had seen by the river Chebar. Then the glory of the Lord entered the temple. The Spirit brought Ezekiel into the inner court and to his amazement "the glory of the Lord filled the temple of the Lord" (43:5; 44:4). The Lord commanded the prophet to portray the temple in full detail as well as to describe the ordinances and laws relating to worship. He was told, "This is the law of the temple: the whole territory round about upon the top of the mountain shall be most holy" (Ezek. 43:12). Through this revelation God purposed that Ezekiel should lead Israel to a genuine worship of the true God. This magnificent scene leads us to understand that the presence of the glory of the Lord in the temple set apart its entire area to be most holy (43:12). As the Lord showed Ezekiel the temple in great detail and elaborated for him all the aspects of the worship centering in the temple, the word "holy" became most descriptive of everything that Ezekiel saw. All this was an enrichment of Israel's worship as depicted in the Book of Leviticus. Through this revelation the command, "You shall be holy; for I the Lord your God am holy," was greatly intensified and enriched (Lev. 19:2).

Contrary to expectation, Daniel did not use the expression "Holy One" with reference to God but it is noteworthy that the word "holy" has a number of significant uses in the book.[8] Thus Nebuchadnezzar and the wife of Belshazzar spoke of Daniel as the one "in whom is the spirit of the holy gods (marginal reading, 'Spirit of the holy God)'." The watchers who came down from heaven were called holy ones. Daniel spoke of God's people, of the hill and mountain of Jerusalem, and of the city itself as being holy. The angelic being who spoke to Daniel referred to the Sinaitic covenant as being the holy covenant. If the marginal reading of 9:24 is correct, then the most significant use of "holy" is in its being ascribed to the coming Anointed One. This captures the cumulative meaning of the attributes ascribed to the coming Messiah. From this we should gather that the Book of Daniel indirectly speaks of God as the Holy One of Israel. Since all the places used for the worship and the people who worshiped there are holy, most emphatically, the God in whom all of this centers is holy.

1. The God of Love and Mercy

In a passage in Ezekiel where the Lord was answering Israel's charge that "The way of the Lord is not just," He said, "If a wicked man turns away from all his sins which he has committed . . . he shall surely live." In a later message the Lord said, "As I live, . . . I have no pleasure in the death of the wicked, but that the wicked turn from his way and live; turn back, turn back from your evil ways; for why will you die, O house of Israel?"[9] Such were the words of love and mercy spoken by God, against whom the people had said, "The way of the Lord is not just."

When the lives of Daniel and his companions were in jeopardy because the magicians and Chaldeans were unable to interpret Nebuchadnezzar's dream, Daniel told his friends, "Seek mercy of the God of heaven concerning this mystery" (2:18). This tells us that according to Daniel's theology God was merciful. Later in his great intercessory prayer for captive Judah and Israel, he spoke of the Lord as the One "who keepest covenant and steadfast love with those who love him and keep his commandments." He confessed, "We have sinned and done wrong and acted wickedly and rebelled, turning aside from thy commandments and ordinances." After this humble confession he could say, "To the Lord our God belong mercy and forgiveness" (9:3-19). Here we see the mercy and love of God in the perspective of His judgment upon His people on account of their rebellion against Him.

e. The God Who Judges Righteously

It may seem strange that the prophet Ezekiel at no place said anything about God's righteousness, especially in view of the Lord's having spoken frequently of righteous people. Alongside this are the frequent occurrences of the words "anger," "fury," and "wrath," usually in dual combination, which the Lord used in expressing His attitude toward the wickedness of His people.[10] God's use of these words has an important bearing on our understanding of His nature. The reasons for His anger, fury, and wrath become apparent when we study His judgments. Many times the purpose of judgment was given by God Himself in the words, "You shall know that I am the Lord."[11]

Much of what the Lord said in chapters 5 — 9 gave the reason for His anger and wrath. God had set Jerusalem in the center of the sinful nations in order that they might see in Israel a God-fearing and holy people. But Israel had wickedly rebelled against God's ordinance and statutes and this led the surrounding nations to do likewise. On that account the Lord would execute judgments upon His people in the sight of the nations. By spending His anger and fury upon Israel the other nations would know that He had spoken in His jealousy. Israel would become a reproach, a taunt, a warning, and a horror to the nations round about them. God expressly declared that through these judgments Israel and the nations would know that He was Lord (Ezek. 6:7). The Lord continued to predict imminent judgments, as in this pronouncement: "Disaster after disaster! Behold, it comes. An end has come, the end has come. . . . Your doom has come to you. . . . Now I will soon pour out my wrath upon you, . . . and judge you according to your ways; and I will punish you for all your abominations. . . . Then you will know that I am the Lord, who smite" (7:5-9).[12]

In the midst of these judgments Israel charged, "The way of the Lord is not just" (18:25). In response the Lord said, "Repent and turn from all your transgressions . . . and get yourselves a new heart and a new spirit! Why will you die. . . ? For I have no pleasure in the death of anyone, says the Lord God; so turn, and live" (18:30-32). Space forbids considering the contexts of this often-repeated statement, but one (20:3-28) may suffice to give the real import of these words. In this instance the Lord drew lessons from Israel's history. He had chosen Israel out of Egypt in order that they would become His people. In a covenant context God had said, "I am the Lord your God" (20:5). In order to be true to this covenant relation with the Lord God, Israel needed to cast away the idols of Egypt, but in their wilderness wanderings they did not cast away the detestable things gotten from that nation. The Lord had made clear Israel's involvements with Him through their covenant relation expressed in the statutes and ordinances. By observing these ordinances Israel would live. But they rebelled against Him in the wilderness. For the sake of His name the Lord did not pour out His wrath upon them. He continued to command them to walk in His statutes. He said to them, "Hallow my sabbaths that they may be a sign between me and you, that you may know that I the Lord am your God." In spite of this Israel continued to rebel against the Lord. They failed to see that by keeping His ordinances they would live. Because of their rebellion the Lord declared that He would scatter Israel among the nations. He gave them statutes that were not good and ordinances by which they could not have life. He did this, He said, "that they might know that I am the Lord" (20:25, 26).

The first part of verse 26 offers some problems of interpretation. The law gave no command that Israel should offer by fire all their firstborn. The Lord had commanded Israel to consecrate to Him all the firstborn (Ex. 13:2, 12, 13). This included the firstlings of their cattle and asses as well as the firstborn of their sons. The firstborn animals were given in sacrifice to the Lord, but the firstborn of their sons were redeemed. Influenced by pagan practices, many of the Israelites actually offered their firstborn by fire. God allowed this perversion of His commandment in order to horrify them, and as He said, "I did it that they might know that I am the Lord." Through offering the firstborn by fire Israel was blaspheming the Lord. By dealing treacherously

with Him they were defiling themselves with all their idols. The Lord
brought this lesson from Israel's history to a climax by showing that
the judgments He brought upon them in the wilderness would be repeated among those who had returned from captivity. The purpose
of this extended illustration was, "Then you will know that I am the
Lord."

The settings of all these pointed statements reveal the great
purpose of the Book of Ezekiel. Having restored Israel to their land,
the Lord would have them know that unless they were obedient to
Him the judgments experienced by their forefathers would again come
upon them. It was time that Israel should know that God was the Lord
and it was He who judged righteously. God's righteous judgments presented in these contexts of Israel's abominable practices, wicked re-
bellions, and idol worship, revealed the real nature of His attributes.

The prophet Daniel was also keenly conscious of God as the One
who judges righteously. He interpreted Nebuchadnezzar's dream-vision
which by its nature revealed God's judgment to be brought upon the
proud monarch. Daniel said, "Break off your sins by practicing righteousness, and your iniquities by showing mercy to the oppressed, that
there may perhaps be a lengthening to your tranquillity" (4:27). By
this counsel Daniel showed Nebuchadnezzar that the Lord, to whom he
was responsible, judged righteously. Therefore he also needed to demonstrate these godly traits. Nebuchadnezzar's experience of insanity, which
brought him to repentance and the return of his reason, led him to say
"Now I Nebuchadnezzar, praise and extol and honor the King of
heaven; for all his works are right and his ways are just; and those who
walk in pride he is able to abase" (4:37). Perhaps the reason for
Daniel's recounting this experience lay in the fact that he would have
his people know that even the great monarch of Babylon could give
such a wonderful prophetic word relating to God's righteousness and
justice.

Daniel's personal recognition of God who judges righteously became
most clear in his great intercessory prayer: "O Lord, the great and
terrible God, who keepest covenant and steadfast love with those who
love him and keep his commandments. . . . To thee, O Lord, belong
righteousness. . . . To the Lord our God belong mercy and forgiveness
because we have rebelled against him, and have not obeyed the voice
of the Lord our God by following his laws. . . . Therefore the Lord has
kept ready the calamity and has brought it upon us; for the Lord our
God is righteous in all the works which he has done, and we have not
obeyed his voice. . . . O Lord, according to all thy righteous acts, let
thy anger and thy wrath turn away from thy city Jerusalem, thy ho-

hill" (9:4-16). These excerpts from Daniel's prayer show how the sinfulness of his people was so deplorable in view of their righteous God, who kept the covenant and continued to show steadfast love, mercy, and forgiveness toward His people. Thus he shared with Ezekiel the profound and exalted understanding of the Lord, who judges righteously and also displays steadfast love, mercy, and forgiveness. These two aspects of God's nature, according to their understanding, were not contradictory. Daniel's exalted concept of the Lord God may well be regarded as the highest peak in Old Testament revelation concerning the nature of God.

f. The God Who Acts in History

This facet of my discussion follows so closely on the preceding that duplication of materials is almost unavoidable. It is very pertinent nevertheless for us to grasp the interlocking ideas involved in these expressions concerning God.

(1) Ezekiel. In Ezekiel's disclosures concerning God's acts in history several purposes of his works become evident. First are the often-repeated words of the Lord, "You shall know that I am the Lord" (6:7). As noted above, this is the most meaningful purpose of God's acting in history. By this He demonstrated His absolute sovereignty over the world. Second, God acted in order to manifest and vindicate His holiness (20:41); 36:20-24; 39:7). This became necessary when Israel argued that "The way of the Lord is not just" (18:25). God's vindication would become evident to the nations as well as to Israel. Third, God's ultimate purpose for these actions in history was to lead Israel to a change of heart and to put His Spirit within them (36:25-28).

The largest portions of the Book of Ezekiel have to do with God's dealings with Israel.[13] Briefly, the Lord predicted that He would execute judgments in their midst in the sight of the nations. A third of the nation would die of pestilence, another third by the sword, and the remainder would be scattered to all the winds. God would loose against them deadly arrows of famine and they would become the prey of wild beasts. God would destroy their idolatrous places of worship. Their end had come upon them and the Lord would loose His anger upon them and punish them for all their abominations. The Lord would bring the worst of the nations to take possession of their house. In a later portion the picture changed and God promised to gather them from the peoples and take them to their own land. God's providential acts would lead to His giving them a new heart and to putting His Spirit within them. Metaphorically, He would take away the stony heart and give them a heart of flesh.

In another setting the Lord likened Israel to a deserted baby girl who grew to maidenhood and to womanhood and gave herself over to harlotry with the Egyptians and the Assyrians. On this account the Lord would use these adulterers to bring judgment upon Israel, the adulterous wife, and to expose Israel's sin. In like manner Sodom and Samaria would be judged but the Lord would restore their fortunes together with that of Israel in order that Israel, Sodom, and Samaria would bear their disgrace and be ashamed of all that they had done. All this came to pass in due time. Looking again at chapter 20, we note another recital of Israel's history in which the Lord explained His dealings with them: "I acted for the sake of my name, that it should not be profaned in the sight of the nations among whom [you dwell]" (20:9, 14, 22).

Through these references to Israel's history the Lord made clear that every detail of their history took place through God's sovereign action. The Lord intended that all this should speak most forcefully to captive Israel. The Lord used another allegorical approach, with a harlot, Oholah, representing Samaria, and another harlot, Oholibah, representing Jerusalem (23). The Lord would bring against Samaria and Jerusalem their lovers — the Babylonians, the Chaldeans, and the Assyrians, who would destroy these cities. A study of secular history gives no idea that God had anything to do with these conquests. Secular history sees the nations of Canaan as lying in the pathway between Mesopotamia and Egypt. The empire which had the nation of Canaan under its control had the military advantage in such conquests. But the Lord would have Israel know that He was using these nations as instruments of chastisement and judgment upon His people.

Also, there were redemptive purposes in God's dealings with Israel (33, 34). The Lord had no pleasure in the death of the wicked but He designed that these judgments would lead His people to repentance. He besought Israel in the words, "Turn back, turn back from your evil ways; for why will you die" (33:11)? Because Israel's leaders were not faithful shepherds the Lord promised that He would save His flock by setting over them "one shepherd, my servant David, and he shall feed them" (34:23). This would be the most glorious note of God's acting in history. In the fulfillment of this promise God would make with His people a covenant of peace. In a graphic figure the Lord made clear to Israel through the vision of the valley of dry bones how He would resurrect Israel to a new spiritual life. He said, "I will put my Spirit within you, and you shall live" (37:14). By the use of another figure, that of two sticks, the Lord showed how Judah and Ephraim would again become one people and that His servant David would be king over them. God would accomplish this through the making of a covenant of peace which would be an everlasting covenant.

Descriptive of God's relation to His people are the words, "My dwelling place shall be with them; and I will be their God, and they shall be my people" (37:26, 27). The spiritual change on the part of Israel presented a new dimension in God's working in history, which was as real as His activity in directing the course of world events. The New Testament verified the fulfillment of this act of God through Christ's mediation of the new covenant and of the church becoming His people. The Book of Revelation, however, gives the prediction of the still more glorious act of God to be fulfilled in the world to come (21:3). If we may consider history as continuing in the new heavens and the new earth, we may regard chapters 40 — 48 as predicting the consummation of God's acts in history. The name of the glorious city in this new creation will be "The Lord is there" (48:35).

The Lord spoke also of His kingly power as being manifested among other nations. He directed attention, first, to the nations who were Israel's nearest neighbors (25 — 32). These were the nations which influenced Israel in their rebellion against the Lord. Thus the Lord acted in the affairs of the Ammonites, the Moabites, the Edomites, the Philistines, the city of Tyre, and the Egyptians. In each instance He used the language which plainly described how He was exercising His sovereign power over the nations. These are some samples: "I have stretched out my hand against you, and will hand you over as spoil to the nations; and I will cut you off from the peoples and will make you perish out of the countries; I will destroy you." "I will stretch out my hand against Edom, and cut off from it man and beast; and I will make it desolate." "I will execute great vengeance upon them with wrathful chastisements." "They shall destroy the walls of Tyre, and break down her towers; and I will scrape her soil from her, and make her a bare rock." "I will bring you to a dreadful end, and you shall be no more; . . . you will never be found again." "I will bring a sword upon you, and will cut off from you man and beast; and the land of Egypt shall be a desolation and a waste."[14] In all these instances the Lord was guiding the affairs of these nations so that these judgments came upon them through neighboring nations, chiefly Babylon. But none of these conquering nations were aware that God was using them as the instruments for executing judgments. We should observe also that the Lord brought punishment upon Babylon for all her wicked conquests even though He used these conquests as the means of bringing judgment upon the nations. If these acts of God present a moral problem, let us reflect on the words of the Lord, "I have no pleasure in the death of the wicked, but that the wicked turn from his way and live; turn back, turn back from your evil ways; for why will you die" (Ezek. 33:11)?

The mysterious prophecies against Gog bear the same character as those against the heathen nations mentioned earlier (38). Since these predictions have to do with end time events, the fulfillment of which presents real problems of interpretation, my interest at this point is to observe that the Lord would deal with Gog in the same manner that He would deal with the other nations. Thus God's actions will continue until the consummation of all things, until the Lord's ultimate purposes will have been fulfilled. To this the Book of Revelation gives positive witness (Rev. 20:7-10).

Since chapters 40 — 48 constitute a magnificent presentation of Ezekiel's temple vision, an effort to describe God's actions in history as embodied in this vision is almost impossible. The only sure lead that we get in probing this problem is found in the Book of Revelation, which alone in the New Testament quotes from it. This would lead us to believe that Ezekiel's vision of the temple will have its fulfillment in the new heaven and the new earth (Rev. 21). This points to a sublime concept of Ezekiel's vision, namely, that God's greatest act of history will come to pass in the new creation, in which it can be said most truthfully, "The Lord is there" (Ezek. 48:35). How could the majesty of God's direction of history be more gloriously foretold!

(2) Daniel. Turning now to the Book of Daniel we observe that almost the entire book sets forth God as acting in history. In a most remarkable way God's sovereign power becomes manifest. After praying that the mystery bound up in Nebuchadnezzar's dream might be revealed to him, Daniel spoke of God in the words, "He changes times and seasons; he removes kings and sets up kings" (2:21). When Daniel was called by Nebuchadnezzar to explain the dream, he told the monarch that there was a God in heaven who revealed mysteries and was making known to him what would be in the latter days. The great image seen by Nebuchadnezzar was prophetic of what God would accomplish in history. The image represented four great kingdoms, the last of which would become a kingdom divided into ten small ones, representing a deterioration of kingdom power. God had given the first kingdom, noted for its power and might, to Nebuchadnezzar. By implication it was God who set up the other kingdoms.

The climax to the dream, as interpreted by Daniel, pictured the God of heaven setting up a kingdom which would never be destroyed. Its sovereignty would not be left to another people. This kingdom would break in pieces all the other kingdoms and bring them to an end. Here we see the relation of God's kingdom to the kingdoms of the world. The interpretation of this dream was not merely a prediction of future events; rather, it was a disclosure of what God in His own time will bring to pass. World history has its focus in the kingdom which God will establish. This asserts the supernatural or miraculous aspect of God's intervention in the affairs of men leading to the setting up of His kingdom. This aspect becomes quite distinctive of what the remainder of the book discloses.

In line with this idea, Daniel's three friends could tell Nebuchadnezzar that their God was able to deliver them from the fiery furnace as well as from him. They confidently believed that God could miraculously intervene in their behalf if it were His will (3:16-18). When Nebuchadnezzar saw how God was saving these men from the torture of the fire, he appeared to be genuinely penitent and spoke in impressive prophetic language, "It has seemed good to me to show the signs and wonders that the Most High God has wrought toward me. How great are his signs, how mighty his wonders! His kingdom is an everlasting kingdom, and his dominion is from generation to generation" (4:2, 3). The king used two distinctive words, "signs" and "wonders," to describe God's miraculous intervention.

In another dream-vision God disclosed to Nebuchadnezzar an imminent intervention in the life of the proud monarch himself. Daniel told the king that his kingdom had departed from him and that he would be further humbled by being driven from men to live among the beasts of the field. This would continue until he would learn that "the Most High rules the kingdom of men and gives it to whom he will" (Dan. 4: 25). On Nebuchadnezzar's return to normal life he gave prophetic words similar to what he had spoken earlier in recognizing God's kingdom as enduring forever (4:34, 35).

When Belshazzar made a great feast in which he desecrated the sacred vessels taken from the temple in Jerusalem, God intervened with the handwriting on the wall. The king asked Daniel to interpret this most extraordinary act of God. In response Daniel reminded Belshazzar that the Most High God had given his father kingship, greatness, glory, and majesty, and that when his heart was lifted up in pride, his majesty and glory were taken from him. This continued until he acknowledged that the Most High God rules the kingdom of men and sets over it whom He will. Daniel warned the new monarch that his life was in the hand of God. The handwriting on the wall was a revelation that God had numbered the days of his kingdom and brought it to an end. His kingdom would be divided and given to the Medes and Persians. That very night the invading Medes slew Belshazzar. In this scene both the supernatural course of events and the natural revealed God's direction of history. When Daniel was thrown into the den of lions, to the king's utter amazement he was not devoured by them. Daniel explained, "My God sent his angel and shut the lions' mouths, and they have not hurt me" (6:22). Here again is a scene of the natural course of events in which the supernatural work of God's angel intervened to shut the lions' mouths. This led Darius to give recognition to the eternal, living God who delivers and rescues, works signs and wonders in heaven and on earth, and who saved Daniel from the power of the lions.

Daniel also had a dream-vision. It becomes evident at once that a profound similarity as well as a sharp difference exists between the two visions. For our present purpose this is very instructive. The center of this vision was the fourth beast, with its ten horns, among which another horn came up. This horn was defying the enthroned Ancient of Days, who was being served by hundreds of thousands. As the heavenly vision continued, one like the Son of man came to the Ancient of Days and "to him was given dominion and glory and kingdom, that all peoples, nations, and languages should serve him; his dominion is an everlasting dominion, which shall not pass away, and his kingdom one that shall not be destroyed" (7:13, 14). The interpretation of the dream revealed the utter antagonism and conflict between the earthly kingdoms and the heavenly kingdom. An earthly king would arise who would aspire to heavenly kingship. God, by divine intervention, would overthrow this opposing kingdom and establish the everlasting kingdom, in which the saints of the Most High would share. The cumulative significance of Nebuchadnezzar's and Daniel's visions is most pertinent when we realize that these visions predict God's consummating acts in history.

Daniel's vision of a ram, a he-goat, and a horn, along with his great prayer followed by Gabriel's interpretation of the vision (8, 9), led further in the explication of God's control of history. Following the prediction of the overthrow of the sanctuary, a holy one revealed to Daniel that after a given time the sanctuary would be restored to its rightful state. Gabriel clarified for Daniel the truth that the vision had to do with the time of the end. He enlarged on this as it had to do with the kings of Media and Persia, the four kings, and the king of bold countenance, who in his great power would cause fearful destruction and the killing of mighty men, including some of the saints. This led Daniel to his great prayer of confession and intercession for his people. In response, Gabriel again came on the scene and disclosed to him the prediction of the seventy weeks of years. The awful destruction to be brought about by an anointed prince is a graphic portrayal of what God had decreed concerning His people. Our Lord picked up this great prediction and verified God's hand in bringing it to fulfillment in the fall of Jerusalem, with its culmination in the great tribulation preceding His return.[15] In Michael's final message to Daniel he foretold a time of unprecedented trouble, from which the people of God would be delivered. He added, "And many of those who sleep in the dust of the earth shall awake, some to everlasting life, and some to shame and everlasting contempt" (12:2). It was very fitting that this last communication with Daniel should deliver a message of hope to God's people and a warning of everlasting contempt to the ungodly. These revelations of God's working in history are hardly surpassed by any of the remaining books of the Old Testament.

g. The God of Salvation

Several of the contexts in which Ezekiel spoke of repentance also set forth some explicit statements of God's saving acts.[16] Thus when the wicked person turns back from his evil ways and walks in the statutes of life, he shall live. The essential idea taught here was that life is possible only after the wicked person turns back from his sin. Under no other circumstances can the wicked be saved. The metaphor of the shepherd seeking out his sheep and rescuing them from all places where they had been scattered, conveyed the spiritual meaning of being saved from sin. The helplessness of the sheep which had gone astray was indicative of the sinners' lost condition. The ritual of sprinkling clean water on those who were unclean symbolized the inner cleansing of God's saving acts. Still more significant was the figure of God's giving His people a new heart and a new spirit which would cause them to walk in His statutes. In covenant language God said, "You shall be my people, and I will be your God" (36:28).

The vision of the valley of dry bones presented still another aspect of salvation similar to what Paul used (Eph. 2:1-10). God would raise His people from their graves and put His Spirit within them. This raising to spiritual life constitutes the very essence of salvation. Speaking again in covenant terms, God said, "I will make a covenant of peace with them; it shall be an everlasting covenant with them. . . . My dwelling place shall be with them; and I will be their God, and they shall be my people" (37:26, 27). This covenant relationship was abiding; it showed that God's act of saving would not be merely for the moment but would be eternal. This eternal aspect of salvation may not have been as clear to Ezekiel as it was to the New Testament writers, who presented the truth that believers have eternal life. Ezekiel's vision of the new temple may give a figurative presentation of God's saving acts. It showed God's acceptance of those who brought the bloody and the nonbloody sacrifices to Him.

The Book of Daniel also lacks explicit teaching on the saving work of God. In a few settings we may find teachings which underlie God's saving work.[17] Certainly the citizens of the eternal kingdom which the God of heaven will set up are those whom God will have saved. It is conceivable that Daniel's exhortation to Nebuchadnezzar envisioned salvation, with the provision, however, that he break off his sins, practice righteousness, and show mercy. The lengthening of his tranquillity would reach beyond this life. Daniel's vision also lends support to this. The everlasting dominion of the Son of man over all peoples of the world has the potential meaning of their having been saved. Daniel's fervent prayer (9:3-19) may also suggest salvation as being wrought by God. Most certainly all whose names will be found written in the book shall awake to everlasting life and will shine like the brightness of the firmament. In the New Testament this awaking to eternal life is the resurrection.

h. Worship of God

(1) Ezekiel's Understanding of Worship. From one point of view the Book of Ezekiel is not the portion of the Bible to which we turn for teaching on the worship of God. From another point of view, however, this book is exceedingly instructive on this theme. This should become very evident if we reflect again on what this book teaches with regard to the glorious majesty of God and His holiness. In such settings the real nature of worship gains profound meaning. Let us take our stand alongside Ezekiel as he beheld the appearance of the likeness of the glory of the Lord. The most natural thing for the God-fearing prophet to do in such an experience was to fall on his face in humble reverence before the glorious majesty of God. Herein is the true spirit of worship. This act of Ezekiel stood in sharpest contrast with the numerous scenes in his book of Israel's false worship. In Ezekiel's experience with the Lord there was no place for the idolatries practiced by his countrymen. To the Almighty God alone was worship due.

Throughout the book, Ezekiel presented a number of scenes of false worship.[18] Perhaps the most abhorrent of these scenes was the occasion when the Spirit of the Lord brought Ezekiel in vision to Jerusalem (8). There he saw again the glory of God. Then the Spirit brought Ezekiel to a secret chamber, where he saw the elders of the house of Israel committing all manner of abominations. The burning of incense was the only semblance of worship. In another instance certain elders came to Ezekiel and before he entered into conversation with them, the Lord said, "These men have taken their idols into their hearts, and set the stumbling block of their iniquity before their faces" (14:3). Through such conduct all the house of Israel had become estranged from the Lord through their idols. Another scene related to the abominable deeds which Israel performed in their worship (22). They had despised the holy things of the temple and profaned the sabbath. In the name of their religion they were committing all kinds of immorality. In ceremonial worship they made no distinction between the holy and the common, nor between the clean and the unclean. Only through cleansing in which God would give them a new heart and a new spirit would they walk in the Lord's statutes and observe His ordinances. Through such a spiritual transformation alone would Israel be able to worship their God.

Finally the Lord disclosed to Ezekiel in a vision the new temple to which restored Israel would have access for worship. The glory of this temple exceeded that of Solomon's temple to an immeasurable degree. Especially significant were the references to the chambers, the offerings, and all the territory about the top of the mountain as being holy. The glory of the Lord filled the temple. No foreigners or uncircumcised in the flesh could enter the Lord's sanctuary. The Lord said, "I will dwell in the midst of the people of Israel for ever" (43:7). Israel would again bring their sin, burnt, peace, and cereal offerings to the Lord. Throughout the description of this new temple a great truth shone forth. As John D. Davis and Henry S. Gehman say, "In the new theocracy the reality will correspond to the divine ideal."[19] In other words, Israel's worship of God as commanded by Moses would be perfectly realized in the new temple.

There is a real need for us to gain a correct understanding of Israel's worship centering in the tabernacle and Solomon's temple. There is a real liability in our attaching to this worship legalistic connotations which do not express the real spirit and nature of Israel's worship. The Lord dwelt in the holy of holies of the tabernacle, which was located in the midst of their congregation. Representatively all Israel could come into the very presence of the Lord through the high priest. The offerings and sacrifices given to the Lord symbolized atonement for sin, consecration of the individual to God, fellowship through peaceful relations with God, and other significant responses of the people, who were bound together with the Lord in covenant relationship. The true goal of Israel's worship was to be holy even as the Lord their God was holy. The proper approach then to the meaning of the worship experiences to be realized in the new temple is by way of magnifying to the highest degree Israel's worship experiences in the tabernacle. The Israel of God

who will dwell in the new Canaan will experience the closest fellowship
with God since the Lord will be dwelling in His temple. The city itself
shall bear the name, "The Lord is there." Thus the vision closed with
the perfected scene of God's dwelling with His people. The highest
conceivable elements of worship involving prayer, praise, adoration,
reverence, and fellowship will continue throughout eternity. This is the
goal to which the worship of God leads.

(2) Daniel's Involvements in Worship. The worship of God, especially prayer, stood in the very center of Daniel's relation to the Lord.
Confronted with the task of interpreting Nebuchadnezzar's dreams or
of being slain with the wise men of Babylon, Daniel naturally re-
sorted to prayer as his only recourse. He and his friends sought the
mercy of God in this crisis. His approach to God was reverent and
humble. Testifying to the wisdom and might of God, Daniel recognized
His dignity as Creator and supreme Ruler of the world. From his
heart came thanks and praise for the wisdom and strength given to him
by God. Most of all he was grateful for the revelation and interpretation of Nebuchadnezzar's dream to him (2:17-23). Daniel's friends
made a similar response to Nebuchadnezzar in the crisis that arose out
of their refusal to worship the golden image. The test in their prayer
experience was exceedingly severe because they did not know whether
God would deliver them from the fiery furnace. Their worship experiences with the Lord were such that they could humbly yield to the
will of God in such a crisis as this (3:16-18).

Even the pagan monarchs Nebuchadnezzar and Darius had worship
experiences which deserve attention.[20] When Nebuchadnezzar re-
covered from his mental illness, he could bless, praise, and honor the
eternal God. He was able to recognize the supreme rule of God
and the absolute subjection of all the created world to Him. He recognized that all the works of the Lord are right and His ways are just.
On about the same level Darius manifested a spirit of worship when
Daniel was about to be thrown into the den of lions. He breathed a
prayer, "May your God, whom you serve continually, deliver you!" He
"spent the night fasting; no diversions were brought to him, and
sleep fled from him." Daniel's deliverance from the lions led Darius to
make a decree which voiced the same spirit of reverence for God as
that shown by Nebuchadnezzar. In the spirit of true worship he spoke
of the God of Daniel as the living God whose kingdom would have no
end. He recognized God as the One who delivers and rescues, works
signs and wonders in heaven and on earth. We are led to conclude that
these pagan monarchs actually believed in the true God; and when they
saw His mighty works, they worshiped the Lord in all sincerity.

Daniel's prayer stands as a model of worship to be shared by all God's people (9:3-23). His praying was in an atmosphere of fasting and sackcloth and ashes, showing true humility and reverence for God. The dominant theme of his prayer was confession of sin. On behalf of the people he confessed, "We have sinned and done wrong and acted wickedly and rebelled, turning aside from thy commandments and ordinances." He ascribed righteousness to God and recognized that to Him belonged mercy and forgiveness. He pleaded that the Lord's anger and wrath might turn away from Jerusalem. He continued with the petition, "For thy own sake, O Lord, cause thy face to shine upon thy sanctuary, which is desolate. . . . O Lord, hear; O Lord, forgive; O Lord, give heed and act; delay not, for thy own sake, O my God, because thy city and thy people are called by thy name." Such was the worship of this devout man of God.

i. The Spirit of God

The prophet Ezekiel gave some important facts with reference to the Holy Spirit.[21] Concerning the Spirit's activity we should observe that the Spirit entered into Ezekiel, lifted him up, and on other occasions fell upon him. Through Ezekiel the Lord spoke of pouring out His Spirit upon the house of Israel and of putting His Spirit within them. This language is identical with post-Pentecostal descriptions of the Holy Spirit's activity in the believer. While Ezekiel did not give any theological explanation of the person and work of the Holy Spirit, his statements of the Spirit's activity are very explicit. Without any doubt he spoke of the Spirit as a person. Further, the deity aspect of the Spirit is equally clear. Foreshadowing the fulfillment of Joel's prediction, the Lord spoke of pouring His Spirit upon His people. Ezekiel did not question the divine mystery bound up in the fact that the Lord God pours out His Spirit on men.

We should observe that the Book of Daniel made no reference to the Holy Spirit. After noting Ezekiel's words concerning the Spirit, we almost wonder why Daniel did not make any reference to His work. Most assuredly the godly Daniel experienced Holy Spirit activity in his interpretation of dreams and visions.

3. God's Revelation, the Spoken and Written Word

The books of Ezekiel and Daniel made valuable contributions to the idea of God's revelation to man, including the various forms of this revelation. This continues to lay the foundation for the biblical concept of the written word. These two books are especially valuable, both from the angle of the mode of revelation through dreams and visions, and also from the content of the prophetic messages. While there is a predominance of the dream-vision form of revelation, God's speaking directly through the prophets continued. This fact helps us to gain the true perspective of the dream-vision form of God's revelation.

The prophet Ezekiel opened his book with the declaration that the heavens were opened and that he saw visions of God. The writer also claimed that the hand of the Lord was upon him. He then gave a detailed description of what he had seen and concluded with the words, "Such was the appearance of the likeness of the glory of the Lord." Seeing the likeness of the glory of the Lord was exceedingly more expressive than a verbal description could have been. We are concerned at the present time with Ezekiel's account of this vision from the point of view of the mode of revelation. The Lord showed him the likeness of His glory, and Ezekiel saw it and gave a written record of his vision. We have grounds for believing then that since the Lord revealed Himself in this manner, He also empowered the prophet to record accurately what he saw. This phenomenon underscores the claims made by Paul and Peter as to the origin and nature of the written word (2 Tim. 3:16; 2 Pet. 1:21). Ezekiel followed this pattern consistently throughout his book (8 — 11; 40 — 48). Ezekiel frequently intermingled with these visions prophetic messages introduced with expressions such as, "The word of the Lord came to me" and "Say to the house of Israel." The accounts of these visions, together with the words of the Lord which came to him, comprise almost the entire content of his book. There is very little of what the prophet himself says, with the exception of his accounts of the temple-visions (1; 40:1 — 43:5).

From the point of view of God's revelation as it relates to the nature of the written word, the Book of Daniel is quite distinctive. In chapters 1 — 6 someone other than Daniel is the narrator and in chapters 7 — 12 Daniel is the speaker, using the first person frequently. The revelation aspect of visions and the special divine gift of interpreting these visions become manifest throughout the book. Concerning Daniel and his friends we read, "God gave them learning and skill in all letters and wisdom; and Daniel had understanding in all visions and dreams" (1:17). Later Daniel told his companions to seek the mercy of the God of heaven concerning the mystery of Nebuchadnezzar's dream. After they had prayed, the mystery was revealed to Daniel in a vision during the night (2:17-19, 28, 29, 47). Daniel himself had dream-visions which heavenly beings interpreted to him (7:12). We should observe that in all these instances God used supernatural means to give dreams and visions and intensified their revelatory nature by sending heavenly beings to interpret them. Even the godly Daniel was not able to discern the meaning of his dream-visions. We need to observe further the absolute integrity of the written record making up the Book of Daniel.

Of more than incidental significance are the two references to things written in the law of Moses (9:11, 13). The written law of Moses embodied in the oral prayer of Daniel gives grounds for attaching identical values to both the oral and written word of God. We should note further that the dream-visions interpreted throughout the book predicted future events, most of which have already been fulfilled. Fulfilled predictions constitute adequate proof of their supernatural origin. All these facts contribute to the distinctive character of the written word of God.

4. Israel's Election Actualized by Covenant Relation with God

Ezekiel's record of God's confronting Israel with their unfaithfulness brought the nation's election into clear view (16). God had taken pity upon enslaved Israel, delivered them from their bondage, and entered into covenant relation with them. Now after about seven centuries the Lord reminded Israel that He still remembered His covenant, which they had broken. In this circumstance, the Lord in His love and mercy promised that He would establish with them a new and everlasting covenant. In a later message to Ezekiel (34) the Lord brought judgment against the shepherds of Israel and gave the promise of setting up over them one shepherd, His servant David. The Lord would bring this to pass through the institution of a covenant of peace. The Lord added to this prediction the promise of a great spiritual blessing that would accompany the making of this covenant. The Lord would give them a new heart and a new spirit by putting His Spirit within them. Repeating the Sinaitic language, the Lord said, "You shall be my people, and I will be your God" (36:26-28). A formidable problem yet remained — the divided kingdom. The Lord was not unmindful of this tragedy and promised the joining together of the two kingdoms. He confirmed this by repeating His promise of setting up His servant David as king and of making the covenant of peace with them. The actualizing of this election would come to its fullest realization in God's placing His sanctuary in the midst of them forevermore (37:15-28).

To Daniel also the covenant relation of Israel to God was exceedingly precious. He treasured Israel's election as actualized by this covenant, this being evidenced by his great intercessory prayer. Daniel also testified to God's faithfulness in keeping His covenant and steadfast love with those who are faithful to Him (9:4-19). When the angelic being disclosed to Daniel imminent historical events, he mentioned the contemptible person, fulfilled in Antiochus Epiphanes, whose heart would be set against the holy covenant (11:20-30). The expression "holy covenant" likely refers to Israel's religion, which had its foundation in the Sinaitic covenant. It would be very natural to expect that this despicable person would know of Israel's covenant relation to God and would do all in his power to destroy this relationship. If this interprets the language correctly, we see the true perspective of Israel's election actualized by covenant relation with God.

5. The Messiah and the Messianic Kingdom

a. Ezekiel's Messianic Visions

The Lord's revelation to Ezekiel concerning Israel's election very naturally leads to the disclosure of the Messiah and the Messianic kingdom. These themes are built on the basic fact of God's rule. Some Bible students find in the parable of the sprig (17:22-24) a prediction of the Messianic king and His kingdom. God will take a sprig from the lofty top of the cedar and plant it on a high and lofty mountain of Israel. It will become a noble cedar under which all kinds of beasts will dwell and in whose branches every kind of bird will nest. Jesus' quotation of one of these clauses in His parable of the mustard seed may give some support to the Messianic interpretation of the cedar sprig (Mt. 13:32). In a later context the Lord evidently spoke of the last king of Israel whose judgment had come; and at the command of the Lord his turban and crown were removed. The turban and the crown likely suggest the priestly and kingly functions of Israel's kings. The Lord declared that Judah would have no king "until he comes whose right it is; and to him I will give it" (21:24-27). Since this message was prophetic and Christ's enthronement fulfilled the prediction, we have grounds for accepting this interpretation of God's prediction.

In the "Shepherds of Israel" context (34) the Lord predicted the setting up of another shepherd in the person of His servant David. His role will be like that of a shepherd over his sheep. This is a very expressive figure for describing kingly authority. The setting up of this king by the Lord shows the mediatorial character of His rule. On this account the Lord will make a covenant of peace with His people which will lead to showers of blessing. This prediction of the enthronement of David, the Lord's servant, built very clearly on the Messianic predictions given to Israel from the time of David on through the time of the writing prophets, Isaiah in particular.

The Lord gave similar messages centering in the vision of the valley of dry bones and the parable of the two sticks (37). The new element presented here was the Lord's promise that Israel and Judah would again be united and that one king would rule over them. The Lord spoke again of making an everlasting covenant of peace with them and of setting up His servant David on the throne. The joining together of Judah and Israel was a very essential element of this prediction. Only in this way could the covenants with Abraham and Israel, together with all of God's promises to set up a king over Israel, be fulfilled. These strands of prophecy were clear and distinct. When the Lord granted Ezekiel the sublime vision of the temple, He showed him the place of God's throne and declared that He would dwell in the midst of the people of Israel forever (43:6-9). We should note here that the time element of God's rule in this reference appears to be the same as that in the foregoing passages. This fact may have a bearing on the larger problem of interpreting chapters 40 — 48.

b. Daniel, Interpreter of Messianic Dreams

Daniel's interpretation of Nebuchadnezzar's dream showed that it had its setting in the course of world history. Eschatologically, the dream viewed world kingdoms from the time of this great monarch on to an era which Daniel called "The Latter Days." Daniel disclosed to Nebuchadnezzar that in these *Latter Days* the God of heaven would set up a kingdom which would never be destroyed. This kingdom would bring an end to all world kingdoms. We should observe that the prophet did not relate this new kingdom to Israel nor did he name its king. Since the God of heaven would set up this kingdom, the sovereignty of its king would be mediatorial, as indicated in the preceding section. Daniel's dream comprehended the same course of events as the dream of Nebuchadnezzar but it appears to have a different focus. We may be correct in saying that the proud monarch's dream gave expression to his self-glorying sovereignty, while Daniel's dream disclosed the beastly character of these kingdoms. Daniel's dreams revealed the judgment of the Ancient of Days upon the nations of the world. Then he saw one like a son of man coming in the clouds of heaven. The Ancient of Days gave him supreme dominion over all mankind and indicated that his rule would continue forever. The common features in the interpretation of the two dreams are evident. In both God sets up the new king who shall rule the world forever. He reigns under the authority of God. There is no expressed relation between the kingdom of the son of man and that of Israel. The identity of the son of man is of highest importance. If we relate these dreams to the Messianic predictions already noted, it becomes evident that this one is none other than the Messiah. His coming with the clouds of heaven suggests the activity of Deity. Our Lord con-

firmed this interpretation by claiming to be this son of man. He predicted the time when all the tribes of the earth "will see the Son of
man coming on the clouds of heaven with power and great glory" (Mt.
24:30). To the high priest Jesus said, "Hereafter you will see the Son
of man seated at the right hand of Power, and coming on the clouds of
heaven" (Mt. 26:64). In a climactic manner, the Book of Revelation established this interpretation (Rev. 1:7, 13; 14:14).

Gabriel also disclosed to Daniel important aspects of the Messianic
kingship (9:24-27). His message centered in the seventy weeks of years
which were decreed concerning Daniel's people and his holy city.
Leaving the eschatological aspects of this portion for a later section, the
temporal perspective of Gabriel's prophecy appears to extend from the
time he was speaking to the end of time. Gabriel mentioned six purposes to be accomplished during these seventy weeks. Their Messianic
import immediately becomes manifest. The first three of these purposes
disclose what the Messiah will have to do with the matter of sin. They
read, "To finish the transgression, to put an end to sin, and to atone
for iniquity." The infinitives are closely related in meaning. Their
combined significance would point to a definite redemptive work. The
second group of infinitives, "To bring in everlasting righteousness, to
seal both vision and prophet, and to anoint a most holy place [one],"
disclose God's work in accomplishing redemption. The bringing in of
everlasting righteousness is a magnificent positive achievement after
sin has been atoned for. The era of the prophets and their visions
will have to come to a close. All five of these purposes will have been
achieved in the anointing of a most holy one, the Messiah.

While the meaning of the sixfold purposes to be accomplished during
the seventy weeks presents some problems with regard to interpretation, it seems clear that New Testament teaching on the Messiah and
His work, together with the closing of the prophetic era with John
the Baptist, confirms the interpretation given above. Most certainly
our Lord made atonement for sin. He brought in everlasting righteousness. The prophets and the law prophesied until John. Jesus was
exalted at the right hand of God and was made both Lord and
Christ. The statement, "an anointed one shall be cut off, and shall
have nothing," likely refers to the crucifixion of the Anointed One, the
Messiah. This rich Messianic content of Gabriel's message becomes all
the more significant when viewed in the context predicted in the words,
"The people of the prince who is to come shall destroy the city and
the sanctuary. Its end shall come with a flood, and to the end there
shall be war; desolations are decreed. And he shall make a strong covenant with many for one week; and for half of the week he shall cause

sacrifice and offering to cease; and upon the wing of abominations shall come one who makes desolate, until the decreed end is poured out on the desolator" (9:26, 27. Cf. 11:1-32; 12:11). In these verses Gabriel disclosed the coming conflict between the Messiah and the coming prince.

Jesus made reference to this conflict in His Olivet discourse, where it appears that He was predicting an imminent fulfillment centering in the fall of Jerusalem and final fulfillment in relation to His second coming (Mt. 24:15-28). When Jesus spoke of "the desolating sacrilege," He brought the seventy weeks' prediction into the perspective of His Messianic reign. It is the age when the gospel will be preached throughout the whole world, leading to the consummation of all things at His return. This aspect of conflict is very essential to our understanding of the agelong tribulation being experienced by the church.

6. The Day of the Lord -- Judgment

The Lord's message of judgment given through Ezekiel was very severe. He said, "The end has come upon the four corners of the land. Now the end is upon you, and I will let loose my anger upon you, and will judge you according to your ways; and I will punish you for all your abominations."[22] The earlier writing prophets had spoken of the Day of the Lord as being imminent. In Ezekiel's day the end had come upon the nations. In the several contexts dealing with this judgment, we learn that it was a day of doom, of wrath, of indignation. For Egypt as well, the Day of the Lord was near (Ezek. 30:3, 4). While the Book of Ezekiel has much to say concerning God's judgments upon Israel and the nations of the world, the expression, "the day of the Lord," occurs only in this passage. I am not able to determine whether any special significance attaches to this sole use of this great eschatological expression. Undoubtedly the language of judgment used in this book is the most emphatic to be found in all the writing prophets. This may be due to the fact that God's people were already experiencing these outpourings of His wrath. We should yet note the profound purpose bound up with these judgments. Repeatedly we read, "Then they shall know that I am the Lord." In more direct address God said, "As silver is melted in a furnace, so you shall be melted in the midst of it; and you shall know that I the Lord have poured out my wrath upon you" (22:22).

We should observe that the Book of Daniel does not have any prediction of the Day of the Lord. The reason for this becomes evident in Daniel's prayer (9:3-19). Daniel was aware that the curse and oath written in the law of Moses had been poured out upon the people. The Lord had already brought upon them a great calamity. So evident was this that Jerusalem and God's people had become a byword among all the nations. This helps us to realize that the judgments attending the Day of the Lord had taken place. The predictions of the early writing prophets had been fulfilled and the Day of the Lord was now a matter of history. But we shall observe in the next chapter that the prophet Malachi predicted the coming of "the great and terrible day of the Lord," which theme both Paul and Peter expanded in their writings.[23]

7. The Latter Days -- Prophetic Eschatology

a. *Ezekiel's Visions of the Latter Days*

The Lord speaking through Ezekiel did not limit His messages to coming judgments but in very meaningful language He disclosed a most glorious future. These messages dealt with (1) the restoration of Israel to their own land, (2) the spiritual change which the Lord would bring about in them, and (3) the outpouring of the Holy Spirit upon them.[24] This regathering of Israel would be from the several peoples and countries among which they had been scattered. The extent of their dispersion is not clear, but it is possible that they had been scattered over the whole Babylonian empire. The regathering of God's people would include the exiles of both Israel and Judah. The Lord described this regathering as raising them from their graves, and of His putting His Spirit within them. Using another figure, He likened the reuniting of Israel and Judah to that of joining together two sticks into one. Of still greater significance would be the spiritual change wrought in His people. The Lord would give them one heart and would put a new spirit within them. Through this inner spiritual change His people would again be bound in covenant relation with Him, as expressed in the words, "You shall be my people, and I will be your God." This would be an everlasting covenant of peace. Pertinent to this spiritual change would be the work of the Spirit of God in the hearts of His people. These Scriptures foreshadow Jesus' teaching on the new birth and that of Paul on the spiritual resurrection (Jn. 3:1-8; Eph. 2:1-10).

The prophecy against Gog of the land of Magog leads us into a new, and until Ezekiel's time an unexplored, era of eschatology. I am not aware that any prophet prior to Ezekiel disclosed anything concerning the conflicts predicted in chapters 38 and 39. Note the following divisions: (1) 38:1-13, which describes Gog's invasion of God's people; (2) 38:14-23, the punishment of Gog; (3) 39:1-16, the destruction of Gog; and (4) 39:17-29, the issue of Gog's ruin, leading to Israel's restoration, redemption, and sanctification. The era of time held in view is that of the Latter Years or the Latter Days (38:8, 16). From this it appears that the time of Gog's invasion lies beyond that of the Day of the Lord mentioned in earlier chapters.

It is very difficult, if not impossible, to identify Gog of the land of Magog. Hence a literal fulfillment of the prediction seems impossible. As J. J. Reeve says, "In general it seems to refer to the last and desperate attempts of a dying heathenism to overturn the true religion of Jehovah, or to make capital out of it, profiting by its great advantages."[25] Accordingly, this prediction appears to have no specific persons or nations in view; rather, it describes a conflict of all the forces of evil against the people of God. The closing verses of section 39:25-29 seem to reflect the restoration predicted in chapters 34 — 37. This would lead us to understand that while the time of the Gog invasion lies beyond the Messianic rule, there appears, nevertheless, to be an involvement of the Messianic kingdom with the forces of evil symbolized by Gog.

The mention of Gog and Magog in Revelation 20:7-10 is of utmost significance. If the thousand-year reign of this chapter is the Messianic reign, then it becomes evident that the Gog-Magog conflict will take place just prior to the return of Christ. It will be Satan who will gather the ungodly people to fight against the saints and the beloved city. It may be correct to interpret Revelation 16:12-16; 19:17-21 as describing the same conflict. It is possible that Jesus' words in Matthew 24:21-28 and those of Paul in 2 Thessalonians 2:3-12 predict the same conflict. If these New Testament references, especially those from Revelation, build on the Gog-Magog prediction of Ezekiel, then we have an unfolding of the future which possesses great meaning. From the point of view of biblical theology this revelation marks a distinct advance in Old Testament eschatology and lays the foundation for its further unfolding in the New Testament.

The prophetic aspects of chapters 40 — 48 confront us with the larger problem of the general interpretation of this portion of the book. First of all, a number of considerations stand against a literal interpretation. The entire section is in vision form including a number of portions in which the Lord spoke to Ezekiel. Further, the description of the temple and the geographical areas allotted to the several tribes goes beyond the bounds of a literal interpretation. Still further, if this portion is prophetic of worship during the Messianic age, we would face the impossibility of reconciling the continued bloody offerings in the temple with the finished work of Christ. For these and other reasons a strictly symbolic interpretation is the only one which does justice to the glorious scenes revealed to Ezekiel.

The purpose of these visions appears manifest in the words, "And you, son of man, describe to the house of Israel the temple and its appearance and plan, that they may be ashamed of their iniquities" (43:10). This statement and others throughout this section support the idea that the Lord was revealing to Ezekiel the most glorious aspects of their temple worship. Instead of revealing progressively the nature of worship during the coming Messianic age, with its vastly superior glory, the Lord was magnifying to the nth degree the glory of worship where the Lord dwelt. The Lord would lead Israel to appropriate its real spiritual nature. In a word, these visions revealed the genuine spiritual character of Israel's worship by picturing a glorious temple with all the offerings and sacrifices, as the dwelling place of the Lord. This revelation would lead Israel into a life of holiness. Israel had the rich privilege of knowing that the Lord was dwelling among them in all His glory.

This interpretation lays chief stress on the exalted spiritual character of Israel's worship under the old covenant. The vision was not cast in a prophetic mold, even though certain typical elements are apparent. The marvelous presence of God in the temple could well typify God's presence with man in the person of Christ, and also the indwelling of the Holy Spirit in the believer. In like manner, all the offerings and sacrifices might well typify the "once for all" sacrifice of Christ on the cross. The holy living to which Israel was being called bore the pattern of the life of the believer in Christ. Of far greater significance for our present inquiry are the seven quotations from this portion in the Book of Revelation, five of which occur in chapters 21 and 22.[26] Thus as John described the New Jerusalem he drew his language and imagery from Ezekiel's vision of the Holy City. Hence we may conclude that Ezekiel's vision, in the large, was prophetic of the New Jerusalem.

b. Daniel's Disclosure of the Latter Days

The prophetic interpretations which Daniel gave throughout his book, together with Gabriel's disclosures to him, provide the grandest panorama of the future that we have from any prophet. He revealed to Nebuchadnezzar that his dream outlined the course of world kingdoms onward until the God of heaven would set up a kingdom which would never be destroyed. Daniel identified this prophetic disclosure as the Latter Days. This definitive expression coined by the early writing prophets identified the temporal aspect of Nebuchadnezzar's dream with that future era culminating in the Messianic kingdom. When Michael revealed to Daniel the historical vista from his time into an indefinite future he also used the expression "the Latter Days." This would lead us to understand that the age to which Michael's disclosure extended was the time of God's setting up the everlasting kingdom. Daniel's dream made clear that the kingdom set up by God was that of the Son of man, the Messiah.

The dreams of Nebuchadnezzar and Daniel set forth the conflict between world kingdoms and the kingdom of the Messiah. This was in reality a spiritual, not merely a political conflict. As Daniel probed further into the meaning of his dream, a heavenly being unfolded to him the meaning of the fourth beast, which had ten horns with still another horn which represented a ruler who would make war with the saints. This ruler would be devilish in character, speaking words against the Most High and attempting to wear out the saints. A heavenly court would sit in judgment of this enemy and take away his dominion from him, and the rule of the world would be given to the saints of the Most High under the dominion of God.

This further disclosure of world history makes still clearer the central burden of the entire book of Daniel. Briefly stated, the kingdoms of the world are under the control of the archenemy of both mankind and God. This foe is doing all in his power to overthrow the rule of God. God's children, the saints, become deeply involved in this conflict. Daniel's mission then was to disclose to captive Israel that their conqueror, Nebuchadnezzar, and all world monarchs after him, are agents of this archenemy, seeking to lead captive the saints of God. Here then is a divine revelation disclosing to the people of God the real meaning of their struggles in this world.

Daniel had another vision of a ram, a he-goat, and a horn, which Gabriel interpreted for him, stating that the vision was for the time of the end (8). The ram with two horns represented the kings of Media and Persia, the he-goat the king of Greece, and the great horn the first king, likely of Greece. This vision finally focused on a king of bold countenance who would seek to destroy the saints. Here again was an archopponent of God's people who was similar to if not the same person whom Daniel had seen in his dream. Evidently the Lord was preparing the people of God for an extraordinary encounter by some archenemy of theirs. We have already noted that the seventy weeks' prediction also focused attention on such a foe. Not to enter into the intricacy of interpreting the time elements of these seventy weeks, it would appear that the prince spoken of was identical with the archenemy earlier disclosed to Daniel. The details of this prediction clearly identify Antiochus Epiphanes as this archenemy. We should note, nevertheless, that the seventy weeks' epoch has still greater eschatological aspects, including the crucifixion of the Messiah, the overthrow of Jerusalem, and a culminating fulfillment centering in the return of Christ. Certainly the people of God could not look forward to a peaceful future. Daniel's dreams and visions depicted mounting struggles throughout the entire course of human history.

The Lord revealed to Daniel still further the course of human history (10, 11). While the interpretation of this vision also presents some almost unsolvable problems, its central message speaks out most forcefully. The heavenly visitor who spoke to Daniel told him that his message would have to do with what would befall his people in the Latter Days. He disclosed the coming conflicts between Persia and Greece and also between the south and the north kingdoms. This message also centered in the rise of a contemptible person who would attack the people of the holy covenant, Israel. His forces would profane the temple and the holy city. He would take away the burnt offerings and establish idol worship in the temple. Unfaithful Jews would be seduced by his flattery, but "the people who know their God" would stand firm and oppose him. This opponent would magnify himself and speak against the God of gods. But finally he would come to his end with none to help him. Again there would be a deliverance of all those whose names are found written in the book. This last presentation of the archopponent of the saints and their God shows yet again the major purpose of the book.

Daniel sought to show his people that the return to their own land at the end of the seventy-year captivity would not be the end of their conflicts. He would brace them for the severest struggle in all their history. This had to do with the deceptive and malignant attitude of Antiochus Epiphanes. So awful and terrifying would be his opposition to restored Israel that New Testament speakers and writers found in him a type of the man of sin who shall oppose the church of Jesus Christ near the time of the end. As a final buttress to the faith of those destined to pass through a time of trouble such as never had been in time past, Michael told Daniel, "At that time your people shall be delivered, every one whose name shall be found written in the book. And many of those who sleep in the dust of the earth shall awake, some to everlasting life, and some to shame and everlasting contempt. And those who are wise shall shine like the brightness of the firmament; and those who turn many to righteousness, like the stars for ever and ever" (12: 1-3). This glorious message showed that the Latter Days would terminate in the resurrection both of the just and the unjust. This prediction would plant a most glorious hope in the hearts of the saints and at the same time stand as a warning to the unfaithful. New Testament teaching built directly on this final message from Daniel.

8. Life of the People of God

Ezekiel's messages dealt very severely with Israel's sins and abominable practices. He wrote very little in a positive manner concerning the life of the people of God. So few were the remaining faithful of Israel that the Lord commanded Ezekiel, "Go through the city, through Jerusalem, and put a mark upon the foreheads of the men who sigh and groan over all the abominations that are committed in it" (Ezek. 9:4). The Lord had made it clear through Ezekiel that his people bore individual responsibility for responding to the warning given through the prophet (3:16-21). The manner of life of the people of God becomes very evident in the several contexts which describe the spiritual change which the Lord would effect in their lives.[27] From these we gain the idea that the pattern of living of His people becomes possible when they receive a new heart and a new spirit, this being accomplished through the inner working of the Holy Spirit.

This body of teaching made clear that people were not able of themselves to achieve the holy living required of them. Walking in His statutes and observing His ordinances were not merely external standards of legalism but had to do with Israel's heart response, since they were the covenant people of God.

In one of the contexts where the Lord was rebuking His people, the lives of three men — Noah, Daniel, and Job — were held up before them as men of righteousness (14:12-20). Through the centuries from Noah to Abraham and onward, the word "righteousness" had gained a definitive and normative meaning. It had laid hold of the most significant aspect of God's perfection. Undoubtedly the chief purpose of Ezekiel's temple vision lay in the portrayal of God's holiness. As Ezekiel pictured the temple as the perfect symbol of worship the people would inevitably be led to probe the depths of the Lord's command through Moses, "You shall be holy; for I the Lord your God am holy" (Lev. 19:2). The word "holy" had also acquired profound meaning through the centuries. It showed the manner of life of God's people as it stood opposed to all the forms of wickedness found among the nations of Canaan and later also among the people of God. In a positive way holiness stood for separation and aloofness from sin, which a righteous people would manifest in their way of life (18:5-9, 19-29).

The Book of Daniel presents the prophet and his friends in all their nobility of character.[28] Here we see the lives of godly men under test as they served in the king's palace. Daniel faced the problem of using temperately the king's rich food and wine. His strength of character kept him from indulging in food and drink which would be harmful to his physical health. At the price of being thrown into the fiery furnace his three friends refused to obey Nebuchadnezzar's command to fall down and worship the golden image. Daniel was a man of prayer and remained faithful to God, even though he knew that practicing his faith would result in his being thrown into the den of lions. His lengthy prayer in chapter 9 included personal confession of sin, as well as vicarious confession for his people. Most earnestly he petitioned the Lord to restore the worship in the temple and to restore his people to their own land. Innocent as he was, he had humbled himself before God; and in answer to his prayer, the Lord revealed to him the real meaning of unfolding history. In sharp contrast to the noble character of these men stood the ungodliness of the Babylonian kings.[29] Daniel counseled Nebuchadnezzar to break off his sins and iniquities. In spite of the warning given through the handwriting on the wall, Belshazzar, refusing to humble his heart, instead lifted up himself against the Lord.

More forceful language describing the sinfulness of sin could hardly be found than that which revealed the character of Antiochus Epiphanes and the man of sin whom he typified. He would be a contemptible person, acting deceitfully, setting his heart against the covenant people, profaning the temple, even to setting up the abomination of idol worship in the temple. A final picture of the extremes of character found in this book comes in the words, "Many shall purify themselves, and make themselves white, and be refined; but the wicked shall do wickedly; and none of the wicked shall understand; but those who are wise shall understand" (12:10). The most heinous aspect of this wickedness was its manifestation in stubborn resistance to God. The life of the people of God as shown in Daniel and his friends was on the highest plane of spiritual achievement found in the Old Testament. It stood out in sharp contrast with the wickedness of the archenemy of man.

9. Nature of Sin -- Man's Sinfulness

a. Ezekiel's Exposure of Sin

After Ezekiel had seen the glory of the Lord, the Spirit sent him to the people of Israel, a nation of rebels, transgressors, people who were impudent and stubborn. This sharp contrast between a vision of Israel's holy God and their own sinfulness may be the reason for more than two hundred references to sin based on a vocabulary of twenty or more words used for sin in this book. Most certainly the Lord was seeking to lead Israel to a consciousness of their sins with a view to showing them their guilt before God and leading them to repentance (2:1-5).

Another reason for the frequent references to Israel's sins may be found in their charge against God expressed in the words, "The way of the Lord is not just."[30] This was Israel's rebuttal to God's judgment upon them for their sins.

Another approach to Ezekiel's teaching on sin may be found in the forty-seven occurrences of the words translated abomination (*toebah* and *shiqquts*). These words have reference to "Whatever is ritually or ethically loathsome and repugnant to God and men."[31] In almost all instances *toebah* has reference to objects and practices abhorrent to *Yahweh*, and opposed to the moral requirements and ritual of his religion."[32] Here we have a very meaningful approach to the idea of sin. Sin is that which is loathsome, detestable, repugnant, and abhorrent to the Lord. This furnishes a new slant to the idea of sin. True indeed, evil, violence, iniquity, transgression, pride, and the like are all sinful. But to speak of these things as abominations to the Lord, shows their antagonism to something in God's nature. The holiness of God makes all these sins detestable to Him. Throughout the Book of Ezekiel about all of the named sins are referred to as abominations to the Lord. A special focus of these abominations is the worship of idols, including all the idolatrous practices.

A study of the vocabulary for sin exposes its real nature. The following words occur from ten to forty times in the book: *ra* (badness, wickedness, evil); *hata* (sin, sinner); *avon* (iniquity, perversity, guilt, punishment); *rasha* (wicked, criminal); *pesha* (transgression); *marah* (contentious, refractory); *halal* (pollute, defile, profane); *zanah* (play the harlot). Words less frequently used are: *hamas* (violence, wrongdoing, cruelty, ruthless outrage); *asham* (offense, trespass, fault, guilt); *marad* (be bold, audacious in acts of rebellion); *maas* (reject, despise, refuse); *avel* (injustice, unrighteous); *mishpat* (bloody crimes); *gavah* (lifted up, haughty); *zadon* (pride). While many of these words refer to specific acts of sin, the great majority lay hold of wrong attitudes and dispositions.

This vocabulary shows also the inward nature of man's sins. Man's heart is sinful. This will become all the more apparent in the next section, where we will note the need for heart renewal, which is accomplished alone by the inner working of the Holy Spirit. The whole idea of repentance and turning away from sins has its origin in man's inner being.

b. Daniel's Understanding of Sin

Daniel's counsel to Nebuchadnezzar to break off his sins by practicing righteousness and his iniquities by showing mercy to the oppressed suggests the inner nature of sin. Likewise the commendation that Daniel was faithful and that no error or fault was found in him, expresses the same idea (4:27; 6:4). Most significant are the words of confession in Daniel's prayer (9:4-11). Note especially, "We have sinned and done wrong and acted wickedly and rebelled, turning aside from thy commandments and ordinances; we have not listened to thy servants the prophets." He spoke also of Israel's treachery, disobedience, transgression, and refusal to obey God's voice. This language practically duplicates that of Ezekiel in showing the nature of sin as well as its inward character. Daniel used at least ten words for sin, all of which are found in Ezekiel.

10. Repentance, Faith, and Regeneration

a. Ezekiel's Teaching on Spiritual Renewal

In view of Ezekiel's forceful exposure of sin it is entirely natural that he should show the way back to God. Repeatedly he calls on Israel to repent and to turn away from their idols.[33] The verb *shub* with its manifold nonmoral meanings also carries the ethical sense of *turn back, return, repent.* The verb occurs twice in both 14:6 and 18:30, but it is uniformly translated *repent* and *turn away from.* The Septuagint used the words *epistrepho* and *apostrepho*, respectively, for these two occurrences of *shub.* This suggests two ideas: first, the turning to God; and second, the turning away from idols. This dual action becomes very expressive as it leads to Ezekiel's understanding of repentance.

The element of grace which the Lord extends to the penitent sinner becomes manifest in the statement, "I have no pleasure in the death of the wicked, but that the wicked turn from his way and live; turn back, turn back from your evil ways; for why will you die" (Ezek. 33:11)? Throughout the book the Lord showed Israel each person's responsibility for his sin (3:19-21; 18:1-20). If Ezekiel warned the wicked person and he would not turn from his wicked way, he would die in his iniquity. Likewise if he warned the righteous man and he did not sin, he would surely live. Each individual possesses the freedom to remain faithful or to turn away from God. Likewise the wicked man is free to turn away from sin or to continue in his transgressions. By implication God supplies grace to both the righteous and the wicked according to their respective needs.

These distinctive teachings on repentance and on the individual's responsibility to God, lead to a further unfolding of His saving acts. It is that of God's giving to those who turn away from sin a new heart and a new spirit within them.[34] A slight variation of language among these Scriptures suggests the very important two-sidedness of the change of those who turn to God. In the 18:31 context the Lord added to His call to repentance the words, "Get yourselves a new heart and a new spirit." Whereas in the 11:19; 36:26 passages the Lord said, "A new heart I will give you, and a new spirit I will put within you." We have grounds for believing that this was not an accidental variation in language. In harmony with the personal responsibility involved in the command to repent and turn from transgressions, there was a real point to the added command, "Get yourselves a new heart and a new spirit." This did not mean that the inner spiritual change took place through the individual's own dynamic, but rather that such a person opened his heart to experience the regenerative power of God. As Paul put it, "For by grace you have been saved through faith; and this is not your own doing, it is the gift of God" (Eph. 2:8). The new heart and the new spirit which the Lord puts within those who repent and return from their transgressions describes an inner change wrought by the Holy Spirit. It is a renewal which the New Testament describes as being born of the Holy Spirit and also as being raised to a newness of life (Jn. 3:5-8; Rom. 6:4). This inner transformation of life would enable these changed persons to walk in God's statutes and to observe His ordinances.

The repeated expressions related to walking in God's statutes and keeping His ordinances[35] were far removed from a formal legalism. A spiritual regenerative work of the Holy Spirit alone made possible Israel's walking in His statutes and keeping His ordinances. The Pharisees' attitude toward keeping the law was entirely different from this. They had forgotten the necessity of the spiritual change to enable them to keep the law. Ezekiel, who had seen the glory of the Lord and had experienced the vision of the new temple, was not a legalist.

As A. F. Kirkpatrick reflected on these spiritual renewal passages he said, "This is not the language of a petrified legalism, which expects salvation by its own works, but of absolute and utter dependence on the renewing grace of God, balanced by the recognition of the freedom of the human will and of personal responsibility." Later he commented on the restored vision of the restored temple: "The people have been exonerated. The temple is the earthly abode of Jehovah who returns to dwell in the midst of His people. The ritual is their expression of devotion to His service."[36]

b. Daniel's Direction of the Way to Repentance

The prophet Daniel sought to lead the Babylonian monarch to repentance (4:27; 5:22, 23). He said, "Break off your sins by practicing righteousness, and your iniquities by showing mercy to the oppressed." Belshazzar had not humbled his heart but had lifted himself up against the Lord of heaven. Thus in Daniel's thinking there were two paths in life: the way of sin, and the way of righteousness. The essential ingredient of repentance, namely, humility, was lacking in Belshazzar. Daniel's prayer is a model of repentance and confession of sin, especially so because it was intercessory (9:3-20). He recognized that Israel had sinned, done wrong, acted wickedly, rebelled and turned aside from the Lord's commandments. This unrestrained confession of sin disclosed his genuine repentance. It enabled him to recognize that "to the Lord our God belong mercy and forgiveness." These words also manifested a genuine faith and trust in God. Such a prayer of repentance and asking the Lord for forgiveness indicated that Daniel had experienced an inner renewal of spirit. While not explicitly stated, it was nevertheless real as viewed from the standpoint of the unfolding doctrine of regeneration. Daniel's experience with the Lord presents one of the clearest examples of a changed life found in the Bible.

It becomes very fitting then that Daniel should close his book with a clear note of individual eschatology. Certainly only those who lived in such close relationship with the Lord as Daniel would be able to conclude his message with the words, "Many of those who sleep in the dust of the earth shall awake, some to everlasting life, and some to shame and everlasting contempt. And those who are wise shall shine like the brightness of the firmament; and those who turn many to righteousness, like the stars for ever and ever" (12:2, 3). This is the most clear-cut prediction in the Old Testament having to do with the life in the world to come. From the standpoint of the central idea of repentance, faith, and regeneration we should note that those who have experienced spiritual renewal in this life shall experience everlasting life in the world to come, while those who rejected the mercy and forgiveness of God will be doomed to shame and everlasting contempt. The glory of those who turn many to righteousness becomes manifest in their shining "like the brightness of the firmament."

For Additional Reading and Reference:

International Standard Bible Encyclopaedia, Vol. I:
  "Daniel, Book of," pp. 786 f.
  "Ezekiel," pp. 1073-81.
  "Haggai," p. 1318.
The Interpreter's Bible, Vol. 6:
  "Ezekiel," pp. 41-61.
  "Daniel," pp. 351, 355-59.
The Interpreter's Dictionary of the Bible, E-J, "Ezekiel," pp. 209-12.

Oehler, *Theology of the Old Testament,* pp. 437-536. A general treatment of all the prophets.
Pfeiffer, *Religion in the Old Testament,* pp. 117-58. A doctrinal approach to all the prophets.
von Rad, *Old Testament Theology,* Vol. II, pp. 220-37, "Ezekiel"; 308-15, "Daniel."
Schultz, *Old Testament Theology,* Vol. I, pp. 300-10.
Titcomb, *Revelation in Progress,* pp. 375-425, 455-59.

1. *The International Standard Bible Encyclopaedia,* James Orr, General Editor (Chicago: The Howard Severance Co., 1930, Vol. II, "Book of Daniel," p. 784. *See also* Dr. Wilson's book, *Studies in the Book of Daniel* (New York and London: G. P. Putnam's Sons, 1917.).
2. *The Westminster Dictionary of the Bible,* by John D. Davis, revised and rewritten by Henry Snyder Gehman (Philadelphia: The Westminster Press, 1944), "Daniel," p. 130. Incidentally, I pursued seminary courses under Doctors Wilson and Davis, and was greatly challenged by their scholarly and evangelical approach to biblical criticism.
3. Ezek. 1:24, 28; 3:12, 23; 8:4; 9:3; 10:4, 5, 18, 19; 11:22, 23; 39:21; 43:2-5; 44:4; 48:35.
4. Dan. 2:47; 4:34, 35; 6:26, 27.
5. 5:11; 14:16, 18, 20; 16:48; 17:16, 19; 18:3; 20:3, 31, 35; 33:11, 27; 34:8; 35:6.
6. *The International Critical Commentary, A Critical and Exegetical Commentary of the Book of Ezekiel,* by G. A. Cooke (Edinburgh: T. & T. Clark, 1960), p. 60.
7. Ezek. 20:1-26, 39-44; 22:8, 26; 36:20-23; 39:7, 25.
8. Dan. 4:8, 9, 13, 17, 18, 23; 5:11; 8:24; 9:16, 20, 24; 11:28, 30, 45; 12:7.
9. Ezek. 18:21-24, 30-32; 33:10-20.
10. Consult a concordance for the occurrences of these words.
11. Ezek. 6:7. Von Rad made the interesting observation that these words occur eighty-six times in Ezekiel. See *Old Testament Theology* (New York: Harper and Row, 1965), Vol. II, p. 237.
12. Ezek. 7:5-9. By checking on the word "know" in an exhaustive concordance the remaining occurrences of this expression can be easily located.
13. Ezek. 5 — 7; 11; 12; 16; 20; 23; 33; 34; 36:16 — 37:28; 40 — 48.
14. Ezek. 25:7, 13, 17; 26:4, 21; 29:8, 9.
15. Mt. 24:15-28; Lk. 21:20-24.
16. Ezek. 18:26-28; 33:10-16; 34:11-25; 36:25-33; 37:11-28; 43:27; 45:13-25; 46.
17. Dan. 2:44; 4:27; 7:14-27; 9:4-19; 12:1-3.
18. Ezek. 8; 14:2-5; 20:7-21; 22:6-31, etc.
19. *The Westminster Dictionary of the Bible* (Philadelphia: The Westminster Press, 1944), p. 176.
20. Dan. 4:34-37; 6:16-18, 25-27.
21. Ezek. 2:2; 3:12, 14, 24; 8:3; 11:1, 5, 24; 37:1, 14; 39:29; 43:5.
22. Ezek. 7:2, 3, 10-27; 21:24-32; 22:24-31; 30:1-19.
23. Mal. 4:5; 2 Thess. 2:2; 2 Pet. 3:10, 12.
24. Ezek. 11:16-21; 14:11; 34:11-16; 36:8-36; 37:11-28; 38:39.
25. *The International Standard Bible Encyclopaedia,* James Orr, General Editor (Chicago: The Howard-Severance Co., 1930), Vol. II, "Gog," p. 1273.
26. Ezek. cf. Rev. 40:2 (21:10); 40:3, 5 (21:15); 43:2 (1:15; 14:2; 19:6); 44:4 (15:8); 47:1, 2 (22:1, 2); 48:16 (21:16); 48:31-35 (21:12, 13).
27. Ezek. 11:19-21; 18:5-18, 25-32; 36:25-29.
28. Dan. 1:8; 3:17, 18; 6:10, 22; 9:3-19; 10:12.
29. Dan. 4:27; 5:22, 23; 11:21-32; 12:10.
30. Ezek. 18:25, 29; *See also* 6:9; 14:22; 20:43; 33:17-20.
31. *The Interpreter's Dictionary of the Bible* (New York: Abingdon Press, 1962), Vol. A-D, p. 12 f. "Abomination," by M. H. Lovelace.
32. *Dictionary of the Bible* (New York: Charles Scribner's Sons, 1963), edited by James Hastings. Revised Edition by Frederic C. Grant and H. H. Rowley, p. 5. "Abomination," by A. R. S. Kennedy, revised by H. H. Rowley.
33. Ezek. 14:6; 18:30; 33:11; 36:31, 32.
34. Ezek. 11:19-21; 18:30-32; 36:25-29.
35. Ezek. 5:6, 7; 11:12; 18:1-20; 20:11-21.
36. *The Doctrine of the Prophets* (London: Macmillan and Company, Ltd., 1909), pp. 348 f.

CHAPTER IX
THEOLOGY OF THE PROPHETS
OF THE PERSIAN PERIOD
520-c.450 B.C.

1. The God of History

a. Haggai

The frequency of Haggai's use of the titles "Lord" (19 times) and "Lord of hosts" (14 times) suggests a special significance which he attached to these names of God. Lord (Yahweh) was the covenant name for God (Ex. 24:7). The title "Lord of hosts," which came into use in the time of Eli, carried the meaning, Lord of the heavenly powers and all created beings, or, as P. T. Manley said, it "is used to exhibit Yahweh as at all times the Savior and Protector of His people (Ps. 46:7, 11). The 'hosts' are all the heavenly powers, ready to do the Lord's command."[1] It was this concept of God which led Haggai to insist on the rebuilding of the temple. He repeated God's command to build the house, "that I may take pleasure in it and that I may appear in my glory" (1:8). Because Israel allowed God's house to lie in ruins, the Lord spoke of withdrawing from His people the fruits of the earth, so that they would give the building of the temple its rightful place. The Lord showed His activity by stirring up Zerubbabel and the remnant of the people to move forward with this task. The Lord would have His people take courage in view of all the difficulties involved in rebuilding the temple. Giving expression to His power in the world, the Lord said, "I will shake the heavens and the earth and the sea and the dry land; and I will shake all nations, so that the treasures of all nations shall come in, and I will fill this house with splendor" (2:6, 7, 21, 22). From the standpoint of teaching about the Holy Spirit in the Old Testament note the words, "My Spirit abides among you" (2:5). This statement asserts the personal distinction between God and His Spirit. It also anticipates quite clearly the New Testament teaching on the deity of the Holy Spirit.

b. Zechariah

The Book of Zechariah disclosed two aspects of God's nature which on the surface may appear irreconcilable, but properly understood they are in harmony with the righteousness and justice of God. The passage 1:13-17 shows that the Lord who speaks gracious and comforting words and has compassion on His people, can also be angry. The passage 8:1-15 also brings into contrast the faithfulness, righteousness, and goodness of God, as they stand in opposition to His wrath. The Lord would have His people return to Jerusalem, and He promised, "I will be the glory within her." Later He added: "Sing and rejoice, O daughter of Zion; for lo, I come and I will dwell in the midst of you" (2:5, 10, 11). Through these promises the Lord let His people know that He would continue to dwell with them. The oracle of 9:1 — 11:3 looked to God's continued activity in the affairs of the nations, both present and future. Undoubtedly these heathen nations would not be able to attribute these judgments to God. This followed the pattern of God's activity among the heathen nations throughout biblical history. To faithful Israel, on the other hand, the Lord would bring great and unspeakable blessings centering in their coming king. The creative work of God becomes manifest in the words, "Thus says the Lord, who stretched out the heavens and founded the earth and formed the spirit of man within him" (12:1).

c. Malachi

What Malachi had to say about God is given in a setting of Israel's stubborn rebuttal of God's claims. This situation served to magnify the nature and attributes of God. The Lord stressed His covenant love to Israel in the words, "I have loved you. . . . I have loved Jacob but I have hated Esau" (1:2, 3). This claim stressed the special love of God as it was manifested in His covenant relationship with Israel. This became all the more significant since it appeared in the last book of the Old Testament. From Abraham and Moses on to the last of the prophets, God was faithful to His covenant relationship with His people. At the center of this covenant relationship was God's love. Further, the Lord, who alone is worthy of worship, confronted the priests with the degrading of their worship by offering on their altars polluted food and animals with all sorts of blemishes (1:6-14). The Lord declared that even among the nations His name was great and He was a great King. The Lord reminded the priests that His covenant with Levi was one of life and peace. Levi had responded with fear and awe of God's name, and as the Lord said, "He walked with me in peace and uprightness, and he turned many from iniquity" (2:6). In this manner the Lord reasserted the holiness of His nature. The tabernacle worship instituted by the Lord at Mt. Sinai had the very definite purpose of revealing to Israel this central attribute of holiness symbolized by the Lord's dwelling in the holy of holies.

Malachi also confronted the people with the truth that God had created man. They all had one Father, the Lord of hosts. In still further exaltation of His name, the Lord foretold the sending of the

Messenger of the new covenant. In the fulfillment of this promise the Lord showed Israel that He does not change. The Sun of Righteousness would rise with healing in His wings. God would still act in the unfolding of history. With these great declarations concerning the God of Israel, given largely in a negative setting, the prophet's disclosure of God rose to the heights of the greater prophets who preceded him. In this last presentation of the God of Israel it is exceedingly gratifying to observe that all through the history of His chosen people one grand concept of God as righteous and holy, and as creator and ruler of the world, shone forth in all of its glory.

2. The Spoken and Written Word of God

Haggai's brief book refers frequently to the spoken words of God. The prophet used three forms of expression to introduce his messages: "The word of the Lord came by Haggai the prophet" occurs five times; "Thus says the Lord of hosts," eight times; and "says the Lord," four times. Through these expressions Haggai sought to declare that Israel's God was speaking through him. An interesting buildup of language, through which the author stated the divine source of Haggai's messages, occurs in the words, "Then Haggai, the messenger of the Lord, spoke to the people with the Lord's message, 'I am with you, says the Lord' " (1:13). The Hebrew word for "messenger" (*malak*) is the word commonly used for angel. This suggests the authoritative nature of Haggai's prophetic calling and gives grounds for recognizing the prophetic character of his book. This is another step leading to an understanding of the distinctive nature of the written word.

The prophet Zechariah opened his book by saying, "The word of the Lord came to Zechariah." He repeated this expression throughout the book when he introduced a message from the Lord. In like manner he introduced specific warnings or commands with the expression, "Thus says the Lord of hosts." It is possible that Zechariah felt that the age of the prophets had passed and on this account he may have tended to doubt the reality of his call to the work of a prophet. Recognizing that a long line of prophets had preceded him, he very appropriately buttressed his own prophetic messages by quoting the former prophets. In a very graphic way, Zechariah saw eight visions, each of which was explained to him by an angel (1:7 — 6:8). Through these visions Zechariah experienced a double mode of revelation: first, in the vividness of what he saw; and second, in the angel's explanation of what the Lord was revealing to him. Throughout the Old Testament we have observed the different forms of divine revelation, all possessing the quality of revealed truth and each form adapted to the nature of the message revealed or to the circumstances of the one receiving the revelation. Under no circumstances should we interpret the vision form of revelation as intimating that the Lord was farther removed from the recipient of the vision than when the Lord spoke directly. The Lord was as near to Zechariah when He showed him these things as when He spoke to the prophet. Just as Zechariah wrote the words spoken to him by the Lord, in the same manner he recorded what he saw, including the angelic interpretation of the visions.

In language similar to that of Isaiah, Jeremiah, Habakkuk, and Zechariah, Malachi opened his book with the words, "The oracle of the word of the Lord to Israel by Malachi." The Hebrew word *massa* has the meaning *burden, load, thing lifted up,* or according to the RSV, *oracle.* This variation of the common way of introducing a prophetic book was just as expressive as "The word of the Lord came" to so and so. The contents of this book bear the same prophetic characteristics as those of the other writing prophets. The expressions, "says the Lord" and "says the Lord of hosts," including the direct quotations of the accompanying messages, possess the same meaning as they have in the other prophetic works.

3. Israel's Election Actualized by Covenant Relation with God

The prophet Haggai made no direct reference to Israel's election or to their covenant relation with the Lord. There are, however, three strands of thought in the book which imply this relationship. When the Lord was commanding His people to proceed with building the temple, He stated His purpose: "that I may appear in my glory" (1:8). Underlying this command was the truth of the Lord's dwelling with His covenant people. The reference to the Lord's promise to Israel when they came out of Egypt also reflects the covenant relation made with them at Sinai (2:5). Israel's failure to recognize things clean and unclean in their worship had its basis in the ceremonial law commanded by the Lord at Sinai (3:11-14). These expressions serve as evidence that the Lord had chosen Israel as His covenant people.

Zechariah's third vision pictured Israel's return to Jerusalem. Speaking of the restored city, the Lord said, "I will be the glory within her." He added, "I will dwell in the midst of you . . . and many nations shall join themselves to the Lord in that day, and shall be my people" (2:1-12). These words also testify to Israel's election when the background idea of Israel's being God's covenant people is brought into the picture. The Lord dwelt in the midst of His covenant people. In the setting of the Oracle (9:1 — 11:3) the Lord spoke of the blood of His covenant with Israel (9:11). Since this is a specific reference to the

Sinaitic covenant, it gives additional support to Israel's election as God's covenant people. Even though Israel was in exile through having broken the covenant, the Lord would seek to establish covenant relationship.

The Lord's message to Israel as recorded in Malachi built on the covenant relationship expressed by the words, "I have loved you" (1:2). In a very real way the Lord was the spiritual Father of Israel. The condemnation of the ungodly priests had its basis in their unfaithfulness to the covenant which underlay the ceremonial law. The priestly tribe of Levi had corrupted the spiritual responsibilities to which they had been called. In Malachi's rebuke of the Levites he asked, "Has not one God created us? Why then are we faithless to one another, profaning the covenant of our fathers" (2:8-10)? Through Judah's faithlessness the sanctuary of the Lord had been profaned. These sins were more grievous because they violated the covenant relationship established at Mt. Sinai.

The concluding thoughts in this discussion have to do with the meaning and significance of the Sinaitic covenant seven hundred years after its institution. Very clearly the last prophets viewed this covenant with the same perspective and understanding as had all the prophets from Moses onward. The Lord and Israel continued to be bound by this covenant. Israel was still the chosen people of the Lord. The Lord spurred their hope by the words, "The sun of righteousness shall rise, with healing in its wings" (4:2). The foundation for Israel's hope in the future lay in the closing admonition: "Remember the law of my servant Moses, the statutes and ordinances that I commanded him at Horeb for all Israel" (4:4). Obedience to this covenant gave assurance to faithful Israel of receiving still larger blessings in the future.

4. The Messiah and the Messianic Kingdom

a. The Forward Look of Haggai

For centuries Christians have treasured a prediction made by Haggai: "The desire of all nations shall come" (2:7, KJV). Since this translation is based on the Latin Vulgate and differs from the Hebrew, a formidable problem appears. The correct rendering of the Hebrew says, "The treasures of all nations shall come in." While this change seems to give this passage a non-Messianic meaning, as practically all present-day scholars maintain, von Rad might have laid hold of its real meaning when he said, "It was Haggai himself who envisaged the time when all the nations were to worship Jahweh and to bring him their treasures, and, surprisingly enough, he believed that this time was already imminent (Hag. 2:6-9). It was for this time when Jahwism would throw off its national limitations and become a universal religion — the time of the Messiah — that the temple had to be built. It is to be preceded by a fearful shaking of the heavens and the earth; the nations are to wage internecine war, and Jahweh is to destroy the weapons of war — it is a 'day of Jahweh.' Thereafter, however, the anointed one is to enter upon his office as the signet-ring of Jahweh, i.e., as the one who gives effect to Jahweh's decrees. When Haggai made this prophecy, he was not thinking vaguely of some unspecified anointed one. He clearly and unequivocally designated as the coming anointed one David's descendant, Zerubbabel, the grandson of the unfortunate Jehoiachin."[2]

In a lengthy paragraph following this von Rad proceeded to show that we may have here a veiled Messianic prediction similar to some other predictions, such as the Servant of the Lord passages in the second part of Isaiah, which at the time of their being given were not understood but became clear in the time of Christ. Thus while Haggai regarded Zerubbabel as the coming anointed one, he never came to the throne. Just as a number of the royal psalms were first interpreted as referring to those on the throne of David but later were recognized as being Messianic, so it is possible that the Zerubbabel reference to Haggai's prediction rightly gained Messianic meaning by the time of Christ.

Entering into this picture is the quotation of Haggai 2:6 by the author of Hebrews, who says, "This phrase, 'Yet once more,' indicates the removal of what is shaken, as of what has been made, in order that what cannot be shaken may remain. Therefore let us be grateful for receiving a kingdom that cannot be shaken, and thus let us offer to God acceptable worship, with reverence and awe; for our God is a consuming fire" (Heb. 12:27-29). While the interpretation of some details of this passage offers some problems, the Messianic reference of the Haggai passage is clear. We have received a kingdom which cannot be shaken. This is the kingdom of Him who has been made Lord and Christ.

b. Zechariah's Messianic Predictions

The prophet Zechariah gave five clear predictions of the coming Messiah.[3] The first of these is the familiar prediction of the Branch — "I will bring my servant the Branch" (3:8). The word "servant" may give a clue as to who will be the Branch. The great Servant of the Lord passages in the second part of Isaiah invite consideration of the possibility that Zechariah is identifying the Branch with the Servant of the Lord. Several other "Branch" predictions may also lie back of his prediction. Isaiah had spoken of a shoot coming from the stump of Jesse and a branch growing out of his roots (Is. 11:1). Jeremiah also had given two Messianic predictions in which he had quoted the Lord as saying, "I will raise up for David a righteous Branch, and he shall reign as king and deal wisely, and shall execute justice and righteousness in the land" (Jer. 23:5; 33:15).

The 6:12 reference to the Branch is very significant even though a difficult exegetical problem confronts us in verse 13. The difficulty centers in whether we should follow the Hebrew, "He shall be a priest upon his throne," or whether the Septuagint expresses the thought more accurately, "There shall be a priest by his throne." It seems clear that the Greek rendering of this verse gives the more natural meaning to it. On the other hand, the verses can yield meaning according to the Hebrew. Everything else being equal, the Hebrew text takes priority over the Septuagint translation. While most expositors see fit to follow the Greek, it is significant that most English versions including KJV, ASV, Modern Reader's Bible, The Holy Bible from the Peshitta, and the Berkeley version follow the Hebrew; while Moffatt's translation, the RSV, and the Jerusalem Bible follow the Greek. While my judgment on this point may be influenced by my bias, I believe that the fulfillment of this prediction in Jesus, the Priest-King, after the order of Melchizedek, constitutes the true fulfillment of this prediction (Heb. 7). If this senses the true meaning of Zechariah 6:12, 13, we have here a distinct advance in the prophetic disclosure of the Messiah.

Psalm 110 may have served as the foundation for this prediction. If so, this prepares us to understand how the Branch is at once God's specially chosen Servant, and also the One who shall be enthroned at the right hand of God. The literal rebuilding of the temple, which was soon to take place, foreshadowed the building of a future spiritual temple of the Lord. The profound symbolism of the temple as the dwelling place of God among His people, and of their approach to Him through bloody sacrifices, forecast the priestly work of Christ culminating in the glories of the heavenly temple in the New Jerusalem, where the Lord will dwell forever with His people.

The second Messianic prediction (9:9, 10) disclosed at once the human and divine aspects of Jesus' kingship. Both Matthew and John captured the human aspect of this in Jesus' triumphal entry into Jerusalem (Mt. 21:5; Jn. 12:15). The divine aspect appears in the words, "And he shall command peace to the nations; his dominion shall be from sea to sea, and from the River to the ends of the earth." While there is no explicit New Testament quotation of this prediction, the great body of teachings on Christ's exaltation to the right hand of the

Father confirms its Messianic and deity reference.[4]

The Zechariah 11:4-14 passage possesses Messianic significance, as attested by Matthew 26:15 and 27:3-10.[5] The Lord bade Zechariah become shepherd of the flock which was doomed to slaughter. The language continued in the form of a parable or allegory, likely involving some irony. The prophet became impatient in this shepherd responsibility and refused to continue to be their shepherd. He took the staff, Grace, and broke it. By doing so he annulled his covenant as shepherd which he had made with all the peoples. He then requested that they would pay him wages for his shepherd service. They responded by weighing out thirty shekels of silver which they gave to him. The Lord told the prophet to put it into the treasury. The amount paid was the value of a slave. Then the shepherd Zechariah broke the second staff, Union, which annulled the brotherhood between Judah and Israel. In this manner the Lord directed Zechariah to give a message of warning to the people of Israel. When Matthew spoke of Judas bringing back the thirty pieces of silver to the chief priests, confessing that he had sinned in betraying innocent blood, the priests ignored his apparent penitence; and in the semblance of having regard for the temple they did not put the money into the treasury but used it to buy the potter's field, allegedly for the reason that the pieces of silver were blood money. Matthew then noted that this action was a fulfillment of Zechariah's casting the thirty shekels of silver into the treasury in the house of the Lord. The point of the comparison lay in this, that just as the Lord's people paid off Zechariah in terms of his being a slave, so the chief priests used the thirty pieces of silver, the price of Christ's blood, for the purchasing of the potter's field. The heinousness of Israel's putting a slave value on Zechariah's service was infinitely exceeded by the chief priests' paying a slave's value for Christ's blood.

Giving so much space to this Messianic reference may find justification in a couple of observations. First, this incident reveals a distinctive character of the Scriptures in that certain portions have embedded truths which become evident only in the New Testament. Second, not all prophetic Scripture is avowedly predictive. Fulfillment may signify similarity or identity in meaning between the Old and the New Testaments.

Zechariah 12:10 is clearly predictive but there is a sharp difference of opinion on whether it is Messianic. Many students detect a close relation between this verse and Isaiah 53. Some would even assert that Zechariah consciously borrowed from this source. I do not think that a final answer can be given to these points. We do not know of any fulfillment of this prediction before the time of Christ. As John wrote of

Jesus' crucifixion, he mentioned the fulfillment of this passage in these words: "They shall look on him whom they have pierced" (Jn. 19:37). Evidently the inhabitants of Jerusalem did not have a spirit of compassion and supplication that would cause them to mourn for Him. It is likely that the mourners were limited to the three Marys, the Apostle John, and others who loved Him, but these hardly constitute the mourners spoken of by Zechariah. John's statement may indicate that this incident at the cross is a partial fulfillment of the prediction.

It is noteworthy that in the Revelation John quoted this statement again in the context of the return of Christ: "Behold, he is coming with the clouds, and every eye will see him, every one who pierced him; and all tribes of the earth will wail on account of him" (Rev. 1:7). The added details of this verse evidently assert the culminating fulfillment of Zechariah's prediction. From the angle of the fulfillment of predictive prophecies we should see this as an example of double fulfillment.

In another context of shepherd imagery we read, "Strike the shepherd, that the sheep may be scattered" (Zech. 13:7). This does not appear as a prediction; but when Jesus went to the Mount of Olives with His disciples, He told them that they would all fall away because of Him that night; and then He added, "For it is written, 'I will strike the shepherd, and the sheep of the flock will be scattered'" (Mt. 26:31). Unlike the other Zechariah passages quoted in the New Testament, Jesus did not claim the fulfillment of any Scripture in this case, but instead He used the label commonly introducing a quotation from the Old Testament, "It is written." Hence it may be going beyond the intent of Jesus' words to say that this verse is a Messianic prediction.

Zechariah 14 presents with unmatched grandeur a prediction of a future all the more glorious because of its apocalyptical nature. The Messianic aspect of this portion becomes manifest in the quotations from it in Revelation 22:1-3. There we observe that the living waters flow from the throne of God and of the Lamb. This assures us that Zechariah's prediction foresaw the unspeakable majesty of the enthroned Lamb. All who share in the glories of the New Jerusalem shall see His face and His name shall be on their foreheads. They shall worship Him and shall share in the eternal reign of God and of the Lamb. While these details are not explicitly expressed in Zechariah's prediction, they do fit most perfectly in this New Jerusalem apocalypse.

This detailed study of Zechariah's Messianic predictions may be still further strengthened by looking at them in toto. We may get the impression that they relate by way of rather casual or incidental references to the life of Christ. At the same time these same incidents constitute so many evidences that Jesus was the Christ. Putting it a bit differently these predictions did not have so much to do with Jesus' humanity or deity as with His Messiahship.

c. Malachi's Messenger of the Covenant

Although expositors are divided on this point, it seems clear that Malachi thinks of "the messenger of the covenant" as being the coming Messiah (3:1). The New Testament did identify the messenger who prepared the way before the Lord, and the returning Elijah, as John the Baptist (Mt. 11:10; 17:11). So great would be the messenger of the covenant that this forerunner was needed to prepare the way for the Messiah. A clue for identifying this messenger of the covenant was that he would suddenly come to his temple. Eschatologically, Malachi predicted the coming of the great and terrible day of the Lord. The Lord's messenger and the messenger of the covenant would come before its arrival. This suggests an era of grace and salvation introduced by the messenger of the covenant. It would be offered to all mankind. It is proper to note here that the New Testament confirmed this idea. Thus the messenger of the covenant gave the great commission to his disciples. The gospel should be preached in all the world and then the end would come.

5. The Day of the Lord — Judgment

From the standpoint of progressive revelation the teaching of this group of books on the Day of the Lord is quite distinctive. The earlier writing prophets were distinctive in predicting imminent judgment upon Israel and Judah. They were forecasting the overthrow of these nations. Now that this judgment had come, the postexilic prophets had a different perspective. These prophets, especially Zechariah, present some difficult problems of interpretation. I shall bypass some of the difficult details and seek to gain an understanding of these messages in the large.

The prophet Haggai made no mention of the Day of the Lord, but he did foresee a coming catastrophic event which bore some similarity to the Day of the Lord passages of the earlier prophets. Quoting the words of the Lord, Haggai wrote: "I am about to shake the heavens and the earth, and to overthrow the throne of kingdoms; I am about to destroy the strength of the kingdoms of the nations, and overthrow the chariots and their riders; and the horses and their riders shall go down, everyone by the sword of his fellow" (2:21, 22). The Lord gave a temporal significance to these predictions by declaring that He would take Zerubbabel and make him like a signet ring. To what extent this was prophetic of an exaltation of the then living

Zerubbabel is very difficult to state. If this is a Messianic prediction, as I indicated in the preceding section, it presents a most glorious consummating triumph of the Messiah. Certainly nothing of this dimension took place in the life of the builder of the second temple.

The prophet Zechariah appears to present two different pictures of a coming day, the one bearing the label "in [on] that day" and the other "a (the) day of the Lord," occurring seven times.[6] Whether the absence of the article "the" in the Hebrew possesses any significance, is a debatable question. In view of the fact that "the Day of the Lord" was a well understood expression among the earlier prophets, it is conceivable that Zechariah envisioned another Day of the Lord which lay in the future.

The frequent occurrences of the phrase "in that day" look to a time of blessings common both to the Lord's people and to the nations. Thus the Lord bade the daughter of Zion sing and rejoice, "For lo, I come and I will dwell in the midst of you, says the Lord. And many nations shall join themselves to the Lord in that day, and shall be my people; and I will dwell in the midst of you. . . . And the Lord will inherit Judah as his portion in the holy land" (2:10-12). Significant in this prediction are such ideas as the geographical location of Israel (in the holy land), the Lord's dwelling in the midst of His people, and the universalism of many nations sharing these blessings. The 12:3 context presented a typical Day of the Lord declaration of coming judgment; but if verses 7-14 belong to the same context, this use of "on that day" predicted not only coming judgment but also the subsequent blessings which would issue out of these judgments. To further complicate the problem, verse 10, as I indicated earlier, envisioned the crucifixion of the Messiah, and further, that there would be a fountain opened for Jerusalem "to cleanse them from sin and uncleanness" (13:1).

In view of the Messianic reference of 12:10, there are reasons for believing that 13:1 has the same general setting. Although there is no New Testament quotation to support this, the fountain opened to cleanse the inhabitants of Jerusalem from sin and uncleanness could well forecast the redemptive work of the Messiah, available first of all to the people of Jerusalem. The following verses (2-6) predict a removal of the false prophets, in spite of their deceptive efforts to conceal themselves. With no sure clue as to what Zechariah is predicting, it becomes a sheer guess to say that the hypocritical scribes and Pharisees of Christ's day are thus pictured. Presumably the "on that day" context extends to the end of chapter 13. If the earlier comment on the Messianic interpretation of "Strike the shepherd, that the sheep may be scattered," is correct, verses 8 and 9 may predict the post-Pentecost age. This also is mere speculation, but in its favor it may be noted that the two-thirds portion of Israel who would be cut off and would perish could be quite descriptive of the fall of Jerusalem in A.D. 70. Alongside this the one-third portion who would be refined and tested would constitute the church, concerning whom the Lord would say, "They are my people," and the people would respond, "The Lord is my God" (Zech. 13:9). The bloody persecutions suffered by the church throughout the Christian era, especially during the first three centuries, would be the fulfillment of the refining and testing which came through fiery trials.

To Zechariah a Day of the Lord was still future. As stated earlier, it is possible that he regarded the predictions of the earlier prophets concerning the Day of the Lord as having been fulfilled. He now saw another Day of the Lord yet to come. Similar to the former Day of the Lord predictions, this prediction by Zechariah contained the element of judgment (14:2). The involvement of other nations in a war against Jerusalem, the destruction of the city, the ravishing of women, and the going into exile of half of the city, vividly portrayed what would take place in the future. The Lord would then fight against these nations, punishing them for their attacks against Jerusalem.

The remainder of chapter 14 centers in the Latter Days. There appears to be an amalgamation of the Day of the Lord with the Latter Days concept. While the former prophets viewed the Latter Days as an era far beyond the Day of the Lord, Zechariah, on the other hand, viewed the Latter Days as organically a part of the Day of the Lord. In the remainder of the chapter some very sublime statements appear which evidently portray future events as leading to the final consummation. One of these reads, "Then the Lord your God will come, and all the holy ones with him" (v. 5). This appears to be a quotation from Enoch from whom Jude also quoted (Jude 14). The statement then is evidently Messianic. Verses 6 and 7 also predict a glorious truth, evidently closely related to the preceding in its outlook. Verse 7 reads: "And there shall be continuous day (it is known to the Lord), not day and not night, for at evening time there shall be light." Zechariah appears to be reflecting on Isaiah's words in 30:26, which context also holds in view a glorious future for Jerusalem. It may be that John's message in Revelation 21: 22-27 will fulfill the predictions of Isaiah and Zechariah. It is noteworthy that this part of Zechariah is apocalyptic, similar in nature to Revelation. This fact serves as a guide to their interpretation. Both give a beatific view of the New Jerusalem.

Zechariah continued with his apocalypse, "On that day living waters shall flow out from Jerusalem, half of them to the eastern sea and half of them to the western sea; it shall continue in summer as in winter" (v. 8). This is also a prediction of the New Jerusalem (Rev. 22:1, 2) and should be interpreted as an apocalypse. In this setting is the prediction noted in the preceding section, "And the Lord will become king over all the earth; on that day the Lord will be one and his name one" (14:9). This is Messianic but it is more than that. Its fuller meaning becomes evident in the Revelation, "The kingdom of the world has become the kingdom of our Lord and of his Christ, and he shall reign for ever and ever" (Rev. 11:15). The last apparent example of Zechariah's bringing together the Day of the Lord and the Latter Days appears in verses 10 and 11. The clue for this amalgamation becomes evident in the Revelation 22:3 quotation from Zechariah which reads, "There shall no more be anything accursed, but the throne of God and of the Lamb shall be in it, and his servants shall worship him." This shows yet again the necessity for regarding these portions of Zechariah as apocalyptic in nature and for interpreting them accordingly.

While this approach to interpretation almost confounds the interpreter, no other approach yields meaning, not even a literal one. The problem is the same here as that encountered in Ezekiel 40 — 48. The restoration of Jerusalem, discussed in such literal language, represented the heavenly Jerusalem with all its splendor as pictured in Revelation. It was this kind of language that would speak to Israel in their low state of spirituality. God would have these people ponder the spiritual significance of a literal restoration, and through this approach they would gain an understanding of God's dwelling place. This would lead them to a genuine worship of the King, of the Lord of hosts. The insignia "Holy to the Lord" would express the commitment of all the Lord's people.

The prophet Malachi closed his book with the prediction of "the great and terrible day of the Lord," which still lay in the future. This forecast must have stirred the hearts of God's people, in whose memory persisted the awfulness of the Day of the Lord which had become history. Malachi saw another outpouring of the wrath of God but it would be preceded by the coming again of Elijah. He would "turn the hearts of fathers to their children and the hearts of children to their fathers." If they would not give heed to this prediction, the Lord would come and smite the land with a curse. This was the last prophetic message given to Israel. The sure preventive for such judgment was expressed in the words of the Lord, "Remember the law of my servant Moses, the statutes and ordinances that I commanded him at Horeb for all Israel" (Mal. 4:4). We do not know how much the people of Israel pondered these words through the centuries that followed. It remained for Christ and Paul to speak of coming judgment. Paul, in particular, used the expressions, "the day of the Lord Jesus" and "the day of the Lord."[7]

6. The Latter Days -- Prophetic Eschatology

While the eschatological expression "the Latter Days" is not found in this group of books, yet the Book of Zechariah gave some significant disclosures with reference to the people of Israel. Even though Haggai made no clear prediction of the Messiah, he did make several references to future judgments which bear a close relationship to the Latter Days.[8]

Zechariah's predictions with reference to the Latter Days have to do almost entirely with the nation of Israel.[9] Very significant are the words, "My cities shall again overflow with prosperity, and the Lord will again comfort Zion and again choose Jerusalem" (1:17). This choosing again of Jerusalem suggests a renewal of the Lord's covenant with Israel at Mt. Sinai. They would experience in still greater measure the special blessings coming upon the elect nation. The Lord expressed this idea a bit differently in the words, "I am jealous for Zion with great jealousy, and I am jealous for her with great wrath. . . . I will return to Zion, and will dwell in the midst of Jerusalem" (8:2, 3). The Lord then pictured the joy of the old people as they would sit in the streets of Jerusalem and also of the children playing in the streets. The Lord closed this message with the idea that many from the nations about them would come to seek the Lord of hosts in Jerusalem. This prophecy of the Gentiles partaking of the special blessings which would come upon the people of Israel sounds the same note of universalism as given by the earlier prophets.

In another Messianic context the Lord predicted, "On that day the Lord their God will save them, for they are the flock of his people; for like the jewels of a crown they shall shine on his land" (9:16). In the 10:6-12 context the Lord spoke of regathering His people, and promised, "I will make them strong in the Lord and they shall glory in his name." The apocalyptic chapter 14 received attention in the preceding sections; but in reading it along with the passages just noted, the question of interpretation again arises. The problem must be solved by an intensive study of the vision and the apocalyptic modes of expression as found in the book.

7. Life of the People of God

The Book of Haggai has little to say about the life of the people

of God. The prophet asked the people to consider how they had fared
(1:5-11). They were thinking only of the material things of life, a
pattern of living which for all practical purposes amounted to earning
wages in order "to put them into a bag with holes." This way of life
was all the more lamentable because they were giving little attention
to rebuilding the temple. They had little regard for the precious
spiritual experience of having the Lord appear in His glory. There
were a few, such as Zerubbabel, who "obeyed the voice of the Lord
their God" and who feared before the Lord. But Zerubbabel was a
man whose spirit the Lord could stir up. He could take courage. He
experienced the abiding presence of the Spirit of God. Truly, Zerubbabel was God's servant, chosen of the Lord.

The Lord's message through Zechariah was first of all a call to the
people to return from their evil ways and deeds. To this there was a
response of repentance. The vision of the flying scroll carried the
symbolism of a curse for everyone who stole and swore falsely. The vision
of the ephah symbolized the iniquity and wickedness in the land (5).
Later the Lord gave positive counsel that the people should render
true judgments and show kindness and mercy each to his brother. They
were to refrain from oppressing the widow, the fatherless, the sojourner, or the poor, and from devising evil against others in their
hearts (7:9, 10). Later advice took the form of this admonition: "Speak
the truth to one another, render in your gates judgments that are true
and make for peace, do not devise evil in your hearts against one
another, and love no false oath." The observances of the fasts were to
be "seasons of joy and gladness, and cheerful feasts; therefore love
truth and peace" (8:16-19). While most of these instructions pertained to
elementary aspects of practical ethics, they presented, nevertheless, a
true pattern of life for God's people.

The Book of Malachi opens with a challenge to Israel concerning
God's love for them. Their level of spiritual attainment was so low that
they failed to recognize God's love manifested in His election of them
to be His people. The priests failed to see how they themselves despised the name of the Lord by offering animals unfit for sacrifice. The
Lord reminded the priests that Levi had feared the Lord and had
stood in awe of His name. No wrong was found on his lips. He walked
with the Lord in peace and uprightness and he turned many from iniquity. Judah also had been faithless, had profaned the sanctuary of the
Lord, and had married the daughter of a foreign god. He was thus
faithless to the wife of his youth. Throughout Israel's history many
Israelites became guilty of marital faithlessness. The Lord exhorted,
"Do not be faithless" (2:16). Other sins which came under God's judg-

ment were those of sorcery, false swearing, and oppression of hire-
lings, widows, orphans, and sojourners. Many were also robbing God by
refusing to give their tithes and offerings. Many could say, "It is
vain to serve God. What is the good of our keeping his charge or of
walking as in mourning before the Lord of hosts? Henceforth we
deem the arrogant blessed; evildoers not only prosper but when they
put God to the test they escape." This language did not describe all
Israel. There were those who feared the Lord and thought on His
name. In a future day they would distinguish "between the righteous
and the wicked, between one who serves God and one who does not
serve him" (3:14-18). Thus Malachi also gave witness to the low plane
of living of God's people. His closing exhortation that Israel should
remember the law, the statutes, and the ordinances of Moses was entirely
in order.

8. Nature of Sin -- Man's Sinfulness

About the only point that Haggai gave on the nature of sin had to
do with its being contagious (Hag. 2:10-19). He showed the priests that
just as physical contact with a dead body caused one to become unclean,
so the contact of righteous people with the ungodly caused the godly
to become infected with sin.

At no point did the Lord's message to Zechariah give a formal discussion of sin. Throughout the book, however, at least six words for
sin are used, each expressing an aspect of Israel's sinfulness. Among
these are the following: "Do not devise evil (*ra*) in your hearts against
one another" (8:17; 1:4; 7:10). This statement traced the source of
evil to the heart. In symbolic language an angel asked those standing
near to Joshua to remove the filthy garments from him and then
added: "Behold, I have taken your iniquity (*avon*) away from you" (3:4,
also 9). This suggested the need of divine power for the removal of
sin. When Zechariah was admonishing the people to render true judgments and to show kindness and mercy to one another, they refused
(*ma en*) to hearken, and turned a stubborn (*sarar*) shoulder (7:11). Here
sin showed itself in wrong attitudes of mind. In symbolic language, those
who bought sheep slew them and held themselves not guilty (*asham*)
(11:5). The prophet spoke of a fountain being opened for the people of
Jerusalem to cleanse them from sin (*chattath*) (13:1). The same word translated "punishment" in 14:19 carries the idea of punishment for sin.

The prophet Malachi exposed sin in about the same manner. He
showed that it was evil (*ra*) to offer blind animals in sacrifice (Mal. 1:8;
2:17). More specifically, this sin profaned (*chalal*) the covenant and sanctuary (1:12; 2:10, 11). Malachi noted the integrity of Levi, stating, "True

instruction was in his mouth, and no wrong (*avlah*) was found on his lips . . . and he turned many from iniquity (*avon*)" (2:6). In the context of the Lord's rebuking faithlessness on the part of those who put away their wives, God spoke in symbolic language: "I hate . . . covering one's garment with violence (*chamas*)" (2:16). Note again the sins condemned in Malachi 3:5 ff., such as sorcery, adultery, false swearing, and the failure to bring in the tithes and offerings. These books certainly show that Israel had not amended their ways, but had continued to manifest the inward nature of sin which required the saving grace of God as its only remedy.

9. Repentance, Faith, and Regeneration

The sparsity of references to repentance in these prophetic books is quite indicative of the impenitence of God's people. In Haggai 2:17 the Lord spoke of judgment being brought upon the people and concluded with the words, "Yet you did not return to me, says the Lord." The opening verses of Zechariah gave the Lord's call for Israel to return to Him, reminding the people of what the earlier prophets had spoken: " 'Thus says the Lord of hosts, Return from your evil ways and from your evil deeds.' But they did not hear or heed me, says the Lord" (1:4). When, however, Judah was carried away into captivity, there were those who did repent. Malachi gave similar words from the Lord: "Return to me, and I will return to you" (3:7). The people gave a strong rebuttal, to which the Lord made a response fitting to the occasion. There were those then who feared the Lord and the Lord heeded and heard them. The Lord's forgiving spirit became manifest in the words, "They shall be mine, says the Lord of hosts, my special possession on the day when I act. . . . Then once more you shall distinguish between the righteous and the wicked, between one who serves God and one who does not serve him" (Mal. 3:16-18). This scarcity of material on repentance in these books serves as an index to the spiritual condition of God's people.

For Additional Reading and Reference:

The Interpreter's Bible:
    Vol. 6, "Haggai," p. 1039.
    Vol. 6, "Zechariah," pp. 1054-56.
    Vol. 6, "Malachi," pp. 1118-20.
Oehler, *Theology of the Old Testament*, pp. 437-536. A general treatment of all the prophets.
Pfeiffer, *Religion in the Old Testament*, pp. 117-58. A doctrinal approach to all the prophets.

von Rad, *Old Testament Theology*, Vol. II, pp. 278-300. "Trito-
Isaiah," "Haggai," "Zechariah," "Malachi," "Jonah."
Schultz, *Old Testament Theology*, Vol. I, pp. 320-36.
Titcomb, *Revelation in Progress*, pp. 425-54, 479-92.
Interpreter's Dictionary of the Bible, K-Q, "Malachi," pp. 231 f.
Interpreter's Dictionary of the Bible, R-Z, "Zechariah," pp. 944-47.

1. *The New Bible Dictionary*, J. D. Douglas, Editor (Grand Rapids: William B. Eerdmans Publishing Company), "Names of God," p. 480. Consult other Bible dictionaries and Bible encyclopedias.

2. *Old Testament Theology* (New York: Harper & Row, 1965), Vol. II, pp. 283 ff.

3. Zech. 3:8; 6:12; 9:9, 10; 11:12, 13; 12:10; 13:7; 14:8.

4. Mt. 11:27; 28:18; Jn. 13:3; Acts 2:33-36; 1 Cor. 15:25; Eph. 1:20-23; Phil. 2:9-11.

5. The exegetical difficulties involved in Matthew's quotation from Zechariah seem to be almost insurmountable. A discussion of these points lies beyond my purpose. The reader should consult commentaries on "Zechariah" and "Matthew." From a number of points of view careful study of this problem is very rewarding.

6. Zech. 2:11; 3:10; 9:16; 12:3, 4, 6, 8, 9, 11; 13:1, 2, 4.

7. 2 Cor. 1:14; Phil. 1:6, 10; 2 Thess. 2:2.

8. Hag. 1:9, 10; 2:6, 7, 15-19, 21, 22.

9. Zech. 1:17; 2:12; 3:2; 8:13, 20-23; 9:9-17; 10:6-12.

CHAPTER I
THEOLOGY OF THE PSALMS

1. Introduction

The Psalms was the songbook of Israel. It had its beginning in the days of David, the sweet psalmist of Israel (2 Sam. 23:1). While authorship of the Psalms presents some difficult problems, we may note that at least seventy-three were attributed to David. These psalms and some others of David's time represented the first songbook of Israel. It declared the profound truth that Israel was involving herself very significantly in worship through singing. At least from the time of Moses the people of Israel sang songs of praise to the Lord (Ex. 15:1-18). One of the first and most overwhelming thoughts which come to our minds in reading the Psalms is their exceedingly rich spiritual content, which forms the basis of worship. The Psalms expressed adoration, praise, prayer, and other elements of worship.

Probing more deeply into their content, we discover the wealth of theological truths embedded in these psalms. First of all, they are God-centered. Man's approach to God is very essential for our understanding of the nature of worship. Other prominent themes include God's covenant relation with man, the Messiah and His work, judgment, redemption, salvation, the Holy Spirit, holy living, sin, forgiveness, faith, life renewal, the future life, Satan, and man's nature. A look at these themes leads us to conclude with Martin Luther that the Psalter is a Bible in miniature.

The foregoing facets pose some difficult problems encountered in a biblical theology approach to the Psalms. The fact that there are one hundred and fifty different units in the collection complicates the task of presenting a brief but comprehensive treatment of God's revelation through the Psalms. Since the general content of the Psalms has to do with worship, I shall present first of all a number of theological aspects of worship. This assumes that it is entirely legitimate to think in terms of the theology of worship. In the presentation of these aspects I am leaning quite heavily on headings borrowed from other studies of the Psalms that have almost become common property. Following this discussion I shall pursue the general pattern of theological headings as found in Parts I and II of this work. I have been amazed to discover the abundance of rich teachings which stand out in practically all of these divisions. We may observe that the psalmists were not formally setting forth theological ideas but were almost spontaneously disclosing these rich truths in a worship setting.

2. Theological Aspects of Worship

a. *The Soul's Thirst for God (42, 43, 63, 84)*

Psalms 42 and 43, which constitute one poem, express the soul's longing for God: "As a hart longs for flowing streams, so longs my soul for thee, O God." This presents one of the deepest spiritual experiences in the life of a man of God. The three stanzas of this hymn have a common refrain in which the psalmist chides himself for being cast down. In a firm personal resolution he speaks to himself, "Hope in God; for I shall again praise him, my help and my God." Psalm 63 declares that the soul's thirst for God finds full satisfaction in God's steadfast love. The psalmist (84) observed the blessedness of those whose strength is in God: "They go from strength to strength." He experienced the reality of the Lord God as being a sun and shield and as the One who does not withhold any good thing from those who walk uprightly. He could conclude, "Blessed is the man who trusts in thee!"

b. *Praise and Thanksgiving (34, 95, 103, 105, 106, 107, 136, 145-150)*

One of the largest groups of psalms expresses praise and thanksgiving to God. A hymn of praise renders homage to God in worship and thanksgiving. Many of these psalms express praise to God for His work of creation, redemption, and salvation. In one of David's crises he responded with a hymn of praise (34) in which he expressed joy because of the Lord's care and protection, for the Lord had saved him out of all his trouble. The psalmist (95) expressed himself, "O come, let us sing to the Lord; let us make a joyful noise to the rock of our salvation!" His invocation continued, "O come, let us worship and bow down, let us kneel before the Lord, our Maker! For he is our God, and we are the people of his pasture, and the sheep of his hand." Let us observe that this song leads to humble worship and to a recognition of being sheep of God's hand.

In Psalm 103 David recognized that his entire being needed to be involved in blessing the Lord. In doing this he revealed some of the great blessings from God as the One who forgives iniquity, heals diseases, redeems one's life from the Pit, crowns us with steadfast love and mercy, and satisfies us with good as long as we live. In a word, one's youth is renewed like the eagle's. In addition to these reasons for blessing the Lord, David noted that He is merciful and gracious, slow to anger, and abounding in steadfast love. As David continued to reflect on all that the Lord does for His people, he closed the psalm bidding the angels, His ministers, all His works, and finally his own soul to bless the Lord.

In three of these psalms (105, 106, 136) the writers drew from Israel's history most significant reasons for giving thanks to the Lord. The first of these psalms directed special attention to their earliest history — the call of Abraham, the deliverance from Egypt through the mighty plagues brought upon the Egyptians, and their wilderness wanderings. In all these experiences, whether of deliverance or discipline, the psalmist could close with a note of praise to the Lord. He began with the creation and continued with Israel's experiences in the wilderness, noting many of the events of Israel's history which came to pass through the Lord's direct intervention. After presenting each act of God the psalmist added, "For his steadfast love endures for ever." It is very noteworthy that the last six psalms of the Psalter are definitely songs of praise. Twelve times in Psalm 148 the psalmist called on various parts of God's creation, including all the heavenly host, sun, moon, and stars; sea and land animals; and all people — in a word, all of God's creation — to praise the Lord. Only Deity is worthy of praise and thanksgiving such as described in these psalms.

c. Singing Praises to the Exalted and Enthroned Lord (47, 68, 93, 96, 99)

In Psalm 47 the writer strikes the keynote when he says, "Sing praises to God. . . . Sing praises to our King." God is the King of all the earth; He reigns over the nations; He is highly exalted; He sits on His holy throne. Here we see kingship raised to Deity level. David pictured (68) the solemn processions of the worshipers going into the sanctuary. God, the King, met with the great congregation in their worship. All Israel had the privilege of enjoying fellowship with God, their King. The psalmist noted the majesty of the reigning Lord (93, 96). They would ascribe the glory and strength due to His name. The people were to "Worship the Lord in holy array; tremble before him, all the earth!" In the exercise of His kingship He would "judge the world with righteousness, and the peoples with his truth." There was need then for God's people to bring into close relationship their worship of the King and the fact that it is He who will judge the world. But this judgment will be with righteousness and with truth. The writer of Psalm 99 stressed the holiness of God alongside His kingship. Extolling the Lord and worshiping at His footstool are most appropriate because the Lord is holy.

d. Prayer to the Lord (27, 141, 142, 143)

When David encountered evildoers, adversaries, and foes (27), he knew which way to turn for help. To dwell in the house of the Lord and to behold the beauty of the Lord built up his courage. He knew that the Lord would hear his cries and be gracious to him. Herein are the elements of prayer. Crying to God for help and unburdening one's heart before the Lord are most appropriate. On this account he could say, "Wait for the Lord; be strong, and let your heart take courage; yea, wait for the Lord!" It was David's privilege (141) to believe that his prayer would be counted as incense before the Lord, and the lifting up of his hands as an evening sacrifice. Since prayer moves on this high level, it shows most clearly the supreme place of the prayer aspect of worship. David's prayer life again comes to our attention (142) when he said, "I cry to thee, O Lord; I say, Thou art my refuge. . . . Give heed to my cry. . . . Deliver me from my persecutors. . . . The righteous will surround me; for thou wilt deal bountifully with me." These prayer privileges of David enabled him to say (143), "I stretch out my hands to thee; my soul thirsts for thee like a parched land."

e. Joy of Worship (33, 34, 84, 122)

The psalmist (33) wrote, "Rejoice in the Lord, O you righteous! Praise befits the upright." In expressing the joy of worship he would have praise to be given with instruments, and the people to sing a new song. With the continuing revelation of God to His people and their enriching of fellowship with Him, a new song could certainly be sung. It would reflect God's love for righteousness and justice. It would be enriched by further disclosures of God's acts of creation. David could sing praises (34) because the Lord delivered him from all his fears and saved him from all his troubles. Here then are contributing factors to the joy of worship. The sons of Korah (84) expressed their worship in relation to God's house. The writer said, "My soul longs, yea, faints for the courts of the Lord; my heart and flesh sing for joy to the living God." This experiential description of the inner joy of worship found expression again in the declaration: "For a day in thy courts is better than a thousand elsewhere. I would rather be a doorkeeper in the house of my God than dwell in the tents of wickedness. For the Lord God is a sun and shield; he bestows favor and honor. No good thing does the Lord withhold from those who walk uprightly. O Lord of hosts, blessed is the man who trusts in thee!" One of David's Songs of Ascents (122) expressed his joy in the words, "I was glad when they said to me, 'Let us go to the house of the Lord!' "

f. Living in the Presence of God (23, 46, 91, 139)

David the shepherd boy (23) was best fitted to make an analogy between the life of sheep in the presence of the shepherd and his own living in the presence of God. The sheep were always in the presence of the shepherd. In all the varied experiences of the sheep, whether lying down for rest, going to the stream for water, passing from one pasture field to another through dangerous mountain paths, going to a new pasture within sight of ravenous beasts, or at nightfall receiving the cup of soothing oil on their heads, we see phases of life with the shepherd. David's own experience with the Lord enabled him to move from life with the shepherd to his own personal life with the Lord. There was no situation in which he was away from the Lord's care and protection. Out of real experience he could write, "Surely goodness and mercy shall follow me all the days of my life; and I shall dwell in the house of the Lord for ever." The entire psalm is a sublime picture of a believer's living constantly in the presence of God, an experience extending into eternity.

Another psalmist could write (46), "God is our refuge and strength, a very present help in trouble." Regardless of what might happen in one's life, full confidence could be placed in these words. The Lord would tell us, "Be still, and know that I am God." The author of Psalm 91 could say, "He who dwells in the shelter of the Most High, who abides in the shadow of the Almighty, will say to the Lord, 'My refuge and my fortress; my God, in whom I trust.' " This statement is almost unexcelled in its description of the spiritual privilege of the one who lives in the presence of the Lord. To such He would answer, "Because he cleaves to me in love, I will deliver him; I will protect him, because he knows my name. When he calls to me, I will answer him; I will be with him in trouble, I will rescue him and honor him. With long life I will satisfy him, and show him my salvation." David was aware, nevertheless (139), that the unspeakable privilege of living in the presence of God would necessitate the most thorough heart searching. Out of his personal experience he wrote, "O Lord, thou hast searched

me and known me! Thou knowest when I sit down and when I rise
up; thou discernest my thoughts from afar." Being always in the
presence of God was not only a stimulus to live a holy life but it was
also a most precious experience. He could say, "How precious to me
are thy thoughts, O God! How vast is the sum of them! If I would
count them, they are more than the sand. When I awake, I am still
with thee." In view of all the wickedness about him, he could pray,
"Search me, O God, and know my heart! Try me and know my
thoughts! And see if there be any wicked way in me, and lead me in the
way everlasting!" Perhaps this final section, "Living in the Presence
of God," is the profoundest theological approach to worship. To the
full realization of this experience all the other aspects lead.

3. The God of Israel

a. The Sovereign Majesty of God Most High

As we move into consideration of the doctrinal content of the
Psalms, we should remind ourselves that all of these doctrinal expressions spring from contexts of worship. The severe space limitations
of this discussion restrict the number of psalms reviewed under each
doctrinal heading. Psalm 24, a psalm of David, gives a splendid introduction to the sovereign majesty of God. Stately are the words, "Who
is the King of glory? The Lord, strong and mighty, the Lord, mighty
in battle! Lift up your heads, O gates! and be lifted up, O ancient
doors! that the King of glory may come in! Who is this King of glory?
The Lord of hosts, he is the King of glory!" As David, a man after
the heart of God pondered his own glory as king of Israel, the Spirit
empowered him to envision the infinitely more majestic King of glory,
the Lord. Looking at Psalm 47, we note that the psalmist recognized
the Lord, the Most High, as being the King of all the earth. He
reigns over the nations and sits on His holy throne. The name "Most
High" connotes the dignity, supremacy, and exaltation of the Lord.

The psalmist wrote (74), "God my King is from of old, working salvation in the midst of the earth. Thou didst divide the sea by thy might;
thou didst break the heads of the dragons on the waters." Here he
noted that God's sovereignty extended from the eternal past to eternity
of the future. He was active in the world over which He ruled and had
regard for His covenant. Thus His faithfulness to covenant relationship
was the mark of His sovereign majesty. Another psalm (89) described
God's sovereign majesty in the words, "Righteousness and justice are the
foundation of thy throne; steadfast love and faithfulness go before thee."
Let us observe that God's rule possessed the qualities which alone de-

scribe the exalted dignity and grandeur of His sovereign majesty. The author of Psalm 95 added the proper human response of recognizing the Lord as the great king above all gods when he said, "O come, let us worship and bow down, let us kneel before the Lord, our Maker!" So the devout response of a godly man in the presence of the Lord, the King, is to bow down and worship Him.

b. The Holiness and Righteousness of God

Observe again that the holiness and righteousness of God are brought together very frequently throughout the Scriptures. This obtains in the Psalms. The close relationship of these attributes in the nature of God deserves continued study. Note again that the root idea of holiness is separation. God is separate from all that is sinful and evil. It stands for the central ethical quality of His being, representing His purity and moral excellence. All of God's attributes center in the holiness of His nature. Righteousness has to do with that aspect of God's nature which, according to His holiness, expresses itself in right action. Hence all of God's acts are righteous and just. This idea bears close relationship to God as Judge. He judges righteously. Justice allows no compromise with unfair decisions. Let us note how these two attributes of God stand in such close relationship in the Psalms. When David was pursued by his enemies (17), he took refuge in God. He had the concern that the Lord would recognize his righteousness and integrity. Knowing that the Lord tries the minds and the hearts, David could confidently entrust himself to the righteous God, who, in accordance with His nature, is a righteous judge. From his heart David said, "I will give to the Lord the thanks due to his righteousness, and I will sing praise to the name of the Lord, the Most High." In his mind the attribute of righteousness was most characteristic of the Lord, the Most High.

In another experience (11) David took refuge in the Lord, for he knew that the Lord is in His holy temple, and His throne is in heaven. Accordingly the Lord tests the righteous and the wicked. He was able to commit himself to the Lord, "For the Lord is righteous, he loves righteous deeds; the upright shall behold his face." In this experience he expressed his full confidence that the righteous Lord has regard for the upright. In the midst of Psalm 30, where David was extolling the Lord, he invited the saints to praise the Lord and to give thanks to His holy name. The saints were God's holy people. Therefore only saints could give genuine thanks to God's holy name. David had laid hold of the truth that God's people should be holy, even as He is holy.

A psalm of Asaph (50) noted how the Mighty One, God, the Lord, spoke to all mankind. Out of Zion, the perfection of beauty, God shone forth. He would judge His people. He said, "Gather to me my faithful ones, who made a covenant with me by sacrifice!" The psalmist then added, "The heavens declare his righteousness, for God himself is judge!" The point of significance to be observed here is the bearing of God's righteous judgment upon His covenant people. Israel had committed themselves through this covenant to be obedient to the Lord, their judge. Looking at another great psalm of praise (96) we observe the command, "Worship the Lord in holy array; tremble before him, all the earth!" The psalmist noted that the Lord reigns and that He will judge the people with equity. All creation will sing for joy before the Lord, "for he comes to judge the earth. He will judge the world with righteousness, and the peoples with his truth." Righteousness and truth are synonymous in expressing God's nature. The following psalm (97) speaks again of the reigning Lord. The psalmist said, "Righteousness and justice are the foundation of his throne." In a beautiful figure he added, "The heavens proclaim his righteousness; and all the peoples behold his glory." He closed the psalm with the words, "Rejoice in the Lord, O you righteous, and give thanks to his holy name!"

We should observe how frequently the psalmists described the Lord's kingly work. Most confidently they associate righteousness and justice with His rule. Consequently the righteous may, indeed, rejoice in the Lord and give thanks to His holy name. Still another psalm (99) speaks of the reigning Lord. This is a very rich expression of these treasured attributes of God. Note the words, "Holy is he! Mighty King, lover of justice, thou hast established equity; thou hast executed justice and righteousness in Jacob." The psalm closes, "Extol the Lord our God, and worship at his holy mountain; for the Lord our God is holy!" Note again the intertwining of holiness, justice, equity, and righteousness. On this account worship is the most appropriate response on the part of the Lord's people. Since holiness, as related to God, is so significant, note some other uses of the words "holy" and "holiness" (20:3; 60:6; 89:35; 108:7).

c. *The God of Love and Mercy*

It may shock the reader to learn that only twice in the Book of Psalms is the Hebrew word *aheb* (to love) used with reference to God's love for man, but these examples are very precious. The first one reads: "He chose our heritage for us, the pride of Jacob whom he loves" (47: 4). Undoubtedly this meant a great deal to the people of Israel. The other reads: "The Lord loves the righteous" (146:8). Every faithful Israelite certainly treasured this brief but expressive statement. Many uses of the word "love" in the Psalms give support to its rich meaning. According to F. H. Palmer, "In the Old Testament, love, whether human or divine, is the deepest possible expression of the personality and of the closeness of personal relations."[1]

On the other hand, the word *chesed* (mercy) is found many times in the Psalms and is, on this account, heavily weighted with meaning. With Psalm 136 before us it is interesting to observe how various English translators have sought to capture the meaning of this word. They have rendered it by such words and phrases as love, grace, mercy, steadfast love, kindness, covenant love, and loving-kindness. This word stands very expressively for covenant love, as in 89:28, "My steadfast love I will keep for him for ever, and my covenant will stand firm for him." When David repented of his grievous sin, he said, "Have mercy on me, O God, according to thy steadfast love; according to thy abundant mercy blot out my transgressions. Wash me thoroughly from my iniquity, and cleanse me from my sin" (51:1, 2)! Here the word is surcharged with meaning because it expresses God's attitude toward a penitent sinner. Only through steadfast love, which most abundantly flowed out to David, could there have been a blotting out of his transgressions and the inner cleansing from his iniquity.

In David's cry of distress (69), when he was experiencing insults from the enemies of God, he could pray, "But as for me, my prayer is to thee, O Lord. At an acceptable time, O God, in the abundance of thy steadfast love answer me. . . . Answer me, O Lord, for thy steadfast love is good; according to thy abundant mercy, turn to me. Hide not thy face from thy servant; for I am in distress, make haste to answer me." This illustration serves to show how God's steadfast love expressed itself in David's trying experience. Taking another look at Psalm 89, we observe Ethan's words, "I will sing of thy steadfast love, O Lord, for ever; with my mouth I will proclaim thy faithfulness to all generations. For thy steadfast love was established for ever, thy faithfulness is firm as the heavens." Later we read, "Righteousness and justice are the foundation of thy throne; steadfast love and faithfulness go before thee." And finally, "My faithfulness and my steadfast love shall be with him, and in my name shall his horn be exalted." In this setting the psalmist clearly brought together the close relation between God's steadfast love and His covenant with Israel. Note also how the psalmist expressed God's faithfulness, righteousness, and justice, by an integral relation with steadfast love. The most glorious presentation of the ever enduring quality of God's steadfast love shines forth in Psalm 136. Here he brings into view God's mighty acts manifested in the Creation, His deliverance of Israel out of Egypt, and His giving them the land of Canaan. In response to each of these great manifestations of what the Lord did for Israel, the psalmist responded, "For his steadfast love endures for ever."

d. The Goodness of God

Good (*tob*) is an example of a word gaining unlimited significance when it is used of God. It carries the meaning of pleasant, joyful, agreeable, and signifies primarily "that which gratifies the senses and derivatively that which gives aesthetic or moral satisfaction."[2] Such astute expressions as "the Lord is good" (34:8) give to the word the most profound meaning. As R. Mehl says, "We must say of The Good what St. Augustine declares concerning Eternity. There is no analytical relation between the essence of God and The Good. But, God Himself is The Good and this term has no assignable sense except in God. Good has no existence outside of God, and God does not consider Good as an external and objective reality. For God there is no norm of The Good. And so man has no chance of knowing The Good except by reference to the will of God: What God wills, that is The Good."[3] With this explanation in mind note David's prayer (25:7, 8) that the Lord should not remember the sins of his youth but according to His steadfast love should remember him. The basis for this plea is, "For thy goodness' sake, O Lord!" and then he declares, "Good and upright is the Lord." Observe how David spoke of the goodness of God in relation to his former sins. It was manifested through His steadfast love, for the Lord is at once good and upright. These words are complementary. On another occasion of real danger, David could say, "The angel of the Lord encamps around those who fear him, and delivers them. O taste and see that the Lord is good! Happy is the man who takes refuge in him" (34:7, 8)!

The realization of the Lord's goodness was definitely experiential with David. He realized the protecting care of the Lord. David enriched the meaning of *good* still further in his prayer, "For thou, O Lord, art good and forgiving, abounding in steadfast love to all who call on thee" (86:5). Thus the Lord who is good forgives. This is possible because He abounds in steadfast love. Still another facet of God's goodness comes in these words, "Teach me good judgment and knowledge, for I believe in thy commandments. . . . Thou art good and doest good; teach me thy statutes" (119:66, 68). This suggests that goodness permeates two important aspects of personality, namely, judgment and knowledge. Very naturally the one who is good will do good. Goodness is not an abstract attribute of personality, for by its very nature it reaches outward in the expression of doing good. With full recognition that God is good, David recognized that the Spirit of God is good also. On this account he sought the leading of the Spirit (143:10). David's last reference to the goodness of God appears in the statement, "The Lord is gracious and merciful, slow to anger and abounding in steadfast love. The Lord is good to all, and his compassion is over all that he has made" (145:8, 9). These interrelations of the goodness of God raise its meaning to the highest conceivable level.

e. The God of Judgment

Because so many psalms speak of God as being a righteous judge (7: 11; 50:6; 99:4) it would have been consistent to combine these two sections. My concern in section *b.* was to look at God's holiness and righteousness as they pertain to His attributes and to note their clear interrelation. My purpose in giving separate consideration to the God of judgment is to see God in His great acts of judging. It is consistent then to consider the relation between God's righteousness and His being judge. David lived in a time when many injustices were suffered by God's people. Throughout the preceding centuries Israel had rejected God's rule. As a result, lawlessness reigned in the land.

It was this condition that David reflected (7) when he recognized that the Lord God was the righteous Judge even though He did not appear to be exercising His judgeship in the world. This psalm teaches, nevertheless, that God had appointed a judgment in which the wicked would receive their just dues, and the righteous would be vindicated. Undoubtedly the wicked were exercising certain restraints in their evil doings as the result of an inner recognition that some time they would stand before God, the righteous Judge. We do not know whether this psalm was ever sung in the presence of the wicked, but apparently David's enemies knew that if they did not repent, the inflicting of righteous judgment upon them would be the most terrible ordeal (7:12-16). This shows that God, the righteous Judge, is also God who has indignation every day. God manifests His righteousness most pointedly in the circumstances of man's gross wickedness.

In another of David's psalms (9) he speaks of God's judging the world with righteousness and with equity. The Hebrew word *yashar* carries the ideas of straightness, uprightness, rightness, and equity. We should also observe that the Lord established His throne for judgment. This is the declared purpose of His rule. We gain another very important idea in that the judgment coming upon the wicked condemns them to Sheol. This is one of the leading Old Testament passages which underlies the New Testament unfolding of this truth. Asaph sang of a time in which God will judge with equity (75). In the imagery of a tottering earth, God spoke of keeping its pillars steady. Evidently Asaph was describing man's wickedness in terms of making the earth go to pieces. In this setting he says, "It is God who executes judgment, putting down one and lifting up another."

Using another figure, Asaph spoke of God's pouring foaming water which the wicked would need to drink down to the dregs. This is another graphic way of describing the outpourings of God's wrath in His judgment. He concludes, "All the horns of the wicked he will cut off, but the horns of the righteous shall be exalted." In these figures the equity of God's judgment becomes very clear. In another joyous psalm (96) God's people are bidden to ascribe glory to the Lord. The reason for this call to worship lies in the fact that "The Lord reigns! Yea, the world is established, it shall never be moved; he will judge the peoples with equity." This psalm of joy closes with the words, "For he comes, for he comes to judge the earth. He will judge the world with righteousness, and the peoples with his truth." In this context equity and truth are linked with righteousness as characterizing God's judgment of the world.

f. The God of Creation

As we might expect, this book of worship makes many references to the Creation. The occasions are quite similar to what we find throughout the Old Testament. Many of them are casual allusions to the Creation brought in to magnify the manifold activities of God or to support some important aspect of His nature. Following are some illustrations: "Know that the Lord is God! It is he that made us, and we are his; we are his people, and the sheep of his pasture" (100:3). "May you be blessed by the Lord, who made heaven and earth" (115:15)! "Thy faithfulness endures to all generations; thou hast established the earth, and it stands fast" (119:90). "My help comes from the Lord, who made heaven and earth" (121:2). "Our help is in the name of the Lord, who made heaven and earth" (124:8). "May the Lord bless you from Zion, he who made heaven and earth" (134:3)! "Happy is he whose help is the God of Jacob, whose hope is in the Lord his God, who made heaven and earth, the sea, and all that is in them; who keeps faith for ever; who executes justice for the oppressed; who gives food to the hungry" (146:5-7). In all these examples hardly any details of God's creative work are mentioned. It is the fact of creation which overawed the psalmists.

Let us examine the extensive vocabulary used for describing God's acts of creation. Note the following words, to which I have attached a few examples: create (bara, 89:12; 104:30); formed (yatsar, 90:2); establish (kun, 24:2; 65:6; 93:1; 96:10); make (asah, 95:5; 104:24; 146:6); to found (yasad, 24:1, 2; 78:69; 102:25).

Let us take a hurried look at several psalms in which the writers enlarged to some extent on the idea of the Creation. As David exclaimed, "O Lord, our Lord, how majestic is thy name in all the earth!" (8), he looked to the heavens and saw the moon and the stars which the Lord had established. He then turned his thought to man and marveled that God would be mindful of a being so small as compared to the wonders of the heavenly bodies. But then he observed that the Lord had made him little less than God and crowned him with glory and honor, giving him dominion over all of God's creation. The impact of this meditation on David is seen in the closing line: "O Lord, our Lord, how majestic is thy name in all the earth!" Inspired by the glories of God's creation David sang, "The heavens are telling the glory of God; and the firmament proclaims his handiwork" (19). David allowed his imagination to picture the glories declared by the heavens. He saw the skies as a great tent in which the sun comes forth in all of its glory; its rising and its circuit extend through the expanse of this great tent. This poetic description of the heavens should inspire all of us as we reflect on the twentieth-century knowledge of astronomy.

Psalm 104 sets forth at greatest length the glories of God's creation. All of His activities stand out in simple details as though He were a human artificer. We see the Lord covering Himself with light as with a garment, stretching out the heavens like a tent, laying the beams of His chambers on the waters, making clouds His chariot, and riding on the wings of the wind. All these are acts which to us are most astounding and as some human beings would say, unbelievable. The number of the creative acts mentioned in this psalm fill us with amazement. Such relatively insignificant things as the forming of valleys, making springs gush forth in the valleys, supplying water for man and beasts, the singing of the birds among the branches of the trees, the grass growing for the cattle, plants for man to cultivate, the high mountains for the wild goats, the rocks a refuge for the badgers — all these show that the psalmist related God's creative work to the manifold details of animal and plant life, and to man who goes forth to his work and to his labor until the evening. Perhaps the most significant statement in this psalm is the reference to God's sending forth His Spirit through whom all these creative acts are performed. All this should lead us to worship in the spirit of the psalmist as he expressed himself in the words of verses 33 and 35: "I will sing to the Lord as long as I live; I will sing praise to my God while I have being. . . . Bless the Lord, O my soul! Praise the Lord!"

Taking another look at Psalm 136, let us observe the thrice-repeated request, "O give thanks to the Lord," which leads to the psalmist's observation that it is the Lord alone who does great wonders. Only five details of God's creative work are given. They have to do with the making of the heavens, the spreading out of the earth upon the waters, and the making of the great lights: the sun, moon, and stars. At once we become inquisitive as to why these five creative acts were chosen and no mention is made of life — neither plants nor animals, nor most of all, man. The historical details of the remainder of the psalm have to do chiefly with miraculous acts of God in Israel's history. Whatever may have been the reason, it is very evident that the details just given were physically the greatest among God's creative acts.

Psalm 148, which gives some details of the Creation, is preeminently a song of praise. It is the psalmist's desire that all creation will praise Him. He then specifies the sun, moon, and stars, representing the highest heavens, and the waters above the heavens — all these He established for ever and ever and fixed their bounds, which cannot be passed. This last expression gives recognition to the fixed laws which control the heavenly bodies. The psalmist then looks to the earth, specifying sea monsters, fire and hail, snow and frost, stormy wind, mountains and hills, fir trees and cedars, beasts and cattle, creeping things and flying birds, and finally human beings, including kings and princes, young men and maidens, old men and children. It is significant that all these references to the Creation occur in contexts centering in worship.

g. The God of History

The study of biblical theology makes us keenly aware that all through the Old Testament the writers represented God as directing the course of history. It may not be too much to state that the Book of Psalms climactically sets forth this great truth. Since this book had its focus in Israel's worship, we may anticipate gaining some of the deepest insights as to the meaning of these acts of God. Beginning with Psalm 18, which was penned by David when the Lord delivered him from his enemies, including Saul, we may observe the aspect of divine providence in these acts of God. In fact, these two expressions are practically synonymous. Divine providence is a theological expression of long standing, while the idea of God's acting in history is of more recent origin, having its basis in an attempt to give a Christian interpretation of world history. We could hardly give a better formal definition of divine providence than in the words, "The Lord is my rock, and my fortress, and my deliverer, my God, my rock, in whom I take refuge, my shield, and the horn of my salvation, my stronghold." Throughout this psalm we note a number of expressions which reveal God's providential actions in this particular experience of David. Outstanding among these are his words, "In my distress I called upon the Lord; to my God I cried for help. From his temple he heard my voice and my cry to him reached his ears." Following this (vv. 7-19) David described in highly poetic figures how the Lord delivered him from his strong enemy. David noted that this manifestation of God's providence was on account of his own blameless life (vv. 20-24). An insight of what lies back of God's providence becomes clear in the words, "With the loyal thou dost show thyself loyal; with the blameless man thou dost show thyself blameless; with the pure thou dost show thyself pure; and with the crooked thou dost show thyself perverse. For thou dost deliver a humble people; but the haughty eyes thou dost bring down." The remainder of the psalm gives more details of God's providential care of David.

Psalm 44 presents an instructive picture of God's actions in Israel's history. It is especially valuable as we note the writer's wrestlings with regard to Israel's experience in his own time. He gleaned from their traditions what God had done in driving out the nations of Canaan and had ordained victories for the nation of Israel. Unfortunately the psalmist had not yet understood the meaning of the defeats which Israel was then experiencing. They had become the taunt of their neighbors and a laughingstock among surrounding nations. What perplexed him still more was the fact that Israel had been true to their covenant with the Lord and their hearts had not turned back from the ways of the Lord. He lamented thus: "For thy sake we are slain all the day long, and accounted as sheep for the slaughter." He called on the Lord to rouse Himself and come to their help for the sake of His steadfast love. This psalm leads us to see that in times of life's most trying experiences, we may fail to bear in mind that God has not fallen asleep but that He is accomplishing purposes in the affairs of men, though we may not be aware of their meaning. In sharp contrast with this is Psalm 47, in which the writer testified to God's subduing Israel's foes and choosing their heritage. The psalmist is confident that God is the king of all the earth and reigns over the nations.

Asaph gave a lengthy account of God's acts in Israel's checkered history (78). He would have the coming generation learn of the Lord's glorious deeds and the wonders which He had wrought. Because of Ephraim's failure to keep God's covenant in spite of all that the Lord had done for them, Judah was chosen as the nation in whose land He would build His sanctuary. The Lord had set up David on His throne, a man of the tribe of Judah and not of Ephraim. The psalmist certainly was drawing great spiritual lessons from the Lord's direction of Israel's history.

The writer of Psalm 105 gives another recital of Israel's history in which God's guidance and providential acts had become very meaningful.

The psalm overflows with thanksgiving for the many occasions in which God intervened. He begins with the Lord's covenant with Abraham and shows the outworking of God's promises in Israel's gaining possession of Canaan. This is one grand example of promise and fulfillment on the part of God. Psalm 136 gives another testimony of thanks to the Lord and reflects significant acts of God manifested in Israel's wilderness experience. After naming each of these acts of divine power, the psalmist proclaims his testimony in the statement: "for his steadfast love endures for ever." While these two psalms have much in common, the latter uses every example of God's saving work that he takes up as the reason for giving witness to God's steadfast love. All of these psalms show how the Lord through these supernatural deeds was revealing Himself to His people.

4. God's Spoken and Written Word

One of the most inspiring phenomena of the psalms becomes evident in the frequent references to the law. This is especially true in 19 and 119. It is important to see what bearing these references have upon the significance of God's Word, and ultimately upon the distinctive character of the written Word. These references to the law become the groundwork for our understanding the New Testament expressions, "It is written" and "the holy scriptures." As we read 19:7-9 we become aware of a set of practically synonymous words: law, testimony, precepts, commandments, fear, and ordinances. This feature becomes apparent also in 119. There is little need for making a study of each word because no problem attaches to their respective meanings. It is more essential for us to observe how the psalmist attached spiritual significance to the law. First of all, we should observe that the law is perfect, sure, right, pure, clean, true, and righteous. Then we should seek to understand the spiritual impact of the law of the Lord in reviving the soul, making wise the simple, rejoicing the heart, and enlightening the eyes.

Psalm 119 also sets forth some of the practical aspects of the law as it has to do with one's manner of life. The psalmist declares, "Blessed are those who keep his testimonies, who seek him with their whole heart, who also do no wrong, but walk in his ways!" Further on he asks a pointed question and answers it: "How can a young man keep his way pure? By guarding it according to thy word." And he declares, "I have laid up thy word in my heart, that I might not sin against thee." Nowhere else in all literature do we find this twofold aspect of God's law. On this account God's people came to regard His Word most highly. It is the thought embedded in the word "holy" in the expression "the holy scriptures," in the word "sacred" and in "the sacred writings." On this account Paul could conclude, "All scripture is inspired by God and profitable for teaching, for reproof, for correction, and for training in righteousness, that the man of God may be complete, equipped for every good work" (2 Tim. 3:15-17). These words almost serve as a paraphrase of Psalm 19:7-9, as well as of the corresponding expressions in 119.

5. Israel's Election Actualized by Covenant Relation with God

It is very natural to expect that the Book of Psalms would give special attention to the covenant relation. Several psalms lay hold of God's choosing Israel (33:12; 105:6, 43; 106:5; 135:4). Most expressive is the last reference, "For the Lord has chosen Jacob for himself, Israel as his own possession." From these references we gain the idea that Israel through the years treasured this close relationship with the Lord. Hence there are a dozen or more references to the Mosaic covenant (25:10, 14; 50:5; 74:20; 78:10; 103:18; 105:8-10). Perhaps the last reference captures the truth bound up in all the others. It reads, "He is mindful of his covenant for ever, of the word that he commanded, for a thousand generations, the covenant which he made with Abraham, his sworn promise to Isaac, which he confirmed to Jacob as a statute, to Israel as an everlasting covenant." Let us observe the clear reference to the eternal aspect of the covenant and note that the Abrahamic covenant was essentially one with Israel's covenant at Sinai. The references to Israel's history extending from Abraham to Israel's entrance into the land of Canaan repeated the promise made to Abraham near the end of the psalm, thus showing that the entire psalm is covenant-centered. From this we may conclude that the people of Israel built their worship of God upon their covenant relationship.

6. The Day of the Lord -- Judgment

The expression "Day of the Lord" does not occur in this book. This would support the view that the earliest writing prophets were the first to speak of this Day. We do observe, however, that a number of the psalm writers speak of judgment (1:5; 7:6; 37:13; 69:24; 119:137). This becomes clear in the first psalm, where the writer declares that the wicked will not stand in judgment. The brevity of this prediction leaves some questions unanswered. For instance, when will this judgment take place? What will be the outcome of this judgment for the wicked? We need to hold these questions in mind as we consider other references to the judgment of the wicked. Note the words, "Pour out thy indignation upon them, and let thy burning anger overtake them." This is a grim picture of God's wrath. John quoted the speaker from the heavenly temple whose message referred to the psalmist's words, "Go and pour out on the earth the seven bowls of the wrath of God" (Rev. 16:1). Observe that an angel quoted another verse from the Psalms, when he said, "Yea, Lord God the Almighty, true and just are thy judgments" (Rev. 16:7; Ps. 119: 137)! If these psalms referring to a coming judgment of the wicked were written by David, we have here the foundational truth of the Judgment Day, forecast by the prophets and expanded in the New Testament.

7. The Messiah and His Work

a. Introduction

A number of problems encounter us at this point. For instance, what are the guidelines for determining what psalms are Messianic? In seeking to answer this question, another major problem is that of attempting to determine which psalms, if any, are clearly predictive of the Messiah. In answer to this question there are different opinions. My own judgment leads me to believe that Psalms 2, 22, 45, 72, and 110 clearly predict one to come who would fulfill the prophecy given by the prophet Nathan to David (2 Sam. 7:12-14). While Nathan's words to David had immediate fulfillment in Solomon, it seems evident that David had grounds for believing in their ultimate fulfillment in one who would be God's Son. Quoting God's words, Nathan said, "I will be his father, and he shall be my son." This becomes still more apparent if David wrote Psalms 22 and 110, and Solomon wrote Psalm 72.

In addition to these five psalms there are several others which are quoted in the New Testament as having some fulfillment in Christ. While it lies beyond the purpose of this study to delve at length into these references, I shall allude to some of them with the purpose of discovering what light they shed on the Messianic idea.

b. The Suffering Messiah

Both Peter and Paul quote a psalm of David as having been fulfilled in the death of Christ (Ps. 16:8-11; Acts 2:25-31; 13:35). In this psalm David is the speaker, but when Peter quoted this portion he said that David was speaking concerning Christ. Peter explained his quotation further by noting that the psalmist was not speaking about himself, that David had died and was buried in Jerusalem and therefore could not fulfill the prediction of not having his flesh see corruption. He noted further that David was a prophet and knew that God would set one of his descendants upon his throne. He foresaw and spoke of the resurrection of Christ. Paul made a similar explanation of this psalm, observing also that David had died and had seen corruption, but Christ whom God raised saw no corruption.

Psalm 22 stands out most impressively as the one predicting the suffering Messiah. The New Testament allusions to this psalm very effectively made clear its fulfillment in Christ's suffering (Mt. 27:35, 39, 43, 46; Heb. 2:12). Christ's agonizing cry on the cross, "My God, my God, why hast thou forsaken me?" expressed David's own cry. Apparently at some point in his life he too had an excruciating experience which brought forth these words. Matthew mentioned those who passed by the cross deriding Him and wagging their heads. It appears that Matthew consciously chose these words in order to reflect this psalm. When John stood by the cross and observed the soldiers apportioning Jesus' clothes, he heard their comment when they said of Jesus' tunic, "Let us not tear it, but cast lots for it to see whose it shall be." John wrote that this was to fulfill the Scripture. Since the verb "fulfill" occurs in a *hina* clause of purpose, the incident described here was David's own prediction of this event. It seems quite clear that the writer of Hebrews interpreted this psalm as being predictive of Christ when he noted that those whom Christ sanctified were brethren (v. 22; Heb. 2:11, 12).

It is quite noteworthy that Luke picked up Jesus' words on the cross, "Father, into thy hands I commit my spirit!" and also Stephen's words, "Lord Jesus, receive my spirit" (Ps. 31:5; Lk. 23:46; Acts 7:59). In neither case did Luke refer to the fulfillment of a prediction. The point of significance lies in the fact that it was Luke, the Gentile, and not Matthew, Mark, or John who picked up these words of Jesus which so definitely quoted David's cry to the Lord. John noted another statement of Jesus that fulfilled a portion of a psalm: "I know whom I have chosen; it is that the scripture may be fulfilled, 'He who ate my bread has lifted his heel against me' " (Jn. 13:18; Ps. 41:9). Observe that Jesus Himself noted the fulfillment of the Scripture in a *hina* purposive clause ("that the scripture may be fulfilled"), which tells us that David was again consciously making a prediction.

John noted yet another Davidic psalm, from which the disciples quoted when Jesus was cleansing the temple. They remembered that it was written, "Zeal for thy house will consume me" (Ps. 69:9; Jn. 2:17). It may be going too far to say that the disciples' expression, "It was written," revealed their idea that David had given these words as a prediction, but we should observe that the disciples so easily associated Jesus' act with David's words. When Jesus was encountering the questions of the chief priests and the elders, He said, "Have you never read in the scriptures: 'The very stone which the builders rejected has become the head of the corner; this was the Lord's doing, and it is marvelous in our eyes' " (Mt. 21:42; Ps. 118:22, 23)? The writer of this psalm apparently picked up an incident in the construction of the temple in which the builders rejected a stone which had been cut out for use in the temple. When they came to place the chief cornerstone, they could not find any cut out for this purpose. Then they discovered that this rejected stone had been designed to be the chief cornerstone. The lesson was obvious and Jesus forcefully let it be known that in rejecting Him the Jews were casting aside the chief cornerstone of God's spiritual temple. These words so impressed Peter that he repeated them on two occasions (Acts 4:10-12; 1 Pet. 2:4-7).

c. Rule of the Anointed One

Psalm 2 stands out as the most important Messianic psalm, because it gave birth to the title, "The Anointed One, the Messiah." The early church clearly recognized this as a Messianic psalm, for on the joyous occasion of Peter and John being released by the Jewish authorities, they said, "Sovereign Lord, who didst make the heaven and the earth and the sea and everything in them, who by the mouth of our father David, thy servant, didst say by the Holy Spirit," and proceeded then to quote Psalm 2:1, 2 (Acts 4:24-26). We should observe that the early church ascribed Psalm 2 to David. Further, they recognized the agency of the Holy Spirit, through whom David had written, and of supreme importance for our purpose was their identification of Jesus with this Anointed One. The most conclusive proof of this identification is the message of God spoken from heaven on the occasion of Jesus' baptism. He said, "This is my beloved Son, with whom I am well pleased." (See Ps. 2:7.) This witness was repeated by the voice from heaven at Jesus' transfiguration (Mt. 3:16, 17; 17:5). For other confirmations of this conclusion, note the witness of Paul, of the author of Hebrews, and of Peter (Acts 3:33; Heb. 1:5; 5:5; 2 Pet. 1:17). From the Book of Revelation we see three apocalyptic pictures of the Messianic reign (Rev. 2:26; 12:5; 19:15). While it lies beyond my purpose to explore the meaning of these disclosures, it suffices to say that they give final witness to the Messianic significance of this psalm.

Psalm 45 presents another glorious picture of the Anointed One. The full confirmation of this comes from the letter to the Hebrews, where the writer in quoting verses 4, 6, and 7, definitely identifies this One as the Son (Heb. 1:8, 9). Descriptive of this reign are the words, "In your majesty ride forth victoriously for the cause of truth and to defend the right. . . . Your divine throne endures for ever and ever. Your royal scepter is a scepter of equity; you love righteousness and hate wickedness. Therefore God, your God, has anointed you with the oil of gladness above your fellows." The elements that stand forth in special grandeur and significance are His majesty, His eternal reign, the scepter of equity, the love of righteousness, the hatred of wickedness, and finally, the anointing with the oil of gladness.

In language reflecting the Lord's coming from Sinai into the holy place, David spoke of the Messiah in the words, "Thou didst ascend the high mount, leading captives in thy train, and receiving gifts among men, even among the rebellious, that the Lord God may dwell there" (68:18). Paul laid hold of this majestic Messianic truth when he interpreted these words as describing our Lord's ascension to the right hand of God. He elaborated most meaningfully on the kind of gifts which the glorified Lord gave to the church: "His gifts were that some should be apostles, some prophets, some evangelists, some pastors and teachers" (Eph. 4:7-13). It is apparent that Peter picked up two additional Messianic strands, and by so doing added to the picture of the Messiah (89:3, 4; 132:11; Acts 2:30). From this we should learn that Peter made little distinction among Psalms 16, 89, and 132 as to their Messianic content.

Finally, Psalm 110 challenges our study. Perhaps the most meaningful declaration of Messianic kingship stands forth in the words, "Sit at my right hand, till I make your enemies your footstool" (110:1). The Messiah's sitting at the right hand of God declares the fact that He shares with the Lord in the exercise of His authority and power. The second half of the verse looks to the final overthrow of all the enemies of the Messiah. The New Testament confirmation of this Messianic rule and of Jesus' being this Messiah is positive and final. Jesus' own witness to this fact became clear when He noted that David, inspired by the Spirit, called his son, Lord, and quoted this verse as proof (Mt. 22:43-45). Jesus repeated this claim when He stood before Caiaphas, the high priest (Mt. 26:64). So evident was Jesus' claim to deity through quoting this verse, that His enemies at once accused Him of blasphemy. Peter also quoted it as the capsheaf to his sermon at Pentecost by which he showed that God had made Jesus both Lord and Christ (Acts 2:33-36). Paul repeatedly gave witness to Jesus' Messiahship on the basis of these words (1 Cor. 15:25; Eph. 1:20; Col. 3:1).

In like manner the author of Hebrews by quoting the words, "Thou art a priest for ever, after the order of Melchizedek," gave witness to the most significant truth that Jesus the Messiah is at once King and Priest (Heb. 1:3, 13; 10:12, 13; 12:2). Shining forth through Old Testament history from the time of Abraham onward, Melchizedek was a man who symbolized in himself ever continuing kingly-priestly responsibilities. Here again the author of Hebrews gave witness to this truth as being most gloriously fulfilled in Christ (Heb. 5:6-10; 6:20 — 7:17). Through the extended delineation of Christ's kingly-priestly work, after the order of Melchizedek, the author assured his readers that through Christ we have a better hope by which we draw near to God. This gave the surest foundation for our salvation as expressed in the words, "Where there is forgiveness of these, there is no longer any offering for sin" (Heb. 10:18).

8. Restoration, Redemption, and Salvation of Israel

a. Frequent Occurrences of Salvation Language

One of the amazing phenomena of the Psalms is the frequent appearances of six words almost synonymous in meaning but distinctive in connotation. These words are: restore (*shub*), redeem (*gaal*), salvation (*yeshuah*), deliver (*natsal*), and ransom (*padah, kopher*). While the words for salvation and deliverance occur most frequently, the total number of occurrences of these words, including the derivative forms, is approximately two hundred and twenty-five times. This frequent use obtains significance for these words and deserves careful study. A preliminary observation would show that Israel's deliverance out of Egypt was an experience which made a deep impression upon them. It was the most important event in their history and was referred to most frequently. Their deliverance was interpreted as a redemption and salvation. The nation of Israel from David onward was being involved in wars with other nations and their own society was not free from turmoil. Accordingly, the writers of the Psalms reflected their own experiences of deliverance by the hand of God. Men of God, such as David, began to attach a deeper meaning to these saving acts. They came to see that deliverance from sin was a saving act of God possessing far greater meaning than being saved from their enemies.

b. Psalms of Spiritual Restoration and Deliverance

As we examine a number of these psalms, let us observe that they had as their background innumerable cases of literal or physical deliverances from their enemies, in all of which they attributed their deliverances to God. In Psalm 40, where David was pouring out his heart to God in praise and thanksgiving, he said, "But may all who seek thee rejoice and be glad in thee; may those who love thy salvation say continually, 'Great is the Lord!' As for me, I am poor and needy; but the Lord takes thought for me. Thou art my help and my deliverer; do not tarry, O my God!" The great penitential psalm (51) overflows with an expression of spiritual experiences. Here David prayed that God would create in him a clean heart and put a new and right spirit within him. He was concerned that the Lord would not take the Holy Spirit from him. In such a context he wrote, "Restore to me the joy of thy salvation, and uphold me with a willing spirit. . . . Deliver me from bloodguiltiness, O God, thou God of my salvation, and my tongue will sing aloud of thy deliverance." In a true spirit of repentance he could say, "A broken and contrite heart, O God, thou wilt not despise." In such a setting David was certainly probing into the spiritual aspects of salvation and deliverance.

In another psalm (79) of rich spiritual content Asaph said, "Help us, O God of our salvation, for the glory of thy name; deliver us, and forgive our sins, for thy name's sake!" The prayer for forgiveness would surely suggest that thoughts associated with salvation and forgiveness are also spiritual in nature. In Psalm 80, three times Asaph said, "Restore us, O Lord God of hosts! let thy face shine, that we may be saved!" While a number of details of this psalm deal with temporal matters, this verse considered by itself is certainly very rich in spiritual implication. In Psalm 85, where the writer spoke of God's forgiveness and pardon of sins as well as of His steadfast love, righteousness, and peace, he told of God restoring the fortunes of Jacob. We cannot be too certain of the spiritual content of this last statement but later words seem to speak quite definitely of a spiritual restoration: "Show us thy steadfast love, O Lord, and grant us thy salvation. . . . Surely his salvation is at hand for those who fear him, that glory may dwell in our land."

The author of Psalm 95 broke forth in the joyous words, "O come, let us sing to the Lord; let us make a joyful noise to the rock of our salvation!" The spiritual connotation which the psalmist evidently attached to the expression, "the rock of our salvation," became still more apparent in the words, "O come, let us worship and bow down, let us kneel before the Lord, our Maker! For he is our God, and we are the people of his pasture, and the sheep of his hand." The psalmist (119) who could affirm so confidently that he kept God's commandments, testimonies, and precepts, was surely thinking of the spiritual aspect of salvation when he wrote of hoping for God's salvation, and at the same time could say, "I love . . . [thy testimonies] exceedingly" (119:165-168). The writer of Psalm 130 was crying to God out of the depths. He noted that the Lord forgives sin. He wrote, "O Israel, hope in the Lord! For with the Lord there is steadfast love, and with him is plenteous redemption. And he will redeem Israel from all his iniquities."

These psalms plus a number of others certainly reveal that it is the Lord who restores, redeems, saves, and delivers His people from sin. We cannot be sure that any of these references look beyond this life. Undoubtedly the clearest passage which anticipates life beyond the grave is in Psalm 49. Here the psalmist wrote, "Truly no man can ransom himself, or give to God the price of his life, for the ransom of his life is costly, and can never suffice, that he should continue to live on for

ever, and never see the Pit." Later he noted that the foolish were
appointed for Sheol and that death would be their shepherd. Sheol was to
be their home but he added in full confidence, "But God will ransom my
soul from the power of Sheol, for he will receive me." Assuredly here
is one of the most significant Old Testament passages which look to
life beyond the grave. Two different destinies are held in view: the one,
of the foolish; the other, of the righteous.

9. Life of the People of God

It is entirely natural to anticipate that this book, which centers in the
praise and worship of God, should have much to tell us about the
manner of life of His people. Those who worship Him who is holy,
righteous, and just, cannot escape the conviction that they should be
godlike. Faith in God leads to holy living.

a. Ethical Ideals

Let us observe how a number of the psalm writers set forth high
ethical standards of living. The specific details of life to which they refer
deserve careful study and meditation. Psalm 1 reads, "Blessed is the
man who walks not in the counsel of the wicked, nor stands in the
way of sinners, nor sits in the seat of scoffers; but his delight is in the
law of the Lord, and on his law he meditates day and night." In
Psalm 15 David asked the question, "Who shall dwell on thy holy hill?"
His answer was, "He who walks blamelessly, and does what is right, and
speaks truth from his heart; who does not slander with his tongue, and
does no evil to his friend, nor takes up a reproach against his
neighbor, . . . who does not put out his money at interest, and does
not take a bribe against the innocent." Here he brought into the picture
the common affairs of life in which ethical standards find application.

In Psalm 24 he answered the same question in the words, "He who
has clean hands and a pure heart, who does not lift up his soul to what
is false, and does not swear deceitfully." His expression, "clean hands and
a pure heart," points to both the outward and the inward aspects of
right living. One's entire being is thus involved. Asaph severely re-
proached those who in the names of their gods were judging unjustly
and showing partiality to the wicked (82). Quoting the Lord, he said,
"Give justice to the weak and the fatherless; maintain the right of the
afflicted and the destitute. Rescue the weak and the needy; deliver them
from the hand of the wicked." Here was a realm of life in which many
had failed to recognize what was right and good. The weak, the afflicted,
and the destitute were so often overrun by the wealthy who were in
power. Asaph saw the ethical involvement of this situation. Psalm 133

looked to another area of right living: "Behold, how good and pleasant it is when brothers dwell in unity!" Perhaps the psalmist who wrote these words reflected on a number of instances where brothers failed to fulfill this standard. The reader can fill in the picture.

b. Some Vocabulary for the Ethically Good

Let us give brief attention to the vocabulary used in the Psalms to express the ethically good. First: righteous, upright (*yashar*), 1:5, 6; 7:10; 11:2, 7; second: just, righteous (*tsaddiq*), 7:9; 37:12; 119:121; third: blameless, perfect, complete *(tamim)*, 15:2; 18:23, 25; 37:18, 37; 84:11; 101:2, 6; fourth: good (*tob*), 34:14; 37:3, 27; 112:5; fifth: humble, meek (*anav*), 10:17; 18:27; 25:19; 37:11; 149:4. This vocabulary is not new but these words became greatly enriched by use in contexts of the worship of Israel's holy God. Their association with ethical ideals upheld in the Psalms also enriched their meaning. For reasons which I am not able to explain, the word "holy" (*qodesh*) was not used to describe holy people. It was used for God and His temple.

c. Trusting God in Life's Varied Experiences

We have already noted how many psalms disclose the trying and sometimes excruciating experiences of life. However, in some of these instances the psalmists wove into their accounts exhortations to trust God in the midst of these experiences. This group of psalms very greatly enrich our understanding of the life of God's people. They pierce into the experiences which test most severely continued trust in God. In several cases the psalmists follow a pattern where in the first few verses they pour out their heart burdens and then in following verses they give their answer to the respective problems. This procedure may occur several times in a given psalm. Consider the following examples: In Psalm 22 David poured out his heart to God in language of deepest sorrow (vv. 1, 2); then in verses 3-5 he gave the confident answer that God is holy and that when Israel's fathers trusted in Him, God delivered and saved them. In verses 6-8 he described himself as a worm, and no man. He was scorned, despised, and mocked by his enemies, but in verses 9-11, he found relief in knowing that God was keeping him safe. In confidence he could say, "Thou hast been my God." Verses 12-18 describe still further how enemies encompassed him, opening their mouths like ravening lions, and piercing his hands and feet. Nevertheless David was able to praise God (vv. 22-31) because he had not despised nor abhorred the affliction of the afflicted. The Lord had heard when David cried to Him. Looking to the future, David could conclude, "Men shall tell of the Lord to the coming generation, and proclaim his deliverance to a people yet unborn, that he has wrought it."

Somewhat the same pattern occurs in 25. In 2b and 3 he unloaded his burden in the words, "Let me not be put to shame; let not my enemies exult over me." Verse 7 expressed his burden that his sins and transgressions might not be remembered. Verse 11 repeated his prayer for pardon. In verse 16 he cried, "For I am lonely and afflicted." His prayer continued through verses 17-19, all expressing his heart burdens. On the other hand, verses 1 and 2a expressed his trust in God. In verses 4-6, he looked confidently to the God of his salvation, and so asked the Lord to be mindful of His mercy and steadfast love. Verses 8-10 expressed his witness that God is good and upright; and that "All the paths of the Lord are steadfast love and faithfulness, for those who keep his covenant and his testimonies." In verses 14, 15, he testified that "The friendship of the Lord is for those who fear him, and he makes known to them his covenant." Verses 20-22 continued his prayer that God may guard his life and deliver him. He prayed, "May integrity and uprightness preserve me, for I wait for thee." He looked to God to redeem Israel.

A similar pattern may be found in 31, where among descriptions of other life situations, he said, "I am in distress; my eye is wasted from grief, my soul and my body also. For my life is spent with sorrow, and my years with sighing; my strength fails because of my misery, and my bones waste away." His final answer gave the challenge, "Love the Lord, all you his saints! The Lord preserves the faithful. . . . Be strong, and let your heart take courage, all you who wait for the Lord!" Here, reflecting on other harrowing experiences, David said, "I am overcome by my trouble. I am distraught by the noise of the enemy, because of the oppression of the wicked." In confident trust, however, he was able to say, "Cast your burden on the Lord, and he will sustain you; he will never permit the righteous to be moved" (55:22). The great truth which we gain through these experiences of David is that those who trust in the Lord can always take refuge in Him, regardless of the most heartbreaking experiences of life.

10. Nature of Sin and Man's Sinfulness

One of my early impressions gained from the study of the Psalms is that of the frequent references to sin and the extensive vocabulary of at least twenty-three different words for sin. When we think of this fact alongside the frequent references to the holiness and righteousness of God, we begin to discover what was most fundamental in the perspective of the psalm writers. A number of times in previous chapters I have listed the vocabulary used for sin. Believing that this procedure possesses definite values for our study, I am listing the words found in the Psalms.

The most frequently used words, listed here in the order of their frequency, and including a few references of each, are these:

1. *rasha* (commit wickedness), 37:12, 14, 16; 106:6.
2. *ra* (evil), 10:15; 73:8.
3. *chamas* (violence), 58:2; 72:14.
4. *hata* (sin), 51:13; 59:3.
5. *pesha* (transgression), 25:7; 51:1, 3.
6. *avon* (iniquity), 25:11; 103:9, 10.

   Less frequently used words are:

1. *sarar* (rebel), 78:8.
2. *marah* (rebel), 78:17.
3. *asham* (guilty), 69:5.
4. *qashah* (harden), 95:8.
5. *shagah* (err), 119:21, 118.
6. *shagag* (go astray), 119:67.
7. *maan* (refuse to obey), 78:10.
8. *maas* (despise), 15:14.
9. *rum* (haughty), 18:27.
10. *avah* (commit iniquity), 106:6.
11. *aval* (unjust), 71:4.
12. *sug* (turn back), 78:57.
13. *kazab* (falsehood), 62:4, 9.
14. *sheqer* (lie), 119:69.
15. *naaph* (adultery), 50:18.
16. *gannab* (thief), 50:18.
17. *gazel* (robbery), 62:10.

We may ask, What does this list of sins say to us? Among other answers let us note first the great stress given to sins of the heart. This revealed a deep insight into the nature of sin. Second, the sins listed were the common transgressions of that period of time. We are reminded that the sins of the Israelites were identical in nature with other lists already noted. A third observation is this, that the psalmists laid hold of the spiritual and moral requirements of worship. This becomes apparent when we observe the forty-two uses of the word "holy" with reference to God and His sanctuary, showing how unqualified were sinners to enter into His holy sanctuary. A final observation is that sin stands in direct antagonism to the holiness of God.

11. Repentance, Faith, and Regeneration

In a number of psalms there is a close interweaving of experiences, including confession of sin, repentance, faith, spiritual renewal, and the work of the Holy Spirit. Their inner spiritual meaning gives depth to the entire concept of worship. They also furnish the foundation for the further unfolding of these spiritual experiences in the New Testament. In Psalm 25 David prayed, "Remember not the sins of my youth, or my transgressions; according to thy steadfast love remember me, for thy goodness' sake, O Lord!" He continued, "For thy name's sake, O Lord, pardon my guilt, for it is great." Psalms 32 and 51 are commonly called the penitential psalms because they give expression to David's repentance of the most heinous sin of his life. In 32 he says, "Blessed is he whose transgression is forgiven, whose sin is covered. Blessed is the man to whom the Lord imputes no iniquity, and in whose spirit there is no deceit." Here we observe the spiritual experience of the joy of being forgiven. It stands in sharp contrast to the sense of guilt which a smiting conscience had been bringing upon him (verses 3, 4). His sincere confession reads, "I acknowledged my sin to thee, and I did not hide my iniquity; I said, 'I will confess my transgressions to the Lord'; then thou didst forgive the guilt of my sin." In this way David laid bare before the Lord his past sins. The emotional aspect is clear in the words, "I confess my iniquity, I am sorry for my sin" (38:18).

Psalm 51 probes most deeply into these spiritual experiences. Overwhelmed by the guilt of his sin with Bathsheba, David was aware that only through the steadfast love and mercy of God could he be forgiven. First of all, he realized that his sin was against the Lord. This is an aspect of sin which often escapes attention. His prayer was, "Wash me thoroughly from my iniquity, and cleanse me from my sin!" He was keenly aware that only through a spiritual washing could he be cleansed. His prayer continued, "Purge me with hyssop, and I shall be clean; wash me, and I shall be whiter than snow." His most serious need was an inner spiritual change which God alone could bring about. He expressed this in the words, "Create in me a clean heart, O God, and put a new and right spirit within me. Cast me not away from thy presence, and take not thy holy Spirit from me. Restore to me the joy of thy salvation, and uphold me with a willing spirit." In this prayer we have the most explicit language found in the Old Testament to describe regeneration. Observe that it is an act of creation brought about by God. It involved an internal working effected by the Holy Spirit, who implanted a new spirit within David. The New Testament counterpart to this change becomes clear in Jesus' words of being "born of the Spirit," and also of Paul's language of being made "alive together with Christ" (Jn. 3:5, 6; Eph. 2:1-10). David was aware that God could effect this change only upon one who had a broken spirit and a contrite heart.

12. Individual Eschatology

a. Ideas of Death

The first impression we gain of death is that it does not mean non-existence. While there are certain problem passages, yet there are many others which speak of the state of the dead, both of the wicked and of the righteous. Among these passages which present real problems of interpretation are 6:5; 30:9; 39:13; 88:10-12; 115:17. We cannot be sure what David meant when he said that in death there is no remembrance of God, and asked the question as to who can give God praise in Sheol. Neither do we know what answer David had for his questions raised in 30:9, "What profit is there in my death, if I go down to the Pit? Will the dust praise thee? Will it tell of thy faithfulness?" From his prayer in 39:12, 13 should we gather that David thought of his death as being the end of his existence? Or as we ponder his questions in 88:10-12 do we gather the implication that in death he would be separated from God's works of wonder, His steadfast love, His faithfulness, and saving help? Shall we conclude from the psalmist's assertion in 115:17 that the dead do not actually praise the Lord? Since the meaning of the great body of references to death in the book is clear, I feel that there is little need for attempting to gain the exact import of these problem passages.

In passing we might observe some of the words used with reference to the abode of the departed. The word "Sheol" carried the thought of being in the depth of the earth. The Old Testament writers thought that in Sheol man's spiritual activities ceased, but that God was present there (63:9; 86:13; 88:3-6; 139:8). The word "Abaddon" meant destruction (88:11). The word *qeber* meant grave. It was used along with "Abaddon" in the preceding reference. The word *dumah* meant silence (94:17; 115:17). The former reference read: "If the Lord had not been my help, my soul would soon have dwelt in the land of silence." This is quite descriptive of the abode of the dead. The last word, *bor*, carried the meaning, *Pit*. Since it was used in parallel structure with Sheol (30:3; 88:3-6), we may conclude that these two words were almost synonymous in meaning.

In connection with these words we should observe that the psalm writers paid attention to the brevity of life (90; 91; 102:26, 28; 103; 104). Very expressive of this idea are the words, "For all our days pass away under thy wrath, our years come to an end like a sigh. The years of our life are threescore and ten, or even by reason of strength fourscore; yet their span is but toil and trouble; they are soon gone, and we fly away" (90:9, 10). These words stand in sharp contrast with the eternal existence of God expressed in the statement, "Before the mountains were brought forth, or ever thou hadst formed the earth and the world, from everlasting to everlasting thou art God" (90:2).

b. State of the Wicked Dead (9:17; 31:17, 18; 49:10-14; 55:15)

The clearest statement setting forth the continued existence of the wicked says, "The wicked shall depart to Sheol, all the nations that forget God." The most descriptive language we have of the state of the wicked dead is this: "Let death come upon them; let them go down to Sheol alive; let them go away in terror into their graves."

c. State of the Righteous Dead

In sharp contrast with what was said of the wicked dead, positive statements described the future glory of the righteous. Note the radiant hope of David: "Therefore my heart is glad, and my soul rejoices; my body also dwells secure. For thou dost not give me up to Sheol, or let thy godly one see the Pit. Thou dost show me the path of life; in thy presence there is fullness of joy, in thy right hand are pleasures for evermore" (16:9-11). He also declared, "As for me, I shall behold thy face in righteousness; when I awake, I shall be satisfied with beholding thy form" (17:15). The familiar Twenty-third Psalm closes with the words, "And I shall dwell in the house of the Lord for ever." In definite antithesis to what the psalmist said concerning the future of the wicked, as quoted above, he said, "But God will ransom my soul from the power of Sheol, for he will receive me" (49:15). Still another prayer expressing David's hope is in the words, "Lead me in the way everlasting" (139:24)! These statements assert with clarity and full assurance that the righteous shall dwell eternally with God. The worship-centered character of these psalms makes these declarations of the righteous all the more sublime. For some additional references see: 27:13; 37:18, 28; 73:23-25; 118:17-20.

13. Imprecatory Psalms

Almost everyone who has made a serious study of the Psalms and has thereby experienced great blessings, recognizes some very difficult problems involved in the so-called imprecatory psalms. Some devout readers have become so disturbed by the kind of judgments which David, a man after God's own heart, would bring upon the wicked, that they have almost lost faith in God. Overwhelmed with the depth of David's spiritual experience with God, they find it impossible to see how a person who was so close to God could bring these imprecations upon his enemies. In my effort to solve this problem I am deeply indebted to A.

F. Kirkpatrick for some of the most helpful suggestions toward understanding these psalms.[4]

a. These psalms belong to the Old Testament and should be interpreted in accordance with this part of the Bible. Since the law permitted, even commanded, acts of retribution, these psalms should be interpreted in line with the New Testament explanation of the Old Testament law. Perhaps Psalms 58, 83, and 104 become intelligible and acceptable on this basis.

b. Some of these psalms spring from an intense zeal for God's cause (129). The psalmists had great concern that the laws of God should be maintained. They may have been fearful that the worship of God would be overthrown by man's wickedness. Let us see how some of the writers appear to have been searching after the truth concerning God's government of the world and the relation of this to divine judgment (35, 55, 59, 109, 139). Having full confidence that the Lord was ruling His people and that He would bring judgment upon all ungodliness, these psalm writers could not understand why God was allowing all this wickedness and not bringing judgment upon His enemies.

c. Up to that time there appears to have been no divine revelation of a final judgment (7, 125, 145). We are aware that the writing prophets did give eschatological predictions of final judgment centering in the Day of the Lord. Since God had not revealed anything like this to the psalmists, they may have felt a certain frustration in not being aware of coming judgment. They probably felt that God should immediately bring judgment upon wicked people.

d. The psalmists expressed their thoughts in the usual Hebrew mode of the concrete (50, 69). We may be correct in understanding these descriptions of gory punishments of the wicked, not according to our modern literalism, but rather in accordance with the vividly pictorial language of the Hebrew. These writers identified a man with his wickedness; they seem not to have been able to consider a wicked man as being a person and then to think of his wickedness in relation to him as an individual.

e. The psalmists had a keen sense of the great conflict constantly going on between good and evil, between God and His enemies (79, 83, 101, 137:8). Their problem reached a crisis stage when they thought of the nations which threatened to destroy Israel. The defeat of Israel would be a reproach to God's name. In their judgment the real issue was not merely the existence of the nation, but rather, the cause of truth and righteousness. The psalmists expressed the desire of Israel to vindicate a righteous cause and to punish the wicked.

f. These psalmists were greatly troubled about the suffering of the godly and the prosperity of the ungodly (37, 52, 54, 69, 92). This had been a perplexing problem all through human history, and it was very real in the days of these psalmists. Why should the godly suffer? Why should the ungodly prosper? The psalmists sought the answer in the light of their understanding of God's righteousness and justice.

g. Coming more directly to an attempted solution of these ethical problems, we bring into focus two fundamental aspects of biblical truth. The first is the grand unity and harmony of the Bible. The second is the progress and unfolding of divine revelation. In the above discussion I have sought to show how these imprecatory psalms can be harmonized with the rest of the Old Testament. These psalms properly understood do not stand in antagonism to the worship experiences described by these psalm writers. The progress of divine revelation becomes clear in Jesus' teaching. The Sermon on the Mount, for instance, shows how Jesus came to fulfill the law and the prophets. Observe how the Beatitudes show the real blessedness of the poor in spirit, of those who mourn, of the meek, the merciful, the peacemakers, in a word, those who have exemplified the kind of love which Jesus taught. In the sixfold contrast between Jesus' teaching and the pharisaical perversion of the law, we come to realize that the law was frequently misunderstood and misinterpreted. We need to recognize the fact that God was leading His people from spiritual immaturity to a larger understanding of divine truth. Throughout the Old Testament we become aware of how the Lord dealt gently, mercifully, and compassionately with His people. Step by step He was leading them to love their enemies as well as their neighbors, but this goal was being realized very slowly.

Jesus made it very clear that He was introducing a new era of divine revelation. In parabolic language He said that no one puts a piece of unshrunk cloth on an old garment, neither does he put new wine in old wineskins. By this He said that He was inaugurating a new age of divine revelation which could not be added to the old revelation as a mere appendage. Looking back then to the Old Testament, we may understand more clearly why the Lord, in His forbearing grace, permitted sub-Christian standards among His people.

There has always been, and likewise always will be, a problem for human beings to hold in clear view God's mercy and justice. When we look at the former, there is a problem of understanding the latter, and vice versa. This is perhaps the chief theological concern in the imprecatory psalms and thus they become a formidable problem for theodicy. It assumed such dimensions because the psalmists were not able to comprehend the interrelation of these divine attributes. Just as we may overstress God's mercy, they may have overdrawn God's justice.

For Additional Reading and Reference:

von Rad, *Old Testament Theology*, Vol. I, pp. 318-24, 356-70, 396-406.
Raven, *The History of the Religion of Israel*, pp. 514-77.
Ringgren, *The Messiah in the Old Testament*, pp. 11-24.
————, *Israelite Religion*. See Psalms in Index.
Sampey, *The Heart of the Old Testament*, pp. 105-25.
Titcomb, *Revelation in Progress*, pp. 153-99.
The Anchor Bible, 16, "Psalms I," pp. XXXV-XXXVII.
The Cambridge Bible, "The Psalms," pp. LXXVI-XCVII.
The International Standard Bible Encyclopaedia, IV, pp. 2492-94.
The Interpreter's Bible, Vol. 4, pp. 12-14.
The Interpreter's Dictionary of the Bible, K-Q, pp. 954-58.
The New Bible Dictionary, pp. 1056-59.

1. *The New Bible Dictionary* (Grand Rapids: William B. Eerdmans Publishing Company, 1962), "Love, Beloved," p. 752.

2. *Op. cit.*, "Good" by J. I. Packer, p. 481.

3. *A Companion to the Bible* (New York: Oxford University Press, 1958), J. J. von Allmen, General Editor, "Good," p. 152.

4. *The Cambridge Bible for Schools and Colleges*, General Editor for the Old Testament, A. F. Kirkpatrick, "The Book of Psalms," edited by Kirkpatrick (Cambridge: At the University Press, 1903). Introduction, Chapter IX, "On Some Points in the Theology of the Psalms," pp. LXXXVIII-XCIII.

CHAPTER II
PROVERBS, ECCLESIASTES,
SONG OF SONGS

1. The Proverbs

a. Introduction

The Book of Proverbs stands in a different category from the Prophets and the Psalms. This becomes apparent when we recall that the prophets claimed to be giving the word of the Lord and the Psalms gave us hymns of praise and worship.

The Book of Proverbs, on the other hand, lays before us a new aspect of life, bound up in the word "wisdom." This word occurs only a few times in the Old Testament before the time of Solomon. In the closing messages which Moses gave to Israel, he reminded them of the statutes and ordinances which had been given to them. He then said, "Keep them and do them; for that will be your wisdom and your understanding in the sight of the peoples" (Deut. 4:6). When Joshua took over the leadership of Israel, the record says that he was "full of the spirit of wisdom, for Moses had laid his hands upon him" (Deut. 34:9). These two uses of wisdom suggest that implicit obedience to all of God's commandments would constitute wisdom. The close association of *understanding* and *wisdom* in this connection suggests a very close relationship in their meaning.

When Solomon came to the throne of Israel he already had the reputation of being a wise man. The author of 2 Chronicles recorded Solomon's prayer to the Lord in which he asked, "Give me now wisdom and knowledge to go out and come in before this people," and to which the Lord responded that He was giving him these gifts (2 Chron. 1: 8-12). The author of 1 Kings gave a similar note in the words, "And God gave Solomon wisdom and understanding beyond measure, and largeness of mind like the sand on the seashore, so that Solomon's wisdom surpassed the wisdom of all the people of the east, and all the wisdom of Egypt." The writer observed also that Solomon "uttered three thousand proverbs; and his songs were a thousand and five" (1 Kings 4:29-32). Later in the book he referred to Solomon's wisdom in connection with the visit of the queen of Sheba and noted also that "King Solomon excelled all the kings of the earth in riches and in wisdom. And the whole earth sought the presence of Solomon to hear his wisdom, which God had put into his mind" (1 Kings 10:1-25). This information discloses Solomon's qualifications for writing the Proverbs and introduces us to the rich spiritual connotation of the word "wisdom." Most significantly, it was a spiritual gift from the Lord.

b. Meaning of Wisdom

The opening verses of The Proverbs at once make clear the meaning of this word. Note the words, "That men may know wisdom and instruction, understand words of insight, receive instruction in wise dealing, righteousness, justice, and equity; that prudence may be given to the simple, knowledge and discretion to the youth — the wise man also may hear and increase in learning, and the man of understanding acquire skill, to understand a proverb and a figure, the words of the wise and their riddles." After giving these introductory ideas, Solomon disclosed the definitive idea bound up in the word "wisdom": "The fear of the Lord is the beginning of knowledge; fools despise wisdom and instruction" (Prov. 1:1-7). When he repeated this definition he added: "and the knowledge of the Holy One is insight" (Prov. 9:10).

Section 8:12-21 states very clearly the nature and origin of wisdom. Solomon added great emphasis to its meaning by personifying wisdom. Among other significant expressions he had wisdom speak thus, "I . . . dwell in prudence, and I find knowledge and discretion. The fear of the Lord is hatred of evil. Pride and arrogance and the way of evil and perverted speech I hate. I have counsel and sound wisdom, I have insight, I have strength." The clarity of this language hardly requires further explanation. The spiritual character of wisdom appears most evident. It enters vitally into the everyday affairs of life. No thought, word, or deed lies beyond its domain. Obedience to God's laws, commandments, and statutes takes on a new look in this concept of wisdom.

Verses 22-31 carry this concept still higher in disclosing wisdom's relation to God. Here we learn that the Lord had created wisdom at the beginning of creation. She was present when God created the earth and established the heavens. Most fascinating are the words, "When he marked out the foundations of the earth, then I was beside him, like a master workman; and I was daily his delight, rejoicing before him always, rejoicing in his inhabited world and delighting in the sons of men." Charles T. Fritsch directed attention to the profound meaning of this section when he wrote, "One of the most perfect pictures of Christ to be found in the Old Testament is in Proverbs 8:22-31."[1] Dr. Fritsch noted further that Jesus identified Himself with wisdom when He said, "The queen of the South will arise at the judgment with the men of this generation and condemn them; for she came from the ends of the earth to hear the wisdom of Solomon, and behold, something greater than Solomon is here" (Lk. 11:31; Mt. 12:42). Fritsch added the comment, "Jesus is not making a simple comparison here, but rather He is saying that the wisdom of the Old Testament, so imperfectly manifested in the character and teaching of Solomon, is now perfectly revealed in the matchless life and words of Him who is David's greater Son."[2]

With this exalted view of wisdom in mind, let us note briefly the contribution which this book makes to biblical theology. It centers in this concept of wisdom. As Solomon expanded its thought content, he showed that the fear of the Lord manifests itself in a befitting manner of life. A fundamental unity exists between wisdom and its expression in an upright, integrated way of life. James, who wrote the New Testament book of wisdom, expressed the same thought in the words, "Faith apart from works is dead." In line with this he said, "The wisdom from above is first pure, then peaceable, gentle, open to reason, full of mercy and good fruits, without uncertainty or insincerity" (Jas. 2:18-26; 3:13-18). Paul dwelt on this unity in a different setting when he showed that the kind of faith which justifies a person leads to a walk in newness of life (Rom. 5:1; 6:4).

c. Fear of the Lord

It should now be evident that wisdom declares very clearly the manner of life for all mankind. It is the outworking of one's living in the fear of the Lord. The countless details of life to which Solomon referred showed how the fear of the Lord permeates the everyday affairs of one's life. For my purpose an enumeration of these graces and virtues must suffice. R. B. Y. Scott most accurately and effectively summarized them as follows. "His typical virtues are diligence, prudence, integrity, forthrightness, calm restraint in speech, trustworthiness, steadfastness, patience, generosity, modesty, peaceableness, self-discipline, kindness to the weak and the unfortunate."[3]

Let us note some further observations made by Dr. Fritsch: "Anyone who reads Proverbs is impressed with the high ethical standard of its teachings. The highest type of family life is extolled; monogamy is taken for granted; the respect for mother and wife is emphasized throughout; chastity and marital fidelity are enjoined for all. The glutton, drunkard, and sluggard, the robber and the oppressor of the poor are all roundly condemned. Those who live in accordance with wisdom's laws are prosperous and happy. A belief in the one true and living God who rewards the righteous and punishes the wicked permeates the book from cover to cover."[4]

Essential to these ethical ideals is Solomon's teaching on one's relation to his enemies (17:5; 20:22; 24:17, 18, 29; 25:21, 22). Solomon expressed a clear insight when he wrote, "Do not say, 'I will repay evil'; wait for the Lord, and he will help you." Obviously it is very difficult for a person to leave evil brought on by one's enemies to the Lord for His settlement. Only a wise man knows the measure of grace and forbearance which are needed when he sees trouble come upon his enemy. This certainly anticipated Jesus' instruction in these words, "Love your enemies and pray for those who persecute you, so that you may be sons of your Father who is in heaven; for he makes his sun rise on the evil and on the good, and sends rain on the just and on the unjust" (Mt. 5:44, 45). Yet another most significant Old Testament statement comes in the words, "If your enemy is hungry, give him bread to eat; and if he is thirsty, give him water to drink; for you will heap coals of fire on his head, and the Lord will reward you" (Prov. 25:21, 22). Paul also quoted these words when he gave some very practical teaching on genuine love (Rom. 12:19-21).

d. The Proverbs, Foundation for New Testament Ethics

A final approach to the contribution of The Proverbs to ethical truth becomes evident in the New Testament quotations from this book. It is all the more remarkable when we observe that these quotations or allusions were made in the portions of these books dealing with practical ethics. Note the following: Prov. 3:4 (Rom. 12:17); 3:7a (Rom. 12:16b); 3:11, 12 (Heb. 12:5, 6); 3:34 (Jas. 4:6; 1 Pet. 5:5b); 4:26a (Heb. 12: 13a); 8:15 (Rom. 13:1); 10:12b (1 Pet. 4:8b); 11:31 (1 Pet. 4:18); 20:17 (Rom. 12:17); 24:29 (Mt. 5:39-42); 25:21, 22 (Rom. 12:20); 26:11a (2 Pet. 2:22b). From these quotations we see how New Testament writers appropriated ethical principles and practices from The Proverbs. Observe the following: never-failing love, humility, returning good for evil, loving conduct toward one's enemies, enduring the Lord's discipline, refraining from swerving back and forth between right and wrong, righteousness that allows no compromise, and refraining from becoming entangled again in sin with all its defilements after having known and experienced the way of righteousness. In conclusion, let us note the supporting evidence these quotations give to the fundamental ideas of progressive revelation and progress of doctrine in the Bible. It is soul-refreshing to observe how Solomon's wisdom related so definitely to practical Christian living, in brief, to living in the fear of the Lord.

e. Life Beyond the Grave

In a number of proverbs the wise man gave glimpses of man's existence beyond the grave (5:5; 7:27; ·9:18; 15:11, 24; 23:14). When Solomon gave advice to his son he added a pertinent warning against his being influenced by a loose woman. He noted that her feet go down to death, and her steps follow the path to Sheol. He also gave advice against being ensnared by the iniquities of the wicked. As to the end of the wicked person he wrote, "He dies for lack of discipline, and because of his great folly he is lost" (5:23). How much meaning we may attach to the word "lost" is not clear. We do know that in the New Testament this word became descriptive of the unsaved after death. In chapter 15, where he mentions both Sheol and Abaddon as lying open before the Lord, he gave a very significant expression in the words, "The wise man's path leads upward to life, that he may avoid Sheol beneath." This suggests two different destinies for mankind, Life and Sheol. We may note a difference here between Solomon's expression and that of other Old Testament references. We gather that a wise man does not enter Sheol. Only the wicked do so. Of greater significance is the word "life," which in the New Testament described the state of the righteous after death. In my effort to garner the meaning of this verse, part of the greatest verse in all the Bible came to my mind, "That whoever believes in him should not perish but have eternal life." It is conceivable that Jesus was reflecting on this proverb when He spoke those matchless words.

2. Ecclesiastes

a. Introduction

The speaker of this book is the Preacher (Ecclesiastes). He is the son of David, undoubtedly Solomon. The unexplained meaning of this title imposes on us the problem of determining its meaning and the reason for its use. With the declaration, "Vanity of vanities! All is vanity," we become aware that Solomon was giving a verdict on the meaning of his experiences in life. Evidently some things had happened which had completely revolutionized his outlook on life from that which was plainly evident in The Proverbs. This suggests a clue to the interpretation of this book which I am presenting for careful thought.

In The Proverbs, Solomon had so nobly presented the guiding principle for right living. It was the fear of the Lord. This is the beginning of wisdom and the knowledge of the Holy One. Evidently something tragic had happened in Solomon's own spiritual experiences. Turning to 1 Kings 11 we become aware that Solomon had failed to live up to the high ethical standards of life upheld in The Proverbs. He had allowed himself to love foreign women, whom the Lord had explicitly commanded Israelite men not to marry. The reason for this prohibition lay in the inevitable outcome that these women would turn the hearts of Israel to idol worship. This is exactly what happened to Solomon. His heart turned after other gods and was not wholly true to the Lord. He even departed to the extent of building a high place for Chemosh, the abomination of Moab, and for Molech, the abomination of the Ammonites. This departure from holy and righteous living, which the fear of the Lord required, resulted in spiritual catastrophe. Now he evaluated all of life as vanity. Having had the rich spiritual experience of living in the fear of the Lord and then of having come to drink the dregs of his sinful conduct, he completely reversed his outlook on life. I have come to believe that this experience of Solomon is the key to the interpretation of this book. His probing insights into the vanities of life were all the more revealing because he still remembered the way of wisdom. He had now come to be the Preacher against all these vanities.

b. Voice of Experience — All Is Vanity

A number of times throughout the book the Preacher laid bare the life of vanity. It had become meaningless (1). There were no gains for man's toil. A generation goes, a generation comes, neither one making any impact upon the earth. The forces of nature follow their course without any meaning; in a word, all things are full of weariness. Nothing takes place which is worth remembering. The Preacher's explanation continues (2). He subjected life to the test of pleasure but in the final reckoning all this was vanity. He subjected wisdom, madness, and folly to the same sort of test, only to discover that all of these were vanity. He came to hate life because what was done under the sun was grievous to him. Another situation in life which led to his desperation was that while the man who pleases God is entrusted with wisdom, knowledge, and joy, the sinner who works through gathering and reaping must give all this to the one who pleases God. This was as futile as trying to catch the wind.

Later he proceeded to call attention to various experiences of life which according to his judgment showed how unjust and hopeless they were (5). He saw in all toil and skill in work the motivation of a man who is envious of his neighbor. He observed that "He who loves money will not be satisfied with money; nor he who loves wealth, with gain: this also is vanity." He noted further, "When goods increase, they increase who eat them; and what gain has their owner but to see them with his eyes?"

He gave other illustrations of the inequalities of life (8). He asserted, "There is a vanity which takes place on earth, that there are righteous men to whom it happens according to the deeds of the wicked, and there are wicked men to whom it happens according to the deeds of the righteous." This, to him, was vanity.

Finally, the Preacher seemed to take hold of himself and pointed to the way of wisdom (12). He gave the advice, "Remember also your Creator in the days of your youth, before the evil days come, and the years draw nigh, when you will say, 'I have no pleasure in them'" After giving this counsel he reiterated what is bound to take place if one fails to follow it. Looking backward over life, he could say, "The sayings of the wise are like goads, and like nails firmly fixed are the collected sayings which are given by one Shepherd. My son, beware of anything beyond these. . . . Fear God, and keep his commandments; for this is the whole duty of man. For God will bring every deed into judgment, with every secret thing, whether good or evil." These words lead us to believe that the Preacher was returning to the manner of life he had upheld in The Proverbs. It would seem that the wise counsel given in these closing statements would be possible only to one who had at an earlier time in his life tried to fulfill the whole duty of man.

I have had two purposes in the foregoing discussion. The first concerns the problems of authorship. Following the lead that this book constitutes the words of the Preacher, the son of David, I have sought to discover whether the skeptical attitudes given throughout the book are descriptive of his own viewpoint of life or that of another. This study has led me to believe that the words of the Preacher were descriptive of his own experiences. The spiritual expressions which appear a number of times throughout the book and become so satisfying at its close, would appear to be explained by the author's turning back from a life of uncontrolled passion to that of prudence, knowledge, and discretion. If this elucidates the problem of authorship, then we have here something of a spiritual autobiography of Solomon.

This leads to my second purpose. If this book serves as an evaluation of Solomon's sinful life given after he had repented and turned back to God, its values for a biblical theology approach become apparent. Throughout this work I have sought to draw attention to the experiential aspects of godly living, under the heading "The Life of the People of God." The Book of Ecclesiastes presents an important facet of this practical topic. Its values become apparent from a negative rather than a positive approach to how God's people should live.

c. Values of Wisdom

In view of Solomon's experiences, what he has to say with reference to wisdom possesses distinctive values (8:16 — 10:12). When he sought again to apply his mind to know wisdom, he realized that the work of God far surpasses man's power to comprehend its meaning. He was able to see that the righteous and the wise, together with their deeds, are in the hand of God. But even at this point he was still unable to pass beyond the verdict that "everything before them is vanity." Referring to the natural enjoyments of life, he was able to say, "Whatever your hand finds to do, do it with your might; for there is no work or thought or knowledge or wisdom in Sheol, to which you are going" (9:10). He was able also to discover a worthy example in the despised poor man who was, nevertheless, wise. Through this poor man's counsel a small city was saved from being overthrown by a powerful king. The Preacher was able to see that wisdom is better than weapons of war. He could testify, "A wise man's heart inclines him toward the right, but a fool's heart toward the left" (10:2). This leads us to see that wisdom does not merely lead one to evaluate matters of right and wrong but it gives him the incentive to do the right. The Preacher came to realize more fully the ethical values of wisdom as they stand in contrast to the foolishness and madness of the fool. The culminating values of wisdom stand out in the words, "The sayings of the wise are like goads, and like nails firmly fixed are the collected sayings which are given by one Shepherd." Just as goads spur oxen to pull their load, and as nails pounded deeply into a piece of wood hold it securely, so do the sayings of the wise. They spur one on to carry forward the heavy load of responsibilities required in wise living and to hold fast to the kind of activities in life consistent with the fear of the Lord. This was the noble commitment of the penitent Preacher.

d. Wholesome Advice

Solomon's return to the way of wisdom enabled him to give sound advice to those who were in danger of leaving wisdom's paths. He set forth worthy counsel for worship (5:1-6). Going to the house of God for worship imposes a spiritual requirement expressed in the words, "Guard your steps." The worship of God involves far more than merely offering sacrifices. In genuine worship the bringing of sacrifices symbolizes the atoning for sin in one's life — involving repentance and confession of sin — as well as consecration and commitment to God. Only persons of such life could fellowship with God in worship. Even though Solomon had built the temple, he had come to realize more fully through his sinful life the spiritual requisites for coming into the presence of God. Herein was manifested genuine wisdom.

In 7:1-14 the Preacher gave some additional wholesome advice which pointed again to the manner of life which should characterize one who guards his steps when he goes into the house of God. Such a person acquires a good name and is known as a wise person by his manner of life. More examples of the Preacher's good advice are these: The wise man shares in the sorrows of the mourning. His way of life reaches far above that of the fool, whose heart is in the house of mirth. One gains a good name in not being quick to anger. Anger belongs to fools. In the varied experiences of life a person comes to realize that "wisdom preserves the life of him who has it." So he gives the counsel, "Consider the work of God; who can make straight what he has made crooked?"

Some additional instruction relating to daily responsibilities came in the words, "Cast your bread upon the waters, for you will find it after many days" (11:1). Inability to understand and evaluate the work of God as displayed in His world, should prompt us to be active in sowing seed in the morning even though we cannot tell whether it will grow. On this account he could advise the young man to rejoice in his youth and to walk in the ways of his heart, but he added solemn counsel in the words, "But know that for all these things God will bring you into judgment." Evidently Solomon was bearing witness to the judgment God had brought upon him on account of his failures to discipline himself in the midst of temptations. The climactic advice then follows, "Remember also your Creator in the days of your youth, before the evil days come, and the years draw nigh, when you will say, 'I have no pleasure in them.'" These words constitute the highest point of Solomon's counsel. They sprang from his own personal experience in discovering the havoc which came in the wake of his own sinful life. He sought to advise youths to avoid such experiences in life.

As a summary exhortation bringing to a climax the entire lesson to be gained from his preaching, Solomon said, "Fear God, and keep his commandments; for this is the whole duty of man. For God will bring every deed into judgment, with every secret thing, whether good or evil." This certainly was the end of the matter. All the noble things of which he had spoken in The Proverbs are thus brought together in one view. He supported this counsel with the very sober warning of the coming judgment of God upon one's entire life, whether good or evil.

e. Value of Ecclesiastes in the Perspective of Biblical Theology

Let us draw together the several strands of thought already presented in this discussion so that their value in the unfolding of divine revelation may be properly evaluated. While we do not have here any statement of a message being given by God to man as through a prophet, we have noted that in 1 Kings God had given Solomon wisdom and understanding beyond measure. This was a spiritual gift equivalent to that acclaimed by the prophets in their declarations that the word of the Lord had come to them. Just as the words of the prophet came from God, so Solomon's wisdom and understanding also came from God. This truth undergirds the biblical concept of the Holy Scriptures, the Sacred Writings. Further, since this book unquestionably belongs to the biblical canon, there are adequate grounds for believing that it does make a contribution to the content of progressive revelation. Throughout the discussion I have attempted to bring these ideas into focus: upon a life that had been saturated with the pleasures of sinfulness Solomon gave the verdict, "Vanity of vanities! All is vanity." He wrote this book after having experienced all these empty pleasures and had returned to God to walk again in the fear of the Lord. Wisdom's diagnosis of a sinful world was that "All is vanity." The way of wisdom was to fear God and keep His commandments. In this was bound up the whole duty of man. This obtained still greater meaning in view of God's bringing "every deed into judgment, with every secret thing, whether good or evil." I am not aware that this divine truth received as clear expression anywhere else in the Old Testament.

3. The Song of Songs

a. Introduction

Here we face a problem still more difficult than that encountered in the Book of Ecclesiastes. At first thought we might conclude that the picture of love given in this book possesses no spiritual value. Since there appears to have been no problem relating to the inclusion of this book in the biblical canon, we may assume that it is the word of God with the same certainty that we recognize other Old Testament books as being Holy Scripture. Hence we may probe into its contents in order to lay hold of what God revealed to us in this book.

We have the right to believe that since God created man a sexual being, the expression of sexual love is entirely good. Knowing only too well what degenerate thinking has done to the divinely ordered expression of sexual love, Christian people from a sense of purity and modesty have exercised wholesome restraint in giving forthright discussions of this subject. We may begin then with the fundamental truth that what God created and ordained in marriage is pure and holy. This is fundamental to the whole body of theological teaching on the nature of man.

With this conclusion in mind we may very properly inquire what spiritual and theological teaching it gives. In answer we may state that even though difficult problems of interpretation do confront us, the book possesses values by reason of its being a part of the Holy Writ.

b. Theological Import of the Book

To begin, the book gives a pure and noble presentation of marriage and sexual love. Since God ordained marriage, a description of its fulfillment in physical union is in order. Nowhere in the book is there a scene of illicit love. We see the joy, beauty, exclusiveness, and binding power in the expression of sexual love. We are aware that the expression of marriage love is implied in the creation account, which reads, "A man leaves his father and his mother and cleaves to his wife, and they become one flesh" (Gen. 2:24). The description of marriage love in this book stands in sharp contrast with the scenes of immorality described in The Proverbs (Prov. 2:16-19; 5:3-20; 6:23-33; 7:5-27; 9:13-18; 23:27, 28).

Since this book is historical, we have grounds for believing that its first message pertains to the beauty of marriage love. This is a legitimate lesson to be gained. But there are grounds also for seeking to discover spiritual values in this book. Going back into Jewish history, we discover that the rabbis interpreted the book allegorically. They saw here an expression of God's love for Israel throughout their history. The early church fathers gave a different allegorical interpretation by finding here a picture of Christ's love for the church. Throughout church history many students have had a problem to accept an allegorical sense and consequently have modified it by attributing a typical significance to the book. Origen and Milton gave it a dramatic interpretation. These various approaches show how difficult the problem really is. Dr. Edward J. Young suggests that the book may be regarded as a tacit parable.[5] I am inclined to believe that this approach comes nearest to being correct. A parabolic interpretation attempts to avoid certain difficulties involved in the allegorical and typical explanations and at the same time seems to be most consistent with the historical basis of the book. Just as Jesus did not explain a number of His parables, so we may see in this book an uninterpreted parable.

In conclusion, the approaches to this book may be summarized as follows: To begin, the story gives a picture of natural human love. Before the coming of Christ some Jews saw in this book a picture of God's love for Israel. From the time of Christ many Christians have found here a picture of Christ's love for the church. From the point of view of hermeneutics the parable mode of interpretation is justifiable.

From the angle of the great spiritual metaphors given in the Bible, there is entire consistency in seeing this story as a tacit parable or a picture of divine love: first, of God's love for Israel; and second, of Christ's love for the church. By this approach the Song of Solomon makes a profound contribution to Old Testament theology.

For Additional Reading and Reference:

Payne, *The Theology of the Older Testament,* pp. 338-46.
von Rad, *Old Testament Theology,* Vol. I, pp. 418-59.
Ringgren, *Israelite Religion.* See Index.
Sampey, ***The Heart of the Old Testament,*** pp. 126-136.
————, *Syllabus for Old Testament Study,* pp. 143-50.
Titcomb, *Revelation in Progress,* pp. 199-222, 271-75.
The Anchor Bible, 18.
  "Proverbs," pp. 22-27.
  "Ecclesiastes," pp. 191-207.
The International Standard Bible Encyclopaedia:
  Vol. IV, "Proverbs," pp. 2473-76.
  Vol. V, "Song of Songs," pp. 2831-34.
The Interpreter's Bible:
  Vol. 4, "Proverbs," pp. 776-78.
  Vol. 5, "Ecclesiastes," pp. 17-20.
  Vol. 5, "Song of Songs," pp. 92-96.
The Interpreter's Dictionary of the Bible:
  K-Q - pp. 938-41.
  E-J - pp. 10-13.
  R-Z - pp. 422-25.
The New Bible Dictionary, pp. 1049 f.; 331 f.; 1205 f.
Theology Today, Vol. VII, No. 2, pp. 169-83.

1. Article, "The Gospel in the Book of Proverbs" (Princeton: *Theology Today,* Vol. VII, 1950), p. 181. See also his *Introduction and Exegesis of the Book of Proverbs* (New York: Abingdon Press, The Interpreter's Bible, 1955), Vol. 4, pp. 776-78.
2. *Ibid.,* p. 180.
3. *The Anchor Bible* (Garden City: Doubleday & Company, Inc., 1965), Vol. 18, "Proverbs," "Ecclesiastes," p. 26.
4. *The Interpreter's Bible,* p. 777.
5. *An Introduction to the Old Testament* (Grand Rapids: William B. Eerdmans Publishing Company, 1949), p. 327.

CHAPTER III
THE BOOK OF JOB

1. Introduction

The manner in which this book presents the man Job gives us grounds for believing that he was a historical character who lived in the land of Uz. The nature and circumstances of his life offer no problems in this respect. The unusual experiences described in this book have led many students to look at it as a dramatic poem, rather than as a historical record. The value of the book need not depend on the solution of this question.

The historical era apparently reflected in this book is likely the age of the patriarchs. It is possible that Job was one of the earliest of the Hebrews. Evidence for this would be the references to God Almighty, the use of the terms "blameless" and "upright" as describing a faithful Hebrew, the use of the terms "sin" and "transgression," and also the references to burnt offerings. Neither Job nor his friends make any reference to being in covenant relation with God.

The general message of the book and its contribution to God's unfolding revelation call for careful study. There is first of all the need for understanding the scene in the spiritual realm, where God encounters Satan on the point of the religious motivation of the blameless and upright man, Job. This conversation was unknown to Job, and thus all that follows in his experiences needs to be understood in relation to the outworking of this scene of which Job was ignorant.

It is essential to be aware of Job's limited knowledge of God. By way of comparison we might ask the question, What was Abraham's knowledge of God when he was still in Ur of the Chaldees? Just as Abraham's life was a school of faith, so Job's experiences may be regarded as a school of tests and trials. The blameless and upright Job was undoubtedly ignorant of God's providential actions in the world. God had not revealed Himself to Job as He had to Abraham. Only through recognizing this difference between the experiences of Abraham and of Job can we rightly appraise the latter's frustration. Job and his friends shared in the common idea that affliction comes only upon those who have sinned. Consequently he and they believed that his affliction was positive proof that he, Job, had sinned. Obviously, there was a certain degree of truth in their thinking because it is a matter of common knowledge that people bring illnesses upon themselves as the result of sinful living. Out of this background the story of Job unfolds.

2. Dramatic Presentation of the Story

For my purpose there is no need to give many details of the story. I shall refer to those factors which prepare us to understand what the book discloses to us from the angle of an unfolding revelation of God. God's confrontation of Satan with reference to the blameless and upright Job accounts for the calamity which came to Job's family, the loss of his possessions, and his bodily affliction. Job and his friends were entirely ignorant of what the Lord had permitted to take place. Job had to face his experience totally unaware of God's purposes lying back of it. His limited knowledge of God prevented him from knowing that God could test in this manner.

Miserable with loathsome sores and rebuked by his wife, whose understanding of this situation was still more limited than Job's, he felt that his way was hid. He could not understand why a man of integrity should suffer. This feeling became immeasurably intensified when his friends attempted to convince him that his afflictions were proofs of his sinfulness. As each of them endeavored to get him to acknowledge supposed wrongs, Job pleaded that he might have an umpire who would stand between him and God and give him the opportunity of proving his life blameless. As the intensity of the interchange increased, Job's inner struggle grew in severity. He had full confidence that if he could lay his case before the Lord, he would be acquitted. He had complete assurance that if God would hear his case, he would come forth with his integrity intact. Along the way Job gave some noble statements which expressed his deep spiritual insights. He said, "Behold, the fear of the Lord, that is wisdom; and to depart from evil is understanding" (28: 28).

When Elihu came on the scene, he rebuked Job still more severely but he seemed to have a larger understanding of God than Job's friends. Climactic were these words of his: "God is clothed with terrible majesty. The Almighty — we cannot find him; he is great in power and justice, and abundant righteousness he will not violate. Therefore men fear him; he does not regard any who are wise in their own conceit" (37:22-24).

Finally the Lord began to question Job. He asked, "Where were you when I laid the foundation of the earth? Tell me, if you have understanding" (38:4). As God continued to confront Job with questions relating to the wonders of the universe, he became speechless. The Lord pointedly asked him, "Will you even put me in the wrong? Will you condemn me that you may be justified" (40:8)? And then the Lord continued to draw Job's attention still further to the wonders of

His creation, all of which revealed the greatness, the majesty, and the power of the Lord. Finally Job admitted that he had uttered what he did not understand. Now that he had actually seen the Lord, he despised himself and repented in dust and ashes.

The scene then changed. The Lord rebuked Job's friends for not speaking what was right and required them to offer a burnt offering for their own sins. Job prayed for them and the Lord accepted Job's prayer. Then the Lord restored the fortunes of Job and blessed his latter days. After a long time Job died, an old man and full of days.

3. The Book of Job -- A Disclosure of Divine Providence

The foregoing account leads to the conclusion that the chief motif of the book is an explication of God's providence. Throughout these Old Testament studies, God's providential acts have repeatedly come into view. God has been seen as directing the course of history in order to accomplish His manifold purposes. It is the overall viewpoint depicted in this book that has led me to conclude that its historical setting was early in Hebrew history, at least pre-Davidic, when God's people were not yet aware of His entering into the affairs of men. God had not yet disclosed to man His activities in human history. It was on this account that Job was unable to reconcile himself to his most grievous affliction.

Let us probe into the meaning of this scene. In the spiritual realm there is need for us to avoid a literal interpretation of this scene lest we be compelled to conclude that God and Satan were at a bargaining table. Rather, this is a dramatic presentation of the way in which God allowed Satan to bring all these troubles upon Job. The experiences of Job were not meaningless events. The unfolding of this scene discloses the avowed purpose of God to test a person such as Job, the blameless and upright man who feared God and turned away from evil. Would Job hold fast his integrity, or would he curse God and die? The Lord would demonstrate to Satan that such a blameless and upright man would under no circumstances lose his integrity of character. This is the test aspect of this particular providential act of God. It becomes all the more vivid to us in view of the fact that Job knew nothing of its purpose and in view of his limited knowledge of God's relationship to His people. In Job's thinking, bodily affliction was due solely to man's sin.

Another aspect of God's providence begins to become evident when Job encountered the rebuke of his wife and the reproaches brought upon him by his friends. This became a severe temptation to Job, especially when he felt himself hedged in by God and rebuked by his friends for despising the chastening of the Almighty. It became all the more severe when no umpire was available to whom he could present his case for being innocent. All the words of his friends and of Elihu accentuated this temptation. In his deep misery there was no one to support him. God had taken away his right and made his soul bitter. Why not curse God and die?

Here we have an experiential approach to the providence of God. Because God's ways are above man's ways and His thoughts above man's thoughts, Job was unable to lay hold of the divine side of his experiences. His own thinking, that of his wife and friends, and also that of Elihu, moved on the low human level of regarding God only as the Almighty One, great in power and justice, One who does not violate righteousness. He saw in God One who brought affliction upon the wicked, but he knew very little of God's personal relations with the godly. He had not yet learned that God has wise purposes in all that He does and that man should trust God even though he may not understand these purposes. The story of Job, then, whether he was a historical character or an actor in the dramatic epic, has the purpose of disclosing the providence of God. While there is much to confirm the time of Job as pre-Mosaic, it is also possible to think of him as living in a later period, between Moses and the time of David. In any event he appears to have had little connection with the unfolding revelation of God during those centuries. In view of the outreaching influences of God's work among His people from the time of David onward, it would seem to be an anachronism to place Job so late. The story does not seem to fit at all into the times of the writing prophets, who expounded so effectively God's providence and in whose time the Psalms were being sung by all Israel.

We need to observe how the Book of Job held forth God's providence as it was interwoven with other attributes of His nature (4:17; 12:13; 13:3; 23:7; 25:2; 33:4, 26; 34:17; 35:10; 36:3, 5, 22; 38:4 — 41:34). We have already noted God's supremacy over Satan and all the forces of evil. Throughout the book God's righteousness stands forth in all clarity. God the righteous One is Judge of all mankind. He is the Redeemer (Vindicator) of man, and this gives us the true perspective of the chastenings experienced by Job. God is the all-knowing One; with Him are wisdom and might, counsel and understanding. Most gloriously God stands forth as the Creator of the world. Nowhere else in the Bible does His creative work shine before us in all its glory and majesty. We have observed how the psalmist and a number of the prophets wrote of God's creation, but here it is God Himself who presented in such wondrous majesty, the irrefutable work of His hands. All this enhances our understanding of God's providential acts.

In closing, let us observe James's comment on Job. In a context where he was exhorting his readers to be patient and to establish their hearts, he noted the suffering and patience of the prophets, and then continues with the words, "Behold, we call those happy who were steadfast. You have heard of the steadfastness of Job, and you have seen the purpose of the Lord, how the Lord is compassionate and merciful" (Jas. 5:8-11).

For Additional Reading and Reference:

Cambridge Bible, "Job," pp. XXIII-XXIX.
Davis-Gehman, *The Westminster Dictionary of the Bible,* pp. 314-16.
Payne, *The Theology of the Older Testament,* pp. 437-42, 452-58.
von Rad, *Old Testament Theology,* Vol. I, pp. 408-418.
Raven, *The History of the Religion of Israel,* pp. 578-639.
Robinson, *The Cross in the Old Testament,* pp. 19-54.
Sampey, *Syllabus for Old Testament Study,* pp. 116-25.
————, *The Heart of the Old Testament,* pp. 42-55.
Titcomb, *Revelation in Progress,* pp. 41-52.
The Anchor Bible, 15, "Job," pp. LXVIII-LXXVIII.
The International Standard Bible Encyclopaedia, Vol. III, "Job," pp. 1685-87.
The Interpreter's Bible, Vol. 3, "Job," pp. 897-902.
The Interpreter's Dictionary of the Bible, E-J, pp. 922-24.
The New Bible Dictionary, p. 637.
The Torch Bible Commentary, "Job," pp. 14-29.

SELECTED BIBLIOGRAPHY

I. GENERAL WORKS

Baab, Otto J., *Theology of the Old Testament* (New York: Abingdon Press, 1949).

Burrows, Millar, *An Outline of Biblical Theology* (Philadelphia: The Westminster Press, 1946).

Davidson, A. B., *The Theology of the Old Testament* (Edinburgh: T. & T. Clark, 1904).

Eichrodt, Walther, *The Theology of the Old Testament*, Vols. I, II (Philadelphia: The Westminster Press, 1961, 1967).

Heinisch — Heidt, *Theology of the Old Testament* (St. Paul: The North Central Publishing Company, 1957).

Jacob, Edmond, *Theology of the Old Testament* (New York: Harper Brothers, Publishers, 1958).

Kaufmann, Yehezkel, *The Religion of Israel* (Chicago: The University of Chicago Press, 1960).

Knight, George A. F., *A Christian Theology of the Old Testament* (Richmond: John Knox Press, 1959).

Knudson, Albert C., *The Religious Teaching of the Old Testament* (New York: Abingdon Press, 1918).

Kohler, K., *Jewish Theology* (New York: The Macmillan Company, 1923).

Köhler, Ludwig, *Old Testament Theology* (Philadelphia: The Westminster Press, 1957).

Mowinckel, S., *He That Cometh* (New York: Abingdon Press, 1954).

Napier, B. Davie, *Song of the Vineyard* (New York: Harper and Brothers, 1962).

Oehler, Gustav Friedrich, *Theology of the Old Testament* (New York: Funk and Wagnalls Company, 1870).

Payne, J. Barton, *The Theology of the Older Testament* (Grand Rapids: Zondervan Publishing House, 1962).

Pfeiffer, Robert H., *Religion in the Old Testament* (New York: Harper and Brothers, 1961).

von Rad, Gerhard, *Old Testament Theology*, I, II (New York: Harper and Brothers, 1962, 1965).

Raven, John Howard, *The History of the Religion of Israel* (New Brunswick Theological Seminary, 1933).

Rust, Eric C., *Salvation History* (Richmond: John Knox Press, 1962).

Schultz, Hermann, *Old Testament Theology*, I, II (Edinburgh: T. & T. Clark, 1892).

Titcomb, J. H., *Revelation in Progress* (London: The Religious Tract Society, 1871).

Vischer, Wilhelm, *The Witness of the Old Testament to Christ*, I (London: Lutterworth Press, 1949).

Vos, Geerhardus, *Biblical Theology — Old and New Testaments* (Grand Rapids: Wm. B. Eerdmans Publishing Co., 1948).

Vriezen, Th. C., *An Outline of Old Testament Theology* (Boston: Charles T. Branford Company, 1958).

Weidner, Revere Franklin, *Biblical Theology of the Old Testament* (New York: Fleming H. Revell Co., 1896).

II. THEOLOGIES OF THE PROPHETS

Anderson, Bernhard W., and Harrelson, Walter, Edited by, *Israel's Prophet Heritage* (New York: Harper and Brothers, 1962).

Davidson, A. B., *Old Testament Prophecy* (Edinburgh: T. & T. Clark, 1912).

Henshaw, T., *The Latter Prophets* (London: George Allen & Unwin, 1958).

Heschel, Abraham J., *The Prophets* (New York: Harper & Row, 1962).

Kirkpatrick, A. F., *The Doctrine of the Prophets* (London: Macmillan and Co., 1909).

Lindblom, J., *Prophecy in Ancient Israel* (Philadelphia: Muhlenberg Press, 1962).

Smart, James D., *Servants of the Word* (Philadelphia: The Westminster Press, 1960).

Young, Edward J., *My Servants the Prophets* (Grand Rapids: Wm. B. Eerdmans Publishing Co., 1955).

III. MONOGRAPHS

Anderson, Bernhard W., Ed., *The Old Testament and Christian Faith* (New York: Harper & Row, 1963).

Bright, John, *The Kingdom of God* (New York: Abingdon-Cokesbury Press, 1953).

Buber, Martin, *Moses — The Revelation and the Covenant* (New York: Harper. and Brothers, 1958).

Childs, Brevard S., *Myth and Reality in the Old Testament* (Naperville: Allenson, Inc., 1960).

Clements, R. E., *God and Temple* (Philadelphia: Fortress Press, 1965).

Eichrodt, Walther, *Man in the Old Testament* (London: SCM Press, Ltd., 1959).

Ellis, E. Earle, *Paul's Use of the Old Testament* (Grand Rapids: Wm. B. Eerdmans Publishing Co., 1960).

Hanke, Howard A., *From Eden to Eternity* (Grand Rapids: Wm. B. Eerdmans Publishing Co., 1960).

Herbert, Gabriel, *The Old Testament from Within* (New York: Oxford University Press, 1962).

Heim, Karl, *The World: Its Creation and Consummation* (Philadelphia: Muhlenberg Press, 1962).

Knight, George A. F., *Law and Grace* (Philadelphia: The Westminster Press, 1962).

Meek, Theophile James, *Hebrew Origins* (New York: Harper & Row, 1960).

Mowinckel, Sigmund, *The Old Testament as Word of God* (New York: Abingdon Press, 1959).

Nielson, Eduard, *Oral Tradition* (London: SCM Press, Ltd., 1955).

von Rad, Gerhard, *Studies in Deuteronomy* (London: SCM Press, Ltd., 1956).

Ringgren, Helmer, *Israelite Religion* (Philadelphia: Fortress Press, 1966).

———, *The Messiah in the Old Testament* (London: SCM Press, Ltd., 1956).

Robinson, H. Wheeler, *The Cross in the Old Testament* (Philadelphia: The Westminster Press, 1955).

————, *Inspiration and Revelation in the Old Testament* (Oxford: At the Clarendon Press, 1960).

————, *The Religious Ideas of the Old Testament* (New York: Charles Scribner's Sons, 1913).

Rowley, H. H., *The Faith of Israel* (Philadelphia: The Westminster Press, 1956).

————, Editor, *The Old Testament and Modern Study* (Oxford: At the Clarendon Press, 1961).

————, *The Re-Discovery of the Old Testament* (Philadelphia: The Westminster Press, 1946).

Sanders, J. A., *The Old Testament in the Cross* (New York: Harper and Brothers, 1961).

Sauer, Erich, *From Eternity to Eternity* (Grand Rapids: Wm. B. Eerdmans Publishing Co., 1954).

————, *The Dawn of World Redemption* (Grand Rapids: Wm. B. Eerdmans Publishing Co., 1953).

Snaith, Norman H., *The Distinctive Ideas of the Old Testament* (Philadelphia: The Westminster Press, 1946).

Stokes, Mack B., *The Epic of Revelation* (New York: McGraw-Hill Book Company, Inc., 1961).

Thielicke, Helmut, *How the World Began* (Philadelphia: Muhlenburg Press, 1961).

Thomson, James G. S. S., *The Old Testament View of Revelation* (Grand Rapids: Wm. B. Eerdmans Publishing Co., 1960).

Wahlstrom, Eric H., *God Who Redeems* (Philadelphia: Muhlenberg Press, 1962).

Westerman, Claus, Editor, *Essays on Old Testament Hermeneutics* (Richmond: John Knox Press, 1963).

Wingren, Gustaf, *Creation and Law* (Philadelphia: Muhlenberg Press, 1961).

Wright, G. Ernest, *God Who Acts* (London: SCM Press, Ltd., 1956).

————, *The Old Testament Against Its Environment* (London: SCM Press, Ltd., 1955).

————, *The Rule of God* (New York: Doubleday & Company, Inc., 1960).

Young, Edward J., *The Study of Old Testament Theology Today* (Fleming H. Revell, 1959).

Zimmerli, W., and Jeremias, J., *The Servant of God* (Naperville: Alec R. Allenson, Inc., 1957).

IV. BIBLE DICTIONARIES AND ENCYCLOPEDIAS

Dictionary of the Bible, James Hastings, Ed., Frederick C. Grant and H. H. Rowley, Rev. Ed. (New York: Charles Scribner's Sons, 1963).

A Dictionary of the Bible, James Hastings, Ed. (New York: Charles Scribner's Sons, 1905).

The International Standard Bible Encyclopaedia, James Orr, Gen. Ed., Melvin Grove Kyle, Rev. Ed. (Chicago: The Howard-Severance Company, 1930).

The Interpreter's Dictionary of the Bible, George Arthur Buttrick, Ed. (New York: Abingdon Press, 1962).

The New Bible Dictionary, J. D. Douglas, Ed. (Grand Rapids: Wm. B. Eerdmans Publishing Company, 1962).

The Westminster Dictionary of the Bible, John D. Davis and Henry Snyder Gehman (Philadelphia: The Westminster Press, 1944).

V. THEOLOGICAL WORD STUDIES

von Allmen, J. J., *A Companion to the Bible* (New York: Oxford University Press, 1958).

Baker's Dictionary of the Bible, Everett F. Harrison, Ed., (Grand Rapids: Baker Book House, 1960).

A Theological Word Book of the Bible, Alan Richardson, Ed. (New York: Macmillan Company, 1955).

VI. BIBLE COMMENTARY

The Interpreter's Bible, George Arthur Buttrick, Commentary Ed.; Walter Russell Bowie, Asst. Ed. of Exposition; Paul Scherer, Assoc. Ed. of Exposition; Samuel Terrien, Assoc. Ed., O. T. Intro. and Ex. (New York; Abingdon-Cokesbury Press, 1952). See introductions to Old Testament and to each of its books for articles or sections dealing with theological content.

INDEX OF BIBLICAL PASSAGES

GENESIS
1 . . . . 47, 49, 50
1; 2 . . . . 48, 50, 51, 53
1:1 ff. 51, 86
1:2 51
1:5 ff. . . . . 50 n. 8
1:7 ff. . . . . 49 n. 5
1:21, 27 . 48 n. l, 49 n. 4
1:26 f. 48
1:28 53
2 50
2; 3 61
2:1-3 . . . . 54, 55
2:2-4 . . . . 49 n. 5
2:3 f. . . . . 48 n. 1
2:4 . . . . 50 n. 8
2:8 59
2:9, 17 187
2:17 61
2:22 49
2:24 . . . . . 53, 130, 452
3:1 . . . 49 n. 5, 62, 63
3:4, 5 63
3:5 83
3:5, 22 187
3:15 . . . . . 65, 70, 81
3:19 62
3:22 . . . . 59, 61
4 — 6 69
4:7 . . . . 69, 187
4:13 188
4:26 . . . . 71, 72
5:1 . . . . 49 n. 5
5:1, 2 . . 48 n. 1, 49 n. 4
5:5 62
5:24 115
5:29 72
6:1-4 72
6:5 . . . . . . 69, 71, 187
6:6 . . . . 49 n. 5
6:6, 7 73
6:7 . . 48 n. 1, 49 n. 5
6:9 74
6:11 188
6:11, 12 72
6:13 73
8:20-22 75
8:21, 22 76
9:1-7 77
9:6 130
9:20-27 79
9:26 80
10 82
11:1-9 83

11:4-6 83
11:10-26 82
11:10-33 84
12:1-4 . . . . . 101 n. 20
12:1-3 . . . 24 n. 1, 89
12:3 . . . . 82, 89, 91
12:7 . . . . 92 n. 3, 101 n. 21,
         102 n. 22
13:4 . . . . . . 102 n. 24
13:10 . . . . . . 59 n. 18
13:14 . . . . . . 101 n. 20
13:15 . . . . 92 n. 3
14:19, 20 . . . . . . 90, 91
14:19, 22 49
15 . . . . 99, 102
15:1 . . . 101 n. 20, 102 n. 25
15:1-8 198
15:6 . . . . . . 93, 97, 194
15:7-21 93
15:16 . . . . . . 80 n. 5
15:18-21 174
16:7 ff. . . . . . 103 n. 28
17:1 94, 97, 100, 101 n. 21,
         126, 192
17:1 ff. . . . . . . 24 n. 1
17:3 99
17:4 82
17:7 . . . . 92 n. 3
17:9-14 94
18:1 . . . . . . 101 n. 21
18:17-32 198
18:18 91
18:19 . . . . . . 100, 198
18:20 188
18:22-33 . . . . . 99, 100
18:23, 25 189
19:5 . . . . 80 n. 5
20:3 . . . . . . 102 n. 27
21:17 . . . . . 103 n. 28
22:11 ff. . . . . 103 n. 28
22:18 . . . . . . 92 n. 3
24:4 92
24:7 . . . . 92 n. 3
24:7, 40 . . . . 103 n. 28
26:2-5, 24 . . . 101 n. 21
26:4 92
26:10 189
27:27-29, 39, 40 . 198 n. 1
28:13 105
28:14 91
28:20 f. 86, 106
31:10, 11, 24 . 102 n. 27
31:11, 13 . . . 103 n. 28
31:19 . . . . . 100 n. 18

31:36 . . . . . . 188, 189
32:10 106
32:24-30 . 103 n. 28, 107
35:1, 7, 9-15 . 102 n. 22
35:1-7 . . . . . 102 n. 24
37.5-20 . . . . 102 n. 27
39:3, 9 108
39:9 187
39:21 108
40:1 ff. 109
40:5 ff. . . . . . 102 n. 27
41:2, 4, 7 220
41:7-32 . . . . 102 n. 27
41:32 108
42:7, 30 190
42:21 189
44:16 188
45:7 f. 109
46:2 . . . . . . 102 n. 25
48:15 f. . . . . 103 n. 28
49 . . . . 198 n. 1
49:4 . . . . 190 n. 5
49:5 188
49:7 190
49:18 192 n. 8, 324 n. 16
50:15, 17, 20 187
50:17 188
50:24 198

EXODUS
1:14 190
3:2 ff. . . . . . . 24 n. 1
3:6, 15 f. . . . . 88 n. 1
3:20 . . . . 114 n. 7
4:2-8 195
4:2-9, 21 . . . 114 n. 7
4:10 . . . . 112 n. 3
4:10-16 199
4:12, 15 f. 218
4:14-16 . . . . 200 n. 2
4:22 115
5:5, 23 . . . . 113 n. 5
6:2 f. 86
6:2-4 . . . 24 n. 1, 88 n. l
6:3 f. 87
6:6 f. . . . . . . 114 n. 7
6:6-9 . . . . . . 113 n. 5
6:7 114
6:12, 30 . . . . . 95 n. 7
6:12-30 . . . . 60 n. 20
7:1 . . . . 200 n. 2
7:3, 9 ff. . . . 114 n. 7
8:19 . . . . 114 n. 7

9:15 f. . . . . . . 114 n. 7
9:16 . . . . 78, 114
9:27 188
10:16 188
11:3 112
12:1-13 . . . . 116 n. 14
12:2 f. 281
12:8 117
12:14 118
12:33-36 168
12:46 117
13:2, 12 f. 359
14:13 . . . 98, 324 n. 16
14:13, 30 . . 192 n. 8, 281
14:22, 31 . . . . . 114 n. 7
14:31 . . . 112 n. 3, 207
                    n. 2, 316
15:1-18 409
15:2 . . . . 192 n. 8
15:8, 11 . . . . . 114 n. 7
15:13 . . . . . . 116 n. 13
15:17, 18 122
15:20 f. . . . . . 200 n. 2
16:7, 10 180
16:22-30 128
17:7 . . . . 180 n. 7
17:14 . . . . . . 36 n. 29
18:19 199
19 — 24 . . . . . 199, 255
19:4 119
19:4 f. 126, 193
19:4-6 138
19:5 f. 175, 179
19:6 122
19:7 f. 120
19:10-14 . . . 162 n. 20
20 — 23 . . . . . 125, 192
20:4-6 127
20:5 188
20:11 51
20:12 125
20:25 . . . . . . 190 n. 4
21:15-17 . . . . 130 n. 25
23:1 . . . . 128 n. 22, 188
24 . . . . . . 112 n. 4, 123
24:1-10 120
24:3, 7 120
24:4 . . . . 36 n. 29, 125
24:7 . . . . 192, 290
24:8 121
24:11 121
24:17 93
25 — 30 166
25 — 31, 35 — 40 . . . 134
25:8 . . . . 134, 168
25:8 f. 281
25:9 138
25:30 140
26:1 138
28:38 . . . . . . 149 n. 15
29:42-45 . . . . . 138 n. 4
30:10 . . . . . . 159 n. 19
30:22-29 107

31:3 . . . . . 226 n. 6
31:3-5 168
31:14 . . . . . 190 n. 4
31:17 51
32:8 . . . . . . 190 n. 6
32:9 190
32:11-14 . . . . 112 n. 4
32:13 317
32:30 ff. 188
33:3, 5 190
33:7 167
33:7 ff. . . . . . . 138 n. 4
33:12-16 . . . . 112 n. 4
34:1-9 . . . . . . 112 n. 4
34:7 . . . . 188, 189
34:9 . . . . . . 188, 190
34:10 . . 114 n. 7, 115
                    n. 10
34:27 . . . . . . 36 n. 29
35 — 39 167
35:31 . . . . . 226 n. 6
39:32 f. . . . . 138 n. 4
40 167
40:17 168
40:34 143
40:34 f. 168
40:36-38 168

LEVITICUS
1:2 f. . . . . . . 149 n. 14
1:4 155
1:5-15 157
2:1 . . . . 149 n. 14
3:1 . . . . 149 n. 14
3:2, 8, 12 155
3:2-13 157
3:11, 16 . . . . 149 n. 16
4:2, 13, 22, 27 . . 190 n. 7
4:5-7, 16-19, 25, 29, 30,
34 . . . . 157 n. 7
4:20, 26, 31, 35 . 158 n. 18
5:6, 10, 13, 18 . . 158 n. 18
5:9 . . . . 157 n. 17
5:15, 18 . . . . . 190 n. 7
5:17 . . . . 188 n. 2
6:2 189
6:27 . . . . 162 n. 20
7:18 . . . . 188 n. 2
8:10 f. . . . . . . 169 n. 22
10:10 161
10:17 . . . . 188 n. 2
11:25, 28, 40 . . 162 n. 20
11:43, 44, 47 162
13:6, 34, 54, 58 . . . . .
                    162 n. 20
14:4, 6, 49-52 117
14:8 f., 47 . . 162 n. 20
15:5-8, 10, 13, 21 f., 27 . .
                    . . . 162 n. 20
15:31 . . . . . 169 n. 22
16 . . . . 159 n. 19
16:2 143

16:6, 11, 16, 18, 24, 32 . .
                    . . . 158 n. 18
16:14 f. 157
16:16 157
16:21 f. 155
16:22 . . . . 188 n. 2
16:26, 28 . . . . 162 n. 20
16:29-31 159
17:10 f. 77
17:11 . . . . 147, 148, 156,
                    157, 158 n. 18
17:14-16 162
17:15 . . . . . 162 n. 20
18:3 . . . . 80 n. 5
18:5 123
18:23 . . . . 190 n. 5
19:2 . . . . 139, 170,
          192, 193, 280, 357, 383
19:8, 12 . . . . . . 190 n. 4
19:12 . . . . . . 128 n. 22
19:15 191
19:17, 18 130
19:18 . . . . 126, 164
19:29 . . . 54 n. 13, 190 n. 5
19:36 165
20:3 . . . . 190 n. 4
20:7, 26 130
20:7, 8, 26 164
20:9 . . . . 130 n. 25
21:6, 8, 17, 21 f. . . . . .
                    . . . 149 n. 16
21:6, 12, 23 . . . 190 n. 4
21:14 f. . . . . . 190 n. 5
21:17-23 149
22:2 . . . . 190 n. 4
22:14 . . . . 190 n. 7
22:24 . . . . 80 n. 5
22:25 . . . . . . 149 n. 16
23:38 . . . . . . 149 n. 15
24:5-9 140
25:42, 55 317
26:40 189
26:41 . . . 60 n. 20, 95 n. 7

NUMBERS
1:50, 53 138
1:50-53 . . . . 169 n. 22
3:7 f., 21 ff. . . 169 n. 12
4:16, 24-33 . . . 169 n. 22
5:5 ff. 194
7:1-11 . . . . . 169 n. 22
7:12 ff. . . . . . 149 n. 14
8:7, 21 . . . . . 162 n. 20
8:10 f. 155
9:12 117
9:15 138
9:15-23 . . . . 169 n. 22
10:11 ff. . . . . . 169 n. 22
11:11 . . . . . . 112 n. 3
11:16 f. 113
11:17-29 113
11:20 . . . . 191, 226 n. 6
11:24, 29 . . . . 206 n. 2

11:26-29 113
12:2, 6 . . . . . . 206 n. 2
12:6 . . . . 102 n. 25
12:6 ff. 101
12:7 . . . . . . 112 n. 3
12:7 f. . . 207 n. 2, 316
12:8 . . 101 n. 20, 200, 207
12:9 113
12:11 199
14:9 191
14:11 195
14:29 f. . . . . . . 61 n. 21
15:22, 24-29 . . 190 n. 7
15:30 191
16:1-28 . . . . 169 n. 22
16:26 188
18:6, 29 . . . . 149 n. 15
19:7, 8, 10, 19, 21, 22 . . .
. . . 162 n. 20
20:12 195
20:24 . . . . . . 189 n. 3
21:1-3 . . . . 176 n. 4
22 — 24 . . . . . 26 n. 2
23:21 122
23:26-32 . . . . . 159 n. 19
24:2 . . . 218 n. 2, 226 n. 6
24:4, 16 . . . . 102 n. 25
24:14-20 183
25:16-18 . . . . 176 n. 4
27:14 . . . . . . 189 n. 3
27:18 . . . . . . 226 n. 6
27:18-20 . . . . . 155, 200
28:2 . . . . 149 n. 16
29:7-11 . . . . . 159 n. 19
31:21-24 . . . . 162 n. 20
32:23 188
33:2 . . . . 36 n. 29
35:11, 15 . . . . . 190 n. 7

DEUTERONOMY
1:1-5 173
1:8 . . 174 n. 2, 222 n. 1
1:8, 21 . . . . . . 174 n. 3
1:26, 43 . . . . . 189 n. 3
1:32 195
1:39 . . . . 61 n. 21
2:3, 8, 9, 19, 22, 37 . . .
. . 174 n. 3
2:36 . . . . 176 n. 4
3:2, 3, 18-21 . . 174 n. 3
3:6 . . . . 176 n. 4
3:24 . . . . . 112 n. 3, 177
4:3, 20 . . . . . . 174 n. 3
4:1-8 123
4:4 173
4:6 442
4:10 . . . . . . 113 n. 5
4:12 121
4:15-24 127
4:15-40 177
4:16 122
4:29, 30 194
4:29-31 183

4:31 . . . 174 n. 2, 222
4:32 . . . . 48 n. 1
4:32-35 44
4:37 . . . . 179 n. 5
5:1-21 129
5:10 181
5:12-15 128
5:15 125
6:1-15 123
6:4 . . . . 126, 331
6:5 . . . . 181, 192
6:6-9 178
6:10 . . . . 88 n. 1
6:10-19 . . . . 179 n. 6
6:10, 23 . . 174 n. 2,
222 n. 1
6:16-19 . . . . . 180 n. 7
7:1, 2, 16-26 . . 174 n. 3
7:2, 16, 22, 23 . . 176 n. 4
7:6 175
7:6-10 . . . . 116 n. 11
7:6, 7 . . . . . . 179 n. 5
7:6, 11 192
7:8 . . . . . . 116 n. 13
7:8, 12 . . 174 n. 2, 222
n. 1
7:9 . . . . 116, 174
8:1-10 . . . . . 123, 179
8:1-20 . . . . . . 179 n. 6
8:2-6 179
8:14 191
8:18 . . 174 n. 2, 222 n. 1
9:4, 5 . . 80 n. 5, 175,
189
9:4-6 . . 116 n. 11, 176
n. 4
9:6, 13 190
9:12, 16 . . . . . 190 n. 6
9:13-21 . . . . . . 112 n. 4
9:18 188
9:22-24 . . . . . . 180 n. 7
9:23 . . . 189 n. 3, 195
9:26 . . . . . . 116 n. 13
9:27 . . . . . . 188, 317
10:10, 11 . . . . 112 n. 4
10:12 182
10:12-22 . . . . 123, 173
10:15 . . 116 n. 11, 179
n. 5
10:16 . . . . 95 n. 7
11:8, 9 . . . . . . 174 n. 2
11:8-12, 22-32 . . 222 n. 1
11:16, 28 . . . . . 190 n. 6
11:24 174
12:5-14 . . . . 169 n. 22
12:11-21 . . . . 184 n. 8
12:29-32 . . . . . 80 n. 5
13:3, 4 182
13:5 . . . . 116 n. 13, 190
14:1, 2 115
14:1-21 162
14:2 . . . . 179 n. 5
14:23-25 . . . . 184 n. 8

15:5 173
15:15 . . . . . . 116 n. 13
16:1-8 . . . . . . 116 n. 14
17:7, 12 187
17:20 . . . . 190 n. 6
18:9-14 182
18:13 . . . . . . 100, 182
18:15 . . . . . . 113 n. 5
18:15-20 199
18:18 210
19:19 187
20:1-4 . . . . . . 176 n. 4
21:8 . . . . . . 116 n. 13
21:18, 20 189
21:18, 21 . . . . 130 n. 25
21:21 187
23.5 200
23:18 . . . . . . 54 n. 13
24:18 . . . . . . 116 n. 13
25:1 189
25:15 191
26:1-15 . . . . . 184 n. 8
26:15 . . . . . . 143 n. 8
27:2-8 224
27:16 . . . . . . 130 n. 25
28 183
28:1-19 124
28:53 183
28:59 183
29:9, 29 192
29:13 . . . 174, 174 n. 2,
222
30:2, 8, 10 194
30:6 . . . . 95 n. 7
30:15-20 124
31:9, 22 . . . . . 36 n. 29
31:24-26 173
31:27 . . . 189, 189 n. 3
31:29 . . . . 190 n. 6
32:6 . . . . 49, 116 n. 11
32:15 . . . 192 n. 4, 324
n. 16
32:44-46 173
32:51 189
33:2-5 122
33.8 . . . . 180 n. 7
33:29 . . . . . . 192 n. 8
34 207
34:1-12 173
34:4 . . 174 n. 2, 222 n. 1
34:5 . . . 112 n. 3, 207
n. 2
34:9 . . 155, 200, 226 n. 6,
442

JOSHUA
1:1-8 . . . . 24 n. 1
1:2, 7, 13, 15 . . 207 n. 2
1:3 . . . . 222 n. 2
1:7 . . . . 40 n. 26
1:8 . . . . 224 n. 4
5:6 224
5:9 224

5:14, 15 229
7:20, 21 227
8:30-35 . . . . 24 n. 1, 224
8:31 . . . . 40 n. 26, 224
18:1 224
22:4 . . . . . . 222 n. 2
22:5 225
23; 24 200
23:5, 14, 15 . . . 222 n. 2
23:6 . . . . 224, 227
23:6-13 223
24:1 f. . . . . . . 85 n. 15
24:2, 3 . . . . 100 n. 18
24:2, 6 . . . 224 n. 4
24:2-4 . . . . . . 88 n. 1
24:2-13 . . . . 222 n. 2
24:3-13 222
24:4-7 . . . . . 115 n. 10
24:14 227
24:19, 20 225
24:19-24 223
24:29 . . . . . . 207 n. 2

JUDGES
2:1 226
2:11-15, 16-23 . 223 n. 3
3:7, 12 . . . . . 227 n. 7
3:7-9, 12-15 . . 223 n. 3
3:10 . . . . 226 n. 5
3:15 226
4:1-3 . . . . . . 223 n. 3
4:5 200
6:1, 2 . . . . . . 223 n. 3
6:7-10 200
6:34 . . . . 226 n. 5
9:56, 57 . . . . 223 n. 3
10:6 . . . . 227 n. 7
10:6-16 . . . . . 223 n. 3
11:29 . . . . . . 226 n. 5
13:25 . . . . . . 226 n. 5
14:6, 19 . . . . 226 n. 5
15:14 . . . . . . 226 n. 5
17:6 . . . 226, 227 n. 7
21:25 . . . 226, 227 n. 7

RUTH
2:4 225

1 SAMUEL
1:3, 9, 19, 24 . . . 169 n. 23
1:3, 11 . . . . . 229 n. 10
1:5, 19, 20 231
1:9 . . . . 143 n. 9
1:28 228
2:1-10 228
2:11, 12 . . . . 169 n. 23
2:22-25 . . . . . 54 n. 13
2:27 . . . . 207 n. 1
2:27-36 200
2:29, 32 . . . . 143 n. 4
3:3 . . 143 n. 9, 169 n. 23
3:19-21 201
4:4 . . . . . . 229 n. 10

6:19, 20 231
8:5-7 122
9:6 201
9:9 201
9:9, 11, 18, 19 . . . . . .
. . . . . . 209 n. 5
10:1-13 234
10:10 202
12:6-18 231
13:14 235
15:2 . . 229 n. 10, n. 11
15:10 228
16:13 234
16:14 234
17:45 . . . . 229 n. 10
19:11, 12 . . . 235 n. 15
21:1-6 . . . . 169 n. 24
22:1 . . . . . 235 n. 15
23:14 . . . . . 235 n. 15
24:5 . . . . . . 235 n. 15

2 SAMUEL
5:2 230
6:2, 18 . . . . 229 n. 10
7:4-11 231
7:8 . . . 229 n. 11, 230
7:12-14 426
7:16 320
11:2-27 . . . 235 n. 16
12:13 235
15:27 . . . . 209 n. 5
22:23 230
23:1 409
23:2 234
23:2, 3 203
24:1-9 . . . . . 235 n. 16
24:11 . 201, 203, 209 n. 6

1 KINGS
2:3 . . . . 40 n. 26
3:6 235
4:29-32 442
8:4 . . . . 169 n. 25
8:13 . . . . . 143 n. 10
8:53 . . . . . . 40 n. 26
10:1-25 442
11 446
11:26-40 232
11:29-39 203
12:15 232
12:24 203
13:1 . . . . 207 n. 1
14:8 . . . . 207 n. 2
15:12 . . . . . . 54 n. 13
17:18, 24 . . . . 217 n. 1
18:36 . . . . 88 n. 1
19:14 . . . . . 229 n. 10
20:13, 22, 28 205
20:28 . . . . . . 207 n. 1
22:5-28 205
22:24 . . . . . 218 n. 2
22:46 . . . . . . 54 n. 13
32:40 203

2 KINGS
4:6, 16, 22, 25, 40, 42 . . .
. . . 207 n. 1
5:20 . . . . 207 n. 1
6:9, 10, 15 . . . . 207 n. 1
7:17-19 . . . . . 207 n. 1
9:7-36 . . . . . . 207 n. 2
13:23 . . . . 88 n. 1
14:6 . . . . 40 n. 26
14:25 . . . . 207 n. 2
17:7-18 . . 205, 210, 232
17:13 . . . . 209 n. 6
21:8 . . . . 40 n. 26
22:8 — 23:3 172
23:21-23 224
23:25 . . . . . . 40 n. 26
24:1-7 232

1 CHRONICLES
1:3 . . . . . . 169 n. 25
6:49 . . . . 40 n. 26
9:22 . . . . . . 209 n. 5
12:18 . . . . . 218 n. 2
17:7 . . . 229 n. 11, 230
21:1-17 . . . . 235 n. 16
21:8 235
21:9 . . . . . . 209 n. 6
22:13 . . . . . 40 n. 26
25:5 . . . . . . 209 n. 6
26:28 . . . . . 209 n. 5
29:3 . . . . . . 119 n. 15
29:11, 17 . . . . 228, 229
29:29 . . . 201, 209 n. 5,
n. 6

2 CHRONICLES
1:8-12 442
5:25 . . . . . . 169 n. 25
6:2 . . . . . . 143 n. 10
6:14 . . . . . . 232, 233
8:13 . . . . . . 40 n. 26
9:29 . . . . . . 209 n. 6
12:15 . . . . . 209 n. 6
15:1 . . . . . . 218 n. 2
16:7, 10 . . . . 209 n. 5
19:2 . . . . . . 209 n. 6
20:7 . . 93 n. 4, 99 n. 16
20:13-17 234
20:14 . . . . . 218 n. 2
23:18 . . . . . 40 n. 26
24:20 . . . . . 218 n. 2
25:4 . . . . . . 40 n. 26
29:25 203
29:25, 30 . . . . 209 n. 6
30 224
30:6 . . . . 88 n. 1
30:16 . . . . . 40 n. 26
32:27-31 229
33:8 . . . . . . 40 n. 26
33:18, 19 . . . 209 n. 6
34:14 . . . . . 40 n. 26
34:14-33 172
35:12 . . . . . 40 n. 26

35:15 . . . . . . 209 n. 6
36:15 . . . . 208 n. 3

EZRA
3:7 325
6:18 . . . . 40 n. 26
7:6 . . . . 40 n. 26

NEHEMIAH
1:7, 8 . . . . . . 40 n. 26
3:1, 14 . . . . . . 40 n. 26
9:6 47
9:7 . . . . 88 n. 1
9:13, 14 . . . . . 40 n. 26
9:20, 30 . . . . . . 218 n. 2
9:30 234
10:29 . . . . . . 40 n. 26
13:1 . . . . 40 n. 26

JOB
4:17 457
12:13 457
13:13 457
23:7 457
25:2 457
28:28 455
33:4-26 457
34:17 457
35:10 457
36:3, 5, 22 457
37:22-24 455
38:4 455
38:4-7 44
38:4 — 41:34 457
40:8 455

PSALMS
1 432
1:5 425
1:5, 6 433
2 . . . . 231, 320
2:1, 2, 7 . . . . 426, 428
3:8 . . . . 324 n. 16
5:7 . . . . 143 n. 9
6:15 437
7 . . . . 419, 439
7:6 425
7:9 433
7:10 433
7:11 419
7:12-16 419
8 420
8:3 . . . . . 44, 49 n. 3
8:5, 6 52
9 419
9:17 438
10:15 435
10:17 433
11 415
11:2, 7 433
11:4 . . . . 143 n. 9
12:2 . . . . . . 128 n. 22
15 432

15:2 433
15:3 . . . . 128 n. 22
16 429
16:8-11 426
16:9, 10 438
17 415
17:3 . . . . 229 n. 9
17:15 438
18 422
18:7-19, 20-24 423
18:8 . . . . 93 n. 5
18:25 433
18:27 . . . . . . 433, 435
19 431
19:1 44
19:7 . . . . . 139, 139 n. 5
19:7-9 . . . . . . 424, 425
19:9 . . . . 163 n. 21
20:3 416
22 . . . 420, 426, 427, 433
23 413
24 . . . . 414, 432
24:1, 2 420
24:2 . . 49 n. 2, n. 3, 420
24:3, 4 . . . 163, 163 n. 21
24:4 . . . . 128 n. 22
24:10 . . . . . 229 n. 10
25 . . . . 434, 436
25:7 435
25:7, 8 418
25:10, 14 425
25:11 435
25:19 433
26:2 . . . . 229 n. 9
26:8 . . . . 143 n. 8
27 412
27:13 438
30 415
30:3 437
30:9 437
31 434
31:5 427
31:17, 18 438
32 . . . . 435, 436
32:1, 2 235
33 412
33:6 229
33:6-9 . . . . . . 44, 47
33:9 . . . . 49 n. 7
33:12 425
34 . . 235 n. 15, 410, 412
34:8 418
34:14 433
35 439
37 440
37:3, 27 433
37:7, 8 418
37:11 433
37:12 433
37:12, 14, 16 435
37:13 425
37:18 433
37:18, 28 438

38:18 436
39:12, 13 437
41:6 . . . . 128 n. 22
41:9 427
42; 43 410
44 423
45 . . . . 320, 426, 428
46 431
46:7, 10 . . . . 229 n. 10
46:7, 11 390
47 . . . . 411, 423
47:4 416
49 431
49:10-14 438
49:15 438
50 . . . . 415, 416, 439
50:5 425
50:6 419
50:18 435
51 . . . . . 235, 430, 436
51:1 235
51:1, 2 417
51:1, 3 435
51:2, 7, 10 . . 163 n. 21
51:7 117
51:13 435
52 440
54 440
55 439
55:15 438
55:22 434
57 . . . . 235 n. 15
58 439
58:2 435
59 . . . 235 n. 15, 439
59:3 435
60:6 416
62:2 . . . . . 324 n. 16
62:4, 9 435
62:10 435
63 . . . . . 235 n. 15, 410
63:9 437
65:6 . . . . 49 n. 3, 420
66:10 . . . . . 229 n. 9
68 411
68:18 429
68:19 . . . . . 324 n. 16
69 . . . . 417, 439, 440
69:5 435
69:9 427
69:24 425
71:4 435
72 . . . . 320, 426
72:14 435
73:8 435
73:23-25 438
74 414
74:20 425
75 419
78 423
78:4 . . . . 139 n. 5
78:8 435
78:10 . . . . . 425, 435

78:17 435	106:5 425	**PROVERBS**
78:42-51 . . . . 114 n. 7	106:6 435	1:1-7 443
78:57 435	106:7-33 . . . . 115 n. 10	2:16-19 452
78:69 . . . . 49 n. 2, 420	107 410	3:4 445
79 . . . . 431, 439	108:7 416	3:7 a 445
80 431	109 439	3:11, 12 445
82 432	110 . 231, 320, 426, 429	3:18 . . . . . . 59 n. 19
82:6 56	110:4 91	3:19 . . . . 49 n. 2
83 439	112:5 433	3:34 445
84 . . . . . . 410, 412, 413	115:15 420	4:26 a 445
84:11 433	115:17 437	5:3-20 452
85 431	118:17-20 438	5:5 445
86:5 418	118:22 . . . . . 146 n. 11	5:23 446
86:13 437	118:22, 23 428	6:23-33 452
88:3-6 437	119 . . . . 24 n. 1, 425	7:5-27 452
88:10-12 437	119:14 139	7:27 445
88:11 437	119:14, 31, 46, 88,	8:12-21 443
89 . . . . . . 414, 417, 429	99, 111, 129, 144,	8:15 445
89:2-18 45	157 . . . . 139 n. 5	8:22-31 443
89:3, 4 429	119:21, 118 435	9:10 443
89:11 . . . . 49 n. 2	119:66, 68 418	9:13-18 452
89:12 420	119:67 435	9:18 445
89:28 417	119:73, 90 . . . . 49 n. 3	10:12b 445
89:35 416	119:88 139	11:30 . . . . . . 59 n. 19
90 437	119:90 420	11:31 445
90:2 . . . . 420, 437	119:121 433	13:12 . . . . . . 59 n. 19
90:9, 10 437	119:129 139	14:5 131
91 . . . . 413, 437	119:137 425	15 446
92 440	119:144 139	15:4 . . . . . . 59 n. 19
93 411	119:165-168 431	15:11, 24 445
93:1 . . . . . 49 n. 3, 420	121:2 420	17:5 444
94:17 437	122 . . . . 396, 413	19:5 131
95 . . . . . 410, 415, 431	124:8 420	20:17 445
95:5 420	125 439	20:22 444
95:8 435	129 439	22:6 130
95:11 . . . . 55, 129	130 431	23:14 445
96 . . . . . . 411, 416, 420	132 429	23:27, 28 452
96:10 . . . . 49 n. 3, 420	132:11 429	24:17, 18, 29 444
97 416	133 . . . . 432, 433	24:29 445
99 . . . . 412, 416	134:3 420	25:18 131
99:4 419	135 119	25:21 445
100:3 420	135:4 425	25:21, 22 . . . . 444, 445
101 439	136 . . 411, 417, 421, 424	26:11a 445
101:2, 6 437	136:1, 5-8 45	
102:25 . . . . 49 n. 2, 420	136:10-16 . . . . 115 n. 10	**ECCLESIASTES**
102:25-27 47	137:8 439	1 447
102:26, 28 437	139 . . . . 413, 414, 439	2 447
103 . . . 113, 410, 411, 437	139:8 437	2:8 . . . . 119 n. 15
103:9, 10 435	139:24 438	5 447
103:18 425	141 412	5:1-6 449
104 . . . . 437, 439	142 . . . . 235 n. 15	7:1-14 449
104:5 . . . . 49 n. 2	143 412	8 447
104:24 420	143:10 418	8:16 — 10:12 448
104:24 bf, 30 45	145 439	9:10 449
104:30 420	145-150 411	10:2 449
104:33, 35 421	145:8, 9 419	11:1 450
105 . . . 113, 411, 423	146:5-7 420	12 448
105:6, 9 . . . . . 88 n. 1	146:6 420	
105:6, 43 425	146:8 416	**ISAIAH**
105:8-10 425	147:19 . . . . . . 101 n. 20	1:1 . . . . 24 n. 1, 218,
105:19 . . . . . 229 n. 9	148 422	220, 258 n. 12
105:23-42 . . . . 115 n. 10	148:5 . . . . 49 n. 7	1:2 253
106 . . . . 113, 411	149:4 433	1:2-17 212

1:3 291
1:4 . . . . 245, 287, 291
1:4-6 280
1:5, 6 . . . . . 287, 291
1:7-9 263
1:10 253
1:11, 13, 14 169
1:16, 17 . . . . . 287, 291
1:16-18 280
1:18-20 . . . . . 247, 253
1:21-23 291
1:24, 25 263
1:27, 28 . . 249, 263, 292
2:1 218
2:1, 5 . . . . . . 258 n. 12
2:1-4 . . . . . 258 n. 13
2:2 275
2:2-4 . . . . 82, 251 n. 5
2:2-5 271
2:10-21 244
2:11, 12, 17 . . 263, 264
3:1 . . . . . . 258 n. 12
3:13, 14 247
3:15 . . . . 230 n. 12
4:2 339
4:2-6 . . 248, 258 n.13, 268, 280
4:3, 4 280
4:4 296
5:1-30 . . . . . 258 n. 12
5:5, 6 264
5:8-23 264
5:12 246
5:13, 14 300
5:16 . . . . 245, 246
5:18 291
5:24 253
5:25 247
5:26 249
6 280
6:1 . . . . 143 n. 9
6:1-3 . . . . 24 n. 1, 140
6:1-13 216
6:3 140
6:3, 5 163
6:5 . . . . . . 163 n. 21
6:5, 7 296
6:9, 10 287
6:11-13 264
6:13 276
7:1-9 . . . . . . 288, 296
7:2-17 . . . . . . 218 n. 3
7:3 218
7:9 249
7:13-16 . . . . . 61 n. 21
7:14 . 249, 258 n. 13, 269
7:14-17 268
7:15-17 269
7:17 264
7:18-25 264
8:1, 5, 11 218
8:5-10 269
8:11-15 297

8:14, 15 . 146 n. 11, 269, 270
8:17, 18 297
8:18, 19 300
8:19, 20 297
8:20 253
9 320
9:1-7 . 258 n. 13, 270, 297
9:1, 6, 7 250
9:8 — 10:27 . 258 n. 12
9:11 250
9; 11 339
9:12, 17, 21 . 247 n. 3, 297 n. 29
10:4 . 247 n. 3, 297 n. 29
10:20-22 245
10:20-23 276
11 320
11:1 396
11:1-10 . . . . 258 n. 13
11:3-10 271
11:6-9 . . . . . . 77, 271
11:9, 10 272
11:10, 11 250
11:11 276
12 246
12:1, 2 297
12:2 . . . . . 324 n. 16
13 — 23 265
13:1-11 288
13:4, 5 264
13:9-11 . . . . 291, 292
13:9, 13 265
13:10 . . . . . . 248, 264
14:1 246
14:1, 2 . . 258 n. 13, 276
14:1, 32 . . . . 258 n. 12
14:1-14 288
14:3-20 301
15:1 218
16:1-5 . . . . . 258 n. 13
16:5 . . 258 n. 12, 272 n. 18
17:1 218
17:4-8 . . . . . . 258 n. 12
17:7 248
18:7 . . . . 258 n. 12
20 . . . . 221 n. 5
20:3 . . . . 207 n. 2
21:6, 8 . . . . . . 209 n. 7
21:11, 12 . . . . 209 n. 8
24 — 27 265
24:5 . . 253, 258, 265, 288, 292
24:14 244
24:14-16 245
24:17-23 265
24:23 . . 258 n. 13, 272 n. 18
25:8 300
25:8, 9 . . . . . 246, 247
25:9 297
26:1-4 . . . . . . 281, 298
26:1-9 288

26:10 244
26:14 302
26:19 . . . . 302 n. 33
26:21 248
27:6 276
27:9 291
27:12, 13 276
28:14, 15 301
28:16 . . 14 n. 11, 258 n. 13, 272 n. 18, 298
28:16, 17 . . . . . 245, 272
28:29 270
29:10 209
29:13-15 288
29:18, 19 . . . . 272 n. 18
29:22, 23 . . . . . 88 n. 1
29:22-24 . . . 258 n. 12
30:10 . . . . . 209 n. 5
30:10, 11 209
30:18, 19 247
30:26 401
32:1-5, 15-20 . . 272 n. 18
32:15, 16 282
32:15-17 298
33:2 . . . . . . 324 n. 16
33:5, 6, 17, 20-22 . . 272 n. 18
34:2-8 265
34:8 248
34:16 . . . . . . 254, 283
35 . . . . . . 272 n. 18
35:1, 2 245
35:5, 6 273
35:5-10 298
35:8-10 . 258 n. 13, 273
36 . . . . 218 n. 3
37:13-16 45
38:17-19 301
39 . . . . 218 n. 3
40:1 308
40:3-5 313
40:3-8 314
40:5 313
40:5-31 304
40:9 339
40:10 314
40:12-28 312
40:15, 17 310
40:20, 21 45
40:25 305
40:28 305
40:31 . . . . . . 305 n. 1
41:2 307
41:2-4 311
41:4 323
41:8 . . 93 n. 4, 99 n. 16
41:8 ff. 317
41:14 306
41:17-20 . . . . 312, 324
41:20 48
41:22, 23 . . . 323 n. 14
42:1-4 . . 318, 318 n. 12
42:1-5 312

42:1-7 . . 322, 323 n. 15
42:1-9 45
42:5 . . . . 49 n. 4
42:6 320
42:6, 7 306
42:9 . . . . . . 323 n. 14
42:18-25 . . . . 317 n. 11
43:1 . . . . . . 48, 49 n. 4
43:1-4 308
43:3 305
43:3-14 311
43:7 52
43:8 . . . . 317 n. 11
43:8-28 308
43:14 . . . . . . 306 n. 4
43:14, 15 312
43:14-21 . . . . 324 n. 18
43:15 . . . . . . 305, 322
43:15-21 . . . . . 305 n. 1
43:18, 19 . . 323 n. 14
43:27 208
43:28 309
44:6 . . . . 322, 323
44:6, 7 314
44:6-17 . . . . . . 305 n. 1
44:21 ff. . . . . . 317 n. 11
44:22 317
44:24-28 . . . . . 306 n. 4
44:24 — 45:8 311
44:26, 28 . . . . 324 n. 18
44:28 309
45:1 ff. 309
45:5, 7, 12, 18 . . . 45, 46
45:7, 18 . . . . . . 49 n. 4
45:8 307
45:12 . . . . 49 n. 7
45:13 311
45:15-17 307
45:17 323
45:18 . . . . . . 48, 312
46:5-11 . . . . . 305 n. 1
46:9-13 . . . . 323 n. 15
46:12 307
46:12, 13 . . . . . 308 n. 6
47:3 310
47:5-9 311
47:6 304
47:7 305
48:1 ff. . . . . . 317 n. 11
48:3-7 . . . . 323 n. 14
48:4 317
48:9, 10 317
48:9-11 310
48:12 323
48:12, 13 313
48:13 . . . . 49 n. 2
48:16 . . . . . . 218 n. 2
48:17-20 . . . . 304 n. 4
48:20, 21 . . . 324 n. 18
49:1-6 . . . 318, 318 n. 12
49:1-13 306
49:6 . . . 82, 312, 317, 320,
                323 n. 15

49:6, 7 314
49:6, 8 . . . . . . 324 n. 16
49:8 . . . . 129, 314, 321
50:4-9 . . . 318, 318 n. 12
51:1, 5, 6, 8 307
51:1-6 . . . . . . 308 n. 6
51:2 . . . . 88 n. 1
51:2, 3 324
51:3 . . . . 59 n. 18
51:6, 8 . . . . 324 n. 16
51:10, 11 . . . 324 n. 18
51:11 325
51:13, 16 . . . . . . 49 n. 2
52 — 55 193
52:1-10 304
52:7 . . . . 323, 339
52:7-12 321
52:7, 10 . . . . . 324 n. 16
52:8 . . . . 209 n. 7
52:9, 10 . . . . 323 n. 15
52:11. 12 . . . . 324 n. 18
52:13 — 53:12 . . 315, 318
                 n. 12, 319, 321
52:15 . . . . 321, 322
53 . . . 151, 154, 156, 397
53:1 . . . . 313, 321
53:4 321
53:4-12 . . . . . 151, 152
53:5, 6 163
53:5, 6, 9 321
53:7, 8 321
53:12 322
54:5-10 306
54:7, 8 . . . . . 324 n. 18
54:7, 10 . . . . . 304, 308
54:9, 10 79
54:10 306
55:3 . . . . . . 306, 324
55:3-7 308
55:5 . . . . . . 324, 325
55:12, 13 . . . 324 n. 18
56:1 313
56:6-8 . . . . . 324 n. 18
56:7 325
56:10 . . . . . 209 n. 7
57:15 . . . . . . 305 n. 1
58:12-14 . . . . 324 n. 18
59:16, 17 307
59:20, 21 . . 324 n. 18, 325
60:3-5 82
60:17, 18 307
61 325
61:1, 2 322
61:1-4 . . 315, 318 n. 12,
                          319
61:9 326
61:11 326
62:1 . . . . 308 n. 6, 326
62:1, 2 307
62:6 . . . . 209 n. 8
62:11, 12 326
62:12 306
63:1-6 310

63:7-9 309
63:15 . . . . . . 143 n. 10
63:15, 16 . . . . . 305 n. 1
64:8-12 310
65:17 . . 54, 128, 323
65:17-25 . . . . . 323, 327
65:17 ff. . . . . . 323 n. 14
65:18 327
65:25 77
66:10-23 327
66:22, 23 323

JEREMIAH
1:1-12 216
1:2 218
1:2, 4, 11, 13, 14
                       337 n. 8
1:4, 7, 9, 11, 13 . . 331 n. 1
1:4-10 24
1:5 333
1:5-10 337
2 — 4 338
2:1, 4 . . 331 n. 1, 337
                         n. 8
2:3 . . . . 345, 347
2:4-25 348
2:5-32 331
2:5, 17, 19 348
2:8, 29 348
2:13 331
2:19 . . . . 341, 348
2:20 348
2:20, 25 348
2:21 348
2:22 . . 163 n. 2, 348, 351
                         n. 16
2:27, 28 . . . . 336 n. 6
2:28 331
3:1-10 348
3:1, 6-8 348
3:3 348
3:6, 11 . . 331 n. 1, 337
                         n. 8
3:6-12 348
3:7, 8, 10, 11, 20 . . . 348
3:8, 9 348
3:10, 17 332
3:12, 13 332
3:12-14, 22, 23 . . 339 n. 13
3:13 348
3:13, 20 348
3:17, 19 343
3:21 348
3:22, 23 . . 332, 336 n. 7
3:25 350
4:1-4, 14 . . . . . 349 n. 13
4:3, 4, 14 . . . . . 351 n. 16
4:4 . . . . 95 n. 8
4:14 . . . 163 n. 21, 348
4:16-27 341
5:2 . . . . 128 n. 22
5:3 348
5:3, 19 348

5:6 348
5:7 348
5:7, 8 348
5:11 348
5:12-14 337
5:17 . . . . . . 351 n. 15
5:22, 24 332
5:23 348
5:27 348
5:30, 31 348
6; 7 338
6:7 348
6:9 . . . . 230 n. 12
6:10 . . . . 95 n. 8
6:12, 13 396
6:13-15 348
6:17 . . . . 209 n. 7
6:20 . . . . 345 n. 12
7:3-7 . . . . 349 n. 13
7:4, 8, 14 . . . . 351 n. 15
7:9 . . . . . 128 n. 22, 348
7:21 218
7:21-26 . . 169, 212, 345
        n. 12
7:23 345
7:23, 24 120
7:24 348
7:26 348
7:28 348
7:32-34 341
8:3 341
8:5 348
8:7 . . . . 332 n. 3
8:8 ff. 348
9:2 348
9:4, 5 . . . . . . 351 n. 15
9:6 348
9:14, 26 348
9:23, 24 332
9:24 332
9:25, 26 . . . . . . 95 n. 8
9:26 . . . . 35 n. 16
10:6, 7 331
10:10 331
10:11 331
10:12 . . . 49 n. 3, 331
10:12, 13 332
10:23 348
11:1-10 338
11:8 348
11:10 348
11:15 . . . . . 345 n. 12
11:18 . . . 333 n. 4, 348
11:20 . . . . 333 n. 5
12:1 332
12:3 . . . . 333 n. 5
12:3, 4 . . . . . . 333 n. 4
12:15-17 344
13:1-7 . . . . . 221 n. 5
13:9 348
13:10 348
13:15 348
13:22 348

13:23 . . 348, 351 n. 16
13:25 . . . . 351 n. 15
13:26, 27 348
13:27 . . . . . . 163 n. 21
14:7 . . . . 348, 350
14:8, 9 . . . . . . 336 n. 7
14:14 348
14:20 350
14:22 . . . . . 332 n. 2, 3
15:3, 4 341
15:15 . . . . 333 n. 4
15:19, 20 . . . . . 336 n. 7
16:10 348
16:10-13 348
16:12 348
16:14, 15 344
16:17 . . . . 333 n. 5
16:21 . . . 332 n. 2, 333
17:1, 9 348
17:5 . . . . 351, 351 n. 15
17:5, 13 348
17:6-8 351
17:9, 10 . . . . . 333 n. 5
17:13 . . . . . . 332 •n. 2
17:13, 14 . . . . 336 n. 7
17:16 . . . . 333 n. 4
17:23 348
18:5-11 . . . 332 n. 2, 334
18:12 348
18:18 348
18:23 . . . . 333 n. 4
19 . . . . 221 n. 5
19:15 348
20:3-6 . . . . . . 218 n. 3
20:8 348
20:12 . . . . 333 n. 5
21:2, 3 . . . . . . 218 n. 3
21:4-10 334
22:3, 17 348
23:5 . . 268 n. 15, 332,
        396
23:5, 6 339
23:7, 8 344
23:10 . . . . . 343 n. 10
23:17 348
23:23, 24 . . . . 331, 333
23:23-32 337
23:29 333
23:36 348
24:4-7 . . . . . 344 n. 11
24:7 . . 345, 351 n. 16
25:8 348
25:13 337
25:15-26 334
26:13 . . . . 349 n. 13
27 335
27:5 . . 46, 332 n. 3, 336
28:5-11 . . . . . 218 n. 3
28:16 348
29:1-9 . . . 218 n. 3, 335
29:10-14 . . . . 335, 350
29:23 . . . . 333, 333 n. 4
29:32 348

30:3-24 . . . . . . 344 n. 11
30:10, 11 . . . . 336 n. 6
30:24 . . . . . . 343 n. 10
31:1-25 . . . . 344 n. 11
31:3 332
31:3, 10 335
31:7-9 . . . . . . 336 n. 6
31:31-34 . . 24 n. 1, 338
        n. 9, 350
31:33, 34 . . . 351 n. 16
31:35-37 . . . 46, 332 n. 3
32:17 . . . . 332 n. 3
32:17-20 333
32:17-25 332
32:18 332
32:27 333
32:32-35 348
32:37-41 . . . . . . 338 n. 9
32:42 335
33:7 . . . . 209 n. 7
33:8 348-351
33:14-16 339
33:15 . . . 268 n. 15, 396
33:17, 18 339
33:19-22 . . . . . 332 n. 2
33:20-22 . 338 n. 9, 344
33:25, 26 78
33:26 . . . . 88 n. 1
34:13-18 348
34:18 348
34:18-20 93
35:15 . . . . . . 349 n. 13
36:3 . . . 342, 351 n. 14
36:11-19 . . . 218 n. 3
38:4-28 . . . . 218 n. 3
42:11 . . . . . . 336 n. 6
43:2 348
46:10, 21 342
46:16 348
48:29 348
48:29, 30 348
48:47 . . . . . . 343 n. 10
49:39 . . . . . 343 n. 10
50; 51 342
50:5 . . . . 338 n. 9
50:13, 27 342
50:20 . . . . . . 351 n. 14
50:31, 32 348
50:34 . . . . . . 336 n. 7
51:15 . . . . 49 n. 3
51:15, 16 . 332 n. 2, n. 3
51:20 335
51:35, 46 348

LAMENTATIONS
3:22, 23 332
3:40-42 . . . . 351 n. 14

EZEKIEL
1 372
1:1 . . . . 218, 220
1:2 217
1:24, 28 . . . . . 354 n. 3

1:28 . . . . . . 220, 355
1:28, 29 79
2:1 218
2:1-5 384
2:2 . . . . 371 n. 21
3:1, 4 218
3:12, 14, 24 . . 371 n. 21
3:12, 23 . . . . . 354 n. 3
3:16-21 383
3:17 . . . . 209, 209 n. 7
3:19-21 386
3:26 . . . . 221 n. 5
4:1-3 . . . . . . 221 n. 5
5:6, 7 . . . . . . 387 n. 35
5:11 . . . . 355 n. 5
6:7 . . . 358, 358 n. 11,
361
6:9 . . . . 385 n. 30
6:11 218
7:2, 3, 10-27 . . . 377 n. 2
7:5-9 . . . . . . 359 n. 12
8 . . . . 368 n. 18
8:3 . . . . 371 n. 21
9:3 . . . . 354 n. 3
9:4 383
10:4, 5, 18, 19 . . 354 n. 3
11:1, 5, 24 . . . 371 n. 21
11:12 . . . . 387 n. 35
11:19 387
11:19-21 . . 383 n. 27,
386 n. 34
11:22, 23 . . . . . 354 n. 3
12:1 ff. . . . . . . 221 n. 5
13:2, 12, 13 359
14:2-5 . . . . . . 368 n. 18
14:3 369
14:6 . . . 386, 386 n. 33
14:12-20 383
14:16, 18, 20 . . . 355 n. 5
14:22 . . . . . 385 n. 30
16 373
16:48 . . . . . . 355 n. 5
17:16, 19 . . . 355 n. 5
17:22-24 374
18:1-20 . . . 386, 387 n. 35
18:3 . . . . . . 355 n. 5
18:4 62
18:5-9, 19-29 383
18:5-18, 25-32 . . 383 n. 27
18:21-24 . . . . . 358 n. 9
18:25 . . . . . . 359, 361
18:25, 29 . . . 385 n. 30
18:26-28 . . . . 367 n. 16
18:30 . . . 386, 386 n. 33
18:30-32 . . 359, 386 n. 34
18:31 387
20:1-26, 39-44 . . 356 n. 7
20:3, 31, 35 . . . . 355 n. 5
20:3-28 359
20:5 359
20:7-21 . . . . . . 368 n. 18
20:9, 14, 22 362
20:11-21 . . . 387 n. 35

20:25, 26 359
20:26, 31 . . . . 149 n. 15
20:41 361
20:43 . . . . . . 385 n. 30
21:24-27 374
21:24-32 . . . . 377 n. 22
22 369
22:6-31 . . . . 368 n. 18
22:8, 26 . . . . . 356 n. 7
22:22 377
22:24-31 . . . 377 n. 22
23 362
23:19, 21, 27 116
24:15 . . . . . . 221 n. 5
25:7, 13, 17 . . 363 n. 14
26:4, 21 . . . 363 n. 14
28:13 . . 48, 49 n. 3, 59
n. 18
29:8, 9 . . . . 363 n. 14
30:1-19 . . . . 377 n. 22
30:3, 4 377
30:32 . . . . . . 358 n. 9
31:8, 9 . . . . 59 n. 18
33:7 . . . . 209 n. 7
33:10-16 . . . . 367 n. 16
33:10-20 . . . 358 n. 9
33:11 . . 362, 364, 386,
386 n. 33
33:11, 27 . . . . 355 n. 5
33:17-20 . . . 385 n. 30
33:34 . . . . . . 361 n. 13
34 . . . . 373, 374
34:8 . . . . . . 355 n. 5
34:11-25 . . . 367 n. 16
34:23 362
35:6 . . . . . . 355 n. 5
36:20-23 . . . 365 n. 7
36:20-24 361
36:25-28 361
36:25-29 . . . 383 n. 27,
386 n. 34
36:25-33 . . . 367 n. 16
36:26 387
36:26-28 373
36:28 367
36:31, 32 . . . 386 n. 33
37 374
37:1, 14 . . . 371 n. 21
37:11-28 . . . 367 n. 16
37:14 362
37:15-28 373
37:26, 27 . . . 363, 367
38:8, 16 379
39:7 361
39:7, 25 . . . . 356 n. 7
39:21 . . . . . . 354 n. 3
39:25-29 379
39:29 . . . . . 371 n. 21
40 — 48 402
40:1 — 43:5 372
40:2 . . . . 380 n. 26
40:3, 5 . . . . 380 n. 26
43:2 . . . . . 380 n. 26

43:2-5 . . . . 354 n. 3
43:5 . . 357, 371 n. 21
43:6-9 375
43:7 369
43:10 380
43:12 357
43:27 . . . . . 367 n. 16
44:4 . . 354 n. 3, 357, 380
n. 26
44:7 . . 95 n. 8, 49 n. 16
44:7, 9 . . . . . 60 n. 20
45:13-25 . . . . 367 n. 16
46 . . . . 367 n. 16
47:1, 2 . . . . 380 n. 26
48:31-35 . . . . 380 n. 26
48:35 . . 354 n. 3, 355,
363, 364

DANIEL
1:8 . . . . 383 n. 28
1:17 372
2:17-23 370
2:17-19, 28, 29, 47 . . 372
2:18 358
2:20-23 355
2:21 364
2:44 . . . . . . 368 n. 17
2:47 . . . . 355 n. 4
3:16-18 . . . . . 365, 370
3:17, 18 . . . . 383 n. 28
4:2, 3 365
4:8, 9, 13, 17, 18, 23
357 n. 8
4:8-12 365
4:12, 21 . . . . . 220 n. 4
4:17 78
4:25 365
4:27 . . 360, 368 n. 17,
384 n. 29, 386, 387
4:34, 35 . . 355 n. 4, 365
4:34-37 . . . . . 370 n. 20
5:11 . . . . 357 n. 8
5:21-23 355
5:22, 23 . . 384 n. 29, 387
6:4 386
6:10, 22 . . . . 383 n. 28
6:16-18, 25-27 . . 370 n. 20
6:22 366
6:26 356
6:26, 27 . . . . . 355 n. 4
7:12 372
7:13, 14 . . . 220 n. 4, 366
7:14-27 . . . . 368 n. 17
8 381
8; 9 366
8:24 . . . . 357 n. 8
9:3-19 . . 358, 368, 383
n. 28
9:3-20 388
9:3-23 371
9:4-11 386
9:4-16 361
9:4-19 . . . 368 n. 17, 373

9:10, 11 . . . . . . 207 n. 2
9:11, 13 . . 40 n. 26, 373
9:16, 20, 24 . . . 357 n. 8
9:24 357
9:24-27 376
9:26, 27 377
10:11 382
10:12 . . . . . . 383 n. 28
11:1-32 377
11:20-30 274
11:21-32 . . . 384 n. 29
11:28, 30, 45 . . 357 n. 8
12:1-3 . . . 368 n. 17, 382
12:2 . . . . 302, 367
12:2, 3 388
12:7 . . . 356, 356 n. 8
12:10 . . . 384, 384 n. 29
12:11 377

HOSEA
1:1 217
1:2, 4 218
1:3 . . . . 221 n. 5
1:4-8 242
1:4-9 254
1:10 f. . . . . 279 n. 21
1:10, 11 . . . . . . 255 n. 8
1:10 — 2:1 254
1:11 . . . . 267, 275
2:1 . . . . 257, 294
2:1, 19, 20 . . . 257 n. 10
2:2 285
2:7, 15, 16, 23 . . 255 n. 8
2:14, 19, 20 255
2:15 f. . . . . . 279 n. 21
2:18 . . . . 255 n. 7
2:19 242
2:19, 20 255
3:1 218
3:5 . . . 265, 279 n. 21,
                        294
4:1, 2 285
4:2-6 256
4:2, 6 . . . . 252 n. 6
4:6 290
4:7, 8 290
4:12-19 285
4:13 290
4:16 290
5:6, 7 294
5:15 290
6:1-3 . . . . . 255 n. 9
6:6 . . . . 255, 257 n. 10,
                        285
6:7 . . . . 255 n. 7
6:6, 7 . . . . . . 290, 294
7:1, 2, 3, 15 . . . 290 n. 25
7:7-10 294
7:14 290
7:16 256
8:1 . . 255 n. 7, 256, 257,
                        290
8:1, 12 . . . . . . 252 n. 6

8:1-10 . . . . . . 255 n. 9
8:8 290
8:11 256
8:11-14 285
8:13 290
9:7 . . . . . . 218 n. 2, 290
9:9 290
9:15 . . . . . 290, 290 n. 25
10:2 . . . . 285, 290
10:4 . . . . 255 n. 7
10:8 290
10:12 . . . . 256, 285, 295
10:13 290
11:1 . . . . . 242, 256, 268
11:1-9 . . . 257 n. 10
11:8 242
12:3-6 107
12:5 242
12:6 . . . . 285, 295
12:10-13 252
13:1 291
13:2 290
13:2, 4 . . . . . . 252 n. 6
13:4, 5 . . . 256, 257 n. 10
13:6, 16 290
13:12 290
13:14 . . . . 278, 299, 300
14:1-4 295
14:1-7 . . . . . 255 n. 9
14:1, 4 242
14:4 . . . . 256, 257
14:4-7 . . 257 n. 10, 268
14:4-8 . . . . 279 n. 21
14:9 . . . . 256, 285, 290

JOEL
1:1 . . . . 217 n. 1
1:15 . . . . 241, 260
2:1, 2 260
2:2-11 260
2:12, 13 . . 214, 284, 294
2:13 . . . . 241, 260
2:20 260
2:28 241
2:28, 29 282
2:28-32 . . . . 261, 278
2:30-32 261
2:32 267
3:4, 19 260
3:9-15 . . . . . 261, 262
3:13, 19 289
3:16-21 275
3:18-21 267
3:20 275

AMOS
1:1 . . . . 217, 220
1:2 242
1:3 . . . 218, 262, 286,
                        291 n. 26
2:1, 3, 6 . . . 291 n. 26
2:4 . . . . 253, 257
2:10, 11 243

2:11 253
3:1 . . . . 218, 243
3:1-3 . . . . . 257 n. 11
3:7 . . . . 207 n. 2, 253
4:2 243
4:12 . 257 n. 11, 262, 295
4:12, 13 . . . 46, 243, 286
4:13 48
5:1, 4, 25 . . . . 257 n. 11
5:4 263
5:4, 6, 14, 15 295
5:6-8 46
5:8, 9 244
5:12 291
5:14, 15 . . . 262, 286, 291
5:15 243
5:18-20 262
5:21, 22, 25 169
5:24 . . . . . 243, 286, 295
6:1 . . . . 257 n. 11
6:1-7 286
6:1-8 243
7:1 218
7:4-6 243
7:8, 15 . . . . 257 n. 11
7:12 . . . . 209 n. 6
7:14 216
8:2 . . . . 257 n. 11, 263
8:9, 10 263
8:11, 12 253
9:1 218
9:5, 6 244
9:6 . . . . . . 49, 49 n. 2
9:7 243
9:11, 12 279
9:11, 15 . . . 243, 258, 268
9:14 . . . . . . 257 n. 11
9:14, 15 . . . . 243, 275

OBADIAH
1 . . . . 218, 251
10 289
15 259
17 — 21 267
18 . . . . 251, 252
21 . . . . 254, 260

JONAH
1:1 . . . . 217 n. 1
1:2 289
2:9 284
3:8 . . . . 289, 295
4:2 . . . . 242, 284

MICAH
1:1 217
1:2-9 250
1:5, 13 292
2:1, 2 289
2:1-3 292
2:7 283
2:10 . . . . . . 163 n. 21
2:12, 13 . . . . . 273, 277

3:2 292
3:2, 3 289
3:5 218
3:7 . . . . 209 n. 6
3:8 . 218 n. 2, 283, 292
3:9 293
3:9-12 266
3:12 . . . . 250, 251
4:5 293
4:1-7 266
4:1, 2 259
4:7 273
4:10 277
5:2-4 273
5:4 274
5:10-15 . . . . . 266, 293
6:4 . . . . 116 n. 11
6:4-8 259
6:7 292
6:8 . . . . 289, 298
6:10-12 . . . . . 289, 293
6:13-15 266
7:1-7 299
7:2 293
7:18-20 . . . . . 251, 293
7:20 . . . . 88 n. 1

NAHUM
1:1 218
1:7 329
1:15 339
3:1-4 345

HABAKKUK
1:1 218
1:2-4 347
1:13 . . 163 n. 21, 330
2:1, 2 209
2:4 . . . 152, 330, 339,
        340, 343, 345, 349
2:4, 5 347
2:4, 5, 6-19 341
2:14 . . . . . 77, 343, 349
2:18, 19 219
2:19, 20 330
2:20 341
3:3b-6 330
3:13 343
3:13, 14 349
3:18 . . . . 339, 349
3:18, 19 343

ZEPHANIAH
1:1 . . . . 217 n. 1
1:1-6 340
1:2-6 346
1:9-13 346
1:10 218
1:14, 18 346
1:14-18 340
1:15-18 329
2:1-3 346
2:3 . . . . 345, 349

2:7 328
2:8-11 346
2:11 . . . . 329, 342
3:2-4 346
3:5 329
3:5-7 346
3:8-20 340
3:9 . . . . 342, 349
3:9-13 346
3:9, 14, 15, 17, 20 . 342
3:11-13, 17 349
3:12, 13 345
3:14-20 339
3:17 329

HAGGAI
1:2 218
1:5, 7 . . . . . 230 n. 12
1:5-11 404
1:8 . . . . 390, 393
1:9, 10 . . . . . 403 n. 8
1:13 392
2:5 . . . . 390, 393
2:6 395
2:6-9 395
2:6, 7, 21, 22 390
2:6, 7, 15-19, 21, 22
                403 n. 8
2:7 394
2:10-19 405
2:17 406
2:21, 22 399
3:11-14 393

ZECHARIAH
1:3, 4 . . . . 230 n. 12
1:4 . . . . 405, 406
1:6 . . . . 207 n. 2
1:7 — 6:8 392
1:13-17 390
1:17 . . . 403, 403 n. 9
2:1-12 393
2:5, 10, 11 391
2:10-12 400
2:11 . . . . . . 400 n. 6
2:12 . . . . . 403 n. 9
3:2 . . . . 403 n. 9
3:4, 9 405
3:8 . . 207 n. 2, 268 n. 15,
        339, 395, 395 n. 3
3:10 . . . . . 400 n. 6
4:1-6 141
5 404
5:4 . . . . 128 n. 22
6:12 . . . 268 n. 15, 339,
                395 n. 3
6:12, 13 396
7:9, 10 404
7:10 405
7:11 405
7:12 . . . . . . 218 n. 2
8:1-15 390
8:2, 3 403

8:13, 20, 23 . . . 403 n. 9
8:16-19 404
8:17 405
9:1 — 11:3 . . . 391, 393
9:9, 10 . . . 359 n. 3, 396
9:9-17 . . . . 403 n. 9
9:11 393
9:16 . . . 400 n. 6, 403
10:6-12 . . 403, 403 n. 9
11:4 218
11:4-14 397
11:5 405
11:12, 13 . . . 395 n. 3
12:1 . . . . . 46, 49 n. 2,
                218, 391
12:3 400
12:3, 4, 6, 8, 9, 11
                400 n. 6
12:7-14 400
12:10 . . . . . . 397, 400
13:1 . . . . . . 400, 405
13:1, 2, 4 . . . . 400 n. 6
13:2-6 400
13:7 . . . 395 n. 31, 398
13:8, 9 400
13:9 401
14 . . . 398, 401, 403
14:2 401
14:5 401
14:6, 7 401
14:8 . . . 395 n. 3, 402
14:9 402
14:10, 11 402
14:19 405

MALACHI
1:1 218
1:2 394
1:2, 3 391
1:4 . . . . . . 230 n. 12
1:6-14 391
1:7, 12 . . . 149 n. 16
1:8 405
1:12 405
2:6 . . . . 391, 406
2:8-10 394
2:10 46
2:10, 11 405
2:16 . . . . 404, 406
2:17 405
3:1 399
3:5 . . . . 128 n. 22
3:5 ff. 406
3:7 406
3:14-18 405
3:16-18 406
4:2 394
4:4 . . 40 n. 26, 394, 402
4:5 . . . . 378 n. 23

MATTHEW
1:12 . . . . 88 n. 1
1:21 193

1:22 269
2:1-6 274
2:15 268
3:13-17 . . . 271 n. 17
3:16, 17 . . . . . 180, 428
4:1-11 . . . . . . 179 n. 6
4:23, 24 . . . . 322 n. 13
5:14-16 142
5:17-20 . . . . 24 n. 1
5:39-42 445
5:44 176
5:44, 45 445
7:1 131
8:11 . . . . 88 n. 1
8:17 321
9:21, 22 273
11:5, 6 273
11:10 399
11:27 . . . . 397 n. 4
11:27-30 . . . . 322 n. 13
12:15-21 . . 319, 322 n. 13
12:17-21 320
12:18-21 318
12:42 443
13:14, 15 . . . 281 n. 22,
287 n. 24
13:32 . . 220 n. 4, 374
13:39 63
15:3-20 . . . . 163 n. 21
15:17-20 164
15:19 71
16:24 . . . . 322 n. 13
17:5 428
17:11 399
19:4-6 47
20:28 116
21:5 396
21:42 428
22:36-40 126
22:43-45 429
24:15-28 . . 367 n. 15, 377
24:21-28 379
24:29-31 264
24:30 . . . 220 n. 4, 376
24:37-39 76
26:15 397
26:26-29 . . . 322 n. 13
26:28 344
26:31 398
26:54 . . . . 24 n. 1
26:64 . . 220 n. 4, 376, 429
26:67 319
27:3-10 397
27:30 319
27:35, 39, 43, 46 . . 427
28:18 . . . . 397 n. 4

MARK
1:9-11 . . . . . 271 n. 17
7:6, 10 . . . . . 24 n. 1
7:6-23 . . . . . 163 n. 21
7:11 . . . . . 149 n. 14
7:21, 22 131

12:19, 26 . . . . . 40 n. 26
12:36, 37 . . . . . 24 n. 1
13:19 47

LUKE
2:30 321
2:32 . . . . 314, 320
2:55 . . . . 24 n. 1
3:4-6 . . . . 314, 321
3:21, 22 . . . . . 271 n. 17
3:34 . . . . 88 n. 1
4:16-21 . . 319, 322, 325
9:20-23 . . . . . 322 n. 13
11:31 443
16:16, 17 . . . . . 24 n. 1
18:31-33 . . . . . 24 n. 1
20:28 . . . . . . 40 n. 26
21:20-24 . . . . . 367 n. 15
22:37 . 24 n. 1, 319, 323
22:37, 69 . . . . 322 n. 13
23:46 427
24:27, 44 . . . . 40 n. 26
24:46, 47 . . . . 322 n. 13

JOHN
1:1-4 47
1:1-18 . . . . 24 n. 1
1:14 . . . . 143, 144
1:17 113
1:29 . . . . 322 n. 13
1:45 . . . . 40 n. 26
1:50, 51 106
1:51 144
2:17 427
2:19 145
3:1-8 378
3:3-8 . . . . 296 n. 28
3:5, 6 436
3:5-8 387
3:16 65
5:39 . . . . 24 n. 1
5:46 . . . . 40 n. 26
7:19, 22, 23 . . 40 n. 26
8:5 . . . . 40 n. 26
8:33 . . . . 116 n. 12
8:33-58 . . . . . 88 n. 1
8:44 63
8:56 99
10:1-18 274
10:16 . . . . . . 325 n. 19
10:35 427
12:15 396
12:36-38 321
12:37-50 . . . . . 24 n. 1
12:39-41 . . 281 n. 22, 287
n. 24
13:3 . . . . . . 397 n. 4
13:18 427
15:1 339
17:24 48
19:36 117
19:37 398

ACTS
2:1-36 241
2:5-11 84
2:21 278
2:25-31 426
2:30 429
2:33-36 . . 397 n. 4, 429
3:13, 25 . . . . . . 88 n. 1
3:17-26 . . . . . 24 n. 1
3:22 . . . . 40 n. 26
3:22, 23 199
3:25 92
3:33 428
4:10-12 428
4:24-26 428
4:25 . . . . 24 n. 1
7:1-5 . . . . . . 85 n. 15
7:2, 3 . . . . 95, 96
7:2-4 89
7:2-10 . . . . 88 n. 1
7:20-44 . . . . . 116 n. 11
7:22 . . . . 36, 112
7:37 199
7:38 200
7:44-47 170
7:59 427
8:28-35 321
10:36 321
10:38 234
13:17 . . . . . . 85 n. 15
13:17, 18 . . . . 116 n. 11
13:26 . . . . 88 n. 1
13:32, 33 24
13:35 426
13:45-49 318
13:47 . . . . 314, 321
15:12-18 258
15:16-18 279
21:20-26 . . . . 163 n. 21
26:18 324
26:22, 23 318
26:26, 27 . . . . 281 n. 22
28:23 . . . . . . 40 n. 26
28:23-25 . . . . . 24 n. 1
28:25 . . . . 218 n. 2
28:26, 27 . . . . 287 n. 24

ROMANS
1:1, 2 24
1:2 . . . . 34, 214
1:16 . . . . 193, 324
1:16, 17 . . . . . 24 n. 1
1:17 343
2:5, 16 . . . . . 261 n. 14
2:25-29 95
3:2, 4 . . . . 24 n. 1
3:21-25 152
3:25 158
4 . . . . 88 n. 1
4:1-12 . . . . 94 n. 6
4:1-21 . . . . . . 98 n. 13
4:3 152
4:11, 12 95

4:17 50
4:18, 20, 21 98
5:1 444
5:12 . . . . 57, 62
5:12-14 136
5:12-21 . . . . 95, 163
5:14 . . . . 54 n. 14
5:18 57
6:4 . . . . 387, 444
6:23 . . . . 62 n. 23
7:7-20 . . . . . . 124 n. 17
7:7b-10 . . . . . 131, 132
8:1-17 . . . . . . 296 n. 28
8:13 234
8:20, 21 . . . . . 116 n. 12
8:28 — 11:36 179
9:4-13 90
9:6-13 92
9:11 104
9:17 . . . . 116 n. 11
9:22-26 257
9:30-33 270
9:33 . . . 245 n. 2, 272
10:1-5 . . . . . . 124 n. 17
10:4 124
10:11 . . . . 245 n. 2
10:13 278
10:15, 16 321
11:5, 6 90
11:26, 27 . . . . 325 n. 19
12:1 148
12:16b 445
12:17 445
12:19 176
12:19-21 445
12:20 445
13:1 445
13:1-7 78
14:10-12 309
14:14-23 . . . . . 163 n. 21
15:1-6 . . . . 24 n. 1
15:8-13 272
15:21 321
16:20 63
16:25-27 . . . . . . 24 n. 1

1 CORINTHIANS
3:9, 16, 17 . . . 233 n. 14
3:13-15 . . . . 261 n. 14
5:7, 8 117
6:19, 20 . . . . . 233 n. 14
9:9 . . . . 40 n. 26
10:1-11 . . . . 24 n. 1
10:14-22 159
10:21 . . . . 149 n. 16
11:7 . . . . 52, 53
15:3 . . . . 322 n. 13
15:5-8 . . . . . . 89, 143
15:22, 45 . . . . 54 n. 14
15:25 . . . 397 n. 4, 429
15:54 281
15:54, 55 300

2 CORINTHIANS
1:14 . . 261 n. 14, 403 n. 7
3:4-18 . . . . 24 n. 1
3:15 . . . . 40 n. 26
5:17 . . . . 325 n. 19
5:21 152
6:1, 2 . . 314, 315, 321
6:2 129
6:14 — 7:1 . . . 233 n. 14
6:17 . . . . 325 n. 19
11:3 . . . . 54 n. 14
11:3, 14 63

GALATIANS
2:20 158
3:6-8 . . . . 94 n. 6
3:6-14 . . . . . . 98 n. 13
3:6-18 . . . . . . 85 n. 15
3:8 92
3:11 343
3:12-24 . . . . 124 n. 17
3:15-18 24
3:16 92
3:19, 20 . . . . 230 n. 13
3:24 124
3:28, 29 84
3:29 92

EPHESIANS
1:7 158
1:20 429
1:20-23 . . . . . 397 n. 4
2:1-6 . . . . 62 n. 23
2:1-10 . . 296 n. 28, 367,
                  378, 436
2:8 387
2:11 . . . . 95 n. 9
2:19-22 . . 145, 233 n. 14
4:7-13 429
4:24 52
5:2 159
6:15 321

PHILIPPIANS
1:6-10 . . . . . . 403 n. 7
1:6-11 . . . . . 261 n. 14
2:9-11 . . 309, 397 n. 4
3:3 . . . . 95 n. 9

COLOSSIANS
1:16, 17 47
1:21, 22 156
2:9 145
2:11-13 . . . . . . 95 n. 9
2:13 . . . . 62 n. 23
2:17 129
3:1 429
3:5 234
3:10 . . . . 52, 53

1 THESSALONIANS
4:13 — 5:11 . . 261 n. 14
5:9 266

2 THESSALONIANS
1:8 320
2:2 . . 378 n. 23, 403 n. 7
2:2-12 262
2:3-12 379

1 TIMOTHY
2:5 . . . . 230 n. 13
2:5, 6 . . . . . . 322 n. 13
2:13, 14 . . . . . 54 n. 14
3:15 146

2 TIMOTHY
3:15 34
3:15, 16 214
3:15-17 . . . . . 24, 425
3:16 372

HEBREWS
1:1 23
1:1-3 56
1:2 47
1:3, 13 429
1:5 . . . 231, 269, 428
1:8, 9 428
2:9, 14, 15 156
2:11, 12 427
2:17 153
3:1-5 114
3:1-6 . . . 146, 233 n. 14
3:4 129
3:5 208
4:1-13 . . . . 24 n. 1
4:3, 4 48
5:1-3 153
5:5 428
5:6-10 . . . . . . 91, 429
6:13-18 . . . . . . 88 n. 1
6:20 — 7:17 429
7 369
7:1-19 91
8 — 10 136
8:1-4 145
8:1 — 10:18 338
8:2 145
8:5 . . . . 138, 147, 233
                        n. 14
8:6 . . . 123, 230, n. 13
9:1-22 153
9:2-5 170
9:6-14 158
9:8-10 137
9:12-15 116
9:14 154
9:15 . . . . 123, 230 n. 13
9:15-17 156
9:19 . . . . 40 n. 26
9:23, 24 137
9:23-28 . . 145, 233 n. 14
10:1 138
10:12, 13 429
10:15-18 . . . . . . 24 n. 1
10:16-18 344

10:18 . . . . 118, 430
10:19-25 146
10:28 . . . . 40 n. 26
10:37-39 343
11 343
11:1 70
11:1, 2 66
11:3 . . . 48, 49 n. 7, 50
11:4 70
11:7 75
11:8 . . . . 85 n. 15, 89
11:8-10 99
11:8-18 198
11:17 95
11:19 . . . . 96, 98
11:20, 21 . . . . 198 n. 1
11:21 108
11:22 198
11:29-32 227
11:39, 40 67
12:2 429
12:5, 6 445
12:13a 445
12:24 . . 123, 230 n. 13
12:27-29 395

JAMES
2:18-26 444
2:21-23 . . . . . . 88 n. 1
2:22 99
2:23 . . 93 n. 4, 99 n. 16
3:13-18 444
4:6 445
4:11 131
5:8-11 458

1 PETER
1:10-12 . 24 n. 1, 218
n. 2
1:14-16 140
1:18, 19 155
1:24, 25 314
2:4, 5 146
2:4-6 . . 245 n. 2, 270
2:4-7 428
2:4-8 272
2:4-10 . . . . 233 n. 14
2:5, 9 326

2:9 . . . 119, 120, 146,
179, 325 n. 19
2:10 257
2:21-25 . . . 322 n. 13
2:22-25 321
2:24 156
3:6 . . . . 88 n. 1
3:20, 21 76
4:8b 445
4:18 445
5:5b 445

2 PETER
1:17 428
1:19-21 . . . . . 218 n. 2
1:20, 21 24
1:21 . 207, 214, 234, 283,
372
2:5 . . . . 74, 76, 198
2:22b 445
3:5, 6 . . . . . 49 n. 7
3:10 261
3:10-12 . . . 378 n. 23
3:10-13 262
3:11-13 266
3:13 . . 55, 128 n. 24, 327

1 JOHN
2:2 158
3:8 63
3:12 70
4:10 158

JUDE
14 . . . . 54 n. 14, 401
14, 15 198

REVELATION
1:1-3 . . . . 24 n. 1
1:7 398
1:7, 13 376
1:12-20 142
1:15 . . . . . . 380 n. 26
1:17 314
2:7 60
2:8 314

2:26 428
3:9 325
3:12 . . . . 233 n. 14
3:14 48
3:20 . . . . . 149 n. 16
6:12-17 264
7:9 84
7:15 . . . . . . 233 n. 14
7:17 281
11:1-19 . . . 233 n. 14
11:15 . . . . . . 265, 402
12:5 428
12:9 63
13:8 48
14:2 . . . . . . 380 n. 26
14:14 376
14:14-20 262
15:8 . . . . . . 380 n. 26
16:1, 7 426
16:12-16 379
17:8 48
18:4 . . . . . . 325 n. 19
18:21 83
19:6 . . . . . . 380 n. 26
19:15 428
19:17-21 379
20:2 63
20:7-10 . . . . 364, 379
21:1 . . . 55, 128 n. 24
21:1-4 327
21:2-4 273
21:3 . . . . . . 59, 363
21:3, 22 146
21:4 281
21:10 . . . . . 380 n. 26
21:12, 13 . . . 380 n. 26
21:15 . . . . . 380 n. 26
21:16 . . . . . 380 n. 26
21:22 . . . . . 233 n. 14
21:22-27 401
21:25, 26 325
21:27 280
22:1, 2 . 60, 380 n. 26,
402
22:1-3 398
22:3 402
22:7, 12 314
22:13 314

INDEX OF SUBJECTS

Abraham, promises to, 24, 82, 83, 91, 92, 174
God's call, 89-91
God's covenant, 93-95
Tested by God, 95, 96
Faith, 97-100
Friend of God, 99
Ethical aspect of his faith, 100, 126
Prophet, 198
Adam and Eve, 25
Historical persons, 54
Adultery, 130
Ahaz, 249
Amos, witness to the Creator, 46
Call to office, 216
God's nature and acts, 242-244
Mosaic law, 257
Messianic kingdom, 258
Day of the Lord, 262, 263
Anointing with oil, 234
Asa, godly life, 236
Assyria, conquest, 232

Balaam, 122, 200
Biblical revelation, 25, 93
Biblical theology, definition, 26-29
Other approaches, 29-32
Relation to other disciplines, 36-38
Blameless, 74, 94, 100
Blood, not for food, 77
Bread of the Presence, 140, 141

Canaan, Canaanites, 79, 80, 82
Canaan (land of), conquest, 129
Inheritance, 174, 175
Ethics of conquest, 176
Canon (O.T.), 210, 211
Church (The), type fulfilled, 145
Circumcision, 94, 95, 100
Confession of sin, 194
Congregation, 122
Consecration, 117
Covenant, Book of, 120
Covenant, 24, 25, 77-79, 93-95, 118-123, 125, 192, 193
Sinaitic covenant, 192, 193, 199, 357
Israel, God's people, 254
Election, 255
Binding quality, 256
Love relationship, 257
Everlasting, 258
Israel's covenant relation, 259, 337 ff.
God faithful to His covenant, 391

Covenant implied, 393 f.
The Messiah and the covenant, 399, 425
Covet, 131
Creation, "foundation," 48
Act of God, 48
Anthropomorphic language, 49
Time element, 50
Theocentric, 51, of man, 52
Cessation of, 54
Religious aspect, 55-58
Preservation and providence, 56
Unity of human race, 57
Basis of man's relation to God, 57

David prays, 228, 229
His kingdom, 230
His godly life, 235
Day of Atonement, 159-161
Day of the Lord, 214, 221, 241, 248
Near, 259
Imminent judgment, 260
Future aspect, 261
Peter's testimony, 261
Judgment, 262, 263
Judah and nations, 264-266
Day of wrath, imminent, 340-342
Judgment upon nations, 377, 378
Coming catastrophe, 399, 400
Day of the Lord and judgment, 401-403, 425, 426
Death and Sheol, 61-64, 300, 301
Resurrection, 302
Decalogue, 124-132
Deuteronomy, critical views, 172
Internal evidence of origin, 173
Authentic record, 173
God's redeeming love, 178
Dreams, 219, 220

Ecclesiastes, Solomon's view of life, 446, 447
Voice of experience, 447, 448
Values of wisdom, 448, 449
Wholesome advice, 449, 450
Values of book, 450, 451
Eldad, 113
Election, Israel's election, 119, 254-259
Actualized by a new covenant, 338, 339
Through covenant of peace, 373, 374
Implied, 393, 394
Elijah, 113
Esau, 104, 106
Eschatology, 25, 71, 79, 83, 129, 231, 245,

246, 249, 250, 297, 298, 322-327
Restoration of Israel, 274-277
Redemption and salvation, 278-281
Outpouring of the Holy Spirit, 282, 283
Future glory of Zion, 325-327
Restoration blessings, 342-344
Latter Days, 378-382
Individual, 388
Israel and nations, 403
Righteous and wicked dead, 437, 438
Ezekiel, 217

Faith, 70, 72, 96
Ingredients of, 98-100, 108, 179-181
Eschatological aspect, 183
Strengthened by central place of worship, 184, 194, 195, 297, 349-351, 388, 435, 436
False witness, 131
Fellowship, 117, 138, 139 (covenant)
Flood, 71, 76
Form criticism, 32
Former and Latter Prophets, 113

Garden of Eden, 25, 58-67, 87
Genealogy, 71
Gideon, 122
God, 73, 74, 81, 225, 226, 241, 336, 355, 391
Almighty, 97, 105, 333, 334
Only true God, 177
Creator, 43-48, 241, 248, 249, 312, 313, 332, 420-422
Election, 84, 85, 90, 103, 104, 115, 116, 254
Goodness, 418, 419
Grace, 84, 90
Holiness, 139, 140, 231, 245, 246, 305, 306, 356, 357, 415, 416
Judgment, 25, 233, 243, 247, 248, 309, 310, 419, 420
Justice and mercy, 65, 66, 73, 296, 332, 416
Love and mercy, 177, 178, 242, 243, 246, 247, 308, 309, 332, 337, 358, 416, 417
Omniscience, 80, 333
Promises, 25
Providence, 80
Purpose, 82
Redeemer, 305, 306
Repents, 228
Revelation, 23, 24, 25, 58-67, 93, 100-103, 125, 126, 177, 178, 218-220, 253
Sovereign majesty, 244, 245, 304, 305, 354, 355, 414, 415
Speaks, 23, 24, 101, 177, 178
Righteousness and salvation, 306-308, 358-361, 415, 416
Rule, 122-124
Salvation, 336-338
Theophany, 101, 102, 121, 122

Tries hearts, 333, 334
Son, 23
Godly living, 74, 75, 164, 165, 226, 227, 234-236, 284-289, 344, 345, 383, 384, 403-405, 432-434
Gospel, 25, 193

Hannah (her prayer), 228
Haran, 105, 106
Hebrew syntax, 91, 92
Hebrews (author), 89-91, 98, 99, 108, 114
Hezekiah, 45, 236
Historical books, 197
Historicism, 30
History directed by God, 79, 174-176, 213, 223, 231, 232, 243, 249-251, 310-312, 334-336, 361-367, 390-392, 422-424
Holy, 161-164
Hope, 25
Hosea, 217, 242

Isaac, 105, 198
Isaiah (1 — 39), 216, 244-246, 250, 263-266
Israel, election, 115, 116, 119, 175, 176, 178-180
Faith and obedience, 181-183
Worship, 184
History, 205
Covenant, 254-257
Restoration, 274-277, 337-339
Chosen by God, 425

Jacob, 103-108, 192, 198
James (letter), 99
Japheth, 79, 81, 82, 85
Jeremiah, 46, 216, 217
Jesus Christ, 24, 47, 63, 64, 105, 106, 113, 144-146, 180, 181
Job (Book of), 454-458
Joel, 241
John, 47, 113
Jonah, 241, 242
Joseph, 108, 109, 223
Josiah, 236
Joshua, 200, 223, 224
Jubilee, Year of, 129
Just Balances, 165

King, kingdom, 25, 201, 202

Lampstand, 141, 142
Latter days, see eschatology
Law, the, 23, 24, 123, 124, 164, 165, 253-257
Leviticus, 139
Literary criticism, 238, 239, 304, 353, 354
Lord, 43, 44, 46, 86, 87, 390
Lord of hosts, 229, 230, 390

Man, 52, 53, 56, 80, 95
Man of God, 200, 201, 207
Marriage, 53, 164

Medad, 113
Mediator, 208, 230
Melchizedek, 90, 91
Messenger of the Lord, 208
Messiah, 91, 92, 231, 268-273, 298, 299,
    320-323, 339, 340, 374-377, 394-399,
    426, 428-430
Micah, 250, 251, 266, 273, 274
Miracles, 114, 115, 221
Monotheism, 42, 330-332
Moses, 44, 112-114, 122-124, 126, 146,
    192, 199, 200
Murder, 77, 78, 130

Nations, 82
Nebuchadnezzar, 232, 381
Neighbor relations, 164
Neoorthodox, 32
Nephilim, 73
New Testament, 23, 24, 124, 147
Noah, 72-81, 118, 119, 198

Obadiah, 251, 252, 254
Offerings and sacrifices, 69, 70, 75, 76, 93,
    94, 96, 117, 120, 121, 147-159, 163,
    164
Old Testament, 23, 24

Parents, 129, 130
Passover, 116-118, 193, 224, 225
Paschal Lamb, 117
Paul, 24, 47, 84, 90, 95, 98, 104, 117, 131
Pentateuch, 34-36, 88, 89, 97, 124, 125
Pentecost, 84
Peter, 24, 119, 120
Poor, the, 164, 165
Prayer, 228
Promises fulfilled, 223, 224
Prophecy, 79, 80
Prophet, 209-211, 213, 220, 221
Prophets, 23-25, 197, 199-205, 212, 214,
    216, 217, 230
Prophetic revelation, 239, 240
Prophetism, 197-199, 202-204, 207-215
Proverbs, 442-446
Psalms, 44, 45, 409, 410, 438-441

Rebecca, 104
Redemption, 114-118, 430-432

Regeneration, 294-298, 349, 351, 352, 386,
    387, 435, 436
Repentance, 194, 228, 293-299, 349, 350,
    386-388, 406, 435, 436
Revelation, 103-108, 213-215, 217-219,
    230, 231, 371, 372
Righteous, 74

Sabbath, 54, 128, 129
Salvation, 25, 26, 192, 193, 294, 295, 297,
    430-432
Samuel, 201, 202
Satan, 61-64
Seer, 201, 209
Septuagint, 97
Servant of the Lord, 45, 151, 207, 208,
    315, 322
Shem, Shemites, 79-82, 84, 85
Sin and Transgression, 25, 64, 65, 70, 71,
    116, 186-192, 242, 243, 289-293, 345-
    348, 384-386, 405, 406, 434, 435
Song of Songs, The, 451-453
Spirit of the Lord, 226, 233, 234, 371
Stealing, 131
Stephen, 89, 200
Symbolism, 142, 143

Tabernacle, 134-147, 166-171
Temple, 232, 233
Temptation, 62-64
Tent of meeting, 167
Terah, 82
Theocracy, 122, 123
Tower of Babel, 83
Tree of knowledge of good and evil, 60-62
Tree of life, 59, 60
Type, 143-147

Universalism, 90
Unleavened bread, 117

Visions, 219-221

Watchman, 209
Word of God, 251-254, 313-315, 336, 337,
    371-373, 392, 393, 424, 425
Worship, 72, 75, 134, 140-142, 165, 223-
    225, 368-371, 410-414

Zechariah, 46